D0511608

2

Principles of Microeconomics

FIFTH EDITION

Principles of Microeconomics

EDWIN MANSFIELD

DIRECTOR, CENTER FOR ECONOMICS AND TECHNOLOGY
UNIVERSITY OF PENNSYLVANIA

FIFTH EDITION

W · W · NORTON & COMPANY · NEW YORK · LONDON

(Photograph credits and acknowledgments appear on page A41.)

To Edward Deering Mansfield (1801–1880)
and his brother-in-law Charles Davies (1798–1876)
neither of whom should be held responsible
for the views expressed here.

The text of this book is composed in Times Roman, with
display type set in Times Roman Bold. Composition by New England
Typographic Service, Inc. Manufacturing by The Murray Printing Company.
Book design by Antonina Krass. Page makeup by Ben Gamit.
Cover design by Mike McIver.

Library of Congress Cataloging-in-Publication Data

Mansfield, Edwin.
    Principles of microeconomics, fifth edition.

    Includes index.
    1. Microeconomics. I. Title.
HB172.M363 1986   338.5   85-29818

ISBN 0-393-95488-9

W. W. Norton & Company, Inc., 500 Fifth Avenue, New York, N. Y. 10110
W. W. Norton & Company Ltd., 37 Great Russell Street, London WCIB 3NU

2 3 4 5 6 7 8 9 0

Contents

Preface   xiii

PART ONE   Introduction to Economics

CHAPTER 1   Economic Problems and Analysis   1

CHAPTER 2   Economic Models and Capitalism, American-Style   18

PART FIVE

Distribution of Income

CHAPTER 14

Determinants of Wages 277

CHAPTER 15

Interest, Rent, and Profits 302

CHAPTER 16

Income Inequality, Poverty, and Discrimination 322

PART SIX | Energy and the Environment

CHAPTER 17 | Environmental and Energy Problems 347

PART SEVEN | International Economics

CHAPTER 18 | International Trade 369

CHAPTER 19 | The Communist Countries and Marxism 394

Preface

Any principles text must keep current with the state of economic knowledge, especially as it applies to the economic issues of the day. The fifth edition of *Principles of Microeconomics* does this, in ways I outline below. But the most fundamental change in this edition is not one of organization or style: it involves a new emphasis which, I believe, will lead to far greater understanding and retention of the core material of the introductory course.

To students, perhaps the biggest defect in most textbooks is their failure to sift through the many details, and present a reasonably small number of basic propositions that should be given central attention. Thus students find it difficult to separate the essential and basic from the less important, and a few years after graduation their recollection of economics is often a smudge.

Almost as formidable a barrier to learning is the tendency of textbooks to treat each topic as a separate entity, with the connections among them either unstated or mentioned in passing. Because the topics are not brought together, the student is like a chef who has the ingredients spread on the counter but lacks the recipe for blending them.

The fifth edition attempts to remedy the twin problems of excessive detail and missing linkages:

Basic Ideas. To provide direction finders through the text, the present edition focuses on 38 Basic Ideas, two highlighted per chapter, which students are encouraged to think through carefully. One can reasonably expect these 38 Basic Ideas to stick with students. If so, their time will have been well spent, because these ideas really constitute the heart of elementary microeconomics, stripped of frills and details. Based on classroom experience, this simple pedagogical aid helps students to see (and remember) the forest, as distinct from a hodgepodge of trees. (Besides presenting each of these 38 Basic Ideas in the relevant chapters in the text, a summary of them is printed in the front and back inside covers of the book, where students can readily refer to them.)

Cross-Chapter Cases. To make connections clear—connections not only between aspects of theory but also between theory and the uses to which it is put—this edition introduces six Cross-Chapter Cases. Appearing near the end of each part (other than the introduction), each takes up a major issue cutting across material contained in various chapters of the part. Among the issues developed in detail are the pros and cons of America's adopting an industrial policy, how robots affect firms' cost curves, the antitrust case involving Berkey Photo and Eastman Kodak, the effects of the minimum wage on teenage unemployment, and the debt problems of Argentina, Brazil and Mexico. These Cross-Chapter Cases are not mere appendages. They require students to draw on a number of tools and techniques to which they have just been exposed in the entire part.

Other New Material. While the 38 Basic Ideas and the Cross-Chapter Cases are the principal innovations in the Fifth Edition, much else has been changed. New inserts, for example, come in two varieties: some on new developments in economics (such as the role of time in economics, market signaling, contestable markets, and laboratory experimentation) while others deal with mistakes and fallacies (such as the discussion of sunk costs in Chapter 8). In addition, new materials have been introduced on such aspects of the current policy scene as tax reform and protectionism. Also, the IBM Corporation is now used to explain the operation of a giant corporation, significantly one with a strong entrepreneurial bent, in Chapter 5. Additional space is also devoted to relatively new theoretical developments.

Glossary of Terms. Another new feature of the Fifth Edition is a Glossary of Terms, which is placed at the end of the book. I am grateful to Nariman Behravesh, who supervised much of the work underlying this glossary, for permission to include it here. This new section should make it easier for students to refresh their memories concerning the definition of economic terms.

Emphasis on Doing Economics. Most textbooks do not encourage the student to get involved in the subject. They simply lay out the material, leaving the student to absorb it passively. In the previous edition, I invited students to *do* economics in order to understand it better. Scores of examples were provided, each describing a real (or realistic) situation and then calling on the student to work through the solution. Within each chapter there were two problem sets, both designated "Test Yourself," that enabled students to check their comprehension of what they had just read. The reaction of instructors and students was very favorable, and the emphasis on doing economics is maintained in this fifth edition. One new feature is that the answers for the odd-numbered Test Yourself questions are now provided at the end of the book. Many students and instructors urged me to include them in this way.

Organizational Changes. Although many new features have been included in the present edition, the book is shorter than the previous edition, due to a tough (even ruthless) editing process. A very determined effort has been made to drop extraneous material and to keep the number of words to a minimum. This edition, while leaner than its predecessor, manages, I believe, to be clearer, both theoretically and empirically.

Updating. All of the empirical and policy-oriented chapters have been updated. Since a text should reflect current conditions and concerns, the government policies in all the major economic areas—farm, energy, environmental, antitrust, and international—are reviewed in depth. The latest data available have been incorporated in the tables, diagrams, and discussions, while revisions in sections on Social Security and a variety of other topics have brought them into line with current developments.

As supplements to the text, I have prepared both a book of readings and a study guide containing problems and exercises. The book of readings is *Principles of Microeconomics: Readings, Issues, and Cases,* fourth edition. It provides a substantial set of supplementary articles, carefully correlated with the text for instructors who want to introduce their students to the writings of major contemporary economists. It is designed to acquaint the student with a wide range of economic analysis, spanning the spectrum from classics to the present-day radicals. The emphasis, as in the text, is on integrating theory, measurement, and applications.

The *Study Guide,* fifth edition, contains, in addition to problems, review questions, and tests, a large number of cases that require the student to work with quantitative material in applying concepts to practical situations. In practically every chapter of the study guide, a new case study has been added. Both students and instructor have reported that such cases are important in motivating students and illuminating economic theory.

An *Instructor's Manual* has been prepared by Michael Claudon of Middlebury College to accompany the text. A *Test Item File,* prepared by Herbert Gishlick of Rider College, is available both in printed form and on computer disk and tape. *Transparency Masters* are also available to instructors who adopt the text.

Finally, it is a pleasure to acknowledge the debts that I owe to the many teachers at various colleges and universities who have commented in detail on various parts of the manuscript. The first, second, and third editions benefited greatly from the advice I received from the following distinguished economists, none of whom is responsible, of course, for the outcome: Wallace Atherton, California State University at Long Beach; Bela Balassa, Johns Hopkins; Robert Baldwin, University of Wisconsin (Madison); Arthur Benavie, North Carolina; Lee Biggs, Montgomery College; Donald Billings, Boise State; William Branson, Princeton; Martin Bronfenbrenner, Duke; Edward Budd, Penn State; Phillip Burstein, Purdue; Wade Chio, U.S. Air Force Academy; Michael Claudon, Middlebury; Warren Coates, Federal Reserve; Richard Cooper, Yale; Alan Deardorff, Michigan; William Desvousges, Missouri (Rolla); F. Trenery Dolbear, Brandeis; Robert Dorfman, Harvard; James Duesenberry, Harvard; William Dugger, North Texas State University; Richard Easterlin, University of Southern California; Jonathan Eaton, Princeton; David Fand, Wayne State; Judith Fernandez, University of California (Berkeley); David Gay, University of Arkansas; Howard A. Gilbert, South Dakota State University; Gerald Goldstein, Northwestern; Robert Gordon, Northwestern; Edward Gramlich, Michigan; Herschel Grossman, Brown; William Gunther, Alabama; Jerry Gustafson, Beloit; Judith Herman, Queens College; Alan Heston, University of Pennsylvania; Albert Hirschman, Harvard; Ronald Jones, Rochester; John Kareken, Minnesota; Ann Krueger, World Bank; Robert Kuenne, Princeton; Simon Kuznets, Harvard; William Leonard, St. Joseph's; Richard Levin, Yale; Raymond Lubitz, Columbia and the Federal Reserve; John F. MacDonald, Illinois (Chicago Circle); Sherman Maisel, University of California (Berkeley); Leonard Martin, Cleveland State University; Thomas Mayer, University of California (Davis); William McEachern, University of Connecticut; Joseph McKinney, Baylor; Edward McNertney, Texas Christian University; Steven Morrison, University of California (Berkeley); John Murphy, Canisius; Arthur Okun, Brookings Institution; Lloyd Orr, Indiana; R.D. Peterson, Markenomics Associates (Fort Collins); E. Dwight Phaup, Union College; Roger Ransom, University of California (Berkeley); Charles Ratliff, Davidson College; Albert Rees, Princeton; Edward Renshaw, State University of New York (Albany); Anthony Romeo, University of Connecticut; Vernon Ruttan, Minnesota; Warren St. James, Nassau County Community College; Steven Sacks, University of Connecticut; Allen Sanderson, William and Mary; David Schulze, Florida; Edward Shapiro, University of Toledo; William Shugart, Arizona; Paul Sommers, Middlebury; Nicolas Spulber, Indiana; Charles Stone, Swarthmore; Richard Sutch, University of California (Berkeley); Frank Tansey, City University of New York; Michael Taussig, Rutgers; Thomas Tidrick, Clayton Junior College; Fred Westfield, Vanderbilt; Simon Whitney, Iona College; William Whitney, University of Pennsylvania; and Harold Williams, Kent State University.

Among the teachers who contributed comments and suggestions for the changes in subsequent editions are: Otis Gilley, University of Texas at Austin; Marvin E. Goodstein, University of the South; William Keeton, Yale; Walter Misiolek, University of Alabama; and Jennifer Roback, Yale.

I would like to thank Elisabeth Allison of Harvard University for contributing the inserts that appear (over her initials) in various chapters, Donald S. Lamm and Nancy K. Palmquist of W.W. Norton for their efficient handling of the publishing end of the work, and Edward D. Mansfield and Elizabeth D. Mansfield for editorial help. As always, my wife, Lucile, has contributed an enormous amount to the completion of this book.

Philadelphia, 1985.   E.M.

PART ONE

Introduction to Economics

CHAPTER 1

Economic Problems and Analysis

A recent national survey concluded that "the American public's knowledge of basic ... economic facts of life is sadly deficient." This is a disturbing discovery, but it is not altogether surprising. Most of us grow up unaware that economics enters into nearly every activity that we engage in. To help you understand the pervasive importance of economics, we begin by looking at a sample of the major problems economists deal with. Each of these problems could have a big effect on your life.

Economic Problems: A Sampler

UNEMPLOYMENT AND INFLATION

The history of the American economy is for the most part a story of growth. Our output—the amount of goods and services we produce annually—has grown rapidly over the years, giving us a standard of living that could not have been imagined a century ago. For example, output per person in the United States was about $15,000 in 1984; in 1900, it was about $3,000. Nonetheless, the growth of output has not been steady or uninterrupted; instead, our output has tended to fluctuate—and so has unemployment. In periods when output has fallen, thousands, even millions, of people have been thrown out of work. In the Great Depression of the 1930s over 20 percent of the labor force was unemployed (see Figure 1.1). Unemployment on this scale results in enormous economic waste and social misery.

The first of our sample of economic problems is: *What determines the extent of **unemployment** in the American economy, and what can be done to reduce it?* This problem is complicated by a related phenomenon: The level of prices may rise when we reduce the level of unemployment. In other words, inflation may occur. Thus the problem is not only to curb unem-

1

Figure 1.1
Unemployment Rates, United States,
1929–84 *The unemployment rate has varied substantially from year to year. In the Great Depression, it reached a high of over 24 percent. In 1984, it exceeded 7 percent.*

ployment, but to do this without producing an inflation so ruinous to the nation's economic health that the cure proves more dangerous than the ailment. Consequently, another major accompanying question is: *What determines the rate of* **inflation** *and how can it be reduced?* As Figure 1.2 shows, we have experienced considerable inflation since 1929; the dollar has lost over four-fifths of its purchasing power during this period. Moreover, in the 1970s and early 1980s, our economy often has been bedeviled by "stagflation": a combination of high unemployment and high inflation.

During the past 50 years, economists have learned a great deal about the factors that determine the extent of unemployment and inflation, and about the ways in which the government can promote high employment with reasonably stable prices. Any responsible citizen needs to know what economists have learned—and to be aware of the differences of opinion among leading economists on this score. To understand many of the central political issues of the day, and to vote intelligently, this knowledge is essential. Also, to understand the fallacies in many apparently simple remedies for the complex economic problems in this area, you need to know some economics.

Economics is divided into two parts: microeconomics and macroeconomics. **Microeconomics** *deals with the economic behavior of individual units like consumers, firms, and resource owners, while* **macroeconomics** *deals with the behavior of economic aggregates like national output, the price level, and the level of unemployment.* This volume is concerned primarily with microeconomics, but since one must know some macroeconomics to understand microeconomics, we include some macroeconomics as well. However, the economic problem cited in this section is too purely macroeconomic in nature to be taken up in detail here. For a more intensive discussion of this sort of problem, see the companion volume to this one, *Principles of Macroeconomics*.

THE PRODUCTIVITY SLOWDOWN AND THE COMPETITIVENESS OF U.S. GOODS

Labor productivity is defined as the amount of output that can be obtained per hour of labor. All nations are interested in increasing labor productivity, since it is intimately related to a nation's standard of living. Many factors, including new technologies like microelectronics and biotechnology, influence the rate of increase of labor productivity. Historically, labor productivity has increased relatively rapidly in the United States.

Figure 1.2

Changes in Price Level, United States, 1929-84 *The price level has increased steadily since the 1930s, and is now over eight times as high as it was in 1933.*

However, beginning in the late 1960s, U.S. labor productivity rose at a slower pace. At first, it was unclear whether this slowdown was only temporary, but during the 1970s the situation got worse, not better. Between 1977 and 1980, labor productivity in the United States actually declined. (In other words, less was produced per hour of labor in 1980 than in 1977!) During the early 1980s, productivity growth picked up, but whether it would reach its old level—and stay there—was by no means obvious.

Many observers regard this productivity slowdown as being a very ominous sign for the U.S. economy. Moreover, they worry too about the fact that labor productivity in the United States has been increasing less rapidly than in many other countries like Japan and West Germany. For this and other reasons, there are questions regarding the ability of American firms to compete with their foreign rivals in industries like autos and machine tools.

Our second example of an economic problem is: *What determines the rate of increase of labor productivity? Why has this productivity slowdown occurred in the United States? What measures can and should be adopted to cope with it?* Economics provides a considerable amount of information on this score. Not only does economics tell us a good deal about the broad factors influencing national productivity levels; in addition, it provides rules and principles that are useful in increasing the productivity and efficiency of individual firms (and government agencies).

GOVERNMENT REGULATION OF BUSINESS

The 100 largest manufacturing firms control about half of all manufacturing assets in the United States (and their share of total assets seems to have increased since World War II). In certain industries, like automobiles, the 4 largest firms have accounted for over 90 percent of the market (see Table 1.1). Nonetheless, although the large corporations obviously wield considerable power in their markets, the American economic system is built on the idea that firms should compete with one another. In particular, the producers of steel, automobiles, oil, toothpicks, and other goods are expected to set their prices independently and not to collude. Certain acts of Congress, often referred to as the antitrust laws, make it illegal for firms to get together and set the price of a product.

Our third example of an economic problem is: *Why is competition of this sort socially desirable?* More specifically, why should we be in favor of the antitrust laws? What reasons are there to believe that such laws will result in a more efficient economic system? (And what do we mean by "efficient"?) To a business executive, lawyer, government official, or judge, these questions are very important, since it is likely that at one time or another these people will be concerned with an antitrust case. But these issues also matter to every citizen, because they deal with the basic rules of the game for firms in our economy. Of course, one reason why Americans have traditionally favored competition over collusion, and relatively small firms over giant ones, is that they have mistrusted the concentration of economic power, and obviously, this mistrust was based on both political and economic considerations. But beyond this, you should know when competition generally benefits society, and when it does not.

One way that society has attempted to control the economic power of corporations that dominate an entire industry is through ***government regulation.*** Take the case of radio and TV. The Federal Communications Commission, a government agency, monitors the activities of broadcasting stations and networks to prevent misuse of the airwaves. Other regulatory commissions supervise the activities of the power companies, the telephone companies, and other industries where it has been felt that competition cannot be relied on to produce socially desirable results.

During the late 1970s and early 1980s, there was a notable movement in the United States toward deregulation. At first, the movement was confined largely to the airlines, but then it spread to railroads, trucking, oil, and other industries. In part, this movement reflected a widespread feeling that the regulatory commissions tended to be lax or, worse still, to be captured by the industries they were supposed to regulate. In addition, it was felt that many aspects of regulation have contributed to inefficiency, both in the regulated industries themselves and in other parts of the economy. Since regulated industries produce about 10 percent of national output, we all have a big stake in understanding how they operate and whether they should be regulated and if so, how. This is another aspect of the same general problem of how industries should be organized.

THE ELIMINATION OF POVERTY

As pointed out by Philip Wicksteed, a prominent twentieth-century British economist, "A man can be neither a saint, nor a lover, nor a poet, unless he

Table 1.1

MARKET SHARE OF FOUR LARGEST FIRMS, SELECTED MANUFACTURING PRODUCT MARKETS, UNITED STATES, 1977

Industry	Market share of four largest firms (percent)
Automobiles	93
Photographic equipment	72
Soap	59
Tires	70
Aircraft	59
Construction machinery	47
Blast furnaces and steel plants	45

Source: Statistical Abstract of the United States.

Table 1.2
PERCENTAGE DISTRIBUTION OF PEOPLE,
BY HOUSEHOLD MONTHLY CASH
INCOME, UNITED STATES, 1983

Money income (dollars)	Percent of all people
Under 300	4.7
300– 599	7.8
600– 899	8.0
900–1,199	8.2
1,200–1,599	11.4
1,600–1,999	10.7
2,000–2,999	22.1
3,000–3,999	13.1
4,000 and over	14.1
Total	100[a]

[a] Because of rounding errors, the figures do not sum to total.
Source: U.S. Bureau of the Census. The data pertain to the third quarter of the year.

has comparatively recently had something to eat." Although relatively few people in the United States lack food desperately, about 35 million American people, approximately 15 percent of the population of the United States, live in what is officially designated as *poverty.* These people have frequently been called invisible in a nation where the average yearly income per family is over $25,000; but the poor are invisible only to those who shut their eyes, since they exist in ghettos in the wealthiest American cities like New York, Chicago, and Los Angeles, as well as near Main Street in thousands of small towns. They can also be found in areas where industry has come and gone, as in the former coal-mining towns of Pennsylvania and West Virginia, and in areas where decades of farming have depleted the soil.

Table 1.2 shows the distribution of income in the United States in 1983. Clearly, there are very substantial differences among families in income level. You as a citizen and a human being need to understand the social mechanisms underlying the distribution of income, both in the United States and in other countries, and how reasonable and just they are. Our fourth economic problem is: *Why does poverty exist in the world today, and what can be done to abolish it?* To help the poor effectively, we must understand the causes of poverty.

Since poverty is intimately bound up with our racial problems and the decay of our cities, the success or failure of measures designed to eradicate poverty may also help us determine whether we can achieve a society where equality of opportunity is more than a slogan and where people do not have to escape to the suburbs to enjoy green space and fresh air. Nor does the economist's concern with poverty stop at our shoreline. One of the biggest problems of the world today is the plight of the poor countries of Asia, Africa, and Latin America—the so-called less developed countries. The industrialized countries of the world, like the United States, Western Europe, Japan, and the Soviet Union, are really just rich little islands surrounded by seas of poverty. Over half of the world's population lives in countries where per capita income is less than $3,000 per year. These countries lack equipment, technology, and education; sometimes (but by no means always) they also suffer from overpopulation. Economists have devoted considerable attention to the problems of the less developed countries, and to developing techniques to assist them.

What Is Economics?

HUMAN WANTS AND RESOURCES

Now that we have looked at a number of specific economic problems, we must provide a definition of economics, as well as a description of the basic questions regarding any economic system that are of particular interest to economists. According to one standard definition, *economics is concerned with the way resources are allocated among alternative uses to satisfy human wants.* This definition is fine, but it does not mean much unless we define what is meant by *human wants* and by *resources.* What do these terms mean?

Human wants are the things, services, goods, and circumstances that people desire. Wants vary greatly among individuals and over time for the

Land

Labor

same individual. Some people like sports, others like books; some want to travel, others want to putter in the yard. An individual's desire for a particular good during a particular period of time is not infinite, but, in the aggregate, human wants seem to be insatiable. Besides the basic desires for food, shelter, and clothing, which must be fulfilled to some extent if the human organism is to maintain its existence, wants stem from cultural factors. For example, society, often helped along by advertising and other devices to modify tastes, promotes certain images of "the good life," which frequently entails owning an expensive car and living in a $150,000 split-level house in the suburbs.

Resources are the things or services used to produce goods which then can be used to satisfy wants. *Economic resources* are scarce, while *free resources,* such as air, are so abundant that they can be obtained without charge. The test of whether a resource is an economic resource or a free resource is price: economic resources command a nonzero price, but free resources do not. The number of free resources is actually quite limited. For instance, although the earth contains a huge amount of water, it is not a free resource to the typical urban or suburban home owner, who must pay a local water authority for providing and maintaining his or her water supply. In a world where all resources were free, there would be no economic problem, since all wants could be satisfied.

Economic resources can be classified into three categories, each of which is described below:

1. Land. A shorthand expression for natural resources, land includes minerals as well as plots of ground. Clearly, land is an important and valuable resource in both agriculture and industry. Think of the fertile soil of Iowa or Kansas, from which are obtained such abundant crops. Or consider Manhattan island, which supports the skyscrapers, shops, and theaters in the heart of New York. In addition, land is an important part of our environment, and it provides enjoyment above and beyond its contribution to agricultual and industrial output.

2. Labor. Human efforts, both physical and mental, are included in the category of labor. Thus, when you study for a final examination or make out an income tax return, this is as much labor as if you were to dig a ditch. In 1985, over 100 million people were employed (or looking for work) in the United States. This vast labor supply is, of course, an extremely important resource, without which our nation could not maintain its current output level.

3. Capital. Buildings, equipment, inventories, and other nonhuman producible resources that contribute to the production, marketing, and distribution of goods and services all fall within the economist's definition of capital. Examples are machine tools and warehouses; but not all types of capital are big or bulky: for example, a hand calculator, or a pencil for that matter, is a type of capital. American workers have an enormous amount of capital to work with. Think of the oil refineries in New Jersey and Philadelphia, the blast furnaces and open hearths in Pittsburgh and Cleveland, the aircraft plants in California and Georgia, and the host of additional types of capital we have and use in this country. Without this capital, the nation's output level would be a great deal less than it is.

Capital

TECHNOLOGY AND CHOICE

As pointed out above, economics is concerned with the way resources are allocated among alternative uses to satisfy human wants. An important determinant of the extent to which human wants can be satisfied from the amount of resources at hand is technology. *Technology* is society's pool of knowledge concerning the industrial arts. It includes the knowledge of engineers, scientists, craftsmen, managers, and others concerning how goods and services can be produced. For example, it includes the best existing knowledge regarding the ways in which an automobile plant or a synthetic rubber plant should be designed and operated. The level of technology sets limits on the amount and types of goods and services that can be derived from a given amount of resources.

To see this, suppose that engineers and craftsmen do not know how an automobile can be produced with less than 500 hours of labor being used in its manufacture. Clearly, this sets limits on the number of automobiles that can be produced with the available labor force. Or suppose that scientists and engineers do not know how to produce a ton of synthetic rubber with less than a certain amount of capital being used in its manufacture. This sets limits on the amount of synthetic rubber that can be produced with the available quantity of capital.

Given the existing technology, the fact that resources are scarce means that only a limited amount of goods and services can be produced from them. In other words, the capacity to produce goods and services is limited — *far more limited than human wants*. Thus there arises the necessity for *choice.* Somehow or other, a choice must be made as to how the available resources will be used (or if they will be used at all). And somehow or other a choice must be made as to how the output produced from these resources will be distributed among the population.

Economics is concerned with how such choices are made. Economists have spent a great deal of time, energy, and talent trying to determine how such choices *are* made in various circumstances, and how they *should* be made. Indeed, as we shall see in the next section, the basic questions that economics deals with are problems of choice of this sort. Note that these problems of choice go beyond the problems of particular individuals in choosing how to allocate their resources; they are problems of social choice.

CENTRAL QUESTIONS IN ECONOMICS

Basic Idea #1: Any economic system must determine what (and how much) is produced, how it is produced, how the output is distributed among the members of society, and what provision is made for growth of per capita income. To understand how a country's economy really works, one must look carefully at how these vital decisions are made.

Economists are particularly concerned with four basic questions regarding the working of any economic system—ours or any other. These questions are: (1) What determines what (and how much) is produced? (2) What determines how it is produced? (3) What determines how the society's output is distributed among the members? (4) What determines the rate at which the society's per capita income will grow? These questions lie at the core of economics, because they are directed at the most fundamental characteristics of economic systems. And as stressed in the previous section, they are problems of choice.

To illustrate the nature and basic importance of these questions, suppose that, because of war or natural catastrophe, your town is isolated from the adjoining territory. No longer is it possible for the town's inhabitants to leave, or for people or goods to enter. (Lest you regard this as fanciful, it is perhaps worthwhile to note that Leningrad was under siege in World War II for over two years.) In this situation, you and your fellow townspeople must somehow resolve each of these questions. You must decide what goods and services will be produced, how each will be produced, who will receive what, and how much provision there will be for increased output in the future.

In a situation of this sort, your very survival will depend on how effectively you answer these questions. If a decision is made to produce too much clothing and too little food, some of the townspeople may starve. If a decision is made to produce wheat from soil that is inappropriate for wheat, but excellent for potatoes, much the same result may occur. If a decision is made to allot practically all of the town's output to friends and political cronies of the mayor, those who oppose him may have a very rough time. And if a decision is made to eat, drink, and be merry today, and not to worry about tomorrow, life may be very meager in the days ahead.

Because we are considering a relatively small and isolated population, the importance of these questions may seem more obvious than in a huge country like the United States, which is constantly communicating, trading, and interacting with the rest of the world. But the truth is that these questions are every bit as important to the United States as to the isolated town. And, for this reason, it is important that we understand how these decisions are made, and whether they are being made effectively. Just as in the hypothetical case of the isolated town, your survival depends on these decisions—but in the United States the situation isn't hypothetical!

Test Yourself

1. Explain why each of the following resources is or is not capital: (a) iron ore in Minnesota that is still in the ground; (b) a Boeing 747 airplane operated by TWA Airlines; (c) a Chrysler dealer's inventory of unsold cars; (d) a telephone used by the University of Oklahoma.

2. Alfred Marshall, the great British economist, defined economics as follows: "Economics is a study of men as they live and move and think in the ordinary business of life. But it concerns itself chiefly with those motives which affect, most powerfully and most steadily, man's conduct *in the business part of life*. . . . [The] steadiest motive to ordinary business work is the desire for the pay which is the material reward of work."* Does this definition encompass all of the examples of economic analysis and problems contained so far in this chapter?

* A. Marshall, *Principles of Economics*, London: Macmillan, 1920.

3. C. J. Blank and E. Rosinski of Mobil Research and Development Corporation invented a new type of catalyst which enables oil refiners to save an estimated 200 million barrels of crude oil per year. Has this invention altered the technology of the oil refining industry? Has it changed the amount of goods and services that can be derived from a given amount of resources? Were resources used to obtain this invention? If so, what types of resources were used?

4. We described four basic questions that any economic system must answer. Which of these questions is involved in each of the following specific problems: (a) Should the United States use natural gas to produce ammonia? (b) Should taxes on the poor be lower? (c) Should American consumers save more? (d) Should more of our nation's industry be used to produce food?

Opportunity Cost: A Fundamental Concept

In previous sections, we have emphasized that economics is concerned with the way resources are allocated among alternative uses to satisfy human wants. To help determine how resources should be allocated, economists often use the concept of **opportunity cost.** We turn now to an introductory discussion of this concept, which should help to acquaint you with how it is used.

Since a specific case is more interesting than abstract discussion, let's return to the case of the town that is isolated from the adjoining territory, because of a war or natural catastrophe. Suppose that you are a member of the town council that is organized to determine how the town's resources should be utilized. To keep things simple, suppose that only two goods—food and clothing—can be produced. (This is an innocuous assumption that allows us to strip the problem to its essentials.) You must somehow figure out how much of each good should be produced. How can you go about solving this problem?

Clearly, the first step toward a solution is to list the various resources contained within the town. Using the technology available to the townspeople, each of these resources can be used to produce either food or clothing. Some of these resources are much more effective at producing one good than the other. For example, a tailor probably is better able to produce clothing than to produce food. But nonetheless most resources can be adapted to produce either good. For example, the tailor can be put to work on a farm, even though he may not be very good at farming.

After listing the various available resources and having determined how effective each is at producing food or clothing, the next step is to see how much food the town could produce per year, if it produced nothing but food, and how much clothing it could produce per year, if it produced nothing but clothing. Also, you should determine, if various amounts of food are produced per year, the maximum amount of clothing that the town can produce per year. For example, if the town produces 100 tons of food per year, what is the maximum amount of clothing it can produce per year? If the town produces 200 tons of food per year, what is the maximum amount of clothing it can produce per year? And so on.

Having carried out this step, suppose that the results are as shown in Table 1.3. According to this table, the town can produce (at most) 200 tons of clothing per year if it produces nothing but clothing (possibility A). Or it can produce (at most) 400 tons of food per year if it produces nothing but food (possibility E). Other possible combinations (labeled B, C, and D) of food output and clothing output are specified in Table 1.3.

The data in Table 1.3 put in bold relief the basic problem of choice facing you and the other members of the town council. Because the town's resources are limited, the town can only produce limited amounts of each good. There is no way, for example, that the town can produce 200 tons of clothing per year and 200 tons of food per year. This is beyond the capacity of the town's resources. If the town wants to produce 200 tons of clothing, it can produce no food—which is hardly a pleasant prospect. And if the town wants to produce 200 tons of food, it can produce 150 (not 200) tons of clothing per year. Table 1.3 shows what combinations of food and clothing outputs are attainable.

Table 1.3

COMBINATIONS OF OUTPUT OF FOOD AND CLOTHING THAT THE TOWN CAN PRODUCE PER YEAR

Possibility	Amount of food produced per year (tons)	Amount of clothing produced per year (tons)
A	0	200
B	100	180
C	200	150
D	300	100
E	400	0

Basic Idea #2: *The cost of using resources in a particular way is the value of what these resources could have produced if they had been used in the best alternative way. Thus the cost of producing a particular commodity is the value of what could have been produced instead. In other words, it is the value of what had to be given up to produce this commodity.*

MORE FOOD MEANS LESS CLOTHING

A very important fact illustrated by Table 1.3 is that, whenever the town increases its production of one good, it must cut back its production of the other good. For example, if the town increases its production of food from 100 to 200 tons per year, it must cut back its production of clothing from 180 to 150 tons per year. Thus *the cost to the town of increasing its food output from 100 to 200 tons per year is that it must reduce its clothing output from 180 to 150 tons per year.*

Economists refer to this cost as **opportunity cost** (or **alternative cost**); it is one of the most fundamental concepts in economics. *The opportunity cost of using resources in a certain way is the value of what these resources could have produced if they had been used in the best alternative way.* In this case, the opportunity cost of the extra 100 tons of food per year is the 30 tons of clothing per year that must be forgone. This is what the town must give up in order to get the extra 100 tons of food.

Why is opportunity cost so important? Because for you and the other members of the town council to determine which combination of food and clothing is best, you should compare the value of increases in food output with the opportunity costs of such increases. For example, suppose that the town council is considering whether or not to increase food output from 100 to 200 tons per year. To decide this question, the council should compare the value of the extra 100 tons of food with the opportunity cost of the extra food (which is the 30 tons of clothing that must be given up). If the town council feels that the extra 100 tons of food are worth more to the town's welfare than the 30 tons of clothing that are given up, the extra food should be produced. Otherwise it should not be produced.

Parks and Opportunity Costs. As we have just seen, the concept of opportunity cost can be used to help solve the hypothetical problem of the town council described above. Used in a similar way, the concept of opportunity cost can throw significant light on many important real problems as well. For example, suppose that a bill is presented to Congress to set aside certain wilderness areas as national parks. At first glance, it may appear that such a step entails no cost to society, since the land is not being utilized and the resources required to designate the areas as national parks are trivial. But using the concept of opportunity cost, it is clear that this step may have very substantial costs to society. For instance, if these lands are made part of the national parks system, the minerals, timber, and other natural resources contained within the areas cannot be extracted nor can the lands be used as sites for factories or processing plants. As pointed out above, the opportunity cost of using resources in one way is the value of what these resources could have produced had they been used in the best alternative way. Suppose that if these lands are not turned into national parks, their most valuable alternative use is for development of copper mines which would produce benefits amounting to $25 million per year to the society. Then the actual cost to society of using these lands as parks is $25 million per year, since this is the amount that society is giving up when it uses them in this way (rather than selecting the most valuable alternative). Thus, whether these lands should be used as parks depends on whether the society believes that it is worth $25 million or more to do so.

The concept of opportunity cost is very important in analyzing personal, managerial, and judicial issues, as well as questions involving government policy. Example 1.1 shows how this concept can be applied to determine the true costs to a student of going to college. Example 1.2 indicates how this concept was used in a legal case to assess damages. Like the examples in subsequent chapters, they should be studied carefully.

The Impact of Economics on Society

In previous sections, we described some of the questions that concern economists. Now we must consider how much influence economics has had. The answer is that economics has influenced generations of statesmen, philosophers, and ordinary citizens, and has played a significant role in shaping our society today.

Example 1.1   How Much Does It Cost to Go to College?

According to the College Board, the average college student incurred the following annual costs in 1984:

	Private College (dollars)	Public College
Tuition and fees	5,016	1,126
Meals, room, books, travel, and other expenses	4,006	3,755
Total	9,022	4,881

(a) Is $9,022 the total cost to the student of a year at a private college? (*Hint:* Are there opportunity costs?) (b) John Martin is a 40-year-old executive; James Miller is an 18-year-old with no job experience. They are both full-time students. Although both must pay the same costs (given above), the true cost to Martin is more than the true cost to Miller. Why? (c) Is $1,126 the total cost to the typical public college of a student's going there for a year? (d) Is $9,022 the total cost to society of a student's going to a private college for a year?

SOLUTION

(a) No, the true cost of going to college is considerably in excess of the out-of-pocket expenses because one can obtain wages by working rather than attending classes and studying. In other words, the time spent in school has opportunity costs, since it could be devoted to a job rather than to education. For example, if the student could earn $8,000 during a school year if he or she worked rather than going to college, the true total annual cost of a college education is $9,022 + $8,000 = $17,022. (b) Martin can earn much more than Miller if, rather than going to school, he were to work. Thus the opportunity cost of his time spent in school is greater than for Miller. (c) No. Tuition and fees cover only part of the public college's costs; the rest are covered by government support, alumni contributions, and other payments. (d) No. The cost to society equals the value to society of the resources used to teach, house, feed, and maintain the student, as well as the opportunity cost to society of his or her time. Although it is not easy to pin down all of the social costs, they clearly do not equal $9,022.

ADAM SMITH, FATHER OF MODERN ECONOMICS

To illustrate the importance of economic ideas, let's consider some of the precepts of Adam Smith (1723–90), the man who is often called the father of modern economics. Much of his masterpiece *The Wealth of Nations*[1] seems trite today, because it has been absorbed so thoroughly into modern thought, but it was not trite when it was written. On the contrary, Smith's ideas were revolutionary. *He was among the first to describe how a free, competitive economy can function—without central planning or government interference—to allocate resources efficiently. He recognized the virtues of the "invisible hand" that leads the private interest of firms and individuals toward socially desirable ends, and he was properly suspicious of firms that are sheltered from competition, since he recognized the potentially undesirable effects on resource allocation.*

In addition, Smith—with the dire poverty of his times staring him in the face—was interested in the forces that determined the evolution of the economy—that is, the forces determining the rate of growth of average income per person. Although Smith did not approve of avarice, he felt that saving was good because it enabled society to invest in machinery and other forms of capital. Accumulating more and more capital would, according to Smith, allow output to grow. In addition, he emphasized the importance of increased specialization and division of labor in bringing about economic progress. By specializing, people can concentrate on the tasks they do best, with the result that society's total output is raised.

All in all, Smith's views were relatively optimistic, in keeping with the intellectual climate of his time—the era of Voltaire, Diderot, Franklin, and Jefferson, the age of the Enlightenment, when men believed so strongly in rationality. Leave markets alone, said Smith, and beware of firms with too much economic power and government meddling. If this is done, there is no reason why considerable economic progress cannot be achieved. Smith's work has been modified and extended in a variety of ways in the past 200 years. Some of his ideas have been challenged and, in some cases, discarded. But his influence on modern society has been enormous.

THE INFLUENCE OF ECONOMICS TODAY

Turning from Adam Smith's day to the present, economics continues to have an enormous influence over the shape of our society. Economics, and economists, play an extremely important part in the formulation of public policy. Skim through the articles in a daily newspaper. Chances are that you will find a report of an economist testifying before Congress, perhaps on the costs and benefits of a program to reduce unemployment among black teenagers in the Bedford-Stuyvesant area of New York City, or on the steps to be taken to make American goods more competitive with those of Japan or West Germany. Still another economist may crop up on the editorial page, discussing the pros and cons of various proposed ways to reduce the federal deficit.

Economics and economists play a key role at the highest levels of our government. The president, whether a Democrat or a Republican, relies

---

[1] Adam Smith, *The Wealth of Nations,* New York: Modern Library, 1937. Originally published in 1776.

ADAM SMITH ON THE "INVISIBLE HAND"

Adam Smith (1723–90) lived during the Industrial Revolution and was one of the first scholars to understand many of the central mechanisms of a free, or unplanned, economy. Much of his life was spent as professor of moral philosophy at the University of Glasgow in Scotland. In 1759, he published *The Theory of Moral Sentiments,* which established him as one of Britain's foremost philosophers, but this was not the book for which he is famous today. His masterpiece, published in 1776 (while the American colonists were brewing rebellion), was *The Wealth of Nations,* a long encyclopedic book 12 years in the writing. It was not an instant success, but the laurels it eventually won undoubtedly compensated for its early neglect.

One of Smith's central contentions was that firms and individuals, by pursuing their own objectives, often will promote the general welfare. In a famous passage, he stated that:

"It is only for the sake of profit that any man employs [his] capital in the support of industry, and he will always, therefore, endeavor to employ it in the support of that industry of which the produce is likely to be of greatest value, or to exchange the greatest quantity either of money or of other goods. But the annual revenue of every society is always precisely equal to the exchangeable value of the whole annual produce of its industry, or rather is precisely the same thing with that exchangeable value. As every individual, therefore, endeavors as much as he can both to employ his capital in the support of domestic industry, and so to direct that industry that its produce may be of the greatest value, every individual necessarily labors to render the annual revenue of the society as great as he can: He generally, indeed, neither intends to promote the public interest, nor knows how much he is promoting it. . . . He intends only his own security; and by directing that industry in such a manner as its produce may be of the greatest value, he intends only his own gain, and *he is in this, as in many other cases, led by an invisible hand to promote an end which was no part of his intention.* Nor is it always the worse for the society that it was no part of it. *By pursuing his own interest he frequently promotes that of the society more effectually than when he really intends to promote it.* I have never known much good done by those who affected to trade for the public good. It is an affectation, indeed, not very common among merchants, and very few words need be employed in dissuading them from it. . . ."

Adam Smith, *The Wealth of Nations,* London: George Routledge, 1900, p. 345. Originally published in 1776. (Italics added.)

heavily on his economic advisers in making the decisions that help to shape the future of the country. In Congress, too, economics plays a major role. Economists are frequent witnesses before congressional committees, staff members for the committees, and advisers to individual congressmen and senators. Many congressional committees focus largely on economic matters. For example, in 1985, many congressmen spent large chunks of their time wrestling with budgetary and tax questions.

Perhaps the most dramatic evidence of the importance of economics in the formulation of public policy is provided during presidential elections, when each candidate—with his or her own cadre of economic advisers supplying ideas and reports—stakes out a position on the major economic issues of the day. This position can be of crucial importance in determining victory or defeat, and you, the citizen, must know some economics to understand whether a candidate is talking sense or nonsense (or merely evading an issue). For example, if a candidate promises to increase government expenditures, lower taxes, and reduce the federal deficit, you can be pretty certain that he is talking through his hat. This may not be obvious to you now, but it should be later on.

Also, economics and economists play an extremely important role in private decision making. Their role in the decision-making process in business firms is particularly great, since many of the nation's larger corporations hire professional economists to forecast their sales, reduce their costs, increase their efficiency, negotiate with labor and government, and carry out a host of other tasks. Judging from the fancy salaries business economists are paid, the firms seem to think they can deliver the goods; and in fact, the available evidence seems to indicate that they do provide important guidance to firms in many areas of their operations.

POSITIVE ECONOMICS VERSUS NORMATIVE ECONOMICS

Before concluding this chapter, it is essential that we recognize the distinction between positive economics and normative economics. *Positive economics contains descriptive statements, propositions, and predictions about the world.* For instance, an economic theory may predict that the price of copper will increase by $.01 a pound if income per person in the United States rises by 10 percent; this is positive economics. Positive economics tells us only what will happen under certain circumstances. It says nothing about whether the results are good or bad—or about what we should do. *Normative economics,* on the other hand, *makes statements about what ought to be, or about what a person, organization, or nation ought to do.* For instance, a theory might say that Chile should introduce new technology more quickly in many of its copper mines; this is normative economics.

Clearly, positive economics and normative economics must be treated differently. Positive economics is science in the ordinary sense of the word. Propositions in positive economics can be tested by an appeal to the facts. In a nonexperimental science like economics, it is sometimes difficult to get the facts you need to test particular propositions. For example, if income per person in the United States does not rise by 10 percent, it may be difficult to tell what the effect of such an increase would be on the price of copper. Moreover, even if per capita income does increase by this amount, it may be difficult to separate the effect of the increase in income per person on the price of copper from the effect of other factors. But nonetheless, we can, in principle, test propositions in positive economics by an appeal to the facts.

In normative economics, however, this is not the case. *In normative economics, the results you get depend on your values or preferences.* For example, if you believe that reducing unemployment is more important than maintaining the purchasing power of the dollar, you will get one answer to certain questions; whereas if you believe that maintaining the purchasing power of the dollar is more important than reducing unem-

---

Example 1.2   The Assessment of Damages

In a well-known legal case, the United States was sued by O'Brien Bros., Inc., the owner of a Brooklyn-bound barge that was sunk by a U.S. Navy tug that collided with the barge. O'Brien Bros. received damages stemming from the collision. The calculation of the damages was turned over to a commissioner, who found them to be as follows:

	dollars
Costs of raising the wreck	7,732.21
Repairs	43,245.22
Compensation for loss of earnings from the barge during the time it was unavailable for work	6,620.25
Miscellaneous costs	3,423.91
Total	61,021.59

(a) Why should O'Brien Bros. be compensated for the loss of earnings? It did not pay out $6,620.25 to anyone. Why should it receive this amount in damages? (b) The United States appealed the decision. Government attorneys introduced evidence that a similar barge could have been built new for $33,000. Does this mean that the damages should have been $33,000? (c) Suppose that O'Brien Bros. could have bought a similar barge for $25,000 and that its forgone earnings during the time elapsing from the sinking of the old barge to the availability of the new barge was $5,000. If the sunk barge would cause no problems either to O'Brien Bros. or anyone else, should it have been raised and repaired? (d) Suppose that O'Brien Bros. could have obtained $8,500 for the wreck (for scrap metal, salvageable parts, and so forth) if it was raised? Should it have been raised?

SOLUTION

(a) If the barge had not been sunk, O'Brien Bros. would have earned this amount. It is the opportunity cost of the barge's being sunk. (b) No. The barge that was sunk may have been worth less than $33,000, since it was not new. On the other hand, the figure of $33,000 takes no account of lost earnings in the time interval until the barge was replaced. (c) No. The cost of raising and repairing it exceeded the cost of buying a similar barge. (d) Yes, because the amount that could be obtained for the wreck would exceed the cost of raising it.*

---

*For further description of this case, see "O'Brien Bros., Inc. v. The Helen B. Moran et al." in R. Byrns and G. Stone, Jr., *An Economics Casebook: Applications from the Law,* Santa Monica: Goodyear, 1980.

ployment, you are likely to get a different answer to the same questions. This is not at all strange. After all, if people desire different things (which is another way of saying that they have different values), they may well make different decisions and advocate different policies. It would be strange if they did not.

This book will spend a lot of time on the principles of positive economics—the principles and propositions concerning the workings of the economic system about which practically all economists tend to agree. Normative economics will also be treated, since we must discuss questions of policy—and all policy discussions involve individual preferences, not solely hard facts. In these discussions, we shall try to indicate how the conclusions depend on one's values. Then you can let your own values be your guide. The purpose of this book is not to convert you to a particular set of values. It is to teach you how to obtain better solutions to economic problems, whatever set of values you may have.

Test Yourself

1. In a famous passage from *The Wealth of Nations,* Adam Smith said that: "It is the maxim of every prudent master of a family, never to make at home what it will cost him more to make than to buy." Suppose that Mrs. Harris spends an hour preparing a meal. She is a psychologist in private practice and can obtain $25 per hour for her services. What is the cost to the Harris family of her preparing this meal? Explain.

2. "Resources are scarce and once a decision is made to use them for one purpose, they are no longer available for another. One opportunity cost of reading [an] . . . article, for example, is not simultaneously being able to read [another article]."* Explain, and relate to the question of how a student should allocate his time among various course assignments.

3. Suppose that it costs a college student $1,000 per year more for room and board than if he or she works (and lives at home). If this assumption is correct, why is this amount, rather than the full cost of room and board, the proper amount to use in Example 1.1?

4. On the basis of positive economics alone, which of the following statements can be determined to be true or false? (a) The tax cut of 1975 reduced unemployment in the United States by 1 percent. (b) The tax cut was timed improperly. (c) The tax cut was a less equitable way of reducing unemployment than a program whereby the unemployed were hired by the government to perform important social functions.

* D. Eastburn, "Economic Man in Conflict with His Economic Self," *New York Times Magazine,* July 26, 1970.

Summary

1. According to one standard definition, economics is concerned with the way resources are allocated among alternative uses to satisfy human wants. A resource is a thing or service used to produce goods (or services) which can satisfy wants. Not all resources are scarce. Free resources, such as air, are so abundant that they can be obtained without charge.

2. Those resources that are scarce are called economic resources. The test of whether a resource is an economic resource or a free resource is price: economic resources command a nonzero price but free resources do not. Economists often classify economic resources into three categories: land, labor, and capital.

3. Since economic resources are scarce, only a limited amount of goods and services can be produced from them, and there arises the necessity for choice. For example, if an isolated town has a certain amount of resources, it must choose how much of each good it will produce from these resources. If it increases the amount produced of one good, it must reduce the amount produced of another good.

4. The opportunity cost (or alternative cost) of using a resource to increase the production of one good is the value of what the resource could have produced had it been used in the best alternative way. To illustrate the use of the concept of opportunity cost, which is one of the most important in economics, we discussed the cases of public parks and a college education.

5. Economists are particularly concerned with four basic questions regarding the working of any economic system, ours or any other. These questions are (1) What determines what (and how much) is produced? (2) What determines how it is produced? (3) What determines how the society's output is distributed among the members? (4) What determines the rate at which the society's per capita income will grow?

6. Economists often distinguish between positive economics and normative economics. Positive economics contains descriptive statements, propositions, and predictions about the world; whereas normative economics contains statements about what ought to be, or about what a person, organization, or nation ought to do.

7. In normative economics, the results you get depend on your basic values and preferences; in positive economics, the results are testable, at least in principle, by an appeal to the facts.

Concepts for Review

Unemployment	Resources	Technology
Inflation	Economic resources	Choice
Labor productivity	Free resources	Opportunity cost
Government regulation	Land	Alternative cost
Poverty	Labor	Positive economics
Economics	Capital	Normative economics
Human wants		

CHAPTER 2

Economic Models and Capitalism, American-Style

The United States, like all other nations, is beset by many economic problems. As pointed out in Chapter 1, the 1970s and early 1980s were a period of bewildering inflation and excessive unemployment. We have also been confronted by serious productivity and environmental problems. Yet, despite these problems, the American economy is among the most prosperous in the world. The average American family has plenty of food, clothing, housing, appliances, and luxuries of many kinds, and the average American worker is well educated and well trained. The tremendous strength and vitality of the American economy should be recognized, as well as its shortcomings. Nothing is gained by overlooking either the successes or the faults of our system.

As a first step toward understanding why we are so well-off in some respects and so lacking in others, we need to understand how our economy works. Of course, this is a big task. Indeed, you could say that this whole book is devoted to discussing this subject. So we will not try to present a detailed picture of the operation of the American economy at this point. All we will do now is give a preliminary sketch, a basic blueprint of what an economic system must do and how our mixed capitalistic system works.

First, however, we must provide a brief description of the role of model building in economics, since this will introduce you to the methods used by economists. Without such an introduction to economic methodology, it would be difficult, if not impossible, for you to understand fully much of the material that follows in this and succeeding chapters. Only after these preliminary matters are covered will we be able to turn to a discussion of the tasks of an economic system and the way our economy functions.

The Methodology of Economics

MODEL BUILDING IN ECONOMICS

Like other types of scientific analysis, economics is based on the formulation of **models**. *A model is a theory. It is composed of a number of assumptions from which conclusions—or predictions—are deduced.* An astronomer who wants to formulate a model of the solar system might represent each planet by a point in space and assume that each would change position in accord with certain mathematical equations. Based on this model, the astronomer might predict when an eclipse would occur, or estimate the probability of a planetary collision. The economist proceeds along similar lines when he sets forth a model of economic behavior.

There are several important points to be noted concerning models:

1. To be useful, a model must simplify the real situation. The assumptions made by a model need not be exact replicas of reality. If they were, the model would be too complicated to use. The basic reason for using a model is that the real world is so complex that masses of detail often obscure underlying patterns. The economist faces the familiar problem of seeing the forest as distinct from just the trees. Other scientists must do the same; physicists work with simplified models of atoms, just as economists work with simplified models of markets. However, this does not mean that *all* models are good or useful. A model may be so oversimplified and distorted that it is utterly useless. The trick is to construct a model so that irrelevant and unimportant considerations and variables are neglected, but the major factors—those that seriously affect the phenomena the model is designed to predict—are included.

2. The purpose of a model is to make predictions about the real world; and in many respects the most important test of a model is how well it predicts. In this sense, a model that predicts the price of copper within plus or minus $.01 a pound is better than a model that predicts it within plus or minus $.02 a pound. Of course, this does not mean that a model is useless if it cannot predict very accurately. We do not always need a very accurate prediction. For example, a road map is a model that can be used to make predictions about the route a driver should take to get to a particular destination. Sometimes, a very crude map is good enough to get you where you want to go, but such a map would not, for instance, serve the hiker who needs to know the characteristics of the terrain through which he plans to walk. How detailed a map you need depends on where you are going and how you want to get there.

3. A person who wants to predict the outcome of a particular event will be forced to use the model that predicts best, even if this model does not predict very well. The choice is not between a model and no model; it is between one model and another. After all, a person who must make a forecast will use the most accurate device available—and any such device is a model of some sort. Consequently, when economists make simplifying assumptions and derive conclusions that are only approximately true, it is somewhat beside the point to complain that the assumptions are simpler than reality or that the predictions are not always accurate. This may be true, but if the predictions based on the economists' model are better than those obtained on the basis of other models, their model must, and will, be used until something better comes along. Thus, if a model can predict the price of

Figure 2.1
Relationship between Annual Clothing Expenditures and Annual Household Income *Each family is represented by a dot. The line shows the average relationship. The line does not fit all families exactly, since all the points do not fall on it. The line does, however, show average clothing expenditure for each income level.*

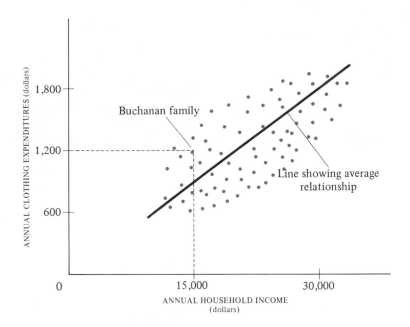

copper to within plus or minus $.01 per pound, and no other model can do better, this model will be used even if those interested in the predictions bewail the model's limitations and wish it could be improved.

ECONOMIC MEASUREMENT

To utilize and test their models, economists need facts of many sorts. For example, suppose that an economist constructs a model which predicts that a household's annual clothing expenditure tends to increase by $60 when its income increases by $1,000. To see whether this model is correct, he must gather data concerning the incomes and clothing expenditures of a large number of households and study the relationship between them. Suppose that the relationship he finds is as shown in Figure 2.1. The line represents an average relationship between household income and household consumption expenditure. Judging by Figure 2.1, his model is reasonably accurate, at least for households with incomes between $15,000 and $30,000 per year.[1]

Measurements like those in Figure 2.1 enable economists to *quantify* their models; in other words, they enable them to construct models that predict *how much* effect one variable has on another. If economists did not quantify their models, they (and their models) would be much less useful. For example, the economist in the previous paragraph might have been content with a model that predicts that higher household income results in higher household clothing expenditures; but this model would not have been interesting or useful, since you do not need an economist to tell you that. A more valuable model is one that is quantitative, that predicts how much clothing expenditure will increase if household income rises by a certain amount. This is the sort of model that economists usually try to construct.

[1] It is worth noting that, although it is useful to see how well a model would have fit the historical facts, this is no substitute for seeing how well it will predict the future. As a distinguished mentor of mine once observed, "It's a darned poor person who can't predict the past."

Graphs and Relationships

To conclude our brief discussion of economic methodology, we must describe the construction and interpretation of graphs, such as Figure 2.1, which economists use to present data and relationships. Such graphs are used repeatedly throughout this book, and it is essential that the following three points be understood:

1. A graph has a horizontal axis and a vertical axis, each of which has a scale of numerical values. For example, in Figure 2.1, the horizontal axis shows a household's annual income, and the vertical axis shows the annual amount spent by the household on clothing. The intersection of the two axes is called the origin and is the point where both the variable measured along the horizontal axis and the variable measured along the vertical axis are zero. In Figure 2.1, the origin is at the lower lefthand corner of the figure, labeled "0."

2. To show the relationship between two variables, one can plot the value of one variable against the value of the other variable. Thus, in Figure 2.1, each family is represented by a dot. For example, the dot for the Buchanan family is in the position shown in Figure 2.1 because its income was $15,000 and its clothing expenditure was $1,200. Clearly, the line showing the average relationship does not fit all the families exactly, since all the points do not fall on the line. This line does, however, give the average clothing expenditure for each level of income: it is an average relationship.

3. The relationship between two variables is *direct* if, as in Figure 2.1, the line of average relationship is upward sloping. In other words, if the variable measured along the vertical axis tends to increase (decrease) in response to increases (decreases) in the variable measured along the horizontal axis, the relationship is direct. On the other hand, if the line of average relationship is downward sloping, as in Figure 2.2, the relationship is *inverse.* In other words, if the variable measured along the vertical axis tends to decrease (increase) in response to increases (decreases) in the variable measured along the horizontal axis, the relationship is inverse.

To illustrate how one can graph a relationship between two variables,

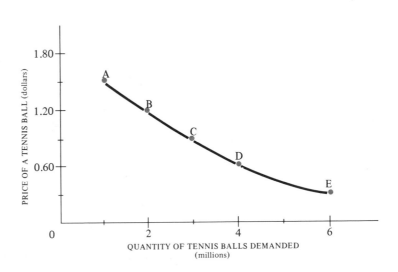

Figure 2.2

Relationship between Quantity Demanded and Price of Tennis Balls (as shown in Table 2.1)

Table 2.1

QUANTITY OF TENNIS BALLS DEMANDED
IN A PARTICULAR MARKET AT VARIOUS
PRICES

Price of a tennis ball (dollars)	Quantity of tennis balls demanded (millions)
1.50	1
1.20	2
0.90	3
0.60	4
0.30	6

consider Table 2.1, which shows the amount of tennis balls demanded in a particular market at various prices. Putting price on the vertical axis and quantity demanded on the horizontal axis, one can plot each combination of price and quantity in this table as a point on a graph; and that is precisely what has been done in Figure 2.2 (points *A* to *E*).

The Tasks of an Economic System

Having discussed the nature and quantification of economic models, we now can turn to the primary purpose of this chapter, which is to provide a preliminary sketch of what an economic system must do and how our mixed capitalistic system works. In this section, we describe what an economic system—*ours or any other*—must do. Basically, as we saw in Chapter 1, there are four tasks that any economic system must perform:

1. An economic system must determine the level and composition of society's output. That is, it must answer questions like: To what extent should society's resources be used to produce new aircraft carriers and missiles? To what extent should they be used to produce sewage plants to reduce water pollution? To what extent should they be used to produce swimming pools for the rich? To what extent should they be used to produce low-cost housing for the poor? Pause for a moment to think about how important—and how vast—this function is. Most people simply take for granted that somehow it is decided what we as a society are going to produce, and far too few people really think about the social mechanisms that determine the answers to such questions.

2. An economic system must determine how each good and service is to be produced. Given existing technology, a society's resources can be used in various ways. Should the skilled labor in Birmingham, Alabama, be used to produce cotton or steel? Should a particular machine tool be used to produce aircraft or automobiles? The way questions of this sort are answered will determine the way each good and service is produced. In other words, it will determine which resources are used to produce which goods and services. If this function is performed badly, society's resources are put to the wrong uses, resulting in less output than if this function is performed well.

3. An economic system must determine how the goods and services that are produced are to be distributed among the members of society. In other words, how much of each type of good and service should each person receive? Should there be a considerable amount of income inequality, the rich receiving much more than the poor? Or should incomes be relatively equal? Take your own case. Somehow or other, the economic system determines how much income you will receive. In our economic system, your income depends on your skills, the property you own, how hard you work, and prevailing prices, as we shall see in succeeding chapters. But in other economic systems, your income might depend on quite different factors. This function of the economic system has generated, and will continue to generate, heated controversy. Some people favor a relatively egalitarian society where the amount received by one family varies little from that received by another family of the same size. Other people favor a society where the amount a family or person receives can vary a great deal. Few people favor a thoroughly egalitarian society, if for no other reason than that some differences in income are required to stimulate workers to do certain types of work.

4. An economic system must determine the rate of growth of per capita income. An adequate growth rate has come to be regarded as an important economic goal, particularly in the less developed countries of Africa, Asia, and Latin America. There is very strong pressure in these countries for changes in technology, the adoption of superior techniques, increases in the stock of capital resources, and better and more extensive education and training of the labor force. These are viewed as some of the major ways to promote the growth of per capita income.

Test Yourself

1. Suppose that the quantity of corn demanded annually by American consumers at each price of corn is as follows:

Price (dollars per bushel)	Quantity of corn (millions of bushels)
1	2.0
2	1.0
3	0.5
4	0.4

How much will farmers receive for their corn crop if it is 2 million bushels? If it is 1 million bushels? If you owned all of the farms producing corn, would you produce 2 million bushels? Why or why not?

2. Plot the relationship between price and quantity demanded in Question 1 in a graph. Is the relationship direct or inverse? Based on your graph, estimate how much corn is likely to be demanded if the price is (a) $1.50, (b) $2.50, and (c) $3.50.

3. Suppose that Americans begin to take up tennis in much larger numbers. Will the curve in Figure 2.2 shift? If so, will it shift to the right or to the left? Explain.

4. Suppose that you wanted to construct a model to explain and predict the breakfast food that your neighbor will choose tomorrow. What factors would you include? How well do you think you could predict?

The Economic System: A Simple Introductory Model

THE PRODUCTION POSSIBILITIES CURVE AND THE DETERMINATION OF WHAT IS PRODUCED

In a previous section, we said that economists use models to throw light on economic problems. At this point, let's try our hand at constructing a simple model to illuminate the basic functions any economic system, ours included, must perform. To keep things simple, suppose that society produces only two goods, food and tractors. This, of course, is unrealistic, but, as we stressed in a previous section, a model does not have to be realistic to be useful. Here, by assuming that there are only two goods, we eliminate a lot of unnecessary complexity and lay bare the essentials. In addition, we suppose that society has at its disposal a certain amount of resources, and that this amount is fixed for the duration of the period in question. This assumption is quite realistic. So long as the period is relatively short, the amount of a society's resources is relatively fixed (except, of course, under unusual circumstances, such as if a country annexes additional land). Finally, we suppose as well that society's technology is fixed. So long as the period is relatively short, this assumption too is realistic.

Under these circumstances, it is possible to figure out the various amounts of food and tractors that society can produce. Specifically, we can proceed as in Chapter 1, where we determined the amounts of food and clothing that an isolated town could produce. Let's begin with how many tractors society can produce if all resources are devoted to tractor production. According to Table 2.2, the answer is 15 million tractors. Next, let's consider the opposite extreme, where society devotes all its resources to food production. According to Table 2.2, it can produce 12 million tons of food in this case. Next, let's consider cases where both products are being produced. Such cases are represented by possibilities *B* to *F* in the table. As emphasized in Chapter 1, the more of one good that is produced, the less of the other good that can be produced. Why? Because to produce more of one good, resources must be taken away from the production of the other good, lessening the amount of the other good produced.

Figure 2.3 shows how we can use a graph to show the various production possibilities society can attain. It is merely a different way of presenting the data in Table 2.2; the output of food is plotted on the horizontal axis and the output of tractors on the vertical axis. The curve in Figure 2.3, which shows the various combinations of output of food and tractors that society can produce, is called a ***production possibilities curve.***

The production possibilities curve sheds considerable light on the economic tasks facing any society. It shows the various production possibilities open to society. In Figure 2.3, society can choose to produce 4 million tons of food and 12 million tractors (point *C*), or 6 million tons of food and 10 million tractors (point *D*), but it cannot choose to produce 6 million tons of food and 12 million tractors (point *H*). Point *H* is inaccessible with this society's resources and technology. Perhaps it will become accessible if the society's resources increase or if its technology improves, but for the present, point *H* is out of reach.

Table 2.2

ALTERNATIVE COMBINATIONS OF OUTPUTS OF FOOD AND TRACTORS THAT CAN BE PRODUCED

Possibility	Food (millions of tons)	Tractors (millions)
A	0	15
B	2	14
C	4	12
D	6	10
E	8	7
F	10	4
G	12	0

Figure 2.3

Production Possibilities Curve *This curve shows the various combinations of tractors and food that can be produced efficiently with given resources and technology. Point* H *is unattainable.*

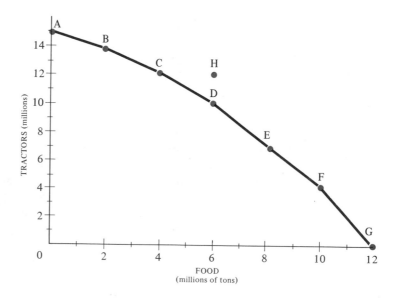

24

Example 2.1   Hay and Grain in Iowa

According to studies carried out at Iowa State University,* the following combinations of grain and hay could be produced in the 1940s from 100 acres of land in a particular part of Iowa:

Number of acres devoted to each use		Total production (pounds)	
Hay	Grain	Grain	Hay
0	100	224,000	0
25	75	212,920	89,600
33	67	166,194	96,400

That is, if all 100 acres were devoted to grain, 224,000 pounds of grain could be produced; if 75 of the 100 acres were devoted to grain, 212,920 pounds of grain and 89,600 pounds of hay could be produced; and so on.

(a) If a 100-acre farm in this part of Iowa was producing 212,920 pounds of grain and 89,600 pounds of hay, what was the approximate cost of increasing its production of grain by 1 pound? (b) Suppose that the profit to be made from a pound of grain was five times the profit to be made from a pound of hay, and that the owner of this farm claimed that, because this was the case, he should produce no hay. Would he be correct? (c) Suppose that, if hay production was increased from zero to about 100,000 pounds, the production of grain *increased*, not *decreased* (because hay contributed elements to the soil needed in the production of grain). Under these circumstances, would the slope of the production possibilities curve be negative at all points? Would it be rational for a farmer to produce no hay? (d) Would the production possibilities curve for a farm of this sort be the same now as in the 1940s?

SOLUTION

(a) If it increased its grain output by 11,080 pounds (from 212,920 to 224,000 pounds), it had to reduce its hay output by 89,600 pounds. Thus an extra pound of grain output cost the farm about 89,600 ÷ 11,080, or 8.09 pounds of hay. (b) No. If he produced 212,920 pounds of grain and 89,600 pounds of hay, his profits would be larger than if he produced no hay, because the profit from the extra 89,600 pounds of hay was greater than the profit from the 11,080 pounds of grain forgone. (c) No. No, because by producing up to 100,000 pounds of hay, the farmer increased the output of grain too. (d) No, because of changes in technology.

* E. Heady, *Economics of Agricultural Production and Resource Use,* New York: Prentice-Hall, 1952.

If resources are fully and efficiently utilized, *the first function of any economic system—to determine the level and composition of society's output—is really a problem of determining at what point along the production possibilities curve society should be.* Should society choose point *A, B, C, D, E, F,* or *G*? In making this choice, one thing is obvious from the production possibilities curve: *you cannot get more of one good without giving up some of the other good.* In other words, you cannot escape the problem of choice. So long as resources are limited and technology is less than magic, you must reckon with the fact (emphasized in Chapter 1) that more of one thing means less of another. The old saw that you don't "get something for nothing" is hackneyed but true, so long as resources are fully and efficiently utilized.

THE LAW OF INCREASING COST

In the previous section, we stressed that an increased output of one good (say, food) means a decreased output of the other good (say, tractors). This amounts to saying (in the language of Chapter 1) that the opportunity cost of producing more food is the output of tractors that must be forgone. In this section, we go a step further; we point out that, *as more and more of a good is produced, the production of yet another unit of this good is likely to entail a larger and larger opportunity cost* and we explain why this is true.

This so-called law of increasing cost can be demonstrated in Figure 2.3. As more and more food is produced, the cost of increasing food output by 2 million tons increases. To see this, note that the *first* 2 million tons of food cost 1 million tractors (because this is the amount that tractor output must be reduced if food output increases from 0 to 2 million tons). The *second* 2 million tons of food cost 2 million tractors (because this is the amount that tractor output must be reduced if food output increases from 2 to 4 million tons). Skipping to the *sixth* 2 million tons of food, the cost of this additional food output is 4 million tractors (because this is the amount that tractor output must be reduced if food output increases from 10 to 12 million tons). Clearly, the more food that is already being produced, the greater the cost of producing an additional 2 million tons.

Why is this the case? Basically, it is because resources are not as effective in producing one good as in producing the other. When society only produces a small amount of food, it can use in food production those resources that are well suited to producing food and not so well suited to producing tractors. But as society produces more and more food, it tends to run out of such resources, and must absorb into food production those resources that are less suited to producing food and better suited to producing tractors. To increase food output by 2 million tons with the latter type of resources, a greater reduction must occur in tractor output than when the 2-million-ton increase in food output occurred with the resources that were well suited to food production (and not so well suited to producing tractors). Thus the cost of producing an additional 2 million tons of food tends to increase as more food is already being produced.

This law of increasing cost explains why a production possibilities curve has the shape shown in Figure 2.3. That is, it explains why the production possibilities curve has the "bowed out" shape (rather than the "bowed in" shape) indicated in Figure 2.4. Because the cost of increasing food output

"Bowed out" shape

"Bowed in" shape

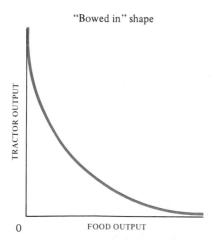

Figure 2.4

Shape of the Production Possibilities Curve So long as the law of increasing cost holds true, the production possibilities curve will have the shape at the top ("bowed out"), not the shape at the bottom ("bowed in").

by a certain amount increases as more of it is already produced, the production possibilities curve tends to fall more steeply as one moves from left to right along the horizontal axis—which explains why the production possibilities curve has the "bowed out" shape.

THE PRODUCTION POSSIBILITIES CURVE AND THE DETERMINATION OF HOW GOODS ARE PRODUCED

Let's turn now to the second basic function of any economic system: to determine how each good and service should be produced. In Table 2.2, we assumed implicitly that society's resources would be fully utilized and that the available technology would be applied in a way that would get the most out of the available resources. In other words, we assumed that the firms making food and tractors were as efficient as possible and that there was no unemployment of resources. But if there is widespread unemployment of people and machines, will society still be able to choose a point on the production possibilities curve? Clearly, the answer is no. Since society is not using all of its resources, it will not be able to produce as much as if it used them all. Thus, *if there is less than full employment of resources, society will have to settle for points inside the production possibilities curve.* For example, the best society may be able to do under these circumstances is to attain point *K* in Figure 2.5. *K* is a less desirable point than *C* or *D*—but that is the price of unemployment.

Suppose, on the other hand, that there is full employment of resources but that firms are inefficient. Perhaps they promote relatives of the boss, regardless of their ability; perhaps the managers are lazy or not much interested in efficiency; or perhaps the workers like to take long coffee breaks and are unwilling to work hard. Whatever the reason, will society still be able to choose a point on the production possibilities curve? Again, the answer is no. Since society is not getting as much as it could out of its resources, it will not be able to produce as much as it would if its resources were used efficiently. Thus, *if resources are used inefficiently, society will*

Basic Idea #3: If there is unemployment of resources or inefficiency, society may be able to increase its output of one good (say guns) without producing less of another good (say butter). In the absence of unemployment or inefficiency, this cannot be done (so long as the quantity of resources and technology are fixed). As pointed out below, this is why the United States, but not the Soviet Union, could increase the output of guns without cutting the output of butter at the outset of World War II.

Figure 2.5

Production Possibilities Curve *This curve, like Figure 2.3, shows the various combinations of tractors and food that can be produced efficiently with given resources and technology. Point K is less desirable than points C or D, because less output is produced at this point. But because of unemployment or inefficiency, society may wind up at point K.*

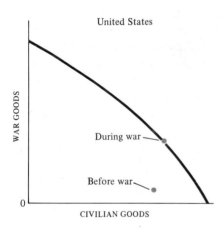

Figure 2.6

Effect of Increased Production of War Goods at the Beginning of World War II *Because the United States was at a point inside its production possibilities curve, we could increase our production of war goods without reducing production of civilian goods. Because the Russians were on their production possibilities curve, they could increase their output of war goods only by reducing output of civilian goods.*

have to settle for points inside the production possibilities curve. Perhaps in these circumstances, too, the best society can do may be point *K* in Figure 2.5. This less desirable position is the price of inefficiency.

At this point, it should be obvious that our model at least partially answers the question of how each good and service should be produced. The answer is to *produce each good and service in such a way that you wind up on the production possibilities curve, not on a point inside it.* Of course, this is easier said than done, but at least our model indicates a couple of villains to watch out for: unemployment of resources and inefficiency. When these villains are present, we can be sure that society is not on the production possibilities curve. Also, the old saw is wrong, and it is possible to "get something for nothing" when society is inside the production possibilities curve. That is, society can increase the output of one good without reducing the output of another good in such a situation. Society need not give up anything—in the way of production of other goods—to increase the production of this good under these circumstances.

The U.S. and the USSR in World War II. This simple model helps illuminate the sequence of events in various countries at the beginning of World War II. In certain countries, like the Soviet Union, the war effort meant a substantial decrease in the standard of living on the home front. Resources had to be diverted from the production of civilian goods to the production of military goods, and the war struck a severe blow at the living standards of the civilian population. In other countries, like the United States, it was possible to increase the production of military goods without making such a dent in the living standards of the civilian population. This happened because the United States at the beginning of World War II was still struggling to emerge from the Great Depression, and several million people were still unemployed. The same was not true in the Soviet Union. Thus we could increase the production of both guns and butter, whereas they could not.

Suppose that we divide all goods into two classes: war goods and civilian goods. Then, as shown in Figure 2.6, *we were inside our production possibilities curve at the beginning of the war, while the Russians were not.* Consequently, for the reasons discussed above, we could increase our production of war goods without reducing our production of civilian goods, while the Russians could not. (Note that in Figure 2.6 the two goods are war goods and civilian goods, not food and tractors.)

THE PRODUCTION POSSIBILITIES CURVE, INCOME DISTRIBUTION, AND GROWTH

Let's return now to the case where our economy produces food and tractors. The third basic function of any economic system is to distribute the goods and services that are produced among the members of society. Each point on the production possibilities curve in Figure 2.5 represents society's total pie, but to deal with the third function, we must know how the pie is divided up among society's members. Since the production possibilities curve does not tell us this, it cannot shed light on this third function.

Fortunately, the production possibilities curve is of more use in analyzing the fourth basic function of any economic system: to determine the society's rate of growth of per capita income. Suppose that the society in

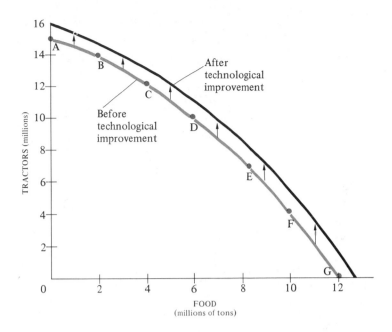

Figure 2.7

Effect of Improvement in Technology on Production Possibilities Curve *An improvement in technology results in an outward shift of the production possibilities curve.*

Figure 2.5 invests a considerable amount of its resources in developing improved processes and products. It might establish agricultural experiment stations to improve farming techniques and industrial research laboratories to improve tractor designs. As shown in Figure 2.7, the production possibilities curve will be pushed outward. This will be the result of improved technology, enabling more food and/or more tractors to be produced from the same amount of resources. Thus one way for an economy to increase its output—and its per capita income—may be to invest in research and development.

Another way is by devoting more of its resources to the production of capital goods rather than consumers' goods. *Capital goods* consist of plant and equipment that are used to make other goods; *consumers' goods* are items that consumers purchase like clothing, food, and drink. Since capital goods are themselves resources, a society that chooses to produce lots of capital goods and few consumers' goods will push out its production possibilities curve much farther than a society that chooses to produce lots of consumers' goods and few capital goods.

To illustrate this point, consider our simple society that produces food and tractors. The more tractors (and the less food) this society produces, the more tractors it will have in the next period; and the more tractors it has in the next period, the more of both goods—food and tractors—it will be able to produce then. Thus the more tractors (and the less food) this society produces, the farther out it will push its production possibilities curve—and the greater the increase in output (and per capita income) that it will achieve in the next period. If this society chooses point *F* (shown in Figures 2.7, 2.5, or 2.3), the effect will be entirely different than if it chooses point *C*. If it chooses point *F*, it produces 4 million tractors, which we assume to be the number of tractors worn out each year. Thus, if it chooses point *F*, it adds nothing to its stock of tractors: it merely replaces those that wear out. Since it has no more tractors in the next period than

29

One of the most remarkable developments in human history was the Industrial Revolution. Until the middle of the eighteenth century, industry (as distinct from agriculture or commerce) played a small role in the economies of Europe or America. But during the late eighteenth and early nineteenth centuries a host of important technological innovations, such as James Watt's steam engine and Richard Arkwright's spinning jenny, made possible a very rapid growth in the output of industrial goods (like textiles and pig iron). And accompanying this growth of industrial output was the advent of the factory—a social and economic institution that is taken for granted today, but which was largely unknown prior to the Industrial Revolution.

The Industrial Revolution was characterized by major improvements in technology and by large increases in the amount of capital resources available to society. Both the improvements in technology and the additional capital resulted in an outward shift in the production possibilities curve in England, where the Industrial Revolution first took hold. (See Figures 2.7 and 2.8.) Due to this shift, the standard of living in England, as measured by per capita income (total income divided by population), grew at an unprecedented rate. As the Industrial Revolution spread, this rise in living standards occurred too on the European continent and in the United States; it remained one of the lasting effects of industrialization.

As stressed above, the Industrial Revolution was characterized by considerable increases in capital. How did England (and other countries) bring about this increase in capital? By saving and investing. In other words, the English people had to set aside some of their resources, and to say in effect, "These resources will *not* be used to satisfy the current needs of our population for food, clothing, and other forms of consumption. Instead, they will be used to produce capital—factories, machines, equipment, railroads, and canals—which will increase our future productive capacity." Much more will be said about this saving process in subsequent chapters. For now, the essential point is that this saving process was one of the necessary conditions that made possible the Industrial Revolution.

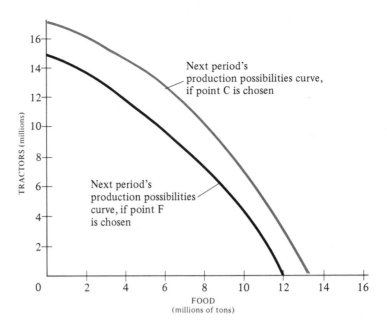

Figure 2.8

Effect of Increase in Capital Goods on Production Possibilities Curve *An increase in the amount of capital goods results in an outward shift of the production possibilities curve. The choice of point C means the production of more capital goods than the choice of point F.*

in the current period, the production possibilities curve does not shift out at all if point *F* is chosen. On the other hand, if point *C* is chosen, the society produces 12 million tractors, which means that it has 8 million additional tractors at the beginning of the next period. Thus, as shown in Figure 2.8, the production possibilities curve is pushed outward. By producing more capital goods (and less consumers' goods) our society has increased its production possibilities and its per capita income.

Capitalism: An Economic System

WHAT IS CAPITALISM?

In previous sections we have discussed the basic tasks that any economic system must perform. Now we must look at how our own economic system performs these tasks. The particular kind of economic system adopted by the United States is *capitalism.* Capitalism is one of those terms that is frequently used but seldom defined, and even less frequently understood. Its operation is complex, but its principal characteristics can be lumped into four major categories.

1. Private Ownership of Capital. Under capitalism you or I can buy the tools of production. We can own factories, equipment, inventories, and other forms of capital. In a capitalistic system, somebody owns each piece of capital—and receives the income from it. Each piece of equipment has some sort of legal instrument indicating to whom it belongs. (If it belongs to a corporation, its owners basically are the stockholders who own the corporation.) Moreover, each piece of capital has a market value. This system is in marked contrast to a Communist or socialist state where the government owns the capital. In these states, the government decides how much and what kinds of capital goods will be produced; it owns the capital goods; and it receives and distributes the income they produce. In the Soviet Union or China, no one can buy or put up a new steel plant; it simply isn't allowed.

The United States is basically a capitalistic system, but there are certain areas where the government, not individuals, owns capital, and where individual property rights are limited in various ways by the government. The government owns much of the tooling used in the defense industries; it owns dams and the Tennessee Valley Authority; and it owns research laboratories in such diverse fields as atomic energy, space exploration, and health. Further, the government determines how much of a deceased person's assets can go to his or her heirs. (The rest goes to the government in the form of estate and inheritance taxes.) Also, the government can make a person sell his or her property to allow a road or other public project to be built. There are many such limitations on property rights. Ours is basically a capitalistic system, but it must be recognized that the government's role is important. More will be said about this in subsequent sections.

2. Freedom of Choice and Enterprise. Another important characteristic of capitalism is freedom of choice and freedom of enterprise. **Freedom of choice** means that consumers are free to buy what they please and reject what they please; that laborers are free to work where, when, and if they please; and that investors are free to invest in whatever property they please. By **freedom of enterprise,** we mean that firms are free to enter whatever markets they please, obtain resources in whatever ways they can, and organize their affairs as best they can. Needless to say, this does not mean that firms can run roughshod over consumers and workers. Even the strongest champions of capitalism are quick to admit that the government must set "rules of the game" to prevent firms from engaging in sharp or unfair practices. But granting such limitations, the name of the game under capitalism is economic freedom.

Freedom to do what? Under capitalism, individuals and firms are free to pursue their own self-interest. Put in today's idiom, each individual or firm can do his, her, or its own thing. However, it is important to note that this freedom is circumscribed by one's financial resources. Consumers in a capitalistic system can buy practically anything they like—if they have the money to pay for it. Similarly, workers can work wherever or whenever they please—if they don't mind the wages. And a firm can run its business as it likes—if it remains solvent. Thus an important regulator of economic activity under capitalism is the pattern of income and prices that emerges in the market place.

3. Competition. Still another important characteristic of capitalism is **competition.** Firms compete with one another for sales. Under perfect competition, there are a large number of firms producing each product; indeed, there are so many that no firm controls the product's price. Because of this competition, firms are forced to jump to the tune of the consumer. If a firm doesn't produce what consumers want—at a price at least as low as other firms are charging—it will lose sales to other firms. Eventually, unless it mends its ways, such a firm will go out of business. Of course, in real-life American markets, the number of producers is not always so large that no firm has any control over price. (Much more will be said about this below.) But in the purest form of capitalism, such imperfections do not exist. Also, lest you think that competition under capitalism is confined to producers, it must be remembered that owners of resources also compete. They are expected to offer their resources—including labor—to the buyer who gives them the best deal, and buyers of resources and products are supposed to compete openly and freely.

4. Reliance upon Markets. Finally, another very important characteristic of capitalism is its reliance upon markets. *Under pure capitalism, the market—the free market—plays a central role.* Firms and individuals buy and sell products and resources in competitive markets. Some firms and individuals make money and prosper; others lose money and fail. Each firm or individual is allowed freedom to pursue its or his or her interests in the market place, while the government guards against shady and dishonest dealings. Such is the nature of the economic system under pure capitalism.

HOW DOES CAPITALISM PERFORM THE FOUR BASIC ECONOMIC TASKS?

The **price system** lies at the heart of any capitalist economy. In a purely capitalist economy, it is used to carry out the four basic economic functions discussed above. The price system is a way to organize an economy. Under such a system, every commodity and every service, including labor, has a price. We all receive money for what we sell, including labor, and we use this money to buy the goods and services we want. If more is wanted of a certain good, the price of this good tends to rise; if less is wanted, the price of the good tends to fall. Producers base their production decisions on the prices of commodities and inputs. Thus increases in a commodity's price generally tend to increase the amount of it produced, and decreases generally tend to decrease the amount produced. In this way, firms' output decisions are brought into balance with consumers' desires.

The very important question of how the price system performs the basic economic functions we discussed above will be answered in some detail in the next chapter. All we can do here is provide a preliminary sketch of the way the price system carries out each of these four tasks.

1. How does the price system determine what society will produce? In a substantially capitalistic economy, such as ours, consumers choose the amount of each good that they want, and producers act in accord with these decisions. The importance consumers attach to a good is indicated by the price they are willing to pay for it. Of course, the principle of **consumer sovereignty**—producers dancing to the tune of consumers' tastes—should not be viewed as always and completely true, since producers do attempt to manipulate the tastes of consumers through advertising and other devices, but it is certainly a reasonable first approximation.

2. How does the price system determine how each good and service will be produced? Prices indicate the desires of workers and the relative value of various types of materials and equipment as well as the desires of consumers. For example, if plumbers are scarce relative to the demand for them, their price in the labor market—their wage—will be bid up, and they will tend to be used only in the places where they are productive enough so that their employers can afford to pay them the higher wages. The forces that push firms toward actually carrying out the proper decisions are profits and losses. Profits are the carrot and losses are the stick used to eliminate the less efficient and less alert firms and to increase the more efficient and the more alert.

3. How does the price system determine how much in the way of goods and services each member of the society is to receive? In general, an individual's income depends largely on the quantities of resources of various kinds that he or she owns and the prices he or she gets for them. For example, if a man both works and rents out farm land he owns, his income is the number of hours he works per year times his hourly wage rate plus the number of acres of land he owns times the annual rental per acre. Thus the distribution of income depends on the way resource ownership—including talent, intelligence, training, work habits, and, yes, even character—is distributed among the population. Also, to be candid, it depends on just plain luck.

4. How does the price system determine the nation's rate of growth of per capita income? A nation's rate of growth of per capita income depends on the rate of growth of its resources and the rate of increase of the efficiency with which they are used. In our economy, the rate at which labor and capital resources are increased is motivated, at least in part, through the price system. Higher wages for more skilled work are an incentive for an individual to undergo further education and training. Capital accumulation occurs in response to the expectation of profit. Increases in efficiency, due in considerable measure to the advance of technology, are also stimulated by the price system.

Our Mixed Capitalist System

Basic Idea #4: The price system is a surprisingly effective way to organize an economy. Even though there is no small group of people directing the workings of the economy (as in the Soviet Union and other planned economies), the result is not chaos, as you might expect. Instead, prices provide the information needed for decentralized decision making.

Since the days of Adam Smith, economists have been fascinated by the features of a purely capitalistic economic system—an economy that relies entirely on the price system. Smith, and many generations of economists since, have gone to great pains to explain that in such an economic system, *the price system, although it is not controlled by any person or small group, results in economic order, not chaos.* The basic economic tasks any economy must perform can, as we have said, be carried out in such an economic system by the price system. It is an effective means of coordinating economic activity through decentralized decision making based on information disseminated through prices and related data.

But does this mean that the American economy is purely capitalistic? As we have noted repeatedly in previous sections, the answer is no. A purely capitalistic system is a useful model of reality, not a description of our economy as it exists now or existed in the past. It is useful because a purely capitalistic economy is, for some purposes, a reasonably close fit to our own. However, this does not mean that such a model is useful for all purposes. Many American markets are not perfectly competitive and never will be; they are dominated by a few producers or buyers who can influence price and thus distort the workings of the price system. Moreover, *the American economy is a mixed capitalistic economy, an economy where both government and private decisions are important.* The role of the government in American economic activity is very large indeed. Although it is essential to understand the workings of a purely capitalistic system, any model that omits the government entirely cannot purport to be adequate for the analysis of many major present-day economic issues.

To create a more balanced picture of the workings of the American economy, we must recognize that, although the price system plays an extremely important role, it is not permitted to solve all of the basic economic problems of our society. Consumer sovereignty does not extend—and cannot realistically be extended—to all areas of society. For example, certain public services cannot be left to private enterprise. The provision of fire protection, the operation of schools, and the development of weapons systems are examples of areas where we rely on political decision making, not the price system alone. Moreover, with regard to the consumption of commodities like drugs, society imposes limits on the decisions of individuals.

In addition, certain consequences of the price system are, by general agreement, unacceptable. Reliance on the price system alone does not assure a just or equitable or optimal distribution of income. It is possible, for example, that one person will have money to burn while another person will live in degrading poverty. Consequently, society empowers the government to modify the distribution of income by imposing taxes that take more from the rich than the poor, and by welfare programs that try to keep the poor from reaching the point where they lack decent food, adequate clothing, or shelter. Besides providing public services and maintaining certain minimum income standards, the government also carries out a variety of regulatory functions. Industries do not police the actions of their constituent firms, so it falls to the government to establish laws that impose limits on the economic behavior of firms. For example, these laws say that firms must not misrepresent their products, that child labor must not be employed, and that firms must not collude and form monopolies to interfere with the proper functioning of the price system. In this way, the government tries, with varying degrees of effectiveness, to establish the "rules of the game"—the limits within which the economic behavior of firms (and consumers) should lie.

Test Yourself

1. Suppose that a society's production possibilities curve is as follows:

	Output (per year)	
Possibility	Food (millions of tons)	Tractors (millions)
A	0	30
B	4	28
C	8	24
D	12	20
E	16	14
F	20	8
G	24	0

(a) Is it possible for the society to produce 30 million tons of food per year? (b) Can it produce 30 million tractors per year? (c) Suppose this society produces 20 million tons of food and 6 million tractors per year. Is it operating on the production possibilities curve? If not, what factors might account for this?

2. Plot the production possibilities curve in Question 1 in a graph. At what point along the horizontal axis does the curve cut the axis? At what point along the vertical axis does the curve cut the axis?

3. Suppose that, because of important technological improvements, the society in Question 1 can double its production of tractors at each level of food production. If so, is this society on its new production possibilities curve if it produces 20 million tons of food

and 16 million tractors? Plot the new production possibilities curve. At what point along the horizontal axis does the new curve cut the axis? At what point along the vertical axis does it cut the axis?

4. "[Some people] . . . fail to realize that the price system is, and ought to be, a method of coercion. . . . The very term 'rationing by the purse' illustrates the point. Economists defend such forms of rationing, but they have to do so primarily in terms of its efficiency and its fairness."* Comment.

5. "The great advantage of the [price system] . . . is that it permits wide diversity. It is, in political terms, a system of proportional representation. Each man can vote, as it were, for the color of tie he wants and get it; he does not have to see what color the majority wants and then, if he is in the minority, submit."** Comment.

* P. Samuelson, "The Economic Role of Private Activity," *A Dialogue on the Proper Economic Role of the State,* Chicago: University of Chicago Press, 1963.
** M. Friedman, *Capitalism and Freedom,* Chicago: University of Chicago Press, 1962, p. 15.

Summary

1. The methodology used by economists is much the same as that used in any other kind of scientific analysis. The basic procedure is the formulation and testing of models. A model must in general simplify and abstract from the real world. Its purpose is to make predictions, and in many respects the most important test of a model is how well it predicts. To test and quantify their models, economists gather data and utilize various statistical techniques.

2. The production possibilities curve, which shows the various production possibilities a society can attain, is useful in indicating the nature of the economic tasks any society faces. The task of determining the level and composition of society's output is really a problem of determining at what point along the production possibilities curve society should be.

3. Society has to recognize that it cannot get more of one good without giving up some of another good, if resources are fully and efficiently used. However, if they are not fully and efficiently used, society will have to settle for points inside the production possibilities curve—and it will be possible to obtain more of one good without giving up some of another good.

4. The task of determining how each good and service should be produced is, to a considerable extent, a problem of keeping society on its production possibilities curve, rather than at points inside the curve. The production possibilities curve does not tell us anything about the distribution of income, but it does indicate various ways that a society can promote growth in per capita income. By doing research and development, or by producing capital goods (rather than consumers' goods), society may push its production possibilities curve outward, thus increasing per capita income.

5. The American economy is a capitalistic economy, an economic system in which there is private ownership of capital, freedom of choice, freedom of enterprise, competition, and reliance upon markets.

6. Under pure capitalism, the price system is used to perform the four basic economic tasks. Although it is not controlled by any person or small group, the price system results in order, not chaos.

7. A purely capitalistic system is a useful model of reality, not a description of our economy as it exists now or in the past. The American economy is a mixed capitalistic economy, in which both government and private decisions are important.

8. Many public services (like defense and environmental protection) cannot be left to private enterprise, and society has said that certain consequences of the price system (like the existence of abject poverty) are unacceptable. For these reasons and others, the government carries out a long and impressive array of functions, many of which are discussed in subsequent chapters.

Concepts for Review

Model	Consumers' goods	Competition
Production possibilities curve	Capitalism	Price system
Capital goods	Freedom of choice	Consumer sovereignty
	Freedom of enterprise	

PART TWO

The Private Sector and the Public Sector: An Overview

CHAPTER 3

The Price System

Capitalist economies use the price system to perform the four basic tasks any economic system must carry out. Of course, as we pointed out in the previous chapter, the American economy is a mixed capitalist system, not a pure one. But this does not mean that the price system is unimportant. On the contrary, the price system plays a vital role in the American economy, and to obtain even a minimal grasp of the workings of our economic system, one must understand how the price system operates. This chapter takes up the nature and functions of the price system, as well as some applications of our theoretical results to real-life problems. For example, we show how the price system determines the quantity produced of a commodity like wheat, and how the pricing policies of the Broadway theater have hurt show business in a variety of ways. These applications should help illustrate the basic theory and indicate its usefulness.

Consumers, Firms, and Markets

We begin by describing and discussing consumers and firms, the basic building blocks that make up the private, or nongovernmental, sector of the economy.

Consumers. Sometimes—for example, when a person buys a beer on a warm day—the consumer is an individual. In other cases—for example, when a family buys a new car—the consumer may be an entire household. **Consumers** purchase the goods and services that are the ultimate end products of the economic system. When a man buys tickets to a ball game, he is a consumer; when he buys himself a Coke at the game, he is a consumer; and when he buys his wife a book on baseball for their twentieth wedding anniversary, he is a consumer.

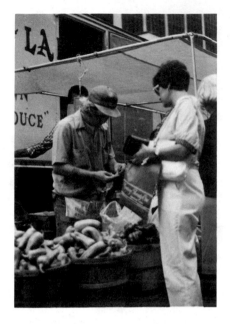

Firms. There are about 16 million firms in the United States. About nine-tenths of the goods and services produced in this country are produced by firms. (The rest are provided by government and not-for-profit institutions like universities and hospitals.) A *firm* is an organization that produces a good or service for sale. In contrast to not-for-profit organizations, firms attempt to make a profit. It is obvious that our economy is centered around the activities of firms.

Markets. Consumers and firms come together in a market. The concept of a market is not quite as straightforward as it may seem, since most markets are not well defined geographically or physically. For example, the New York Stock Exchange is an atypical market because it is located principally in a particular building. For present purposes, a *market* can be defined as a group of firms and individuals that are in touch with each other in order to buy or sell some good. Of course, not every person in a market has to be in contact with every other person in the market. A person or firm is part of a market even if it is in contact with only a subset of the other persons or firms in the market.

Markets vary enormously in their size and procedures. For some goods like toothpaste, most people who have their own teeth (and are interested in keeping them) are members of the same market; while for other goods like Picasso paintings, only a few dealers, collectors, and museums in certain parts of the world may be members of the market. And for still other goods, like lemonade sold by neighborhood children for a nickel a glass at a sidewalk stand, only people who walk by the stand—and are brave enough to drink the stuff—are members of the market. Basically, however, all markets consist primarily of buyers and sellers, although third parties like brokers and agents may be present as well.

Markets also vary in the extent to which they are dominated by a few large buyers or sellers. For example, in the United States, there was for many years only one producer of aluminum. This firm, the Aluminum Corporation of America, had great power in the market for aluminum. In contrast, the number of buyers and sellers in some other markets is so large that no single buyer or seller has any power over the price of the product. This is true in various agricultural markets, for example. When a market for a product contains so many buyers and sellers that none of them can influence the price, economists call the market *perfectly competitive.* In these introductory chapters, we make the simplifying assumption that markets are perfectly competitive. We will relax that assumption later.

The Demand Side of a Market

Every market has a demand side and a supply side. The *demand* side can be represented by a *market demand curve,* which shows the amount of the commodity buyers would like to purchase at various prices. Consider Figure 3.1, which shows the demand curve for wheat in the American market during the mid-1980s.[1] The figure shows that about 2.7 billion bushels of wheat

---

[1] I am indebted to officials of the U.S. Department of Agriculture for providing me with this information. Of course, these estimates are only rough approximations, but they are good enough for present purposes.

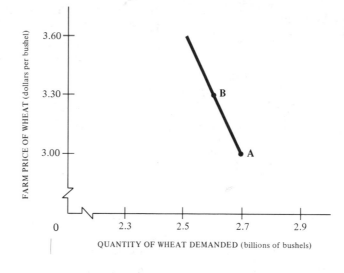

Figure 3.1

Market Demand Curve for Wheat, Mid-1980s *The curve shows the amount of wheat buyers would demand at various prices. At $3.00 per bushel, about 8 percent more wheat can be sold than at $3.60 per bushel.*

will be demanded annually if the farm price is $3.00 per bushel, about 2.6 billion bushels will be demanded annually if the farm price is $3.30 per bushel, and about 2.5 billion bushels will be demanded annually if the farm price is $3.60 per bushel. The total demand for wheat is of several types: to produce bread and other food products for domestic use, as well as for feed use, for export purposes, and for industrial uses. The demand curve in Figure 3.1 shows the total demand—including all these components—at each price. Any demand curve pertains to a particular period of time, and its shape and position depend on the length of this period.

Take a good look at the demand curve for wheat in Figure 3.1. This simple, innocent-looking curve influences a great many people's lives. After all, wheat is the principal grain used for direct human consumption in the United States. To states like Kansas, North Dakota, Oklahoma, Montana, Washington, Nebraska, Texas, Illinois, Indiana, and Ohio, wheat is a mighty important cash crop. Note that the demand curve for wheat slopes downward to the right. In other words, the quantity of wheat demanded increases as the price falls. This is true of the demand curve for most commodities: they almost always slope downward to the right. This makes sense; one would expect increases in a good's price to result in a smaller quantity demanded.

Any demand curve is based on the assumption that the tastes, incomes, and number of consumers, as well as the prices of other commodities, are held constant. Changes in any of these factors are likely to shift the position of a commodity's demand curve, as indicated below.

Consumer Tastes. If consumers show an increasing preference for a product, the demand curve will shift to the right; that is, at each price, consumers will desire to buy more than previously. On the other hand, if consumers show a decreasing preference for a product, the demand curve will shift to the left, since, at each price, consumers will desire to buy less than previously. Take wheat. If consumers become convinced that foods containing wheat prolong life and promote happiness, the demand curve may shift, as shown in Figure 3.2; and the greater the shift in preferences, the larger the shift in the demand curve.

Figure 3.2

Effect of Increased Preference for Wheat on Market Demand Curve *An increased preference for wheat would shift the demand curve to the right.*

Figure 3.3

Effect of Increase in Income on Market Demand Curve for Wheat *An increase in income would shift the demand curve for wheat to the right, but only slightly.*

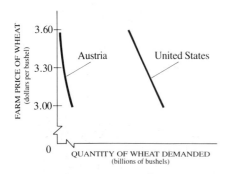

Figure 3.4

Market Demand Curve for Wheat, Austria and the United States *Since the United States has far more consumers than Austria, the demand curve in the United States is far to the right of Austria's.*

Income Level of Consumers. For some types of products, the demand curve shifts to the right if per capita income increases; whereas for other types of commodities, the demand curve shifts to the left if per capita income rises. Economists can explain why some goods fall into one category and other goods fall into the other, but, at present, this need not concern us. All that is important here is that changes in per capita income affect the demand curve, the size and direction of this effect varying from product to product. In the case of wheat, a 10 percent increase in per capita income would probably have a relatively small effect on the demand curve, as shown in Figure 3.3.

Number of Consumers in the Market. Compare Austria's demand for wheat with the United States'. Austria is a small country with a population of less than 8 million; the United States is a huge country with a population of over 200 million. Clearly, at a given price of wheat, the quantity demanded by American consumers will greatly exceed the quantity demanded by Austrian consumers, as shown in Figure 3.4. Even if consumer tastes, income, and other factors were held constant, this would still be true simply because the United States has so many more consumers in the relevant market.[2]

Level of Other Prices. A commodity's demand curve can be shifted by a change in the price of other commodities. Whether an increase in the price of good B will shift the demand curve for good A to the right or the left depends on the relationship between the two goods. If they are substitutes, such an increase will shift the demand curve for good A to the right. Consider the case of corn and wheat. If the price of corn goes up, more wheat will be demanded since it will be profitable to substitute wheat for corn. If the price of corn drops, less wheat will be demanded since it will be profitable to substitute corn for wheat. Thus, as shown in Figure 3.5, increases in the price of corn will shift the demand curve for wheat to the right, and decreases in the price of corn will shift it to the left.[3]

THE DISTINCTION BETWEEN CHANGES IN DEMAND AND CHANGES IN THE QUANTITY DEMANDED

It is essential to distinguish between a *shift in a commodity's demand curve* and a change in the *quantity demanded of the commodity.* A shift in a commodity's demand curve is a change in the *relationship* between price and quantity demanded. Figures 3.2, 3.3, and 3.5 show cases where such a change occurs. A change in the quantity demanded of a commodity may occur even if *no* shift occurs in the commodity's demand curve. For example, in Figure 3.1, if the price of wheat increases from $3.00 to $3.30 per bushel, the quantity demanded falls from 2.7 to 2.6 billion bushels. This change in the quantity demanded is due to a *movement along* the demand

[2] Note that no figures are given along the horizontal axis in Figure 3.4. This is because we do not have reasonably precise estimates of the demand curve in Austria. Nonetheless, the hypothetical demand curves in Figure 3.4 are close enough to the mark for present purposes.

[3] If goods A and B are complements, an increase in the price of good B will shift the demand curve for good A to the left. Thus an increase in the price of gin is likely to shift the demand curve for tonic to the left. Why? Because gin and tonic tend to be used together. The increase in gin's price will reduce the quantity of gin demanded, which in turn will reduce the amount of tonic that will be demanded at each price of tonic.

Figure 3.5

Effect of Price of Corn on Market Demand Curve for Wheat *Price increases for corn will shift the demand curve for wheat to the right.*

Figure 3.6

Market Supply Curve for Wheat, Mid-1980s *The curve shows the amount of wheat sellers would supply at various prices. At $3.60 per bushel, about 17 percent more wheat would be supplied than at $3.00 per bushel.*

curve (from point *A* to point *B* in Figure 3.1), not to a *shift* in the demand curve.

When economists refer to an *increase in demand,* they mean a *rightward shift* in the demand curve. Thus Figures 3.2, 3.3, and 3.5 show increases in demand for wheat. When economists refer to a *decrease in demand,* they mean a *leftward shift* in the demand curve. An increase in demand for a commodity is not the same as an increase in the quantity demanded of the commodity. In Figure 3.1, the quantity demanded of wheat *increases* if the price falls from $3.30 to $3.00 per bushel, but this is not due to an increase in demand, since there is no rightward shift of the demand curve. Similarly, a decrease in demand for a commodity is not the same as a decrease in the quantity demanded of the commodity. In Figure 3.1, the quantity demanded of wheat *decreases* if the price rises from $3.00 to $3.30 per bushel, but this is not due to a decrease in demand, since there is no leftward shift of the demand curve.

The Supply Side of a Market

So much for our first look at demand. What about the other side of the market: supply? *The **supply** side of a market can be represented by a **market supply curve** that shows the amount of the commodity sellers would offer at various prices.* Let's continue with the case of wheat. Figure 3.6 shows the supply curve for wheat in the United States in the mid-1980s, based on estimates made informally by government experts.[4] According to the figure, about 2.4 billion bushels of wheat would be supplied if the farm price were $3.00 per bushel, about 2.6 billion bushels if the farm price were $3.30 per bushel, and about 2.8 billion bushels if the farm price were $3.60 per bushel.

Look carefully at the supply curve shown in Figure 3.6. Although it looks innocuous enough, it summarizes the potential behavior of thousands of American wheat farmers—and their behavior plays an important role in determining the prosperity of many states and communities. Note that the supply curve for wheat slopes upward to the right. In other words, the quantity of wheat supplied increases as the price increases. This seems plausible, since increases in price give a greater incentive for farms to produce wheat and offer it for sale. Empirical studies indicate that the supply curves for a great many commodities share this characteristic of sloping upward to the right.

Any supply curve is based on the assumption that technology and input prices are held constant. Changes in these factors are likely to shift the position of a commodity's supply curve, as indicated below.

Technology. Recall that technology was defined in Chapter 1 as society's pool of knowledge concerning the industrial arts. As technology progresses, it becomes possible to produce commodities more cheaply, so that firms often are willing to supply a given amount at a lower price than formerly. Thus technological change often causes the supply curve to shift

[4] Officials of the U.S. Department of Agriculture provided me with these estimates. Although rough approximations, they are good enough for present purposes.

43

Figure 3.7

Effect of Technological Change on Market Supply Curve for Wheat *Improvements in technology often shift the supply curve to the right.*

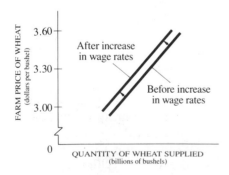

Figure 3.8

Effect of Increase in Farm Wage Rates on Market Supply Curve for Wheat *An increase in the wage rate might shift the supply curve to the left.*

to the right. This certainly has occurred in the case of wheat, as shown in Figure 3.7. There have been many important technological changes in wheat production, ranging from advances in tractors to the development of improved varieties, like semi-dwarf wheats.

Input Prices. The supply curve for a commodity is affected by the prices of the resources (labor, capital, and land) used to produce it. Decreases in the price of these inputs make it possible to produce commodities more cheaply, so that firms may be willing to supply a given amount at a lower price than they formerly would. Thus decreases in the price of inputs may cause the supply curve to shift to the right. On the other hand, increases in the price of inputs may cause it to shift to the left. For example, if the wage rates of farm labor increase, the supply curve for wheat may shift to the left, as shown in Figure 3.8.

An *increase in supply* is defined to be a *rightward shift* in the supply curve; a *decrease in supply* is defined to be a *leftward shift* in the supply curve. A change in supply should be distinguished from a change in the quantity supplied. In Figure 3.6, the quantity supplied of wheat will increase from 2.4 to 2.6 billion bushels if the price increases from $3.00 to $3.30 per bushel, but this is not due to an increase in supply, since there is no rightward shift of the supply curve in Figure 3.6.

Equilibrium Price

The two sides of a market, demand and supply, interact to determine the price of a commodity. Recall from the previous chapter that prices in a capitalistic system are important determinants of what is produced, how it is produced, who receives it, and how rapidly per capita income grows. It behooves us, therefore, to look carefully at how prices themselves are determined in a capitalist system. As a first step toward describing this process, we must define the equilibrium price of a product. At various points in this book, you will encounter the concept of an equilibrium, which is very important in economics, as in many other scientific fields.

Put briefly, an **equilibrium** is a situation where there is no tendency for change; in other words, it is a situation that can persist. Thus an **equilibrium price** is a price that can be maintained. Any price that is not an equilibrium price cannot be maintained for long, since there are basic forces at work to stimulate a change in price. The best way to understand what we mean by an equilibrium price is to take a particular case, such as the wheat market. Let's put both the demand curve for wheat (in Figure 3.1) and the supply curve for wheat (in Figure 3.6) together in the same diagram. The result, shown in Figure 3.9, will help us determine the equilibrium price of wheat.

We begin by seeing what would happen if various prices were established in the market. For example, if the price were $3.60 per bushel, the demand curve indicates that 2.5 billion bushels of wheat would be demanded, while the supply curve indicates that 2.8 billion bushels would be supplied. Thus, if the price were $3.60 a bushel, there would be a mismatch between the quantity supplied and the quantity demanded per year, since the rate at which wheat is supplied would be greater than the rate at which it is demanded. Specifically, as shown in Figure 3.9, there would be an *excess sup-*

Figure 3.9

Determination of the Equilibrium Price of Wheat, Mid-1980s *The equilibrium price is $3.30 per bushel, and the equilibrium quantity is 2.6 billion bushels. At a price of $3.60 per bushel, there would be an excess supply of 300 million bushels. At a price of $3.00 per bushel, there would be an excess demand of 300 million bushels.*

ply of 300 million bushels. Under these circumstances, some of the wheat supplied by farmers could not be sold, and, as inventories of wheat built up, suppliers would tend to cut their prices in order to get rid of unwanted inventories. Thus a price of $3.60 per bushel would not be maintained for long—and for this reason, $3.60 per bushel is not an equilibrium price.

If the price were $3.00 per bushel, on the other hand, the demand curve indicates that 2.7 billion bushels would be demanded, while the supply curve indicates that 2.4 billion bushels would be supplied. Again we find a mismatch between the quantity supplied and the quantity demanded per year, since the rate at which wheat is supplied would be less than the rate at which it is demanded. Specifically, as shown in Figure 3.9, there would be an *excess demand* of 300 million bushels. Under these circumstances, some of the consumers who want wheat at this price would have to be turned away empty-handed. There would be a shortage. And given this shortage, suppliers would find it profitable to increase the price, and competition among buyers would bid the price up. Thus a price of $3.00 per bushel could not be maintained for long—so $3.00 per bushel is not an equilibrium price.

Under these circumstances, the equilibrium price must be the price where the quantity demanded equals the quantity supplied. Obviously, this is the only price at which there is no mismatch between the quantity demanded and the quantity supplied; and consequently the only price that can be maintained for long. In Figure 3.9, the price at which the quantity supplied equals the quantity demanded is $3.30 per bushel, the price where the demand curve intersects the supply curve. Thus $3.30 per bushel is the equilibrium price of wheat under the circumstances visualized in Figure 3.9, and 2.6 billion bushels is the equilibrium quantity.

Actual Price

The price that counts in the real world, however, is the **actual price,** not the equilibrium price, and it is the actual price that we set out to explain. In

Example 3.1   It's Not Just for Breakfast Anymore

In recent years, many oranges grown in California and Arizona have been provided to cattle for feed or given away to juicing plants. An 11-member committee of farmers and shippers establishes the number and size of oranges that can be sold. Anyone selling oranges without the committee's permission can face civil and criminal prosecution by the Department of Justice. Although some industry spokesmen claim that the oranges held off the market are too small to be sold, it is reported that the industry's figures show that some of these oranges are as large as those sent to market.*

(a) In the absence of government intervention, suppose that the demand and supply curves for oranges would be as shown below:

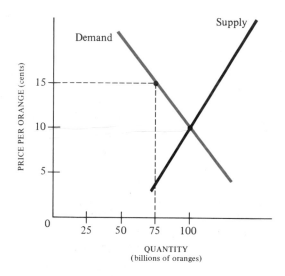

What would be the equilibrium price under these circumstances? (b) If the committee says that the quantity of oranges that can be sold must be 25 percent less than what would be sold in a free market, what will be the equilibrium price? (c) Under the committee's edict, will the growers receive more or less for their crop than under the free market? How much more or less? (d) How are consumers affected by the committee's edict?

SOLUTION

(a) 10 cents per orange. (b) In a free market, 100 billion oranges would be sold. If this quantity is reduced by 25 percent, only 75 billion oranges can be sold. Based on the demand curve, this amount can be sold for 15 cents per orange. Thus this will be the price. (c) Under the committee's edict, growers will sell 75 billion oranges at 15 cents each, so they will receive $11.25 billion. Under the free market, they will sell 100 billion oranges at 10 cents each, so they will receive $10 billion. Thus they will receive $1.25 billion more under the committee's edict than under the free market. (d) They consume fewer oranges and pay more for those they do consume.

* "Growers Bar Oranges from Market as Prices Dip," *New York Times,* February 15, 1981.

Basic Idea #5: An equilibrium price is one that can be maintained. The basic forces at work tend to push the actual price toward the equilibrium price. Once the actual price reaches the equilibrium price, there is no tendency for it to change. To find the equilibrium price, see where the demand curve intersects the supply curve.

general, economists simply assume that the actual price will approximate the equilibrium price, which seems reasonable enough, since the basic forces at work tend to push the actual price toward the equilibrium price. Thus, if conditions remain fairly stable for a time, the actual price should move toward the equilibrium price.

To see that this is the case, consider the market for wheat, as described in Figure 3.9. What if the price somehow is set at $3.60 per bushel? As we saw in the previous section, there is downward pressure on the price of wheat under these conditions. Suppose the price, responding to this pressure, falls to $3.50. Comparing the quantity demanded with the quantity supplied at $3.50, we find that there is still downward pressure on price, since the quantity supplied exceeds the quantity demanded at $3.50. The price, responding to this pressure, may fall to $3.40, but comparing the quantity demanded with the quantity supplied at this price, we find that there is still a downward pressure on price, since the quantity supplied exceeds the quantity demanded at $3.40.

So long as the actual price exceeds the equilibrium price, there will be a downward pressure on price. Similarly, so long as the actual price is less than the equilibrium price, there will be an upward pressure on price. Thus there is always a tendency for the actual price to move toward the equilibrium price. But it should not be assumed that this movement is always rapid. Sometimes it takes a long time for the actual price to get close to the equilibrium price. Sometimes the actual price never gets to the equilibrium price because by the time it gets close, the equilibrium price changes (because of shifts in either the demand curve or the supply curve or both). All that safely can be said is that the actual price will move toward the equilibrium price. But of course this information is of great value, both theoretically and practically. For many purposes, all that is needed is a correct prediction of the direction in which the price will move.

Test Yourself

1. Assume that the market for electric toasters is competitive and that the quantity supplied per year depends as follows on the price of a toaster:

Price of a toaster (dollars)	Number of toasters supplied (millions)
6	4.0
8	5.0
10	5.5
12	6.0
14	6.3

Plot the supply curve for toasters. Is this a direct or inverse relationship? Are supply curves generally direct or inverse relationships?

2. Suppose that the quantity of toasters demanded per year depends as follows on the price of a toaster:

Price of a toaster (dollars)	Number of toasters demanded (millions)
6	7.0
8	6.5
10	6.2
12	6.0
14	5.8

Plot the demand curve for toasters. If the price is $8, will there be an excess demand of toasters? If the price is $14, will there be an excess demand? What is the equilibrium price of a toaster? What is the equilibrium quantity? (Use the data in Question 1.)

3. Suppose that the government imposes a price ceiling on toasters. In particular, suppose that it decrees that a toaster cannot sell for more than $8. Will the quantity supplied equal the quantity demanded? What sorts of devices may come into being to allocate the available supply of toasters to consumers? What problems will the government encounter in keeping the price at $8? What social purposes, if any, might such a price ceiling serve? (Use the data in Questions 1 and 2.)

4. Suppose that the government imposes a price floor on toasters. In particular, suppose that it decrees that a toaster cannot sell for less than $14. Will the quantity supplied equal the quantity demanded? How will the resulting supply of toasters be taken off the market? What problems will the government encounter in keeping the price at $14? What social purposes, if any, might such a price floor serve? (Use the data above.)

5. If the demand curve for butter is $Q_D = 20 - 4P$ (where Q_D is the quantity demanded and P is the price of butter) and the supply curve for butter is $Q_S = 2P$ (where Q_S is the quantity supplied), what is the equilibrium price? What is the equilibrium quantity? (Both Q_D and Q_S are measured in millions of pounds, and price is measured in dollars per pound.)

The Effects of Shifts in the Demand Curve

Heraclitus, the ancient Greek philosopher, said you cannot step in the same stream twice: everything changes, sooner or later. One need not be a disciple of Heraclitus to recognize that demand curves shift. Indeed, we have already seen that demand curves shift in response to changes in tastes, income, population, and prices of other products, and that supply curves shift in response to changes in technology and input prices. Any supply-and-demand diagram like Figure 3.9 is essentially a snapshot of the situation during a particular period of time. The results in Figure 3.9 are limited to a particular period because the demand and supply curves in the figure, like any demand and supply curves, pertain only to a certain period.

What happens to the equilibrium price of a product when its demand curve changes? This is an important question because it sheds a good deal of light on how the price system works. Suppose that consumer tastes shift in favor of foods containing wheat, causing the demand curve for wheat to shift *to the right,* as shown in Figure 3.10. It is not hard to see the effect on the equilibrium price of wheat. Before the shift, the equilibrium price is OP. But when the demand curve shifts to the right, a shortage develops at this price: that is, the quantity demanded exceeds the quantity supplied at this price.[5] Consequently, suppliers raise their prices. After some testing of market reactions and trial-and-error adjustments, the price will tend to settle at OP_1, the new equilibrium price, and quantity will tend to settle at OQ_1.

On the other hand, suppose that consumer demand for wheat products falls off, perhaps because of a great drop in the price of corn products. The demand for wheat now shifts *to the left,* as shown in Figure 3.11. What will be the effect on the equilibrium price of wheat? Clearly, the equilibrium price falls to OP_2, where the new demand curve intersects the supply curve.

In general, *a shift to the right in the demand curve results in an increase in the equilibrium price, and a shift to the left in the demand curve results in a*

---

[5] This shortage is equal to $OQ_1' - OQ$ in Figure 3.10.

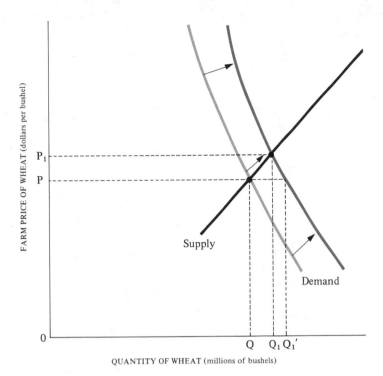

P_1

P

Supply

Demand

0

Q Q_1 Q_1'

QUANTITY OF WHEAT (millions of bushels)

Figure 3.10

Effect on the Equilibrium Price of a Shift to the Right of the Market Demand Curve *This shift of the demand curve to the right results in an increase in the equilibrium price from OP to OP_1 and an increase in the equilibrium quantity from OQ to OQ_1.*

Demand

FARM PRICE OF WHEAT (dollars per bushel)

P
P_2

Supply

$Q_2 Q$

QUANTITY OF WHEAT
(millions of bushels)

Figure 3.11

Effect on the Equilibrium Price of a Shift to the Left of the Market Demand Curve *This shift of the demand curve to the left results in a decrease in the equilibrium price from OP to OP_2 and a decrease in the equilibrium quantity from OQ to OQ_2.*

decrease in the equilibrium price. This is the lesson of Figures 3.10 and 3.11. Of course, this conclusion depends on the assumption that the supply curve slopes upward to the right, but, as we noted in a previous section, this assumption is generally true.

At this point, since all of this is theory, you may be wondering how well this theory works in practice. In 1972 and 1973, there was a vivid demonstration of the accuracy of this model in various agricultural markets, including wheat. Because of poor harvests abroad and greatly increased foreign demand for American wheat, the demand curve for wheat shifted markedly to the right. What happened to the price of wheat? In accord with our model, the price increased spectacularly, from about $1.35 a bushel in the early summer of 1972 to over $4.00 a year later. Anyone who witnessed this phenomenon could not help but be impressed by the usefulness of this model.

The Effects of Shifts in the Supply Curve

What happens to the equilibrium price of a product when its supply curve changes? For example, suppose that, because of technological advances in wheat production, wheat farmers are willing and able to supply more wheat at a given price than they used to, with the result that the supply curve shifts *to the right,* as shown in Figure 3.12. What will be the effect on the equilibrium price? Clearly, it will fall from *OP* (where the original supply curve intersects the demand curve) to OP_3 (where the new supply curve intersects the demand curve).

On the other hand, suppose that the weather is poor, with the result that the supply curve shifts *to the left,* as shown in Figure 3.12. What will be the

49

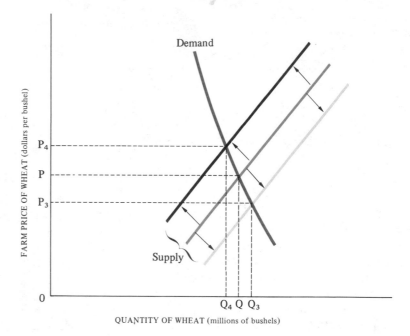

Figure 3.12

Effects on the Equilibrium Price of Shifts in the Market Supply Curve *The shift of the supply curve to the right results in a decrease in the equilibrium price from OP to OP₃. The shift of the supply curve to the left increases the equilibrium price from OP to OP₄.*

effect? The equilibrium price will increase from *OP* (where the original supply curve intersects the demand curve) to *OP₄* (where the new supply curve intersects the demand curve).

In 1984, law enforcement officers concerned with narcotics consumption in the United States were shown vividly what a shift to the right in the supply curve of a commodity will do. Because of a massive increase in the amount of coca production in South America, the supply curve for cocaine shifted dramatically to the right. The result was just what our theory would predict: a big drop in the price of cocaine. In some parts of the United States, cocaine sold in 1984 for one-half to one-third the price of a year before. According to one federal official, "At no time in the modern history of international drug control has the price of a drug dropped by half so quickly."

In general, a shift to the right in the supply curve results in a decrease in the equilibrium price, and a shift to the left in the supply curve results in an increase in the equilibrium price. Of course, this conclusion depends on the assumption that the demand curve slopes downward to the right, but, as we noted in a previous section, this assumption is generally true.

The Price System and the Determination of What Is Produced

Having described how prices are determined in free markets, we can now describe somewhat more fully how the price system goes about performing the four basic tasks that face any economic system. Let's begin by considering the determination of what society will produce: How does the price system carry out this task? Consumers indicate what goods and services they want in the market place, and producers try to meet these wants. More specifically, the demand curve for a product shows how much of that product consumers want at various prices. If consumers don't want much of it at a certain price, its demand curve will indicate that fact by being positioned close to the vertical axis at that price. In other words, the demand curve will show that, at this price for the product, the amount consumers will buy is small. On the other hand, if consumers want lots of the product at this price, its demand curve will be far from the vertical axis.

A product's demand curve is an important determinant of how much firms will produce of the product, since it indicates the amount of the product that will be demanded at each price. From the point of view of the producers, the demand curve indicates the amount they can sell at each price. In a capitalist economy, firms are in business to make money. Thus the manufacturers of any product will turn it out only if the amount of money they receive from consumers exceeds the cost of putting the product on the market. Acting in accord with the profit motive, firms are led to produce what the consumers desire. We saw in a previous section that if consumers' tastes shift in favor of foods containing wheat, the demand curve for wheat will shift to the right, which will result in an increase in the price of wheat. This increase will stimulate farmers to produce more wheat. For example, when the demand curve shifts to the right in Figure 3.10, the equilibrium quantity produced increases from OQ to OQ_1. Given the shift in the demand curve, it is profitable for firms to step up their production. Acting in their own self-interest, they are led to make production decisions geared to the wants of the consumers.

Thus the price system uses the self-interest of the producers to get them to produce what consumers want. Consumers register what they want in the market place by their purchasing decisions—shown by their demand curves. Producers can make more money by responding to consumer wants than by ignoring them. Consequently, they are led to produce what consumers want—and are willing to pay enough for to cover the producers' costs. Note that costs as well as demand determine what will be produced, and that producers are not forced by anyone to do anything. They can produce air conditioners for Eskimos if they like and if they are prepared to absorb the losses. The price system uses prices to communicate the relevant signals to producers, and metes out the penalties and rewards in the form of losses or profits.

The Price System and the Determination of How Goods Are Produced

Next, consider how society determines how each good and service is produced. How does the price system carry out this task? The price of each resource gives producers an indication of how scarce this resource is, and how valuable it is in other uses. Clearly, firms should produce goods and services at minimum cost. Suppose that there are two ways of producing tables: Technique A and Technique B. Technique A requires 4 man-hours of labor and $10 worth of wood per table, whereas Technique B requires 5 man-hours of labor and $8 worth of wood. If the price of a man-hour of labor is $4, Technique A should be used since a table costs $26 with this

Example 3.2   Tennis Anyone?

In the early 1970s, the American public turned to tennis in droves, and many indoor tennis courts were built. In the late 1970s and early 1980s, the tennis fad began to fade. One indication: sales of tennis rackets fell by 20 percent in 1980. Also, during the late 1970s and early 1980s, the costs of operating an indoor tennis court increased markedly because of ballooning prices of electricity needed to light, heat, and air-condition the courts. For example, a 12-court facility near Philadelphia paid $8,600 a month for electricity in early 1981.*

(a) What sort of shift occurred during the late 1970s and early 1980s in the demand curve for playing time at indoor tennis courts? (b) Taken by itself, what effect did this shift in the demand curve have on the price per hour of playing time at indoor tennis courts? (c) Did the shift in the supply curve for playing time offset or reinforce this effect on price? (d) Based on the above facts, would you expect that the total amount of playing time sold by indoor tennis courts increased or decreased during the early 1980s? Why?

SOLUTION

(a) The demand curve shifted to the left because consumers demanded fewer hours of playing time at a given price. (b) Holding the supply curve constant, the leftward shift in the demand curve tended to reduce the price. (c) The supply curve shifted upward and to the left because of the increased price of electricity, a major input. Taken by itself, this shift in the supply curve tended to increase the price. Thus its effect was to offset the effect of the shift in the demand curve. (d) A leftward shift in both the demand curve and the supply curve would result in a decrease in the total amount of playing time sold (from $0Q$ to $0Q'$), as shown below:

* See "As Racquet Fads Fade, Clubs Are Scrambling," *Philadelphia Inquirer,* May 4, 1981.

technique, as opposed to $28 with Technique B.[6] In other words, Technique A uses fewer resources per table.

The price system nudges producers to opt for Technique A rather than Technique B through profits and losses. If each table commands a price of $35, then by using Technique A, producers make a profit of $35 − $26 = $9 per table. If they use Technique B, they make a profit of $35 − $28 = $7 per table. Thus producers, if they maximize profit, will be led to adopt Technique A. Their desire for profit leads them to adopt the techniques that will enable society to get the most out of its resources. No one commands firms to use particular techniques. Washington officials do not order steel plants to substitute the basic oxygen process for open hearths, or petroleum refineries to substitute catalytic cracking for thermal cracking. It is all done through the impersonal market place.

You should not, however, get the idea that the price system operates with kid gloves. Suppose all firms producing tables used Technique B until this past year, when Technique A was developed: in other words, Technique A is based on a new technology. Given this technological change, the supply curve for tables will shift to the right, as we saw in a previous section, and the price of a table will fall. Suppose it drops to $27. If some firm insists on sticking with Technique B, it will lose money at the rate of $1 a table; and as these losses mount, the firm's owners will become increasingly uncomfortable. The firm will either switch to Technique A or go bankrupt. The price system leans awfully hard on producers who try to ignore its signals.

The Price System and the Determination of Who Gets What

Let's turn now to how society's output will be distributed among the people: How does the price system carry out this task? How much people receive in goods and services depends on their money income, which in turn is determined under the price system by the amount of various resources that they own and by the price of each resource. Thus, under the price system, each person's income is determined in the market place: the person comes to the market place with certain resources to sell, and his or her income depends on how much he or she can get for them.

The question of who gets what is solved at two levels by the price system. Consider an individual product—for example, the tables discussed in the previous section. For the individual product, the question of who gets what is solved by the equality of quantity demanded and quantity supplied. If the price of these tables is at its equilibrium level, the quantity demanded will equal the quantity supplied. Consumers who are willing and able to pay the equilibrium price (or more) get the tables, while those who are unwilling or unable to pay it do not get them. It is just as simple—and as impersonal—as that. It doesn't matter whether you are a nice guy or a scoundrel, or whether you are a connoisseur of tables or someone who doesn't know good workmanship from poor: all that matters is whether you are able and willing to pay the equilibrium price.

---

[6] To obtain these figures, note that the cost with Technique A is 4 man-hours times $4 plus $10, or $26, while the cost with Technique B is 5 man-hours times $4 plus $8, or $28.

Next, consider the question of who gets what at a somewhat more fundamental level. After all, whether a consumer is able and willing to pay the equilibrium price for a good depends on his money income. Thus the super-rich can pay the equilibrium price for an astonishing variety of things, whereas those in abject poverty can scrape up the equilibrium price for very little. As we have already seen, a consumer's money income depends on the amount of resources of various kinds that he or she owns and the price that he or she can get for them. Some people have lots of resources: they are endowed with skill and intelligence and industry, or they have lots of capital or land. Other people have little in the way of resources. Moreover, some people have resources that command a high price, while others have resources that are of little monetary value. The result is that, under the price system, some consumers get a lot more of society's output than do other consumers.

The Price System and Economic Growth

Let's turn now to the task of determining a society's rate of growth of per capita income. How does the price system do this? As pointed out in the previous chapter, a nation's rate of increase of per capita income depends on the rate of growth of its resources and the rate of increase of the efficiency with which they are used. First, consider the rate of growth of society's resources. The price system controls the amount of new capital goods produced much as it controls the amount of consumer goods produced. Similarly, the price system influences the amount society invests in educating, training, and upgrading its labor resources. To a considerable extent, the amount invested in such resource-augmenting activities is determined by the profitability of such investments, which is determined in turn by the pattern of prices.

Next, consider the rate of increase of the efficiency with which a society's resources are used. Clearly, this factor depends heavily on the rate of technological change. If technology is advancing at a rapid rate, it should be possible to get more and more out of a society's resources. But if technology is advancing rather slowly, it is likely to be difficult to get much more out of them. The price system affects the rate of technological change in a variety of ways: it influences the profitability of investing in research and development, the profitability of introducing new processes and products into commercial practice, and the profitability of accepting technological change—as well as the losses involved in spurning it.

The price system establishes strong incentives for firms to introduce new technology. Any firm that can find a cheaper way to produce an existing product, or a way to produce a better product, will have a profitable jump on its competitors. Until its competitors can do the same thing, this firm can reap higher profits than it otherwise could. Of course, these higher profits will eventually be competed away, as other firms begin to imitate this firm's innovation. But lots of money can be made in the period during which this firm has a lead over its competitors. These profits are an important incentive for the introduction of new technology.

Two Case Studies

THE PRICE SYSTEM IN ACTION BEHIND ENEMY LINES

Just as general discussions of tennis will take a neophyte only so far, after which he or she must watch and participate in a few matches, so a general discussion of the price system will take a student only so far. Then he or she should look at real-life examples of the price system at work. Our first illustration of the price system in operation is a prisoner-of-war camp in World War II. This case is not chosen because of its inherent importance, but because of its simplicity. Just as certain elementary forms of life illustrate important biological principles in a simple way, so the economic organization of a prisoner-of-war camp is an elementary form of economic system that illustrates certain important economic principles simply and well.

The prisoner-of-war camp was so elementary because no goods were produced there. All commodities were provided by the country running the camp, by the Red Cross, and by other outside donors. Each prisoner received an equal amount of food and supplies—canned milk, jam, butter, cookies, cigarettes, and so on. In addition, private parcels of clothing, cigarettes, and other supplies were received, with different prisoners, of course, receiving different quantities. Because no goods were produced in the prisoner-of-war camp, the first two tasks of an economic system (What will be produced? How will it be produced?) were not relevant; neither was the fourth task (What provision is to be made for growth?).

All that did matter in this elementary economic system was the third task: to determine who would consume the various available goods. At first blush, the answer may seem obvious: each prisoner would consume the goods he received from the detaining country, the Red Cross, and private packages. But this assumes that prisoners would not trade goods back and forth ("I'll swap you a cigarette for some milk"), which is clearly unrealistic. After all, some prisoners smoked cigarettes, others did not; some liked jam and didn't like canned beef, others liked canned beef and didn't like jam. Thus there was bound to be exchange of this sort, and the real question is in what way and on what terms such exchange took place.

How did the prisoners go about exchanging goods? According to one observer, the process developed as follows:

> Starting with simple direct barter, such as a nonsmoker giving a smoker friend his cigarette issue in exchange for a chocolate ration, more complex exchanges soon became an accepted custom. . . . Within a week or two, as the volume of trade grew, rough scales of exchange values came into existence. [Some prisoners], who had at first exchanged tinned beef for practically any other foodstuff, began to insist on jam and margarine. It was realized that a tin of jam was worth one-half pound of margarine plus something else, that a cigarette issue was worth several chocolate issues, and a tin of diced carrots was worth practically nothing. . . . By the end of the month, there was a lively trade in all commodities and their relative values were well known, and expressed not in terms of one another—one didn't quote [jam] in terms of sugar—but in terms of cigarettes. The cigarette became the standard of value.[7]

[7] R. A. Radford, "The Economic Organization of a P.O.W. Camp," reprinted in E. Mansfield, *Principles of Microeconomics: Readings, Issues, and Cases,* 4th ed., New York: Norton, 1983.

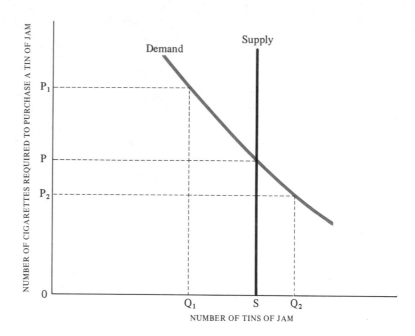

Figure 3.13

Determinants of Equilibrium Price of a Tin of Jam (in terms of cigarettes) in a P.O.W. Camp *The market supply for jam is fixed at OS tins. Thus the equilibrium price of a tin of jam is OP cigarettes. If the price were OP$_1$, OQ$_1$ tins would be demanded; if the price were OP$_2$, OQ$_2$ tins would be demanded.*

Thus the prisoners used the price system to solve the problem of allocating the available supply of goods among consumers. A market developed for each good. This market had, of course, both a demand and a supply side. Each good had its price—but this price was quoted in cigarettes, not dollars and cents. These markets were not started in a self-conscious, deliberate way. No one said, "Let's adopt the price system to allocate available supplies," or "Let's vote on whether or not to adopt the price system." Instead, the system just evolved . . . and it worked.

To see how the supply of a particular good—jam, say—was allocated, look at Figure 3.13, which shows the market supply curve for jam. In the short run, this supply was fixed, so this supply curve is a vertical line. Figure 3.13 also provides the market demand curve for jam, which shows the amount of jam the prisoners wanted to consume at various prices of jam—expressed in terms of cigarettes. For example, the prisoners wanted OQ_1 tins of jam when a tin of jam cost OP_1 cigarettes, and OQ_2 tins of jam when a tin of jam cost OP_2 cigarettes. For the quantity demanded to equal the available supply, the price of a tin of jam had to be OP cigarettes; one tin of jam had to exchange for OP cigarettes. At this price, the available supply of jam was rationed, without resort to fights among prisoners or intervention by the prison authorities. Those prisoners who could and would pay the price had the jam—and there were just enough such consumers to exhaust the available supply. Moreover, this held true for each of the other goods (including cigarettes) as well.

THE PRICE SYSTEM IN ACTION ON THE GREAT WHITE WAY

It is a long way from a prisoner-of-war camp to the Broadway theater, but economics, like any good tool of analysis, applies to a very wide variety of problems. In this section, we discuss the theater's pricing problems—and the role of the price system in helping to solve these problems. Prices for tickets to Broadway shows are established at levels that are much the same whether the show is a success or a flop. An orchestra ticket to *Kelly* (which managed to hold out for one performance before closing) cost about as much as an orchestra ticket to such hits as *Fiddler on the Roof* or *Cats*. And once a play opens, the price of a ticket remains much the same whether the play is greeted with universal praise or with discontented critics and customers.

Because of these pricing methods, the Broadway theater has been beset for many years by serious problems. Here they are described by two veteran observers of the Broadway stage:

> For centuries the sale of theater tickets has brought on corruption and confusion. When there are more buyers than sellers, a black market results. The so-called "retail" price, the price printed on the ticket, becomes meaningless. Speculation doubles, triples, or quadruples the "real" as opposed to the "legal" asking price. A smash hit on Broadway means "ice"—the difference between the real and legal prices—a well-hidden but substantial cash flow that is divided among shadowy middlemen. Ticket scandals break out in New York as regularly as the flu. The scenario is familiar. A play opens and becomes a superhit. Tickets become difficult, then impossible, to obtain. There are letters to the newspapers.... Shocking corruption is discovered. Someone ... is convicted of overcharging and accepting illegal gratuities. Someone may even go to jail. The black market, valiantly scotched, *never stops for a single moment.*[8]

Besides enriching crooked box-office men and managers, as well as other shadowy elements of society, the black market for theater tickets has the additional undesirable effect of excluding the authors, composers, directors, and stars of the play from participation in the premium revenue. Almost all of these people receive a percentage of the play's revenues; and if the revenues at the box office are less than what customers pay for their seats (because of "ice"), these people receive less than they would if no black market existed. The amount of "ice" can be substantial. For example, Rodgers and Hammerstein estimated that, at one performance of their play, *South Pacific,* the public probably paid about $25,000 for tickets with a face value of $7,000, the amount turned in at the box office.

To focus on the problem here, let's look at the market for tickets to a particular performance of *A Chorus Line* (one of Broadway's all-time big hits) when it was at the height of its popularity. Since the supply of tickets to a given performance of this play is fixed, the market supply curve, shown in Figure 3.14, is a vertical line at the quantity of tickets corresponding to the capacity of the theater. The price set officially on a ticket was about $20. But because the show was enormously popular, the market demand curve was *D* in Figure 3.14, and the equilibrium price for a ticket was $50.[9]

Figure 3.14 makes the nature of the problem apparent: at the official price of $20, the quantity of tickets demanded is much greater than the quantity supplied. Supply and demand don't match. Obviously, there is an incentive for people to buy the tickets from the box office at $20 and sell

---

[8] S. Little and A. Cantor, *The Playmakers,* New York: Norton, 1970, p. 220.

[9] This figure is only a rough estimate, but it is good enough for present purposes.

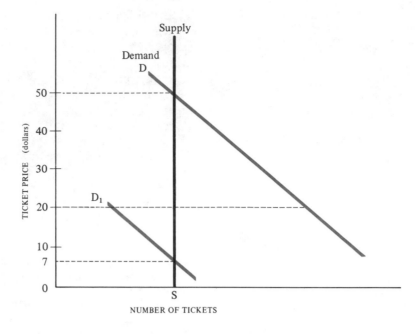

Figure 3.14
Equilibrium Price for Tickets to A Chorus Line *The market supply for tickets is fixed at OS per performance. If the demand curve is D, the equilibrium price of a ticket is $50. (If the demand curve is D_1, the equilibrium price is $7.) If the demand curve is D and the price of a ticket is $20, the quantity of tickets demanded will far exceed the quantity supplied.*

them at the higher prices customers are willing to pay. There is also an incentive for box-office men to sell them surreptitiously at higher prices and turn in only $20. The price system cannot play the role it did in the prisoner-of-war camp for jam and other goods. It cannot act as an effective rationing device because, to do so, the price of tickets would have to increase to its equilibrium level, $50.

Many theater experts believe that the solution to Broadway's pricing problems lies in allowing the price system to work more effectively by permitting ticket prices to vary depending on a show's popularity. For example, the official ticket price would be allowed to rise to $50 for *A Chorus Line*. On the other hand, if *A Chorus Line* had been much less popular and its market demand curve had been D_1 in Figure 3.14, its official ticket price would have been allowed to fall to $7. In this way, the black market for tickets would be eliminated, since the equilibrium price—which equates supply and demand—would be the official price. "Ice" would also be eliminated, since there would be no difference between the official and the actual price paid, and the people responsible for the show would receive its full receipts, not share them with crooked box-office men and illegal operators.[10]

Price Ceilings and Price Supports

During national emergencies, the government sometimes puts a lid on prices, not allowing them to reach their equilibrium levels. For example,

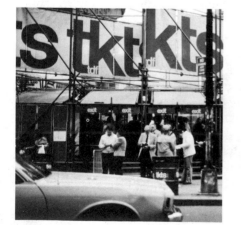

[10] Steps have been taken toward somewhat greater price flexibility for Broadway shows. For example, in the mid-1970s, a booth was established in Times Square where tickets to some shows were on sale at (approximately) half of the official ticket price. In this way, a show was enabled to cut its price, if it was unable to fill the theater at the official ticket price. Apparently, this innovation has worked quite well, both for the producers of the shows and the theatergoing public.

Basic Idea #6: Governments frequently establish price ceilings or price floors in an attempt to help particular parts of the population. Such intervention prevents the price system from doing the job expected of it. Price ceilings tend to result in shortages, and price floors tend to result in surpluses. Both can cause serious social waste.

during World War II, the government did not allow the prices of various foodstuffs to rise to their equilibrium levels, because it felt that this would have been inequitable (and highly unpopular). Under such circumstances, the quantity demanded of a product exceeds the quantity supplied. In other words, the situation is like that in Figure 3.14, where the quantity of tickets demanded for *A Chorus Line* exceeds the quantity supplied at a price of $20. There is a shortage.

Since the price system is not allowed to perform its rationing function, some formal system of rationing or allocating the available supply of the product may be required. Thus, in World War II, families were issued ration coupons which determined how much they could buy of various commodities. And in 1979, when the Organization of Petroleum Exporting Countries cut back oil production and reduced exports of oil to the United States, there was serious talk that gasoline and oil might be rationed in a similar way. Such rationing schemes may be justified in emergencies (of reasonably short duration), but they can result eventually in serious distortions, since prices are not allowed to do the job normally expected of them.

To illustrate the sorts of problems that can arise when price ceilings are imposed, consider the rent ceilings that exist on some apartments in New York City. Originally imposed to prevent dwelling costs from soaring during World War II, these ceilings have been defended on the ground that they help the poor, at least in the short run. Although this may be so, they have also resulted in a shortage of housing in New York City. Because they have pushed the price of housing below the equilibrium price, less housing has been supplied than has been demanded. The depressed price of housing has discouraged investors from building new housing, and has made it unprofitable for some owners of existing housing to maintain their buildings. Thus, although it would be socially desirable to channel more resources into New York housing, the rent ceilings have prevented this from occurring.

Government authorities may also impose price floors—or price supports, as they often are called. These floors are generally defended on the ground that they enable the producers of the good in question to make a better living. For example, the federal government has imposed price supports on a wide range of agricultural commodities, the purpose being to increase farm incomes. Just as in the case in Figure 3.14 where the demand curve is D_1 and where a price floor of $20 exists, the result is that the quantity supplied exceeds the quantity demanded at the support price. Thus there is a surplus of the commodity—and, in the case of agricultural commodities, the government has to buy up and store these surpluses. As in the case of a price ceiling, the result is that the price system is not allowed to do the job expected of it.

Whether price ceilings or floors are socially desirable depends on whether the loss in social efficiency resulting from them is exceeded by the gain in equity they achieve. As indicated above, their purpose is to help or protect particular parts of the population which would be treated inequitably by the unfettered price system. Since one person's view of what is equitable differ from another person's, this is an area of considerable controversy. More will be said about both price ceilings and floors in subsequent chapters, particularly Chapters 4 and 6.

The Circular Flows of Money and Products

So far we have been concerned largely with the workings of a single market—the market for wheat or tables or jam or tickets to *A Chorus Line*. But how do all of the various markets fit together? This is a very important question. Perhaps the best way to begin answering it is to distinguish between product markets and resource markets. As their names indicate, **product markets** *are markets where products are bought and sold; and* **resource markets** *are markets where resources are bought and sold.* Let's first consider product markets. As shown in Figure 3.15, firms provide products to consumers in product markets, and receive money in return. The money the firms receive is their receipts; to consumers, on the other hand, it represents their expenditures.

Next, let's consider resource markets. Figure 3.15 shows that consumers provide resources—including labor—to firms in resource markets, and they receive money in return. The money the consumers receive is their income; to firms, on the other hand, it represents their costs. Note that the flow of resources and products in Figure 3.15 is counterclockwise: that is, *consumers provide resources to firms which in turn provide goods and services to consumers.* On the other hand, the flow of money in Figure 3.15 is clockwise: that is, *firms pay money for resources to consumers who in turn use the money to buy goods and services from the firms.* Both flows—that of resources and products, and that of money—go on simultaneously and repeatedly.

So long as consumers spend all their income, the flow of money income from firms to consumers is exactly equal to the flow of expenditure from consumers to firms. Thus these circular flows, like Ole' Man River, just keep rolling along. As a first approximation, this is a perfectly good model. But as we pointed out in Chapter 1, capitalist economies have experienced periods of widespread unemployment and severe inflation that this model cannot explain. Also, note that our simple economy in Figure 3.15 has no

Figure 3.15
The Circular Flows of Money and Products *In product markets, consumers exchange money for products and firms exchange products for money. In resource markets, consumers exchange resources for money and firms exchange money for resources.*

government sector. In the following chapter, we shall bring the government into the picture. Under pure capitalism, the government would play a limited role in the economic system, but in the mixed capitalistic system we have in the United States, the government plays an important role indeed.

Test Yourself

1. Will each of the following tend to shift the demand curve for toasters to the right, to the left, or not at all? (a) Consumer incomes rise by 20 percent. (b) The price of bread falls by 10 percent. (c) The price of electricity increases by 5 percent. (d) Medical reports indicate that toast prevents heart attacks. (e) The cost of producing a toaster increases by 10 percent.

2. Will each of the following tend to shift the supply curve for toasters to the right, to the left, or not at all? (a) The wage of workers producing toasters increases by 5 percent. (b) The price of the metal used to make toasters falls by 10 percent. (c) The price of bread falls by 10 percent. (d) Consumer incomes rise by 20 percent. (e) New technology makes toaster production much more efficient.

3. If both the demand and supply curve for a product shift to the right, can one predict whether the product's equilibrium price will increase or decrease? Can one predict whether its equilibrium quantity will increase or decrease?

4. In most years, New Jersey blueberry farmers can get up to 80 cents a pint. In the summer of 1984, prices were pushed to as low as 30 cents a pint. (a) Why do you think this happened? (b) New Jersey farmers complained that they couldn't make money at the 30-cent price. Should the government establish a price floor for blueberries? Explain.

5. Suppose that the American public becomes convinced that beets are more desirable than they have been, and string beans are less so. Describe the shifts that will occur in the demand and supply curves in the relevant markets, and the mechanisms that will signal and trigger a redeployment of resources.

Summary

1. There are two sides of every market: the demand side and the supply side. The demand side can be represented by the market demand curve, which almost always slopes downward to the right and whose location depends on consumer tastes, the number and income of consumers, and the prices of other commodities.

2. The supply side of the market can be represented by the market supply curve, which generally slopes upward to the right and whose location depends on technology and resource prices.

3. The equilibrium price and equilibrium quantity of the commodity are given by the intersection of the market demand and supply curves. If conditions remain reasonably stable for a time, the actual price and quantity should move close to the equilibrium price and quantity.

4. Changes in the position and shape of the demand curve—in response to changes in consumer tastes, income, population, and prices of other commodities—result in changes in the equilibrium price and equilibrium output of a product. Similarly, changes in the position and shape of the supply curve—in response to changes in technology and resource prices, among other things—also result in changes in the equilibrium price and equilibrium output of a product.

5. To determine what goods and services society will produce, the price system sets up incentives for firms to produce what consumers want. To the extent that they produce what consumers want and are willing to pay for, firms reap profits; to the extent that they don't, they experience losses.

6. The price system sets up strong incentives for firms to produce goods at minimum cost. These incentives take the form of profits for firms that minimize costs and losses for firms that operate with relatively high costs.

7. To determine who gets what, the price system results in each person's receiving an income that depends on the quantity of resources he or she owns and the prices that they command.

8. The price system establishes incentives for activities that result in increases in a society's per capita income. For example, it influences the amount of new capital goods produced, as well as the amount society spends on educating its labor force and improving its technology.

9. There are circular flows of money and products in a capitalist economy. In product markets, firms provide products to consumers and receive money in return. In resource markets, consumers provide resources to firms, and receive money in return.

Concepts for Review

Consumers	**Market demand curve**	**Equilibrium price**
Firms	**Supply**	**Actual price**
Markets	**Market supply curve**	**Product market**
Perfect competition	**Equilibrium**	**Resource market**
Demand		

CHAPTER 4

The Economic Role
of the Government

To state that the United States is a mixed capitalist system, in which both government decisions and the price system play important roles, is hardly to provoke a controversy. But going a step beyond takes us into areas where viewpoints often diverge. The proper functions of government and the desirable size and nature of government expenditures and taxes are not matters on which all agree. Indeed, the question of how big government should be, and what its proper functions are, is hotly debated by conservatives and liberals throughout the land. This is only a preliminary airing of many of these issues. As the base of economic analysis is broadened in subsequent chapters, much more will be said on these matters, and you will be in a far better position to judge them for yourself.

Limitations of the Price System

Despite its many advantages, the price system suffers from limitations. Because these limitations are both prominent and well known, no one believes that the price system, left to its own devices, can be trusted to solve all society's basic economic problems. To a considerable extent, the government's role in the economy has developed in response to the limitations of the price system, which are described below.

Distribution of Income. There is *no* reason to believe that the distribution of income generated by the price system is *fair* or, in some sense, *best*. Most people feel that the distribution of income generated by the price system should be altered to suit humanitarian needs; in particular, that help should be given to the poor. Both liberals and conservatives tend to agree on this score, although there are arguments over the extent to which the poor should be helped and the conditions under which they should be eligible for help. But the general principle that the government should step in to redistribute income in favor of the poor is generally accepted in the United States today.[1]

Public Goods. Some goods and services *cannot be provided through the price system because there is no way to exclude citizens from consuming the goods whether they pay for them or not.* For example, there is no way to prevent citizens from benefiting from national expenditures on defense, whether they pay money toward defense or not. Consequently, the price system cannot be used to provide such goods; no one will pay for them since they will receive them whether they pay or not. Further, some goods, like the quality of the environment and national defense (and others cited below), *can be enjoyed by one person without depriving others of the same enjoyment.* Such goods are called ***public goods.*** The government provides many public goods. Such goods are consumed collectively, or jointly, and it is inefficient to try to price them in a market. They tend to be indivisible; thus they frequently cannot be split into pieces and be bought and sold in a market.

External Economies and Diseconomies. In cases where *the production or consumption of a good by one firm or consumer has adverse or beneficial uncompensated effects on other firms or consumers, the price system will not operate effectively.* An ***external economy*** is said to occur when consumption or production by one person or firm results in uncompensated benefits to another person or firm. A good example of an external economy exists where fundamental research carried out by one firm is used by another firm. (To cite one such case, there were external economies from the Bell Telephone Laboratories' invention of the transistor. Many electronics firms, such as Texas Instruments and Fairchild, benefited considerably from Bell's research.) Where external economies exist, it is generally agreed that the price system will produce too little of the good in question and that the government should supplement the amount produced by private enterprise. This is the basic rationale for much of the government's huge investment in basic science. An ***external diseconomy*** is said to occur when consumption or production by one person or firm results in uncompensated costs to another person or firm. A good example of an external diseconomy occurs when a firm dumps pollutants into a stream and makes the water unfit for use by firms and people downstream. Where activities result in external diseconomies, it is generally agreed that the price system will tolerate too much of the activity and that the government should curb it. For example, as we shall see in Chapter 17, the government, in keeping with this doctrine, has involved itself in environmental protection and the reduction of air and water pollution.[2]

---

[1] Also, because the wealthy have more "dollar votes" than the poor, the sorts of goods and services that society produces will reflect this fact. Thus luxuries for the rich may be produced in larger amounts and necessities for the poor may be produced in smaller amounts than some critics regard as sensible and equitable. This is another frequently encountered criticism of the price system.

[2] The effects of external economies and diseconomies can also be taken care of by legal arrangements that assign liabilities for damages and compensate for benefits. However, such arrangements often are impractical or too costly to be used.

What Functions Should the Government Perform?

There are wide differences of opinion on the proper role of government in economic affairs. Although it is generally agreed that the government should redistribute income in favor of the poor, provide public goods, and offset the effects of external economies and diseconomies, there is considerable disagreement over how far the government should go in these areas, and what additional areas the government should be responsible for. Some people feel that "big government" is already a problem; that government is doing too much. Others believe that the public sector of the economy is being undernourished and that government should be allowed to do more. This is a fundamental question, and one that involves a great deal more than economics.

Conservative View. On the one hand, conservatives, such as Stanford University's Nobel laureate, Milton Friedman, believe that the government's role should be limited severely. They feel that economic and political freedom is likely to be undermined by excessive reliance on the state. Moreover, they tend to be skeptical about the government's ability to solve the social and economic problems at hand. They feel that the prevailing faith in the government's power to make a substantial dent in these problems is unreasonable, and they call for more and better information concerning the sorts of tasks government can reasonably be expected to do—and do well. They point to the slowness of the government bureaucracy, the difficulty in controlling huge government organizations, the inefficiencies political considerations can breed, and the difficulties in telling whether government programs are successful or not. On the basis of these considerations, they argue that the government's role should be carefully circumscribed.

Liberal View. To such arguments, liberals like Nobel laureate Paul Samuelson of the Massachusetts Institute of Technology respond with telling salvos of their own. Just as conservatives tend to be skeptical of the government's ability to solve important social and economic problems, so liberals tend to be skeptical about the price system's ability to solve these problems. They point to the limitations of the price system, discussed above, and they assert that the government can do a great deal to overcome these limitations, by regulating private activity and by subsidizing and providing goods and services that the private sector produces too little of. Liberals tend to be less concerned than conservatives about the effects on personal freedom of greater governmental intervention in the economy. They point out that the price system also involves coercion, since the fact that the price system awards the available goods and services to those who can pay their equilibrium price can be viewed as a form of coercion. In their view, people who are awarded only a pittance by the price system are coerced into discomfort and malnutrition.[3]

[3] See P. Samuelson, "The Economic Role of Private Activity," and G. Stigler, "The Government of the Economy," *A Dialogue on the Proper Economic Role of the State,* University of Chicago, Graduate School of Business, Selected Paper no. 7, in E. Mansfield, *Principles of Microeconomics: Readings, Issues, and Cases,* 4th ed.

FDA inspectors

Establishing "Rules of the Game"

Although there is considerable disagreement over the proper role of the government, both conservatives and liberals agree that it must do certain things. The first of these is to establish the "rules of the game"—that is, a legal, social, and competitive framework enabling the price system to function as it should. Specifically, *the government must see to it that contracts are enforced, that private ownership is protected, and that fraud is prevented.* Clearly, these matters must be tended to if the price system is to work properly. Also, *the government must maintain order (through the establishment of police and other forces), establish a monetary system (so that money can be used to facilitate trade and exchange), and provide standards for the weight and quality of products.*

As an example of this sort of government intervention, consider the Pure Food and Drug Act. This act, originally passed in 1906 and subsequently amended in various ways, protects the consumer against improper and fraudulent activities on the part of producers of foods and drugs. It prohibits the merchandising of impure or falsely labeled food or drugs, and it forces producers to specify the quantity and quality of the contents on labels. These requirements strengthen the price system. Without them, the typical consumer would be unable to tell whether food or drugs are pure or properly labeled. Unless consumers can be sure that they are getting what they pay for, the basic logic underlying the price system breaks down. Similar regulation and legislation have been instituted in fields other than food and drugs—and for similar reasons.

MAINTAINING A COMPETITIVE FRAMEWORK

Besides establishing a legal and social framework that will enable the price system to do its job, *the government must also see to it that markets remain reasonably competitive.* Only if they are will prices reflect consumer desires properly. If, on the other hand, markets are dominated by a few sellers (or a few buyers), prices may be "rigged" by these sellers (or buyers) to promote their own interests. For example, if a single firm is the sole producer of aluminum, it is a safe bet that this firm will establish a higher price than if there were many aluminum producers competing among themselves. The unfortunate thing about prices determined in noncompetitive markets—rigged prices, if you will—is that they give incorrect signals concerning what consumers want and how scarce resources and commodities are. Producers, responding to these incorrect signals, do not produce the right things in the right quantities. Consumers respond to these incorrect signals by not supplying the right resources in the right amounts, and by not consuming the proper amounts of the goods that are produced. Thus the price system is not permitted to solve the four basic economic problems properly in the absence of reasonable competition.

To try to encourage and preserve competition, the Congress has enacted a series of **antitrust laws,** such as the Sherman Antitrust Act and the Clayton Act, and it has established the Federal Trade Commission. The antitrust laws make it illegal for firms to collude or to attempt to monopolize the sale of a product. Both conservative and liberal economists, with some notable exceptions, tend to favor the intent and operation of the antitrust laws.

Redistribution of Income

We have already noted at several points the general agreement that the government should redistribute income in favor of the poor. In other words, *it is usually felt that help should be given to people who are ill, handicapped, old and infirm, disabled, and unable for other reasons to provide for themselves.* To some extent, the nation has decided that income—or at least a certain minimum income—should be divorced from productive services. Of course, this doesn't mean that people who are too lazy to work should be given a handout. It does mean that people who cannot provide for themselves should be helped. To implement this principle, various payments are made by the government to needy people—including the aged, the handicapped, the unemployed, and pensioners.

These ***welfare payments*** are to some extent a "depression baby," for they grew substantially during the Great Depression of the 1930s, when relief payments became a necessity. But they also represent a feeling shared by a large segment of the population that human beings should be assured that, however the wheel of fortune spins and whatever number comes up, they will not starve and their children will not be deprived of a healthy environment and basic schooling. Of course, someone has to pay for this. Welfare payments allow the poor to take more from the nation's output than they produce. In general, the more affluent members of society contribute some of their claims on output to pay for these programs, their contributions being in the form of taxes. By using its expenditures to help certain groups and by taxing other groups to pay for these programs, the government accomplishes each year, without revolt and without bayonets, a substantial redistribution of income. This is a crucial aspect of the government's role in our economy.

Stabilizing the Economy

It is also generally agreed that *the government should promote the maintenance of reasonably full employment with reasonably stable prices.* Capitalist economies have tended to alternate between booms and depressions in the past. The Great Depression of the 1930s hit the American economy—and the world economy—a particularly devastating blow, putting millions of people out of work and in desperate shape. When World War II ended, the American people vowed that they would not let a depression of this sort occur again. Congress passed the Employment Act of 1946, which stated that it was the responsibility of the federal government to maintain full employment in the United States. In particular, the federal government was not supposed to tolerate unemployment of the sort that materialized during severe depressions in the past.

Besides trying to maintain full employment, the government must also try to maintain a reasonably stable price level. No economy can function well if prices are gyrating wildly. Through its control of the money supply and its decisions regarding expenditures and taxation, the government has considerable impact on the price level, as well as on the level of employment. Unfortunately, during the 1970s in particular, the government was not very successful in maintaining price stability. According to many economists, the government's own policies contributed to this inflation.

Providing Public Goods

As we have indicated, the government provides many public goods. Let's consider the nature of public goods in more detail.

What Is a Public Good? One hallmark of a public good is that it can be consumed by one person without diminishing the amount that other people consume of it. Public goods tend to be relatively indivisible; they often come in such large units that they cannot be broken into pieces that can be bought or sold in ordinary markets. *Once such goods are produced, there often is no way to bar certain citizens from consuming them.* Whether or not citizens contribute toward their cost, they benefit from them. As pointed out in a previous section, this means that the price system cannot be used to handle effectively the production and distribution of such goods.

National Defense: A Public Good. National defense is a public good. The benefits of expenditure on national defense extend to the entire nation. Extension of the benefits of national defense to an additional citizen does not mean that any other citizen gets less of these benefits. Also, there is no way of preventing citizens from benefiting from them, whether they contribute to their cost or not. Thus there is no way to use the price system to provide for national defense. Since it is a public good, national defense, if it is to reach an adequate level, must be provided by the government. Similarly with flood control, environmental protection, and a host of other such services.

Decision Making Regarding Public Goods. Essentially, deciding how much to produce of a public good is a political decision. The citizens of the United States elect senators and congressmen who decide how much should be spent on national defense, and how it should be spent. These elected representatives are responsive to special-interest groups, as well as to the people as a whole. Many special-interest groups lobby hard for the production of certain public goods. For example, an alliance of military and industrial groups presses for increased defense expenditures, and other interested groups promote expenditures on other functions.

The tax system is used to pay for the production of public goods. In effect, the government says to each citizen, "Fork over a certain amount of money to pay for the expenses incurred by the government." The amount a particular citizen is assessed may depend on his or her income (as in the income tax), the value of all or specific types of his or her property (as in the property tax), the amount he or she spends on certain types of goods and services (as in the sales tax), or on still other criteria. In the 1980s, the tax system has often been the object of enormous controversy. Much more will be said about the tax system, and the controversies swirling around it, in a later section of this chapter

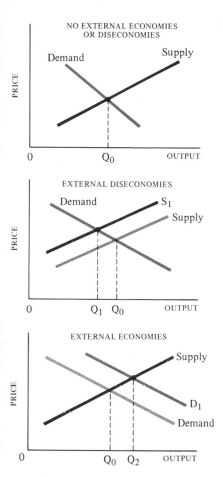

NO EXTERNAL ECONOMIES
OR DISECONOMIES

EXTERNAL DISECONOMIES

EXTERNAL ECONOMIES

***Effect of External Economies and
Diseconomies on the Optimal Output of
a Competitive Industry*** *The optimal
output is* OQ$_0$ *if neither external
economies nor diseconomies are present.
If there are external diseconomies, curve*
S$_1$ *reflects the true social costs of
producing the product, and* OQ$_1$ *is the
optimal output. If there are external
economies, curve* D$_1$ *reflects the true social benefits of producing the product,
and* OQ$_2$ *is the optimal output.*

Externalities

It is generally agreed that *the government should encourage the production
of goods and services that entail external economies and discourage the
production of those that entail external diseconomies.* Take the pollution of
air and water. When a firm or individual dumps wastes into the water or
air, other firms or individuals often must pay all or part of the cost of
putting the water or air back into a usable condition. Thus the disposal of
these wastes entails external diseconomies. Unless the government prohibits certain kinds of pollution, or enforces air and water quality standards, or charges polluters in accord with the amount of waste they dump
into the environment, there will be socially undesirable levels of pollution.

Effects of External Diseconomies. To see how such externalities affect the
social desirability of the output of a competitive industry, consider Figure
4.1, where the industry's demand and supply curves are contained in the
top panel. As shown there, the equilibrium output of the industry is OQ_0. If
the industry results in no external economies or diseconomies, this is likely
to be the socially optimal output. But what if the industry results in external
diseconomies, such as the pollution described above? Then the industry's
supply curve does not fully reflect the true social costs of producing the
product. The supply curve that reflects these social costs is S_1, which, as
shown in the middle panel of Figure 4.1, lies to the left of the industry's
supply curve. The optimal output of the good is OQ_1, which is less than the
competitive output, OQ_0.

What can the government do to correct the situation? There are a variety
of ways that it can intervene to reduce the industry's output from OQ_0 to
OQ_1. For example, it can impose taxes on the industry. If these taxes are of
the right type and amount, they will result in the desired reduction of output.

Effects of External Economies. What if the industry results in external
economies? For example, what if the manufacture of one industrial product
makes it cheaper to produce other products? Then the industry's demand
curve underestimates the true social benefits of producing the product. The
demand curve that reflects these social benefits correctly is D_1, which, as
shown in the bottom panel of Figure 4.1, lies to the right of the industry's
demand curve. The optimal output of the good is OQ_2, which is greater
than the competitive output, OQ_0.

As in the case where the industry results in external diseconomies, the
government can intervene in various ways to change the industry's output.
But in this case, the object is to increase, not decrease, its output. To accomplish this, the government can, among other things, grant subsidies to
the industry. If they are of the right type and amount, they can be used to
increase the industry's output from OQ_0 to OQ_2.

Size and Nature of Government Activities

HOW BIG IS THE GOVERNMENT?

Up to this point, we have been concerned primarily with the reasons why
the government must intervene in our economy—and the types of role it

Example 4.1 The Economics of Urban Blight

During the past 30 years, the federal government has promoted and encouraged the redevelopment of the inner core of our major cities. Consider two adjacent urban properties. Suppose that the two owners, Mr. Lombardi and Mr. Moore, are each trying to determine whether to invest $100,000 to redevelop their properties. If they do not invest the $100,000 in redevelopment, each can get a 10 percent return from other forms of investment. The rate of return on the $100,000 investment by each owner (which depends on whether the other owner redevelops his property as well) is shown below:

	Other Owner Redevelops	Other Owner Does Not Redevelop
	(percent)	
Redevelop	12	5
Do not redevelop	15	10

(a) If Mr. Lombardi redevelops his property, is Mr. Moore better off by redeveloping his property as well? (b) If Mr. Lombardi does not redevelop his property, is Mr. Moore better off by redeveloping his property? (c) Will either owner redevelop his property? (d) In a situation of this sort, can social gains be achieved by government intervention?

SOLUTION

(a) No, because the rate of return Mr. Moore receives if he redevelops is 12 percent, whereas the rate of return he receives if he does not redevelop is 15 percent (because his property benefits from Mr. Lombardi's investment in redevelopment even though he pays nothing). (b) No, because the rate of return Mr. Moore receives if he redevelops is only 5 percent (because little is accomplished so long as Mr. Lombardi does not redevelop too), whereas the rate of return he receives if he does not redevelop is 10 percent (which is what he can obtain from other investments). (c) No. Consider Mr. Moore. As pointed out in (a) and (b), whether or not Mr. Lombardi redevelops, Mr. Moore receives a higher return if he does not redevelop than if he does. Thus he will not redevelop. Neither will Mr. Lombardi, for the same reasons. (d) Yes. From society's point of view, or from the point of view of the two owners acting together as a unit, redevelopment may be desirable. If carried out properly, government intervention may bring this about.

should play—but we have made little or no attempt to describe its role in quantitative terms. It is time now to turn to some of the relevant facts. One useful measure of the extent of the government's role in the American economy is the size of government expenditures, both in absolute terms and as a percent of our nation's total output.

The sum total of government expenditures—federal, state, and local—was about $1.2 trillion in 1983. Since the nation's total output was about $3.3 trillion, this means that government expenditures were about one-third of our total output. The ratio of government expenditures to total output in

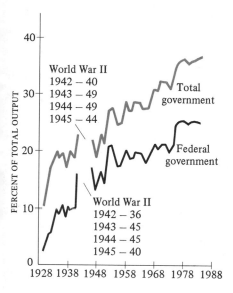

Figure 4.2

Government Spending as a Percent of Total Output, United States *Government expenditures—federal, state, and local—totaled about $1.2 trillion in 1983. These expenditures, which include transfer payments, have grown more rapidly than total output in this period.*

the United States has not always been this large, as Figure 4.2 shows. In 1929, the ratio was about 10 percent, as contrasted with over 30 percent in 1983. (Of course, the ratio of government spending to total output is smaller now than during World War II, but in a wartime economy, one would expect this ratio to be abnormally high.)

There are many reasons why government expenditures have grown so much faster than total output. Three of these are particularly important. First, *the United States did not maintain anything like the kind of military force in pre-World War II days that it does now.* In earlier days, when weapons were relatively simple and cheap, and when we viewed our military and political responsibilities much more narrowly than we do now, our military budget was relatively small. The cost of being a superpower in the days of nuclear weaponry is high by any standards. Second, *there has been a long-term increase in the demand for the services provided by government,* like more and better schooling, more extensive highways, more complete police and fire protection, and so forth. As incomes rise, people want more of these services. Third, ***government transfer payments**—payments in return for no products or services—have grown substantially.* For example, various types of welfare payments have increased markedly. (Another transfer payment, social security, increased from about $20 billion in 1965 to about $180 billion in 1984.) Since transfer payments do not entail any reallocation of resources from private to public goods, but a transfer of income from one private citizen or group to another, Figure 4.2 is, in some respects, an overstatement of the role of the public sector.

WHAT THE FEDERAL, STATE, AND LOCAL GOVERNMENTS SPEND MONEY ON

There are three levels of government in the United States—federal, state, and local. The state governments spend the least, while the federal government spends the most. This was not always the case. Before World War I, the local governments spent more than the federal government. In those days, the federal government did not maintain the large military establishment it does now, nor did it engage in the many programs in health, education, welfare, and other areas that it currently does. Figure 4.2 shows that federal spending is now a much larger percentage of the total than it was 40 years ago. Table 4.1 shows how the federal government spends its money. *About one-third of the federal expenditures goes for the defense and other items connected with international relations and national security. About one-half goes for social security, welfare (and other income security) programs, health, and education. The rest goes to support farm, transportation, housing, and other such programs,* as well as to run Congress, the courts, and the executive branch of the federal government.

What about the local and state governments? On what do they spend their money? Table 4.2 shows that *the biggest expenditure of the state and local governments is on schools.* After the end of World War II, these expenditures increased greatly because of the baby boom—the increase in number of school-age children. Traditionally, schools in the United States have been a responsibility of local governments—cities and towns. *State governments spend most of their money on education; welfare, old age, and unemployment benefits; and highways.* (Besides supporting education directly, they help localities to cover the costs of schooling.) In addition, the

Table 4.1

FEDERAL EXPENDITURES, FISCAL 1986

Purpose	Amount (billions of dollars)	Percent of total	Purpose	Amount (billions of dollars)	Percent of total
National defense	286	29	Transportation	26	3
International affairs	18	2	Community and		
Energy	5	1	regional		
Veterans' benefits	27	3	development	7	1
General science,			Interest	143	15
space, and			General government	5	1
technology	9	1	Income security	116	12
Agriculture	13	1	Administration of		
Education, training,			justice	5	1
employment, and			General purpose		
social services	29	3	fiscal assistance	3	b
Health	35	4	Social security		
Natural resources			and medicare	269	28
and environment	12	1	Offsetting receipts	−37	−4
Commerce and			Total[a]	974	100
housing credit	2	b			

[a] Because of rounding errors, the figures may not sum to totals.
[b] Less than ½ of 1 percent.

Source: Economic Report of the President, 1985. These are estimates made in 1985.

Table 4.2

EXPENDITURES OF STATE AND LOCAL
GOVERNMENTS, UNITED STATES, 1983

Type of expenditure	Amount (billions of dollars)	Percent of total
Education	164	35
Highways	37	8
Public welfare	60	13
Other	205	44
Total	466	100

Source: Economic Report of the President,
1985.

local and state governments support hospitals, redevelopment programs, courts, and police and fire departments.

Changes in View of Government Responsibilities

We have already seen that government expenditures in the United States have grown considerably, both in absolute amount and as a percentage of our total output. This growth in government expenditures was part of a general trend in the United States toward a more extensive role of government in the economy. Two hundred years ago, there was considerable suspicion of government interference and meddling, freedom was the watchword, and governments were viewed as potential tyrants. In the nineteenth century, the United States prospered mightily under this *laissez-faire* system, but gradually—and not without considerable protest—the nation began to interpret the role of the government differently.

INCREASES IN GOVERNMENT ROLE

Responding to the dangers of noncompetitive markets, states were given the power to regulate public utilities and railroads. The Interstate Commerce Commission was established in 1887 to regulate railroads operating across state lines; and the Sherman Antitrust Act was passed in 1890 to curb monopoly and promote competition. To help control recurring business fluctuations and financial panics, banking and finance were regulated. In 1913, the Federal Reserve System was established as a central bank controlling the

About 29 percent of the federal budget goes for defense. Decisions concerning how much to spend on what kinds of weapons systems are enormously complex and involve a mixture of military, political, and economic considerations. To illustrate some of these considerations, take the case of the B-1 bomber. As early as 1954, the Air Force began to think about a replacement for the B-52 bomber, but both Presidents Kennedy and Johnson were not impressed with the need for it, since they felt that strategic missiles would be more efficient and accurate than a new manned bomber.

Nonetheless, the Air Force and its contractors did not give up on the idea of the new bomber, and even after President Carter blocked the production of such a bomber in 1977, they continued to push for it. Moreover, the Armed Services Committee of the House of Representatives approved more than $300 million for research and development on this airplane between 1977 and 1980. Within the Pentagon, a group of Air Force officers, led by General Kelly Burke, worked hard to make the bomber a reality. When the Reagan administration was elected in 1980, the political climate was much more favorable, and in January 1982 Congress voted approval of the B-1 program.

To help build political support for the B-1 program, Rockwell, the builder of the B-1, farmed out the airplane's production among thousands of subcontractors. For example, the prototype engines were built in Lynn, Massachusetts; the actuators were built in Kalamazoo, Michigan; and so on. Nearly every member of Congress had a firm in his or her district that had a stake in the B-1 program.

The B-1 program is likely to cost at least $20 billion. But the costs of weapons systems are often underestimated, since this makes it easier to sell them to Congress. For a long time, the B-1 systems program office at Wright-Patterson Air Force Base made two different cost estimates, according to one report. "One [estimate] showed what we'd said the B-1 would cost. The other showed what we really thought it would cost."*

Whether the B-1 will be an effective weapons system has been the subject of great controversy. Some argue that it will be slow, sluggish, and limited in range. Like the B-52, the B-1 would need mid-air refueling both going to and returning from the Soviet Union. According to some experts, it makes more sense to modernize the existing B-52 bombers until Stealth (a new bomber that is claimed to be more effective in avoiding enemy defenses than the B-1) comes along. In 1984, the first Stealth was tentatively scheduled to appear in 1991–92.

The amount of resources devoted to military programs of this sort is nothing less than mammoth. (In the case of the B-1, at least $20 billion will be spent for 100 airplanes!) Few people would question the need for a strong and effective national defense, but there is a widespread feeling that the weapons acquisition process is not as efficient as it might be. In August 1984, one of the first B-1 bombers crashed in the Mojave Desert, thus provoking more controversy concerning this already controversial military procurement program.

* "Is the B-1 a Plane Whose Time Has Come?" *Philadelphia Inquirer,* March 18, 1984.

member commercial banks. In 1933, the Federal Deposit Insurance Corporation was established to insure bank deposits. And in 1934, the Securities and Exchange Commission was established to watch over the financial markets.

In addition, the government's role in the fields of labor and welfare expanded considerably. For example, in the 1930s minimum-wage laws were enacted, old-age pensions and unemployment insurance were established, and the government became an important force in collective bargaining and labor relations. Furthermore, the power of government was used increasingly to ensure that citizens did not fall below a certain economic level. Food-stamp programs and programs to provide aid to dependent children were established. *In general, the broad trend in the United States in the century up to about 1975 or 1980 was for the government to be used to a greater and greater extent to achieve social objectives.*

RECENT CHANGES IN ATTITUDE

However, during the 1970s and early 1980s there was a pronounced change in the public's attitude toward the government. People seemed more inclined to question the government's capacity to solve the difficult social problems that confront our nation. In part, this seemed to be due to the apparent failure of large and expensive government programs initiated to solve a variety of social ills, such as poverty. In part, it seemed to reflect a general cynicism concerning government and politicians. One public-opinion poll after another showed that the public was irritated by the payment of what it regarded as excessively high taxes.

In 1978, California's voters supported Proposition 13 by nearly a 2-to-1 margin. Proposition 13 called for a 57 percent cut in the property tax and decreed that no local tax may increase by more than 2 percent per year. Californians were angry at the rapid increase in their property taxes during the 1970s. One Los Angeles family bought a house for $64,000 in 1968 and its property tax then was $1,800. By 1976, it had increased to $3,500, and without Proposition 13, it soon would have gone to $7,000. Californians supported Proposition 13 as a way to offset past increases and limit future increases in the property tax.

In the 1980 elections, Ronald Reagan won the presidency in part by promising to get government "off the backs" of citizens. In his first years in office, he cut back the rate of growth of federal expenditure and reduced many government programs. In 1984, he ran again on a platform that emphasized the reduction of government's role (but an increase in defense expenditure). Again he won. Certainly, the prevailing attitude was different than in the 1960s. How long this change in attitude will persist is hard to say, but while it lasts, conservatives tend to be happy and liberals tend to be concerned.

What the Federal, State, and Local Governments Receive in Taxes

To get the money to cover most of the expenditures discussed in previous sections, governments collect taxes from individuals and firms. As Table 4.3

Table 4.3
FEDERAL RECEIPTS BY TAX, FISCAL 1986

Type of tax	Amount (billions of dollars)	Percent of total
Personal income tax	359	45
Corporation income tax	74	9
Employment taxes	289	36
Excise taxes	35	4
Estate and gift taxes	5	1
Other revenues	31	4
Total[a]	794	100

[a] Because of rounding errors, the figures may not sum to totals.

Source: Economic Report of the President, 1985. These are estimates made in 1985.

FEDERAL, STATE, LOCAL GOV'T TAX
RECEIPTS

Table 4.4

STATE AND LOCAL TAX REVENUES, BY
SOURCE, 1983

Source	Revenues (billions of dollars)	Percent of total
General sales tax	100	25
Property tax	89	22
Personal income tax	55	14
Corporate income tax	14	4
Other taxes	138	35
Total[a]	396	100

[a] Because of rounding errors, the figures may not sum to the totals.

Source: Economic Report of the President, 1985.

shows, *at the federal level the **personal income tax** is the biggest single money raiser.* It brings in almost one-half of the tax revenue collected by the federal government. The next most important taxes at the federal level are the Social Security, payroll, and employment taxes. Other noteworthy taxes are the corporation income tax, excise taxes (levied on the sale of tobacco, liquor, imports, and certain other items), and death and gift taxes. (Even when the Grim Reaper shows up, the Tax Man is not far behind.)

*At the local level, on the other hand, the most important form of taxation and source of revenue is the **property tax.*** This is a tax levied primarily on real estate. Other important local taxes—although dwarfed in importance by the property tax—are local sales taxes and local income taxes. Many cities—for example, New York City—levy a sales tax, equal to a certain percent—4 percent in New York City—of the value of each retail sale. The tax is simply added on to the amount charged the customer. Also, many cities—for example, Philadelphia and Pittsburgh—levy an income (or wage) tax on their residents and even on people who work in the city but live outside it. *At the state level, **sales (and excise) taxes** are the biggest money raisers,* followed by income taxes and highway-user taxes. The latter include taxes on gasoline and license fees for vehicles and drivers. Often they exceed the amount spent on roads, and the balance is used for a variety of nonhighway uses. (See Table 4.4.)

Although some people claim that taxes in the United States are higher than in most other industrialized countries, this really is not true. When we compare taxes in the United States (relative to total output) with those in other countries, we learn that the governments of Sweden, France, West Germany, and the United Kingdom tax more—as a percent of total output—than we do. In part, of course, this is because of the extensive welfare programs in Sweden and the United Kingdom. It is interesting, however, that, despite our huge military programs, our government does not tax and spend more (relative to total output) than these countries.

Test Yourself

1. "I believe the government should do only that which private citizens cannot do for themselves, or which they cannot do so well for themselves." Interpret and comment. Indicate how one might determine in practice what the legitimate functions of government are, according to this proposition.

2. "The ideal public policy, from the viewpoint of the state, is one with identifiable beneficiaries, each of whom is helped appreciably, at the cost of many unidentifiable persons, none of whom is hurt much."* Interpret and comment. Indicate how this proposition might be used to help predict government behavior.

3. Explain why national defense is a public good but a rifle is not a public good.

4. "I cannot get the amount of national defense I want and you, a different amount."** Explain. Is this true of all public goods?

5. According to the 1985 *Economic Report of the President,* the federal government will spend about $8.7 billion on general science, space, and technology in fiscal 1985. Why should the government support each of these activities?

* G. Stigler, "The Government of the Economy," in E. Mansfield, *Principles of Microeconomics: Readings, Issues, and Cases.*

** M. Friedman, *Capitalism and Freedom.*

The Role of Government in American Agriculture

Thus far, we have been discussing the government's role in the American economy in rather general terms. Now we need to consider in some detail a particular example of the economic programs carried out by our government. The government's farm programs are a logical choice, because they illustrate the usefulness of the supply-and-demand analysis presented in the previous chapter. It is important to recognize at the outset that these farm programs are not being held up as a representative sample of what the government does. There are a host of other government economic programs—poverty programs, urban programs, defense programs, research programs, education programs, transportation programs, fiscal programs, monetary programs, and many more. Most of these programs will be discussed at some point in this book.

Agriculture is an enormously important sector of the American economy. Even though its size has been decreasing steadily—and this contraction has been going on for many decades—agriculture still employs about 3 million Americans. Its importance, moreover, cannot be measured entirely by its size. You need only think about how difficult it would be to get along without food to see the strategic role agriculture plays in our economic life. Also, when it comes to technological change, agriculture is one of the most progressive parts of the American economy. The efficiency of American agriculture is admired throughout the world.

The Farm Problem

Nonetheless, it is widely acknowledged that American agriculture has had serious problems. Perhaps the clearest indication of these problems is shown by a comparison of per capita income of American farmers with per capita income among the rest of the population. Until the past ten years, it is clear that farm incomes have tended to be much lower than nonfarm incomes. In 1970, per capita income on the farms was about 20 percent below that for the nonfarm population. Moreover, a large proportion of the rural population is poor. Thus the National Advisory Commission on Rural Poverty found that "rural poverty is so widespread, and so acute, as to be a national disgrace."[4] Of course, this does not mean that all farmers are poor: on the contrary, many do very well indeed. But a large percentage of the nation's farmers are poor by any standard.

This farm problem is nothing new. During the first two decades of the twentieth century, farmers enjoyed relatively high prices and relatively high incomes. But in 1920, the country experienced a sharp depression that jolted agriculture as well as the rest of the economy. Whereas the Roaring Twenties saw a recovery and boom in the nonfarm sector of the economy, agriculture did not recover as completely, and the 1930s were dreadful years; the Great Depression resulted in a sickening decline in farm prices and farm incomes. World War II brought prosperity to agriculture, but in

[4] National Advisory Committee on Rural Poverty, *The People Left Behind*, Washington, D.C., 1967.

the postwar period, farm incomes continually have been well below non-farm incomes. In 1973 to 1975, prosperity returned to the farms, but the late 1970s and 1980s saw renewed complaints by farmers about prices and incomes. All in all, agriculture has had difficulties for several decades.

CAUSES OF THE FARM PROBLEM

In Chapter 1, we claimed that relatively simple economic models are of considerable use in understanding important public and private problems. To back up this claim, we will apply the simple models of market behavior presented in the previous chapter—the models involving market demand curves and market supply curves—to explain the basic causes of the problems that have tended to besiege agriculture.

Characteristics of Demand and Supply. Let's start with the market demand curve for farm products. If you think about it for a moment, you will agree that this market demand curve must have two important characteristics. First, *its shape must reflect the fact that food is a necessity and that the quantity demanded will not vary much with the price of food.* Second, *the market demand curve for food is unlikely to shift to the right very much as per capita income rises,* because consumption of food per capita faces natural biological and other limitations.

Next, consider the market supply curve for farm products. Again, you should be aware of two important characteristics of this market supply curve. First, *the quantity of farm products supplied tends to be relatively insensitive to price,* because the farmers have only limited control over their output. (Weather, floods, insects, and other such factors are very important.) Second, because of the rapid technological change emphasized in a previous section, *the market supply curve has been shifting markedly and rapidly to the right.*

Decline in Relative Food Prices. If you understand these simple characteristics of the market demand curve and market supply curve for farm products, it is no trick at all to understand why we have had the sort of farm problem just described. Figure 4.3 shows the market demand and market supply curves for farm products at various points in time. As you would expect, the market demand curve for farm products shifts rather slowly to the right as incomes (and population) grow over time. Specifically, the market demand curve shifted from D in the first period to D_1 in the second period to D_2 in the third period. On the other hand, the market supply curve for farm products shifted rapidly to the right as technology improved over time. Specifically, it shifted from S in the first period to S_1 in the second period to S_2 in the third period.

What was the consequence of these shifts in the market demand and supply curves for food products? Clearly, *the equilibrium price of food products fell (relative to other products).* Specifically, the equilibrium price fell from OP to OP_1 to OP_2 in Figure 4.3. This price decrease was, of course, a large part of the farm problem. If we correct for changes in the general level of prices (which have tended to rise over time), there was, in general, a declining trend in farm prices. That is, agricultural prices generally fell, relative to other prices, in the last 60 years. Moreover, *given this fall in farm prices, farm incomes tended to fall, because, although lower prices were as-*

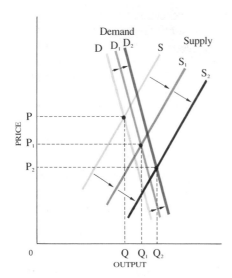

Figure 4.3

**Shifts over Time in Market Demand and
Supply Curves for Farm Products**   *The
market demand curve has shifted rather
slowly to the right (from* D *to* D₁ *to* D₂*),
whereas the market supply curve has
shifted rapidly to the right (from* S *to* S₁
to S₂*), with the result that the equilibrium
price has declined (from* OP *to* OP₁ *to*
OP₂*).*

*sociated with greater amounts sold, the reduction was much greater
than the increase in quantity sold,* as shown in Figure 4.3.[5]

Thus the simple model of market behavior described in the previous
chapter makes it possible to explain the fact that, in real terms, farm prices
and farm incomes have tended to fall in the United States. Certainly there is
nothing mysterious about these trends. Given the nature and characteristics
of the market demand curve and market supply curve for farm products,
our simple model shows that these trends are as much to be expected as
parades on the Fourth of July.

SLOW EXIT OF RESOURCES

However, one additional fact must be noted to understand the farm problem: *people and nonhuman resources have been relatively slow to move out
of agriculture in response to these trends.* Recall from the previous chapter
that the price system uses such trends—lower prices and lower incomes—to
signal producers that they should use their resources elsewhere. Farmers
have been loath to move out of agriculture (even though they often could
make more money elsewhere)—and this has been a primary cause of the
farm problem that has existed over most of the past 40 years. If more people and resources had left farming, agricultural prices and incomes would
have risen, and ultimately farm incomes would have come closer to nonfarm incomes. (Poor education and color were, of course, significant barriers to migration.)

Nonetheless, even though farmers have been slow to move out of agriculture, they have left the farm in the long run. In 1930 the farm population
was about 30 million, or 25 percent of the total population; in 1950, it was
about 23 million, or 15 percent of the total population; and in 1983, it was
about 6 million, or 3 percent of the total population. Thus the price system
has had its way. Resources have been moving out of agriculture in response
to the signals and pressures of the price system. This movement of people
and nonhuman resources unquestionably has contributed to greater efficiency and production for the nation as a whole. But during most of the
past 40 years, we have continued to have a "surplus" of farmers—and this
has been the root of the farm problem.

Government Aid to Agriculture

Traditionally, farmers have had a disproportionately large influence in
Congress; and faced with declining economic fortunes, they appealed to
the government for help. They extolled the virtues of rural life, emphasized that agriculture is a competitive industry, and claimed that it was
unfair for their prices to fall relative to the prices they have had to pay. In
addition, they pointed out that the movement of resources out of agriculture has entailed large human costs, since this movement, although bene-

---

[5] The amount farmers receive is the amount they sell times the price. Thus, in Figure 4.3, the
amount farmers receive in income is $OP \times OQ$ in the first period, $OP_1 \times OQ_1$ in the second
period, and $OP_2 \times OQ_2$ in the third period. Clearly, since the price is decreasing much more
rapidly than the quantity is increasing, farm incomes are falling.

ficial to the nation as a whole, has been traumatic for the farm population. For reasons of this sort, they argued that the government should help farmers; and in particular, that the government should act to bolster farm prices and farm incomes.

THE CONCEPT OF PARITY

Their voices were heard. In the Agricultural Adjustment Act of 1933, the Congress announced the concept of parity as the major objective of American farm policy. This concept acquired great importance—and must be clearly understood. Put in its simplest terms, the concept of *parity* says that a farmer should be able to exchange a given quantity of his output for as much in the way of nonfarm goods and services as he could at some time in the past. For example, if a farmer could take a bushel of wheat to market in 1912 and get enough money to buy a pair of gloves, today he should be able to get enough money for a bushel of wheat to buy a pair of gloves.

To see what the concept of parity implies for farm prices, suppose that the price of gloves triples. Obviously, if parity is to be maintained, the price of wheat must triple too. Thus the concept of parity implies that farm prices must increase at the same rate as the prices of the goods and services farmers buy. Of course, farmers buy lots of things besides gloves, so in actual practice the parity price of wheat or other farm products is determined by the changes over time in the average price of all the goods and services farmers buy.

Two major points should be noted about parity. First, to use this concept, one must agree on some base period, such as 1912 in the example above, during which the relationship of farm to nonfarm prices is regarded as equitable. Obviously, the higher farm prices were relative to nonfarm prices in the base period, the higher farm prices will be in subsequent periods if parity is maintained. It is interesting to note that 1910–14 was used for many years as the base period. Since this was a period of relatively high farm prices and of agricultural prosperity, the farm bloc must have wielded considerable political clout on this issue. Second, note that the concept of parity is an ethical, not a scientific proposition. It states what the relative economic position of a bushel of wheat ought to be—or more precisely, it states one particular view of what the relative economic position of a bushel of wheat should be. Based on purely scientific considerations, there is no way to prove (or disprove) this proposition, since it is based on one's values and political preferences. Using the terminology of Chapter 1, it is a proposition in normative, not positive economics.

Price Supports and Surplus Controls

During the four decades up to 1973, the concept of parity was the cornerstone of a system of government price supports. In many cases, the government did not support farm prices at the full 100 percent of parity. For example, Congress may have enacted a bill saying that the secretary of agriculture could establish a price of wheat, corn, cotton, or some other

Figure 4.4
Effects of Farm Price-Support Program
The support price, OP', *is above the equilibrium price,* OP, *so the public buys* OQ₂, *farmers supply* OQ₁ *units of output, and the government buys the difference* (OQ₁ − OQ₂).

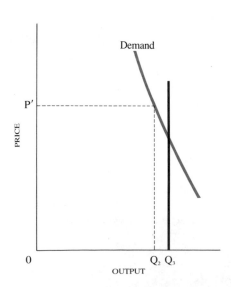

Figure 4.5
Effects of Price Supports and Output Restrictions *The government restricts output to* OQ₃, *with the result that it buys* (OQ₃ − OQ₂) *units of output.*

product that is between 65 and 90 percent of parity. But whatever the exact level of the price supports, the idea behind them was perfectly simple: it was to maintain farm prices above the level that would result in a free market.

Using the simple supply-and-demand model developed in the previous chapter, we can see more clearly the effects of these price supports. The situation is shown in Figure 4.4. A support price, OP', was set by the government. Since this support price was above the equilibrium price, OP, the public bought *less* of farm products (OQ_2 rather than OQ) and paid a *higher* price for them. Farmers gained from the price supports, since the amount they received for their crop under the price support was equal to $OP' \times OQ_1$, a greater amount than what they would have received in a free market, which was $OP \times OQ$.

Note, however, that since the support price exceeded the equilibrium price, the quantity supplied of the farm product, OQ_1, exceeded the quantity demanded, OQ_2. That is, *there was a surplus of the farm product in question*, which the government had to purchase, since no one else would. These surpluses were an embarrassment, both economically and politically. They showed that society's scarce resources were being utilized to produce products consumers simply did not want at existing prices. Moreover the cost of storing these surpluses was very large indeed: in some years, these storage costs alone hit the $1-billion mark.

POLICIES TO CUT SURPLUSES

To help reduce these surpluses, the government followed two basic strategies: First, *it tried to restrict output of farm products.* In particular, the government established an acreage allotment program, which said that farmers had to limit the number of acres they planted in order to get price supports on their crops. The Department of Agriculture estimated how much of each product would be demanded by buyers (other than the government) at the support price, and tried to cut back the total acreage planted with this crop to the point where the quantity supplied equaled the quantity demanded. These output restrictions did not eliminate the surpluses, because farmers managed to increase the yields from acreage they were allowed to plant, but undoubtedly they reduced the surpluses. With these restrictions, the situation was as shown in Figure 4.5, where OQ_3 was the total output that could be grown on the acreage that could be planted with the crop. Because of the imposition of this output control, the surplus—which the government had to purchase—was reduced from $(OQ_1 − OQ_2)$ to $(OQ_3 − OQ_2)$. Farmers continued to benefit from price supports because the amount they received for their crop—$OP' \times OQ_3$—was still greater than they would have received in a free market, because the amount demanded of farm products was not very sensitive to their price.

Second, *the government tried to shift the demand curve for farm products to the right.* An effort was made to find new uses for various farm products. Also, various antipoverty programs, such as the food-stamp program, used our farm surpluses to help the poor. In addition, the government tried to expand the export markets for American farm products. Western Europe and Japan increased their demand for food, and the Communist countries

Figure 4.6
Effects of Price Supports, Output Restrictions, and a Shift to the Right in the Demand Curve for Farm Products
By shifting the demand curve to the right, the government reduces the surplus from (OQ₃ − OQ₂) to (OQ₃ − OQ₄) units of output.

purchased our farm products to offset their own agricultural deficiencies. Moreover, the less developed countries were permitted by Public Law 480 to buy our farm products with their own currencies, rather than dollars. The result was a reduction in farm surpluses, as shown in Figure 4.6. Since the market demand curve for farm products shifted to the right, the surplus was reduced from $(OQ_3 - OQ_2)$ to $(OQ_3 - OQ_4)$. Because of these demand-augmenting and output-restricting measures, surpluses during the late 1960s and early 1970s were considerably smaller than they were during the late 1950s and early 1960s.

The 1973 Farm Bill and More Recent Developments

In 1973, farm prices increased markedly, due partly to very great increases in foreign demand for American agricultural products. This increase in foreign demand was due partly to poor harvests in the Soviet Union, Australia, Argentina, and elsewhere, as well as to devaluations of the dollar. (In 1972–73, the Soviet Union alone bought over $1 billion of grain—on terms that provoked considerable controversy in the United States.) As a result, farm incomes reached very high levels, farm surpluses disappeared, and for the first time in 30 years the government was trying to stimulate farm production rather than restrict it.

THE 1973 BILL

Taking advantage of this new climate, Congress passed a new farm bill which ended price supports. This bill, the Agriculture and Consumer Protection Act of 1973, aimed at reducing government involvement in agriculture and at a return to freer markets. Specifically, agricultural prices were allowed to fluctuate freely in accord with supply and demand. However, the government made cash payments to farmers if prices fell below certain "target" levels established by the law. These target levels were above the prices that generally prevailed in the past, but they were below the high levels of prices prevailing in 1973. A program of this kind was originally proposed in 1949 by Charles F. Brannan, who was secretary of agriculture under President Harry Truman. More will be said about the Brannan plan in Chapter 6.

Besides establishing these new forms of subsidies, the 1973 farm bill limited total subsidy payments to any individual farmer to $20,000 per year. This provision was meant to deal more effectively than did the prior law with the problem of very large subsidies being paid to wealthy farmers. Also, the 1973 law stated that whether or not land is taken out of production is at the discretion of the secretary of agriculture. In 1974, Secretary Earl Butz said that none should be taken out of production, and encouraged farmers to produce as much as they wanted. Nonetheless, in 1974, American crop production as a whole suffered its biggest setback in almost 40 years, due primarily to bad weather. Coupled with continued strong foreign demand for farm products, as well as domestic demand, the result was another year of high farm prices.

CHANGES IN GOVERNMENT INVOLVEMENT

By 1975 it appeared to many knowledgeable observers that the farm sector no longer was suffering from overcapacity, and that, in this respect at least, an equilibrium had been achieved. However, this attitude did not last long. During 1976 and 1977 U.S. farmers harvested bumper crops, with the result that prices fell considerably. The price of wheat, which had been about $3.50 per bushel in 1975, fell to about $2.30 per bushel in 1977. Farmers protested, and exerted political pressure for increased government price and income supports.

In 1977 Congress passed the Food and Agricultural Act, which contained flexible price-support levels and income supports. And in the late 1970s Secretary of Agriculture Bob Bergland said that a substantial amount of farmland had to be taken out of production. No longer was there much talk about a return to freer markets. Instead, the emphasis seemed to be on more support for farm prices and incomes.

In 1983 the Reagan administration adopted the $9 billion payment-in-kind program (PIK) in response to large grain harvests—the idea being to pay farmers for idling acreage by giving them crops stored by the government. Although this program was supposed to hold down government cash payments, expenditures soared to about $19 billion. Faced with huge government deficits, the Reagan administration announced in 1985 that it would try to persuade Congress to slash farm subsidy programs. However, many congressmen and senators (particularly from farm states) were skeptical about the chances that such a dramatic policy shift would be adopted.

Indeed, in late 1985, the trend seemed to be in the other direction. A substantial number of farmers were reported to be unable to pay their debts, and farm groups (and banks) were pressing for government help. Congress passed a bill calling for about $169 billion in spending over five years.

Evaluation of Government Farm Programs

It is obviously hard to evaluate the success of the government's farm programs. Farmers will certainly take a different view of price supports and other measures than their city cousins. Nonetheless, from the point of view of the nation as a whole, these farm programs have received considerable criticism. To understand these criticisms, we must hark back to our discussion earlier in this chapter of the proper functions of government, and ask what justification there is for the government's intervening in this way in agriculture. Perhaps the most convincing justification is that the government ought to help the rural poor. As we saw in previous sections, most people agree that the government should redistribute income in this way.

Have the Poor Been Helped? Unfortunately, however, *our farm programs have done little for the farmers most in need of help,* because the amount of money a farmer has gotten from these programs has depended on how much he produced. Thus the big farmers have gotten the lion's share of the subsidies—and they, of course, needed help least. On the other hand, the small farmers, the farmers who are mired mostly deeply in poverty, have received little from these programs. Recognizing this fact, many observers have pointed out that, if these programs are really aimed at helping the rural poor, it would be more sensible to channel the money to them through direct subsidies, than to finance programs where much of the benefits goes to prosperous commercial farmers.

Has the Farm Problem Been Solved? It must also be recognized that *our farm programs have not dealt with the basic causes of the farm problem.* In the past at least, we have had too many people and resources in agriculture. This, as we stressed in previous sections, is why farmers' incomes have tended to be low. Yet the government's farm programs have been directed more toward supporting farm prices and incomes (and stabilizing a sector of the economy that historically has been unstable), rather than toward promoting the needed movement of people and resources out of agriculture. Indeed, some people would say that the government's farm programs have made it more difficult for the necessary adjustments to take place.

Given these defects, many proposals have been made to alter our farm programs. In the view of many observers, agriculture should return to something more closely approximating free markets, and the price system should be allowed to work more freely. The changes that occurred in 1973 were in that direction, but it is important to note that the government is still intervening heavily in agriculture.

A BASIC MORAL

Basic Idea #8: *Just because the price system has well-known limitations, it does not follow that the task of organizing the nation's economic activities should be turned over to the government. As illustrated by our agricultural policies, the government has limitations of its own. Neither the price system nor the government is a panacea.*

Finally, before closing this chapter, we must point out a fundamental moral of our farm programs:

The government, like the price system, can bungle the job of organizing a nation's economic activities. We began this chapter by stressing the fact that the price system breaks down under some circumstances, and that the government must intervene. It is also worth stressing that the government sometimes intervenes when it shouldn't—and that even when it should intervene, it sometimes does so in a way that wastes resources. This, of course, doesn't mean that the government should play no part in the American economy. On the contrary, the government must—and does—play an important role. What it does mean is that, just as the price system is no all-purpose cure-all, neither is the government.

Test Yourself

1. Suppose that the demand and supply curves for paper are as shown on the right. If paper production results in serious pollution of rivers and streams, is the socially optimal output of paper less than, greater than, or equal to *OQ?* Does the supply curve reflecting the true social costs of producing paper lie to the right or to the left of the supply curve shown on the right? Why?

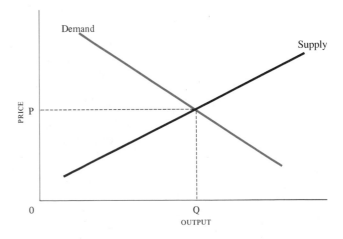

2. Suppose that paper production results in some important uncompensated benefits to other industries. If there are major external economies of this sort (and if paper production no longer results in any pollution), is the socially optimal output of paper less than, greater than, or equal to OQ in Question 1? Does the demand curve reflecting the true social benefits from paper output lie to the right or to the left of the demand curve shown in Question 1? Why?

3. Explain the nature of America's farm problem. To what extent have government policies solved the problem?

4. Suppose that the demand curve for corn is as follows:

Price (dollars per bushel)	Quantity demanded per year (millions of bushels)
1	70
2	65
3	60
4	55
5	50
6	45

If the government supports the price of corn at $4 per bushel, and if it restricts output to 60 million bushels per year, how much corn will the government have to buy each year? If the government stopped supporting the price of corn, what would its price be?

5. On August 8, 1982, David Stockman, director of President Reagan's Office of Management and Budget, wrote that, "There is ... [an] asymmetry between powerful and persuasive interest groups on the one hand and the general taxpayer on the other. For example, dairy subsidies are $7,000 per dairy producer but the individual taxpayer pays only about $18 a year for dairy subsidies." Explain how such an asymmetry can result in high levels of government spending.

6. "The sharp increases in the price of wheat during the mid-1970s were due primarily to shifts in the supply curve for wheat." Comment.

Summary

1. The price system, despite its many virtues, suffers from serious limitations. There is no reason to believe that the distribution of income generated by the price system is equitable or optimal. Also, there is no way for the price system to handle public goods properly, and because of external economies or diseconomies, the price system may result in too little or too much of certain goods being produced.

2. To a considerable extent, the government's role in the economy has developed in response to these limitations of the price system. There is considerable agreement that the government should redistribute income in favor of the poor, provide public goods, and offset the effects of external economies and diseconomies. Also, it is generally felt that the government should establish a proper legal, social and competitive framework for the price system, and that it should promote the maintenance of relatively full employment with reasonably stable prices.

3. Beyond this, however, there are wide differences of opinion on the proper role of government in economic affairs. Conservatives tend to be suspicious of "big government" while liberals are inclined to believe that the government should do more.

4. In the past 50 years, government spending has increased considerably, both in absolute terms and as a percent of total output. (It is now about one-third of our total output.) To a large extent, this increase has been due to our greater military responsibilities, as well as to the fact that, as their incomes have risen, our citizens have demanded more schools, highways, and other goods and services provided by government. Also, government transfer payments have grown substantially.

5. To get the money to cover most of these expenditures, governments collect taxes from individuals and firms. At the federal level, the most important form of taxation is the personal income tax; at the local level, the property tax is very important; and at the state level, sales (and excise) taxes are the biggest money raisers.

6. One example of the role of government in the American economy is the farm program. American agriculture has been plagued by relatively low incomes. In general, the demand for farm products grew slowly, while rapid technological change meant that the people and resources currently in agriculture could supply more and more farm products. Because people and resources did not move out of agriculture as rapidly as the price system dictated, farm incomes tended to be relatively low.

7. In response to political pressures from the farm blocs, the government set in motion a series of programs to aid farmers. A cornerstone of these programs was the concept of parity, which said that the prices farmers receive should increase at the same rate as the prices of the goods and services farmers buy. The government instituted price supports to keep farm prices above their equilibrium level. But since the support prices exceeded the equilibrium prices, there was a surplus of the commodities that the government had to purchase and store. To help reduce these surpluses, the government tried to restrict the output of farm products and expand the demand for them.

8. These farm programs received considerable criticism. From the point of view of income redistribution, they suffered from the fact that they did little for the farmers most in need of help. As tools of resource allocation, they suffered because they dealt more with the symptoms of the farm problem than with its basic causes. In 1973, price supports were ended, but the government pledged to make cash payments to farmers if farm prices fall below certain target levels. During the late 1970s and 1980s, the government continued to intervene heavily in agriculture.

9. The government's farm programs illustrate the fact that government intervention, like the price system, has plenty of limitations. Neither the price system nor government intervention is an all-purpose cure-all.

Concepts for Review

Public goods	Welfare payments	Property tax
External economy	Transfer payments	Sales tax
External diseconomy	Personal income tax	Parity
Antitrust laws		

CHAPTER 5

The Business Firm: Organization, Motivation, and Technology

It is hard to overstate the importance of business firms in the American economy. They produce the bulk of our goods and services, hire most of the nation's workers, and issue stocks and bonds that represent a large percentage of the nation's wealth. Judged by any yardstick—even less complimentary ones like the responsibility for environmental pollution—business firms are an extremely important part of the American economy. In this chapter, we discuss the various types of business firms, such as proprietorships and corporations. Then we describe the various types of securities—common stock, bonds, and so forth—issued by firms, and discuss the workings of the stock market. Next, we take up the motivation and structure of firms, as well as their technology. Finally, we provide some essential elements of accounting. This material is a necessary introduction to the workings of the business enterprise, absolutely essential to anyone who works for, manages, or invests in a firm.

The IBM Corporation: A Case Study

To begin with, let's look in some detail at one of America's biggest firms: the IBM Corporation. A description of its history and vicissitudes should give you a better feel for what firms do and the sorts of problems they face.

ELECTRONIC COMPUTERS: COMING FROM BEHIND

The IBM Corporation operated under the strong leadership of Thomas Watson, Sr., until his death in 1956. Watson joined the Computing-Tabulating-Recording Corporation in 1914, and renamed it International Business Machines in 1924. The firm became a very successful and fast-growing office-equipment company. In the late 1940s and early 1950s, the first electronic computers were developed, but IBM did not then appreciate the commercial potential of such equipment. According to Watson's son:

> During these really earth-shaking developments in the accounting machine industry, IBM slept soundly. We had put the first electronically-operated punched card calculator on the market in 1947. We clearly knew that electronic computing even in those days was so fast that the machine waited 9/10 of every card cycle for the mechanical portions of the machine to feed the next card. In spite of this, we didn't jump to the obvious conclusion that if we could feed data more rapidly, we could increase speeds by 900 percent. Remington Rand and Univac drew this conclusion and were off to the races.
>
> Finally we awoke and began to act. We took one of our most competent operating executives with a reputation for fearlessness and competence and put him in charge of all phases of the development of an IBM large-scale electronic computer. He and we were successful.
>
> How did we come from behind? First, we had enough cash to carry loads of engineering, research, and production, which were heavy. Second, we had a sales force which enabled us to tailor our machine very closely to the market. Finally, and most important, we had good company morale. All concerned realized that this was a mutual challenge to us as an industry leader. We had to respond with all that we had to win, and we did.[1]

SNOW WHITE AND THE SEVEN DWARFS

Although IBM was a slow starter, it soon became the dominant producer of electronic computers. By 1956, it had over 80 percent of the market. According to many observers, its success was due particularly to its marketing skills. In the 1960s, it became known as Snow White, while its rivals—Burroughs, Univac, NCR, Control Data, Honeywell, GE, and RCA—were referred to as the Seven Dwarfs. In the 1970s, after GE and RCA left the computer industry, only five dwarfs remained.

On January 17, 1969, the federal government brought a massive antitrust case against IBM, accusing it of monopolistic practices. The case went on for thirteen years. According to IBM's former chairman, Frank Cary, "The suit was a tremendous cloud that was over the company. . . . It couldn't help influencing us in a whole variety of ways. Ending it lifted a huge burden from management's shoulders." In January 1982, the Justice Department dropped the case, saying that it was "without merit."

Since the settlement of the case, IBM has been selling aggressively and entering new markets. Some observers are worried that it is becoming too big and powerful; others feel that it has plenty of competition from the Japanese, among others. In 1983, its net income of $5.5 billion made IBM the

---

[1] T. Belden and M. Belden, *The Lengthening Shadow: The Life of Thomas J. Watson,* Boston: Little, Brown, 1962.

world's most profitable industrial corporation, although sales of $40.2 billion made it only the world's seventh largest. In 1984, its profits were over $6.5 billion.

THE IBM PERSONAL COMPUTER

One of IBM's most dramatic recent moves was its entrance into the personal computer market in 1981. The job of overseeing the development of IBM's personal computer (PC) was entrusted to a twelve-member group, which worked for about a year on the project. The group broke with tradition by making the PC's technical specifications available to other firms, thus allowing outsiders to write software and make peripheral equipment for the PC that would extend its appeal. Within a few months after its introduction, the IBM PC was setting the standard for the industry. By 1983, IBM had garnered about 28 percent of the market for personal computers.

According to some observers, IBM will eventually gain a much larger share of the personal computer market, thus cutting into the sales of Apple Computer and others. Only time will tell whether this is true. But without question IBM's very successful entrance into the personal computer market during the early 1980s has transformed the computer industry.

Characteristics of American Firms: Some Salient Facts

IBM world headquarters

IBM is an economic colossus—a huge organization with over 300,000 employees. Of course it is not typical of American business firms. If we broaden our focus to take in the entire population of business firms in the United States, the first thing we note is their tremendous number; according to government statistics, there are about 16 million. The vast majority of these firms, as one would expect, is very small. There are lots of grocery stores, gas stations, auto dealers, drugstores, clothing shops, restaurants, and so on. You see hundreds of them as you walk along practically any downtown city street. But these small firms, although numerous, do not control the bulk of the nation's productive capacity. The several hundred largest firms have great economic power, measured by their sales, assets, employment, or other such indices. The small firms tend to be weak and short-lived. Although some prosper, many small firms go out of business after only a few years of existence.

The next thing to note is that *most of the nation's business firms are engaged in agriculture, services, and retail trade.* Table 5.1 shows that about three-quarters of the firms in the United States are in these industries, an understandable figure since these industries tend to have lots and lots of small businesses. *Although manufacturing firms constitute only about 3 percent of all American firms, they account for more than one-third of all business receipts.* On the other hand, agriculture (including forestry and fisheries) includes about 25 percent of the nation's business firms, but accounts for only 3 percent of the total receipts. Clearly, this is because manufacturing firms tend to be much bigger, in terms of receipts, employment, and assets, than agricultural firms. Think, for example, of the steel plants in Pittsburgh or Cleveland, or of the aircraft plants in California or

Table 5.1

NUMBER AND RECEIPTS OF BUSINESS FIRMS, BY INDUSTRY, UNITED STATES[a]

Industry	Number of firms (millions)	Receipts of firms (billions of dollars)
Agriculture, forestry, and fisheries	4.0	170
Mining	0.1	143
Construction	1.4	318
Manufacturing	0.5	2,099
Transportation, communication[b]	0.5	456
Wholesale and retail trade	3.4	1,968
Financial	2.1	353
Services	4.5	368
Total	16.2	5,877

[a] Figures may not sum to total due to rounding.
[b] Includes electric and gas.
Source: *Statistical Abstract of the United States.*

Georgia. They dwarf the typical farm—and they are only parts of a manufacturing firm.

Finally, note that *most of the nation's business firms are proprietorships;* indeed, almost four-fifths fall into this category, while about 14 percent are corporations, and about 8 percent are partnerships. You often hear the terms *proprietorship, partnership, corporation.* What do these terms mean?

Proprietorships

A proprietorship is a legal form of business organization—the most common form, as we saw in the previous section, and also the simplest. Specifically, a **proprietorship** is a firm owned by a single individual. A great many of the nation's small businesses are proprietorships. For example, the corner drugstore may well be one. If so, it has a single owner. He hires the people he needs to wait on customers, deliver orders, do the bookkeeping, and so forth. He borrows, if he can, whatever money he feels he needs. He reaps the profits, or incurs the losses. All his personal assets—his house, his furniture, his car—can be taken by creditors to meet the drugstore's bills; that is, he has unlimited liability for the debts of the business.

Pros. What Lincoln said about the common man applies as well to proprietorships: God must love them, or He wouldn't have created so many of them. If proprietorships didn't have advantages over other legal forms of business organization under many sorts of circumstances, there wouldn't be so many of them. What are these advantages? First, *owners of proprietorships have complete control over their businesses.* They don't have to negotiate with partners or other co-owners. They are the boss—and the only boss. Anyone who has been in a position of complete authority knows the joy it can bring. Many proprietors treasure this feeling of independence. Second, *a proprietorship is easy and inexpensive to establish:* all you have to do is hang out your shingle and announce you are in business. This too is a great advantage.

Cons. But proprietorships have important disadvantages as well—and for this reason, they are seldom found in many important industries. One disadvantage is that *it is difficult for a proprietor to put together enough financial resources to enter industries like automobiles, steel, or computers.* No one in the world has enough money to establish, by himself or herself, a firm of IBM's present size. Another disadvantage is that *proprietors are liable for all of the debts of the firm.* If their business fails, their personal assets can be taken by their creditors, and they can be completely wiped out.

Partnerships

A ***partnership*** is somewhat more complicated than a proprietorship. As its name implies, it is a form of business organization where two or more people agree to own and conduct a business. Each partner agrees to contribute some proportion of the capital and labor used by the business, and to receive some proportion of the profits or losses. There are a variety of types of partnerships. In some cases, one or more of the partners may be "silent partners," who put up some of the money, but have little or nothing to do with the operations of the firm. The partnership is a common form of business organization in some industries and professions, like the law. But as we saw in a previous section, partnerships are found less frequently than proprietorships or corporations in the United States.

Pros. A partnership has certain advantages. Like a proprietorship, *it can be established without great expense or legal red tape.* (However, if you ever go into a partnership with someone, you would be well advised to have a good lawyer draw up a written agreement establishing such things as the salaries of each partner and how profits are to be shared.) In addition, a partnership can avoid some of the problems involved in a proprietorship. *It can usually put together more financial resources and specialized know-how than a proprietorship*—and this can be an important advantage.

Cons. But the partnership also has certain drawbacks. First, *each partner is liable without limit for the bills of the firm.* For example, even if one partner of a law firm has only a 30 percent share of the firm, he or she may be called upon to pay all the firm's debts if the other partners cannot do so. Second, *there is some red tape in keeping a partnership in existence.* Whenever a partner dies or withdraws, or whenever a new partner is admitted, a new partnership must be established. Third, like the proprietorship, *the partnership is not a very effective way to obtain the large amounts of capital required for some modern industries.* A modern automobile plant may cost $500 million, and not many partnerships could assemble that much capital. For these reasons, as well as others discussed in the next section, the corporation has become the dominant form of business organization.

Corporations

A far more complicated form of business organization than either the proprietorship or partnership, the ***corporation*** is a fictitious legal person, separate and distinct from its owners. A corporation is formed by having lawyers draw up the necessary papers stating (in general terms) what sorts of activities the owners of the corporation intended to engage in. The owners of the corporation are the stockholders. **Stock,** pieces of paper signifying ownership of the corporation, is issued to the owners, generally in exchange for their cash. Ordinarily, each *share* of stock gives its owner one vote. The corporation's **board of directors,** which is responsible for setting overall policy for the firm, is elected by the stockholders. The firm's owners can, if they are dissatisfied with the company's policies or think they have better opportunities elsewhere, sell their stock to someone else, assuming, of course, that they can find a buyer.

Pros. The corporation has many advantages over the partnership or proprietorship. In particular, *each of the corporation's owners has limited, not unlimited, liability.* If I decide to become one of the owners of IBM and if a share of IBM stock sells for $125 a share, I can buy ten shares of IBM stock for $1,250. And I can be sure that, if IBM falls on hard times, I cannot lose more than $1,250 I paid for the stock. There is no way that I can be assessed beyond this. Moreover, *the corporation, unlike the partnership or proprietorship, has unlimited life.* If several stockholders want to withdraw from the firm, they simply sell their stock. The corporation goes on, although the identity of the owners changes. For these reasons, *the corporation is clearly a better device for raising large sums of money than the partnership or proprietorship.* This is an enormous advantage of the corporation, particularly in industries like automobiles and steel, which could not otherwise finance their operations.

Cons. Without question, the corporation is a very important social invention. It permits people to assemble the large quantities of capital required for efficient production in many industries. Without limited liability and the other advantages of the corporation, it is doubtful that the opportunities and benefits of large-scale production could have been reaped. However, this does not mean that the corporate form will work for all firms. In many cases, a firm requires only a modest amount of capital, and there is no reason to go to the extra trouble and expense of establishing a corporation. Moreover, one disadvantage of the corporation is **double taxation of income,** since corporations pay income taxes—and the tax rate is often almost one-half of every extra dollar earned. Thus every dollar earned by a corporation and distributed to stockholders is taxed twice by the federal government—once when it is counted as income by the corporation, and once when the remainder is counted as income by the stockholders.

Corporate Securities

The corporation raises money by issuing various kinds of securities; of these, three kinds—common stock, preferred stock, and bonds—are particularly significant. Each of these types of securities is important to the workings of the corporation and to people's investment decisions.

Common Stock. **Common Stock** is the ordinary certificate of ownership of the corporation. Holders of common stock are owners of the firm. They share in the firm's profits—if there are any profits. At frequent intervals, the board of directors of the firm may declare a dividend of so much per share for the common stockholders. For example, the common stockholders of IBM received dividends of $4.40 per share in 1984. *Dividends* are thus the income the owners of common stock receive. (In addition, of course, common stockholders may make money by selling their stock for more than they paid for it; as noted in the previous chapter, such income is called *capital gains.*) Common stock is generally regarded as more risky than preferred stock or bonds, for reasons that will be explained.

Preferred Stock. **Preferred stock** is a special kind of certificate of ownership that pays at most a stated dividend. For example, consider the General Motors Corporation, the huge auto maker. Owners of one type of General Motors preferred stock receive $5 a share per year, as long as the firm makes enough to pay this dividend. To protect the owners of preferred stock, it is stipulated that no dividends can be paid on the common stock unless the dividends on the preferred stock are paid in full. Since the common stockholders cannot receive their dividends unless the preferred stock's dividends have been paid, common stock is obviously more risky than preferred stock. But by the same token, the amount preferred stockholders have to gain if the company prospers is less than the amount common stockholders have to gain, since however high its profits may be, the firm will pay only the stated dividend—for example, $5 per share per year in the case of General Motors—to the owners of preferred stock.

Bonds. Bonds are quite different from both common and preferred stocks. **Bonds** are debts of the firm; in other words, they are IOUs issued by the firm. In contrast to stockholders, the bondholders are not owners of a firm: they are its creditors, and receive interest, not dividends. Specifically, a bond is a certificate bearing the firm's promise to pay the interest every six months until the bond matures, at which time the firm also promises to pay the bondholders the principal (the amount they lent the firm) as well. Often bonds are sold in $1,000 denominations. For example, one type of bond issued by IBM is a 9⅜ percent bond, due in 2004. The owner of each such bond receives $93.75 per year in interest, and IBM promises to pay him or her the principal of $1,000 when the bond falls due in 2004. A firm must pay the interest on the bonds and the principal when it is due, or it can be declared bankrupt. In other words, the bondholders are legally entitled to receive what is due them before the stockholders can get anything.

Thus, from the point of view of the investor, bonds are generally considered less risky than preferred stock, and preferred stocks are considered less risky than common stock. But we have ignored another fact: inflation. The tendency for the price level in the United States to increase over time has meant that bondholders have been paid off with dollars that were worth less than those they lent. For this reason, together with the fact that owners of common stocks reaped substantial capital gains during the 1960s and early 1970s, many investors tended to favor common stocks. Indeed, during the 1960s, a "cult of equities" developed; these were the years when it appeared that stock prices were headed only one way—even higher. It became very fashionable to buy common stock. But in the middle 1970s, the public's infatuation with common stocks seemed to fade, as stock prices fell; and the 1980s have seen considerable variation in stock prices. To understand why the value of stocks can gyrate so considerably, it is necessary to look briefly at the workings of the stock market.

The Stock Market

In general, large corporations do not sell stock directly to the investor. Instead, the investor buys stock on the stock market. Two major stock exchanges in the United States are the New York Stock Exchange and the American Stock Exchange, both in New York City. On these and similar exchanges in other cities, the common stocks of thousands of corporations are bought and sold.

Price Fluctuations. The price of each common stock fluctuates from day to day, indeed from minute to minute. Basically, the factors responsible for these price fluctuations are the shifts in the demand curve and supply curve for each kind of common stock. For example, if a strike breaks out at a General Motors plant, this may cause the demand curve for General Motors stock to shift downward to the left, since the strike is liable to mean lower profits for General Motors. Because of this downward, or leftward, shift in the demand curve, the price of General Motors common stock will tend to fall, as in fact happened during a United Auto Workers strike in 1974.

The Great Crash. Occasionally, the stock market gets a case of the jitters over economic conditions, stock prices tumble, and old investors think back to the Great Crash of 1929. The 1920s witnessed a feverish interest in investing in the stock market. Along with raccoon coats, Stutz Bearcats, and the Charleston, common stocks were the rage. Both the professionals on Wall Street and the neophytes on Main Street bought common stocks and more common stocks. Naturally, as the demand curves for common stocks shifted upward to the right, their prices rose, thus whetting the appetites of investors for still more common stocks. This upward spiral continued until 1929, when the bubble burst. Suddenly the prices of common stocks fell precipitously—and continued to drop during the early 1930s. The most famous average of industrial stock prices, the Dow-Jones average, fell from 381 in 1929 to 41 in 1933. Many investors, large and small, were wiped out.

Stocks Come Back. The Great Crash made investors wary of common stocks for many years. But by the 1960s confidence in them was fully restored, and there certainly was no tendency for investors to shy away from them. In the 1970s and 1980s, although many small investors (and some large ones) lost their shirts, the stock market remained a major outlet for savings. Judging from historical experience, the public's taste for common stocks seems to be justified. Studies show that, during the course of a lifetime, the typical investor would have done better to invest in common stocks than in the best-quality bonds, because stock prices have tended to rise. This tended to apply in a great many cases, even for investors who lived through the Great Crash. And it has certainly been borne out over the past 40 or 50 years. Thus, although common stocks are riskier in some respects than bonds or preferred stocks, they seem to have performed better, on the average, at least in recent times.

MAKING MONEY ON STOCKS

During periods when the average of stock prices is going up, such as the 1920s and much of the 1950s and 1960s (as well as in more recent bull markets), it is relatively easy to be a financial wizard, whether by luck or calculation. A much more exacting test of your financial acumen is how

Over 30 million Americans own common stocks, which indicates that you don't have to be wealthy to be an investor. Suppose that you are interested in buying IBM stock. To determine its current price, you need only look at the financial pages of any major newspaper. For example, on April 1, 1985, the *Wall Street Journal* showed the following information concerning IBM common stock:

52-week				Sales				Net
High	Low	Stock	Div	100s	High	Low	Last	Change
138¼	99	IBM	4.40	6950	127⅛	125⅝	127	+⅜

Reading from left to right, $138.25 and $99 are the highest and lowest prices of IBM stock in the previous year, and $4.40 is the level of IBM's dividends in the previous year. The last five figures show the number of shares sold (695,000), the highest price (127.12½), the lowest price (125.62½), and the final price ($127) of a share on the previous day, as well as the change in the price from the day before (up $.37½ per share).

To determine whether IBM common stock is a good buy, you would be well advised to look at IBM's recent earnings record and to obtain as much information as you can concerning the firm's earnings prospects. This is because, as a firm's earnings (per share of common stock) go up, the price of its stock tends to go up too. Some economists and business analysts have gone so far as to publish formulas by which one can determine, on the basis of forecasts of what a firm's earnings will be, how much the stock is worth. They believe that one should buy if the current price of the stock is below this measure of the stock's intrinsic value and sell if the price is above it.

In contrast, other economists believe that the movement of stock prices has more to do with psychology than with financial valuation of this sort. As John Maynard Keynes put it, "[Most persons] are concerned, not with what an investment is really worth to a man who buys it 'for keeps,' but with what the market will value it at, under the influence of mass psychology, three months or a year hence. . . . For it is not sensible to pay 25 for an investment of which you believe the prospective yields to justify a value of 30, if you also believe that the market will value it at 20 three months hence." As Yale's Burton Malkiel observes, "This theory might . . . be called the 'greater-fool theory.' It's perfectly all right to pay three times what a stock is worth as long as later on you can find some innocent to pay five times what it's worth."*

There is no simple, foolproof way to determine whether IBM common stock is a good buy. Since even the most astute traders on Wall Street frequently do no better than one could do by buying the Dow-Jones average, you would do well to approach the stock market with caution. More than one economic savant has lost his or her shirt.

* B. Malkiel, *A Random Walk down Wall Street,* 4th ed., New York: Norton, 1985.

well you can pick which stocks will outperform the averages. If you can predict that increases will occur in a certain firm's profits, and if other people don't predict the same thing, you may be able to pass this test. However, the sobering truth is that "playing the stock market" is much more an art than a science. The stock market is affected by psychological as well as economic considerations. Moreover, when you try to spot stocks that will increase in price, you are pitting your knowledge and experience against those of skilled professionals with big research staffs and with friends and acquaintances working for the companies in question. And even these professionals can do surprisingly poorly at times.

Do economists have a nose for good investments? John Maynard Keynes was an extremely successful speculator who made millions of dollars. Other economists have been far less successful. Certainly, a knowledge of basic economics is not sufficient to enable you to make money on the stock market, but insofar as the market reflects economic realities, a knowledge of basic economics should be helpful.

The Giant Corporation

Much of the trading on the stock market centers around the relatively small number of giant corporations that control a very substantial percentage of the total assets and employment in the American economy. And well it might, for the largest 100 manufacturing corporations control about half of this country's manufacturing assets. These firms have tremendous economic and political power. They include the giant automobile manufacturers (General Motors, Ford), the big oil firms (Exxon, Standard Oil of Indiana, Mobil, Standard Oil of California, Texaco, Atlantic Richfield), the big steel firms (U.S. Steel, Bethlehem, Armco), the big computer and office machinery producers (IBM and Xerox), the leading tobacco firms (American Brands, R. J. Reynolds, Philip Morris), the electrical equipment producers (General Electric, Westinghouse), and many others.

MANAGEMENT

Usually, the president is the chief operations officer in the firm, although sometimes the chairman of the board of directors fills this role. As for the board of directors, some members are chosen for their reputations and contacts, while others are chosen for their knowledge of the firm, the industry, or some profession or specialty.

The board generally contains at least one representative of the financial community, and a university president or former government official is often included to show that the firm is responsive to broad social issues. Members of IBM's board include Harold Brown, a former Secretary of Defense; Patricia Harris, a professor at George Washington University; and Richard Lyman, president of the Rockefeller Foundation.

The board of directors is concerned with overall policy. Since it meets only a few times a year, it seldom becomes involved in day-to-day decisions; and it usually goes along with management's policies, so long as management retains the board's confidence.

SEPARATION OF OWNERSHIP FROM CONTROL

An interesting and important feature of the large corporation is the fact that it is owned by many people, practically all of whom have little or no detailed information about the firm's operations. The owners of IBM number over 700,000, but most of them know relatively little about what is going on in the firm. Moreover, because of the wide diffusion of ownership, working control of a large corporation can often be maintained by a group with only one-fifth or less of all the voting stock. The result is a *separation of ownership from control.* In other words, the owners control the firm in only a limited and somewhat sporadic sense.

So long as a firm's management is not obviously incompetent or corrupt, it is difficult for insurgent stockholders to remove the management from office. Most stockholders do not go to the annual meetings to vote for members of the firm's board of directors. Instead, they receive *proxies,* which, if returned, permit the management to exercise their votes. Usually enough shareholders mail in their proxies to give management the votes it needs to elect a friendly board of directors. In recent years, the Securities and Exchange Commission, which oversees and regulates the financial markets, has attempted to make the giant corporations more democratic by enabling insurgent groups to gain access to mailing lists of stockholders and so forth. But there is still a noteworthy and widespread separation of ownership from control.

Test Yourself

1. In its 1979 annual report, the Exxon Corporation reported that it was building a new olefins plant (costing $500 million) in Baytown, Texas. Is this plant a firm? Why or why not? Do you think that a proprietorship would be likely to build and own such a plant? Why or why not?

2. Assume that a partnership wanted to enter the automobile industry. What problems would such a legal form of organization impose upon the potential entrants? Are any of the Big Three in the U.S automobile industry (General Motors, Ford, and Chrysler) partnerships?

3. Explain why each of the following statements is true or false. (a) The University of Texas is a firm. (b) Massachusetts General Hospital is a firm. (c) A firm must be owned by more than one person. (d) The owner of a firm must participate in its management.

4. On February 19, 1985, the common stock of Exxon Corporation closed at $47.25 per share. What effect would each of the following have on its price? (a) A marked increase in the demand for gasoline. (b) A prolonged strike at a major Exxon refinery. (c) Price ceilings on gas and oil.

5. Explain why bondholders do not vote for a corporation's board of directors and why common stockholders are not guaranteed a particular dividend rate.

Motivation of the Firm

What determines the behavior of the business firm? As a first approximation, *economists generally assume that firms attempt to maximize* **profits,** which are defined as the difference between the firm's revenue and its costs.

Basic Idea #9: Economists frequently assume that firms maximize profit. Although this is an oversimplification, models based on this assumption have proved very useful, both in explaining why firms and markets behave as they do and in indicating rules of business behavior for firms that want to try to maximize profit.

In other words, economists generally assume that firms try to make as much money as possible. This assumption certainly does not seem unreasonable; most businessmen appear to be interested in making money. Nonetheless, the assumption of profit maximization oversimplifies the situation. Although businessmen certainly want profits, they are interested in other things as well. Some firms claim that they want to promote better cultural activities or better racial relations in their community. At a less lofty level, other firms say that their aim is to increase their share of the market. Whether or not one takes these self-proclaimed goals very seriously, it is clear that firms are not interested *only* in making money—often for the same reason that Dr. Johnson gave for not becoming a philosopher: "because cheerfulness keeps breaking in."[2]

Intrafirm Politics. In a large corporation, there are some fairly obvious reasons why firms may not maximize profits. Various groups within such firms develop their own party lines, and intrafirm politics is an important part of the process determining firm behavior. Whereas in a small firm it may be fairly accurate to regard the goals of the firm as being the goals of the proprietor, in the large corporation the decision on the goals of the firm is a matter of politics, with various groups within the organization struggling for power. In addition, because of the separation of ownership from control, top management usually has a great deal of freedom as long as it seems to be performing reasonably well. Under these circumstances, the behavior of the firm may be dictated in part by the interests of the management group, resulting in higher salaries, more perquisites, and a bigger staff for their own benefit than would otherwise be the case.

Risk and Uncertainty. Also, in a world full of risk and uncertainty, it is difficult to know exactly what profit maximization means, since the firm cannot be sure that a certain level of profit will result from a certain action. Instead, the best the firm can do is to estimate that a certain probability distribution of profit levels will result from a certain action. Under these circumstances, the firm may choose less risky actions, even though they have a lower expectation of profit than other actions. In a world where ruin is ruinous, this may be perfectly rational policy.

PROFIT MAXIMIZATION IS THE STANDARD ASSUMPTION

Nonetheless, profit maximization remains the standard assumption in economics. As we agreed in our discussion of model building in Chapter 2, to be useful models need not be exact replicas of reality. Economic models based on profit maximization have been very useful indeed. For one thing, they help to show how the price system functions. For another, in the real world, they suggest how a firm should operate if it wants to make as much money as possible. Even if a firm does not want to maximize profit, these theories can be utilized. For example, they can show how much profit the firm is forgoing by taking certain courses of action. In recent years, the theory of the profit-maximizing firm has been studied more and more for the sake of determining profit-maximizing rules of business behavior.

[2] This quote is taken from R. Solow, "The New Industrial State, or Son of Affluence," *The Public Interest,* Fall 1967. Since footnotes are so often used to cite dreary material, it seems worthwhile to use them occasionally to cite humor as well.

Technology, Inputs, and the Production Function

The decisions a firm should make in order to maximize its profits are determined by the current state of technology. Technology, it will be recalled from Chapter 1, is the sum total of society's knowledge concerning the industrial arts. Just as consumers are limited by their income, firms are limited by the current state of technology. If the current state of technology is such that we do not know how to produce more than 40 bushels of corn per year from an acre of land and 2 man-years of labor, then this is as much as the firm can produce from this combination of land and labor. In making its decisions, the firm must take this into account.

INPUTS

In constructing a model of the profit-maximizing firm, economists must somehow represent the state of technology and include it in their model. As a first step toward this end, we must define an **input.** Perhaps the simplest definition of an input is that it is anything the firm uses in its production process. Some of the inputs of a farm producing corn might be seed, land, labor, water, fertilizer, various types of machinery, as well as the time of the people managing the farm.

PRODUCTION FUNCTION

Having defined an input, we can now describe how economists represent the state of technology. The basic concept economists use for this purpose is the production function.

For any commodity, *the **production function** is the relationship between the quantities of various inputs used per period of time and the maximum quantity of the commodity that can be produced per period of time.* More specifically, the production function is a table, a graph, or an equation showing the maximum output rate that can be achieved from any specified set of usage rates of inputs. The production function summarizes the characteristics of existing technology at a given point in time. It reflects the technological constraints the firm must reckon with.

To see more clearly what we mean by a production function, consider the Milwaukee Machine Company, a hypothetical machine shop that produces a simple metal part. Suppose that we are dealing with a period of time that is so short that the firm's basic plant and equipment cannot be altered. For simplicity, suppose that the only input whose quantity can be altered in this period is the amount of labor used by the machine shop. Suppose that the firm collects data showing the relationship between the quantity of its output and the quantity of labor it uses. This relationship, given in Table 5.2, is the firm's production function. It shows that, when 1 worker is employed, 100 parts are produced per month; when 2 workers are employed, 210 parts are produced per month; and so on. Information concerning a firm's production function is often obtained from the firm's engineers, as well as its craftsmen and technicians. Much more will be said about production functions in later chapters. All that we want to do here is to introduce the concept of the production function.

Table 5.2

PRODUCTION FUNCTION, MILWAUKEE MACHINE COMPANY

Quantity of labor used per month (number of men employed)	Output per month (number of parts)
0	0
1	100
2	210
3	315
4	415
5	500

Elements of Accounting: The Firm's Balance Sheet

Having touched on the firm's technology, we must return to the motivation of the firm. In a previous section, we stated that economists generally assume that firms attempt to maximize profits. Viewed as a first approximation, this assumption does not seem too hard to swallow, but exactly what do we mean by profit? This is an important question, of interest to businessmen and investors as well as to economists. The accounting profession provides the basic figures that are reported in the newspapers and in a firm's annual reports to its stockholders. If IBM reports that it made $5.5 billion last year, this figure is provided by IBM's accountants. How do the accountants obtain this figure? What are its limitations?

Basically, accounting concepts are built around two very important statements: the balance sheet and the income statement. A *firm's balance sheet shows the nature of its assets, tangible and intangible, at a certain point in time.*

LEFT-HAND SIDE OF THE BALANCE SHEET

Let us return to the Milwaukee Machine Company. Its balance sheet might be as shown in Table 5.3. The left-hand side of the balance sheet shows the assets of the firm as of December 31, 1985. *Current assets* are assets that will be converted into cash relatively quickly (generally within a year), whereas *fixed assets* generally will not be liquidated quickly. The firm has $20,000 in cash, $120,000 in inventory, $160,000 in equipment, and $180,000 in buildings. At first glance, these figures may seem more accurate than they are likely to be. It is very difficult to know how to value various assets. For example, should they be valued at what the firm paid for them, or at what it would cost to replace them? More will be said about these problems below.

RIGHT-HAND SIDE OF THE BALANCE SHEET

The right-hand side of the firm's balance sheet shows the claims by creditors on the firm's assets and the value of the firm's ownership. In Table 5.3,

Table 5.3

BALANCE SHEET, MILWAUKEE MACHINE COMPANY, AS OF DECEMBER 31, 1985

Assets (dollars)		Liabilities and net worth (dollars)	
Current assets		Current liabilities	
Cash	20,000	Accounts payable	20,000
Inventory	120,000	Notes payable	40,000
Fixed assets		Long-term liabilities	
Equipment	160,000	Bonds	160,000
Buildings	180,000		
		Net worth	
		Preferred stock	100,000
		Common stock	100,000
		Retained earnings	60,000
Total	480,000	Total	480,000

the Milwaukee Machine Company has total liabilities—or debts—of $220,000. There is $60,000 in *current liabilities,* which come due in less than a year; and $160,000 in *long-term liabilities,* which come due in a year or more. Specifically, there is $20,000 in *accounts payable,* which are bills owed for goods and services that the firm bought; $40,000 in *notes payable,* short-term notes owed to banks, finance companies, or other creditors; and $160,000 in *bonds payable,* or bonds outstanding.

LEFT-HAND SIDE = RIGHT-HAND SIDE

The difference between the value of a firm's assets and the value of its liabilities is its *net worth,* which is the value of the firm's owners' claims against the firm's assets. In other words, the value of the firm to its owners is the total value of its assets less the value of the debts owed by the firm. Since

total value of assets − total liabilities = net worth,

it follows that

total value of assets = total liabilities + net worth.

That is, *the sum of the items on the left-hand side of the balance sheet must equal the sum of the items on the right-hand side.* This, of course, must be true because of the way we define net worth.

In the case of the Milwaukee Machine Company, the firm's net worth—the difference between its assets and its liabilities—is $260,000. Specifically, there is $100,000 worth of preferred stock and $100,000 worth of common stock; there is also $60,000 in retained earnings. *Retained earnings* is the total amount of profit that the stockholders have reinvested in the business. In other words, the stockholders of the Milwaukee Machine Company have reinvested $60,000 of their profits in the business. Rather than withdrawing this sum as dividends, they have kept it invested in the firm.

The Firm's Income Statement

A firm's income statement shows its sales during a particular period, its costs incurred in connection with these sales, and its profits during this period. Table 5.4 shows the Milwaukee Machine Company's income statement during the period January 1, 1986 to December 31, 1986. Sales during this period were $240,000. The cost of manufacturing the items made during this period was $110,000, which includes $30,000 for materials, $40,000 for labor, $34,000 for depreciation (discussed below), and $6,000 for miscellaneous operating expenses.

However, because the firm has reduced its inventory from $120,000 to $110,000 during the period, the cost of manufacturing the items *made* during the period does not equal the cost of manufacturing the items *sold* during the period. To find the *cost of goods sold*—which is the amount that logically should be deducted from sales to get the profits made from the sale of these goods—we must add the decrease in the value of inventory to

Table 5.4

INCOME STATEMENT, MILWAUKEE MACHINE COMPANY, JANUARY 1, 1986, TO
DECEMBER 31, 1986 (DOLLARS)

Net Sales		240,000
Manufacturing cost of goods sold		120,000
Materials	30,000	
Labor	40,000	
Depreciation	34,000	
Miscellaneous operating cost	6,000	
Total	110,000	
Plus beginning inventory	120,000	
Less closing inventory	−110,000	
Adjusted total	120,000	
Selling and administrative costs		20,000
Fixed interest charges and state and local taxes		10,000
Net earnings before income taxes		90,000
Corporation income taxes		40,000
Net earnings after taxes		50,000
Dividends on preferred stock		4,000
Net profits of common stockholders		46,000
Dividends paid on common stock		20,000
Addition to retained earnings		26,000

the total manufacturing cost. (Why? Because the firm sold more items than it produced during this period. Thus the cost of the items it sold equals the cost of the items it produced during this period plus the cost of the items it sold from its inventory. Since the cost of the items it sold from its inventory equals the decrease in the value of its inventory, the cost of the items it sold equals the cost of the items it produced during this period plus the decrease in inventory.) Putting it another way, we must add the beginning inventory and subtract the closing inventory, as shown in Table 5.4. The resulting figure for cost of goods sold is $120,000.

But manufacturing costs are not the only costs the firm incurs. To estimate the firm's profits, we must also deduct from sales its selling and administrative expenses, its interest charges, and its state and local taxes, as well as its federal income taxes. Table 5.4 shows that the Milwaukee Machine Company's after tax earnings during 1986 were $50,000. This is the amount left for the owners of the business. The income statement also shows what the owners do with what is left. Table 5.4 shows that the Milwaukee Machine Company used $4,000 to pay dividends to holders of preferred stock. When this was done, the holders of common stock were free to distribute some of the profits to themselves. According to Table 5.4, they distributed $20,000 to themselves in dividends on the common stock, and plowed the rest—$26,000—back into the business as retained earnings.

DEPRECIATION

Before leaving the income statement, we should explain one element of manufacturing cost—*depreciation.* While the other elements of manufacturing cost are self-explanatory, this one is not. The idea behind depreciation is that the buildings and equipment will not last forever; eventually

Cross-Chapter Case/Part Two

SHOULD AMERICA ADOPT AN INDUSTRIAL POLICY?

In Chapters 3–5, we have been concerned primarily with the role of the price system and of firms and the government in the American economy. In the mid-1980s, one of the leading questions in this area has been: Should the United States adopt an industrial policy? It is difficult to define an "industrial policy" with precision, since economists do not all use the same definition. But all industrial policies involve some form of government action designed to stimulate and revitalize a nation's industry. In particular, according to many advocates of an industrial policy, the government should encourage new high-technology industries and help older, declining industries to adjust to lower output and employment levels.

In the United States, those favoring the adoption of an industrial policy have proposed a variety of ways in which the government's role in directing the allocation of resources might be expanded. For example, there might be a central agency to formulate the government's industrial policy. Councils including representatives of business, labor, and government might obtain data on particular industries and construct a consensus strategy. A government development bank might invest money in sectors and industries that are regarded as receiving too little capital from private financial sources. Declining industries (so-called "sunset" industries) might get protection from imports and other government help to ease the adjustment to new economic realities.

Advocates of an industrial policy argue that the United States already has an industrial policy of sorts, but that it is largely uncoordinated. For example, the U.S. government spends large amounts on research, sets import quotas, and subsidizes many kinds of firms, just as other countries do. Moreover, this is nothing new. In 1643, Massachusetts granted a fledgling firm exclusive iron-making privileges for 21 years in order to encourage the industry. More recently, the federal government provided a loan guarantee to the Chrysler Corporation to help keep the auto maker in business. Since the U.S. government is already engaged in many of the activities encompassed under the broad heading of "industrial policy," the real question, according to the proponents of an industrial policy, is whether these activities should be better coordinated. In their view, councils of business, labor, and government could do a better job than is now being done of coordinating these far-flung activities of the government, many of which conflict with one another.

Many proponents of an industrial policy also argue that a government-financed industrial development bank should provide industrial firms with money for high-risk, long-term projects. One reason why such a bank is needed, in their opinion, is that private investors tend to be averse to risk and too inclined to want quick pay-backs. Consequently, they invest too little in risky ventures extending for 5 or 10 years or more. Moreover, according to Felix Rohatyn, chairman of New York City's Municipal Assistance Corporation, such a federal bank "could make sure that the aid would be conditional on management and labor concessions needed to make the business viable." In other words, it could force firms to make tough decisions.

Many advocates of an industrial policy feel that the government should act to slow the decline in "basic" industries like steel. Besides providing loans and special tax benefits, the government would sponsor plans to spread adjustment burdens among labor, management, stockholders, creditors, and suppliers. If the industry faces competition from imports, industry commitments to restructure would be the price of protection from imports. Retraining and compensation programs would be employed to help workers whose jobs are lost.

Whereas some economists are strong advocates of an industrial policy for the United States, others feel that it would be a mistaken, and even dangerous, step to take. To begin with, they feel that councils of business, labor, and government experts would be no more effective in improving coordination of various policies of the government than the existing coordinating mechanisms. In particular, they point out that other countries with industrial policies continue to have coordination problems of this sort.

As for the creation of a government-supported industrial bank, many economists react negatively to this proposal, because they feel that political considerations would inevitably enter into the allocation of funds and that money would be wasted on "targeted growth" industries with no commercial future. According to President Reagan's Council of Economic Advisers:

> The proposal to target emerging industries suggests that government can obtain better information than the private sector. It is difficult to understand how government officials, together with private business and labor leaders, will be able to gather more accurate information and use the information more wisely than the private sector. The United States has numerous investors willing to finance new ventures through equity or bank loans. Private investment analysts spend a great deal of time and effort evaluating new technologies and advising private investors on the most promising firms. Information on emerging industries is also exchanged by job shifting among scientists and engineers who are close to the development of new technologies. Ties between industry and the academic community also contribute to the spread of new ideas. In the United States the private sector already has information at least as good as the proposed government councils and banks could expect to gather.
>
> In any event, a government agency is more likely to be short-sighted and risk averse than private investors. Since politicians face frequent elections, they often have very short time horizons. A government agency is also more likely to make decisions based on the shared expectations that are the conventional wisdom of the time; these processes tend to neglect or reject the idiosyncratic information that is the basis for decisions by the most successful private entrepreneurs.
>
> Finally, government officials will often make investments based on politics rather than economics. One country tries to develop a computer industry before it has sufficient technical workers. Other countries invest in highly visible but wasteful energy projects that private firms think are likely to fail.[1]

[1] Council of Economic Advisers, *1984 Annual Report,* Washington, D.C.: Government Printing Office, 1984.

they will have to be replaced. Clearly, it would be foolish to charge the entire cost of replacing them to the year when they are replaced. Instead, a better picture of the firm's true profitability will be drawn if the cost of replacing them is spread gradually over the life of buildings and equipment, thus recognizing that each year's output has a hand in wearing them out. One frequently used technique is so-called *straight-line depreciation,* which spreads the cost of buildings and equipment (less their scrap value) evenly over their life. Thus, if the Milwaukee Machine Company buys a piece of equipment for $20,000 and if it is expected to last ten years (its scrap value being zero), it would charge depreciation of $2,000 per year

---

Example 5.1   How to Depreciate a Baseball Club

Suppose that you decide to buy the Philadelphia Phillies for $30 million. There are some important tax advantages you should understand. According to Bill Veeck, former owner of the Chicago White Sox, "It is almost impossible not to make money on a baseball club when you are buying it new, because, unless you are inordinately successful, you pay no income tax."* In particular, half of the purchase price of the team can be regarded as the cost of the players, which are depreciable assets like machinery or breeding cattle. Suppose that you regard 5 years as being the "useful life" of the players, and that you use straight-line depreciation.

(a) How much depreciation (of the players) can you deduct from the Phillies' receipts each year to figure your profits? (b) Suppose that you pay $3 million in cash and borrow the remaining $27 million to pay for the Phillies. If you pay 15 percent interest, how much interest expense do you deduct from the Phillies' receipts each year to figure your profits? (c) Suppose that this year the Phillies' receipts equal $35 million and their operating expenses (excluding depreciation of the players and the interest on your loan) equal $28 million. Must you pay any income tax? (Assume that you have no income from sources other than the Phillies.)

SOLUTION

(a) Since the cost of the players can be regarded as one-half of the purchase price of the team, it equals one-half of $30 million, or $15 million. Since the life of the players is 5 years, annual depreciation equals $15 million divided by 5, or $3 million. (b) $27 million times 15 percent, or $4.05 million. (c) Your income from the Phillies is as follows:

Earnings (before depreciation and interest)	$7 million
Less depreciation	−3 million
Less interest	−4.05 million
	−$.05 million

Since you incurred a loss (because of the depreciation of the players), you pay no income tax.

* *Philadelphia Inquirer,* March 15, 1981.

for this machine (for ten years after its purchase). The $34,000 charge for depreciation in Table 5.4 is the sum of such charges. Clearly, this is only a rough way to estimate the true depreciation charges, but it is good enough for many purposes.

Economic versus Accounting Profits

The previous section described the nature of profit, as defined by accountants. This is the concept on which practically all published figures in business reports are based. But economists define profits somewhat differently. In particular, economists do not assume that the firm attempts to maximize the current, short-run profits measured by the accountant. Instead they assume that the firm will attempt to maximize the sum of profits over a long period of time.[3] Also, when economists speak of profit, they mean profit after taking account of the capital and labor provided by the owners. Thus, suppose that the owners of the Milwaukee Machine Company, who receive profits but no salary or wages, put in long hours for which they could receive $30,000 in 1986 if they worked for someone else. Also suppose that if they invested their capital somewhere other than in this firm, they could obtain a return of $22,000 on it in 1986. Under these circumstances, economists would say that the firm's after-tax profits in 1986 were $50,000 − $30,000 − 22,000, or −$2,000, rather than the $50,000 shown in Table 5.4. In other words, the economists' concept of profit includes only what the owners make above and beyond what their labor and capital employed in the business could have earned elsewhere. In this case, that amount is negative.

To a considerable extent, the differences between the concepts used by the accountant and the economist reflect the difference in their functions. The accountant is concerned with controlling the firm's day-to-day operations, detecting fraud or embezzlement, satisfying tax and other laws, and producing records for various interested groups. On the other hand, the economist is concerned primarily with decision making and rational choice among prospective alternatives. Although the figures published on profits almost always conform to the accountant's, not the economist's, concept, the economist's concept is the more relevant one for many kinds of decisions. (And this, of course, is recognized by sophisticated accountants.) For example, suppose the owners of the Milwaukee Machine Company are trying to decide whether they should continue in business. If they are interested in making as much money as possible, the answer depends on the firm's profits as measured by the economist, not the accountant. If the firm's economic profits are greater than (or equal to) zero, the firm should continue in existence; otherwise, it should not. Thus the Milwaukee Machine Company should not stay in existence if 1986 is a good indicator of its future profitability.

Basic Idea #10: To economists, profit is the amount that a firm's owners receive over and above what they could make from the capital and labor they provide, if this capital and labor were used outside the firm. Only if profit in this sense is non-negative should the firm stay in existence. (Note that this is closely related to Basic Idea #2 on p. 10.)

---

[3] The profits earned at various points in time should be *discounted* before being added together, but, for simplicity's sake, we neglect this point here. For some relevant discussion, see Chapter 15.

Test Yourself

1. Which of the following are inputs in the steel industry? (a) coke, (b) iron ore, (c) labor, (d) land, (e) capital, (f) water, (g) oxygen, (h) food eaten by U.S. Steel's workers.

2. The 1981 tax law allowed firms to depreciate assets more quickly. For example, they could depreciate some types of assets over 3 years, rather than 5 years. If a firm depreciates an asset more quickly, will its accounting profits in the first year after it buys the asset be increased or decreased?

3. Suppose that a firm's balance sheet is as follows:

Assets (dollars)		Liabilities and net worth (dollars)	
Current assets		Current liabilities	
Cash	200,000	Accounts payable	100,000
Inventory	300,000	Notes payable	_____
Fixed assets		Long-term liabilities	
Equipment	_____	Bonds	400,000
Buildings	800,000		
		Net worth	400,000
Total	2,000,000	Total	_____

Fill in the three blanks. What is the total amount that the firm owes? How much have the owners contributed? What is the difference between current assets and fixed assets?

4. Suppose that a firm's accounting profits for 1986 are $20,000. The firm is a proprietorship, and the owner worked 500 hours managing the business during 1986, for which she received no compensation other than the profits. If she could have gotten $10 an hour working for someone else, how much were her economic profits during 1986? Suppose that she also contributed $50,000 in capital to the firm, and that she could have obtained 6 percent interest on this capital if she had invested it elsewhere. In this case, how much were her economic profits?

Summary

1. There are three principal types of business firms: proprietorships, partnerships, and corporations. The corporation has many advantages over the other two—limited liability, unlimited life, and greater ability to raise large sums of money. Nonetheless, because the corporation also has disadvantages, many firms are not corporations.

2. The corporation raises money by issuing various kinds of securities, of which three kinds—common stock, preferred stock, and bonds—are particularly important.

3. A relatively small number of giant corporations control a very substantial proportion of the total assets and employment in the American economy. In the large corporation, ownership and control tend to be separated.

4. As a first approximation, economists generally assume that firms attempt to maximize profits. In large part, this is because it is a close enough approximation to reality for many of the most important purposes of economics. Also, economists are interested in the theory of the profit-maximizing firm because it provides rules of behavior for firms that do want to maximize profits.

5. To summarize the characteristics of existing technology at a given point in time, the economist uses the concept of the production function, which shows the maximum output rate of a given commodity that can be achieved from any specified set of usage rates of inputs.

6. Accounting concepts are built around two very important statements: the balance sheet and the income statement. The balance sheet shows the nature of the firm's assets and liabilities at a given point in time. The difference between its assets and its liabilities is its net worth, which is the value of the firm's owners' claims against its assets.

7. A firm's income statement shows its sales during a particular period, its costs incurred in connection with these sales, and its profits during the period.

8. Economists define profits somewhat differently than accountants do. In defining profit, economists deduct the amount the owners could receive from the capital and labor they provide, if this capital and labor were used outside the firm. Also, economists are interested in longer periods than those to which accounting statements apply. Although the profit figures that are published almost always conform to the accountant's concept, the economist's concept is the more relevant one for many kinds of decisions.

Concepts for Review

Proprietorship	Dividends	Balance sheet
Partnership	Preferred stock	Current assets
Corporation	Bonds	Fixed assets
Board of directors	Profits	Net worth
Double taxation of income	Input	Income statement
Common stock	Production function	Depreciation

PART THREE

Consumer Behavior and Business Decision Making

CHAPTER 6

Market Demand and Price Elasticity

What do Corfam (Du Pont's synthetic leather) and the Edsel (the new make of automobile Ford introduced in the 1950s) have in common? Both were new products that were unsuccessful because the market demand for them was too small. In a capitalist economy, market demand is a fundamental determinant of what is produced and how. The market demand curve for a commodity plays an important role in the decision-making process within each firm producing the commodity, as well as in the economy as a whole. It is no exaggeration to say that firms spend enormous time and effort trying to cater to, estimate, and influence market demand.

In this chapter, we discuss the factors influencing the market demand curve for a commodity, as well as the measurement of market demand curves and their role in decision making by private business firms and government agencies. We consider questions like: How can we measure market demand curves? What is the price elasticity of demand? What role does the price elasticity of demand play in various practical problems facing the private and public sectors of the economy? What factors underlie the market demand curve for a commodity? These are important questions, from both a theoretical and a practical point of view.

Market Demand Curves

Let's review what a market demand curve is. You will recall from Chapter 3 that a commodity's market demand curve shows how much of the commodity will be purchased during a particular period of time at various

Figure 6.1

Market Demand Curve for Wheat, Mid-1980s *This curve shows how much wheat would be purchased per year at various prices.*

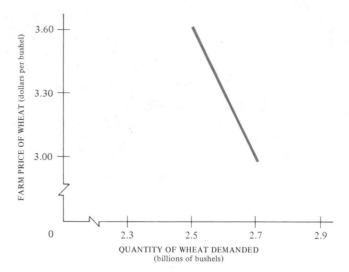

prices. Figure 6.1 ought to be familiar; it is the **market demand curve** for wheat in the mid-1980s, which figured prominently in our discussion of the price system in Chapter 3. Among other things, it shows that during the mid-1980s about 2.7 billion bushels of American wheat would have been purchased per year if the price was $3.00 per bushel, that about 2.6 billion bushels would have been purchased per year if the price was $3.30 per bushel, and that about 2.5 billion bushels would have been purchased if the price was $3.60 per bushel.

Since the market demand curve reflects what consumers want and are willing to pay for, when the market demand curve for wheat shifts upward to the right, this indicates that consumers want more wheat at the existing price. On the other hand, when the curve shifts downward to the left, this indicates that consumers want less wheat at the existing price. Such shifts in the market demand curve for a commodity trigger changes in the behavior of the commodity's producers. When the market demand curve shifts upward to the right, the price of wheat will tend to rise, thus inducing farmers to produce more wheat, because they will find that, given the price increase, their profits will increase if they raise their output levels. The same process occurs in other parts of the economy. Shifts in the demand curve reflecting the fact that consumers want more (less) of a commodity set in motion a sequence of events leading to more (less) production of the commodity.

MEASURING MARKET DEMAND CURVES

To be of practical use, market demand curves must be based on careful measurements. Let's look briefly at some of the techniques used to estimate the market demand curve for particular commodities. At first glance, a quick and easy way to estimate the demand curve might seem to be interviewing consumers about their buying habits and intentions. However, although more subtle variants of this approach sometimes may pay off, simply asking people how much they would buy of a certain commodity at particular prices does not usually seem very useful, since off-the-cuff answers to such questions are rarely very accurate. Thus marketing researchers and econometricians interested in measuring market demand curves have been forced to use more complex procedures.

PRICE OF SLINGSHOTS

AMOUNT SOLD OF SLINGSHOTS

Figure 6.2
Estimated Demand Curve for Slingshots
One very crude way to estimate the
market demand curve is to plot the
amount sold of a commodity in each
year against its price in that year, and
draw a curve that seems to fit the points
reasonably well. However, this technique
is generally too crude to be reliable.

One such procedure is the ***direct market experiment.*** Although the designs of such experiments vary greatly and are often quite complicated, the basic idea is simple—to see the effects on the quantity demanded of actual variations in the price of the product. (Researchers attempt to hold other market factors constant or to take into account whatever changes may occur.) The Parker Pen Company conducted an experiment a number of years ago to estimate the demand curve for their ink, Quink. They increased the price from \$.15 to \$.25 in four cities, and found that the quantity demanded was quite insensitive to the price. Experiments like this are frequently made to try to estimate a product's market demand curve.

Still another technique is to use statistical methods to estimate demand curves from historical data on price and quantity purchased of the commodity. For example, one might plot the price of slingshots in various periods in the past against the quantity sold, as shown in Figure 6.2. Judging from the results, curve *D* in Figure 6.2 seems a reasonable approximation to the demand curve. Although this simple analysis provides some insight into how statistical methods are used to estimate demand curves from historical data, it is a vast oversimplification. For one thing, the market demand curve may have shifted over time, so that curve *D* is not a proper estimate. Fortunately, modern statistical techniques recognize this possibility and allow us to estimate the position and shape of this curve (at each point in time) in spite of it.

Hundreds, perhaps thousands, of studies have been made to estimate the demand curves for particular commodities. In view of the importance of the results for decision making, this is not surprising. To illustrate the role played by such studies in the formulation of public policy, let's consider the following case involving the Boston and Maine Railroad.

RAILROAD TRANSPORTATION IN METROPOLITAN
BOSTON: A CASE STUDY

In the early 1960s the Boston and Maine Railroad wanted to discontinue passenger commuter service into Boston because it felt such service was unprofitable. In 1963, the Mass Transportation Commission of Massachusetts contracted with the Boston and Maine to establish a demonstration project to estimate the effect of a lowering of fares on the quantity of commuter tickets sold. The Boston and Maine was requested not to file a petition for the discontinuance of commuter service into Boston until after the experiment. During the experiment, which lasted about a year, fares were reduced about 28 percent on the average. The result was, of course, an increase in the number of tickets sold. However, the more important thing to the railroad and the commission was the *extent* to which the fare cut would increase the number of tickets sold. *How great* would be the resulting increase in the number of tickets sold? This was the important question because to increase the railroad's profits, a fare cut had to increase the railroad's revenues more than it increased its costs. And unless the price cut increased the number of tickets sold by a greater percentage than the reduction in price, it would not increase the railroad's revenues at all.

A comparison of the Boston and Maine's commuter revenues in 1963 with those in 1962 showed that this large fare reduction resulted in only a

0.6 percent increase in the railroad's revenues. Thus the price reduction increased the railroad's revenues by little or nothing. Since the reduction in fares increased the railroad's costs—because it was more costly to handle the larger volume of traffic—and increased its revenues scarcely at all, it did not increase the railroad's profits. Thus, after the experiment, the Boston and Maine decided to continue with its petition to terminate com-

Example 6.1   Speculation and the Demand Curve

In many markets, speculators buy and sell, hoping to make money in the process. Suppose that the demand and supply curves for corn this year and next year are as shown below. Speculators, seeing that the price of corn is likely to rise (from OA to OH), decide to buy corn this year and sell it next year. Thus, including the speculators, the demand curve shifts to the right this year, and the supply curve shifts to the right next year, as shown below:

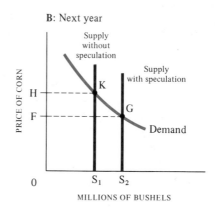

(a) In this case, do speculators even out the consumption of corn over time, thus avoiding famine-feast cycles? (b) In this case, do speculators raise the total value of the corn sold in the two periods? (c) In this case, speculators guessed correctly that the price of corn would rise. If they guess incorrectly, can they make more uneven the consumption of corn over time? (d) Once speculation is included in the analysis, does the demand curve for a product depend on its expected future price?

SOLUTION

(a) Yes. Without the speculators, much less corn would be consumed next year than this year. With them, consumption of corn is relatively constant. (b) Yes. The value (price times quantity) of the corn sold this year is increased considerably (from area $OABS_0$ to area $OCES_0$). The value of the corn sold next year does not change very much, based on the above diagram. (It is area $OHKS_1$ without speculation and area $OFGS_2$ with speculation.) Thus the total value of the corn sold in the two periods is raised. (c) Yes. (d) Yes. If there is a general feeling that the price of a product is going to increase substantially, the demand curve for this product may shift to the right.

muter service.[1] (Eventually, however, public subsidies were instituted to keep the service going.)

This is a fairly typical example of a direct market experiment designed to obtain information on relevant aspects of a market demand curve. Note the problems experiments of this sort must face. First, *the experiment can be very costly if it alienates customers or reduces the firm's profits.* Second, *it is difficult to hold other relevant variables constant.* For example, the effect of price changes was mixed up, to some extent, with the effect of increased service in the Boston and Maine case. Third, *it is hard to conduct an experiment of this sort over a long enough period to estimate long-run effects.* Thus, in the Boston and Maine case, the effect of the fare reduction on the number of tickets sold might have been much greater if the experiment had lasted longer. Nonetheless, despite these problems, experiments of this sort can produce useful evidence on the location and shape of a product's market demand curve. They are an important supplement to statistical analysis of historical data to estimate market demand curves.

The Price Elasticity of Demand

The quantity demanded of some commodities, like beef in Figure 6.3, is fairly sensitive to changes in the commodity's price. That is, changes in price result in significant changes in quantity demanded. On the other hand, the quantity demanded of other commodities, like cotton in Figure 6.3, is very insensitive to changes in the price. Large changes in price result in small changes in the quantity demanded.

To promote unambiguous discussion of this subject, we must have some measure of the sensitivity of quantity demanded to changes in price. The measure customarily used for this purpose is the *price elasticity of demand,* defined as the percentage change in quantity demanded resulting from a 1 percent change in price.[2] For example, suppose that a 1 percent reduction in the price of slingshots results in a 2 percent increase in quantity demanded. Then, using this definition, the price elasticity of demand for slingshots is 2. (Convention dictates that we give the elasticity a positive sign even though the change in price is negative and the change in quantity demanded is positive.) The price elasticity of demand is likely to vary from one point to another on the market demand curve. For example, the price elasticity of demand for slingshots may be higher when a slingshot costs $1.00 than when it costs $0.25.

Note that the price elasticity of demand is expressed in terms of *relative*—i.e., proportional or percentage—changes in price and quantity demanded, not *absolute* changes in price and quantity demanded. Thus, in

Figure 6.3

Market Demand Curves, Beef and Cotton *The quantity demanded of beef is much more sensitive to price than is the quantity demanded of cotton.*

---

[1] See *Mass Transportation in Massachusetts,* Boston: Mass Transportation Commission, 1964.

[2] What if price does not change by 1 percent? Then the price elasticity of demand is defined as the *percentage change in quantity demanded divided by the percentage change in price.* This definition will be used in the next section. Put in terms of symbols, the price elasticity of demand equals $\dfrac{-\Delta Q}{\Delta P} \times \dfrac{P}{Q}$, where P is price, ΔP is the change in price, Q is quantity demanded, and ΔQ is the change in the quantity demanded.

studying the slingshot market, we looked at the *percentage* change in quantity demanded resulting from a 1 *percent* change in price. This is because absolute changes depend on the units in which price and quantity are measured. Suppose that a reduction in the price of good *Y* from $100 to $99 results in an increase in the quantity demanded from 200 to 210 pounds per month. If price is measured in dollars, the quantity demanded of good *Y* seems quite sensitive to price changes, since a decrease in price of "1" results in an increase in quantity demanded of "10." On the other hand, if price is measured in cents, the quantity demanded of good *Y* seems quite insensitive to price changes, since a decrease in price of "100" results in an increase in quantity demanded of "10." By using relative changes, we do not encounter this problem. Relative changes do not depend on the units of measurement. Thus the percentage reduction in the price of good *Y* is 1 percent, regardless of whether price is measured in dollars or cents. And the percentage increase in the quantity demanded of good *Y* is 5 percent, regardless of whether it is measured in pounds or tons.

CALCULATING THE PRICE ELASTICITY OF DEMAND

The price elasticity of demand is a very important concept and one that economists use often, so it is worthwhile to spend some time explaining exactly how it is computed. Suppose that you have a table showing various points on a market demand curve. For example, Table 6.1 shows the quantity of wheat demanded at various prices, as estimated by Professor Karl Fox of Iowa State University during the early 1960s.[3] Given these data, how do you go about computing the price elasticity of demand for wheat? Since the price elasticity of demand for any product generally varies from point to point on its market demand curve, you must first determine at what point on the demand curve you want to measure the price elasticity of demand.

Let us assume that you want to estimate the price elasticity of demand for wheat when the price of wheat is between $2.00 and $2.20 per bushel. To do this, you can use the following formula:

price elasticity =

$$\frac{\text{percentage change}}{\text{in quantity demanded}} \div \frac{\text{percentage change}}{\text{in price}} =$$

$$\frac{\text{change in quantity demanded}}{\text{original quantity demanded}} \div \frac{\text{change in price}}{\text{original price}}.$$

Table 6.1 shows that the quantity demanded equals 700 million bushels when the price is $2.00, and that it equals 675 million bushels when the price is $2.20. But should we use $2.00 and 700 million bushels as the original price and quantity? Or should we use $2.20 and 675 million bushels as the original price and quantity? If we choose the former,

Table 6.1

MARKET DEMAND FOR WHEAT, EARLY 1960s

Farm price of wheat (dollars per bushel)	Quantity of wheat demanded (millions of bushels)
1.00	1,500
1.20	1,300
1.40	1,100
1.60	900
1.80	800
2.00	700
2.20	675

Source: K. Fox, V. Ruttan, and L. Witt, *Farming, Farmers, and Markets for Farm Goods.* New York: Committee for Economic Development, 1962.

[3] Note that Table 6.1 pertains to the early 1960s whereas Figure 6.1 pertains to the mid-1980s. Consequently, the demand curves are quite different, as you can see.

price elasticity =

$$-\frac{675 - 700}{700} \div \frac{2.20 - 2.00}{2.00} = .36.$$

The price elasticity of demand is estimated to be .36. (The minus sign at the beginning of this equation is due to the fact, noted above, that convention dictates that the elasticity be given a positive sign.)

But we could just as well have used $2.20 and 675 million bushels as the original price and quantity. If this had been our choice, the answer would be

price elasticity =

$$-\frac{700 - 675}{675} \div \frac{2.00 - 2.20}{2.20} = .41,$$

which is somewhat different from the answer we got in the previous paragraph.

To get around this difficulty, the generally accepted procedure is to use the average values of price and quantity as the original price and quantity. In other words, we use as an estimate of the price elasticity of demand:

price elasticity =

$$\frac{\text{change in quantity demanded}}{\text{sum of quantities}/2} \div \frac{\text{change in price}}{\text{sum of prices}/2}.$$

This is the so-called **arc elasticity of demand.** In the specific case we are considering, the arc elasticity is

price elasticity =

$$-\frac{(675 - 700)}{\dfrac{(675 + 700)}{2}} \div \frac{(2.20 - 2.00)}{\dfrac{(2.20 + 2.00)}{2}} = .38.$$

This is the answer to our problem.

Determinants of the Price Elasticity of Demand

Many studies have been made of the price elasticity of demand for particular commodities, Table 6.2 reproduces the results of some of them. Note the substantial differences among products. For example, the estimated price elasticity of demand for women's hats is about 3.00, while for cotton it is only about 0.12. Think for a few minutes about these results, and try to figure out why these differences exist. If you rack your brains for a while, chances are that you will agree that the following factors are important determinants of whether the price elasticity of demand is high or low.

Number and Closeness of Available Substitutes. If a commodity has many close substitutes, its demand is likely to be highly elastic, i.e., the price elasticity is likely to be high. If the price of the product increases, a large proportion of its buyers will turn to the close substitutes that are available.

Table 6.2

ESTIMATED PRICE ELASTICITIES OF
DEMAND FOR SELECTED COMMODITIES,
UNITED STATES

Commodity	Price elasticity
Women's hats	3.00
Gasoline	0.30
Sugar	0.31
Corn	0.49
Cotton	0.12
Hay	0.43
Potatoes	0.31
Oats	0.56
Barley	0.39
Buckwheat	0.99
Refrigerators	1.40
Airline travel	2.40
Radio and TV sets	1.20
Legal services	0.50
Pleasure boats	1.30
Canned tomatoes	2.50
Newspapers	0.10
Tires	0.60
Beef	0.92
Shoes	0.40

Source: H. Schultz, *Theory and Measurement of Demand.* Chicago: University of Chicago Press. 1938; M. Spencer and L. Siegelman, *Managerial Economics,* Homewood, Ill.: Irwin, 1959; H. Houthakker and L. Taylor, *Consumer Demand in the United States, 1929–1970.* Cambridge, Mass.: Harvard, 1966; and U.S. Department of Agriculture.

WHY WASHINGTON'S GASOLINE TAX BIT THE DUST

In August 1980, Washington, D.C. imposed a tax on gasoline, which increased the price of gasoline by 6 percent. Estimates of the price elasticity of demand for gasoline in the United States as a whole generally are about 0.3. Thus, based on such an estimate of the price elasticity of demand, one would expect that the amount of gasoline sold in Washington, D.C. would decrease by about 0.3 times 6 percent, or about 1.8 percent. In fact, there was a 33 percent drop in the amount of gasoline sold in Washington, D.C. Why was the drop so much larger than the 1.8 percent decrease forecasted above?

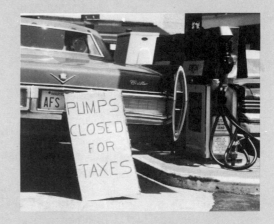

The answer is that the price elasticity of demand for gasoline in Washington, D.C. (when the price of gasoline outside Washington is held constant) is much higher than the price elasticity of demand for gasoline in the nation as a whole. Gasoline sold in Virginia and Maryland is a very good substitute for gasoline sold in Washington. A price increase in Washington, when no such price increase occurs in Virginia or Maryland, will induce many customers to buy their gasoline outside the nation's capital. Although this seems obvious (with hindsight), it was a surprise to Washington officials, who repealed the tax in December 1980.

One important moral of this tale is that one cannot assume that the price elasticity of demand for a good is the same, regardless of the market. Perhaps a rose is a rose is a rose; but a price elasticity can vary a lot, depending on what market you are talking about. To grab a price elasticity for a particular good off the shelf and apply it, regardless of the market to which it pertains, can be a formula for disaster.

If its price decreases, a great many buyers of substitutes will switch to this product. Naturally, the closeness of the substitutes depends on how narrowly the commodity is defined. In general, one would expect that, as the definition of the product becomes narrower and more specific, the product has more close substitutes and its price elasticity of demand is higher. Thus the demand for a particular brand of oil is more price elastic than the overall demand for oil, and the demand for oil is more price elastic than the demand for fuel as a whole. If a commodity is defined so that it has perfect substitutes, its price elasticity of demand approaches infinity. Thus, if one farmer's wheat is exactly like that grown by other farmers and if the farmer raises the price slightly (to a point above the market level), the farmer's sales will be reduced to nothing.

Importance in Consumers' Budgets. It is often asserted that the price elasticity of demand for a commodity is likely to depend on the importance of the commodity in consumers' budgets. The elasticity of demand for commodities like pepper and salt may be quite low. Typical consumers spend a very small portion of their income on pepper and salt, and the quantity they demand may not be influenced much by changes in price within a reasonable range. However, although a tendency of this sort is often hypothesized, there is no guarantee that it always exists.

Length of the Period. Every market demand curve pertains, you will recall, to a certain time interval. In general, *demand is likely to be more sensitive to price over a long period than over a short one.* The longer the period, the easier it is for consumers and business firms to substitute one good for another. If, for example, the price of oil should decline relative to other fuels, oil consumption in the month after the price decline would probably increase very little. But over a period of several years, people would have an opportunity to take account of the price decline in choosing the type of fuel to be used in new and renovated houses and businesses. In the longer period of several years, the price decline would have a greater effect on the consumption of oil than in the shorter period of one month.

Price Elasticity and Total Money Expenditure

Basic Idea #11: People commonly assume that a price reduction will lower the amount spent on a commodity, and that a price increase will raise it. The truth is that, whether the price is raised or lowered, the effect may be either an increase or decrease in the amount spent on the commodity: It all depends on the price elasticity of demand.

Many important decisions hinge on the price elasticity of demand for a commodity. One reason why this is so is that the price elasticity of demand determines whether a given change in price will increase or decrease the amount of money spent on a commodity—often a matter of basic importance to firms and government agencies. (Recall the case of the Boston and Maine Railroad.) In this section, we show how the price elasticity of demand determines the effect of a price change on the total amount spent on a commodity.

As a first step, we must define three terms—price elastic, price inelastic, and unitary elasticity. The demand for a commodity is **price elastic** if the price elasticity of demand is *greater than 1*. The demand for a commodity is **price inelastic** if the price elasticity of demand is *less than 1*. And the demand for a commodity is of **unitary elasticity** if the price elasticity of demand *equals 1*. As indicated below, the effect of a price change on the total amount spent on a commodity depends on whether the demand for

117

In 1905 the average automobile produced in the United States cost more than the average Datsun seventy years later. Many of the firms in the auto industry were warmed-over buggy makers who hand-crafted rich men's toys. But change was in the air. *Motor Age,* the industry's first trade magazine, prophesied that "the simple car is the car of the future—. A golden opportunity awaits some bold manufacturer of a simple car."

It remained for Henry Ford, the son of a Wisconsin farmer, to translate these words into a car—the Model T. Ford, commenting on his rural youth, declared, "It was life on the farm that drove me into devising ways and means to better transportation." Turning from the kid glove and checkbook set, he saw the potential market—at the right price—for car sales in the agricultural community.

Henry Ford in his first automobile, 1903

The Model T was introduced in 1909. A few numbers indicate its phenomenal progress.

Year	Price (dollars)	Cars Sold
1909	900	58,022
1914	440	472,350
1916	360	730,041

However, all good things come to an end. By the twenties, Ford's unwillingness to alter the Model T in any fashion (cosmetic or mechanical), as well as increased competition from other manufacturers, and the development of trade-in and installment buying (which reduced the price elasticity of demand for automobiles) brought the Model T to an end. But the record profits of the Ford Motor Company between 1910 and 1920 vindicated Henry Ford in his belief that "it is better to sell a large number of cars at a reasonably small margin than to sell fewer cars at a larger margin of profit. Bear in mind that when you reduce the price of the car without reducing the quality you increase the possible number of purchases. There are many men who will pay $360 for a car who would not pay $440. I figure that on the $360 basis we can increase the sales to 800,000 cars for the year—less profit on each car, but more cars, more employment of labor and in the end, we get all the profit we ought to make." Needless to say, price reductions do not always result in higher profits. But in his appraisal of the auto market between 1910 and 1920, Henry Ford seemed right.*

E.A.

*Henry Ford, ed. John B. Rae, Englewood Cliffs, N.J.: Prentice-Hall, 1969, p. 112.

the commodity is price elastic, price inelastic, or of unitary elasticity. Let's consider each case.

CASE 1: DEMAND IS PRICE ELASTIC

In this case, if the price of the commodity is *reduced,* the total amount spent on the commodity will *increase.* To see why, suppose that the price elasticity of demand for hi-fi sets is 2 and that the price of the hi-fi sets is reduced by 1 percent. Because the price elasticity of demand is 2, the 1 percent reduction in price results in a 2 percent increase in quantity of hi-fi sets demanded. Since the total amount spent on hi-fi sets equals the quantity demanded times the price, the 1 percent reduction in price will be more than offset by the 2 percent increase in quantity demanded. The result of the price cut will be an increase in the total amount spent on hi-fi sets.

On the other hand, if the price of the commodity is *increased,* the total amount spent on the commodity will *fall.* For example, if the price of hi-fi sets is raised by 1 percent, this will reduce the quantity demanded by 2 percent. The 2 percent reduction in the quantity demanded will more than offset the 1 percent increase in price, the result being a decrease in the total amount spent on hi-fi sets.

CASE 2: DEMAND IS PRICE INELASTIC

In this case, if the price is *reduced,* the total amount spent on the commodity will *decrease.* To see why, suppose that the price elasticity of demand for corn is 0.5 and the price of corn is reduced by 1 percent. Because the price elasticity of demand is 0.5, the 1 percent price reduction results in a ½ percent increase in the quantity demanded of corn. Since the total amount spent on corn equals the quantity demanded times the price, the ½ percent increase in the quantity demanded will be more than offset by the 1 percent reduction in price. The result of the price cut will be a decrease in the total amount spent on corn.

On the other hand, if the price of the commodity is *increased,* the total amount spent on the commodity will *increase.* For example, if the price of corn is raised by 1 percent, this will reduce quantity demanded by ½ percent. The 1 percent price increase will more than offset the ½ percent reduction in quantity demanded, the result being an increase in the total amount spent on corn.

CASE 3: DEMAND IS OF UNITARY ELASTICITY

In this case, a price increase or decrease results in no difference in the total amount spent on the commodity. Why? Because a price decrease (increase) of a certain percentage always results in a quantity increase (decrease) of the same percentage, so that the product of the price and quantity is unaffected.

Table 6.3 summarizes the result of this section. It should help you review our findings.

Table 6.3

EFFECT OF AN INCREASE OR DECREASE IN THE PRICE OF A COMMODITY ON THE TOTAL EXPENDITURE ON THE COMMODITY

Commodity's price elasticity of demand	Effect on total expenditure of:	
	Price decrease	Price increase
Price elastic (which means that elasticity is greater than 1)	Increase	Decrease
Price inelastic (which means that elasticity is less than 1)	Decrease	Increase
Unitary elasticity (which means that elasticity equals 1)	No change	No change

Test Yourself

1. Professor Kenneth Warner of the University of Michigan estimated in 1984 that a 10 percent increase in the price of cigarettes results in a 4 percent decline in the quantity of cigarettes consumed. For teenagers, he estimated that a 10 percent price increase results in a 14 percent decline in cigarette consumption. Based on his estimates, what is the price elasticity of demand for cigarettes? Among teenagers, what is the price elasticity of demand? Why is the price elasticity different among teenagers than for the public as a whole?

2. Suppose that each of the four corners of an intersection contains a gas station, and that the gasoline is essentially the same. Do you think that the price elasticity of demand for each station's gasoline is above or below 1? Why? Do you think that it is less than or greater than the price elasticity of demand for all gasoline in the U.S.?

3. The Bugsbane Music Box Company is convinced that an increase in its price will reduce the total amount of money spent on its product. Can you tell from this whether the demand for its product is price elastic or price inelastic?

4. Suppose that the relationship between the price of aluminum and the quantity of aluminum demanded is as follows:

Price (dollars)	Quantity
1	8
2	7
3	6
4	5
5	4

What is the arc elasticity of demand when price is between $1 and $2? Between $4 and $5?

The Farm Problem and the Price Elasticity of Demand

To illustrate the importance of the price elasticity of demand, let's return to the nation's farm problems. One of the most difficult problems for farmers is that, under a free market, farm incomes vary enormously between good times and bad, the variation being much greater than for nonfarm incomes. This is so because farm prices vary a great deal between good times and bad, whereas farm output is much more stable than industrial output. Why is agriculture like this?

The answer lies in considerable part with the price elasticity of demand for farm products. As we emphasized in Chapter 4, food is a necessity with few good substitutes. Thus we would expect the demand for farm products to be price inelastic. And as Table 6.2 suggests, this expectation is borne out by the facts. Given that the demand curve for farm products is price inelastic—and that the quantity supplied of farm products is also relatively insensitive to price—it follows that relatively small shifts in either the supply curve or the demand curve result in big changes in price. This is why farm prices are so unstable. Panel A of Figure 6.4 shows a market where the demand curve is much more inelastic than in panel B. As you can see, a small shift to the left in the demand curve results in a much larger drop in price in panel A than in panel B.

PRICE ELASTICITY AND THE BRANNAN PLAN

This is not the only role the price elasticity of demand plays in our farm problems. Many other questions involve it. Consider the plan proposed after World War II by Charles Brannan who served as President Truman's secretary of agriculture. The plan was later supported in somewhat modified form by Ezra Taft Benson, secretary of agriculture in the Eisenhower administration. But it drew fire from many farmers, and not until 1973,

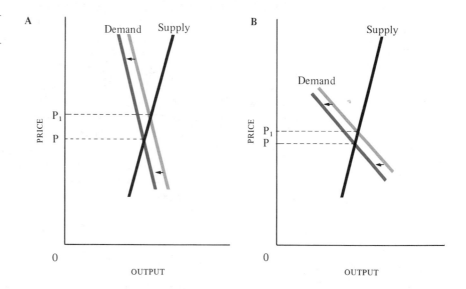

Figure 6.4

Instability of Farm Prices and Incomes
Because the demand curve in panel A is much less elastic than in panel B, a small shift in the demand curve has a much bigger impact on price in panel A than in panel B.

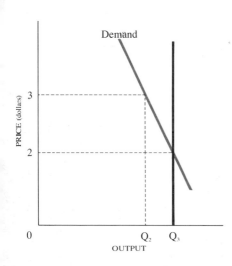

Figure 6.5

Effect of the Brannan Plan   *Under the Brannan plan, the competitive market would be let alone, so that, if output were OQ_3, the price would be $2. Then the government would pay farmers the difference between this price and the target price, $3.*

after nearly three decades of controversy, was the plan approved by Congress.

According to the **Brannan plan,** a floor is established under the price received by farmers. Suppose that the market price is below this target level. If the target level is $3 in Figure 6.5, and if the output quota is OQ_3, this plan lets the competitive market alone, so that the output of OQ_3 is sold at a price of $2. Then according to this plan, the government issues subsidy checks to farmers to cover the difference between the market price ($2) and the target price ($3).

The cost to the Treasury under the Brannan plan is $(\$3 - \$2) \times OQ_3$. Why? Because the Treasury pays a subsidy of $(\$3 - \$2)$ per bushel, and OQ_3 bushels are grown; thus the total subsidy is $(\$3 - \$2) \times OQ_3$. Before the Brannan plan was adopted, the government supported the price at $3, and bought the amount—$(OQ_3 - OQ_2)$—that private buyers would not purchase at that price. The cost to the Treasury under this system is $3 $(OQ_3 - OQ_2)$. Why? Because the Treasury buys $(OQ_3 - OQ_2)$ bushels at $3 per bushel.

An important question is: Will the cost to the U.S Treasury under the Brannan plan be greater than under the previous system? The answer can be shown to depend on the price elasticity of demand. As demonstrated in footnote 4, the cost under the Brannan plan is greater than under the previous system[4] if $\$2 \times OQ_3 < \$3 \times OQ_2$. But since $\$2 \times OQ_3$ is the total money expenditure at a price of $2 and $\$3 \times OQ_2$ is the total money expenditure at a price of $3, it follows from the previous section that $\$2 \times OQ_3$ will be less than $\$3 \times OQ_2$ if the price elasticity of demand is less than 1. (Why? Because the total amount spent on a commodity will be less at a lower price [such as $2] than at a higher price [such as $3] if demand is price inelastic.) Thus, since the elasticity of demand for farm

[4] The cost to the government under the Brannan plan is $(\$3 - \$2) \times OQ_3 = \$3 \times OQ_3 - \$2 \times OQ_3$, while the cost under the other system is $\$3 \times (OQ_3 - OQ_2) = \$3 \times OQ_3 - \$3 \times OQ_2$. Thus the difference between the former cost and the latter is $\$3 \times OQ_2 - \$2 \times OQ_3$, which means that the cost under the Brannan plan would be greater than under the other system if $\$2 \times OQ_3 < \$3 \times OQ_2$.

121

products is in fact less than 1, the cost to the Treasury will be greater under the Brannan plan than under a system whereby the price is supported at $3, with the government clearing the market of the farm products not purchased by the private sector at that price.[5]

Our purpose here is not to decide whether the Brannan plan is good or bad. To make such a decision, we would have to take account of many factors besides the cost to the Treasury. Instead, our point is that the price elasticity of demand is an important concept in discussing the effects of the Brannan plan, just as in discussing the instability of farm income and prices. Moreover, as we shall see in subsequent sections, the price elasticity of demand is equally as important in problems concerning the industrial sector of the economy as in problems concerning agriculture.

Industry and Firm Demand Curves

Up to this point, we have been dealing with the market demand curve for a commodity. *The market demand curve for a commodity is not the same as the market demand curve for the output of a single firm that produces the commodity, unless, of course, the industry is composed of only a single firm.* If the industry is composed of more than one firm, as is usually the case, the demand curve for the output of each firm producing the commodity will usually be quite different from the demand curve for the commodity. The demand curve for the output of Farmer Brown's wheat is quite different from the market demand curve for wheat.

In particular, the demand curve for the output of a particular firm is generally more price elastic than the market demand curve for the commodity, because the products of other firms in the industry are close substitutes for the product of this firm. As pointed out earlier, products with many close substitutes have relatively high price elasticities of demand.

If there are many, many firms selling a homogeneous product, the individual firm's demand curve becomes *horizontal,* or essentially so. To see this, suppose that 100,000 firms sell a particular commodity and that each of these firms is of equal size. If any one of these firms were to triple its output and sales, the total industry output would change by only .002 percent—too small a change to have any perceptible effect on the price of the commodity. Consequently, each firm can act as if variations in its output—within the range of its capabilities—will have no real impact on market price. In other words, the demand curve facing the individual firm is horizontal, as in Figure 6.6.

Income Elasticity of Demand

So far this chapter has dealt almost exclusively with the effect of a commodity's price on the quantity demanded of it in the market. But price is not, of course, the only factor that influences the quantity demanded of

Figure 6.6

Demand Curve for Output of an Individual Firm: The Case of a Great Many Sellers of a Homogeneous Commodity *If there are many firms selling a homogeneous product, the demand curve facing an individual firm is horizontal.*

Basic Idea #12: *Be careful to distinguish between the market demand curve for a commodity and the market demand curve for the output of a single firm producing the commodity. The latter is generally much more price elastic than the former. Indeed, if there are a great many firms selling a homogeneous product, the individual firm's demand curve becomes horizontal, or close to it.*

---

[5] Note that this result does not depend on our choice of $3 as the target price and of $2 as the market price. Regardless of what the target price and market price may be, this result will hold, if the price elasticity of demand is less than 1.

the commodity. Another important factor is the level of money income among the consumers in the market. The sensitivity of the quantity demanded to the total money income of all of the consumers in the market is measured by the ***income elasticity of demand,*** *which is defined as the percentage change in the quantity demanded resulting from a 1 percent increase in total money income (all prices being held constant).*

A commodity's income elasticity of demand may be positive or negative. For many commodities, increases in income result in increases in the amount demanded. Such commodities, like steak or caviar, have positive income elasticities of demand. For other commodities, increases in income result in decreases in the amount demanded. These commodities, like margarine and poor grades of vegetables, have negative income elasticities of demand. However, be careful to note that the income elasticity of demand of a commodity is likely to vary with the level of income under consideration. For example, if only families at the lowest income levels are considered, the income elasticity of demand for margarine may be positive.

Luxury items tend to have higher income elasticities of demand than necessities. Indeed, one way to define luxuries and necessities is to say that luxuries are commodities with high income elasticities of demand, and necessities are commodities with low income elasticities of demand.

EMPIRICAL STUDIES

Many studies have been made to estimate the income elasticity of demand for particular commodities, since, like the price elasticity of demand, it is of great importance to decision makers. In making long-term forecasts of industry sales, for example, firms must take the income elasticity of demand into account. Thus, if the income elasticity of demand for a product is high, and if incomes increase considerably during the next 20 years, the product's sales will tend to increase greatly during that period. On the other hand, if the income elasticity of demand for a product is close to zero, one would expect the product's sales not to increase very much on account of such increases in income.

To illustrate the findings of empirical studies in this area, consider the following results obtained by Herman Wold, a distinguished Swedish economist. According to his estimates, the income elasticity of demand is 0.37 for eggs, 0.34 for cheese, 0.42 for butter, 1.00 for liquor,—0.20 for margarine, 0.07 for milk and cream, and 1.48 for restaurant consumption of food. Certainly, these estimates seem reasonable. One would expect the income elasticity of demand to be negative for margarine, because consumers tend to view margarine as an inferior good, and as their incomes rise, they tend to switch from margarine to butter. Also, it is not surprising that the income elasticity of demand for milk and cream is close to zero, since people tend to view milk and cream as necessities, particularly for children. In addition, it is quite reasonable that the income elasticity of demand for liquor and restaurant consumption of food is higher than for the other commodities. Liquor and restaurant meals tend to be luxury items for most people.

Example 6.2   The Demand for "Suds"

According to Thomas Fogarty and Kenneth Elzinga,* the price elasticity of demand for beer in the United States is about 0.8, and the income elasticity of demand for beer is about 0.4.

(a) Is the demand curve shown above consistent with their findings? Why or why not? (b) If the price of a case of beer increases, will this result in an increase or decrease in the amount of money spent per year on beer? (c) If consumer income increases by 15 percent, while the price of beer remains constant, what will be the effect on the amount of money spent per year on beer? (d) Holding the prices of other goods and income constant, do you think that the market demand curve for beer varies from month to month? From state to state? If so, why? (e) If Budweiser lowers the price of its beer by 1 percent, can it expect to increase the quantity it sells by 0.8 percent? Why or why not? (f) At the close of 1953, Budweiser was selling for 58 cents per case more than its rivals in the St. Louis market and had 12 percent of the market. In early 1955, Budweiser sold its beer at the same price as its rivals and had 39 percent of the market. Suppose that other brewers held their price constant at $2 per case during this period, and that the total amount of beer sold in this market was constant during this period. What was the price elasticity of demand for Budweiser beer in this market?

SOLUTION

(a) No. According to this demand curve, the price elasticity of demand for beer is 1, since the amount spent on beer is the same ($8 billion) regardless of the price. (b) Increase. (c) It will increase by about 6 percent. (d) Yes, because of differences among months and states in temperature, tastes, and other factors. (e) No. Because Budweiser is only one firm in the market, the percentage increase in the quantity it sells is likely to be greater than 0.8 percent, if other firms hold their price constant. (f) $- (.39X - .12X)/.255X \div (\$2.00 - \$2.58)/\$2.29 = 4.2$. ($X$ is the total amount of beer sold in this market then.)

* T. Fogarty and K. Elzinga, "The Demand for Beer," *Review of Economics and Statistics,* May 1972.

Cross Elasticity of Demand

Besides the price of the commodity and the level of total money income—the factors discussed primarily in previous sections of this chapter—the quantity demanded of a commodity also depends on the prices of other commodities. Suppose the price of butter is held constant. The amount of butter demanded will be influenced by the price of margarine. The *cross elasticity of demand, defined as the percentage change in the quantity demanded of one commodity resulting from a 1 percent change in the price of another commodity, is used to measure the sensitivity of the former commodity's quantity demanded to changes in the latter commodity's price.*

Pairs of commodities are classified as **substitutes** or **complements,** depending on the sign of the cross elasticity of demand. *If the cross elasticity of demand is positive, two commodities are substitutes.* Butter and margarine are substitutes because a decrease in the price of butter will result in a decrease in the quantity demanded of margarine—many margarine eaters really prefer the "higher-priced spread." *On the other hand, if the cross elasticity of demand is negative, two commodities are complements.* For example, gin and tonic may be complements since a decrease in the price of gin may increase the quantity demanded of tonic. The reduction in the price of gin will increase the quantity demanded of gin, thus increasing the quantity demanded of tonic since gin and tonic tend to be used together.

Many studies have been made of the cross elasticity of demand for various pairs of commodities. After all, it frequently is very important to know how a change in the price of one commodity will affect the sales of another commodity. For example, what would be the effect of a 1 percent increase in the price of pork on the quantity demanded of beef? According to Herman Wold's estimates, the effect would be a .28 percent increase in the quantity demanded of beef—since he estimates that the cross elasticity of demand for these two commodities is 0.28. What effect would a 1 percent increase in the price of butter have on the quantity demanded of margarine? According to Wold, the effect would be a .81 percent increase in the quantity demanded of margarine—since he estimates that the cross elasticity of demand for these two commodities is 0.81.

Test Yourself

1. Is each of the following statements true, partly true, or false? Explain. (a) If a good's income elasticity of demand is less than one, an increase in the price of the good will increase the amount spent on it. (b) The income elasticity of demand will have the same sign regardless of the level of income at which it is measured. (c) If Mr. Miller spends all of his income on steak (regardless of his income or the price of steak), Mr. Miller's cross elasticity of demand between steak and any other good is zero.

2. What is the sign of the cross elasticity of demand for each of the following pairs of commodities: (a) tea and coffee, (b) tennis rackets and tennis balls, (c) whiskey and gin, (d) fishing licenses and fishing poles, (e) nylon rugs and wool rugs?

3. On page 118, we saw the quantity of Model T's sold increased from about 472,000 to about 730,000 when its price was reduced from $440 in 1914 to $360 in 1916. How can this fact be reconciled with recent studies which indicate that the price elasticity of demand for automobiles is about 1.2 to 1.5?

4. According to the U.S. Department of Agriculture, the income elasticity of demand for coffee is about 0.23. If incomes rose by 1 percent, what effect would this have on the quantity demanded of coffee?

Summary

1. The market demand curve, which is the relationship between the price of a commodity and the amount of the commodity demanded in the market, is one of the most important and frequently used concepts in economics. The shape and position of a product's market demand curve depend on consumers' tastes, consumer incomes, the price of other goods, and the number of consumers in the market.

2. The market demand curve for a commodity is not the same as the demand curve for the output of a single firm that produces the commodity, unless the industry is composed of only one firm. In general, the demand curve for the output of a single firm will be more elastic than the market demand curve for the commodity. Indeed, if there are many firms selling a homogeneous commodity, the individual firm's demand curve becomes horizontal.

3. There are many techniques for measuring demand curves, such as interview studies, direct experiments, and the statistical analysis of historical data. An example of a direct experiment was the project carried out by the Boston and Maine Railroad.

4. The price elasticity of demand, defined as the percentage change in quantity demanded resulting from a 1 percent change in price, measures the sensitivity of the amount demanded to changes in price. Whether a price increase results in an increase or decrease in the total amount spent on a commodity depends on the price elasticity of demand.

5. The income elasticity of demand, defined as the percentage change in quantity demanded resulting from a 1 percent increase in total money income, measures the sensitivity of the amount demanded to changes in total income. A commodity's income elasticity of demand may be positive or negative. Luxury items are generally assumed to have higher income elasticities of demand than necessities.

6. The cross elasticity of demand, defined as the percentage change in the quantity demanded resulting from a 1 percent change in the price of another commodity, measures the sensitivity of the amount demanded to changes in the price of another commodity. If the cross elasticity of demand is positive, two commodities are substitutes; if it is negative, they are complements.

Concepts for Review

Market demand curve	**Price elastic**	**Cross elasticity of**
Direct market experiment	**Price inelastic**	**demand**
Price elasticity of	**Unitary elasticity**	**Substitute**
demand	**Brannan plan**	**Complement**
Arc elasticity of	**Income elasticity**	
demand	**of demand**	

CHAPTER 7

Getting behind the Demand Curve: Consumer Behavior

To a considerable extent, consumers, voting with their pocketbooks, are the masters of our economic system. No wonder, then, that economists spend much of their time describing and analyzing how consumers act. In this chapter, we present the basic model economists use to analyze consumer behavior.

Consumer Expenditures

THE WALTERS OF SAN DIEGO

Since we are concerned here with consumer behavior, perhaps the best way to begin is to look at the behavior of a particular consumer. It is hard to find any consumer who is "typical." There are hundreds of millions of consumers in the United States, and they vary enormously. Nonetheless, it is instructive to look at how a particular American family—the Walters of San Diego[1]—spends its money. The Walters are in their mid-thirties, have two children (ages 8 and 6), and have Mrs. Walter's younger brother living with them. They own their own home, and both work. Mr. Walter manages a small clothing firm in San Diego, and Mrs. Walter is a designer at the same firm. Together, the Walters make about $43,000 a year.

[1] For obvious reasons, we have changed the name and residence of the family in question. Otherwise, however, the facts given in the following paragraphs are as they were stated in a national magazine. To correct for inflation, we have increased the figures in the article by the (approximate) percentage by which the price level has risen since the article appeared.

Table 7.1

MONTHLY SPENDING PATTERN OF MR. AND MRS. WALTER OF SAN DIEGO, CALIFORNIA

Item	Amount (dollars)	Percent of income
Housing	1,250	35
Food and drink	500	14
Domestic help	250	7
Private school and education	260	7
Entertainment and clothing	260	7
Medical, dental, and insurance expenses	250	7
Transportation	85	2
Taxes and savings[a]	745	21
Monthly income	3,600	100

[a]Estimated by deducting other items from monthly income.

How do the Walters spend their money? For most consumers, we cannot answer this question with any accuracy, because the people in question simply do not tell anyone what they do with their money. But because the Walters and their buying habits were scrutinized in a series of articles in a national magazine, it is possible to describe quite accurately where their money goes. As shown in Table 7.1, the Walters, who own their own home, spend about $1,250 a month—about 35 percent of their income—on housing. In addition, they spend about $500 a month—about 14 percent of their income—on food and drink. Also, they spend about $250 a month—about 7 percent of their income—on domestic help, which is needed since both parents work.

In addition, as shown in Table 7.1, the Walters spend about $260 a month—about 7 percent of their income—on private schools and other lessons for their children. Another $260 a month goes for entertainment and clothing. Because of the mild weather in San Diego (and perhaps because they can get clothing at a discount since they are in the clothing business), their expenditures on clothing are not very large. Medical, dental, and insurance expenses consume about $250 a month—again, about 7 percent of income—and $85 a month—or about 2 percent of their income—is spent on transportation. Finally, the Walters allocate about $745 a month—about 21 percent of their income—for taxes and savings.

This, in a nutshell, is how the Walters spend their money. The Walters exchange their resources—mostly labor—in the resource markets for $43,000 a year. They take this money into the product markets and spend about four-fifths of it for the goods and services described above. The remaining one-fifth of their income goes for taxes and saving. The Walters, like practically every family, keep a watchful eye on where their money goes and what they are getting in exchange for their labor and other resources. As stressed in Chapter 2, the basic purpose of our economic system is to satisfy the wants of consumers.

AGGREGATE DATA FOR THE UNITED STATES

How does the way that the Walters spend their money compare with consumer behavior in general? In Table 7.2, we provide data on how all con-

Table 7.2

ALLOCATION OF INCOME BY U.S. HOUSEHOLDS, 1983

	Percent of total[a]
Personal taxes	15
Personal saving	4
Interest payments	2
Consumption expenditures	
Autos and parts	5
Furniture and household equipment	4
Other durable goods	2
Food and drink	15
Clothing and shoes	5
Gasoline and oil	3
Other nondurable goods	6
Housing	13
Household operations	6
Transportation	3
Other services	18
Total income	100

[a]Because of rounding errors, figures do not sum to total.

Source: Survey of Current Business, July 1984.

sumers allocated their aggregate income in 1983. These data tell us much more about the typical behavior of American consumers than our case study of the Walters. Note first of all that American households paid about 15 percent of their income in taxes. This, of course, is the price of governments services we described in Chapter 4. In addition, American households saved about 4 percent of their income. In other words, they refrained from spending 4 percent of their income on goods and services; instead, they put this amount into stocks, bonds, bank accounts, or other such channels for saving. Also, about 2 percent of their income went for interest payments to banks and other institutions from which they had borrowed money.

American consumers spent the remaining 79 percent of their income on goods and services. Table 7.2 makes it clear that they allocated much of their expenditures to housing, food and drink, and transportation. Spending on housing, household operations, and furniture and other durable household equipment accounted for about 23 percent of American consumers' total income. Spending on food and beverages accounted for about 15 percent of total income. Spending on automobiles and parts, gasoline and oil, and other transportation accounted for about 11 percent of total income. Thus taxes, savings, housing, food and drink, and transportation accounted for about 70 percent of the total income of all households in the United States.

The data in Table 7.2 make it obvious that the Walter family is not very typical of American consumers. For example, it spends a much larger percentage of its income on housing, domestic help, and education than do consumers as a whole. To some degree, this is because the Walters are more affluent than most American families, but this is only part of the reason. To a large extent, it simply reflects the fact that people want different things. Looking around you, you see considerable diversity in the way consumers spend their money. Take your own family as an example. It is a good bet that your family spends its money quite differently than the nation as a whole. If your parents like to live in a big house, your family may spend much more than the average on housing. Or if they like to go to sports events, their expenditures on such entertainment may be much higher than average.

A Model of Consumer Behavior

Why do consumers spend their money the way they do? The economist answers this question with the aid of a *model of consumer behavior,* which is useful both for analysis and for decision making. To construct this model, the economist obviously must consider the tastes of the consumer. As Henry Adams put it, "Everyone carries his own inch-rule of taste, and amuses himself by applying it, triumphantly, wherever he travels." Certainly one would expect that the amount a consumer purchases of a particular commodity is influenced by his or her tastes. Some people like beef, others like pork. Some people like the opera, others would trade a ticket to hear Luciano Pavarotti for a ticket to the Dallas Cowboys game any day of the week. Three assumptions, which seem reasonable for most purposes, underlie the economist's model of consumer preferences.

Alfred Marshall (1842–1924) played a major role in the construction of theories of consumer demand, and pioneered in many other areas of economics as well. His Principles of Economics *(1890), which had eight editions, was a leading economics text for many years.*

1. We assume that *consumers, when confronted with two alternative market baskets, can decide whether they prefer the first to the second, the second to the first, or whether they are indifferent between them.* For example, suppose Mrs. Walter, the San Diego designer, is confronted with a choice between a market basket containing 3 chocolate bars and a ticket to the movies and another market basket containing 2 chocolate bars and a record of the Tabernacle Choir singing Chopin's Minute Waltz. Despite the rather bizarre composition of these two market baskets, we assume that she can somehow decide whether she prefers the first market basket to the second, the second market basket to the first, or whether she is indifferent between them.

2. We assume that *the consumer's preferences are transitive.* The meaning of transitive in this context is simple enough. Suppose that Mrs. Walter prefers an ounce of Chanel No. 5 perfume to an ounce of Blue Grass perfume, and that she prefers an ounce of Blue Grass perfume to an ounce of Sortilège perfume. Then, if her preferences are transitive, she must prefer an ounce of Chanel No. 5 perfume to an ounce of Sortilège perfume. The reason for this assumption is clear. If the consumer's preferences were not transitive, the consumer would have inconsistent or contradictory preferences. Although some people may have preferences that are not transitive, this assumption seems to be a reasonable first approximation—for the noninstitutionalized part of the population at least.

3. We assume that *the consumer always prefers more of a commodity to less.* For example, if one market basket contains 3 bars of soap and 2 monkey wrenches and a second contains 3 bars of soap and 3 monkey wrenches, it is assumed that the second market basket is preferred to the first. To a large extent, this assumption is justified by the definition of a commodity as something the consumer desires.[2] This does not mean that certain things are not a nuisance. If one market basket contains 3 bars of soap and 2 rattlesnakes, we would not be at all surprised if the consumer did *not* prefer this market basket to one containing 3 bars of soap and no rattlesnakes. But to such a consumer, a rattlesnake would not be desired—and thus would not be a commodity. Instead, the absence of a rattlesnake would be desired—and would be a commodity.

TOTAL UTILITY

In Chapter 2, we pointed out that a model, to be useful, must omit many unimportant factors, concentrate on the basic factors at work, and simplify in order to illuminate. So that we focus on the important factors at work here, let's assume that there are only two goods, food and clothing. This is an innocuous assumption, since the results we shall obtain can be generalized to include cases where any number of goods exists. For simplicity, food is measured in pounds, and clothing is measured in number of pieces of clothing.

Consider Mrs. Walter, making choices for her family. Undoubtedly, she

[2] An individual's desire for a particular good during a particular period of time is not infinite but in the aggregate human wants seem to be insatiable. Besides the basic desires for food, shelter, and clothing, which must be fulfilled to some extent if the human organism is to survive, wants arise from cultural factors. Advertising and the emulation of social leaders stimulate and extend a person's wants.

regards certain market baskets—that is, certain combinations of food and clothing (the only commodities)—to be more desirable than others. She certainly regards 2 pounds of food and 1 piece of clothing to be more desirable than 1 pound of food and 1 piece of clothing. For simplicity, suppose that it is possible to measure the amount of satisfaction that she gets from each market basket by its utility. *A **utility** is a number that represents the level of satisfaction that the consumer derives from a particular market basket.* For example, the utility attached to the market basket containing 2 pounds of food and 1 piece of clothing may be 10 utils, and the utility attached to the market basket containing 1 pound of food and 1 piece of clothing may be 6 utils. (A util is the traditional unit in which utility is expressed.)

MARGINAL UTILITY

It is important to distinguish between total utility and marginal utility. The total utility of a market basket is the number described in the previous paragraph, whereas *the **marginal utility** measures the additional satisfaction derived from an additional unit of a commodity.* To see how marginal utility is obtained, let's take a close look at Table 7.3. The total utility the Walter family derives from the consumption of various amounts of food is given in the middle column of this table. (For simplicity, we assume for the moment that the Walters consume only food.) The marginal utility, shown in the right-hand column, is the extra utility derived from each amount of food over and above the utility derived from 1 less pound of food. Thus it equals the difference between the total utility of a certain amount of food and the total utility of 1 less pound of food.

For example, as shown in Table 7.3, the *total* utility of 3 pounds of food is 9 utils, which is a measure of the total amount of satisfaction that the Walters get from this much food. In contrast, the *marginal* utility of 3 pounds of food is the extra utility obtained from the third pound of food— that is, the total utility of 3 pounds of food less the total utility of 2 pounds of food. Specifically, as shown in Table 7.3, it is 2 utils. Similarly, the *total* utility of 2 pounds of food is 7 utils, which is a measure of the total amount of satisfaction that the Walters get from this much food. In contrast, the *marginal* utility of 2 pounds of food is the extra utility from the second pound of food—that is, the total utility of 2 pounds of food less the total utility of 1 pound of food. Specifically, as shown in Table 7.3, it is 4 utils.

THE LAW OF DIMINISHING MARGINAL UTILITY

Economists generally assume that, as a person consumes more and more of a particular commodity, there is, beyond some point, a decline in the extra satisfaction derived from the last unit of the commodity consumed. For example, if the Walters consume 2 pounds of food in a particular period of time, it may be just enough to meet their basic physical needs. If they consume 3 pounds of food in the same period of time, the third pound of food is likely to yield less satisfaction than the second. If they consume 4 pounds of food in the same period of time, the fourth pound of food is likely to yield less satisfaction than the third. And so on.

This assumption or hypothesis is often called the **law of diminishing marginal utility.** This law states that, *as a person consumes more and more*

Table 7.3

TOTAL UTILITY AND MARGINAL UTILITY DERIVED BY THE WALTERS FROM CONSUMING VARIOUS AMOUNTS OF FOOD PER DAY[a]

Pounds of food	Total utility	Marginal utility
0	0	
1	3	3 (=3–0)
2	7	4 (=7–3)
3	9	2 (=9–7)
4	10	1 (=10–9)

[a]This table assumes that no clothing is consumed. If a nonzero amount of clothing is consumed, the figures in this table will probably be altered since the marginal utility of a certain amount of food is likely to depend on the amount of clothing consumed.

of a given commodity (the consumption of other commodities being held constant), the marginal utility of the commodity eventually will tend to decline. The figures concerning the Walter family in Table 7.3 are in accord with this law, as shown in Figure 7.1, which plots the marginal utility of food against the amount consumed. Once the consumption of food exceeds about 1½ pounds, marginal utility of food declines.

The Equilibrium Market Basket

Preferences alone do not determine the consumer's actions. *Besides knowing the consumer's preferences, we must also know his or her income and the prices of commodities to predict which market basket he or she will buy.* The consumer's money income is the amount of money he or she can spend per unit of time. A consumer's choice of a market basket is constrained by the size of his or her money income. For example, although Mr. Walter may regard a Hickey Freeman as his favorite suit, he may not buy it because he may have insufficient funds (as the bankers delicately put it). Also, the market basket the consumer chooses is influenced by the prices of commodities. If the Hickey Freeman suit were offered by a discount store at $100, rather than its list price of $350, Mr. Walter might purchase it after all.

Given the consumer's tastes, economists assume that he or she attempts to maximize utility. In other words, *consumers are assumed to be rational in the sense that they choose the market basket—or more generally, the course of action—that is most to their liking.* As previously noted, consumers cannot choose whatever market basket they please. Instead, they must maximize their utility subject to the constraints imposed by the size of their money income and the nature of commodity prices.

What is the optimal market basket, the one that maximizes utility subject to these constraints? It is the one where *the consumer's income is allocated among commodities so that, for every commodity purchased, the marginal utility of the commodity is proportional to its price.* Thus, in the case of the Walter family, the optimal market basket is the one where

$$\frac{MU_F}{P_F} = \frac{MU_C}{P_C}, \tag{7.1}$$

where MU_F is the marginal utility of food, MU_C is the marginal utility of clothing, P_F is the price of a pound of food, and P_C is the price of a piece of clothing.

WHY IS THIS RULE CORRECT?

To understand why the rule in Equation (7.1) is correct, it is convenient to begin by pointing out that $MU_F \div P_F$ is the marginal utility of the *last dollar's worth* of food and that $MU_C \div P_C$ is the marginal utility of the *last dollar's worth* of clothing. To see why this is so, take the case of food. Since MU_F is the extra utility of the *last pound* of food bought, and since P_F is the price of this *last pound*, the extra utility of the *last dollar's worth* of food must be $MU_F \div P_F$. For example, if the last pound of food results in

Figure 7.1

Total and Marginal Utility from Food Consumption, Walter Family *The marginal utility of the first pound of food (which, according to Table 7.3, equals 3 utils) is plotted at the midpoint between 0 and 1 pounds of food. The marginal utility of the second pound of food (which, according to Table 7.3, equals 4 utils) is plotted at the midpoint between 1 and 2 pounds of food. The marginal-utility curve connects these and other points showing the marginal utility of various amounts of food consumed.*

Beyond some point, the marginal utility curve of any commodity would be expected to fall, because of the law of diminishing marginal utility (which states that, as a person consumes more and more of a given commodity, the marginal utility of the commodity eventually will tend to decline). In the case shown here, the marginal utility curve falls when the Walter family's consumption of food exceeds about 1½ pounds per day.

Table 7.4

MARGINAL UTILITY DERIVED BY THE
WALTERS FROM VARIOUS QUANTITIES OF
FOOD AND CLOTHING

Commodity	Dollars worth				
	1	2	3	4	5
	Marginal utility (utils)				
Food	20	16	12	10	7
Clothing	12	10	7	5	3

Basic Idea #13: If any person or organization has a fixed sum of money which must be allocated among a variety of uses, the money should be allocated so that the marginal utility of the last dollar spent on each use is the same. The marginal utility of the last dollar spent on each use is the critically important factor.

an extra utility of 4 utils and this pound costs $2, then the extra utility from the last dollar's worth of food must be 4 ÷ 2, or 2 utils. In other words, the marginal utility of the last dollar's worth of food is 2 utils.

Since $MU_F \div P_F$ is the marginal utility of the last dollar's worth of food and $MU_C \div P_C$ is the marginal utility of the last dollar's worth of clothing, what Equation (7.1) really says is that *the rational consumer will choose a market basket where the marginal utility of the last dollar spent on all commodities purchased is the same.* To see why this must be so, consider the numerical example in Table 7.4, which shows the marginal utility the Walters derive from various amounts of food and clothing. Rather than measuring food and clothing in physical units, we measure them in Table 7.4 in terms of the amount of money spent on them.

Given the information in Table 7.4, how much of each commodity should Mrs. Walter buy if her money income is only $4 (a ridiculous assumption but one that will help to make our point)? Clearly, the first dollar she spends should be on food since it will yield her a marginal utility of 20. The second dollar she spends should also be on food since a second dollar's worth of food has a marginal utility of 16. (Thus the total utility derived from the $2 of expenditure is 20 + 16 = 36.)[3] The marginal utility of the third dollar is 12 if it is spent on more food—and 12 too if it is spent on clothing. Suppose that she chooses more food. (The total utility derived from the $3 of expenditure is 20 + 16 + 12 = 48.) What about the final dollar? Its marginal utility is 10 if it is spent on more food and 12 if it is spent on clothing; thus she will spend it on clothing. (The total utility derived from all $4 of expenditure is then 20 + 16 + 12 + 12 = 60.)

Thus Mrs. Walter, if she is rational, will allocate $3 of her income to food and $1 to clothing. This is the **equilibrium market basket,** the market basket that maximizes consumer satisfaction. The important thing to note is that this market basket demonstrates the principle set forth earlier in Equation (7.1). As shown in Table 7.4, the marginal utility derived from the last dollar spent on food is equal to the marginal utility derived from the last dollar spent on clothing. (Both are 12.) Thus this market basket has the characteristic described above: the marginal utility of the last dollar spent on all commodities purchased is the same. In the next section, we show that this will always be the case for market baskets that maximize the consumer's utility. If it were not true, the consumer could obtain a higher level of utility by changing the composition of his or her market basket.

FURTHER PROOF OF THE BUDGET ALLOCATION RULE

In the previous section, we stated the proposition that the consumer, to maximize utility, will choose a market basket where the marginal utility of the last dollar spent on all commodities purchased is the same. In this section, we show that, if this budget allocation rule is not followed, the consumer cannot be maximizing utility. This is offered as further proof of the proposition in the previous section. For simplicity, we assume that the consumer buys only two commodities, food and clothing.

---

[3] Since the marginal utility is the extra utility obtained from each dollar spent, the total utility from the total expenditure must be the sum of the marginal utilities of the individual dollars of expenditure.

Suppose that the marginal utility of the last dollar spent on food is 5 utils whereas the marginal utility of the last dollar spent on clothing is 3 utils. The consumer is not maximizing utility, because spending $1 more on food will increase total utility by 5 utils,[4] and spending $1 less on clothing will reduce total utility by 3 utils. Thus the transfer of $1 of expenditure from clothing to food will increase total utility by 2 utils—which

---

[4] We assume here that the extra utility from an *extra* dollar spent on food equals the extra utility from the *last* dollar spent on food. This is an innocuous assumption.

Example 7.1 The Diamond-Water Paradox

In 1985, a perfect blue-white diamond sold for over $10,000 per carat, while a gallon of water sold for about 2 cents per hundred gallons. For centuries, people have been fascinated by this fact. Diamonds, after all, are hardly essential to life, whereas water *is* essential. How is it, then, that people are willing to buy diamonds at a price that seems so much higher than that of water? Suppose that the typical consumer's marginal utility curves for diamonds and water are as shown below:

AMOUNT OF DIAMONDS

HUNDREDS OF GALLONS
OF WATER

(a) If the price per carat of a diamond is 500,000 times as great as the price per hundred gallons of water, and if the consumer buys both diamonds and water, does it follow that the total utility that the consumer receives from the diamonds is 500,000 times as great as the total utility received from the water? (b) Does it follow that the marginal utility of a carat of diamonds is 500,000 times as great as the marginal utility of a hundred gallons of water? (c) If the consumer buys a great deal of water and practically no diamonds, is it possible that the marginal utility of a carat of diamonds will be 500,000 times as great as the marginal utility of a hundred gallons of water? (d) Describe in your own words why people are willing to buy diamonds at a price that seems so much higher than that of water?

SOLUTION

(a) No. If the consumer is maximizing utility, the *marginal* utility of a carat of diamonds must be 500,000 times as great as the *marginal* utility of a hundred gallons of water. But there is no reason to believe that this is true of the *total* utilities. (b) Yes. (c) Yes. (d) They buy practically no diamonds and very large quantities of water. The marginal utility of diamonds is so much higher than the marginal utility of water that the marginal utility of the last dollar spent on diamonds is equal to the marginal utility of the last dollar spent on water.

means that the consumer currently isn't maximizing utility. More generally, a transfer of expenditure from clothing to food will always increase a consumer's utility so long as the marginal utility of the last dollar spent on food exceeds the marginal utility of the last dollar spent on clothing. Thus *the consumer will not be maximizing utility if the marginal utility of the last dollar spent on food exceeds the marginal utility of the last dollar spent on clothing.*

Suppose that the situation is reversed, the marginal utility of the last dollar spent on food being 3 utils and the marginal utility of the last dollar spent on clothing being 5 utils. The consumer is not maximizing utility, because spending $1 more on clothing will increase total utility by 5 utils,[5] and spending $1 less on food will reduce total utility by 3 utils. Thus the transfer of $1 of expenditure from food to clothing will result in a net increase of utility of 2 utils—which means that the consumer currently isn't maximizing utility. More generally, a transfer of expenditure from food to clothing will always increase total utility so long as the marginal utility of the last dollar spent on clothing exceeds the marginal utility of the last dollar spent on food. Thus *the consumer will not be maximizing utility if the marginal utility of the last dollar spent on clothing exceeds the marginal utility of the last dollar spent on food.*

In the previous paragraph, we showed that the consumer will *not* be maximizing utility if the marginal utility of the last dollar spent on food *is less than* the marginal utility of the last dollar spent on clothing. In the paragraph before last, we showed that the consumer will *not* be maximizing utility if the marginal utility of the last dollar spent on food *exceeds* the marginal utility of the last dollar spent on clothing. It follows that the consumer will be maximizing utility only when the marginal utility of the last dollar spent on food *equals* the marginal utility of the last dollar spent on clothing. This is what we set out to prove.

[5] We assume here that the extra utility from an *extra* dollar spent on clothing equals the extra utility from the *last* dollar spent on clothing. This, like the assumption in footnote 4, is innocuous.

Test Yourself

1. Suppose that the total utility attached by Ms. Johnson to various quantities of hamburgers consumed (per day) is as follows:

Numbers of hamburgers	Total utility (utils)
0	0
1	5
2	12
3	15
4	17
5	18

Between 3 and 4 hamburgers, what is the marginal utility of a hamburger? Between 4 and 5 hamburgers, what is the marginal utility of a hamburger? Do these results conform to the law of diminishing marginal utility?

2. If Ms. Johnson is maximizing her satisfaction, and if the marginal utility of a hot dog is twice that of a bottle of beer, what must the price of a hot dog be if (a) the price of a bottle of beer is $.75, (b) the price of a bottle of beer is $1. (Assume that Ms. Johnson consumes both beer and hot dogs.)

3. "A good's price is related to its marginal utility, not its total utility. Thus a good like water or air may be cheap, even though its total utility is high." Comment and evaluate.

4. If the marginal utility of one good is 3 and its price is $1, while the marginal utility of another good is 6 and its price is $3, is the consumer maximizing his or her satisfaction, given that he or she is consuming both goods? Why or why not?

The Consumer's Demand Curve

In analyzing consumer behavior, economists often use the concept of an *individual demand curve.* Like the market demand curve (discussed at length in Chapter 6), the individual demand curve is the relationship between the quantity demanded of a good and the good's price. But whereas the market demand curve shows the quantity demanded in the *entire market* at various prices, the individual demand curve shows the quantity demanded by a *particular consumer* at various prices. Applying the theory of consumer behavior presented earlier in this chapter, one can derive a particular consumer's demand curve for a particular good. To see how this can be done, let's turn to Mrs. Walter and show how we can derive the relationship between the price of food and the amount of food she will buy per month.

Assuming that food and clothing are the only goods, that Mrs. Walter's monthly income is $400, and that the price of clothing is $40 per piece of clothing, we confront Mrs. Walter with a variety of prices of food. First, we confront her with a price of $1 per pound of food. How much food will she buy? Next, we confront her with a price of $2 per pound of food. How much food will she buy? The theory of consumer behavior shows how, under each of these sets of circumstances, she will allocate her income between food and clothing. (From Equation (7.1), we know that she will choose an allocation where the marginal utility of the last dollar spent on food will equal the marginal utility of the last dollar spent on clothing.) Suppose that she will buy 200 pounds of food when the price is $1 per pound, and 100 pounds of food when the price is $2 per pound. These are two points on Mrs. Walter's individual demand curve for food—those corresponding to prices of $1 and $2 per pound. Figure 7.2 shows these two points, *X* and *Y*.

It is no trick to obtain more points on her individual demand curve for food. All that we have to do is confront her with other prices of food, and see how much food she buys at each price. Plotting the amount of food she buys against the price, we obtain new points on her individual demand curve for food. Connecting up all these points, we get her complete individual demand curve for food, shown in Figure 7.2.

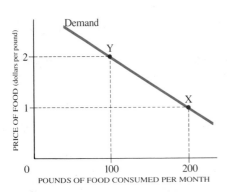

Figure 7.2

Mrs. Walter's Individual Demand Curve for Food *The consumer's individual demand curve for a commodity shows the amount of the commodity the consumer will buy at various prices. (Points* X *and* Y *on Mrs. Walter's individual demand curve for food are derived in Figure 7.13.)*

FACTORS INFLUENCING THE DEMAND CURVE

The location and shape of an individual demand curve depend on the tastes of the consumer. For example, if Mrs. Walter values food so much that she is determined to maintain her family's consumption of this commodity regardless of its price, her individual demand curve for food may look like demand curve *B* in Figure 7.3. But if she is less determined to maintain her family's food consumption, it may look like demand curve *A* in Figure 7.3.

Besides the consumer's tastes, other factors determining the location and shape of the consumer's individual demand curve are the income of the consumer and the prices of other goods. For example, Mrs. Walter's individual demand curve for food in Figure 7.2 is based on the assumption that her income is $400 per month and that the price of a piece of clothing is $40. If her income or the price of clothing changes, her individual demand curve

Figure 7.3

Hypothetical Individual Demand Curves *If Mrs. Walter values food so much that she is determined to buy much the same amount regardless of its price, her individual demand curve for food may look like demand curve B; but if she is less determined to maintain her family's food consumption, her individual demand curve for food may look like demand curve A.*

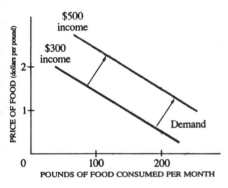

Figure 7.4

Effect of a Change in Income (from $300 to $500 per Month) on Mrs. Walter's Individual Demand Curve for Food *If Mrs. Walter's income increases from $300 to $500 per month (and if the price of a piece of clothing remains at $40), her demand curve will shift upward and to the right.*

for food will change as well. Figure 7.4 shows how her individual demand curve for food may change if her income increases from $300 to $500 per month (assuming that the price of a piece of clothing remains fixed at $40). Figure 7.5 shows how her individual demand curve for food may change if the price of a piece of clothing increases from $40 to $50 (assuming that her income remains constant at $500 per month).

In Chapter 3, we pointed out the importance of distinguishing between *changes in the quantity demanded* and *changes in demand.* This is just as true for individual consumers as for the market as a whole. The shifts in Mrs. Walter's demand curve for food shown in Figure 7.4 and 7.5 are *changes in demand.* In other words, they are changes in the relationship between the quantity demanded and price. Even if there is no change in demand—that is, even if there is no shift in the demand curve—the quantity demanded may change because of a change in price. For example, in Figure 7.2, the quantity of food demanded by Mrs. Walter increases from 100 to 200 pounds per month if the price of food declines from $2 to $1 per pound. Yet Mrs. Walter's demand curve for food is unchanged in Figure 7.2, so there is no increase in demand. Instead, there has been a *movement along* Mrs. Walter's demand curve from point *Y* to point *X.* The quantity of food demanded by Mrs. Walter has changed even though her demand for food has *not* changed.

Figure 7.5

Effect of a Change in the Price of a Piece of Clothing (from $40 to $50) on Mrs. Walter's Individual Demand Curve for Food *If the price of a piece of clothing increases from $40 to $50 (and if her income remains at $500 per month), her demand curve for food will shift upward and to the right.*

Why Do Individual Demand Curves Generally Slope Downward?[7]

Individual demand curves almost always slope downward to the right. That is, consumers almost always respond to an increase in a commodity's price by reducing the amount of it they consume. Or, put the other way around, a commodity's price almost always must be reduced to persuade the consumer to buy more of it. One way to explain this fact is by an appeal to the law of diminishing marginal utility, which (you will recall) states that, as a person consumes more and more of a particular commodity, the commodity's marginal utility declines. *Since the marginal utility— the extra utility derived from an extra unit of the commodity—declines, the price the consumer is willing to pay for an extra unit of the commodity must decline too.* This explanation relies on the assumption that marginal utility is measurable. Another way to explain the same thing makes no such assumption. According to this explanation, an increase in a commodity's price has two kinds of effects on the consumer—a substitution effect and an income effect.

SUBSTITUTION EFFECT

Basic Idea #14: Individual demand curves almost always slope downward to the right. Holding other factors (like tastes and income) constant, a commodity's price almost always must be lowered to induce the consumer to purchase more of it. This is because, as a person consumes more and more of a particular commodity, its marginal utility eventually falls.

*If the price of a commodity increases, the **substitution effect** of this price increase is the change in the quantity demanded of the commodity resulting from the commodity's becoming dearer relative to other commodities, if the consumer's level of utility is held constant.* Suppose that the price of chicken increases. Because of this price increase, the consumer may not be able to achieve as high a level of utility as he or she achieved before the price increase. Nonetheless, let's see what effect the price increase would have on the amount of chicken consumed by the consumer, *even if his or her level of utility were unchanged.* This effect is the substitution effect. *The substitution effect of a price increase always is a reduction in the quantity demanded of the commodity.* Suppose the price of chicken increases, while other prices and the consumer's level of utility are held constant. Because chicken becomes more expensive relative to other goods, the consumer will substitute other goods for chicken. Thus the substitution effect would be a *reduction* in the quantity demanded of chicken.

INCOME EFFECT

If the price of a commodity increases, the consumer's level of utility may be reduced, as pointed out above. *The **income effect** of the price increase is the change in the quantity demanded of the commodity due to this change in the consumer's utility level.* If an increase in the price of chicken cuts the consumer's level of utility by a particular amount, which in turn reduces the quantity of chicken demanded by the consumer, this reduction in the quantity demanded is the income effect. *The income effect of a price increase can be either a reduction or increase in the quantity demanded.* For

---

[7] This section is optional. Some instructors may want to skip it. The reader can go to the next section without losing the thread of the argument.

some commodities, like steak and probably chicken, a reduction in the consumer's utility level will result in the consumer's demanding *less* of them; thus the income effect of a price increase is a *reduction* in the quantity demanded of these commodities. For other commodities like margarine and poorer grades of food products, a reduction in the consumer's utility level may result in the consumer's demanding *more* of them; thus the income effect of a price increase is an *increase* in the quantity demanded of these commodities.

Example 7.2   Meat and Consumers' Surplus

It is important to recognize that consumers generally would be willing to pay more than in fact they pay for a particular good. Suppose that a consumer's demand curve for meat is as shown below, and that the price of a pound of meat is $2.

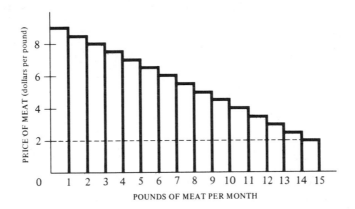

(a) What is the maximum amount that the consumer would pay for the first pound of meat per month? By how much does this exceed the actual price? (b) What is the maximum amount that the consumer would pay for the second pound of meat per month? By how much does this exceed the actual price? (c) What is the maximum amount that the consumer would pay for the 15 pounds of meat consumed per month? By how much does this exceed the actual amount paid? (d) Returning to Example 7.1, do you think that the actual amount paid for water is much less than the maximum amount that would be paid? Does this help to explain the diamond–water paradox?

SOLUTION

(a) $9. $7. (b) $8.50. $6.50. (c) $82.50. $52.50. (d) Yes. Yes, the actual amount paid for water is not a good indicator of the importance to the consumer (that is, the total utility) of water, since the actual amount paid is much less than the maximum amount that would be paid for it. *Economists use the term,* **consumer's surplus,** *to mean the difference between the maximum amount that the consumer would pay and what he or she actually pays.* For example, the consumer's surplus for the first pound of meat is $7.

RECENT DEVELOPMENTS IN ECONOMICS: THE ROLE OF TIME IN CONSUMPTION DECISIONS

In recent years, economists, led by Gary Becker of the University of Chicago, have begun to view a household as similar to a firm, in the sense that a household uses inputs of various kinds to produce outputs, like meals or recreation. Some of the inputs that the household uses are food, chairs, tables, and beds, but another input of great importance is *time*. The consumer has only a limited amount of time, and this time limitation, as well as his or her limited income, must be taken into account in making decisions.

To illustrate the importance of time to the consumer, take the case of a haircut. The cost to the consumer of a haircut is not only the $5 he must pay the barber; it is also the value of the time it takes for the barber to cut his hair, and, often more important, the value of the time he must wait before the barber is free to begin to cut his hair.

Gary Becker

Similarly, the cost of a vacation in Florida is not just the amount of money that must be paid for air tickets, hotels, meals, and entertainment; it is also the value placed on the reduced amount of time available to engage in non-vacation activities.

How does the economist measure the value of the time that is used up in consuming a particular item like a vacation? By the opportunity cost of the time. Thus the value of the time spent on the Florida vacation is the value of that time in its best alternative use. For example, if the consumer could have used this time to earn $100 a day, and if this would have been the best alternative use of this time to the consumer, then the value of the time spent on this vacation is $100 per day to this consumer.

Some economists have calculated the elasticity of demand for particular services with respect to the time they consume. In other words, they have estimated the percentage reduction in quantity demanded resulting from a 1 percent increase in the time taken by the service. For example, Jan Acton of the RAND Corporation studied the relationship between the number of visits to free sources of medical care by Brooklyn residents and the length of time, on the average, that such residents had to spend traveling and waiting for service. He found that a 1 percent increase in travel time was associated with slightly less than a 1 percent fall in number of visits.[1]

Of course, the value of time is not the same for all people. For example, the alternative cost of time to a teenager is generally lower than for an adult. This helps to explain the fact that teenagers frequently are more willing than adults to wait in line for tickets to various kinds of sports and musical events. Further, it has been suggested that the rise of fast-food chains has been due to an increase in the opportunity cost of time. Because of the increase in wage rates, there has been a rise in the value of time, according to this argument.

[1] Jan Acton, "Demand for Health Care among the Urban Poor," The New York City RAND Institute, April 1973.

THE TOTAL EFFECT OF A PRICE INCREASE

The *total* effect of a price increase is the *sum* of the income effect and the substitution effect. That is, the total change in the quantity demanded is the change in the quantity demanded due to the change in the consumer's utility level (the income effect) plus the change in the quantity demanded that would have occurred even if the consumer's utility level had not changed (the substitution effect). If (as is frequently the case) the income effect of a price increase is a reduction in the quantity demanded, the demand curve must slope downward. Why? Because both the income effect and the substitution effect are reductions in the quantity demanded, so the total effect of a price increase must be a reduction in the quantity demanded. Even if the income effect of a price increase is an increase in the quantity demanded, the demand curve may slope downward. Why? Because the increase in the quantity demanded due to the income effect may be more than offset by the substitution effect, which is always a reduction in the quantity demanded. Thus the demand curve will slope upward only in those *rare* cases where the income effect is an increase in the quantity demanded and where the income effect is big enough to offset the substitution effect.

Deriving the Market Demand Curve

In previous sections, we have described how each consumer's individual demand curve for a commodity can be derived, given the consumer's tastes and income, as well as the prices of other commodities. Suppose that we have obtained the individual demand curve for each of the consumers in the market. How can these individual demand curves be used to derive the market demand curve?

The answer is simple. *To derive the market demand curve, we obtain the horizontal sum of all the individual demand curves.* In other words, to find the total quantity demanded in the market at a certain price, we add up the quantities demanded by the individual consumers at that price.

Table 7.5 shows the individual demand curves for food of four families: the Walters, Joneses, Smiths, and Kleins. For simplicity, suppose that these

Table 7.5
INDIVIDUAL DEMAND CURVES AND MARKET DEMAND CURVE FOR FOOD

Price of food (dollars per pound)	Individual demand				Market demand
	Jones	Klein	Smith	Walter	
		(hundreds of pounds per month)			
1.00	50.0	45.0	5.0	2.0	102
1.20	43.0	44.0	4.2	1.8	93
1.40	36.0	43.0	3.4	1.6	84
1.60	30.0	42.0	2.6	1.4	76
1.80	25.0	41.4	2.4	1.2	70
2.00	20.0	41.0	2.0	1.0	64

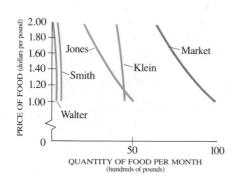

Figure 7.6

Individual Demand Curves and Market Demand Curve for Food *The market demand curve is the horizontal sum of all the individual demand curves.*

four families constitute the entire market for food. (This assumption can easily be relaxed; it just makes things simple.) Then the market demand curve for food is shown in the last column of Table 7.5. Figure 7.6 shows the families' individual demand curves for food, as well as the resulting market demand curve. To illustrate how the market demand curve is derived from the individual demand curves, suppose that the price of food is $1 per pound. Then the total quantity demanded in the market is 102 hundreds of pounds per month, since this is the sum of the quantities demanded at this price by the four families. (As shown in Table 7.5, this sum equals 50.0 + 45.0 + 5.0 + 2.0, or 102.)

Since individual demand curves for a commodity almost always slope downward to the right it follows that *market demand curves too almost always slope downward to the right.* (Why? Because, as stressed above, the market demand curve is the horizontal sum of all of the individual demand curves.) However, as emphasized in Chapter 6, the shape and location of the market demand curve vary greatly from commodity to commodity and from market to market. Market demand curves, like people, do not look alike.

Test Yourself

1. Suppose that there are five people who are the only members of a particular market. The amount that each person will buy of the product in question (at each price) is shown below. Determine five points on the market demand curve for the product.

Price (dollars)	Quantity demanded				
	First person	Second person	Third person	Fourth person	Fifth person
1	5	4	2	8	7
2	4	4	2	7	6
3	3	4	1	6	5
4	2	3	0	5	4
5	1	3	0	5	2

2. Some people judge the quality of a good by its price. If a consumer does this, how does it affect the model presented in this chapter? (*Hint:* Is utility independent of price?)

3. Bill Thompson would be willing to pay 30 cents for the first apple he consumes per day and 24 cents for the second apple he consumes per day. The current price of an apple is 24 cents. How great is Bill Thompson's consumer's surplus? What does this number mean? How might such a number be used?

4. Mrs. Moriarty (the Professor's wife) learns that the price of turkey has fallen. (a) What is the substitution effect? Do you think that it will be positive or negative? Why? (b) What is the income effect? Do you think that it will be positive or negative? Why? (c) Do you think that the Moriarty family's demand curve for turkey slopes downward to the right? Why or why not?

Summary

1. The amount of a particular commodity a consumer purchases is clearly influenced by his or her preferences. The model of consumer behavior assumes that the consumer's preferences are transitive and that commodities are defined so that more of them is preferred to less.

2. Utility is a number that represents the level of satisfaction derived by the consumer from a particular market basket. Market baskets with higher utilities are preferred over market baskets with lower utilities.

3. The model of consumer behavior recognizes that preferences alone do not determine the consumer's actions. The choices open to the consumer are dictated by the size of his or her money income and the nature of commodity prices. These factors, as well as the consumer's preferences, determine his or her choice.

4. If the consumer maximizes utility, his or her income is allocated among commodities so that, for every commodity purchased, the marginal utility of the commodity is proportional to its price. In other words, the marginal utility of the last dollar spent on each commodity is made equal for all commodities purchased.

5. The individual demand curve shows the quantity of a good demanded by a particular consumer at various prices of the good. The individual demand curve for practically all goods slopes downward and to the right. Its location depends on the consumer's income and tastes and the prices of other goods.

6. To derive the market demand curve, we obtain the horizontal sum of all the individual demand curves of the people in the market. Since individual demand curves for a commodity almost always slope downward to the right, it follows that market demand curves too almost always slope downward to the right.

Concepts for Review

Model of consumer behavior	**Law of diminishing marginal utility**	**Individual demand curve**
Utility	**Equilibrium market basket**	**Consumer's surplus**
Marginal utility		**Substitution effect**
		Income effect

Appendix: How Indifference Curves Can Be Used to Analyze Consumer Behavior

In this Appendix, we show how the theory of consumer behavior can be used in cases where one is not willing to assume that marginal utility is measurable. Generally, it is exceedingly difficult to formulate meaningful measures of a person's extra satisfaction from an extra amount of a particular good. We shall show that the theory remains useful even if such measures cannot be obtained. Once again, we assume for simplicity that there are only two goods, food and clothing, since this allows us to use simple two-dimensional diagrams to illustrate the model. Since there are only these two commodities, we can represent every possible combination of goods purchased by a consumer by a point in Figure 7.7, which measures the amount of food purchased along the vertical axis and the amount of clothing purchased along the horizontal axis.

INDIFFERENCE CURVES

*An **indifference curve** contains points representing market baskets among which the consumer is indifferent.* To illustrate, consider Mrs. Walter, making choices for her family. Certain market baskets—that is, certain combinations of food and clothing (the only commodities)—will be equally desirable to her. For example, she may be indifferent between a market basket containing 100 pounds of food and 5 pieces of clothing and a market basket containing 200 pounds of food and 2 pieces of clothing. These two market baskets can be represented by two points, U and V, in Figure 7.7. In addition, other market baskets—each of which can be represented by a point in Figure 7.7—are just as desirable to Mrs. Walter as those represented by

Figure 7.7

Two of Mrs. Walter's Indifference Curves I_1 and I_2 are two of Mrs. Walter's indifference curves. Each shows market baskets that are equally desirable to Mrs. Walter. For example, she is indifferent between 200 pounds of food and 2 pieces of clothing (point **V**) and 100 pounds of food and 5 pieces of clothing (point **U**).

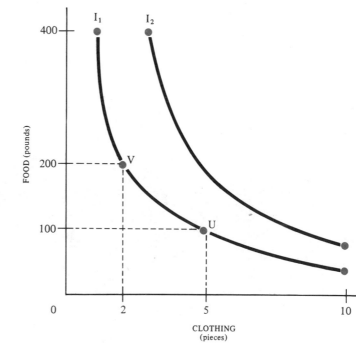

points U and V. If we connect all of these points, we get a curve that represents market baskets that are equally desirable to the consumer. In our case, Mrs. Walter is indifferent among all of the market baskets represented by points on curve I_1 in Figure 7.7. I_1 is therefore called an indifference curve.

There are three important things to note about any consumer's indifference curves:

1. Any consumer has lots of indifference curves, not just one. If Mrs. Walter is indifferent among all the market baskets represented by points on I_2 in Figure 7.7, I_2 is another of her indifference curves. Moreover, one thing is certain. She prefers any market basket on I_2 to any market basket on I_1, since I_2 includes market baskets with as much clothing and more food (or as much food and more clothing) than the market baskets on I_1. (Remember that commodities are defined so that more of them is preferred to less.) Consequently, it must always be true that market baskets on higher indifference curves like I_2 must be preferred to market baskets on lower indifference curves like I_1.

2. Every indifference curve must slope downward and to the right, to reflect the fact that commodities are defined so that more of them is preferred to less. If one market basket has more of one commodity than a second market basket, it must have less of the other commodity than the second market basket—assuming that the two market baskets are to yield equal satisfaction to the consumer. You can prove this to yourself. Suppose that you have a choice between two snacks and that you are indifferent between them. One snack consists of 1 piece of apple pie and 2 glasses of milk. The other consists of 2 pieces of apple pie and a certain number of glasses of milk. If you prefer more apple pie to less, and if you prefer more milk to less, can the number of glasses of milk in the latter snack be as large as 2? Clearly, the answer must be no.

3. Indifference curves cannot intersect. If they did, this would contradict the assumption that more of a commodity is preferred to less. For example, suppose that I_1 and I_2 in Figure 7.8 are two indifference curves and that they intersect. If this is the case, the market basket represented by point D is equivalent in the eyes of the consumer to the one represented

Figure 7.8

***Intersecting Indifference Curves: A
Contradiction*** *Indifference curves cannot
intersect. If they did, the consumer would
be indifferent between D and E, since
both are on indifference curve* I_1; *and between F and E, since both are on
indifference curve* I_2. *But this implies that
he or she must be indifferent between D
and F, which is impossible since F
contains the same amount of food and 6
more pieces of clothing than D.*

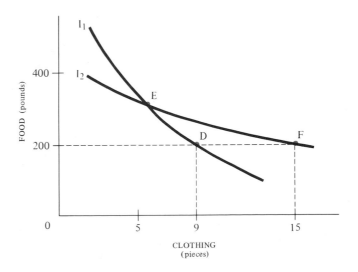

145

by point *E*, since both are on indifference curve I_1. Moreover, the market basket represented by point *F* is equivalent in the eyes of the consumer to the one represented by point *E*, since both are on indifference curve I_2. And this means that the market basket represented by point *F* must be equivalent in the eyes of the consumer to the one represented by point *D*. (Remember that consumer preferences are assumed to be transitive!) But this is impossible because market basket *F* contains the same amount of food and 6 more pieces of clothing than does market basket *D*. Since more of a commodity is preferred to less, market basket *F* must be preferred to market basket *D*.

INDIFFERENCE CURVES AND UTILITY

To continue building this new version of our model of consumer behavior, we need to return to the concept of utility. Since all market baskets on a particular indifference curve yield the same satisfaction to the consumer, they all must have the same utility. For example, all market baskets on indifference curve I_1 in Figure 7.7 must have the same utility. Moreover, market baskets on higher indifference curves must have higher utilities than market baskets on lower indifference curves. For example, all market baskets on indifference curve I_2 in Figure 7.7 must have higher utilities than market baskets on indifference curve I_1.

Given a group of indifference curves for a certain consumer, it is easy to establish an index of the utility obtained from any market basket by this consumer. *All that we have to do is attach a number to each indifference curve, this number being larger for higher indifference curves than for lower indifference curves. The utility index for any market basket is then the number attached to the indifference curve on which this market basket is located.* The resulting utility index shows at a glance which market baskets the consumer will pick over other market baskets. The rational consumer will, of course, try to pick the market basket that maximizes this index of utility.

Note that this utility index is not unique. Any set of numbers that increases as one goes from successively lower to higher indifference curves will constitute a suitable set of indices. Thus no assumption is made that we can obtain a meaningful measure of marginal utility. But it is possible to construct a utility index of this sort, so long as the three basic assumptions underlying the theory of consumer demand (described in the earlier section on "A Model of Consumer Behavior") are met.

Figure 7.9

Mrs. Walter's Budget Line The *consumer's budget line shows the market baskets that can be purchased, given the consumer's income and prevailing commodity prices. This budget line assumes that Mrs. Walter's income is $400 per month, that the price of a pound of food is $1, and that the price of a piece of clothing is $40.*

THE BUDGET LINE

The consumer wants to maximize his or her utility, which means that he or she wants to achieve the highest possible indifference curve. But whether or not a particular indifference curve is attainable depends on the consumer's money income and on commodity prices. Exactly what constraints are imposed on the consumer by the size of his or her money income and the nature of commodity prices? To make things concrete, let's return to Mrs. Walter. Suppose that her total income is $400 per month, and that she can spend this amount only on two commodities, food and clothing. Needless to say, it is unrealistic to assume that there are only two com-

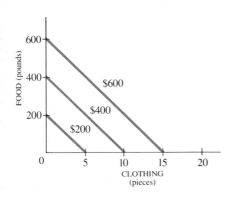

Figure 7.10

Mrs. Walter's Budget Line at Money Incomes of $200, $400, and $600 per Month *The higher the consumer's money income, the higher the budget line. Holding commodity prices constant, the budget line's slope remains constant.*

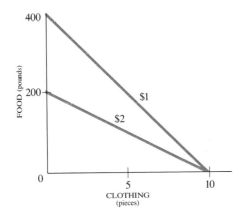

Figure 7.11

Mrs. Walter's Budget Line at Food Prices of $1 and $2 per Pound *Holding constant Mrs. Walter's money income at $400 per month and the price of a piece of clothing at $40, the budget line cuts the vertical axis farther from the origin when the price of food is $1 than when it is $2.*

modities in existence, but, to repeat what was said earlier, this makes it easier to present the model, and the results can easily be generalized to cases where more than two commodities exist.

Given these conditions, the answer to how much of each commodity Mrs. Walter can buy depends on the price of a pound of food and the price of a piece of clothing. Suppose the price of a pound of food is $1 and the price of a piece of clothing is $40. Then if she spent all of her income on food, she could buy 400 pounds of food per month. On the other hand, if she spent all of her income on clothing, she could buy 10 pieces of clothing per month. Or she could, if she wished, buy some food and some clothing. There are a large number of combinations of amounts of food and clothing that she could buy, and each such combination can be represented by a point on the line in Figure 7.9. This line is called her budget line. *A consumer's **budget line** shows the market baskets that he or she can purchase, given the consumer's income and prevailing market prices.*

The consumer's budget line will shift if changes occur in the consumer's money income or in commodity prices. In particular, an increase in money income means that the budget line rises, and a decrease in money income means that the budget line falls. This is illustrated in Figure 7.10, which shows Mrs. Walter's budget line at money incomes of $200, $400, and $600 per month. As you can see, her budget line moves upward as her income rises.

Commodity prices too affect the budget line. A decrease in a commodity's price causes the budget line to cut this commodity's axis at a point farther from the origin. Figure 7.11 shows Mrs. Walter's budget line when the price of a pound of food is $1 and when it is $2. You can see that the budget line cuts the vertical, or food, axis farther from the origin when the price of food is $1 per pound.

THE EQUILIBRIUM MARKET BASKET

With information on the consumer's indifference curves and budget line, we are in a position to determine the consumer's *equilibrium market basket* —the market basket that, among all those that the consumer can purchase, yields the maximum utility. The first step is to combine the indifference curves with the budget line on the same graph. Figure 7.12 brings together Mrs. Walter's indifference curves (from Figure 7.7) and her budget line (from Figure 7.9). Given the information assembled in Figure 7.12, it is a simple matter to determine her equilibrium market basket. *Her indifference curves show what she wants:* specifically, she wants to attain the highest possible indifference curve. Thus she would rather be on indifference curve I_2 than on indifference curve I_1, and on indifference curve I_3 than on indifference curve I_2. But, as we have pointed out repeatedly, she cannot choose any market basket she likes. *The budget line shows which market baskets her income and commodity prices permit her to buy.* Thus she must choose some market basket on her budget line.

Consequently, *the consumer's choice boils down to choosing that market basket on the budget line that is on the highest indifference curve. This is the equilibrium market basket.* For example, Mrs. Walter's equilibrium market basket is clearly at point G in Figure 7.12; it consists of 200 pounds of food and 5 pieces of clothing per month. This is her equilibrium market

147

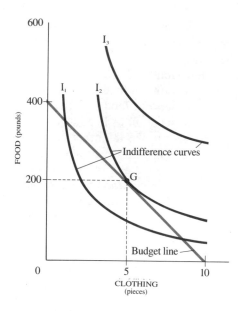

basket because any other market basket on the budget line is on a lower indifference curve than point *G* is. But will the consumer choose this market basket? Admittedly, it may take some time and fumbling for the consumer to find out that this is the best market basket for him or her under the circumstances. Consumers, after all, do make mistakes. But they also learn, and eventually one would expect a consumer to come very close to acting in the predicted way.

DERIVING THE INDIVIDUAL DEMAND CURVE

Finally, we show how indifference curves can be used to derive the consumer's demand curve. In particular, let's return to the case of Mrs. Walter, and show how her demand curve for food can be derived.

Assuming that food and clothing are the only goods, that Mrs. Walter's monthly income is $400, and that the price of clothing is $40 per piece of clothing, Mrs. Walter's budget line is budget line 1 in Figure 7.13, when the price of food is $1 per pound. Thus, as we saw in Figure 7.2, Mrs. Walter will buy 200 pounds of food per month under these conditions.

If, however, the price of food increases to $2 per pound, her income and the price of clothing remaining constant, her budget line will be budget line 2 in Figure 7.13, and she will attain her highest indifference curve, I_1, by choosing the market basket corresponding to point *U*, a market basket containing 100 pounds of food per month. Thus, if the price of food is $2 per pound, she will buy 100 pounds of food per month.

We have derived two points on Mrs. Walter's individual demand curve for food—those corresponding to prices of $1 and $2 per pound. Figure 7.2 shows these two points, *X* and *Y*. To obtain more points on her individual demand curve for food, all we have to do is assume a particular

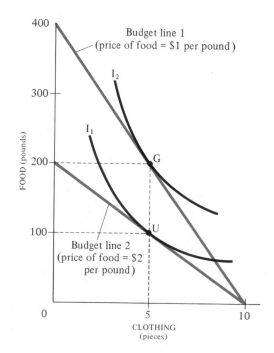

price of food, construct the budget line corresponding to this price (holding her income and the price of clothing constant), and find the market basket on this budget line that is on her highest indifference curve. Plotting the amount of food in this market basket against the assumed price of food, we obtain a new point on her individual demand curve for food. Connecting up all these points, we get her complete individual demand curve for food, shown in Figure 7.2.

CHAPTER 8

Optimal Input Decisions by Business Firms

In economies based largely on free enterprise, like our own, the managers of business firms are given considerable responsibility for deciding where, when, and how various resources are used. Thus the manager's job is a central one, from both a social and private point of view. Fortunately, the United States has been able to develop large cadres of effective managerial talent, in large part because management and business have been highly esteemed professions in the United States. As Calvin Coolidge put it, with characteristic brevity and uncharacteristic overstatement, "The business of America is business." This is quite a different sentiment from that expressed by the ancient Roman historian, Tacitus, who said that Sabinus "had talents equal to business, and aspired no higher."

In this chapter, we shall take a closer look at the decision-making process within the firm. Our discussion builds on Chapter 5, which dealt with the organization, motivation, and technology of the firm. We look in more detail at the firm's technology, and focus particular attention on the following central question: If a firm attempts to maximize profits, what production technique—that is, what combination of inputs—should it choose to produce a particular quantity of output? Two points should be noted at the outset. First, when finding the optimal input combination, we take as given the quantity of output that the firm will produce. In subsequent chapters, we shall discuss how the firm should choose this quantity. Second, just as one purpose of the previous two chapters was to show how a product's market demand curve can be derived, so an important purpose of Chapters 8 through 10 is to show how a product's market supply curve can be derived. In this chapter, we present some of the concepts and findings that are required for this purpose.

The Production Function Revisited

If the United States Steel Corporation decides to produce a certain quantity of steel, it can do so in many ways. It can use open-hearth furnaces, or basic oxygen furnaces, or electric furnaces; it can use various types of iron ore; and it can use various types of coke. Which of these many ways will maximize U.S. Steel's profits? The management of U.S. Steel—and every business firm—devotes considerable time and energy to answering this kind of question. Let's restate it in the economist's terms. Given that a firm is going to produce a certain quantity of output, what production technique—i.e., what combination of inputs—should it choose to maximize its profits?

As a first step toward answering this question, it is wise to review the concept of the production function, taken up in Chapter 5. As you will recall, *the production function shows the most output that existing technology permits the firm to extract from each quantity of inputs.* Consider the hypothetical case of a wheat farm with 1 acre of land. The relationship between the amount of labor used per year by this farm and the farm's output is shown in Table 8.1. This is the farm's production function. It shows that the farm can produce 30 bushels of wheat per year if 1 man-year of labor is used, 70 bushels of wheat per year if 2 man-years of labor are used, and so on.

The production function summarizes the characteristics of existing technology at a given point in time; it shows the technological constraints that a firm must reckon with. Like it or not, the most that the wheat farm in Table 8.1 can produce, if it uses 2 man-years of labor, is 70 bushels per year. This is the best that existing technology permits. Perhaps future advances in technology will permit such a farm (with 2 man-years of labor) to produce more than 70 bushels per year, but this presently cannot be done.

Table 8.1

RELATIONSHIP BETWEEN LABOR INPUT AND OUTPUT ON 1-ACRE WHEAT FARM

Number of man-years of labor	Bushels of wheat produced per year
0	0
1	30
2	70
3	100
4	125
5	145

A CRUDE-OIL PIPELINE: A CASE STUDY

To illustrate what a production function looks like in a real case, let's consider a crude-oil pipeline that transports petroleum from oil fields and storage areas over hundreds of miles to major urban and industrial centers. We begin by noting that the output of such a pipeline is the amount of oil carried per day, and that the two principal inputs are the diameter of the pipeline and the horsepower applied to the oil carried. Both inputs are important. The bigger the diameter of the pipe, the more oil the pipeline can carry, holding constant the horsepower applied. And the greater the horsepower applied, the more oil the pipeline can carry, holding constant the diameter of the pipeline.

The production function shows the maximum output rate that can be derived from each combination of input rates. Thus, in this case, the production function shows the maximum amount of oil carried per day as a function of the pipeline's diameter and the amount of horsepower applied. On the basis of engineering estimates, one can derive the production function for crude-oil pipelines. Leslie Cookenboo of the Exxon Corporation derived such a production function, assuming that the pipeline carries Mid-Continent crude, has ¼-inch pipe throughout the lines, has lines

Table 8.2

PRODUCTION FUNCTION, CRUDE-OIL
PIPELINE[a]

Line diameter (inches)	Horsepower (thousands)				
	20	30	40	50	60
	Output rate (thousands of barrels per day)				
14	70	90	95	100	104
18	115	140	155	165	170
22	160	190	215	235	250
26	220	255	290	320	340

[a] The output rates given in this table are only approximate, since they were read from Cookenboo's graph on p. 16.

Source: Leslie Cookenboo, *Crude Oil Pipe Lines and Competition in the Oil Industry,* Cambridge, Mass.: Harvard University Press, 1955.

1,000 miles in length with a 5 percent terrain variation, and no net gravity flow in the line.[1] Some of his results are shown in Table 8.2. For example, the production function shows that if the diameter of the pipeline is 22 inches and the horsepower is 40,000, the pipeline can carry 215,000 barrels per day. Certainly, any firm operating a pipeline or considering the construction of one is vitally interested in such information. The production function plays a strategic role in the decision making of any firm.

Types of Inputs

As pointed out in Chapter 5, an input is anything that the firm uses in its production process. In analyzing production processes, we suppose that all inputs can be classified into two categories: fixed and variable inputs.

A **fixed input** *is one whose quantity cannot change during the period of time under consideration.* This period will vary. It may be six months in one case, six years in another case. Among the most important inputs often included as fixed are the firm's plant and equipment—that is, its factory and office buildings, its machinery, its tooling, and its transportation facilities. In the simple example of the wheat farm in Table 8.1, land is a fixed input since its quantity is assumed to be fixed at 1 acre.

A **variable input** *is one whose quantity can be changed during the relevant period.* It is generally possible to increase or decrease the number of workers engaged in a particular activity (although this is not always the case, since they may have long-term contracts). Similarly, it frequently is possible to alter the amount of raw material that is used. In the case of the wheat farm in Table 8.1, labor clearly is a variable input since its quantity can be varied from 0 to 5 man-years.

The Short Run and the Long Run

Whether an input is considered variable or fixed depends on the length of the period under consideration. The longer the period, the more inputs are variable, not fixed. Although the length of the period varies from case to case, economists have found it very useful to focus special attention on two time periods: the short run and the long run. *The **short run** is defined as the period of time in which at least one of the firm's inputs is fixed.* More specifically, since the firm's plant and equipment are among the most difficult inputs to change quickly, *the short run is generally understood to mean the length of time during which the firm's plant and equipment are fixed.* On the other hand, *the **long run** is that period of time in which all inputs are variable.* In the long run, the firm can make a complete adjustment to any change in its environment.

To illustrate the distinction between the short run and the long run, let's consider the General Motors Corporation. Any period of time during which GM's plant and equipment cannot be altered freely is the short run.

[1] L. Cookenboo, *Crude Oil Pipe Lines and Competition in the Oil Industry,* Cambridge, Mass.: Harvard University Press, 1955.

A period of one year is certainly a case of the short run, because in a year GM could not vary the quantity of its plant and equipment. It takes longer than a year to construct an automotive plant, or to alter an existing plant to produce a new kind of automobile. For example, the tooling phase of the model changeover cycle currently takes about 2 years. Also, because some of its existing contracts with suppliers and workers extend for more than a year, GM cannot vary all its inputs in a year without violating these contracts. On the other hand, any period of time during which GM can vary the quantity of all inputs is the long run. A period of 50 years is certainly a case of the long run. Whether a shorter period of time—10 years, say—is a long-run situation depends on the problem at hand. If all the relevant inputs can be varied, it is a long-run situation; if not, it is a short-run situation.

A useful way to look at the long run is to consider it a *planning horizon*. While operating in the short run, the firm must continually be planning ahead and deciding its strategy in the long run. Its decisions concerning the long run determine the sort of short-run position the firm will occupy in the future. Before a firm makes the decision to add a new type of product to its line, the firm is in a long-run situation (with regard to the new product), since it can choose among a wide variety of types and sizes of equipment to produce the new product. But once the investment is made, the firm is confronted with a short-run situation, since the type and size of equipment is, to a considerable extent, frozen.

Average Product of an Input

In order to determine which production technique—that is, which combination of inputs—a firm should use, it is necessary to define the average product and marginal product of an input. *The **average product** of an input is the firm's total output divided by the amount of input used to produce this amount of output.* The average product of an input can be calculated from the production function. Consider the wheat farm in Table 8.1. The average product of labor is 30 bushels per man-year of labor when 1 man-year of labor is used, 35 bushels per man-year of labor when 2 man-years are used, 33⅓ bushels per man-year of labor when 3 man-years are used, and so forth.

Marginal Product of an Input

As the amount of labor used on the farm increases, so does the farm's output, but the amount of extra output from the addition of an extra man-year of labor varies depending on how much labor is already being used. The extra output from the addition of the first man-year of labor is $30 - 0 = 30$ bushels per man-year of labor. The extra output due to the addition of the second man-year of labor is $70 - 30 = 40$ bushels per man-year of labor. And the extra output from the addition of the fifth

Table 8.3

AVERAGE AND MARGINAL PRODUCTS OF LABOR, 1-ACRE WHEAT FARM

Number of man-years of labor	Total output (bushels per year)	Marginal product (bushels per man-year)	Average product (bushels per man-year)
0	0		—
		30	
1	30		30
		40	
2	70		35
		30	
3	100		33⅓
		25	
4	125		31¼
		20	
5	145		29

man-year of labor is $145 - 125 = 20$ bushels per man-year of labor. *The marginal product of an input is the addition to total output due to the addition of the last unit of input, the quantity of other inputs used being held constant.* Thus the marginal product of labor is 30 bushels when between 0 and 1 man-years of labor are used, 40 bushels when between 1 and 2 man-years of labor are used, and so on.

The concept of marginal product is analogous to that of marginal utility, which we discussed in Chapter 7. Recall that marginal utility is the extra utility resulting from an additional unit of a commodity. Substitute "output" for "utility" and "an input" for "a commodity" in the previous sentence, and you get a perfectly valid definition of marginal product. Economics is chock full of marginal "thises" and marginal "thats," and it is important that you become aware of their general family traits.

Table 8.3 shows the average and marginal products of labor at various levels of utilization of labor; Figure 8.1 shows the same thing graphically. The data in both Table 8.3 and Figure 8.1 concerning the average and marginal products of labor are derived from the production function. Given

Figure 8.1

Average and Marginal Products of Labor, 1-Acre Wheat Farm *The marginal product of the first man-year of labor (which, according to Table 8.3, equals 30 bushels per man-year) is plotted at the midpoint between 0 and 1 man-year of labor. The marginal product of the second man-year of labor is plotted at the midpoint between 1 and 2 man-years of labor. The marginal product curve connects these and other points showing the marginal product of various amounts of labor.*

The average product curve shows the average product of labor when various amounts of labor are used. As the graph shows, both the average product and the marginal product of labor rise, reach a maximum, and fall.

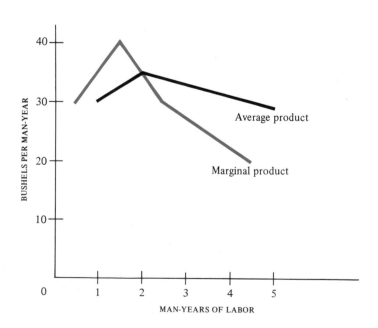

the production function, shown in Table 8.1, and reproduced in Table 8.3, the average and marginal products at each level of utilization of labor can be determined in the way we have indicated.

In Figure 8.1, as in the case of most production processes, the average product of the variable input—labor in this case—rises, reaches a maximum, and then falls. The marginal product of labor also rises, reaches a maximum, and falls. This too is typical of many production processes. Why do average and marginal product behave in this way? Because of the law of diminishing marginal returns, to which we now turn.

The Law of Diminishing Marginal Returns

Basic Idea #15: Suppose that you are the manager of a small farm. You have a fixed amount of capital and land, but you can vary the number of laborers employed. If you hire more and more laborers, there eventually will come a point where the extra output due to hiring still another laborer is less than that due to hiring the last laborer. This is an illustration of the law of diminishing marginal returns.

Perhaps the best-known—and certainly one of the least understood—laws of economics is the so-called *law of diminishing marginal returns.* Put in a single sentence, this law states that *if equal increments of an input are added, the quantities of other inputs being held constant, the resulting increments of product will decrease beyond some point;* that is, the marginal product of the input will diminish.

Suppose that a small factory that manufactures a metal automobile component has eight machine tools. If this firm hires only one or two workers, total output and output per worker will be quite low. These workers will have a number of quite different tasks to perform, and the advantages of specialization will be sacrificed. Workers will spend considerable time switching from one machine to another, and many of the eight machine tools will be idle much of the time. What happens as the firm increases its work force? As more and more workers are added, the marginal product (that is, the extra product) of each will tend to rise, as the work force grows to the point where it can man the fixed amount of equipment effectively. However, if the firm continues to increase the number of workers, the marginal product of a worker will eventually begin to decrease. Why? Because workers will have to wait in line to use the fixed number of machine tools, and because the extra workers will have to be assigned to less and less important tasks. Eventually, if enough workers are hired (and utilized within the plant), they may get in each other's way to such an extent that production may grind to a halt.

Returning to the wheat farm discussed in the previous section, Table 8.3 shows that the law of diminishing marginal returns applies in this case too. The third column of this table indicates that, beyond 2 man-years of labor, the marginal product of labor falls. Certainly, it seems entirely reasonable that, as more and more of a variable input (in this case, labor) is combined with a fixed amount of another input (in this case, land), the additional output to be derived from an additional unit of the variable input will eventually decrease. In the case of a 1-acre wheat farm, one would expect that, as more and more labor is added, the extra workers' functions eventually would become less and less important and productive.

The law of diminishing marginal returns plays a major part in determining the firm's optimal input combination and the shape of the firm's cost functions, as we shall see in this and the next chapter. To prevent misunderstanding and confusion, several points about this law should be stressed. First, *it is assumed that technology remains fixed.* If technology changes, the law of diminishing marginal returns cannot predict the effect of an additional unit of input. Second, *at least one input must be fixed in quantity,* since the law of diminishing marginal returns is not applicable to cases where there is a proportional increase in all inputs. Third, *it must be possible to vary the proportions in which the various inputs are utilized.* This is generally possible in industry and agriculture.

Example 8.1   Production Theory in the Milking Shed

According to the U.S. Department of Agriculture, the relationship between a cow's total output of milk and the amount of grain it is fed is as follows:

Amount of grain (pounds)	Amount of milk (pounds)
1,200	5,917
1,800	7,250
2,400	8,379
3,000	9,371

Forage input is assumed to be fixed at 6,500 pounds of hay.
   (a) What is the average product of grain when each amount is used? (b) Should a milk producer feed a cow the amount of grain that will maximize its average product? Why or why not? (c) What is the marginal product of grain when between 1,200 and 1,800 pounds are fed; when between 1,800 and 2,400 pounds are fed; and when between 2,400 and 3,000 pounds are fed? (d) Does this production function exhibit diminishing marginal returns?

SOLUTION

(a) At 1,200 pounds, it is 4.93; at 1,800 pounds, it is 4.03; at 2,400 pounds, it is 3.49; and at 3,000 pounds, it is 3.12 pounds of milk per pound of grain. (b) No, because this generally will not maximize profit, as we shall see in subsequent discussions. (c) 2.22, 1.88, and 1.65 pounds of milk per pound of grain. (d) Yes. The marginal product of grain decreases as more of it is used.

Test Yourself

1. Suppose that a firm has the following production function:

Man-hours of labor per year (thousands)	Output per year (thousands)
0	0
1	2
2	8
3	12
4	14
5	15

Plot on a graph the marginal product of labor at various levels of utilization of labor.

2. Using the data in Question 1, plot the average product of labor at various levels of utilization of labor.

3. A tool and die shop has three types of inputs: labor, machines, and materials. It cannot obtain additional machines in less than 6 months. In the next month, do you think that labor is a fixed or variable input? Do you think that machines are a fixed or variable input? Explain.

4. The tool and die shop in Question 3 expands its use of all three types of inputs. The owner of the shop worries that by doing so the firm may encounter diminishing marginal returns. Is this a legitimate concern? Why or why not?

The Optimal Input Decision

Basic Idea #16: To minimize the cost of producing a given amount of output, a firm (under competitive conditions) should choose a combination of inputs where the marginal product of a dollar's worth of each input (that is used) is the same. The marginal product of a dollar's worth of each input, not the average product, is the crucially important criterion for this purpose.

Now we are in a position to answer the question posed at the beginning of this chapter: Given that a firm is going to produce a particular quantity of output, what production technique—i.e., what combination of inputs—should it choose to maximize profits? Note first that if the firm maximizes its profits, it must minimize the cost of producing this quantity of output. This seems obvious enough. But what combination of inputs (that will produce the required quantity of output) will minimize the firm's costs? The answer can be stated like this: *The firm will minimize cost by combining inputs in such a way that the marginal product of a dollar's worth of any one input equals the marginal product of a dollar's worth of any other input used.*

Another way to say the same thing is: *The firm will minimize cost by combining inputs in such a way that, for every input used, the marginal product of the input is proportional to its price.* Why does this say the same thing? Because the marginal product of a dollar's worth of an input equals the marginal product of the input divided by its price. If the marginal product of a man-year of labor is 40 units of output, and if the price of labor is $8,000 per man-year, the marginal product of a dollar's worth of labor is $40 \div 8,000 = .005$ units of output. Thus, if the firm is satisfying the rule for cost minimization in the previous paragraph—that is, if it is combining inputs so that the marginal product of a dollar's worth of any one input equals the marginal product of a dollar's worth of any other input used—it must at the same time be combining inputs so that, for every input used, the marginal product of the input is proportional to its price.

THE WHEAT FARM: A NUMERICAL EXAMPLE

To illustrate the application of this rule, let's take a numerical example from the wheat farm cited above. Suppose that the farm can vary the amount of labor and land it uses. Table 8.4 shows the marginal product of

Table 8.4

DETERMINATION OF OPTIMAL INPUT COMBINATION

Amount of input used		Marginal product		Marginal product ÷ price of input		Total cost
Labor (man-years)	Land (acres)	Labor	Land	Labor	Land	(dollars)
0.5	7.0	50	5	50 ÷ 8,000	5 ÷ 2,000	18,000
1.0	4.1	40	10	40 ÷ 8,000	10 ÷ 2,000	16,200
1.5	3.0	30	30	30 ÷ 8,000	30 ÷ 2,000	18,000
2.5	2.0	20	50	20 ÷ 8,000	50 ÷ 2,000	24,000

each input when various combinations of inputs (all combinations being able to produce the specified quantity of output) are used. Suppose that the price of labor is $8,000 per man-year and that the annual price of using land is $2,000 per acre. (We assume that the firm takes the prices of inputs as given and that it can buy all it wants of the inputs at these prices.) For each combination of inputs, Table 8.4 shows the marginal product of each input divided by its price. Based on our rule, the optimal input combination is 4.1 acres of land and 1 man-year of labor, since this is the only combination (capable of producing the required output) where the marginal product of labor divided by the price of labor equals the marginal product of land divided by the price of land. (See Table 8.4.)

Is this rule correct? Does it really result in a least-cost combination of inputs? Let's look at the cost of the various input combinations in Table 8.4. The first combination (0.5 man-years of labor and 7 acres of land) costs $18,000; the second combination (1.0 man-years of labor and 4.1 acres of land) costs $16,200; and so on. An examination of the total cost of each input combination shows that the input combination chosen by our rule— 1.0 man-years of labor and 4.1 acres of land—is indeed the least-cost input combination, the one for the profit-maximizing firm to use.

A More General Proof of the Rule

One example really does not prove that the rule results in minimum costs; it only demonstrates that it does so in this particular case. In this section, we prove that this rule generally is valid. To do so, we show that, if this rule is violated (and the firm combines inputs so that the marginal product of a dollar's worth of one input does *not* equal the marginal product of a dollar's worth of some other input used), the firm is not minimizing its costs. Specifically, we take the case of the wheat farm, and proceed in two steps. (1) We show that if the marginal product of a dollar's worth of labor is *greater* than the marginal product of a dollar's worth of land, the firm is not minimizing costs. (2) We show that if the marginal product of a dollar's worth of labor is *less* than the marginal product of a dollar's worth of land, the firm is not minimizing costs.

Suppose that *the marginal product of a dollar's worth of labor is greater than the marginal product of a dollar's worth of land.* Since the marginal product of a dollar's worth of labor is greater than the marginal product of a dollar's worth of land, it must follow that the wheat farm can increase its output, *without increasing its costs,* if it substitutes a dollar's worth of labor for a dollar's worth of land. Suppose that the marginal product of a dollar's worth of labor is 2 bushels of wheat, whereas the marginal product of a dollar's worth of land is 1 bushel of wheat. Then, if it substitutes a dollar's worth of labor for a dollar's worth of land, the wheat farm can increase its output by 1 bushel of wheat without increasing its costs. (Why? Because the addition of an extra dollar's worth of labor increases output by 2 bushels, while the subtraction of the dollar's worth of land reduces output by 1 bushel—and the net effect is an increase in output of 1 bushel.) Thus, since the firm can increase its output without increasing its costs, it must be able to reduce its costs, if it maintains the same output. In other words, it must not be minimizing its costs.

One of the most common errors made by decision makers is that they do not ignore sunk costs. What is a sunk cost? It is a cost that has been incurred in the past and that cannot be altered or affected by any action the decision maker can take. For example, suppose that a real estate investor signs an agreement to buy a lot. The purchase price is $10,000. He makes a $2,000 down payment and will pay the remaining $8,000 in six months. Under the terms of the agreement, he will not secure title to the lot until he has paid the entire $10,000. If he fails to make the remaining payment of $8,000, the agreement states that he will lose his down payment, but he is not liable for the unpaid balance.

After buying this lot, and making the $2,000 down payment, the real estate investor travels to another city where he finds a lot which is just as desirable from his point of view as the one he has bought. Because

the real estate market in this city is depressed, the price of this lot is $7,000. The real estate investor wishes that he had seen this lot before purchasing the other one, but feels that there is nothing he can do. He only wants one such lot and, if he were to back out of the purchase agreement he signed, he would lose $2,000. Clearly, he doesn't want to incur such a loss!

But the real estate investor is committing a cardinal sin: he is not ignoring a sunk cost. Regardless of which lot he purchases, he loses the $2,000. Thus the $2,000 is a sunk cost. The real question is whether he will pay an *additional* $8,000 for the lot on which he has paid the down payment or whether he will pay an *additional* $7,000 for the lot he has seen more recently. Put in this way, there is no doubt about the proper course of action: he should ignore the $2,000 sunk cost, and buy the lot for $7,000. In this way, the total cost (including the sunk cost) is $9,000, which is less than the price of the lot he originally intended to purchase.

Suppose that *the marginal product of a dollar's worth of labor is less than the marginal product of a dollar's worth of land.* Since the marginal product of a dollar's worth of labor is less than the marginal product of a dollar's worth of land, it must follow that the wheat farm can increase its output, *without increasing its costs,* if it substitutes a dollar's worth of land for a dollar's worth of labor. Suppose that the marginal product of a dollar's worth of labor is 1 bushel of wheat, whereas the marginal product of a dollar's worth of land is 2 bushels of wheat. Then, if it substitutes a dollar's worth of land for a dollar's worth of labor, the wheat farm can increase its output by 1 bushel of wheat without increasing its costs. (Why? Because the addition of an extra dollar's worth of land increases output by 2 bushels, while the subtraction of a dollar's worth of labor reduces output by 1 bushel—and the net effect is an increase in output of 1 bushel.) Thus, since the firm can increase its output without increasing its costs, it must be able to reduce its costs, if it maintains the same output. In other words, it must not be minimizing its costs.

Since the firm is not minimizing the cost of producing its current output when the marginal product of a dollar's worth of labor is greater than, or less than, that of a dollar's worth of land, it must be true that *the firm is minimizing its costs only when the marginal product of a dollar's worth of labor equals that of a dollar's worth of land.* This is what we set out to prove.

Producing Kansas Corn: A Case Study

If by now you wonder about the practical payoff from this sort of analysis, consider how a distinguished agricultural economist, Earl Heady of Iowa State University, has used these methods to help farmers make better production decisions. Table 8.5 shows the various amounts of land and fertilizer that will produce 82.6 bushels of corn on Kansas Verdigras soil. As you can see, this amount of corn can be produced if 1.19 acres of land and no fertilizer are used, or if 1.11 acres of land and 20 pounds of fertilizer are used, or if .99 acres of land and 60 pounds of fertilizer are used, and so forth.

The third column of Table 8.5 shows the ratio of the marginal product of a pound of fertilizer to the marginal product of an acre of land, when each of these input combinations is used. For example, when 1.19 acres of land and no fertilizer are used, this ratio equals .0045. Based on the rule discussed in previous sections, a firm, if it minimizes costs, must set this ratio equal to the ratio of the price of a pound of fertilizer to the price of an acre of land. Why? Because the rule discussed above stipulates that the firm should choose an input combination so that

$$\frac{\text{marginal product of fertilizer}}{\text{price of fertilizer}} = \frac{\text{marginal product of land}}{\text{price of land}}.$$

So if we multiply both sides of this equation by the price of fertilizer, and divide both sides by the marginal product of land, we get

$$\frac{\text{marginal product of fertilizer}}{\text{marginal product of land}} = \frac{\text{price of fertilizer}}{\text{price of land}}.$$

Table 8.5

COMBINATIONS OF FERTILIZER AND LAND REQUIRED TO PRODUCE 82.6 BUSHELS OF CORN, AND RATIO OF MARGINAL PRODUCTS AT EACH SUCH COMBINATION

| Amount of input used | | Marginal product of fertilizer ÷ Marginal product of land |
Fertilizer (pounds)	Land (acres)	
0	1.19	.0045
20	1.11	.0038
40	1.04	.0030
60	0.99	.0019
80	0.96	.0010
100	0.95	.0003

Source: E. Heady and L. Tweeten, *Resource Demand and Structure of the Agricultural Industry,* Ames: Iowa State University Press, 1963, p. 111.

Thus, to minimize costs, a firm should set the ratio in the third column of Table 8.5 equal to the ratio of the price of fertilizer to the price of land.

Heady and his coworkers, having obtained the results in Table 8.5, used this technique to determine the optimal input combination farmers should use to minimize their costs.[2] The optimal input combination depends on the price of land and the price of fertilizer. Suppose that a pound of fertilizer costs .003 times as much as an acre of land. Under these circumstances, the minimum-cost input combination would be 40 pounds of fertilizer and 1.04 acres of land—since, as shown in Table 8.5, this is the input combination where the ratio of the marginal product of fertilizer to the marginal product of land is .003. No matter what the ratio of the price of fertilizer to the price of land may be, the least-cost input combination can be derived this way.

Such results are of considerable practical value to farmers. Moreover, the same kind of analysis can be used by organizations in other sectors of the economy, not just agriculture. Studies of how the Defense Department could reduce its costs have utilized concepts and techniques of essentially this sort. In a more peaceful vein, this same kind of analysis has been used in various kinds of manufacturing firms. For example, steel firms have made many such studies to determine least-cost ways to produce steel, and auto firms have made similar studies to reduce their own costs.

[2] E. Heady and L. Tweeten, *Resource Demand and Structure of the Agricultural Industry,* Ames: Iowa State University Press, 1963. It is assumed that a certain amount of labor is used, this amount being proportional to the number of acres of land.

Test Yourself

1. Suppose that a cost-minimizing firm in a perfectly competitive market uses two inputs: labor and capital. If the marginal product of capital is twice the marginal product of labor, and if the price of a unit of labor is $4, what must be the price of a unit of capital?

2. In Figure 8.1, the marginal product of labor equals its average product when the latter is a maximum. Do you think that this is generally the case? Why or why not? (*Hint:* If the marginal product of an extra amount of labor exceeds the average product, will the average product increase? If it is less than the average product, will the average product decrease?)

3. A firm uses two inputs, capital and labor. The firm's chief engineer says that its output depends in the following way on the amount of labor and capital it uses:

$$Q = 3L + 4C,$$

where Q is the number of units of output produced per day, L is the number of units of labor used per day, and C is the amount of capital used per day. Does this relationship seem sensible? Why or why not?

4. In the previous problem, suppose that the price of using a unit of labor per day is $50 and the price of using a unit of capital per day is $100. What is the optimal input combination for the firm, if the relationship in the previous problem is valid? Does this seem reasonable? Why or why not?

Summary

1. Inputs can be classified into two categories: fixed and variable. A fixed input is one whose quantity cannot be changed during the period of time under consideration. A variable input is one whose quantity can be changed during the relevant period.

2. Whether an input is considered variable or fixed depends on the length of the period under consideration. The longer the period, the more inputs are variable, not fixed. The short run is defined as the period of time in which some of the firm's inputs (generally its plant and equipment) are fixed. The long run is the period of time in which all inputs are variable.

3. The average product of an input is the firm's total output divided by the amount of input used to produce this amount of output. The marginal product of an input is the addition to total output due to the addition of the last unit of input, the quantity of other inputs used being held constant.

4. The law of diminishing marginal returns states that if equal increments of an input are added (and the quantities of other inputs are held constant), the resulting increments of product will decrease beyond some point; that is, the marginal product of the input will diminish.

5. To minimize its costs, a firm must choose its input combination so that the marginal product of a dollar's worth of any one input equals the marginal product of a dollar's worth of any other input used. Put differently, the firm should combine inputs so that, for every input used, the marginal product of the input is proportional to its price. As an illustration, we showed how this sort of model can be used to determine the optimal combination of fertilizer and land in the production of Kansas corn.

Concepts for Review

Production function	**Short run**	**Marginal product**
Fixed input	**Long run**	**Law of diminishing**
Variable input	**Average product**	**marginal returns**

CHAPTER 9

Cost Analysis

The Peabody Coal Company, a huge steam-coal producer, signed many contracts with electric power companies during the 1960s, agreeing to supply coal at stipulated prices to the power companies for a number of years. By the mid-1970s, Peabody regretted these contracts because its costs had risen so much that it could not fulfill the contracts without losing money. Peabody hired McKinsey and Company, a leading management consulting firm, to figure out exactly what Peabody's costs of producing coal were in the mid-1970s. Then it went to the electric power companies and tried to renegotiate the contracts. Sometimes the power companies were willing to renegotiate; sometimes they weren't.

This example illustrates the major role played by a firm's costs in determining both its financial health and its behavior. In this chapter, we discuss the nature of costs, describe the various cost functions of the firm, and indicate some of the ways that these cost functions can be measured and used. Among the major questions taken up are: What do we mean by a firm's costs? How do various types of costs vary with the firm's output rate? Of what significance or use are the relationships between a firm's output and its various types of cost? These questions are of the utmost importance, both for the managers of a firm and for society as a whole.

What Are Costs?

The previous chapter discussed how we can determine the input combination that minimizes costs. But what do we mean by costs?

Although this question may seem foolishly simple, it is in fact tricky. *Fundamentally, the cost of a certain course of action is the value of the best*

163

alternative course of action that could have been adopted instead. The cost of producing automobiles is the value of the goods and services that could be obtained from the resources used currently in automobile production if these resources were no longer used to produce automobiles. In general, the costs of inputs to a firm are their values in their most valuable alternative uses. As we pointed out in Chapter 1, this is the so-called *opportunity cost,* or *alternative cost* doctrine. (Recall Basic Idea #2 on p. 10.)

Suppose that a firm's owner devotes 50 hours a week to the firm's business, and that, because he is the owner, he pays himself no salary. According to the usual rules of accounting, as we saw in Chapter 5, the costs of his labor are not included in the firm's income statement. But according to the economist's opportunity cost doctrine, the cost of his labor is by no means zero! Instead, this cost equals whatever amount he could obtain if he worked 50 hours a week for someone else. Both economists and sophisticated accountants agree that opportunity costs are the relevant costs for many types of problems, and that failure to use the proper concept of cost can result in serious mistakes.

Costs for the individual firm are the necessary payments to the owners of resources to get them to provide these resources to the firm. To obtain these resources as inputs, the firm must bid them away from alternative uses. The payments made to the owners of these resources may be either explicit or implicit costs. If a payment is made to a supplier, laborer, or some other resource owner besides the firm's owner, this is an explicit cost, which is paid for in an explicit way. But if a resource is owned by the firm's owner, there may be no explicit payment for it, as in the case of the labor of the owner who paid himself no salary. *The costs of such owner-supplied resources are called **implicit costs.*** As we stressed above, such implicit costs equal what these resources could bring if they were used in their most valuable alternative employments. And the firm's profits (or losses), as defined by the economist, are the difference between the firm's revenues and its total costs, both explicit and implicit.

Short-Run Cost Functions

In the previous chapter, we showed how to determine the least-cost combination of inputs to produce any quantity of output. With this information at our disposal, it is easy to determine the minimum cost of producing each quantity of output. *Knowing the (minimum) cost of producing each quantity of output, we can define and measure the firm's **cost functions,** which show how various types of costs are related to the firm's output.* A firm's cost functions will vary, depending on whether they are based on the short or long run. In the short run, the firm cannot vary the quantities of plant and equipment it uses. These are the firm's fixed inputs, and they determine the scale of its operations.

TOTAL FIXED COST

Three kinds of costs are important in the short run—total fixed cost, total variable cost, and total cost. *Total fixed cost is the total expenditure per period of time by the firm for fixed inputs.* Since the quantity of the fixed

Figure 9.1

Total Fixed Cost, Bugsbane Music Box Company *The total fixed cost function is always a horizontal line, since fixed costs do not vary with output.*

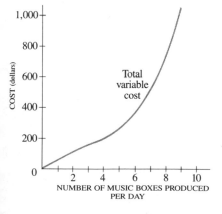

Figure 9.2

Total Variable Cost, Bugsbane Music Box Company *Total variable cost is the total expenditure per period of time on variable inputs. Due to the law of diminishing marginal returns, total variable cost increases first at a decreasing rate, then at an increasing rate.*

Table 9.1

FIXED, VARIABLE, AND TOTAL COSTS, BUGSBANE MUSIC BOX COMPANY

Number of music boxes produced per day	Total fixed cost	Total variable cost (dollars)	Total cost
0	300	0	300
1	300	60	360
2	300	110	410
3	300	160	460
4	300	200	500
5	300	260	560
6	300	360	660
7	300	510	810
8	300	710	1,010
9	300	1,060	1,360

inputs is unvarying (by definition), the total fixed cost will be the same whatever the firm's level of output. Among the firm's fixed costs in the short run are property taxes and interest on bonds issued in the past. If the firm has contracts with suppliers and workers that cannot be renegotiated (without dire consequences) in the short run, the expenses involved in meeting these contracts are also fixed costs.

To inject a whimsical note into a subject not otherwise noted for its amusement value, consider a hypothetical firm—the Bugsbane Music Box Company. This firm produces a high-priced line of music boxes that, when opened, play your favorite aria, show tune, or hymn, and emit a deadly gas that kills all insects, rodents, or pests—and, alas, occasionally a frail Chihuahua—within a 50-foot radius. Table 9.1 shows that Bugsbane's fixed costs are $300 per day; the firm's total fixed cost function is shown in Figure 9.1.

TOTAL VARIABLE COST

Total variable cost *is the firm's total expenditure on variable inputs per period of time.* Since higher output rates require greater utilization of variable inputs, they mean a higher total variable cost. Thus, if Bugsbane increases its daily production of music boxes, it must increase the amount it spends per day on metal (for the components), wood (for the outside of the boxes), labor (for the assembly of the boxes), and other variable inputs. Table 9.1 shows Bugsbane's total variable costs at various output rates; Figure 9.2 shows the firm's total variable cost function.

Up to the output rate of 4 music boxes per day, total variable cost increases at a decreasing rate; beyond that output rate, total variable cost increases at an increasing rate. It is important to understand that this characteristic of the total variable cost function results from the operation of the law of diminishing marginal returns. At small output rates, increases in the utilization of variable inputs may bring about increases in their productivity, causing total variable cost to increase with output, but at a decreasing rate. Beyond a point, however, there are diminishing marginal returns from the variable input, with the result that total variable costs increase at an increasing rate.

165

TOTAL COST

Total cost *is the sum of total fixed cost and total variable cost.* Thus, to obtain the Bugsbane Company's total cost at a given output, we need only add its total fixed cost and its total variable cost at that output. The result is shown in Table 9.1, and the corresponding total cost function is shown in Figure 9.3. Since the total cost function and the total variable cost function differ by only a constant amount (equal to total fixed cost), they have the same shape, as shown in Figure 9.4, which brings together all three of the total cost functions (or cost curves as they are often called).

Average Costs in the Short Run

The president of Bugsbane unquestionably cares about the average cost of a music box as well as the total cost incurred; so do economists. *Average cost tells you how much a product costs per unit of output.* There are three average cost functions, one corresponding to each of the three total cost functions.

Figure 9.3

Total Cost, Bugsbane Music Box Company *Total cost is the sum of total fixed cost and total variable cost. It has the same shape as the total variable cost curve, since they differ by only a constant amount (equal to total fixed cost).*

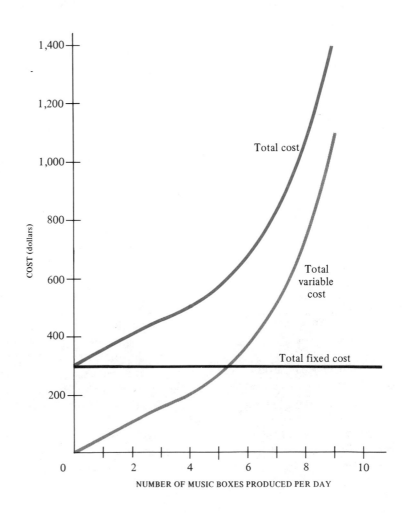

Figure 9.4

Fixed, Variable, and Total Costs, Bugsbane Music Box Company *All three cost functions, presented in Figures 9.1–9.3, are brought back for a curtain call.*

Table 9.2

AVERAGE FIXED COST, AVERAGE VARIABLE COST, AND AVERAGE TOTAL COST, BUGSBANE MUSIC BOX COMPANY

Number of music boxes produced per day	Average fixed cost	Average variable cost (dollars)	Average total cost
1	300(=300 ÷ 1)	60(=60 ÷ 1)	360(=360 ÷ 1)
2	150(=300 ÷ 2)	55(=110 ÷ 2)	205(=410 ÷ 2)
3	100(=300 ÷ 3)	53(=160 ÷ 3)	153(=460 ÷ 3)
4	75(=300 ÷ 4)	50(=200 ÷ 4)	125(=500 ÷ 4)
5	60(=300 ÷ 5)	52(=260 ÷ 5)	112(=560 ÷ 5)
6	50(=300 ÷ 6)	60(=360 ÷ 6)	110(=660 ÷ 6)
7	43(=300 ÷ 7)	73(=510 ÷ 7)	116(=810 ÷ 7)
8	38(=300 ÷ 8)	89(=710 ÷ 8)	126(=1010 ÷ 8)
9	33(=300 ÷ 9)	118(=1060 ÷ 9)	151(=1360 ÷ 9)

Figure 9.5

Average Fixed Cost, Bugsbane Music Box Company *Average fixed cost is total fixed cost divided by the firm's output. Since it equals a constant (total fixed cost) divided by the output rate, it must decline with increases in output.*

Figure 9.6

Average Variable Cost, Bugsbane Music Box Company *Average variable cost is total variable cost divided by the firm's output. Beyond a point (in this case, 4 music boxes per day), average variable cost rises with increases in output because of the law of diminishing marginal returns.*

AVERAGE FIXED COST

Let's begin with **average fixed cost,** *which is simply the total fixed cost divided by the firm's output.* Table 9.2 and Figure 9.5 show the average fixed cost function for the Bugsbane Music Box Company. Average fixed cost must decline with increases in output, since it equals a constant—total fixed cost—divided by the output rate.

AVERAGE VARIABLE COST

The next type of average cost is **average variable cost,** *which is total variable cost divided by output.* For Bugsbane, the average variable cost function is shown in Table 9.2 and Figure 9.6. At first, increases in the output rate result in decreases in average variable cost, but beyond a point, they result in higher average variable cost. This is because the law of diminishing marginal returns is in operation. As more and more of the variable inputs are utilized, the extra output they produce declines beyond some point, so that the amount spent on variable input per unit of output tends to increase.

The third type of average cost is **average total cost,** *which is total cost divided by output.* For Bugsbane, the average total cost function is shown in Table 9.2 and Figure 9.7. At any level of output, *average total cost equals average fixed cost plus average variable cost.* This is easy to prove:

$$\text{average total cost} = \frac{\text{total cost}}{\text{output}} = \frac{\text{total fixed cost} + \text{total variable cost}}{\text{output}},$$

since total cost = total fixed cost + total variable cost. Moreover,

$$\frac{\text{total fixed cost} + \text{total variable cost}}{\text{output}} = \frac{\text{total fixed cost}}{\text{output}} + \frac{\text{total variable cost}}{\text{output}}$$

and the right-hand side of this equation equals average fixed cost plus average variable cost. Thus we have proved what we set out to prove.

The fact that average total cost is the sum of average fixed cost and average variable cost helps explain the shape of the average cost function. If, as the output rate goes up, both average fixed cost and average variable cost decrease, average total cost must decrease too. But beyond some point, average total cost must increase because increases in average variable cost eventually more than offset decreases in average fixed cost. However, average total cost achieves its minimum after average variable cost, because the increases in average variable cost are for a time more than offset by decreases in average fixed cost. All the average cost functions are shown below in Figure 9.9.

Marginal Cost in the Short Run

No one can really understand the operations of a business firm without understanding the concept of **marginal cost,** *the addition to total cost resulting from the addition of the last unit of output.* To see how marginal cost is calculated, look at Table 9.3, which shows the total cost function of the Bugsbane Music Box Company. When output is between 0 and 1 music

Figure 9.7

Average Total Cost, Bugsbane Music Box Company *Average total cost is total cost divided by output. It equals average fixed cost plus average variable cost. When output is 4 music boxes or less per day, both average fixed cost and average variable cost are decreasing, so average total cost must decrease too. When output is 5 or 6 music boxes per day, average total cost decreases because the fall in average fixed cost more than offsets the rise in average variable cost. When output exceeds 6 music boxes per day, the rise in average variable cost more than offsets the fall in average fixed cost, so average total cost increases.*

Table 9.3

CALCULATION OF MARGINAL COST, BUGSBANE MUSIC BOX COMPANY

Number of music boxes produced per day	Total cost	Marginal Cost (dollars)
0	300	
1	360	60 (= 360−300)
2	410	50 (= 410−360)
3	460	50 (= 460−410)
4	500	40 (= 500−460)
5	560	60 (= 560−500)
6	660	100 (= 660−560)
7	810	150 (= 810−660)
8	1,010	200 (= 1,010−810)
9	1,360	350 (= 1,360−1,010)

SHORT RUN MARGINAL COST

Figure 9.8

Marginal Cost, Bugsbane Music Box Company *Marginal cost is the addition to total cost arising from the addition of the last unit of output. The marginal cost of the first unit of output (which according to Table 9.3, is $60) is plotted at the midpoint between 0 and 1 units of output. The marginal cost of the second unit of output is plotted at the midpoint between 1 and 2 units of output. The marginal cost function connects these and other points showing the marginal cost of various amounts of output. Beyond a point (in this case, between 3 and 4 music boxes per day), marginal cost increases because of the law of diminishing marginal returns.*

Basic Idea #17: *Marginal cost is the addition to total cost resulting from the addition of the last unit of output. Beyond some point, a firm's marginal cost rises as more and more is produced —due to the law of diminishing marginal returns (see Basic Idea #15 on p. 155.) To comprehend how firms operate, it is extremely important that you understand the concept of marginal cost.*

box per day, the firm's marginal cost is $60, since this is the *extra cost* of producing the first music box per day. In other words, $60 equals marginal cost in this situation because it is the difference between the total cost of producing 1 music box per day ($360) and the total cost of producing 0 music boxes per day ($300).

In general, marginal cost will vary depending on the firm's output level. Thus Table 9.3 shows that at Bugsbane marginal cost is $50 when the firm produces between 1 and 2 music boxes per day, $100 when the firm produces between 5 and 6 music boxes per day, and $350 when the firm produces between 8 and 9 music boxes per day. Table 9.3—and Figure 9.8, which shows the marginal cost function graphically—indicate that marginal cost, after decreasing with increases in output at low output levels, increases with further increases in output. In other words, *beyond some point it becomes more and more costly for the firm to produce yet another unit of output.*

INCREASING MARGINAL COST AND DIMINISHING RETURNS

The reason why marginal cost increases beyond some output level is to be found in the law of diminishing marginal returns. *If (beyond some point) increases in variable inputs result in less and less extra output, it follows that a larger and larger quantity of variable inputs must be added to produce an extra unit of output. Thus the cost of producing an extra unit of output must increase.*

To illustrate how diminishing marginal returns result in increasing marginal cost, let's return for a moment to the wheat farm in Tables 8.1 and 8.3. (For convenience, the data regarding this farm are reproduced in Table 9.4.) If it is producing 70 bushels of wheat, it requires an extra 1/30 man-year of labor to produce an extra bushel—since Table 9.4 shows that the marginal product of a man-year of labor is 30 bushels. But if it is producing 100 bushels of wheat, an extra 1/25 man-year of labor is needed to produce an extra bushel, since Table 9.4 shows that the marginal product of a man-year of labor is 25 bushels. Thus more of the variable input (specifically, 1/25 man-year of labor rather than 1/30 man-year of labor) is required to produce an extra bushel of wheat. And *since more and more of the variable input is required to produce an extra unit of output, the cost of producing an extra unit of output increases as output rises.*

Table 9.4

AVERAGE AND MARGINAL PRODUCTS OF LABOR, 1-ACRE WHEAT FARM

Number of man-years of labor	Total output	Marginal product (bushels per man-year)	Average product
0	0		—
1	30	30	30
2	70	40	35
3	100	30	33⅓
4	125	25	31¼
5	145	20	29

169

RELATIONSHIP BETWEEN MARGINAL COST AND AVERAGE COST FUNCTIONS

The relationship between the marginal cost function and the average cost functions must be noted. Figure 9.9 shows the marginal cost curve together with the three average cost curves. *The marginal cost curve intersects both the average variable cost curve and the average total cost curve at their minimum points.* The reason for this is simple. If the extra cost of a unit of output is greater (less) than the average cost of the units of output already produced, the addition of the extra unit of output clearly must raise (lower) the average cost of production. Thus, if marginal cost is greater (less) than average cost, average cost must be rising (falling). And if this is so, average cost can be a minimum only when it equals marginal cost. (The same reasoning holds for both average total cost and average variable cost, and for the short and long runs.)

To make sure that you understand this point, consider the following numerical example. Suppose that the average total cost of producing 4 units of output is $10, and that the marginal cost of the fifth unit of output is less than $10. Will the average total cost be less for 5 units of output than for 4 units? It will be less, because the fifth unit's cost will pull down

Figure 9.9

Average Fixed Cost, Average Variable Cost, Average Total Cost, and Marginal Cost, Bugsbane Music Box Company
All of the curves presented in Figures 9.5–9.8 are brought together for review. Note that the marginal cost curve intersects both the average variable cost curve and the average total cost curve at their minimum points.

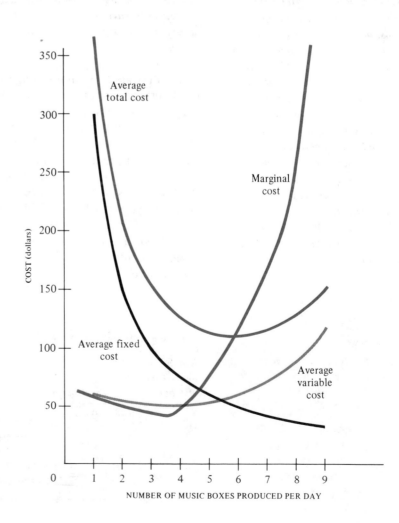

NUMBER OF MUSIC BOXES PRODUCED PER DAY

Figure 9.10

Total Cost Function, Crude-Oil Pipeline, 18-Inch Diameter *This graph shows the total cost function in an actual case. Note that it is shaped as economic theory would predict.*

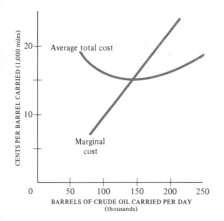

Figure 9.11

Average Total Cost Function and Marginal Cost Function, Crude-Oil Pipeline, 18-Inch Diameter *This graph shows the average cost and marginal cost functions in an actual case. Note that their shape follows economic theory.*

the average. On the other hand, if the marginal cost of the fifth unit of output had been greater than $10, the average total cost for 5 units of output would have been greater than for 4 units of output, because the fifth unit's cost would pull up the average. Thus *average total cost will fall when it is above marginal cost, and it will rise when it is below marginal cost.* Consequently, *when it is a minimum, average total cost must equal marginal cost,* as shown in Figure 9.9.

Short-Run Cost Functions of a Crude-Oil Pipeline: A Case Study

Cost functions are not academic toys, but eminently practical analytical devices that play a major role in decision making by business executives and government agencies. To illustrate the nature and use of short-run cost functions, we will take up the real-world case of crude-oil pipelines where we left off (in the previous chapter). In the short run, it is reasonable to assume that the diameter of a pipeline is fixed. Given the production function in Table 8.2, it is easy to figure out the total cost of carrying various amounts of oil per day, with a pipeline of a given diameter. In other words, we assume that the company that owns the pipeline can vary the horsepower by varying the number and type of pumping stations, but that the diameter of the pipeline is fixed.[1] Under these circumstances, if the diameter of the pipeline is 18 inches, what will the pipeline's cost functions look like?

Figures 9.10 and 9.11 answer this question. Figure 9.10 shows the *total cost function* for an 18-inch pipeline—the total daily cost of operating it, given that it carries various amounts of crude oil per day. If the pipeline carries 200,000 barrels of oil per day, the total daily cost is $33,000; if the amount of oil is increased to 250,000 barrels per day, the total daily cost rises to $48,000.

Figure 9.11 shows the *average total cost function* for an 18-inch pipeline—the total daily cost per barrel for the pipeline, given that it carries various amounts of crude oil per day. According to Figure 9.11, the total daily cost per barrel for this pipeline to carry 200,000 barrels per day is $.16½, and the total daily cost per barrel for it to carry 250,000 barrels per day is $.19⅓. Figure 9.11 also shows the *marginal cost function* for such a pipeline—the additional daily cost of carrying an extra barrel of crude oil per day. When this pipeline is carrying 200,000 barrels per day, the marginal cost runs to about $.23.

To the operators of the pipeline, a knowledge of these cost functions can mean the difference between profit and loss. For example, suppose that the operators of a particular 18-inch pipeline are thinking about increasing the amount of oil the pipeline will carry per day. Specifically, suppose that the pipeline can now carry 200,000 barrels per day and that the operators are thinking about adding enough horsepower so that it can carry 250,000 barrels per day. Suppose that, according to the best esti-

---

[1] Because the number and type of pumping stations must be altered, Leslie Cookenboo refers to this as the "intermediate run." See Cookenboo, *Crude Oil Pipe Lines and Competition in the Oil Industry,* Cambridge, Mass.: Harvard University Press, 1955.

mates available, the pipeline can get $5 million in additional revenue each year if it carries the additional 50,000 barrels per day. Should the operators increase in this way the amount of oil the pipeline can carry?

If they want to increase profits, they should decide against this increase in the amount of horsepower. According to the total cost function in Figure 9.10, the pipeline's daily costs would increase by $15,000 per day if horsepower were increased so that 250,000, rather than 200,000 barrels of oil could be carried per day, while the extra oil carried would increase daily revenues by $5 million ÷ 365, or about $14,000 per day. Thus the extra costs would exceed the extra revenue, which means that the pipeline's profit would be reduced by increasing the amount of horsepower. In making decisions of this sort (and they must make them repeatedly!), managers must rely heavily on information about the relevant cost functions.

Example 9.1   The Costs of a Dairy Farm

According to Leonard Weiss of the University of Wisconsin,* a typical dairy farm with 50 cows located near one of the large cities on the eastern seaboard might have the following relationship between cost and output:

Output (thousands of pounds of milk per year)	Total fixed cost (dollars per year)	Total variable cost (dollars per year)
0	24,000	0
400	24,000	9,000
440	24,000	10,650
480	24,000	13,050
520	24,000	18,000

(a) Included in the fixed cost is $5,600 in interest on the farmer's investment in the farm. If the farmer owns the farm (and does not have to pay interest to anyone else), should this item still be included? (b) Suppose that the farmer and his wife do all the work, and that the opportunity cost of their labor is the same, regardless of the farm's output. Is their labor cost a fixed or variable cost? (c) What is the marginal cost of a pound of milk when output is between 480 and 520 thousands of pounds per year? (d) At which of the above output levels is average total cost a minimum? Is this the output that the farmer should choose?

SOLUTION

(a) Yes, because if he sold this farm, he could lend out the proceeds and get $5,600 in interest. Thus this is the opportunity cost of the farmer's investment in the farm. (b) It is a fixed cost. (c) ($18,000 − $13,050) ÷ 40,000 = 12.4 cents. (d) 480 thousand pounds. In general, as we shall see in the following chapter, the farmer, if he or she wants to maximize profit, should not choose the output in the short run that minimizes average total cost.

* L. Weiss, *Case Studies in American Industry,* New York: John Wiley, 1980.

Test Yourself

1. Suppose that a firm's short-run total cost function is as follows:

Output (number of units per year)	Total cost per year (dollars)
0	20,000
1	20,100
2	20,200
3	20,300
4	20,500
5	20,800

What are the firm's total fixed costs? What are its total variable costs when it produces 4 units per year?

2. In Question 1, what is the firm's marginal cost when between 4 and 5 units are produced per year? Does marginal cost increase beyond some output level?

3. In Question 1, what is the firm's average cost when it produces 1 unit per year? 2 units per year? 3 units per year? 4 units per year? 5 units per year?

4. Fill in the blanks below:

Total output	Total fixed cost	Total variable cost	Average total cost	Average fixed cost	Average variable cost
			(dollars)		
0	500	—			
1	—	20	—	—	—
2	—	—	300	—	—
3	—	—	—	—	133⅓
4	—	1,100	—	—	—

5. In Question 4, does marginal cost increase with increases in output? Explain.

Long-Run Cost Functions

THE LONG-RUN AVERAGE COST FUNCTION

We have held to the last one additional kind of cost function that plays a very important role in economic analysis. This is the firm's *long-run average cost function, which shows the minimum average cost of producing each output level when any desired type or scale of plant can be built.* Unlike the cost functions discussed in the previous sections, this cost function pertains to the long run—*to a period long enough so that all inputs are variable and none is fixed.* As pointed out in the previous chapter, a useful way to look at the long run is to consider it a *planning horizon.* The firm must continually be planning ahead and trying to decide its strategy in the long run.

Suppose a firm can build plants of three sizes—small, medium, and large. The short-run average total cost functions corresponding to these plants are AA', BB', and DD' in Figure 9.12. If the firm is still in the planning stage of plant construction, it can choose whichever plant has the lowest costs. Consequently, the firm will choose the small plant if it believes its output rate will be smaller than OQ_1, the medium plant if it believes its output rate will be above OQ_1, but below OQ_2, and the large plant if it believes that its output rate will be above OQ_2. Thus the long-run average cost curve is $AUVD'$. And if, as is generally the case, there are many possible types of plants, the long-run average cost curve looks like LL' in Figure 9.13. (Only a few of the short-run average cost curves are shown in Figure 9.13.)

The usefulness of the long-run average cost function can be illustrated by the familiar case of crude-oil pipelines. Figure 9.14 shows the long-run average cost function for these pipelines, as well as selected short-run

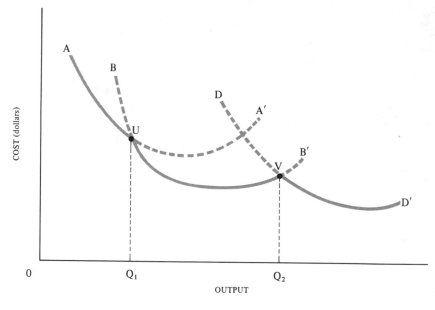

Figure 9.12

**Short-Run Average Cost Curves and
Long-Run Average Cost Curve**   *The
short-run average total cost functions for
three plants—small, medium, and
large—are* AA′, BB′, *and* DD′. *The
long-run average cost function is* AUVD′,
*if these are the only three types of plant
that can be built.*

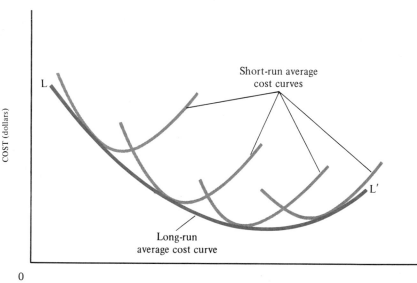

Figure 9.13

Long-Run Average Cost Curve   *If many
possible types of plants can be built, the
long-run average cost function is* LL′.

average cost functions (corresponding to diameters of 8, 10, 12, 14, 16, 18,
20, 24, 26, 30, and 32 inches). Note that long-run average cost—that is, cost
per barrel—decreases as more and more oil is carried per day, at least up
to 400,000 barrels per day. Thus it appears that costs are reduced when the
greatest possible quantities of oil are transported in large-diameter pipelines.

This fact is important in evaluating the effects of various kinds of market structure in the pipeline industry. *If long-run average costs decrease
with increases in output up to an output representing all, or nearly all, of the
market, it is wasteful to force competition in such an industry, since costs
would be greater if the industry output were divided among a number of firms
than if it were produced by only one or two firms.* More will be said on this
score in Chapter 11.

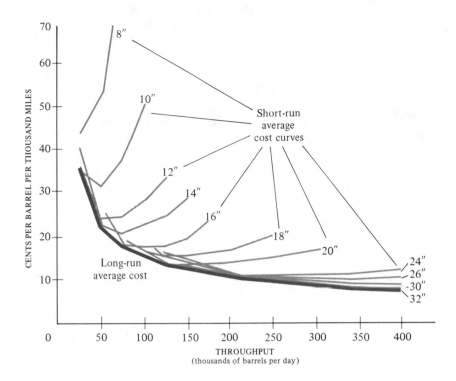

Figure 9.14

Costs per Barrel of Operating Crude-Oil Trunk Pipeline *This graph shows the long-run average cost curve (and the revelant short-run average cost curves) in an actual case. Note that in this range at least, long-run average cost decreases as output increases.*

Returns to Scale

What determines the shape of the long-run average cost function in a particular industry? Its shape must depend upon the characteristics of the production function—specifically, upon whether there are increasing, decreasing, or constant returns to scale. To understand what these terms mean, consider a long-run situation and suppose that the firm increases the amount of all inputs by the same proportion. What will happen to output? *If output increases by a larger proportion than each of the inputs, this is a case of* **increasing returns to scale.** *If output increases by a smaller proportion than each of the inputs, this is a case of* **decreasing returns to scale.** *If output increases by the same proportion as each of the inputs, this is a case of* **constant returns to scale.**

At first glance it may seem that constant returns to scale must always prevail. After all, if two factories are built with the same equipment and use the same type and number of workers, it would seem obvious that they can produce twice as much output as one such factory. But things are not that simple. If a firm doubles its scale, it may be able to *use techniques that could not be used at the smaller scale.* Some inputs are not available in small units; for example, we cannot install half a numerically controlled machine tool. Because of indivisibilities of this sort, increasing returns to scale may occur. Thus, although one could double a firm's size by simply building two small factories, this may be inefficient. One large factory may be more efficient than two smaller factories of the same total capacity because it is large enough to use certain techniques and inputs that the smaller factories cannot use.

Another reason for increasing returns to scale stems from certain *geo-*

metrical relations. For example, since the volume of a box that is 3 × 3 × 3 feet is 27 times as great as the volume of a box that is 1 × 1 × 1 foot, the former box can carry 27 times as much as the latter box. But since the area of the six sides of the 3 × 3 × 3-foot box is 54 square feet and the area of the six sides of the 1 × 1 × 1-foot box is 6 square feet, the former box only requires 9 times as much wood as the latter. Greater *specialization* also can result in increasing returns to scale. As more men and machines are used, it is possible to subdivide tasks and allow various inputs to specialize.

Decreasing returns to scale can also occur; the most frequently cited reason is *the difficulty of coordinating a large enterprise.* It can be difficult even in a small firm to obtain the information required to make important decisions; in a large firm, the difficulties tend to be greater. It can be difficult even in a small firm to be certain that management's wishes are being carried out; in a larger firm these difficulties too tend to be greater. Although the advantages of a large organization seem to have captured the public fancy, there are often very great disadvantages as well.

Whether there are increasing, decreasing, or constant returns to scale in a particular situation must be settled case by case. Moreover, the answer is likely to depend on the particular range of output considered. There frequently are increasing returns to scale up to some level of output, then perhaps constant returns to scale up to a higher level of output, beyond which there may be decreasing returns to scale. This pattern is responsible for the *U*-shaped long-run average cost function in Figure 9.13. At relatively small output levels, there are increasing returns to scale, and long-run average cost decreases as output rises. At relatively high output levels, there are decreasing returns to scale, and long-run average cost increases as output rises.

As we shall see in the following section, this *U*-shaped pattern is not found in all industries. Within the range covered by the available data, there is little or no evidence in many industries that long-run average cost increases as output rises. But this may be because the data do not cover a wide enough range. Eventually, one would expect long-run average cost to rise because of problems of coordination, increased red tape, and reduced flexibility. Firms as large as General Motors or IBM are continually bedeviled by the very real difficulties of enormous size.

Measurement and Application of Cost Functions

MEASUREMENT OF COST FUNCTIONS

Countless studies have been made to estimate cost functions in particular firms and industries. Many of these have been based on the relationship over time between cost and output. Figure 9.15 shows the total costs of a hypothetical firm in various years plotted against the firm's output in these years. Based on the data, a reasonable approximation to the firm's total cost function might be the curve that is drawn in Figure 9.15. However, there are a number of difficulties in this simple procedure. For one thing, the firm's cost function may not have remained fixed throughout this period.

Basic Idea #18: Although it is commonly believed that larger firms enjoy lower average costs than smaller ones, this frequently is not true. Up to some point, increases in scale generally produce lower average costs, but beyond that point (which varies from industry to industry), further increases do not result in lower average costs.

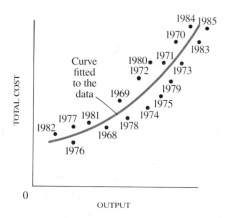

Figure 9.15

Relationship between Total Cost and Output: Time Series for a Particular Firm *One very crude way to estimate the total cost curve is to plot total cost in each year against total output in that year, and draw a curve, like the one shown in the diagram, that fits the points reasonably well. However, this technique is generally too crude to be reliable.*

For another, accounting data on costs may not be as accurate as one would like.[2] For these and other reasons, economists and statisticians have devised more sophisticated techniques to estimate cost functions.

To illustrate the sorts of results that have been obtained, Figure 9.16 shows the total cost function, average total cost function, and marginal cost function for a leather belt shop. Note that the total cost function appears linear, that is, a straight line, in the relevant range.

These results were obtained over 40 years ago by one of the pioneers in this field, Joel Dean of Columbia University.[3] Since that time, a great deal of evidence has been amassed on the shape of the cost functions of individual firms and industries. Two findings are particularly worth noting. First, *within the range of observed data, the long-run average cost curve in many industries seems to be L-shaped* (as in Figure 9.17), *not U-shaped* (as in Figure 9.13). That is, there is little or no evidence that it turns upward, rather than remains horizontal, at high output levels. As pointed out in the previous section, this may be due in part to the limited range of the data. Second, *many empirical studies indicate that marginal cost in the short run tends to be constant in the relevant output range.* However, this really does not contradict our assertions in previous sections, because the data used in these studies often do not cover periods when the firm was operating at peak capacity.

BREAK-EVEN CHARTS

Estimated cost functions are used in a variety of ways by firms and government agencies. One important practical application of cost functions is to so-called **break-even charts.** To construct a break-even chart, *the firm's total revenue must be plotted on the same chart with its total cost function.* It is generally assumed that the price the firm receives for its product will not be influenced by the amount it sells, so that total revenue is proportional

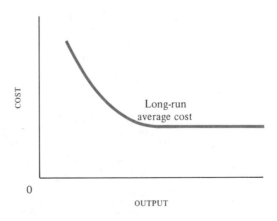

[2] Some of the difficulties are that the depreciation of an asset is often determined by the tax laws rather than economic criteria, many inputs are valued at historical, rather than opportunity cost, and accountants sometimes use arbitrary allocations of overhead and joint costs.

[3] Joel Dean, *The Relation of Cost to Output for a Leather Belt Shop,* New York: National Bureau of Economic Research, 1941.

Although articles in the popular press often exaggerate the abilities and social implications of robots, it certainly is true that they will have a noteworthy effect on production costs, particularly in the metal working industries. According to the Robot Institute of America, a robot is defined as a "reprogrammable, multi-functional manipulator designed to move material parts, tools, or specialized devices through variable programmed motions for the performance of a variety of tasks."[1] The market for robots has been estimated to rise by about 30-35 percent per year over the rest of the 1980s. Many experts expect that the world stock of robots will number about 300,000 by 1990.

Robots are currently used in a variety of processes, such as forging, welding, assembly, painting, and machine tool loading. For example, at John Deere and Company, robots are handling about 80 percent of the painting on each tractor produced, resulting in a considerable saving of labor. Volvo introduced 28 robots into an automobile assembly line to make about 700 spot welds, replacing 67 workers with a handful of key staff. Often, robots are used to do difficult and dangerous jobs in foundries and welding and painting operations.

Firms generally introduce robots to reduce labor inputs. According to recent evidence from Japan, the most advanced robots currently in use sometimes displace 2 to 4 workers per shift. For example, in one Japanese factory, the operation of five die cast machines required five workers before the robot was introduced; after its introduction, only one worker was needed. However, most studies seem to indicate that the average number of workers displaced per shift by a robot is only about 1.5. Moreover, although robots reduce the amount of labor required to do some types of work, they increase the amount of labor required to do other types (such as the maintenance of the robots). Thus the reduction in labor requirements often is not as large as it may seem.

Industrial robots are a key component of flexible manufacturing systems that allow relatively low-cost production of batches of custom-tailored products. For example, John Deere's tractor plant can produce tractors in more than 5,000 configurations. This plant is often cited as a model of modern automation. In the section where transmissions are assembled, a computer identifies which of 10 different models the transmission is to be before its elements start down the assembly line. A lone worker loads the raw castings on carts, and punches a code into a computer terminal. The computer takes over from that point on.

Besides reducing labor requirements, the use of flexible manufacturing systems can reduce capital requirements. At present, machine tools are idle most of the time, because human operators have to set up, inspect, load, and unload their machines. Also, plants are closed for holidays, strikes, and other reasons; and when plants are not closed, there may not be three shifts

---

[1] "Robots: The Users and the Makers," *The OECD Observer*, July 1983, p. 12.

every day of the week. By using robots and computer control, firms can reduce considerably the amount of idle time which has been a prime factor in maintaining relatively low machine productivity. For example, a Japanese firm's flexible manufacturing system enables it to run an unmanned night shift, because the machining of parts is so completely automated.

According to engineers and business executives, the use of robots and flexible manufacturing systems is beginning to have a significant effect on the long-run average cost curve for the production of many products in the metal-working industries. Because they reduce the amount of labor and capital inputs required per unit of output, these new technologies are pushing the long-run average cost curve downward, as shown in panel A of the graph below. However, many observers report that the new long-run average cost curve is not parallel to the old one. Instead, the vertical distance between the new and old cost curves is greater at intermediate than very large output levels, as shown below, because the reduction in average cost is greater for intermediate ranges of output than for very large output levels (where mass production techniques are appropriate).

In the case of automobile production, the Organization for Economic Co-operation and Development (OECD) has reported that these technological changes have resulted in a reduction in the minimum efficient scale for an automobile assembly plant (as well as for an engine and transmission plant). Whereas such a plant formerly had to produce about 400,000 vehicles per year to have reasonably low costs, plants producing 250,000 vehicles now have low enough costs to be competitive. (The situation is shown in panel B of the graph below.) Indeed, Nissan's proposed United Kingdom plant has been planned for 200,000 units per year. Such a change in the minimum efficient scale of plant is regarded as an important development in the automobile industry.

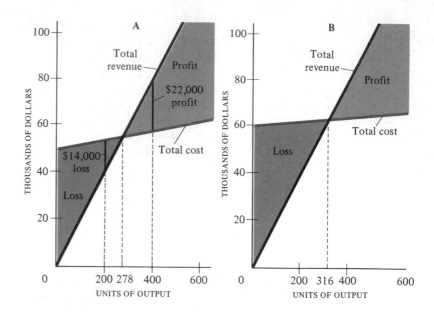

Figure 9.18

Break-Even Chart, Cable Manufacturing Firm In panels A and B, the sales price of each unit of output is $200. In panel A, the firm's fixed costs are $50,000 per month, and its average variable cost per unit of output is $20. In panel B, the firm's fixed costs are $60,000 per month, and its average variable cost per unit of output is $10. In panel A, the firm's break-even point is 278 units of output per month, whereas in panel B it is 316 units of output per month.

to output. Thus the total revenue curve is a straight line through the origin. Also, it is generally assumed that the firm's average variable cost and marginal cost are constant *in the relevant output range,* meaning that the firm's total cost function is also assumed to be a straight line.

Panel A of Figure 9.18 shows the break-even chart for an actual cable manufacturing firm.[4] The sales price of each unit of its output was $200. The firm's fixed costs were $50,000 per month and its average variable cost per unit of output was $20. The break-even chart shows the monthly profit or loss that will result from each sales level. Panel A (Figure 9.18) shows that the firm would have lost $14,000 per month if it had sold 200 units per month. On the other hand, it would have made a profit of $22,000 per month if it had sold 400 units per month. The chart also shows the **break-even point,** *the output level that must be reached if the firm is to avoid losses.* In panel A, the break-even point is 278 units of output per month.

Break-even charts are used very extensively by firms and other groups to estimate the effect of the sales rate on costs, receipts, and profits. A firm may use a break-even chart to determine the effect on profits of a projected increase in sales, or how many units of a particular product it must sell in order to break even. For instance, the cable manufacturing firm wanted to find out, among other things, how its break-even point would be affected if it installed new equipment that would increase its fixed costs to $60,000 per month and reduce its average variable cost to $10. Panel B of Figure 9.18 shows that, under these circumstances, the firm's break-even point would be 316, rather than 278, units of output per month. This information is, of course, of considerable value to the firm. It means that, if the firm installs the new equipment, it must sell at least 316 units of output per month to stay in the black.

[4] See Charles Stokes, *Managerial Economics: A Case Book,* New York: Random House, 1969. However, I have changed the numbers to make them easier to work with.

Test Yourself

1. Explain why each of the following statements is true, partly true, or false. (a) "Decreasing returns to scale occur when increased scale allows efficiencies of various sorts." (b) "The law of diminishing marginal returns is inconsistent with increasing returns to scale." (c) "John Maynard Keynes said, 'In the long run we are all dead.' He was right. What is important for the determination of the optimal number of firms in an industry is the short-run average cost function."

2. As the electronics industry has grown more mature and new technologies have been developed, the costs of many electronic products have fallen dramatically. Is this evidence that the long-run average cost curve slopes downward to the right? Explain.

3. A business analyst uses a break-even chart which assumes that her firm's total cost is a linear function of output (as in Figure 9.18). If the firm's marginal cost increases sharply as its output increases, is this break-even chart likely to be very accurate? Why or why not?

4. Suppose that you were the president of a firm that operates a crude-oil pipeline. Describe in detail the various ways in which the cost functions given in this chapter might be useful to you.

Summary

1. The cost of a certain course of action is the value of the best alternative course of action that could have been pursued instead. This is the doctrine of opportunity, or alternative, cost.

2. Three kinds of total cost functions are important in the short run—total fixed cost, total variable cost, and total cost. In addition, there are three kinds of average cost functions (corresponding to each of the total cost functions)—average fixed cost, average variable cost, and average total cost.

3. Marginal cost—the addition to total cost due to the addition of the last unit of output—is of enormous significance in the firm's decision making process. Because of the law of diminishing marginal returns, marginal cost tends to increase beyond some output level.

4. The firm's long-run average cost curve shows the minimum average cost of producing each output level when any desired type or scale of plant can be built. The shape of the long-run average cost curve is determined in part by whether there are increasing, decreasing, or constant returns to scale.

5. Suppose that a firm increases the amount of all inputs by the same percentage. If output increases by more than this percentage, this is a case of increasing returns to scale. If output increases by less than this percentage, this is a case of decreasing returns to scale. If output increases by this percentage, this is a case of constant returns to scale.

6. If long-run average costs decrease with increases in output up to an output representing all, or nearly all, of the market, it is wasteful to force competition in such an industry, since costs would be greater if the industry output were divided among a number of firms than if it were produced by only one or two firms.

7. Cost functions play a very important practical role in economics and management. There have been countless studies to estimate cost functions in particular firms and industries, based on engineering and accounting data.

8. Cost functions can be used to help solve important sorts of managerial problems, as well as problems of public policy. We have shown how estimates of cost functions have been used to construct break-even charts, commonly employed by firms to promote better decisions.

Concepts for Review

Opportunity cost	Average fixed cost	Long-run average cost function
Alternative cost	Average variable cost	
Implicit cost	Average total cost	Increasing returns to scale
Cost functions	Marginal cost	Decreasing returns to scale
Total fixed cost	Total cost function	Constant returns to scale
Total variable cost	Average total cost function	Break-even chart
Total cost		Break-even point
	Marginal cost function	

PART FOUR

Market Structure and Antitrust Policy

CHAPTER 10

Perfect Competition

Even a country as rich as the United States cannot afford to waste resources, particularly when much of the world is hungry. One of the important determinants of how a society's resources are used is how its markets are organized. Thus, if the market for wheat contained few sellers rather than many, it would certainly use resources quite differently. Or if 20 firms, rather than one, provided local telephone service in Chicago, resources would be used differently. Economists do not have any simple formulas that will eliminate all social waste. But based on existing models and evidence, some forms of market organization tend to minimize social waste, whereas other forms seem to promote it.

In this chapter, we examine the way resources are allocated and prices are set under *perfect competition.* This type of market organization—or market structure, as it is often called—is a polar case which seldom, if ever, occurs in a pure form in the real world. But it is an extremely useful model that sheds much light on a market structure's effects on resource allocation. Anyone who wants to understand how markets work in a capitalistic economy—or why our public policies toward business are what they are—must understand perfect competition, as well as the other market structures taken up in the next two chapters.

Market Structure and Economic Performance

Many economists have come to the conclusion, based on their studies of the workings of markets, that certain kinds of market organization are better, from society's point of view, than others. This is a much stronger

Table 10.1

TYPES OF MARKET STRUCTURE

Market structure	Examples	Number of producers	Type of product	Power of firm over price	Barriers to entry	Nonprice competition
Perfect competition	Parts of agriculture are reasonably close	Many	Standardized	None	Low	None
Monopolistic competition	Retail trade	Many	Differentiated	Some	Low	Advertising and product differentiation
Oligopoly	Autos, steel, machinery	Few	Standardized or differentiated	Some	High	Advertising and product differentiation
Monopoly	Public utilities	One	Unique product	Considerable	Very high	Advertising

statement than merely saying, as we did in the previous section, that market structure influences market behavior. This statement is based on some set of values and preferences, explicit or implicit, and on certain economic models that predict that "better" behavior is more likely if markets are organized in certain ways than in other ways. Although there is considerable controversy on this score, many economists believe that, from society's point of view, market structures should be as close as possible to perfect competition (for reasons given in the next three chapters).

Economists have generally found it useful to classify markets into four broad types: **perfect competition, monopoly, monopolistic competition,** and **oligopoly.** Each of these terms describes a particular type of market structure or organization. Table 10.1 provides a capsule description of each of these types. Before looking in detail at each of them, we must go over this table to see how these market structures differ.

Number of Firms. The economist's classification of market structures is based to an important extent on the number of firms in the industry that supplies the product. In perfect competition and monopolistic competition, there are *many* sellers, each of which produces only a small part of the industry's output. In monopoly, on the other hand, the industry consists of only a *single* seller. Oligopoly is an intermediate case where there are a *few* sellers. Thus Consolidated Edison, if it is the only supplier of electricity in a particular market, is a monopoly. And since there is only a small number of computer manufacturers, the market for computers is an oligopoly.

Control over Price. Market structures differ considerably in the extent to which an individual firm has control over price. A firm under perfect competition has *no control* over price. For example, a wheat farm (which is close to being a perfectly competitive firm) has no control over the price of wheat. On the other hand, a monopolist is likely to have *considerable control* over price. Thus, in the absence of public regulation, Consolidated Edison would have considerable control over the price of electricity in New York City. A firm under monopolistic competition or oligopoly is likely to have *more* control over price than a perfectly competitive firm and *less* control over price than a monopolist.

Type of Product. These market structures also differ in the extent to which the firms in an industry produce standardized (that is, identical) products. Firms in a perfectly competitive market all produce *identical* products. Thus Farmer Brown's corn is essentially the same as Farmer Smith's. In a monopolistic competitive industry like dress manufacturing, firms produce *somewhat different* products. One firm's dresses differ in style and quality from another firm's dresses. In an oligopolistic industry, firms *sometimes,* but not always, produce identical products. And in a monopolistic industry, there can be *no difference* among firms in their products, since there is only one firm.

Barriers to Entry. The ease with which firms can enter the industry differs from one market structure to another. In perfect competition, barriers to entry are *low.* Thus only a small investment is required to enter many parts of agriculture. Similarly, there are *low* barriers to entry in monopolistic competition. But in oligopolies such as autos and steel, there tend to be *very considerable* barriers to entry because it is so expensive to build an auto or steel plant (and for many other reasons too). In monopoly, entry is blocked; once entry occurs, the monopolist is an ex-monopolist.

Nonprice Competition. These market structures also differ in the extent to which firms compete on the basis of advertising and differences in product characteristics, rather than price. In perfect competition, there is *no* nonprice competition. In monopolistic competition, there is *considerable emphasis* on nonprice competition. Thus dress manufacturers compete by trying to develop better styles and by advertising their product lines. Oligopolies also tend to rely *heavily* on nonprice competition. For example, auto firms try to increase their sales by building better and more attractive cars and by advertising. Monopolists also engage in advertising, although this advertising is not directed at reducing the sales of other firms in the industry, since no other firms exist.

Table 10.1 provides a useful summary of some of the key characteristics of each market structure. Before proceeding further, study it carefully.

Perfect Competition

When business executives speak of a highly competitive market, they often mean one in which each firm is keenly aware of its rivalry with a few others and in which advertising, styling, packaging, and other such commercial weapons are used to attract business away from them. In contrast, the basic feature of the economist's definition of **perfect competition** is its *impersonality.* Because there are so many firms in the industry, no firm views another as a competitor, any more than one small tobacco farmer views another small tobacco farmer as a competitor. A market is perfectly competitive if it satisfies the following three conditions.

Homogeneity of Product. The first condition is that *the product of any one seller must be the same as the product of any other seller.* This condition insures that buyers do not care from which seller they purchase the goods, so long as the price is the same. This condition is met in many markets. As pointed out in the previous section, Farmer Brown's corn is likely to be essentially the same as Farmer Smith's.

Many Buyers and Sellers. The second condition is that there must be a

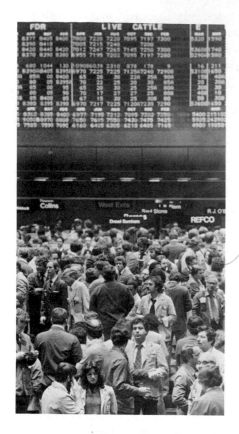

large number of buyers and sellers. *Each participant in the market, whether buyer or seller, must be so small in relation to the entire market that he or she cannot affect the product's price.* That is, all buyers and sellers must be "price takers," not "price makers." As we know from Chapter 6, a firm under perfect competition faces a *horizontal demand curve,* since variations in its output—within the range of its capabilities—will have no effect on market price.

Mobility of Resources. The third condition is that *all resources must be able to switch readily from one use to another, and consumers, firms, and resource owners must have complete knowledge of all relevant economic and technological data.*

No industry in the real world, now or in the past, satisfies all these conditions completely; thus no industry is perfectly competitive. Some agricultural markets may be reasonably close, but even they do not meet all the requirements. But this does not mean that it is useless to study the behavior of a perfectly competitive market. The conclusions derived from the model of perfect competition have proved very helpful in explaining and predicting behavior in the real world. Indeed, as we shall see, they have permitted a reasonably accurate view of resource allocation in many important segments of our economy.

The Output of the Firm

What determines the output rate in the short run of a perfectly competitive firm? Since the firm is perfectly competitive, it cannot affect the price of its product, and it can sell any amount it wants at this price. Since we are concerned with the short run, the firm can expand or contract its output rate by increasing or decreasing its utilization of its variable, but not its fixed, inputs. The situation in the long run will be reserved for a later section.

WHAT IS THE PROFIT AT EACH OUTPUT RATE?

To see how a firm determines its output rate, suppose that your aunt dies and leaves you her business, the Allegro Piano Company. Once you take over the business, your first problem is to decide how many pianos (each of which has a price of $1,000) the firm should produce per week. Having a good deal of economic intuition, you instruct your accountants to estimate the company's *total revenue* (defined as price times output) and total costs (as well as fixed and variable costs) at various output levels. They estimate the firm's total revenue at various output rates and its total cost function (as well as its total fixed cost function and total variable cost function), with the results shown in Table 10.2. Subtracting the total cost at a given output rate from the total revenue at this output rate, you obtain the total profit at each output rate, which is shown in the last column of Table 10.2.

FINDING THE MAXIMUM-PROFIT OUTPUT RATE

As the output rate increases from 0 to 4 pianos per week, the total profit *rises.* As the output rate increases from 5 to 8 pianos per week, the total

Table 10.2
COSTS AND REVENUES, ALLEGRO PIANO COMPANY

Output per week (pianos)	Price	Total revenue (price × output)	Total fixed cost (dollars)	Total variable cost	Total cost	Total profit
0	1,000	0	1,000	0	1,000	−1,000
1	1,000	1,000	1,000	200	1,200	− 200
2	1,000	2,000	1,000	300	1,300	700
3	1,000	3,000	1,000	500	1,500	1,500
4	1,000	4,000	1,000	1,000	2,000	2,000
5	1,000	5,000	1,000	2,000	3,000	2,000
6	1,000	6,000	1,000	3,200	4,200	1,800
7	1,000	7,000	1,000	4,500	5,500	1,500
8	1,000	8,000	1,000	7,200	8,200	− 200

profit *falls.* Thus the *maximum* profit is achieved at an output rate between 4 and 5 pianos per week.[1] (Without more detailed data, one cannot tell precisely where the maximum occurs, but this is close enough for present purposes.) Since the maximum profit is obtained at an output of between 4 and 5 pianos per week, this is the output rate you choose.

Figure 10.1 gives a somewhat more vivid picture of the firm's situation by plotting the relationship between total revenue and total cost, on the one hand, and output on the other. At each output rate, the vertical distance between the total revenue curve and the total cost curve is the amount of profit the firm earns. Below an output rate of about 1 piano per week and above a rate of about 8 pianos per week, the total revenue curve lies *below* the total cost curve, indicating that profits are negative—that is, there are losses. Both Table 10.2 and Figure 10.1 show that the output rate that will maximize the firm's profits is between 4 and 5 pianos per week. At this

Figure 10.1

Costs, Revenues, and Profits, Allegro Piano Company *Profit equals the vertical distance between the total revenue curve and the total cost curve. This distance is maximized when the output rate is between 4 and 5 pianos per week. At this output rate, profit (measured by the vertical distance) is somewhat more than $2,000.*

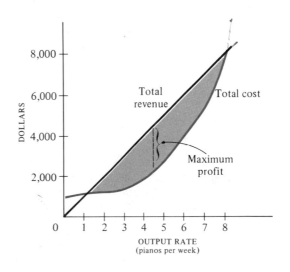

[1] This assumes that the output rate can be varied continuously and that there is a single maximum. These are innocuous assumptions.

187

Table 10.3

MARGINAL COST AND PRICE, ALLEGRO PIANO COMPANY

Output per week (pianos)	Marginal cost (dollars)	Price
0		1,000
	200	
1		1,000
	100	
2		1,000
	200	
3		1,000
	500	
4		1,000
	1,000	
5		1,000
	1,200	
6		1,000
	1,300	
7		1,000
	2,700	
8		1,000

Figure 10.2

Marginal Cost and Price, Allegro Piano Company *At the profit-maximizing output rate of between 4 and 5 pianos per week, marginal cost (which is $1,000 when the output rate is between 4 and 5) equals price ($1,000). Recall from Figure 9.8 that marginal cost is plotted at the mid-point of the range of output to which it pertains.*

output rate, the firm will make a profit of over $2,000 per week, which is more than it can make at any other output rate.

There is an alternative way to analyze the firm's situation. Rather than looking at total revenue and total cost, let's look at price and marginal cost. Table 10.3 and Figure 10.2 show the product price and marginal cost of each output rate. It turns out that the maximum profit is achieved at the output rate where price equals marginal cost. In other words, both Table 10.3 and Figure 10.2 indicate that price equals marginal cost at the profit-maximizing output rate of between 4 and 5 pianos per week. This raises a question. Will price usually equal marginal cost at the profit-maximizing output rate, or is this merely a coincidence?

THE GOLDEN RULE OF OUTPUT DETERMINATION

Readers familiar with television scripts and detective stories will have recognized that the question just posed can only be answered in one way without ruining the plot. The equality of marginal cost and price at the profit-maximizing output rate is no mere coincidence. It will usually be true if the firm takes the price of its product as given. Indeed, the Golden Rule of Output Determination for a perfectly competitive firm is: *Choose the output rate at which marginal cost is equal to price.*

To prove that this rule maximizes profits, consider Figure 10.3, which shows a typical short-run marginal cost function. Suppose that the price is OP_1. At any output rate less than OQ_1, price is greater than marginal cost.[2] This means that increases in output will increase the firm's profits since they will add more to total revenues than to total costs. Why? Because an extra unit of output adds an amount equal to price to total revenue and an amount equal to marginal cost to total cost. Thus, since price exceeds marginal cost, an extra unit of output adds more to total revenue than to total cost. This is the case for the Allegro Piano Company when it is producing 3 pianos per week. As shown in Table 10.3, the extra cost of producing a fourth piano is $500, while the revenue brought in by producing and selling it is $1,000. Consequently, it pays the Allegro Piano Company to produce more than 3 pianos per week.

At any output rate above OQ_1, price is less than marginal cost. This means that decreases in output will increase the firm's profits since they will subtract more from total costs than from total revenue. This happens because one less unit of output subtracts an amount equal to price from total revenue and an amount equal to marginal cost from total cost. Thus, since price is less than marginal cost, one less unit of output subtracts more from total cost than from total revenue. Such a case occurs when the Allegro Piano Company is producing 7 pianos per week. As shown in Table 10.3, the extra cost of producing the seventh piano is $1,300, while the extra revenue it brings in is $1,000. So it pays the Allegro Piano Company to produce less than 7 pianos per week.

Since increases in output will increase profits if output is less than OQ_1, and decreases in output will increase profits if output is greater than OQ_1, it follows that profits must be maximized at OQ_1, the output rate at which

[2] Except perhaps for an irrelevant range where marginal cost decreases with increases in output.

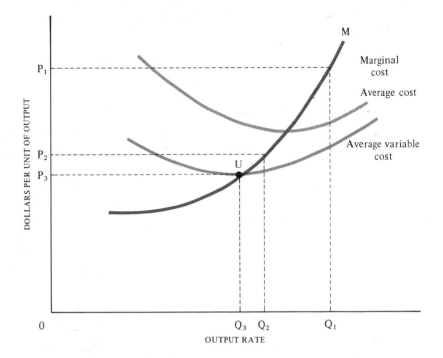

Figure 10.3
Short-Run Average and Marginal Cost Curves *If price is OP₁, the profit-maximizing output rate is OQ₁. If price is OP₂, the profit-maximizing output rate is OQ₂, even though the firm will incur a loss. If the price is below OP₃, the firm will discontinue production. (Note that, regardless of what the price is, the demand curve facing the firm is a horizontal line at this price.)*

Basic Idea #19: *To determine the profit-maximizing output rate of a firm, compare the extra revenue with the extra cost of each additional unit of output. If the extra revenue (which equals price here) is greater than the extra cost (which equals marginal cost), the extra unit should be produced; otherwise it should not be produced. (But if there is no output where price exceeds average variable cost, the firm will be better off producing nothing at all.)*

price equals marginal cost. After all, if increases in output up to this output *(OQ₁)* result in increases in profit and further increases in output result in decreases in profit, *OQ₁* must be the profit-maximizing output rate. For the Allegro Piano Company, this output rate is between 4 and 5 pianos per week, as we saw above.

DOES IT PAY TO BE A DROPOUT?

All rules—even the Golden Rule we just mentioned—have exceptions. Under some circumstances, the perfectly competitive firm will not maximize its profits if it sets marginal cost equal to price. Instead, it will maximize profits only if it becomes an economic dropout by discontinuing production. Let's demonstrate that this is indeed a fact. The first important point is that even if the firm is doing the best it can, it may not be able to earn a profit. If the price is *OP₂* in Figure 10.3, short-run average cost exceeds the price, *OP₂*, at all possible output rates. Thus the firm cannot earn a profit whatever output it produces. Since the short run is too short for the firm to alter the scale of its plant, it cannot liquidate its plant in the short run. Its only choice is to produce at a loss or discontinue production.

Under what conditions will the firm produce at a loss, and under what conditions will it discontinue production? *If there is an output rate where price exceeds average variable costs, it will pay the firm to produce, even though price does not cover average total cost. If there is no such output rate, the firm is better off to produce nothing at all.* This is true because even if the firm produces nothing, it must pay its fixed cost. Thus, if the loss resulting from production is less than the firm's fixed cost, the firm is better off producing than not producing. On the other hand, if the loss resulting from production is greater than the firm's fixed cost, the firm is better off not to produce.

In other words, *the firm will find it advantageous to produce if total losses are less than total fixed cost.* Since

$$\text{total losses} = \text{total cost} - \text{total revenue},$$

this will be the case if

$$\text{total cost} - \text{total revenue} < \text{total fixed cost}.$$

If we subtract total fixed cost from both sides of this inequality, and if we add total revenue to both sides, we find that the firm is better off to produce if

$$\text{total cost} - \text{total fixed cost} < \text{total revenue}.$$

Dividing each side of this inequality by output (and recognizing that total revenue = price × output), we find that the firm is better off to produce if

$$\text{average variable cost} < \text{price},$$

since average variable cost equals average total cost minus average fixed cost.

Once again, we have proved what we set out to prove—that the firm will maximize profits by producing *nothing* if there is no output rate at which price exceeds average variable cost. If such an output rate does exist, the Golden Rule applies. The firm will set its output rate at the point where marginal cost equals price.

DROPPING OUT: ILLUSTRATIVE CASES

To illustrate the conditions under which it pays a firm to drop out, suppose that the cost functions of the Allegro Piano Company are as shown in Table 10.4. In this case, there exists no output rate such that average variable cost is less than price—which, you will recall, is $1,000 per piano. Thus, according to the results of the last paragraphs, the Allegro Piano Company should discontinue production under these conditions. The wisdom of this course of action is shown by the last column of Table 10.4, which demonstrates that the profit-maximizing—or, what amounts to the same thing, the loss-minimizing—output rate is zero.

Table 10.4

COSTS AND REVENUES, ALLEGRO PIANO COMPANY

Output per week (pianos)	Price	Total revenue	Total fixed cost	Total variable cost	Average variable cost	Total cost	Total profit
				(dollars)			
0	1,000	0	1,000	0	—	1,000	−1,000
1	1,000	1,000	1,000	1,200	1,200	2,200	−1,200
2	1,000	2,000	1,000	2,600	1,300	3,600	−1,600
3	1,000	3,000	1,000	4,200	1,400	5,200	−2,200
4	1,000	4,000	1,000	6,000	1,500	7,000	−3,000
5	1,000	5,000	1,000	8,000	1,600	9,000	−4,000
6	1,000	6,000	1,000	10,200	1,700	11,200	−5,200
7	1,000	7,000	1,000	12,600	1,800	13,600	−6,600
8	1,000	8,000	1,000	15,200	1,900	16,200	−8,200

Sometimes, as in the present case, the best thing to produce is nothing. The situation is analogous to the common experience of leaving a movie after the first ten minutes indicate that it is not going to be a good one, even though the admission price is not refundable. One ignores the fixed costs (the admission price), and finding that the variable cost (the pleasure gained from activities that would be forgone by seeing the rest of the show) is going to exceed the benefits of staying, one leaves.

In 1973, many meat-processing plants discontinued production for essentially this reason. The federal government, in an attempt to control inflation, froze the price of their product, but allowed the prices of the inputs they used to go up, with the result that their average variable costs exceeded price at all possible output levels. The consequence, as our theory would predict, was that many plants closed down. In Chicago, the American Meat Institute announced that 16 plants closed down in the second quarter of 1973. As the president of Detroit's Crown Packing Company put it, "Frankly, we closed down so that we would lose less money."

The Market Supply Curve

In Chapter 3, we described some of the factors underlying a commodity's market supply curve, but we could not go into much detail. Now we can, because our Golden Rule of Output Determination underlies the market supply curve. As a first step, let's derive the *firm's supply curve*, which shows how much the firm will want to produce at each price.

THE FIRM'S SUPPLY CURVE

Since the firm takes the price of its product as given (and can sell all it wants at that price), we know from the previous sections that the firm will choose the output level at which price equals marginal cost. Or if the price is below the firm's average variable cost curve at every output level, the firm will produce nothing. These results are all we need to determine the firm's supply curve.

Suppose that the firm's short-run cost curves are as shown in Figure 10.3. The marginal cost curve must intersect the average variable cost curve at the latter's minimum point, U. If the price of the product is less than OP_3, the firm will produce nothing, because there is no output level where price exceeds average variable cost. If the price of the product exceeds OP_3, the firm will set its output rate at the point where price equals marginal cost. Thus, if the price is OP_1, the firm will produce OQ_1; if the price is OP_2, the firm will produce OQ_2; and so forth. Consequently, *the firm's supply curve is exactly the same as the firm's marginal cost curve for prices above the minimum value of average variable cost* (OP_3). For prices at or below the minimum value of average variable cost, the firm's supply curve corresponds to the price axis, the desire to supply at these prices being uniformly zero. Thus the firm's supply curve is OP_3UM.

Deriving the Market Supply Curve

Our next step is to derive the market supply curve from the supply curves of the individual firms. If one assumption holds, the *market supply curve can be regarded as the horizontal summation of the supply curves of all the firms producing the product.* If there were 3 firms in the industry and their supply curves were as shown in Figure 10.4, the market supply curve would be the horizontal summation of their 3 supply curves. Thus, since these 3 supply curves show that firm 1 would supply 25 units of output at a price of $2 per unit, that firm 2 would supply 40 units at this price, and that firm 3 would supply 55 units at this price, the market supply curve shows that 120 units of output will be supplied if the price is $2 per unit. Why? Because the market supply curve shows the *total* amount of the product that all of the firms together would supply at this price—and 25 + 40 + 55 = 120. If there were only 3 firms, the market would not be perfectly competitive, but we can ignore this inconsistency. Figure 10.4 is designed to illustrate the fact that the market supply curve is the horizontal summation of the firm supply curves, at least under one important assumption.

The assumption underlying this construction of the short-run market supply curve is that *increases or decreases in output by all firms simultaneously do not affect input prices.* This is a convenient simplification, but it is not always true. Although changes in the output of one firm alone often cannot affect input prices, the simultaneous expansion or contraction of output by all firms may well alter input prices, so that the individual firm's cost curves—and supply curve—will shift. For instance, an expansion of the whole industry may bid up the price of certain inputs, with the result that the cost curves of the individual firms will be pushed upward. In the aerospace industry, a sudden expansion of the industry might well increase the price of certain inputs like the services of aerospace scientists and engineers.

Figure 10.4

Horizontal Summation of Short-Run Supply Curves of Firms   If each of the three firms' supply curves is as shown here (and if each firm supplies nothing if the price is below OH), the market supply curve is the horizontal summation of the firms' supply curves, assuming that input prices are not influenced by the output of the industry. If the price is $2, firm 1 will supply 25 units, firm 2 will supply 40 units, and firm 3 will supply 55 units; thus, the total amount supplied is 120 units.

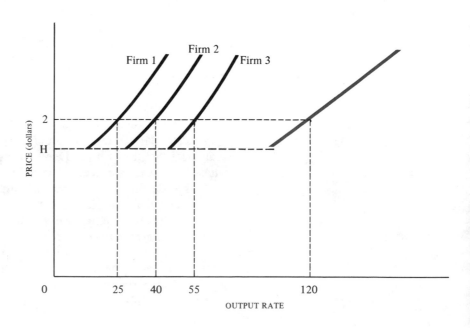

If, contrary to the assumption underlying Figure 10.4, input prices *are* increased by the expansion of the industry, one can still derive the short-run market supply curve by seeing how much the industry will supply in the short run at each price of the product. But it is incorrect to assume that the market supply curve is the horizontal summation of the firm supply curves. More will be said in the chapter Appendix about the effects of industry output on input prices.

Example 10.1   How Much Mercury Do We Have?

According to the U.S. Bureau of Mines,* the quantity of mercury reserves in the United States at selected price levels of mercury is as follows:

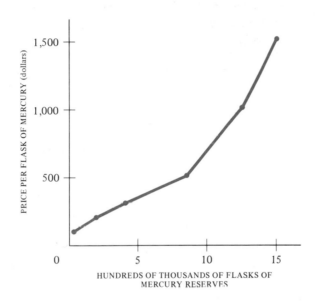

(a) Is this the supply curve for mercury? Why or why not? (b) Does this curve show how much mercury will be supplied per period of time? (c) Why is the quantity of reserves sensitive to price? (d) Does it appear that, as price increases, beyond some point increasing price begins to lose its power to elicit substantially larger supplies? Is this reasonable? Why or why not?

SOLUTION

(a) No. This curve shows how much mercury will be available (not produced) at various prices. (b) No. (c) Because, at higher mercury prices, it becomes profitable to obtain mercury from relatively high-cost sources; whereas at lower mercury prices this is not the case. (d) Yes. This is reasonable because beyond some point it becomes increasingly expensive to find and obtain an extra flask of mercury.

* U.S. Bureau of Mines, *Mercury Potential of the United States*, Washington, D.C.: Government Printing Office, 1965.

DETERMINANTS OF THE LOCATION AND SHAPE OF THE MARKET SUPPLY CURVE

Based on the preceding discussion, we now can identify the basic determinants of the location and shape of a commodity's short-run market supply curve. If increases or decreases in output by all firms do not affect input prices, the short-run market supply curve is the horizontal summation of the firm supply curves. Thus its location and shape are derived from the location and shapes of the marginal cost curves of the firms in the industry, since these marginal cost curves determine the firm supply curves. From previous chapters, we know that the location and shape of each marginal cost curve depend on *the size of the firm's plants, the level of input prices,* and *the state of technology* in particular. Thus these factors play a major role in determining the location and shape of the market supply curve. Also, its location and shape in the short run are determined by the *number of firms* in the industry. The market supply curve in Figure 10.4 would be located farther to the right if there were more firms in the industry. In addition, its location and shape are determined by *the effect of industry output on input prices.*

The short-run market supply curve generally slopes upward and to the right because marginal cost curves (in the relevant range) generally slope upward to the right. If industry output does not affect input prices, the market supply curve is the horizontal sum of the firms' marginal cost curves (in the range where they are rising). Consequently, since each of the marginal cost curves slopes upward and to the right (in this range), this is also true of their horizontal sum, the short-run market supply curve.

Test Yourself

1. Suppose that the total costs of a perfectly competitive firm are as follows:

Output rate	Total cost (dollars)
0	40
1	60
2	90
3	130
4	180
5	240

If the price of the product is $50, what output rate should the firm choose?

2. Suppose that the firm in Question 1 experienced an increase of $30 in its fixed costs. Plot its new total cost function. What effect will this increase in its fixed costs have on the output it will choose?

3. After the increase in fixed costs described in Question 2, what does the firm's marginal cost curve look like? Plot it on a graph. Does it differ from what it was before the increase in fixed costs? Why or why not?

4. After the increase in fixed costs described in Question 2, what output rate would the firm choose if the price of its product were $40? $50? $60? $70?

The Price Elasticity of Supply

Market supply curves vary in their shape. For some commodities, the quantity supplied is very sensitive to changes in the commodity's price. For others, the quantity supplied is not at all sensitive to changes in price.

To measure the sensitivity of quantity supplied to changes in price, economists use the **price elasticity of supply,** *which is defined as the percentage change in quantity supplied resulting from a 1 percent change in price.* Suppose that a 1 percent reduction in the price of slingshots results in a 1.5 percent reduction in the quantity supplied. Then the price elasticity of supply for slingshots (in the neighborhood of the existing price) is 1.5. The price elasticity of supply is likely to vary from one point to another on the market supply curve. Thus the price elasticity of supply for slingshots may be higher when the price of a slingshot is $2 than when it is $1.

The same factors that influence the location and shape of the market supply curve also determine the price elasticity of supply. But to these factors previously mentioned—the number of plants, input prices, and the nature of technology, among others—another important factor should be added—the length of the time period to which the supply curve pertains. *Market supply curves, like market demand curves, tend to be more price elastic if the time period is long rather than short.* Consider the market for watermelons. If we are dealing with a very short period—a few hours or a day—the supply of watermelons may be fixed, as shown in Figure 10.5. That is, the market supply curve may be perfectly inelastic, the price elasticity of supply being zero, because the period is too short to grow any more watermelons or transport any more watermelons into the market.

Suppose now that we lengthen the period of time to a year or so. In this period, farmers can alter the size of their watermelon crop in response to variations in price. Thus the price elasticity of supply will be higher than in the very short period of a few hours or a day. In this longer period, the price elasticity of supply has been estimated to be about .30; and the supply curve may be as shown in Figure 10.5.[3]

Finally, suppose that we lengthen the period further—to 10 years. In this period, farmers will take land out of watermelon production or put land into watermelon production. Indeed, they can make all reasonable adjustments to changes in price. So the price elasticity of supply will be higher than in a period of a year or so—and much higher than in a period of a few hours or a day. The supply curve may be as shown in Figure 10.5.

Figure 10.5
Market Supply Curves for Watermelons, Periods of Varying Length *The left-hand panel shows the market supply curve in a period of a few hours or a day. The middle panel refers to a year or so. The right-hand panel refers to 10 years.*

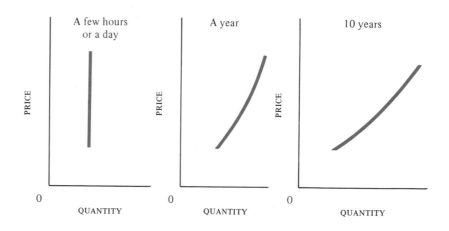

[3] D. Suits, "An Econometric Model of the Watermelon Market," *Journal of Farm Economics,* May 1955; and W. L'Esperance, "A Case Study in Prediction," *Econometrica,* 1964.

195

Price and Output: The Market Period

How much of a particular product will be produced if the market is perfectly competitive, and what will the price be? The answers depend on the length of the time period. To begin with, let's consider the relatively short period of time when the supply of the relevant good is *fixed.* This period of time is called the **market period.** In the market period, as in the short and long runs, the price of a good in a perfectly competitive market is determined by the market demand and market supply curves. However, in the market period, the market supply curve is a vertical line, as shown in Figure 10.6.

Thus, in the market period, output is unaffected by price. In Figure 10.6, output is OQ—and regardless of price, it cannot be changed. The equilibrium price depends on the position of the demand curve. Price is OP_1 if the demand curve is A, and OP_2 if the demand curve is B.

The role of the price as a rationing device is particularly obvious in the market period, where this is the major function of price. Consumers who are willing to pay a relatively high price get some of the product; others do without. The allocation of jam in the prisoner-of-war camp and the allocation of tickets to *A Chorus Line,* both taken up in Chapter 3, are among the examples you have encountered earlier of how price rations output in the market period. These cases can be regarded as taking place in the market period because the supply is fixed in each case.

Figure 10.6

Price Determination in the Market Period *In the market period, supply is fixed at* OQ. *Equilibrium price is* OP₁ *if the demand curve is demand curve* A *and* OP₂ *if the demand curve is demand curve* B.

Price and Output: The Short Run

Let's turn now to the short run, the period during which each firm's plant and equipment are fixed. What determines the price and output of a good in a perfectly competitive market in the short run? The answer once again is the market demand and market supply curves. However, the position and shape of these curves will generally be different in the short run than in the market period. In particular, the market supply curve in the short run will not be a vertical line; it will generally slope upward to the right, as in panel B of Figure 10.7. Thus, *in the short run, price influences, as well as rations, the amount supplied.* In panel B of Figure 10.7, the equilibrium price and output in the short run are OP and OQ.

To illustrate the nature of the short-run supply curve, consider the bituminous coal industry, which in many respects comes reasonably close to perfect competition. According to Hubert Risser of the University of Kansas, the short-run supply curve for bituminous coal is very price elastic, so long as output stays within the range of existing capacity.[4] In other words, if output is less than existing capacity, small variations in price will result in large variations in output. Thus the situation in the short run is quite different from that in the market period, where output is fixed and unaffected by price. But the basic fact remains that equilibrium price and equilibrium output are determined by the intersection of the relevant demand and supply curves, in both the market period and the short run.

[4] H. Risser, *The Economics of the Coal Industry,* Lawrence: University Press of Kansas, 1958, p. 155.

Figure 10.7

Short-Run Competitive Equilibrium *In the short run, equilibrium price is* OP, *and the equilibrium output of the industry is* OQ, *since (as shown in panel* B) *the industry demand and supply curves intersect at this price and output. The demand curve facing the individual firm is a horizontal line at* OP *(as shown in panel* A). *Each firm produces* Oq *units of the product, since this is the output that maximizes its profits. The output of the industry* (OQ) *is the sum of the outputs* (Oq) *of the individual firms. In short-run equilibrium, firms may be making either profits or losses. In this particular case, the individual firm earns a profit equal to the shaded area in panel* A. *(Why? Because the profit* per unit of output *equals the price* [OP] *minus average cost* [OC], *or the vertical distance* CP. *To obtain the firm's* total *profit, this distance must be multiplied by the firm's output* [Oq], *the result being the shaded area.) If firms were making losses rather than profits, the demand curve confronting each firm would intersect the marginal cost curve at a point below (rather than above) the average cost curve.*

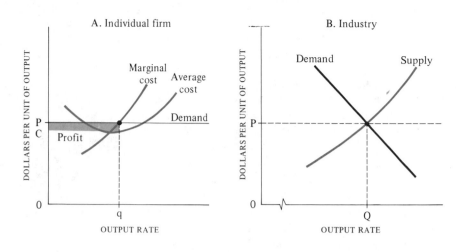

Returning to Figure 10.7, panel A shows the behavior of an individual firm in short-run equilibrium. Since *OP* is the price, the demand curve facing the firm is a horizontal line at *OP,* as shown in panel A. To maximize profit, the firm produces an output of *Oq,* because price equals marginal cost at this output. In short-run equilibrium, firms may be making either profits or losses. In the particular case described in panel A, the firm earns a profit equal to the shaded area shown there. Since the profit per unit of output equals *CP,* total profit equals *CP* multiplied by *Oq,* which is this shaded area.

Taken together, the two panels in Figure 10.7 bring out the following important point. To the *individual* firm, the price of the product is taken as given. If the price is *OP,* the firm in panel A reacts to this price by setting an output rate of *Oq* units. It cannot alter the price; it can only react to it. But *as a group* the reactions of the firms are a major determinant of the price of the product. The supply curve in panel B shows the total amount that the entire group of firms will supply at each price. It summarizes the reactions of the firms to various levels of the price. Put briefly, the equilibrium price is viewed by the individual firm as being beyond its control; yet the supply decisions of all firms taken as a group are a basic determinant of the equilibrium price.

Price and Output: The Long Run

In the long run, what determines the output and price of a good in a perfectly competitive market? In the long run, a firm can change its plant size, which means that established firms may *leave* an industry if it has below-average profits, or that new firms may *enter* an industry with above-average profits. Suppose that textile firms can earn up to (but no more than) a 15 percent rate of return by investing their resources in other industries. If they can earn only 12 percent by keeping these resources invested in the textile industry, they will leave the textile industry. On the other hand, if a rate of return of 18 percent can be earned by investing in the textile industry, firms in other industries, attracted by this relatively high return, will enter the textile industry.

In the past decade or two, economists have begun to use laboratory experiments to understand better how markets work. In an experimental market, the subjects (often college students) trade a commodity (e.g., a scrap of paper) that has no intrinsic value. Buyers make a profit by purchasing the commodity from sellers and reselling it to the experimenter. For example, the rules of the experiment may state that the experimenter will redeem the first unit of the commodity for $2.00, the second unit for $1.50, the third unit for $1.00, and so on. Sellers make a profit by buying units from the experimenter and selling them to the buyers. For example, the experimenter may provide the seller with the first unit of the commodity for $0.25, the second unit for $0.75, the third unit for $1.00, and so on.

Charles Plott

The way in which the market is organized varies from experiment to experiment. Frequently, they are organized as double auctions, which are characterized by public bids to buy units of the commodity and public offers to sell units of it. Any participant is free to accept whatever terms he or she wants. Typically, bids are made verbally. An auctioneer, when hearing a bid or offer, writes it on the blackboard. The last bid and offer remain standing until accepted, cancelled, or replaced.

Based on the work of Caltech's Charles Plott, Arizona's Vernon Smith, and other leaders in this new field, auctions of this type tend to converge to the competitive equilibrium even with relatively few traders. In other words, if one constructs a market demand curve (based on the amount of the commodity that each buyer will purchase at a given price in order to maximize profit) and a market supply curve (based on the amount of the commodity that each seller will sell at a given price in order to maximize profit), the actual price in the experiment generally moves toward the level at which the market demand curve intersects the market supply curve.

This, of course, is an interesting test of the basic model considered in this chapter, which seems to come through with flying colors. Laboratory experiments have also been carried out to test and extend the models of monopoly, monopolistic competition, and oligopoly discussed in succeeding chapters. Without question, such experiments have been and will be useful in a variety of ways. However, as the leading experimenters are quick to point out, one must be very careful in extrapolating behavior from a very simple laboratory setting to a complex industrial environment. The real world is, of course, a lot more complicated than these simple experiments.

EQUILIBRIUM: ZERO ECONOMIC PROFIT

Equilibrium is achieved in the long run when enough firms—no more, no less—are in the industry so that *economic profits—defined as the excess of a firm's profits over what it could make in other industries—are zero.* This condition is necessary for long-run equilibrium because, as we have seen, new firms will enter the industry if there are economic profits, and existing firms will leave if there are economic losses. This process of entry and exit is the key to long-run equilibrium. It is discussed repeatedly in this and subsequent sections.

Note that the existence of economic profits or losses in an industry brings about a shift in the industry's short-run supply curve. If there are economic profits, new firms will enter the industry, and so shift the short-run supply curve to the right. On the other hand, if there are economic losses in the industry (i.e., if the industry's profits are less than could be obtained elsewhere), existing firms will leave the industry, causing the short-run supply curve to shift to the left. Only if economic profits are zero will the number of firms in the industry—and the industry's short-run supply curve—be stable. Putting this equilibrium condition another way, *the long-run equilibrium position of the firm is at the point at which its long-run average costs equal price.* If price exceeds average total costs, economic profits are being earned; and if price is less than average total costs, economic losses are being incurred.

EQUILIBRIUM: MAXIMUM ECONOMIC PROFIT

Going a step further, *long-run equilibrium requires that price equal the lowest value of long-run average total costs.* In other words, firms must be producing at the *minimum point* on their long-run average cost curves, because to maximize their profits they must operate where price equals long-run marginal cost,[5] and at the same time they also have to operate where price equals long-run average cost. But if both these conditions are satisfied, long-run marginal cost must equal long-run average cost since both equal price. And we know that long-run marginal cost equals long-run average cost only at the point at which long-run average cost is a minimum.[6] Consequently, if long-run marginal cost equals long-run average cost, the firm must be producing at the minimum point on the long-run average cost curve.

This equilibrium position is illustrated in Figure 10.8. When all adjustments are made, price equals *OP*. The equilibrium output of the firm is *Oq*, and its plant corresponds to the short-run average and marginal cost curves in Figure 10.8. At this output and with this plant, long-run marginal cost equals short-run marginal cost equals price. This insures that the firm is maximizing profit. Also, long-run average cost equals short-run average cost equals price. This insures that economic profits are zero. Since the long-run marginal cost and long-run average cost must be equal, the firm is producing at the minimum point on its long-run average cost curve.

Basic Idea #20: The big difference between short-run equilibrium and long-run equilibrium is that entry and exit of firms are possible in the long run but not in the short run. For a long-run equilibrium to occur, there must be zero economic profit; otherwise, the number of firms would not be stable. In contrast, in short-run equilibrium, economic profit may be positive or negative, since the time interval is too short for firms to enter or leave the industry.

---

[5] The reasons why marginal cost must be equal to price, if profits are to be maximized, are given in earlier sections of this chapter.

[6] The previous discussion of this point on p. 170 concerned short-run cost functions, but the argument applies just as well to long-run cost functions.

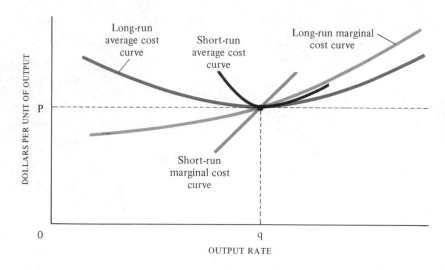

Figure 10.8

Long-Run Equilibrium of a Perfectly Competitive Firm *In long-run equilibrium, output is Oq and the firm's plant corresponds to the short-run average and marginal cost curves shown here. At Oq, long-run marginal cost equals short-run marginal cost equals price; also, long-run average cost equals short-run average cost equals price. These conditions ensure that the firm is maximizing profits and that economic profits are zero.*

To illustrate the process of entry and exit in an industry that approximates perfect competition, let's return to the bituminous coal industry. Entry into this industry is relatively easy, but exit is relatively difficult, for at least two reasons. First, it is costly to shut down a mine and reopen it later. Second, because of corrosion and water damage, it is hard to shut down a mine for longer than two years unless it is to be abandoned entirely. For these reasons, mines tend to stay open and produce even though short-term losses are incurred. In the period before World War II, the demand for coal fell substantially, but although the industry suffered substantial losses, mines were slow to close down. Nonetheless, the competitive process had its way. Slowly, but surely, the number of mines fell markedly in response to these losses.[7] Thus, despite the barriers to rapid exit, firms eventually left the industry, just as the model would predict.

The Allocation of Resources Under Perfect Competition: A More Detailed View

At this point, it is instructive to describe the process by which a perfectly competitive economy—one composed of perfectly competitive industries—would allocate resources. In Chapters 2 and 3, we stressed that the allocation of resources among alternative uses is one of the major functions of any economic system. Equipped with the concepts of this and previous chapters, we can now go much further in describing how a perfectly competitive economy shifts resources in accord with changes in tastes, technology and other factors.

CONSUMERS TURN FROM CORN TO WHEAT

To be specific, suppose that a change occurs in tastes. Consumers become more favorably disposed toward wheat and less favorably disposed toward

[7] J. B. Hendry, "The Bituminous Coal Industry," in W. Adams, *The Structure of American Industry,* New York: Macmillan, 1961.

corn than in the past.[8] In the short run, the increase in the demand for wheat increases the price of wheat, and results in some increase in the output of wheat. However, the output cannot be increased very substantially because the industry's capacity cannot be expanded in the short run. Similarly, the fall in the demand for corn reduces the price of corn, and results in some reduction in output. But the output will not be curtailed greatly because firms will continue to produce as long as they can cover variable costs.

PRICES SIGNAL RESOURCE REALLOCATION

The change in the relative prices of wheat and corn tells producers that a reallocation of resources is called for. Because of the increase in the price of wheat and the decrease in the price of corn, wheat producers are earning economic profits and corn producers are showing economic losses. This will trigger a new deployment of resources. If some variable inputs in corn production can be used as effectively in the production of wheat, they may be switched from corn production to wheat production. Even if no variable inputs are used in both wheat and corn production, adjustment can be made in various interrelated markets, with the result that wheat production gains resources and corn production loses resources. When short-run equilibrium is attained in both the wheat and corn industries, the reallocation of resources is not yet complete since there has not been enough time for producers to build new capacity or liquidate old capacity. In particular, neither industry is operating at minimum average cost. The wheat producers are operating at greater than the output level where average cost is a minimum; and the corn producers are operating at less than this level.

EFFECTS IN THE LONG RUN

What will happen in the long run? The shift in consumer demand from corn to wheat will result in greater adjustments in production and smaller adjustments in price than in the short run. In the long run, existing firms can leave corn production and new firms can enter wheat production. Because of short-run economic losses in corn production, some corn land and related equipment will be allowed to run down, and some firms engaged in corn production will be liquidated. As firms leave corn production, the supply curve shifts to the left, causing the price to rise above its short-run level. The transfer of resources out of corn production will stop when the price has increased, and costs have decreased, to the point where losses are avoided.

While corn production is losing resources, wheat production is gaining them. The prospect of positive economic profits in wheat production will cause new firms to enter the industry. The increased demand for inputs will raise input prices and cost curves in wheat production, and the price of wheat will be depressed by the movement to the right of the supply curve because of the entry of new firms. Entry ceases when economic profits are no longer being earned. At this point, when long-run equilib-

[8] Since we assume here that the markets for wheat and corn are perfectly competitive, it is also assumed that there is no government intervention in these markets.

Example 10.2 How Many Apples Should Be Produced?

Suppose that the demand and supply curves for apples are as shown below:

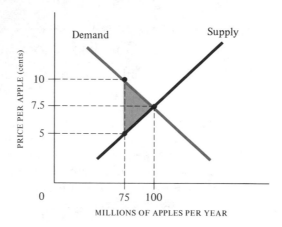

(a) If 75 million apples are produced per year, how much would an additional apple cost to produce? How much would an additional apple be worth to consumers? (b) Under these circumstances, is it socially worthwhile to increase apple production? Why or why not? (c) If 100 million apples are produced per year, how much would an additional apple cost to produce? How much would an additional apple be worth to consumers? (d) If 100 million apples are produced, is it socially worthwhile to increase apple production? Explain. (e) How great is the loss to society if 75 million, rather than 100 million, apples are produced?

SOLUTION

(a) 5 cents, since the supply curve shows marginal cost. 10 cents, because the demand curve shows the maximum amount consumers would pay for an extra apple. (b) Yes, because the extra social cost of producing an extra apple is less than the extra social benefit from doing so. Consumers would be glad to pay producers to produce extra apples. (c) 7½ cents. 7½ cents. (d) No, since the extra social cost of producing an extra apple is no less than the maximum amount that consumers would pay for an extra apple. If private benefits and costs do not differ from social benefits and costs, 100 million apples is the optimal output level. It would not be socially worthwhile to exceed or fall short of it. (e) The vertical distance from the demand curve to the supply curve is the difference between the social benefit and the social cost of an *extra* apple. (For example, if 75 million apples are produced, the social benefit of an extra apple exceeds its social cost by $10 - 5 = 5$ cents.) Thus the difference between the social benefit and social cost of the *extra 25 million apples* equals the sum of these vertical distances for all of the extra apples. This sum equals the shaded area in the above diagram, which amounts to 25 million × 2½ cents = $625,000. This is the loss to society.

rium is achieved, more resources will be used in the industry than in the short run. (Note that, if corn land and equipment can be converted to the production of wheat, some of the "entry" may occur through existing farmers' shifting of their crop mix toward wheat and away from corn.)

Finally, long-run equilibrium is established in both industries, and the reallocation of resources is complete. It is important to note that this reallocation can affect industries other than wheat and corn. If corn land and equipment can be easily adapted to the production of wheat, corn producers can simply change to wheat production. If not, the resources used in corn production are converted to some use other than wheat, and the resources that enter wheat production come from some use other than corn production.

Bituminous Coal: A Case Study

To illustrate how resources are allocated in the long run, we will look in more detail at the bituminous coal industry. Although it does not have all the characteristics of a perfectly competitive industry, it has enough of them so that the perfectly competitive model predicts many aspects of its behavior reasonably well. From the turn of the century until about 1923, the bituminous coal industry expanded rapidly. Between 1903 and 1923, the price of coal increased from $1.24 to $2.68 per ton, in considerable part because of the marked upward shift to the right of the demand curve for coal, an important fuel in this period of general industrial growth. In addition, the high prices of the period were sometimes the result of temporary shortages caused by strikes and insufficient railroad transportation. Thus temporary upward shifts to the left of the supply curve for coal, as well as shifts of the demand curve, were responsible for the increases in price.

Given the very high coal prices of 1917–23, coal mining was very profitable. Indeed, after-tax income in 1920 was about 20 percent of invested capital for all bituminous coal companies—and much higher for particular companies. These high profits signaled that more resources should be invested in the industry. And just as the perfectly competitive model would predict, more resources were invested; the number of bituminous coal firms increased by over 130 percent in nine key states between 1903 and 1923, and the industry's capacity grew by over 50 percent between 1913 and 1923.

Unfortunately, the demand for coal dropped considerably from 1923 to 1933, plunging the industry into a severe economic crisis. The downward shift to the left of the demand curve for coal during the early 1930s was due in considerable part to the fall in national output during the Great Depression. It was accompanied by a marked decrease in the price of coal. From $2.68 in 1923, the price per ton fell to $1.34 in 1933. Needless to say, this tremendous drop meant losses for bituminous coal producers. Indeed, in every year between 1925 and 1940, the bituminous coal industry as a whole showed losses.

These economic losses signaled that resources should be withdrawn from the bituminous coal industry and used elsewhere in the economy where they could be more valuably employed. And as the perfectly competitive model would predict, resources were in fact taken out of bituminous coal. Between 1923 and 1933, there was a reduction of over 40 percent in the number of coal companies operating in nine key states. And the industry's capacity fell by almost 40 percent between 1923 and 1933. Despite the difficulties in exit that we described in a previous section, the competitive process had its way. Its signals were heeded. Consequently, the industry began to move closer and closer to a position of long-run equilibrium, and although the industry remained on the nation's sick list, it began to show much smaller losses. By the onset of World War II, many of the basic adjustments had occurred.

In the postwar period, many important changes have taken place in the bituminous coal industry. Strip mining has become much more important relative to underground mining. The federal government has passed new legislation setting stricter safety requirements for coal. The energy crisis of the 1970s focused new attention on our great coal resources. But from the point of view of the present chapter, perhaps the most interesting development is the increased dominance of the industry by relatively few large firms—and the fact that many big coal companies have been purchased by the major oil firms. About half of the country's 10 biggest coal companies were bought up during the 1960s. Some observers worry that the bituminous coal industry, which tended to be relatively competitive in the past, may be less so in the future.[9]

[9] See T. Duchesneau, *Competition in the U.S. Energy Industry,* Cambridge, Mass.: Ballinger, 1975; R. Moyer, *Competition in the Midwestern Coal Market,* Cambridge, Mass.: Harvard University Press, 1964; and "Out of the Pits," *Barron's,* May 21, 1979.

Test Yourself

1. If the price elasticity of supply for corn is about 0.1 in the short run, as estimated by Marc Nerlove of the University of Pennsylvania, a 1 percent increase in the price of corn would have approximately what impact on the quantity supplied?

2. In Example 10.2, suppose that 125 million apples are produced per year. Under these circumstances, is it socially desirable to reduce apple production? Explain.

3. Suppose that the demand curve for onions is $P = 10 - 3Q$, where P is the price of a pound of onions and Q is the quantity demanded (in millions of pounds). If the supply of onions in the market period is 3⅙ million pounds, what is the equilibrium price of onions in the market period? What does the supply curve for onions look like in the market period?

4. In the short run, suppose that the demand curve for onions is as given in Question 3, and that the supply curve is $P = Q/3$. What is the equilibrium price of onions in the short run? What does the supply curve of onions look like in the short run?

5. In Chapter 3 we pointed out that, in the late 1970s and in the 1980s, consumers seemed to become less interested in playing tennis than in previous years. Describe how the price system reallocated resources in response to this change in tastes.

Summary

1. Economists generally classify markets into four types—perfect competition, monopoly, monopolistic competition, and oligopoly. Perfect competition requires that the product of any seller be the same as the product of any other seller, that no buyer or seller be able to influence the price of the product, and that resources be able to switch readily from one use to another.

2. If it maximizes profit, a perfectly competitive firm should set its output rate in the short run at the level where marginal cost equals price, so long as price exceeds average variable cost. If there is no output rate at which price exceeds average variable cost, the firm should discontinue production.

3. The firm's supply curve coincides with its marginal cost curve for prices exceeding the minimum value of average variable cost. For prices that are less than or equal to the minimum value of average variable cost, the firm's supply curve coincides with the price axis.

4. As a first approximation, the market supply curve can be viewed as the horizontal summation of the supply curves of all of the firms producing the product. This assumes that increases or decreases in output by all firms simultaneously do not affect input prices.

5. The market supply curve of a product is determined by the size of the firms' plants, the level of input prices, the nature of technology, and the other factors determining the shape of the firms' marginal cost curves, as well as by the effect of changes in the industry output on input prices and by the number of firms producing the product.

6. The sensitivity of the quantity supplied to changes in price is measured by the price elasticity of supply, defined as the percentage change in quantity supplied resulting from a 1 percent change in price. In general, the price elasticity of supply is greater if the time interval is long rather than short.

7. Price and output under perfect competition are determined by the intersection of the market supply and demand curves. In the market period, supply is fixed; thus price plays the role of the allocating device. In the short run, price influences as well as rations the amount supplied.

8. In the long run, equilibrium is achieved under perfect competition when enough firms—no more, no less—are in the industry so that economic profits are eliminated. In other words, the long-run equilibrium position of the firm is at the point where its long-run average cost equals price. But since price must also equal marginal cost (to maximize profit), it follows that the firm must be operating at the minimum point on the long-run average cost curve.

9. In a perfectly competitive economy, prices are the signals that are used to guide the reallocation of resources in response to changes in consumer tastes, technology, and other factors.

Concepts for Review

Perfect competition	Oligopoly	Price elasticity of supply
Monopoly	Firm's supply curve	Market period
Monopolistic competition	Market supply curve	Economic profits

Appendix: Constant, Increasing, and Decreasing Cost Industries

Perfectly competitive industries can be categorized into three types—constant cost industries, increasing cost industries, and decreasing cost industries.

CONSTANT COST INDUSTRIES

*In a **constant cost industry** an expansion of output does not result in a change in input prices.* Figure 10.9 shows the long-run equilibrium in a constant cost industry. Panel A shows the short- and long-run cost curves of a typical firm in the industry. Panel B shows the demand and supply curves in the market as a whole. It is assumed that the industry is in long-run equilibrium, with the result that the price line is tangent to the long-run (and short-run) average cost curve at its minimum point. The price is OP.

Let's assume that the demand curve shifts upward and to the right, as shown in panel B. In the short run, with the number of firms fixed, the price of the product will rise from OP to OP_1; each firm will expand output from Oq to Oq_1; and each firm will be making economic profits since OP_1 exceeds the short-run average costs of the firm at Oq_1. The consequence is that firms will enter the industry and shift the short-run supply curve to the right. In a constant cost industry, the entrance of the new firms does not affect the costs of the existing firms. The inputs used by this industry are used by many other industries as well, and the appearance of the new firms in this industry does not bid up the price of inputs (and consequently raise the costs of existing firms). In the long run, the price settles back to OP, the level of (minimum) long-run average cost. Thus *a constant cost industry has a horizontal long-run supply curve.* Since output can be varied by varying the number of firms producing Oq units at an average cost of OP, the long-run supply curve is horizontal at OP.

INCREASING COST INDUSTRIES

Most economists seem to regard increasing, not constant, cost industries as the most prevalent of the three types. *An **increasing cost industry** is one*

Figure 10.9

Long-Run Equilibrium: Constant Cost Industry *If the demand curve shifts upward and to the right, the price will increase in the short run from OP to OP$_1$. Each firm will expand output from Oq to Oq$_1$, and entry will occur, thus shifting the supply curve downward and to the right. The long-run supply curve in a constant cost industry is horizontal.*

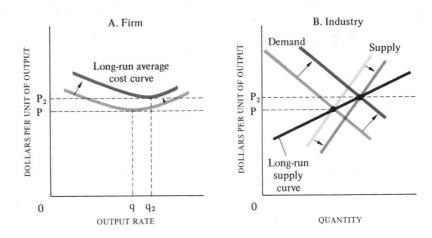

Figure 10.10

Long-Run Equilibrium: Increasing Cost Industry *If the demand curve shifts upward and to the right, the price will increase in the short run. Entry will occur, and the price of inputs will increase, thus pushing the long-run average cost curve upward. The short-run supply curve will shift downward and to the right. The long-run supply curve in an increasing cost industry slopes upward to the right.*

where the price of inputs increases with the amount the industry uses. The situation in such an industry is shown in Figure 10.10. The original conditions are the same as those in Figure 10.9, and we suppose again that the demand curve shifts upward and to the right, with the result that the price of the product increases and firms earn economic profits, thus attracting new entrants. More and more inputs are required by the industry, and in an increasing cost industry the price of inputs increases with the amount the industry uses. Consequently, the cost of inputs increases for the established firms as well as the new entrants. The long-run average cost curve of each firm is pushed up, as shown in panel A. The short-run supply curve shifts downward and to the right, as shown in panel B. Thus the new equilibrium price is OP_2 and each firm produces Oq_2 units. *An increasing cost industry has a positively sloped long-run supply curve,* as shown in Figure 10.10. That is, after long-run equilibrium is achieved, increases in output require increases in the price of the product.

DECREASING COST INDUSTRIES

Decreasing cost industries are the most unusual situation, although quite young industries may sometimes fall into this category. *In a **decreasing cost industry,** the expansion of the industry results in a decrease in the costs of the established firms.*[10] Thus *a decreasing cost industry has a negatively sloped long-run supply curve.* That is, after long-run equilibrium is reached, increases in output are accompanied by decreases in price.

Whether an industry is a constant cost industry, an increasing cost industry, or a decreasing cost industry is an empirical question that must be settled case by case. In trying to determine whether a particular industry is an increasing or constant cost industry, one important consideration is whether or not it is a relatively large user of certain inputs. Because the automobile industry uses a great deal of the nation's steel, an expansion of the automobile industry might well cause an increase in the price of steel; but an expansion of the paper-clip industry, which uses very little of the nation's steel, would be unlikely to raise the price of steel.

[10] Certain *external economies,* which are cost reductions that occur when an industry expands, may be responsible for the existence of decreasing cost industries. An example of such an external economy is an improvement in transportation that is due to the expansion of an industry and that reduces the costs of each firm in the industry (see Chapter 4).

CHAPTER 11

Monopoly and Its Regulation

At the opposite extreme from perfect competition is monopoly. Under a monopolistic market structure, what sorts of behavior can we expect? How much of the product will be produced, and at what level will its price be set? What are the social disadvantages of monopoly? In what ways have government commissions attempted to regulate industries whose market structures approximate monopoly? These are some of the major questions dealt with in this chapter.

To begin with, recall what is meant by *monopoly:* *a market where there exists one, and only one, seller.* Monopoly, like perfect competition, seldom corresponds more than approximately to conditions in real industries, but it is a very useful model. In several respects, monopoly and perfect competition stand as polar opposites. The firm in a perfectly competitive market has so many rivals that competition becomes entirely impersonal. The firm is a price taker, an inconspicuous seller in a sea of inconspicuous sellers. Under monopoly, on the other hand, the firm has no direct competitors at all; it is the sole supplier.

However, even the monopolist is affected by certain indirect and potential forms of competition. Suppose a firm managed to obtain a monopoly on wheat production. It would have to worry about competition from corn and other agricultural commodities that could be substituted for wheat. Moreover, the wheat monopolist would also have to take into account the possibility that new firms might arise to challenge its monopoly if it attempted to extract conspicuously high profits. Thus even the monopolist is subject to some restraint imposed by competitive forces.

Causes of Monopoly

There are many reasons why monopolies, or market structures that closely approximate monopoly, may arise.

Patents. A firm may acquire a monopoly over the production of a good by having patents on the product or on certain basic processes used in its production. The patent laws of the United States give an inventor the exclusive right to make a certain product or to use a certain process for 17 years. The purpose of the patent system is to encourage invention and innovation and to discourage industrial secrecy. Many firms with monopoly power achieved it in considerable part through patents. For example, the United Shoe Machinery Company became the sole supplier of certain important kinds of shoemaking equipment through control of basic patents. United Shoe was free to dominate the market until 1954, when, after prosecution under the antitrust laws, the firm was ordered to license its patents. And in 1968, when this remedy seemed insufficient, a divestiture program was agreed upon.

Control of Input. A firm may become a monopolist by obtaining control over the entire supply of a basic input required to manufacture a product. The International Nickel Company of Canada controls about nine-tenths of the proven nickel reserves in the world. Since it is hard to produce nickel without nickel, the International Nickel Company obviously has a strong monopoly position. Similarly, the Aluminum Company of America (Alcoa) kept its dominant position for a long time by controlling practically all the sources of bauxite, the ore used to make aluminum. However, as we shall see in Chapter 13, Alcoa's monopoly was broken in 1945 when the Supreme Court decided that Alcoa's control of practically all the industry's output violated the antitrust laws.

Government Action. A firm may become a monopolist because it is awarded a market franchise by a government agency. The government may give a particular firm the franchise to sell a particular product in a public facility. Or it may give a particular company the right to provide a service, such as telephone service, to people in a particular area. In exchange for this right, the firm agrees to allow the government to regulate certain aspects of its operations. The form of regulation does not matter here; the important point for now is that the monopoly is created by the government.

Declining Cost of Production. A firm may become a monopolist because the average costs of producing the product reach a minimum at an output rate that is large enough to satisfy the entire market (at a price that is profitable). In a case like this, a firm obviously has an incentive to expand until it produces all the market wants of the good. (Its costs fall as it continues to expand). Thus competition cannot be maintained in this case. If there are a number of firms in the industry, the result is likely to be economic warfare —and the survival of a single victor, the monopolist.[1]

Cases where costs behave like this are called **natural monopolies.** When an industry is a natural monopoly, the public often insists that its behavior be regulated by the government. For example, electric power is an industry where there seem to be great economies of scale—and thus de-

---

[1] Note that economies of scale are different from the external economies discussed in note 10 of the previous chapter. The individual firm has no control over external economies.

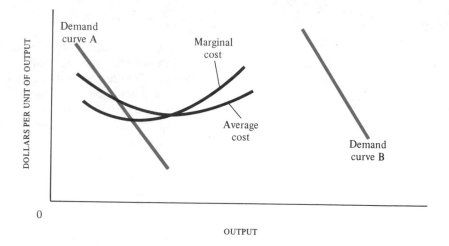

Figure 11.1

Natural Monopoly *The industry is a
natural monopoly if the demand curve is
A,* but not if it is B.

creasing average costs. Fuel consumed per kilowatt hour is lower in larger
power generating units, and there are economies in combining generating
units at a single site. Because of these factors, there has been little attempt
to force competition in the industry, since it would be wasteful. Instead, as
we describe later, the market for electric power in a particular area is a
regulated monopoly.[2]

The likelihood that the long-run average cost curve will decrease up to a
point that satisfies the entire market depends on the size of the market. The
smaller the market, the more likely it is. In Figure 11.1, the industry is a
natural monopoly if the demand curve is *A,* but not if it is *B.* In a large
market like the United States, it is much less likely that an industry will be
a natural monopoly than in a small market like Belgium or Denmark. One
of the advantages claimed for the Common Market in Europe (which was a
step toward integrating Europe into a single market) was that it would
create a larger market that could support more efficient production and
more competitive industries. More will be said on this score in Chapter 18.
For now, the important point to recognize is that, just as stagnant marshes
are the breeding ground for mosquitos, so small, insulated markets are the
breeding ground for monopoly.

Demand Curve and Marginal Revenue under Monopoly

Before we can make any statements about the behavior of a monopolistic
market, we must point out certain important characteristics of the demand
curve facing the monopolist. Since the monopolist is the only seller of the
commodity, the demand curve it faces is the market demand curve for the
product. Since the market demand curve is almost always downward-
sloping to the right, the monopolist's demand curve must also be downward-sloping to the right. This is quite different from perfect competition,

[2] However, it is worth noting that technological developments in this industry may permit
more competition in the future. See L. Weiss, "Antitrust in the Electric Power Industry," in
A. Phillips, *Promoting Competition in Regulated Markets,* Washington, D.C.: The Brookings
Institution, 1975.

DEMAND CURVE AND MARGINAL REVENUE

Table 11.1

DEMAND AND REVENUE OF A
MONOPOLIST

Quantity	Price	Total revenue (dollars)	Marginal revenue
1	100	100	80
2	90	180	60
3	80	240	40
4	70	280	20
5	60	300	0
6	50	300	−20
7	40	280	−40
8	30	240	

Figure 11.2

Marginal Revenue and Demand Curves
The demand curve comes from Table 11.1. Each value of marginal revenue is plotted at the midpoint of the range of output to which it pertains. Since the demand curve is downward-sloping, marginal revenue is always less than price, for reasons discussed in the text. Note that the value of marginal revenue is related to the price elasticity of demand. At outputs where demand is price elastic, marginal revenue is positive; *at outputs where it is price inelastic, marginal revenue is* negative; *and at outputs where it is of unitary elasticity, marginal revenue is* zero.

where the firm's demand curve is horizontal. To illustrate the situation faced by a monopolist, consider the hypothetical case in Table 11.1. The price at which each quantity (shown in column 1) can be sold by the monopolist is shown in column 2. The firm's *total revenue*—its total dollar sales volume—is shown in column 3. Obviously, column 3 is the product of the first two columns. Column 4 contains the firm's *marginal revenue, defined as the addition to total revenue attributable to the addition of one unit to sales.* (Thus if $R(q)$ is total revenue when q units are sold and $R(q-1)$ is total revenue when $(q-1)$ units are sold, the marginal revenue between q units and $(q-1)$ units is $R(q) - R(q-1)$.)

Marginal revenue is very important to the monopolist. We can estimate it from the figures in the first three columns of Table 11.1. The marginal revenue between 1 and 2 units of output per day is $180—$100, or $80; the marginal revenue between 2 and 3 units of output per day is $240—$180, or $60; the marginal revenue between 3 and 4 units of output per day is $280—$240, or $40; and so on. The results are shown in column 4 of the table (and are plotted in Figure 11.2). Note that marginal revenue is analo-

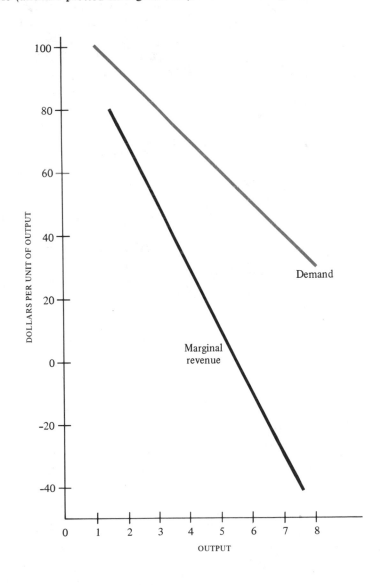

gous to marginal cost (and marginal utility and marginal product, for that matter). Recall that marginal cost is the extra cost resulting from an extra unit of production. Substitute "revenue" for "cost" and "sales" for "production" in the previous sentence, and what do you get? A perfectly acceptable definition of marginal revenue.

Marginal revenue will always be less than price if the firm's demand curve is downward-sloping (as it is under monopoly and other market structures that are not perfectly competitive). In Table 11.1, the extra revenue from the second unit of output is $80 whereas the price of this unit is $90. *The basic reason is that the firm must reduce the price of all units of output, not just the extra unit, in order to sell the extra unit.* Thus, in Table 11.1, the extra revenue from the second unit of output is $80 because, while the price of the second unit is $90, the price of the first unit must be reduced by $10 in order to sell the second unit. Thus the extra revenue (that is, marginal revenue) from selling the second unit of output is $90—$10, or $80, which is less than the price of the second unit.

Similarly, the marginal revenue from selling the third unit of output ($60, according to Table 11.1) is less than the price at which the third unit can be sold ($80, according to Table 11.1). Why? Because, to sell the third unit of output, the price of the first two units of output must be reduced by $10 each (that is, from $90 to $80). Thus the extra revenue (that is, marginal revenue) from selling the third unit is not $80, but $80 less the $20 reduction in the amount received for the first two units.

Price and Output: The Short Run

We are now in a position to determine how output and price behave under monopoly. If the monopolist is free to maximize its profits, it will choose the price and output rate at which the difference between total revenue and total cost is greatest. Suppose that the firm's costs are as shown in Table 11.2 and that the demand curve it faces is as shown in Table 11.1. Based on the data in these two tables, the firm can calculate the profit that it will make at each output rate. To do so, it subtracts its total cost from its total

Table 11.2

COSTS OF A MONOPOLIST

Quantity	Total variable cost	Total fixed cost	Total cost	Marginal cost
		(dollars)		
0	0	100	100	
1	40	100	140	40
2	70	100	170	30
3	110	100	210	40
4	150	100	250	40
5	200	100	300	50
6	260	100	360	60
7	350	100	450	90
8	450	100	550	100

Figure 11.3

Total Revenue, Cost, and Profit of Monopolist *The output rate that will maximize the firm's profit is between 3 and 4 units per day. At this output rate, profit (which equals the vertical distance between the total revenue and total cost curves) is over $30 per day. Based on the demand curve for its product (shown in Table 11.1), the firm must set a price of between $70 and $80 to sell between 3 and 4 units per day.*

Table 11.3

PROFITS OF A MONOPOLIST

Quantity	Total revenue	Total cost	Total profit
	(dollars)		
1	100	140	−40
2	180	170	10
3	240	210	30
4	280	250	30
5	300	300	0
6	300	360	−60
7	280	450	−170
8	240	550	−310

Table 11.4

MARGINAL COST AND MARGINAL REVENUE OF A MONOPOLIST

Quantity	Total profit	Marginal cost	Marginal revenue
	(dollars)		
1	−40	30	80
2	10	40	60
3	30	40	40
4	30	50	20
5	0	60	0
6	−60	90	−20
7	−170	100	−40
8	−310		

revenue, as shown in Table 11.3. What output rate will maximize the firm's profit? According to Table 11.3, profit *rises* as its output rate increases from 1 to 3 units per day, and profit *falls* as its output rate increases from 4 to 8 units per day. Thus the *maximum* profit is achieved at an output rate between 3 and 4 units per day.[3] (Without more detailed data, one cannot tell precisely where the maximum occurs, but this is close enough for present purposes.) Figure 11.3 shows the same thing graphically.

What price will the monopolist charge? To maximize its profit, it must charge the price that results in its selling the profit-maximizing output, which in this case is between 3 and 4 units per day. Thus, according to Table 11.1, it must charge between $70 and $80 per unit. Why? Because if it charges $70, it will sell 4 units per day; and if it charges $80, it will sell 3 units per day. Consequently, to sell the profit-maximizing output of between 3 and 4 units per day, it must charge a price of between $70 and $80 per unit.

THE GOLDEN RULE OF OUTPUT DETERMINATION

In Chapter 10, we set forth the Golden Rule of Output Determination for a perfectly competitive firm. We can now formulate a Golden Rule of Output Determination for a monopolist: *set the output rate at the point where marginal revenue equals marginal cost.* Table 11.4 and Figure 11.4 show that this rule results in a maximum profit in this example. It is evident from Table 11.4 that marginal revenue equals marginal cost at the profit-maximizing output of between 3 and 4 units per day. Figure 11.4 shows the same thing graphically.

Why is this rule generally a necessary condition for profit maximiza-

---

[3] This assumes that the output rate can vary continuously and that there is a single maximum. These are innocuous assumptions.

tion? At any output rate at which marginal revenue *exceeds* marginal cost, profit can be increased by *increasing* output, since the extra revenue will exceed the extra cost. At any output rate at which marginal revenue is *less than* marginal cost, profit can be increased by *reducing* output, since the decrease in cost will exceed the decrease in revenue. Thus, since profit will *not* be a maximum when marginal revenue exceeds marginal cost or falls short of marginal cost, *it must be a maximum only when marginal revenue equals marginal cost.*

THE MONOPOLIST'S EQUILIBRIUM POSITION

Figure 11.5 shows the equilibrium position of a monopolist in the short run. Short-run equilibrium will occur at the output, *OQ,* where the marginal cost curve intersects the marginal revenue curve (the curve that shows the firm's marginal revenue at each output level). And if the monopolist is to sell *OQ* units per period of time, the demand curve shows that it must set a price of *OP.* Thus the equilibrium output and price are *OQ* and *OP,* respectively.

It is interesting to compare the Golden Rule of Output Determination for a monopolist (set the output rate at the point where marginal revenue equals marginal cost) with that for a perfectly competitive firm (set the output rate at the point where price equals marginal cost). The latter is really the same as the former because, *for a perfectly competitive firm, price equals marginal revenue.* Since the perfectly competitive firm can sell all it wants at the market price, each additional unit sold increases the firm's total revenue by the amount of the price. Thus, *for both the monopolist and the perfectly competitive firm, profits are maximized by setting the output rate at the point where marginal revenue equals marginal cost.*

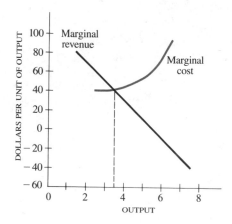

Figure 11.4

Marginal Cost and Marginal Revenue of Monopolist *At the profit-maximizing output rate of between 3 and 4 units per day, marginal cost (which is $40 between an output rate of 3 and 4 units per period) equals marginal revenue (which also is $40 between an output rate of 3 and 4 units per period). Both marginal cost and marginal revenue are plotted at the midpoints of the ranges of output to which they pertain. (See Figures 9.8 and 11.2.)*

Figure 11.5

Equilibrium Position of Monopolist
The monopolist sets its output rate at OQ, where the marginal revenue curve intersects the marginal cost curve. At this output, price must be OP. And profit per unit of output equals CP, since average cost equals OC.

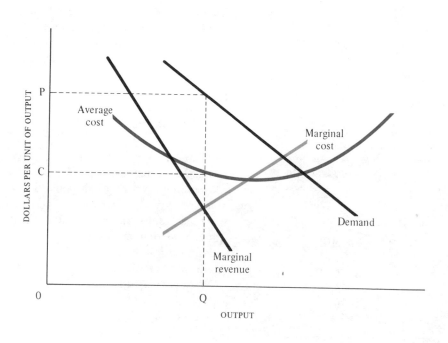

214

WHEN WILL A MONOPOLIST SHUT DOWN?

From the previous chapter, we know that perfectly competitive firms sometimes find it preferable to shut down rather than follow this rule. Is this true for monopolists as well? The answer is yes. *Just as perfectly competitive firms will discontinue production if they will lose more money by producing than by shutting down, so monopolists will do the same thing, and for the same reasons.* In other words, if there is no output such that price exceeds average variable costs, monopolists, like perfect competitors, will discontinue production. This makes sense. If by producing, monopolists incur greater losses than their fixed costs, they will "drop out," i.e., produce nothing.

TWO MISCONCEPTIONS

Finally, note two misconceptions concerning monopoly behavior. First, it is sometimes said that monopolists will charge "as high a price as they can get." This is nonsense. The monopolist in Table 11.1 could charge a higher price than $70 to $80, but to do so would be foolish since it would result in lower profits. Second, it is sometimes said that monopolists will seek to ·maximize their profit per unit of output. This too is nonsense, since monopolists are interested in their total profits and their return on capital, not on the profit per unit of output. Rational monopolists will not sacrifice their total profits to increase their profit per unit of output.

Price and Output: The Long Run

In contrast to the situation under perfect competition, the long-run equilibrium of a monopolistic industry may not be marked by the absence of economic profits. If a monopolist earns a short-run economic profit, it will not be confronted in the long run with competitors, unless the industry ceases to be a monopoly. The entrance of additional firms into the industry is incompatible with the existence of monopoly. Thus the long-run equilibrium of an industry under monopoly may be characterized by economic profits.

On the other hand, if the monopolist incurs a short-run economic loss, it will be forced to look for other, more profitable uses for its resources. One possibility is that the firm's existing plant is not optimal and that it can earn economic profits by appropriate alterations to its scale and characteristics. If so, the firm will make these alterations in the long run and remain in the industry. However, *if there is no scale of plant that will enable the firm to avoid economic losses, it will leave the industry in the long run.* The mere fact of having a monopoly over the production of a certain commodity does not mean that the firm must be profitable. A monopoly over the production of cut-glass spittoons would be unlikely to catapult a firm into financial glory—or even allow it to avoid losses.

To illustrate the long-run behavior of a monopolist, consider the prewar policy of the Aluminum Company of America (Alcoa). Until after World War II, Alcoa was virtually the sole producer of aluminum in the United

States. According to various observers, Alcoa recognized the dangers involved in potential competition, and adopted a policy of keeping its price low enough to ward off potential entrants. Naturally, it wanted to make money—and it did. But it was smart enough to see that, if it charged very high prices, it might encourage other firms to enter the aluminum industry. So it set a price high enough to permit it to make plenty of economic profits, but not so high that it would have to wrestle with competitors. Some other firms with monopoly power think the same way and act accordingly, but by no means all are so clever. On the contrary, some monopolists, like some newlyweds, think the *status quo* will last forever. And just as for newlyweds, sometimes it does, but sometimes it doesn't.

Perfect Competition and Monopoly: A Comparison

At the beginning of the previous chapter, we said that a market's structure would be likely to affect the behavior of the market; in other words, that a market's structure would influence how much was produced and the price that would be set. If we could perform an experiment in which an industry was first operated under conditions of perfect competition and then under conditions of monopoly (assuming that the demand for the industry's product and the industry's cost functions would be the same in either case),[4] we would find that the equilibrium price and output would differ under the two sets of conditions.

HIGHER PRICE AND LESS OUTPUT UNDER MONOPOLY

Specifically, if the product demand curve and the industry's cost functions are the same, *the output of a perfectly competitive industry tends to be greater and the price tends to be lower than under monopoly.* We see this in Figure 11.6, which shows the industry's demand and supply curves, if it is perfectly competitive. Since price and output under perfect competition are given by the intersection of the demand and supply curves, OQ_C is the industry output and OP_C is the price. But what if all of the competitive firms are bought up by a single firm, which operates as a pure monopolist? Under these conditions, what formerly was the industry's supply curve is now the monopolist's marginal cost curve.[5] And what formerly was the industry's demand curve is now the monopolist's demand curve. Since the

---

[4] However, the cost and demand curves need not be the same. For example, the monopolist may spend money on advertising, thus shifting the demand curve. It should be recognized that the assumption that they are the same is stronger than it appears at first glance.

[5] The monopolist will operate the various plants that would be independent under perfect competition as branches of a single firm. The marginal cost curve of a multiplant monopoly is the horizontal sum of the marginal cost curves of the individual plants. (To see why, suppose that a monopoly has two plants, A and B. The total amount that the monopoly can produce at a particular marginal cost is the sum of (1) the amount plant A can produce at this marginal cost, and (2) the amount plant B can produce at this marginal cost.) From the previous chapter, we know that this is also the supply curve of the industry if the plants are operated as separate firms under perfect competition.

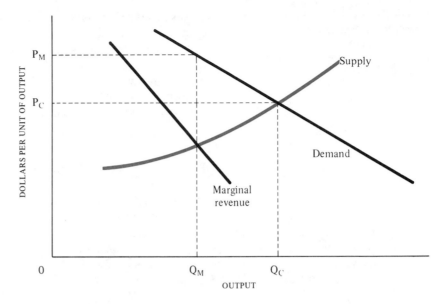

Figure 11.6

Comparison of Long-Run Equilibria:
Perfect Competition and Monopoly
Under perfect competition, OQ_C is the
industry output and OP_C is the price.
Under monopoly, OQ_M is the industry
output, OP_M is the price. Clearly, output
is higher and price is lower under perfect
competition than under monopoly.

monopolist chooses the output where marginal cost equals marginal revenue, the industry output will be OQ_M and the price will be OP_M. Clearly, OQ_M is less than OQ_C, and OP_M is greater than OP_C—which is what we set out to prove.

Of course, all this is theory. But there is plenty of evidence that monopolists restrict output and charge higher prices than under competition. Take the case of tungsten carbide, which sold for $50 per pound until a monopoly was established in 1927 by General Electric. Then the price went to between $225 and $453 per pound, until the monopoly was broken by the antitrust laws in 1945. The price then dropped back to between $27 and $45 per pound.[6] This case was extreme, but by no means unique. Indeed, for centuries people have observed that when monopolies are formed, output tends to be restricted, and price tends to be driven up.

MONOPOLY AND RESOURCE ALLOCATION

Moreover, it has long been felt that the allocation of resources under perfect competition is socially more desirable than under monopoly. Society might be better off if more resources were devoted to producing the monopolized good in Figure 11.6, and if the competitive, not the monopolistic, output were produced. For example, in the *Wealth of Nations,* published about 200 years ago, Adam Smith stressed that when competitive forces are thwarted by "the great engine . . . of monopoly," the tendency for resources to be used "as nearly as possible in the proportion which is most agreeable to the interest of the whole society" is thwarted as well.

Why do many economists believe that the allocation of resources under perfect competition is more socially desirable than that under monopoly? This is not a simple question, and like most hard questions can be answered at various levels of sophistication. Put most simply, many econ-

[6] W. Adams, *The Structure of American Industry,* 5th ed., New York: Macmillan, 1977, p. 485.

omists believe that firms under perfect competition are induced to produce quantities of goods that are more in line with consumer desires, and that firms under perfect competition are induced to use the least costly methods of production. In the following section, we shall indicate in detail why they believe that these things are true. In Chapter 13 (and in Appendix D), we provide a much more complete discussion of the pros and cons of monopoly and competition.

Example 11.1   Another Newspaper for Haverhill?

In Haverhill, Massachusetts, one newspaper had been published for over a century. Then, in the 1950s, another newspaper was founded. In the Haverhill market, suppose that the market demand curve for the town's newspapers, and the demand curve facing each newspaper, were as shown below. Also, each newspaper's cost curves and marginal revenue curve are given below. (Note: In this special case, the firm's demand curve is the same as a monopolist's marginal revenue curve.)

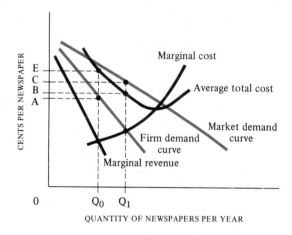

(a) If both firms stay in business, how much will each lose? (b) If only one of them stays in business, can it make a profit? How big a profit? (c) Is this a case of natural monopoly? (d) If entry by one firm may drive the other out of business, is this illegal?

SOLUTION

(a) Each firm will produce OQ_0 newspapers, since this is the output where marginal revenue equals marginal cost. To sell this output, each sets a price of OA, since this is the price on the firm's demand curve corresponding to the sale of OQ_0 newspapers. At an output of OQ_0 newspapers, each firm's average total cost equals OE. Thus it loses $(OE - OA)$ cents per newspaper sold, and since it sells OQ_0 newspapers per year, its total annual loss is $OQ_0 \times (OE - OA)$ cents. (b) The monopolist will produce OQ_1 newspapers, since this is the output where its marginal revenue equals marginal cost. (Recall that in this case the firm's demand curve is the same as the monopolist's marginal revenue curve.) To sell this output, it must charge a price equal to OC cents per newspaper. Since its average total cost is OB cents per newspaper, it makes a profit of $(OC - OB)$ cents per newspaper sold, and its total annual profit is $OQ_1 \times (OC - OB)$ cents. (c) Yes. (d) This question was taken to court by these newspapers. The decision was that it was not illegal.

Test Yourself

1. If you were the president of a firm that has a monopoly on a certain product, would you choose an output level where demand for the product was price inelastic? Explain.

2. Suppose that a monopolist's demand curve is as follows:

Quantity demanded (per year)	Price (dollars)
8	1,000
7	2,000
6	3,000
5	4,000
4	5,000
3	6,000
2	7,000
1	8,000

Plot the firm's marginal revenue curve.

3. Suppose that the monopolist in Question 2 has fixed costs of $10,000 and an average variable cost of $4,000. The average variable cost is the same for outputs of 1 to 10 units per year. What output rate will the firm choose? What price will it set?

4. Plot the marginal cost curve of the firm in Question 3. Where does this curve intersect the marginal revenue curve you drew in Question 2?

5. Suppose that the firm in Question 3 experienced a 50 percent increase in both its fixed and average variable costs. If the demand curve in Question 2 remains valid, what effect will this cost increase have on the output rate and price that the firm will choose?

The Case Against Monopoly

Many people oppose monopolies on the grounds that they "gouge" the consumers by charging a higher price than would otherwise exist—a price that can be sustained only because monopolists artificially limit the supply. In other words, these people claim that monopolists reap higher profits than would be possible under perfect competition and that these profits are at the expense of consumers, who pay higher prices than under perfect competition. Is their claim accurate? As we have just seen, a monopolist will reap higher profits than under perfect competition and consumers will pay higher prices under monopoly than under perfect competition. But is this bad?

To the extent that the monopolist is rich and the consumers are poor, we are likely to answer yes. Also, to the extent that the monopolist is less deserving than the consumers, we are likely to answer the same thing. But suppose the monopolist is a selfless philanthropist who gives to the poor. Is monopoly still socially undesirable? The answer remains yes, because *monopoly imposes a burden on society by misallocating resources. In the presence of monopoly, the price system cannot be relied on to direct the allocation of resources to their most efficient use.*

THE MISALLOCATION OF RESOURCES

To see more precisely how monopoly interferes with the proper functioning of the price system, suppose that all industries other than the shoe industry are perfectly competitive. The shoe industry, however, has been monopolized. How does this cause a misallocation of resources? Under fairly general circumstances, a good's price can be taken as a measure of the social value of an extra unit of the good. Thus, if the price of a pair of socks is $1, the value to the consumer of an extra pair of socks can be taken to be $1. Moreover, under fairly general circumstances, a good's marginal cost can be taken as a measure of the cost to society of an extra unit of the good. Thus, if the marginal cost of a pair of shoes is $30, the cost to society of producing an extra pair of shoes can be taken to be $30.

In perfectly competitive industries, price is set equal to marginal cost, as we saw in Chapter 10. Thus each of the competitive industries produces up to the point where the social value of an extra unit of the good (which equals price) is set equal to the cost to society of producing an extra unit of the good (which equals marginal cost). This is the amount each of these industries should produce—the output rate that will result in an optimal allocation of resources.

WHY IS THE COMPETITIVE OUTPUT OPTIMAL?

To see that this is the optimal output rate, consider what happens when an industry produces up to the point where the social value of an extra unit of the good is *more* than the cost to society of producing an extra unit. This isn't the socially optimal output rate because a one-unit increase in the output rate will increase the social value of output by more than the social cost of production, which means that it will increase social welfare. Thus, since a one-unit increase in the output rate will increase social welfare, the existing output rate cannot be optimal. (Recall Example 10.2.)

Next, consider what happens when an industry produces up to the point where the social value of an extra unit of the good is *less* than the cost to society of producing the extra unit. This isn't the socially optimal output rate because a one-unit decrease in the output rate will decrease the social value of output by less than the social cost of production, which means that it will increase social welfare. Thus, since a one-unit decrease in the output rate will increase social welfare, the existing output rate cannot be optimal.

Putting together the results of the previous two paragraphs, it follows that the socially optimal output rate must be at the point where the social value of an extra unit of the good *equals* the social cost of producing an extra unit of the good. Why? Because if the output rate is not optimal when the social value of an extra unit of the good exceeds or falls short of the cost to society of producing the extra unit, it must be optimal only when the two are equal.

THE MONOPOLIST PRODUCES TOO LITTLE

Now let's return to the shoe industry—the sole monopolist.[7] Is the shoe industry producing the optimal amount of shoes? The answer is no. Like any monopolist, it produces at the point where marginal revenue equals marginal cost. Thus, since marginal revenue is *less* than price (as was proved above), the monopolist produces at a point where price is *greater* than marginal cost. Consequently, *the monopolistic industry produces at a point where the social value of an extra unit of the good (which equals price) is greater than the cost to society of producing the extra unit (which equals marginal cost).* As we saw in a previous paragraph, this means that the

---

[7] Are puns really the lowest form of humor?

Basic Idea #22: Under perfect competition, the social value of an extra unit of the good (which equals price) is set equal to the cost to society of producing an extra unit of the good (which equals marginal cost). Thus economists often argue that perfect competition results in an optimal allocation of resources. In contrast, monopoly results in a misallocation of resources since too little is produced of the monopolized good.

monopolist's output rate is too small. A one-unit increase in the output of shoes will increase the social value of output by more than the social cost of production. (The situation is similar to that in Example 10.2 when 75 million apples are produced.)

Here lies the economist's principal complaint against monopoly: it results in a misallocation of resources. Too little is produced of the monopolized good. Society is less well off—in terms of its own tastes and potentialities—than it could be. The price system, which would not lead to, or tolerate, such waste if all industries were perfectly competitive, is not allowed to perform as it should. (These inefficiencies caused by monopoly are described further and in more detail in Appendix D.)

INCOME DISTRIBUTION, EFFICIENCY, AND TECHNOLOGICAL CHANGE

Misallocation of resources is only part of the economist's brief against monopoly. As we have already pointed out, *monopoly redistributes income in favor of the monopolists.* In other words, monopolists can fatten their own purse by restricting their output and raising their price. Admittedly, there is no scientific way to prove that monopolists are less deserving than the rest of the population, but it is also pretty difficult to see why they are more deserving.

In addition, *since monopolists do not have to face direct competition, they are likely to be less diligent in controlling costs and in using resources efficiently.* As Sir John Hicks put it, "The best of all monopoly profits is a quiet life."[8] Certainly we all dream at times of being able to take life easy. It would be strange if monopolists, having succeeded in insulating themselves from direct competition, did not take advantage of the opportunity—not open to firms in perfectly competitive markets—to relax a bit and worry less about pinching pennies. For this reason, economists fear that, to use Adam Smith's pungent phrase, "Monopoly . . . is a great enemy to good management."

Further, *it is often claimed that monopolists are slow to innovate and adopt new techniques and products.* This lethargy stems from the monopolist's freedom from direct competition. Innovation tends to be disruptive, while old ways, like old shoes, tend to be comfortable. The monopolist may be inclined, therefore, to stick with "time-honored" practices. Without question, competition is an important spur to innovation and to the rapid diffusion of innovations. But there are well-known arguments on the other side as well. Some economists argue that substantial monopoly power promotes innovation and technological change. Much more will be said on this score in Chapter 13.

Public Regulation of Monopoly

One way that society has attempted to reduce the harmful effects of monopoly is through *public regulation.* Suppose that the long-run cost curve in a particular industry is such that competition is not feasible. In such a case, society may permit a monopoly to be established. But a commission

[8] J. Hicks, "Annual Survey of Economic Theory: The Theory of Monopoly," *Econometrica*, 1935.

Figure 11.7

Regulation of Monopoly *The price
established by a commission might be
OP, where the demand curve intersects
the average total cost curve. (Costs here
include what the commission regards as a
fair profit per unit of output.) In the
absence of regulation, the monopolist
would set a price of OP$_M$ (because it
would set its output at the point where
marginal revenue equals marginal cost).
Since OP is less than OP$_M$, regulation
has reduced price in this instance, but not
to the point where price equals marginal
cost (as in perfect competition). For price
to equal marginal cost, price would have
to equal OP$_u$. (For a discussion of
marginal-cost pricing, see the Appendix
to this chapter.)*

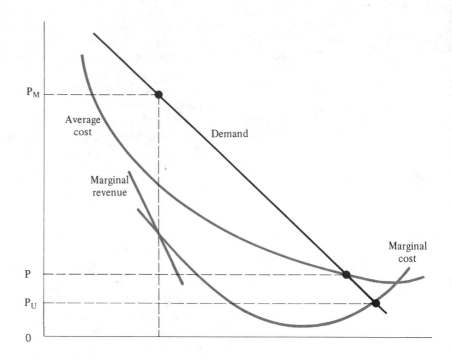

or some other public body is also established to regulate the monopoly's
behavior. Among the many such regulatory commissions in the United
States are the Federal Energy Regulatory Commission, the Federal Communications Commission, and the Interstate Commerce Commission.
They regulate the behavior of firms with monopoly power in the electric
power, communications, transportation, and other industries. These industries are big as well as important, taking in about 10 percent of the national
output. Thus we need to know how these commissions operate and make
decisions on prices and other matters.

*Regulatory commissions often set the price—or the maximum price—at the
level at which it equals average total cost, including a "fair" rate of return on
the firm's investment.* In Figure 11.7, the price would be established by the
commission at *OP*, where the demand curve intersects the average total
cost curve (which includes what the commission regards as a fair profit per
unit of output). Needless to say, there has been considerable controversy
over what constitutes a fair rate of return. Frequently, commissions have
settled on 8 to 10 percent. In addition, there has been a good deal of
controversy over what should be included in the company's "investment"
on which the fair rate of return is to be earned. A company's assets can be
valued at **historical cost** or at **reproduction cost**—at what the company paid
for them or at what it would cost to replace them. If the price level does
not change much, these two approaches yield much the same answer. But
if prices are rising—as they have been during most of the past 40 years—
replacement cost will be greater than historical cost, with the result that
the company will be allowed higher profits and rates if replacement cost is
used. Most commissions now use historical cost.[9]

[9] The use of marginal-cost pricing by regulated industries is discussed in the Appendix to
this chapter.

Does Regulation Affect Prices?

The regulatory commissions and the principles they use have become extremely controversial. *Many observers feel that the commissions are lax, and that they tend to be captured by the industries they are supposed to regulate.* Regulated industries, recognizing the power of such commissions, invest considerable time and money in attempts to influence the commissions. The public, on the other hand, often has only a foggy idea of what the commissions are doing, and of whether or not it is in the public interest. According to some critics like Ralph Nader, "Nobody seriously challenges the fact that the regulatory agencies have made an accommodation with the businesses they are supposed to regulate—and they've done so at the expense of the public." For these and other reasons, some economists believe that regulation has little effect on prices.

It is difficult to isolate and measure the effects of regulation on the average level of prices. Some well-known economists have conducted studies which suggest that regulation has made little or no difference in this regard. Nobel laureate George Stigler and Claire Friedland of the University of Chicago compared the levels of rates charged for electricity by regulated and unregulated electric power companies. They found that there was no significant difference between the average rates charged by the two sets of firms.[10] Other economists challenge Stigler's and Friedland's interpretation of their factual findings, and much more research on this topic is needed. Nonetheless, it seems fair to conclude that, although the simple model of the regulatory process presented in previous sections would predict that regulated prices would be lower, on the average, than unregulated prices (of the same item), the evidence in support of this prediction is much weaker than might be supposed.

Whether or not regulation has a significant effect on the *average* level of prices, it certainly has an effect on *particular* prices charged by regulated firms. In some cases, it has reduced the price of a product. There seems to be general agreement that the Federal Energy Regulatory Commission kept the price of natural gas (in interstate commerce) below what this price would have been during the 1970s in the absence of regulation. In other cases, it has increased the price of a product. Some observers believe that prior to the deregulation of the airlines in the late 1970s, the Civil Aeronautics Board (CAB) increased the airplane fare between New York and Washington. As evidence of this, they compared at that time this fare with the fare from San Francisco to Los Angeles, which was not subject to CAB regulation since the trip was entirely within California. Although the distance from San Francisco to Los Angeles is almost twice as great as that from New York to Washington, the fare from San Francisco to Los Angeles was less than that from New York to Washington.

[10] G. Stigler and C. Friedland, "What Can Regulators Regulate? The Case of Electricity," *The Journal of Law and Economics,* 1962. For another point of view, see H. Trebing, "The Chicago School versus Public Utility Regulation," *Journal of Economic Issues,* March 1976.

Example 11.2   Price Discrimination in Dentistry

An isolated town of 5,000 inhabitants in the Rocky Mountains is looking for a dentist. To simplify matters, we divide the town's inhabitants into two categories: the rich and the poor. The demand curve for dental care among each type of inhabitant is shown below. Adding the two demand curves horizontally, we find that the total demand curve for dental care is *DAB*.

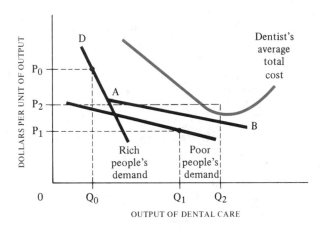

(a) If a dentist charges the same price to all inhabitants (rich or poor), can the dentist cover his or her average total costs? (b) If the dentist charges the rich a higher price than the poor, can the dentist cover his or her average total costs? (c) *Price discrimination* occurs when a producer sells the same commodity or service at more than one price. Thus the dentist in (b) is engaging in price discrimination. In fact, do physicians and dentists engage in price discrimination? (d) In some instances, is it true that a good or service cannot be produced without price discrimination? (e) Is this always the case?

SOLUTION

(a) No. The total demand curve lies below the average total cost curve. Thus, regardless of what output the dentist chooses, price would be less than average total cost. (b) Yes. If the dentist charges rich people a price of OP_0, he or she can sell OQ_0 units of dental care to them. If he or she charges poor people a price of OP_1, he or she can sell OQ_1 units of dental care to them. Thus the total output, which equals OQ_2, brings an average price of OP_2, which is greater than average total cost. (c) Yes. (d) Yes, the situation depicted in the graph is an example. Without price discrimination, this dentist could not cover his or her costs. (e) No. It is important to note that price discrimination frequently occurs in situations where the good or service could be produced without it. Price discrimination is used in these situations to increase the profits of the producer. (From the point of view of society as a whole, price discrimination frequently is objectionable because it violates the conditions for optimal resource allocation described in Appendix D.)

Increase of Prices and Reduction of Competition by Regulators

As pointed out in the previous section, regulatory commissions, far from reducing prices, sometimes actually increase them. This is because *many commissions have been concerned with the regulation of competition as much as with the regulation of monopoly.* Consider the Interstate Commerce Commission (ICC), created in 1887 to regulate the railroads, which had considerable monopoly power at that time. With the advent of the motor truck and the phenomenal growth of highways, the railroads became increasingly vulnerable to competition from trucks; and there were fears that, if the railroads continued to be regulated but the trucks were not regulated, the railroads would be hurt badly by this new competition. In 1935, the ICC and the railroads were successful in bringing most trucking under the ICC's regulation, over the objection of some truckers. Thus, despite the fact that trucking, if unregulated, would be a highly competitive industry, it was brought under the regulatory umbrella.

EFFECTS ON TRUCKING

The results, according to most accounts, were pretty dismal. In interstate trucking, firms were allowed to agree upon rates in secret, through rate-bureau negotiations. These rates were seldom challenged by the ICC except in cases of across-the-board increases. Because of this system, rates tended to be established so as to cover the costs of the less efficient firms, with the consequence that consumers paid higher prices than under a competitive market structure. In markets where only one trucking firm was certificated, this system of rate setting allowed the firm to earn excess profits by offering poorer service (at the regulated price) than if other firms were permitted to compete. In markets where two or more trucking firms were certificated, there were potential excess profits for the more efficient truckers because the rates were set to cover the costs of the less efficient truckers. But these potential excess profits tended to be eliminated by service competition; that is, the firms provided more frequent schedules or larger trucks than otherwise would be the case. This sort of nonprice competition tended to create excess capacity which had a lower value to the shipper than the extra price paid.

Many economists argued that, to help solve the problem of excess capacity in markets with more than one trucking firm and the problem of poor service in markets with only one trucking firm, the ICC should allow entry into the trucking industry and encourage price competition among trucking firms. Why would freer entry and more price competition reduce excess capacity? Because new trucking firms would enter and force rates downward if existing truckers did not reduce their rates. Why would freer entry and more price competition promote better service in markets with only one trucking firm? Because the excess profits earned by the monopolist would attract new firms that would try to take away some of the monopolist's business by offering better service. The monopolist would have to improve its service and/or lower its rates, unless it wanted to lose much of its share of the market.

In 1980, President Carter, responding in part to arguments of this sort, signed a bill to deregulate the trucking industry. The law loosens—to an extent that is open to interpretation—the ICC's regulatory controls over the industry, but does not remove them completely. By 1985, there was considerable evidence of price competition among truckers. Between 1978 and 1985, thousands of small carriers entered the market, and battled with established firms (and among themselves) for a share of the market. The number of business failures in trucking increased considerably. In January 1985 one trucking executive reported: "There's a rate war going on."

EFFECTS ON RAILROADS

The ICC was established originally to regulate railroads, not trucks. How did its policies work in the railroad industry? Unfortunately, there were serious problems here too. With the growth of the trucking industry, many low-density rail lines were used less and less, until now they are no longer economical to operate. Nonetheless, the railroads were prevented by regulatory requirements from discontinuing such services as quickly as would seem warranted. Because of the losses incurred on unprofitable lines, the overall financial position of many railroads was impaired, with the result that needed maintenance and capital investments had to be reduced.

In 1980, President Carter signed a bill to deregulate the railroads, which hoped that greater freedom to change rates would enable them to earn a profit. Opponents of deregulation feared that the railroads would raise the price of hauling coal (and other bulk commodities) very sharply. A compromise was reached which permitted a relaxation of the ICC's rate-approval authority on a prearranged schedule. The purpose was to provide the railroads with significant freedom to alter rates while trying to give the customers of the railroads some protection against abuse of this freedom.

Effects of Regulation on Efficiency

As previous chapters have stressed, competitive markets provide considerable incentives for a firm to increase its efficiency. Firms that are able to push their costs below those of their competitors reap higher profits than their competitors. As a simple illustration, suppose that firms A and B both have contracts to produce 100 airplanes, and that the price they will get for each airplane is $25,000. Firm A's management, which is diligent, imaginative, and innovative, gets the cost per airplane down to $10,000, and thus makes a healthy profit of $1,500,000. Firm B's management which is lazy, unimaginative, and dull, lets the cost per airplane rise to $30,000, and thus loses $500,000. Clearly, firm A is rewarded for its good performance, while firm B is penalized for its poor performance.

NO INCENTIVE FOR EFFICIENCY

One of the primary purposes of regulators is to prevent a monopoly from earning excessive profits. The firm is allowed only a "fair" rate of return on its investment. One problem with this arrangement is that the firm is guaranteed this rate of return, regardless of how well it performs. If the regulators decide that the Sleepy Hollow Electric and Gas Company should receive a 10 percent rate of return on its investment, this is the rate of return it will receive regardless of whether the Sleepy Hollow Electric and Gas Company is managed well or poorly. Why is this a problem? Because unlike the competitive firms discussed in the previous paragraph, there is no incentive for the firm to increase its efficiency.

The available evidence indicates that, if a firm is guaranteed a fixed amount of profit for a job (regardless of how efficiently it does this job), the firm will tend to be less efficient than if the amount of profit it receives is directly related to its efficiency. The Department of Defense has found that, when it bought goods or services on a cost-plus-fixed-fee basis, these goods and services were not produced as cheaply as when it bought them in a competitive market. This is reasonable. It takes time, energy, and lots of trouble to make a firm more efficient. Why should a firm's managers bother to induce added efficiency if the firm's profits are the same, regardless of how efficient or inefficient it is?

REGULATORY LAG AND INCENTIVE FOR EFFICIENCY

The regulatory process is characterized by long delays. In many regulated industries, a proposed rate increase or decrease may be under consideration for months before a decision is made by the commission. In cases where such a price change is strongly contested, it may take years for the required hearings to occur before the commission and for appeals to be made subsequently to the courts. Such a delay between a proposed price change and its ultimate disposition is called a *regulatory lag.* Long regulatory lags are often criticized by those who would like the regulatory process to adapt more quickly to changing conditions and to provide more timely decisions. But one advantage of regulatory lags is that they result in some rewards for efficiency and penalties for inefficiency.

To see why this is so, consider a regulated company whose price is set so that the firm can earn a rate of return of 10 percent (which is what the commission regards as a "fair" rate of return). The firm develops and introduces some improved manufacturing processes which reduce the firm's costs, thus allowing it to earn 13 percent. If it takes 18 months for the commission to review the prices it approved before and to modify them to take account of the new (lower) cost levels, the firm earns a higher rate of return (13 percent rather than 10 percent) during these 18 months than if it had not developed and introduced the improved manufacturing processes. This is a reward for efficiency.

On the other hand, suppose that this firm makes several serious blunders which result in a substantial increase in its costs, the result being that the firm earns only a rate of return of 6 percent. If once again it takes 18 months for the commission to review the prices it set before and to modify them to take account of the changes in firms' cost levels, this firm earns a lower rate of return (6 percent rather than 10 percent) during these 18 months than if it had not made these blunders. This is a penalty for inefficiency.

Although regulatory lag does restore some of the incentives for efficiency (and some of the penalties for inefficiency), it would be a mistake to believe that it results in as strong a set of incentives as does competitive markets. One of the basic problems with regulation is that, *if a regulatory commission prevents a firm from earning higher-than-average profits, there may be relatively little incentive for the firm to increase its efficiency and innovate.*

Test Yourself

1. Compare the long-run equilibrium of a perfectly competitive industry with that which would occur if all the firms were to be merged in a single monopolistic firm. Is there any reason for society to prefer one equilibrium over the other?

2. "No firm has a monopoly since every good competes to some extent with every other good. Thus there is no good that is completely sealed off from competition." Comment and evaluate.

3. "Firms with relatively high profits are bound to be monopolists. If they were competitive, the entry of new firms into the industry would drive economic profits down to zero. Thus the easiest and best way to determine whether a firm is a monopolist is to look at its profits." Comment and evaluate.

4. According to the Council of Economic Advisers, "although exit from an industry via bankruptcy is a normal characteristic of efficient competitive markets, the bankruptcy of a regulated firm tends to be viewed as a sign of regulatory failure." What problems are likely to result from this attitude?

Summary

1. A pure monopoly is a market with one, and only one, seller. Monopolies may occur because of patents, control over basic inputs, and government action, as well as decreasing average costs up to the point where the market is satisfied.

2. If average costs reach their minimum at an output rate large enough to satisfy the entire market, perfect competition cannot be maintained; and the public often insists that the industry (a natural monopoly) be regulated by the government.

3. Since the monopolist is the only seller of the product, the demand curve facing the monopolist is the market demand curve, which slopes downward (rather than being horizontal as in perfect competition).

4. The unregulated monopolist will maximize profit by choosing the output where marginal cost equals marginal revenue, marginal revenue being defined as the addition to total revenue attributable to the addition of one unit to sales. This rule for output determination also holds under perfect competition, since price equals marginal revenue under perfect competition.

5. If monopolists cannot prevent losses from exceeding fixed costs, they, like perfect competitors, will discontinue production. In contrast to the case in perfect competition, the long-run equilibrium of a monopolistic industry may not be marked by the absence of economic profits.

6. The output of a monopoly tends to be smaller and the price tends to be higher than under perfect competition. Economists tend to believe that society would be better off if more resources were devoted to the production of the good than under monopoly, the competitive output often being regarded as best.

7. One way that society has attempted to reduce the harmful effects of monopoly is through public regulation. Commissions often set price at the level at which it equals average total cost, including a "fair rate of return" on the firm's investment.

8. There has been a great deal of controversy over the practices of the regulatory commissions. Many economists have viewed them as lax or ill-conceived. In many areas, like transportation, they have been concerned as much with the regulation of competition as with the regulation of monopoly; and, according to many studies, their decisions have resulted in substantial costs and inefficiencies.

9. Regulatory commissions try to prevent a monopoly from earning excessive profits; the firm is allowed only a "fair rate of return" on its investment. One difficulty with this arrangement is that, since the firm is guaranteed this rate of return (regardless of how well or poorly it performs), there is no incentive for the firm to increase its efficiency. Although regulatory lag results in some incentives of this sort, they often are relatively weak.

10. In some industries (like airlines, trucking, and railroads), the late 1970s and early 1980s saw a strong movement toward deregulation. This has been one of the most significant recent developments in this area.

Concepts for Review

Monopoly	**Marginal revenue**	**Reproduction cost**
Natural monopoly	**Regulation**	**Regulatory lag**
Total revenue	**Historical cost**	

Appendix: Marginal Cost Pricing

In this and the previous chapter, we indicated that, under the assumptions made here, the conditions for optimal resource allocation are satisfied under perfect competition. (See Appendix D for a more detailed discussion of this point.) Economists interested in the functioning of planned, or socialist, economies have pointed out that a price system also could be used to increase social welfare in such economies. Also, it has been argued that government-owned enterprises and public utilities in capitalist economies should set price equal to marginal cost, just as perfectly competitive firms do. In this Appendix, we discuss marginal cost pricing, and how it might be used by government-owned or regulated monopolists, as well as by socialist economies.

SOCIALIST ECONOMIES

According to economists like Abba Lerner[11] of Florida State University, rational economic organization could be achieved in a socialist economy that is decentralized, as well as under perfect competition. The socialist government might solve the system of equations that is solved automatically in a perfectly competitive economy, and obtain the prices that would prevail under perfect competition. Then the government might publish this price list, together with instructions for consumers to maximize their satisfaction and for producers to maximize profit. (Of course, the wording of the instructions to consumers might be a bit less heavy-handed than "Maximize your satisfaction!")

Under a socialist system of this sort, the government does not have to become involved in the intricate and detailed business of setting production targets for each plant. It need only compute the proper set of prices. In following the rules to maximize "profits," plant managers will choose the proper production levels. Thus decentralized decision making, rather than detailed centralized direction, could be used, thus reducing administrative costs and bureaucratic disadvantages, according to Lerner.

GOVERNMENT-OWNED OR REGULATED MONOPOLIES

The prices the government would publish, like those prevailing in a perfectly competitive economy, would equal marginal cost. Many economists have recommended that government-owned enterprises in basically capitalist economies also adopt *marginal cost pricing,* i.e., that they set price equal to marginal cost. Taking the case of a bridge where the marginal cost (the extra cost involved in allowing an additional vehicle to cross) is zero, Harold Hotelling argued in a famous article that the socially optimal price for crossing the bridge is zero, and that its costs should be defrayed by general taxation. If a toll is charged, the conditions for optimal resource use are not met.[12]

Marginal cost pricing has fascinated economists during the 50 years that

[11] Abba Lerner, *The Economics of Control,* New York: Macmillan, 1944.
[12] Harold Hotelling, "The General Welfare in Relation to Problems of Taxation and of Railway and Utility Rates," *Econometrica,* 1938.

have elapsed since Hotelling's article,[13] but there are a number of problems in the application of this idea. One of the most important is that if the firm's average costs decrease with increases in its scale of output (as is frequently the case in public utilities), it follows from the discussion in Chapter 9 that marginal cost must be less than average cost, with the consequence that the firm will not cover its costs if price is set equal to marginal cost.[14] This means that marginal cost pricing must be accompanied by some form of subsidy if the firm is to stay in operation—and the collection of the funds required for the payment of the subsidy may also violate the conditions for optimal resource allocation. This subsidy also means that there is a change in the income distribution favoring users of the firm's output and penalizing nonusers.

THE COMMON SENSE OF MARGINAL COST PRICING

To illustrate the reasoning that underlies marginal cost pricing, consider the case of water supplies. What determines the level at which the price of water should be set?

> Suppose that at a certain moment in time [consumers are willing to pay] $30 per unit. Then, if the community as a whole can acquire and transport another unit of water for, say, $20, it would clearly be desirable to do so; in fact, any of the individual customers to whom the unit of water is worth $30 would be happy to pay the $20 cost, and none of the other members of the community would be made worse off thereby. We may say that, on efficiency grounds, additional units should be made available so long as any members of the community are willing to pay the additional or marginal costs incurred.... So the ... rule is to make the price equal to marginal cost and equal for all customers.[15]

Unfortunately, it seems that water-pricing practices do not often conform to this rule. Some types of water users are commonly charged lower prices than other types of water users, although the marginal cost of the water is the same. According to a study carried out at the RAND Corporation,

> In Los Angeles, for example, there is an exceptionally low rate for irrigation use. Domestic, commercial, and industrial services are not distinguished as such, but they are differentially affected by the promotional volume rates. More serious, because much more common, is the system of block rates, with reductions [in price] for larger quantities used.... [This system leads] to wasteful use of water by large users, since small users would value the same marginal unit of water more highly if delivered to them.... The customer paying the lower price will on the margin be utilizing water for less valuable purposes than it could serve if transferred to the customer paying the higher price.

[13] See J. Nelson, *Marginal Cost Pricing in Practice,* Englewood Cliffs, N.J.: Prentice-Hall, 1964.

[14] Recall from Chapter 9 that an increase in output results in a reduction in average cost only when marginal cost is less than average cost. Since the firm's receipts will cover its costs only if price is at least equal to average cost, it follows that, under these circumstances, the firm cannot cover its costs if it sets price equal to marginal cost.

[15] Hirshleifer, Milliman, and DeHaven, *Water Supply,* Chicago: University of Chicago Press, 1969, pp. 40–41.

CHAPTER 12

Monopolistic Competition and Oligopoly

The industries encountered in the real world are seldom perfectly competitive or monopolistic. Although perfect competition and monopoly are very useful models that shed much valuable light on the behavior of markets, they are polar cases. Economists have developed other models that portray more realistically the behavior of many modern industries. The model of monopolistic competition helps to explain market behavior in such industries as retail drug stores and barber shops, while the model of oligopoly pertains to industries like steel, oil, and automobiles.

In this chapter, we examine how resources are allocated and prices are set under monopolistic competition and oligopoly. We also compare the behavior of monopolistically competitive and oligopolistic markets with the behavior of perfectly competitive and monopolistic markets. The results are of considerable significance, both because they give us a better understanding of how many markets work, and because they provide valuable information on the social desirability of monopolistic competition and oligopoly.

Monopolistic Competition and Oligopoly: Their Major Characteristics

To begin with, we must recall what monopolistic competition and oligopoly are. *Monopolistic competition occurs where there are many sellers (as in perfect competition) but where there is product differentiation. In other words, the firms' products are not the same.* It does not matter whether the differences among products are real or imagined. What is important is that the consumer regards the products as different.

Oligopoly occurs in markets where there are few sellers. There are two types of oligopolies, one where all sellers produce an identical product, and one where the sellers produce somewhat different products. Examples of the first type—*pure oligopoly*—are the markets for steel, cement, tin cans, and petroleum. Examples of the second type—*differentiated oligopoly*—are the markets for automobiles and machinery.

In contrast to the extremes of perfect competition and monopoly, monopolistic competition and oligopoly are intermediate cases that include an element of competition and of monopoly—an advantage from the point of view of realism.

Monopolistic Competition

The key feature of monopolistic competition is *product differentiation.* In contrast to perfect competition, where all firms sell an identical product, firms under monopolistic competition sell somewhat different products. Producers differentiate their product from that of other producers. This is the case in many American markets. In many parts of retail trade, producers try to make their product a little different, by altering the product's physical make-up, the services they offer, and other such variables. Other differences—which may be spurious—are based on brand name, image making, advertising claims, etc. In this way, the producers have some monopoly power, but it usually is small, because the products of other firms are very similar.

In perfect competition, the firms included in an industry are easy to determine because they all produce the same product. But if product differentiation exists, it is no longer easy to define an industry, since each firm produces a somewhat different product. Nevertheless, it may be useful to group together firms that produce similar products and call them a *product group.* We can formulate a product group called "toothpaste" or "toilet soap" or "chocolate bars." The process by which we combine firms into product groups is bound to be somewhat arbitrary, since there is no way to decide how close a pair of substitutes must be to belong to the same product group. But it is assumed that meaningful product groups can be established.

Besides product differentiation, other conditions must be met for an industry to qualify as a case of monopolistic competition. First, *there must be a large number of firms in the product group.* In other words, the product must be produced by perhaps 50 to 100 or more firms, with each firm's product a fairly close substitute for the products of the other firms in the product group. Second, *the number of firms in the product group must be large enough so that each firm expects its actions to go unheeded by its rivals and is unimpeded by possible retaliatory moves on their part.* If there is a large number of firms, this condition will normally be met. Third, *entry into the product group must be relatively easy, and there must be no collu-*

sion, such as price fixing or market sharing, among firms in the product group. If there is a large number of firms, collusion generally is difficult, if not impossible.

Price and Output under Monopolistic Competition

Basic Idea #23: Product differentiation is a hallmark of monopolistic competition. If there is product differentiation, each firm's product is somewhat different from that of other firms, either physically or through the image created in the minds of consumers. Thus the demand curve for each firm's output is downward-sloping, not horizontal (as it is under perfect competition).

Under monopolistic competition, what determines how much output a firm will produce, and what price it will charge? If each firm produces a somewhat different product, it follows that the demand curve facing each firm slopes downward to the right. That is, if the firm raises its price slightly it will lose some, but by no means all, of its customers to other firms. And if it lowers its price slightly, it will gain some, but by no means all, of its competitors' customers. This is in contrast to perfect competition, where the demand curve facing each firm is horizontal.

Figure 12.1 shows the short-run equilibrium of a monopolistically competitive firm. The firm in the short run will set its price at OP_0 and its output rate at OQ_0, since this combination of price and output will maximize its profits. We can be sure that this combination of price and output maximizes profit because marginal cost equals marginal revenue at this output rate. Economic profits will be earned because price, OP_0, exceeds average total costs, OC_0, at this output rate.

What will the equilibrium price and output be in the long run? One condition for long-run equilibrium is that each firm be making no economic profits or losses, since entry or exit of firms will occur otherwise—and entry and exit are incompatible with long-run equilibrium. Another condition for long-run equilibrium is that each firm be maximizing its profits. At what price and output will both these conditions be fulfilled?

Figure 12.1

Short-Run Equilibrium: Monopolistic Competition *The firm will set price at OP_0 and its output rate at OQ_0 since marginal cost equals marginal revenue at this output. It will earn a profit of C_0P_0 per unit of output.*

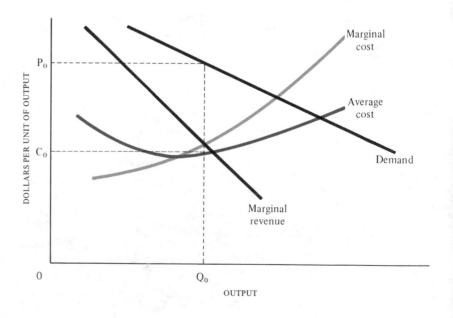

Figure 12.2

Long-Run Equilibrium: Monopolistic Competition *The long-run equilibrium is at a price of* OP$_1$ *and an output of* OQ$_1$. *There are zero profits since long-run average cost equals price. Profits are being maximized since marginal cost equals marginal revenue at this output.*

Figure 12.2 shows that the long-run equilibrium is at a price of OP_1 and an output of OQ_1. The zero-economic-profit condition is met at this combination of price and output since the firm's average cost at this output equals the price, OP_1. And the profit-maximization condition is met since the marginal revenue curve intersects the marginal cost curve at this output rate.

EXCESS CAPACITY

A famous conclusion of the theory of monopolistic competition is that *a firm under this form of market organization will tend to operate with excess capacity.* In other words, the firm will construct a plant smaller than the minimum-cost size of plant and operate it at less than the minimum-cost rate of output. Why? Because, as shown in Figure 12.2, the long-run average cost curve must be tangent in long-run equilibrium to the demand curve. Thus, since the demand curve is *downward-sloping,* the long-run average cost curve must also be *downward-sloping* at the long-run equilibrium output rate. Consequently, the firm's output must be less than OQ_2, the output rate at which long-run average costs are minimized, since the long-run average cost curve slopes downward only at output rates less than OQ_2.

This is a very important conclusion, since it suggests that monopolistically competitive industries will be overcrowded with firms. There will be too many firms (from society's point of view), each of which is smaller than required to minimize its unit costs. For this conclusion, as well as much of the entire theory of monopolistic competition, we are indebted to Edward Chamberlin of Harvard University, whose path-breaking book on the subject first appeared in 1933.[1]

---

[1] E. Chamberlin, *The Theory of Monopolistic Competition,* Cambridge, Mass.: Harvard University Press, 1933.

Edward Chamberlin

Comparisons with Perfect Competition and Monopoly

Market structure is important because it influences market behavior. We need to know how the behavior of a monopolistically competitive industry differs from that of a perfectly competitive industry or a monopoly. Suppose that there exists a magician who can transform an industry's structure by a wave of a wand. (John D. Rockefeller was a real-life magician who transformed the structure of the oil industry in the late 1800s—but he seemed to favor mergers, mixed with some ungentlemanly tactics, over wands.) Suppose that the magician makes an industry monopolistically competitive, rather than perfectly competitive or monopolistic. What difference would it make in the behavior of the industry? Or, to take a less fanciful case, what difference would it make if government action or technological change resulted in such a change in an industry's market structure? It is difficult to say how the industry's behavior would be affected, because output would be heterogeneous in one case and homogeneous in the other, and its cost curves would probably vary with its organization. But many economists seem to believe that differences of the following kind can be expected.

1. The firm under monopolistic competition is likely to produce less, and charge a higher price, than under perfect competition. The demand curve confronting the monopolistic competitor slopes downward to the right. Consequently, as we saw in the previous chapter, marginal revenue must be less than price. Thus, under monopolistic competition, marginal cost must also be less than price, since marginal revenue must equal marginal cost at the firm's profit-maximizing output rate. But if marginal cost is less than price, the firm's output rate must be smaller—and the price higher—than if marginal cost equals price, which is the case under perfect competition. On the other hand, *relative to monopoly, monopolistically competitive firms are likely to have lower profits, greater output, and lower price.* The firms in a product group might obtain positive economic profits if they were to collude and behave as a monopolist. Such an increase in profits resulting from the monopoly would benefit the producers. Consumers would be worse off because of the higher prices and smaller output of goods.

2. As noted in the previous section, *a firm under monopolistic competition may be somewhat inefficient because it tends to operate with excess capacity.* Each firm builds a smaller-than-minimum-cost plant and produces a smaller-than-minimum-cost output. More firms exist than if there were no excess capacity, resulting in some overcrowding of the industry. Inefficiencies of this sort would not be expected under perfect competition. These inefficiencies may not be very great, since the demand curve confronting the monopolistically competitive firm is likely to be highly elastic; and the more elastic it is, the less excess capacity the firm will have. But many observers seem to believe that excess capacity of this sort is a serious problem in many important industries, including textiles.

3. Firms under monopolistic competition will offer a wider variety of styles, brands, and qualities than firms under perfect competition. Moreover, they will spend much more on advertising and other selling expenses than a perfectly competitive firm would. Whether this diversity is worth its cost is hard to say. Some economists are impressed by the apparent waste in monopolistic competition. They think it results in too many firms, too many brands, too much selling effort, and too much spurious product differentiation. But if the differences among products are real and are understood by consumers, the greater variety of alternatives available under monopolistic competition may be very valuable to consumers. The proper evaluation of the social advantages and disadvantages of product differentiation is a problem economists have not solved.

Retailing: A Case Study[2]

To illustrate the case of monopolistic competition, consider retailing in the United States. Each retailer has a certain amount of monopoly power because his location, his product lines, his personality, and his salespeople are somewhat different from those of his competitors. In other words, his product is differentiated. But the extent and strength of his monopoly power is generally quite limited because he faces many competitors reasonably similar to himself in these respects. That is, lots of other firms sell products that are close substitutes for his own product. The goods carried by one drugstore, grocery store, or clothing shop are close substitutes for those carried by another drugstore, grocery store, or clothing shop. Moreover, entry into retail trade tends to be quite easy, as indicated by the fact that firms are continually entering various lines of retailing, and that the capital and skill required for entry are generally rather modest.

All in all, retailing seems to have many of the most important characteristics of monopolistic competition. Assuming that the retail industry can be approximated reasonably well by our model of monopolistic competition, we would expect that there would be some overcrowding of firms, that firms would try hard to differentiate their product through advertising and other selling expenses, and that long-run profits in the industry would tend to be low. Let us see to what extent these conditions do prevail.

There seems to be considerable evidence of overcrowding. More firms exist in retail trade than would be the case if each were operating at a point where unit costs were a minimum. But the extent of this excess capacity may not be very great, since the price elasticity of demand in retailing is normally very high—typically about 5.0, according to Leonard Weiss of the University of Wisconsin. Also, in accord with the model, firms in retail trade spend a great deal on various selling expenses, notably advertising. About one-quarter of the total expenditure on advertising in the United States is spent by retailers. Usually these ads are local and provide a valuable source of information on sales and specials in a particular neighborhood. (It is the exceptional person who does not spend some part of each week scanning the retail ads in a local newspaper.) Retail stores spend a lot on other selling expenses too—attractive décor, free parking, trading stamps, clerks to hover over the customer, and so forth.

[2] For a much more extensive discussion of retailing, see Leonard Weiss, *Case Studies in American Industry,* New York: Wiley, 1967. For further relevant discussion, see W. Shepherd, *The Economics of Industrial Organization,* Englewood Cliffs, N.J.: Prentice-Hall, 1979.

These expenses add to the prices they charge for the products they carry.

The level of profits in retail trade also accords with what theory would lead us to expect. It is low. Except for a few years right after World War II (when there was a relative scarcity of retail outlets), profits seem to have been consistently lower in retailing than in manufacturing. Moreover, this can hardly be attributed to less risk in retailing than in manufacturing, since retailing's bankruptcy rate has been exceptionally high—much higher than in other parts of the nonfarm economy. The facts seem to correspond quite well with the theory's prediction of no economic profits in the industry.[3]

Oligopoly

Oligopoly (domination by a few firms) is a common and important market structure in the United States; many industries, like steel, automobiles, oil, and electrical equipment, are oligopolistic. An example of an oligopolist is IBM, described in Chapter 5. *The key characteristic of oligopoly is interdependence, actual and perceived, among firms.* Each oligopolist formulates its policies with an eye to their effect on its rivals. Since an oligopoly contains a small number of firms, any change in one firm's price or output influences the sales and profits of its competitors. Moreover, since there are only a few firms, each must recognize that changes in its own policies are likely to result in changes in the policies of its rivals as well.

What factors are responsible for oligopoly? First, in some industries, *low production costs cannot be achieved unless a firm is producing an output equal to a substantial portion of the total available market,* with the consequence that the number of firms will tend to be rather small. Second, *there may be economies of scale in sales promotion* in certain industries, and this too may promote oligopoly. Third, entry into some industries may be blocked by *the requirement that a firm build and maintain a large, complicated, and expensive plant, or have access to patents or scarce raw materials.* Only a few firms may be in a position to obtain all these necessary prerequisites for membership in the club.

ECONOMIES OF SCALE

The automobile industry is a good example of the impact of *economies of scale in production.* According to studies made by Joe Bain of the University of California, an automobile plant of minimum efficient size can provide almost 10 percent of the total national market.[4] Thus it simply is not economical to have a great many automobile firms. It might be possible to have a dozen automobile firms rather than the four we currently have without sacrificing productive efficiency, but because of economies of scale, it would not be feasible to have 50 or 100.

The automobile industry is a good example of *economies of scale in sales promotion.* To be effective, advertising must often be carried out on a large

[3] Before leaving the subject of monopolistic competition, it should be recognized that Professor Chamberlin's theory has been subjected to considerable criticism. As a case in point, the definition of the product group is ambiguous. See G. Stigler, *Five Lectures on Economic Problems,* London: Longmans Green, 1949.

[4] J. Bain, *Barriers to New Competition,* Cambridge, Mass.: Harvard University Press, 1956.

scale, the result being that the advertising cost per unit of output decreases with increases in output, at least up to some point. Also, car buyers like to deal with firms with a large, dependable dealer network. Since it takes a lot of money to establish such a network, and since the better dealers are attracted by the more popular brands, the smaller automobile manufacturers are at a substantial disadvantage.

BARRIERS TO ENTRY

In addition, the automobile industry offers a good example of *barriers to entry due to large financial requirements.* An automobile plant of minimum efficient size costs about $500 million to build and put into operation. This is an enormous amount of money, beyond the reach of practically all individuals. It takes the help of major financial interests and financial institutions to break into the automobile business. Since World War II, no new firms have obtained a foothold in the American automobile industry.

The *availability of raw materials* can also be a barrier to entry. Such is the case in the steel industry, where a few big firms have most of the available iron ore, partly through foresight and partly because they were the only organizations that could afford to spend the vast sums required to obtain the ore. Also, *patents* can be a very big barrier to entry. The electric light industry is a famous example. General Electric was able to dominate the industry from 1892 to 1930 through the acquisition of the basic Edison patents and then the acquisition of patents on many of the improvements.[5]

Mergers and Oligopoly

Mergers between firms often contribute to the movement toward oligopoly in particular industries. There have been three major waves of mergers in the American economy. The first occurred between 1887 and 1904, the second between 1916 and 1929, and the third after World War II. The first wave in 1887–1904 saw the formation of such giants as U.S. Steel and John D. Rockefeller's Standard Oil. The mergers in this period tended to be *horizontal,* that is, among firms producing essentially the same product. Such was the case with U.S. Steel, formed in 1901 from a combination of about 785 plants. During the second wave of mergers in 1916–29, the emphasis was more on *vertical mergers* (mergers among firms at various stages in the production process) and *conglomerate mergers* (mergers among firms producing entirely different products). During the third wave of mergers in the 25 years following World War II, a very large number of firms was absorbed and assimilated by others. Of the 1,000 largest manufacturing firms in existence at the end of 1950, 216 had disappeared by merger by 1963.

Mergers of all types (horizontal, vertical, conglomerate) continue to occur. Sometimes they take place to reduce competition. Thomas Edison was forthright when he said in 1892 about the formation of General Elec-

---

[5] F. M. Scherer, *Industrial Market Structure and Economic Performance,* Skokie, Ill.: Rand McNally, 1970, pp. 391–92.

tric, "The consolidation of the companies ... will do away with a competition which has become so sharp that the product of the factories has been worth little more than ordinary hardware."[6] Other mergers are made so that promoters can earn profits from corporate marriages. In still other cases, mergers occur because firms need the people or ideas other firms have, or because the owners want to sell out, or because there appear to be beneficial synergetic effects arising from complementary resources owned by the merging firms.

Oligopoly Behavior and the Stability of Prices

Unlike perfect competition, monopoly, and monopolistic competition, there is no single unified model of oligopoly behavior. Instead, *there are a number of models, each based on a somewhat different set of assumptions concerning the relationships among the firms that make up the oligopoly.* Basically, no single model exists because economists have not yet been able to devise one that would cover all the relevant cases adequately. Economics, like all sciences, continues to grow; perhaps someone—indeed, perhaps someone reading this book—may be able to develop such a model before too long. However, it doesn't exist now.

THE KINKED OLIGOPOLY DEMAND CURVE

Let's start with a model that sheds light on the stability of oligopolistic prices. Empirical studies of pricing in oligopolistic markets have often concluded that prices in such markets tend to be rigid. A classic example occurred in the sulphur industry. From 1926 to 1938, the price of sulphur remained at $18 a ton, despite great shifts in demand and production costs. This example is somewhat extreme, but it illustrates the basic point: Prices in oligopolistic industries commonly remain unchanged for fairly long periods. A well-known model designed to explain this price rigidity was advanced by Paul Sweezy, who asserted that, *if an oligopolist cuts its price, it can be pretty sure that its rivals will meet the reduction. On the other hand, if it increases its price, its rivals may not change theirs.*

Figure 12.3 shows the situation. The oligopolist's demand curve is represented by *DAD'* and the current price is *OP*. There is a "kink" in the demand curve because *under the postulated circumstances the demand curve for the oligopolist's product is much less elastic for price decreases than for price increases.* Why is it less elastic for price decreases than for price increases? Because price decreases will be met by the firm's rivals, which means that the firm will not be able to take any appreciable amount of sales away from its rivals by such decreases. The effect of such decreases will be to increase the quantity demanded of the firm's product, since the total quantity demanded of the entire industry's product will increase due to the price reduction. But the increase in the quantity demanded of the firm's product will be relatively modest. On the other hand, if the firm raises its price, it is assumed that its rivals do not follow suit. Thus the

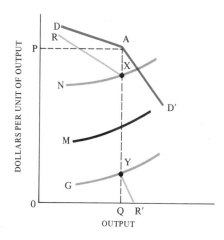

Figure 12.3

The Kinked Oligopoly Demand Curve
The oligopolist's demand curve is DAD', the current price being OP. Because of the kink in the demand curve, the marginal revenue curve consists of two segments RX and YR'. Since the marginal cost curve is M, the most profitable output is OQ. Moreover, it remains the most profitable output—and OP the most profitable price—even if the marginal cost curve shifts to N or to G or if the demand curve shifts considerably (within limits).

---

[6] Ibid., p. 113.

quantity demanded of the firm's product will fall considerably, if it raises its price.

PREDICTION: RIGID PRICES

Because of the kink in the demand curve, the marginal revenue curve in Figure 12.3 is not continuous. It consists of two segments, *RX* and *YR'*. Given that the firm's marginal cost curve is *M,* the most profitable output is *OQ,* where the marginal cost curve intersects the vertical line, *XY.* Moreover, OQ *remains the most profitable output—and* OP *the most profitable price—even if the marginal cost curve shifts considerably (even to* N *or* G*) or if the demand curve shifts (within limits).* One would expect price to be quite rigid under these circumstances, since many types of changes in cost and demand will not alter the price that maximizes profits.

This theory, although useful in explaining why price tends to remain at a certain level (*OP* in Figure 12.3), is of no use at all in explaining why this level, rather than another, currently prevails. It simply takes the current price as given. Thus this theory is an incomplete model of oligopoly pricing. Nonetheless, it seems to explain some of the relevant facts; and for this and other reasons, Sweezy's model has achieved a place in the theory of oligopoly.

Test Yourself

1. In a previous section, it was asserted that, if the demand curve confronting a monopolistically competitive firm is highly elastic, the firm is likely to have less excess capacity than if it is relatively inelastic. Explain why this is true.

2. Explain how a firm's output and price are determined under monopolistic competition in (a) the short run and (b) the long run.

3. "The kinked oligopoly demand curve is not a very effective tool of analysis because oligopolists frequently do raise their price in response to a price increase by a rival." Comment and evaluate.

4. "The Sweezy model is unrealistic because oligopolists seldom take account of how their rivals will respond to their actions. After all, there is no way to tell what their rivals will do in response to a particular action." Comment and evaluate.

Collusion and Cartels

HOW FIRMS COLLUDE

Collusion occurs when firms get together and agree on price and output. Up to this point, we have assumed that oligopolists do not collude, but conditions in oligopolistic industries tend to promote collusion, since the number of firms is small and the firms recognize their interdependence. The advantages of collusion to the firms seem obvious—increased profits, decreased uncertainty, and a better opportunity to prevent entry.

Not all collusion is disguised from the public or secret. In contrast to illicit collusion, a **cartel** is an open, formal collusive arrangement among firms. In many countries in Europe, cartels have been common and legally acceptable. In the United States, most collusive arrangements, whether secret or open cartels, were declared illegal by the Sherman Antitrust Act, which was passed in 1890.

However, this does not mean that such arrangements do not exist. Widespread collusion to fix prices occurred among American electrical equipment manufacturers during the 1950s, and when the collusion was uncovered a number of high executives were tried, convicted, and sent to jail. Moreover, collusion of this sort is not limited to a single industry—or a single country. Some cartels, like that in quinine in the early 1960s or in crude oil in the 1970s and 1980s, are international in scope.

PRICE AND OUTPUT OF A CARTEL

If a cartel is established to set a uniform price for a particular product, what price will it charge? As a first step, the cartel must estimate the marginal cost curve for the cartel as a whole. Then it must find the output where its marginal cost equals its marginal revenue, since this output maximizes the total profit of the cartel members. In Figure 12.4, this output is *OQ.* Thus, if it maximizes cartel profits, the cartel will choose a price of *OP,* which is the monopoly price. In short, *the cartel acts like a monopolist with a number of plants or divisions, each of which is a member firm.*

How will the cartel allocate sales among the member firms? If its aim is to maximize cartel profits, it will allocate sales to firms in such a way that the sum of the firms' costs is minimized. But this allocation is unlikely to occur in reality. The allocation process is a bargaining process, and firms with the most influence and the shrewdest negotiators are likely to receive the largest sales quotas, even though this decreases the total profits of the cartel. Moreover, high-cost firms are likely to receive larger sales quotas than would be the case if total cartel profits were maximized, since they would be unwilling otherwise to stay in the cartel. In practice, it appears that cartels often divide markets geographically or in accord with a firm's level of sales in the past.

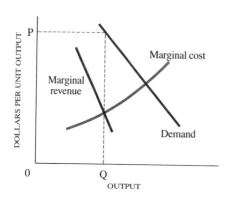

Figure 12.4

Price and Output of a Cartel   *The marginal cost curve shows the marginal cost for the cartel as a whole. Based on the demand curve for the industry's product, the cartel can derive the marginal revenue curve. The output that maximizes the total profit of the cartel members is* OQ. *The corresponding price is* OP.

THE ELECTRICAL CONSPIRACY

To illustrate how firms collude, consider the electrical equipment manufacturers we mentioned above. During the 1950s, there was widespread collusion among about 30 firms selling turbine generators, switchgear, transformers, and other products with total sales of about $1.5 billion per year. Representatives of these firms got together and agreed upon prices for many products. The available evidence indicates that both prices and profits tended to be increased by the collusive agreements—or at least until the firms were prosecuted under the antitrust laws by the Department of Justice. The following statement by F. M. Scherer of Swarthmore College is a good description of some of the procedures used by these firms:

> Some of the most elaborate procedures were devised to handle switchgear pricing. As in the case of generators, book prices served as the initial departure point. Each seller agreed to quote book prices in sales to private buyers,

and meetings were held regularly to compare calculations for forthcoming job quotations. Sealed-bid competitions sponsored by government agencies posed a different set of problems, and new methods were worked out to handle them. Through protracted negotiation, each seller was assigned a specific share of all sealed-bid business, e.g., General Electric's share of the high voltage switchgear field was set at 40.3 per cent in late 1958, and Allis-Chalmers' at 8.8 per cent. Participants then coordinated their bidding so that each firm was low bidder in just enough transactions to gain its predetermined share of the market. In the power switching equipment line, this was achieved for a while by dividing the United States into four quadrants, assigning four sellers to each quadrant, and letting the sellers in a quadrant rotate their bids. A "phases of the moon" system was used to allocate low-bidding privileges in the high voltage switchgear field, with a new seller assuming low-bidding priority every two weeks. The designated bidder subtracted a specified percentage margin from the book price to capture orders during its phase, while others added various margins to the book price. The result was an ostensibly random pattern of quotations, conveying the impression of independent pricing behavior.[7]

Barriers to Collusion

The fact that oligopoly often can lead to collusion is not new. Nor is it newly understood. Back in 1776, Adam Smith warned that "people of the same trade seldom meet together even for merriment and diversion, but the conversation ends in a conspiracy against the public, or in some contrivance to raise prices." However, it must be borne in mind that collusive arrangements are often difficult to accomplish and maintain for long. In particular, there are several important barriers to collusion.

LEGAL PROBLEMS

The antitrust laws forbid outright collusion and price fixing. This does not mean that firms do not break those laws; witness the electrical equipment manufacturers just described. But the antitrust laws are an important obstacle to collusion.

TECHNICAL PROBLEMS

Collusion is often difficult to achieve and maintain because an oligopoly contains an unwieldy number of firms, or the product is quite heterogeneous, or the cost structures of the firms differ considerably. It is clear that a collusive agreement will be more difficult to achieve and maintain if there are a dozen oligopolists than if there are three or four. Moreover, if the products sold by the oligopolists differ substantially, it will probably be more difficult for them to find a common price strategy that will be acceptable to all. Similarly, if the firms' cost structures differ, it will be more difficult to get agreement, since the low-cost firms will be more inclined to cut price. For example, National Steel, after introducing low-cost continuous strip mills in the 1930s, became a price cutter in the steel industry.

[7] F. M. Scherer, *Industrial Market Structure and Economic Performance*, p. 160.

Basic Idea #24: *Because they are few in number, firms in an oligopolistic industry may be tempted to collude to fix price and output. If this occurs, and if the firms try to maximize industry profits, the industry will act like a monopolist with a number of plants or divisions, each of which is a member firm. But there is a strong temptation for oligopolists to cheat on a collusive agreement, so agreements of this sort tend to be unstable.*

CHEATING

There is a constant temptation for oligopolists to cheat on any collusive agreement. If other firms stick to the agreement, any firm that cheats—by cutting its price below that agreed to under the collusive arrangement—can take a lot of business away from the other firms and increase its profits substantially, as least in the short run. This temptation is particularly great when an industry's sales are depressed and its profits are low. Every firm is hungry for business, and it is difficult to resist. Moreover, one firm may be driven to cheating because it hears that another firm is doing so, with the eventual result that the collusive agreement is torn apart.

To illustrate the problems of maintaining a collusive agreement, let's return to the electrical equipment manufacturers. As the *Wall Street Journal* summed it up,

> One of the great ironies of the conspiracies was that no matter how hard the participants schemed, no matter how friendly their meetings and communications might be, there was an innate tendency to compete. Someone was always violating the agreements to get more business and this continually called for new illegal plans. For example, price-cutting in sales of power switching equipment to government agencies was getting out of hand in late 1958. This led to the "quadrant" system of dividing markets [described in the previous section].

As one executive of General Electric complained, "No one was living up to the agreements and we...were being made suckers. On every job someone would cut our throat; we lost confidence in the group." Given that these agreements were illegal, it is remarkable that such a complaint was uttered with a straight face.

Price Leadership

In order to coordinate their behavior without outright collusion, some industries contain a *price leader.* It is quite common in oligopolistic industries for one or a few firms to set the price and for the rest to follow their lead. Two types of price leadership are the dominant-firm model and the barometric-firm model. *The **dominant-firm** model applies to cases where the industry has a single large dominant firm and a number of small firms.* The dominant firm sets the price for the industry, but it lets the small firms sell all they want at that price. *The **barometric-firm** model applies to cases where one firm usually is the first to make changes in price that are generally accepted by other firms in the industry.* The barometric firm may not be the largest, or most powerful, firm. Instead, it is a reasonably accurate interpreter of changes in basic cost and demand conditions in the industry as a whole. According to some authorities, barometric price leadership often occurs as a response to a period of violent price fluctuation in an industry, during which many firms suffer and greater stability is widely sought.

In the past, the steel industry has been a good example of price leadership of the dominant-firm variety. The largest firm in the industry is U.S. Steel, which, as we know, was formed in 1901 by the merger of a number of companies. Judge Elbert Gary, the first chairman of the board of U.S.

Steel, sought the cooperation of the smaller firms in the industry. He inaugurated a series of so-called "Gary dinners," attended by all the major steel producers, which made declarations of industry policy on pricing and other matters. Since any formal pricing agreements would have been illegal, they made no such agreements. But, generally speaking, U.S. Steel set the pricing pattern and other firms followed. Moreover, this relationship continued long after Judge Gary had gone to his reward. According to Walter Adams of Michigan State University, U.S. Steel typically set the

Example 12.1   How Other Sources of Oil Influence OPEC's Price

The Organization of Petroleum Exporting Countries (OPEC) is a cartel that includes many of the world's leading oil producers, such as Saudi Arabia, Nigeria, Venezuela, Indonesia, and others. Nonetheless, OPEC does not supply all of the world's oil. Important oil producers outside OPEC include the United States, Mexico, Canada, Britain, Norway, and Australia. Suppose that the supply curve for non-OPEC oil and the world demand curve for oil are as shown below:

(a) If the price of oil is $30 per barrel, what is the quantity demanded of OPEC oil? (b) If the price of oil is $40 per barrel, what is the quantity demanded of OPEC oil? (c) From the above graph, how can we determine the demand curve for OPEC oil? (d) Given the demand curve for OPEC oil, how can we determine the price that would maximize OPEC's profit?

SOLUTION

(a) $(OQ_3 - OQ_0)$ barrels of oil. (b) $(OQ_2 - OQ_1)$ barrels of oil. (c) To determine the quantity of OPEC oil demanded at each price, subtract the quantity of non-OPEC oil supplied at that price from the quantity of oil demanded in the world as a whole at that price. (d) Find the marginal revenue curve corresponding to the demand curve for OPEC oil, and determine the output at which this marginal revenue curve intersects OPEC's marginal cost curve. The profit-maximizing price is the one that corresponds to this output on the demand curve for OPEC oil. That is, it is the price that results in OPEC's selling this quantity of output.

price "and the other companies follow in lockstep—both in their sales to private customers and in their secret bids on government contracts."[8]

Illustrating the attitude of other firms was the statement by the president of Bethlehem Steel to a congressional committee in 1939 that "in the main we . . . await the [price] schedules of the [U.S.] Steel Corporation." However, there was some secret price cutting, particularly during depressions. On at least one occasion, U.S. Steel responded to such price cutting by announcing publicly that it would meet any price reduction it heard of. In this way, it attempted to discourage under-the-counter price cutting. In more recent times, U.S. Steel no longer seems to be the price leader it once was. In 1962, it drew a great deal of criticism from President Kennedy for being the first steel firm to raise prices. Subsequently, smaller steel firms have often been the first. Indeed, in 1968 the world was treated to the amusing spectacle of Bethlehem announcing a price cut in order to counter some secret price cutting by the former price leader, U.S. Steel.

Cost-Plus Pricing

There is one further model of oligopoly behavior to consider. According to studies of business behavior, *cost-plus pricing* is used by many oligopolists. It occurs in two steps. First, *the firm estimates the cost per unit of output of the product.* Since this cost will generally vary with the output rate, the firm must base this computation on some assumed output rate—often two-thirds or three-quarters of the firm's capacity. Second, *the firm adds a markup to the estimated average cost.* This markup is meant to include certain costs that cannot be allocated to any specific product and to provide a return on the firm's investment. The size of the markup depends on the rate of profit the firm believes it can earn. Some firms, like General Electric and General Motors, have set a *target rate of return* figure they hope to earn, which determines the markup.

Unquestionably, many firms do compute prices on the basis of this sort of procedure. However, the cost-plus pricing model is incomplete unless it specifies more precisely what determines the size of the markup. Although firms may construct these markups to yield a certain target rate of return, the firms' income statements show that these markups do not prevail, since the firms' actual rates of return frequently vary considerably from the target rate of return. Moreover, to many economists this form of pricing seems naïve, since it takes no account, explicitly at least, of the extent or elasticity of demand or of the size of marginal, rather than average, costs.

THE CASE OF GENERAL MOTORS

Consider General Motors, which has often used cost-plus pricing. General Motors has begun by stating an objective of earning a profit of about 15 percent (after taxes) on total invested capital. Then it has assumed that it will sell enough cars in the next year to operate at about 80 percent of its capacity; and on the basis of this assumption, it has figured what its cost per car will be. Then it has added to this cost a markup big enough to pro-

[8] W. Adams, *The Structure of American Industry,* New York: Macmillan, 1961, p. 168.

duce the desired return on investment. The result is the so-called standard price. General Motors' high-echelon price policy committee has taken this standard price as a first approximation, and has made small adjustments to reflect competitive conditions, long-run goals of the firm, and other things. Typically, these adjustments have been quite small, and the actual price has turned out to be close to the standard price.

Needless to say, there is no assurance that General Motors will earn the desired 15 percent of total invested capital. If it sells fewer cars than it needs to sell in order to operate at 80 percent of capacity, its unit costs will be higher than expected and its profits—both total and per unit of output—will be less than expected. On the other hand, if it sells more cars than it needs to sell in order to operate at 80 percent of capacity, its profits will be higher than expected. In general, since World War II, General Motors has achieved sales levels that permitted it to operate at more than 80 percent of capacity, with the result that it has earned substantially more, on the average, than the target rate of 15 percent of invested capital.

But this was not true in 1974 and 1975. And in 1980, General Motors' sales dropped considerably below the 1979 level, and it lost a whopping $762 million. 1981 was not a good year either. With the increased competition from Japanese imported cars, General Motors found it more difficult to use its traditional pricing methods. However, in 1983 and 1984, due partly to quotas on auto imports, General Motors' profits increased substantially.

Nonprice Competition

Oligopolists tend to compete more aggressively through advertising and product differentiation than through direct price reductions. In other words, when we observe the behavior of major oligopolies, we find that firms try hard to get business away from their rivals by outdoing them with better advertising campaigns and with improvements in the product; but it is less common for oligopolists to slug it out, toe to toe, with price reductions. This is an important characteristic of oligopoly. In contrast to the case of perfect competition, nonprice competition plays a central role in oligopoly. It is worthwhile, therefore, to note a few salient points about the advertising and product development strategies of oligopolists.

ADVERTISING

Advertising is a very big business. In 1983 over $75 billion per year was spent on it in the United States. One important purpose of advertising is to convince the consumer that one firm's product is better than another's. In industries where there is less physical differentiation of the product, advertising expenditures often are larger than in industries where the product varies more. Thus the cigarette, liquor, and soap industries spend over 10 percent of their gross revenues (excluding excise taxes) on advertising, whereas the automobile industry spends less than 1 percent of its gross revenues on advertising.

The social desirability of much of this advertising is debatable, and much debated. While advertising can serve an important purpose by keeping the consumer better informed, some advertising is more misleading than informative. Unfortunately, it is difficult to make reliable estimates of the extent to which oligopolists may be overinvesting, from society's point of view, in advertising.[9]

PRODUCT DEVELOPMENT

The development of new and improved products is also a very big business in the United States. Currently firms spend over $40 billion per year on research and development. In many industries, R and D is a central part of oligopolistic competition. For example, a spectacular case in the drug industry was the effect of American Cyanamid's Achromycin tetracycline, introduced in 1953, on sales of Aureomycin chlortetracycline, which had been marketed since late 1948. After an almost continuous upward trend in 1950–53, Aureomycin sales dropped by nearly 40 percent during the first full year of the sale of Achromycin. Hardly a typical case, this nonetheless illustrates how one firm can take sales away from its rivals through new product development.

It is important to add, however, that much of industry's R and D is aimed at fairly minor improvements in products and processes. Moreover, a good deal of the engineering efforts of many important industries is aimed largely at style changes, not basic improvements in the product. A case in point is the automobile industry, which spends an enormous amount to produce the model changes that are familiar to car buyers throughout the land. Specifically, according to three economists—Frank Fisher, Zvi Griliches, and Carl Kaysen—such model changes in the automobile industry cost about $5 billion per year during the late 1950s.[10] From society's point of view, it is not at all clear that such huge expenditures are justifiable.

Perhaps the main reason why oligopolists would rather compete through advertising and product differentiation than through price is that a firm's rivals can easily and quickly match a price reduction, whereas they may find it difficult to match a clever advertising campaign or an attractive product improvement. Eastman Kodak had to work over six years to develop the instant camera it introduced in 1976 to compete with Polaroid's instant camera. Thus oligopolists tend to feel that they have a better chance of improving their long-run profits at the expense of their rivals in the arena of nonprice competition than by price cutting.

Comparison of Oligopoly with Perfect Competition

We have seen that economists have constructed a number of types of models of oligopoly behavior—the Sweezy model, the cartel models, price leadership models, cost-plus pricing models, and others—but there is no

[9] See W. Comanor and T. Wilson, *Advertising and Market Power,* Cambridge: Harvard University Press, 1975.

[10] For more recent data, see L. White, *The Automobile Industry Since 1945,* Cambridge, Mass.: Harvard University Press, 1971.

During the late 1970s and early 1980s, a group of economists at New York and Princeton Universities (and the Bell Laboratories), headed by William Baumol, developed a theory of contestable markets. This theory has received considerable attention. Because it is so new, it is very difficult to predict how significant it will eventually turn out to be. But it has had enough influence to warrant discussion.

What is a contestable market? According to Baumol and his colleagues, it is a market into which entry is absolutely free, *and exit is absolutely costless.* Any firm can leave the market without impediment, and can get back whatever costs it incurred in entering. The key characteristic of a contestable market is its vulnerability to hit-and-run entry. A firm can enter such a market, make a quick profit, and leave without cost, if this seems to be the most profitable course of action.

William Baumol

Just as a perfectly competitive market is only a model, so the same is true of a contestable market. Nonetheless, models of this sort can be very useful and suggestive. At least three characteristics of a contestable market are worth noting. First, it can be shown that profits are zero in equilibrium in a contestable market. If profits were positive, a firm could enter the market, undercut the price of the firm with profits, and make a profit, and leave the market if this seemed desirable. Thus profits will be eroded by such price cutting until they are zero. This is true regardless of how few firms exist in the contestable market. Because each is subject to such hit-and-run tactics, profits are eliminated.

Second, the organization of a contestable market is efficient in the sense that the average cost of production is as low as possible. Again because of the possibility of hit-and-run entry, firms in such a market must maintain their costs at the lowest possible level in the long run. If they do not do so, more efficient firms will enter, undercut their price, and force them to reduce their costs or withdraw from the market.

Third, if a contestable market contains two or more sellers, their prices, in equilibrium, must equal their marginal costs. As pointed out in Chapter 11, there are fundamental reasons why economists favor markets in which price equals marginal cost. One reason why perfect competition is favored by so many economists is that price equals marginal cost. Thus it is very interesting that this desirable feature of perfect competition exists as well in contestable markets.

In the past, it has often been presumed that these three outcomes—zero profits, minimum cost, and price equal to marginal cost—would be very unlikely to occur when there are few sellers. The theory of contestable markets implies that this is not necessarily the case.

agreement that any of these models is an adequate general representation of oligopoly behavior. For this reason, it is difficult to estimate the effects of an oligopolistic market structure on price, output, and profits. Nonetheless, if a perfectly competitive industry were turned overnight into an oligopoly, it seems likely that certain changes would occur.

1. Price would probably be higher than under perfect competition. The difference between the oligopoly price and the perfectly competitive price will depend on the number of firms in the industry and the ease of entry. The larger the number of firms and the easier it is to enter the industry, the closer the oligopoly price will be to the perfectly competitive level. Also, prices will tend to be more inflexible under oligopolistic conditions than under perfect competition.

2. If the demand curve is the same under oligopoly as under perfect competition, it also follows that *output will be less under oligopoly than under perfect competition.* However, it is not always reasonable to assume that the demand curve is the same in both cases, since the large expenditures for advertising and product differentiation incurred by some oligopolies may tend to shift the demand curve to the right. Consequently in some cases both price and output may tend to be higher under oligopoly than under perfect competition.

3. Oligopolistic industries tend to spend more on advertising, product differentiation, and style changes than perfectly competitive industries. The use of some resources for these purposes is certainly worthwhile, since advertising provides buyers with information, and product differentiation allows greater freedom of choice. Whether oligopolies spend too much for these purposes is by no means obvious. However, there is a widespread feeling among economists, based largely on empirical studies (and hunch), that in some oligopolistic industries such expenditures have been expanded beyond socially optimal levels.

4. One might expect on the basis of the models presented in this chapter that the *profits earned by oligopolists would be higher, on the average, than the profits earned by perfectly competitive firms.* This conclusion is supported by some statistical evidence. Joe Bain of the University of California has found that firms in industries in which the largest few firms had a high proportion of total sales tended to have higher rates of return than firms in industries in which the largest few firms had a small proportion of total sales.[11]

---

[11] J. Bain, "Relation of Profit Rate to Industry Concentration: American Manufacturing, 1936–1940," *Quarterly Journal of Economics,* August 1951. However, there has been much disagreement on this score. According to some recent evidence, a firm is likely to have higher-than-average profits if it has a relatively big share of the market, regardless of whether or not the industry as a whole is highly concentrated. For some relevant discussion, see L. Weiss, "The Concentration-Profits Relationship and Antitrust," in H. Goldschmid, H. M. Mann, and J. F. Weston, *Industrial Concentration, The New Learning,* Boston: Little Brown, 1974.

Test Yourself

1. Suppose that a cartel consists of four firms, each of which has a horizontal marginal cost curve. For each firm, marginal cost equals $4. Suppose that the marginal revenue curve for the cartel is $MR = 10 - 2Q$, where MR is marginal revenue (in dollars) and Q is the cartel's output per year (in thousands of units). What output rate will the cartel choose?

2. According to the Senate Subcommittee on Antitrust and Monopoly, "Some system of marketing quotas, whether overt or carefully hidden, must underlie any price-fixing agreement." Comment and evaluate.

3. Discuss the incentives that each firm in Question 1 would have to cheat on the collusive agreement described there.

4. Suppose that a firm engages in cost-plus pricing. Assuming that it will operate next year at 80 percent of capacity, it estimates its average costs at that output rate. Then it adds a certain percentage to this average cost figure to get its price. But suppose that the demand curve shifts to the left during the next year, and that the firm can only operate at 40 percent of capacity if it maintains this price. What factors will govern whether the firm sticks with this price? What does this indicate about cost-plus pricing?

Summary

1. Monopolistic competition occurs where there are many sellers whose products are somewhat different. The demand curve facing each firm slopes downward to the right. The conditions for long-run equilibrium are that each firm is maximizing profits and that economic profits are zero. A famous conclusion of the theory of monopolistic competition is that firms under this form of market organization will tend to operate with excess capacity.

2. The firm under monopolistic competition is likely to produce less, and charge a higher price, than under perfect competition. Relative to pure monopoly, monopolistically competitive firms are likely to have lower profits, greater output, and lower prices. Firms under monopolistic competition will offer a wider variety of styles, brands, and qualities than will firms under perfect competition.

3. Oligopoly is characterized by a small number of firms and a great deal of interdependence, actual and perceived, among them. Oligopoly is a common market structure in the United States.

4. According to empirical studies, prices tend to be rigid in oligopolistic industries. A well-known theory designed to explain this phenomenon is Sweezy's model, based on the kinked demand curve. This theory is an incomplete model of oligopoly pricing, even though it may be of use in explaining the rigidity of prices.

5. Conditions in oligopolistic industries tend to promote collusion. A cartel is an open, formal, collusive arrangement. A profit-maximizing cartel will act like a monopolist with a number of plants or divisions, each of which is a member firm. In practice, it appears that the members of a cartel often divide markets geographically or in accord with each firm's level of sales in the past.

6. Price leadership is quite common in oligopolistic industries, one or a few firms apparently setting the price and the rest following their lead. Two types of price leadership are the dominant-firm model and the barometric-firm model. An example of the former kind of price leadership was the steel industry until a decade or so ago.

7. According to numerous studies of business behavior, cost-plus pricing is used by many oligopolists. However, a cost-plus model of pricing is incomplete unless it specifies more precisely the determinants of the size of the markup.

8. Relative to perfect competition, it seems likely that both price and profits will be higher under oligopoly. Moreover, oligopolistic industries will tend to spend more on advertising, product differentiation, and style changes than perfectly competitive industries.

Concepts for Review

Monopolistic competition	**Horizontal merger**	**Dominant firm**
Oligopoly	**Vertical merger**	**Barometric firm**
Pure oligopoly	**Conglomerate merger**	**Cost-plus pricing**
Differentiated oligopoly	**Collusion**	**Markup**
Product differentiation	**Cartel**	**Target rate of return**
Product group	**Price leader**	

Appendix: The Theory of Games

A useful model of oligopoly is one that stresses its gamelike characteristics. As in a game, in oligopoly each firm must take account of its rivals' reactions to its own actions. For this reason, an oligopolistic firm cannot tell what effect a change in its output will have on the price of its product and on its profits unless it can guess how its rivals will respond to the change. To understand game theory, you have to know what a *game* is. It is a competitive situation where two or more persons pursue their own interests and no person can dictate the outcome. Poker is a game, and so is a situation in which two firms are engaged in competitive advertising campaigns. A game is described in terms of its players, rules, payoffs, and information conditions. These elements are common to all conflict situations.

DEFINITIONS OF TERMS

More specifically, a *player*, whether a single person or an organization, is a decision-making unit. Each player has a certain amount of resources, and the *rules of the game* describe how these resources can be used. Thus the rules of poker indicate how bets can be made and which hands are better than others. A *strategy* is a complete specification of what a player will do under each contingency in the playing of the game. Thus a corporation president might tell his subordinates how she wants an advertising campaign to start, and what should be done at subsequent times in response to various actions of competing firms. The game's outcome clearly depends on each player's strategies. A player's *payoff* varies from game to game. It is win, lose, or draw in checkers, and various sums of money in poker.

For simplicity we will restrict our attention to *two-person games*, i.e., those with only two players, and to *zero-sum games*, in which the amount one player wins exactly equals the amount the other player loses. The relevant features of a two-person, zero-sum game can be shown by constructing a *payoff matrix*. To illustrate, consider the case of two big soap producers, Procter & Gamble and Lever Brothers. Suppose that these two firms are about to stage rival advertising campaigns and that each firm has a choice of strategies. Procter & Gamble can choose to concentrate on either television ads or magazine ads; Lever Brothers has the same choice. Table 12.1 shows what will happen to the profits of each firm when each combination of strategies is chosen. If both firms concentrate on TV ads, Procter & Gamble gains $3 million and Lever Brothers loses $3 million. If Procter & Gamble concentrates on TV ads and Lever Brothers concentrates on magazine ads, Procter & Gamble gains $2 million and Lever Brothers loses $2 million. And so on.

PROCTER AND GAMBLE'S VIEWPOINT

Given the payoff matrix in Table 12.1, there is a definite optimal choice for each firm. To see that this is the case, let's begin by looking at the situation from Procter & Gamble's point of view. If Procter & Gamble concentrates on magazine ads, Lever Brothers will respond by choosing to concentrate on TV ads. Why? Because Lever Brothers will lose less ($1 million) than if it too concentrates on magazine ads (in which case its loss will be $1.5 million). Thus *Procter & Gamble, if it concentrates on magazine ads, will gain $1 million.*

What if Procter & Gamble concentrates on TV ads? In this case, Lever Brothers will respond by choosing to concentrate on magazines. Why? Because Lever Brothers will lose less ($2 million) than if it too concentrates on TV ads (in which case its losses will be $3 million). Thus *Procter & Gamble, if it concentrates on TV ads, will gain $2 million.*

Consequently, if both firms know the payoff matrix, *Procter & Gamble will choose the strategy of concentrating on TV ads, since it provides Procter & Gamble with a greater gain ($2 million) than if it concentrates on magazine ads (in which case the gain is $1 million).*

LEVER BROTHERS' VIEWPOINT

Now let's look at the situation from the point of view of Lever Brothers. If Lever Brothers concentrates on TV ads, Procter & Gamble will respond by

Table 12.1

PAYOFF MATRIX

Possible strategies for Procter & Gamble	Possible strategies for Lever Brothers	
	Concentrate on TV	Concentrate on magazines
Concentrate on TV	P & G gains $3 million, and Lever loses $3 million	P & G gains $2 million, and Lever loses $2 million
Concentrate on magazines	P & G gains $1 million, and Lever loses $1 million	P & G gains $1.5 million, and Lever loses $1.5 million

also concentrating on TV ads. Why? Because Procter & Gamble will gain more ($3 million) than if it concentrates on magazine ads (in which case it will gain $1 million). Thus *Lever Brothers, if it concentrates on TV ads, will lose $3 million.*

What if Lever Brothers concentrates on magazine ads? In this case, Procter & Gamble will respond by choosing to concentrate on TV ads. Why? Because Procter & Gamble will gain more ($2 million) than if it concentrates on magazine ads (in which case it will gain $1.5 million). Thus *Lever Brothers, if it concentrates on magazine ads, will lose $2 million.*

Consequently, if both firms know the payoff matrix, *Lever Brothers will choose the strategy of concentrating on magazine ads, since it provides Lever Brothers with a smaller loss ($2 million) than if it concentrates on TV ads (in which case the loss will be $3 million).*

THE SOLUTION OF THE GAME

At this point, the solution of this game is clear. *Procter & Gamble will concentrate on TV ads, and Lever Brothers will concentrate on magazine ads.* In this way Procter & Gamble gains $2 million, Lever Brothers loses $2 million. By adopting these strategies, Procter & Gamble can guarantee itself a gain of this amount, and Lever Brothers can guarantee that its loss will not exceed this amount.

Note that each firm is assumed to maximize its payoff under the assumption that its opponent will adopt the strategy most damaging to itself. Many economists feel that this is an unnecessarily pessimistic outlook for the firm, and wonder whether such an attitude is a realistic representation of how firms actually view competitive situations. The firm that adopts this viewpoint, while his competitor does not, is likely to forgo considerable profit. Despite this and other limitations, the theory of games is a useful addition to economic theory because it provides a suggestive framework for analysis. One can structure formerly intractable problems and think about them in terms of this theory. However, in its present state, game theory cannot be used to derive specific predictions of the behavior of oligopolists; the world is much more complicated than simple examples like this one.

CHAPTER 13

Industrial Organization and Antitrust Policy

Monopoly and *monopolist* have long been dirty words—or at least slightly derogatory ones. The public has tended to view monopolists with suspicion at least since Adam Smith's famous attack on monopolies in the eighteenth century. Smith preached and generations of economists since have taught that a monopolist charges a price in excess of the price that would prevail under perfect competition. For reasons given in Chapter 11, this is likely to result in a misallocation of society's resources. One way that society has attempted to deal with problems caused by monopoly is through public regulation, discussed in Chapter 11. Another way is through antitrust policy, discussed in the present chapter.

In this chapter we begin by discussing the case against oligopoly and monopolistic competition, after which we take up the defense of monopoly power made by some economists. Then, after describing the extent of industrial concentration in the United States, we discuss the nature, history, and effectiveness of antitrust policy in the United States, together with the problems in constructing standards for antitrust policy. Finally, we describe some laws in this country that restrict, rather than promote, competition.

The Case Against Oligopoly and Monopolistic Competition

Complaints against Oligopoly. In Chapter 11, we discussed the case against monopoly. Although economists are more concerned about monopoly than about oligopoly or monopolistic competition, this does not mean that they give either oligopoly or monopolistic competition a clean bill of health. Even though oligopoly has aroused less public indignation and opposition than out-and-out monopoly, an oligopoly can obviously be just as deleterious to social welfare. After all, *if oligopolists engage in collusion, open or tacit, their behavior with regard to price and output may resemble a monopolist's.* Only if there is real competition among the oligopolists can we expect price to be pushed closer to marginal cost under oligopoly than under monopoly. If oligopolists "cooperate" and "maintain orderly markets," the amount of social waste may be no less than under monopoly.

Also, *the inflexibility of prices under oligopoly tends to interfere with the effective functioning of the price system.* In a perfectly competitive industry, price will decline when the demand curve shifts to the left, thus prompting resources to move out of the industry. (We examined this process in Chapter 10, using coal and corn as examples.) But in an oligopolistic industry, price tends to remain constant when demand shifts to the left, with the result that output falls and much of the industry's plant is left idle. Although resources leave the oligopolistic industry, as they should, the resources that are stuck in the industry in the short run are not utilized adequately. And the fact that prices are not allowed to decline contributes to cost-push inflation.

Complaints against Monopolistic Competition. Monopolistic competition can also be a socially wasteful form of market organization. As we saw in Chapter 12, monopolistically competitive markets are characterized by overcrowding and excess capacity. There are more firms than would exist under perfect competition, and each firm produces less than the minimum-cost output rate. Thus the industry's output is produced inefficiently. More resources are used than are really necessary. The extent of this waste may not be very great if the demand curve facing each firm is very elastic, but there is no reason to believe that the demand curve will always be so elastic as to ensure that the waste is small.

In addition, price under monopolistic competition—as well as under monopoly and oligopoly—will exceed marginal cost, although the difference between price and marginal cost may be smaller than under monopoly or oligopoly. Thus monopolistic competition, like monopoly and oligopoly, results in a misallocation of resources. The argument leading to this conclusion is exactly like that given in Chapter 11 (and Appendix D) for monopoly. Also, monopolistic competition, as well as oligopoly, may allow waste arising from too much being spent (from society's point of view) on product differentiation, advertising, and other selling expenses. This is very difficult to prove, although many economists suspect it is so.

The Bottom Line. The moral is that many economists look with disfavor on serious departures from perfect competition, whether these departures are in the direction of monopoly, oligopoly, or monopolistic competition. Judged against the perfectly competitive model, all may lead to social waste and inefficiency. However, monopoly is generally presumed to be the greatest evil, with the result that economists usually look with most disfavor on markets dominated by one, or a very few, sellers—or buyers.[1]

---

[1] Monopsony, where a single buyer exists, is taken up in Chapter 14.

Joseph Schumpeter

The Defense of Monopoly Power

Not all economists agree that monopoly power is a bad thing. On the contrary, some respected voices in the economics profession have been raised to praise monopoly, not bury it. In discussing the social problems due to monopoly in Chapter 11, we assumed that the rate of technological change is independent of an industry's market structure. Some economists like Joseph Schumpeter and John Kenneth Galbraith challenge this assumption. *They assert that the rate of technological change is likely to be higher in an imperfectly competitive industry (i.e., monopoly, oligopoly, etc.) than in a perfectly competitive industry.* Since the rate of technological change affects productivity and living standards, in their view a perfectly competitive economy is likely to be inferior in a dynamic sense to an economy containing many imperfectly competitive industries.

Arguments by Schumpeter and Galbraith. Schumpeter and Galbraith point out that firms under perfect competition have fewer resources to devote to research and experimentation than do firms under imperfect competition. Because profits are at a relatively low level, it is difficult for firms under perfect competition to support large expenditures on research and development. Moreover, they argue that unless a firm has sufficient control over the market to reap the rewards from an innovation, the introduction of the innovation may not be worthwhile. If competitors can imitate the innovation very quickly, the innovator may be unable to make any money from it.

Rejoinders to Schumpeter and Galbraith. Defenders of perfect competition retort that there is likely to be less pressure for firms in imperfect markets to introduce new techniques and products, since such firms have fewer competitors. Moreover, firms in imperfect markets are better able to drive out entrants who, uncommitted to present techniques, are likely to be relatively quick to adopt new ones. (Entrants, unlike established producers, have no vested interest in maintaining the demand for existing products and the profitability of existing equipment.) Also, there are advantages in having a large number of independent decision-making units. There is less chance that an important technological advance will be blocked by the faulty judgment of a few men or women.

It is very difficult to obtain evidence to help settle the question, if it is posed in this way, since perfect competition is a hypothetical construct that does not exist in the real world. However, it does seem unlikely that a perfectly competitive industry (if such an industry could be constructed) would be able in many areas of the economy to carry out the research and development required to promote a high rate of technological change. Moreover, if entry is free and rapid, firms in a perfectly competitive industry will have little motivation to innovate. Although the evidence is not at all clear-cut, at least this much can be granted the critics of perfect competition.

Monopoly Power, Big Business, and Technological Change

But some economists go much further than the assertion that a certain amount of market imperfection will promote a more rapid rate of techno-

John Kenneth Galbraith

logical change. *They say that an industry composed of or dominated by a few large companies is the best market structure for promoting rapid technological change.* Galbraith has said that the "modern industry of a few large firms [is] an almost perfect instrument for inducing technical change."[2] And in some circles, it is accepted as an obvious fact that giant firms with their financial strength and well-equipped laboratories are absolutely necessary to maintain a rapid rate of technological change.

Suppose that, for a market of given size, we could replace the largest firms by a larger number of somewhat smaller firms—and thus reduce the extent to which the industry is dominated by the largest firms. Is there any evidence that this would decrease the rate of technological change, as is sometimes asserted? The evidence currently available is much more limited than one would like, but the available studies—based on detailed data concerning research expenditures, patents, important inventions and innovations, and the diffusion of innovations—do not indicate that such a decrease in industrial concentration would reduce the rate of technological change in most industries.

Specifically, the available studies do not show that total research and development expenditures in most industries would decrease if the largest firms were replaced by somewhat smaller ones. Nor do they indicate that the research and development expenditures carried out by the largest firms are generally more productive (or more ambitious or more risky) than those carried out by somewhat smaller firms. Moreover, they do not suggest that greater concentration of an industry results in a faster diffusion of innovations. However, if innovations require a large amount of capital, they do suggest that the substitution of a larger number of smaller firms for a few large ones may lead to slower commercial introduction of the innovations.[3]

Thus, *contrary to the allegations of Galbraith and others, there is little evidence that industrial giants are needed in most industries to insure rapid technological change and rapid utilization of new techniques.* This does not mean that industries composed only of small firms would necessarily be optimal for the promotion and diffusion of new techniques. On the contrary, there seem to be considerable advantages in a diversity of firm sizes. Complementarities and interdependencies exist among large and small firms. There is often a division of labor. Smaller firms may focus on areas requiring sophistication and flexibility and cater to specialized needs, while bigger firms concentrate on areas requiring large production, marketing, or technical resources. However, there is little evidence in most industries that firms considerably smaller than the biggest firms are not big enough for these purposes.

How Much Monopoly Power Is Optimal?

The discussion in previous sections makes it clear that the case against monopoly power is not open and shut. On the contrary, a certain amount

---

[2] John Kenneth Galbraith, *American Capitalism*, Boston: Houghton Mifflin, 1952, p. 91.
[3] Edwin Mansfield, *Technological Change*, New York: Norton, 1971, and the literature

of monopoly power is inevitable in practically all real-life situations, since perfect competition is a model that can only be approximated in real life. Moreover, a certain amount of monopoly power may be needed to promote desirable technological change. The difficult problem is to determine how much monopoly power is optimal under various circumstances (and how this power is to be measured). Some economists (like Galbraith) are convinced that a great deal of monopoly power is both inevitable and desirable. Others believe the opposite. And the economic arguments are not strong enough to resolve the differences of opinion.

Concentration of Economic Power

Some critics of monopoly power and big business are concerned with the centralization of power in the hands of a relatively few firms. Although this is only partly an economic matter, it is obviously relevant to public policy makers. Economic power in the United States is distributed very unevenly; a few hundred corporations control a very large share of the total assets of the nonfarm economy. Moreover, within particular industries, there is considerable concentration of ownership and production, as we shall see in the next sections. This concentration of power has been viewed with concern by observers like A. A. Berle, who asserted that the largest several hundred firms "each with its own dominating pyramid within it—represent a concentration of power over economies which makes the medieval feudal system look like a Sunday School party. In sheer economic power this has gone far beyond anything we have yet seen."[4]

It is important to note that this distrust of power leads to a distrust of giant firms, whether or not they have substantial monopoly power. Even if General Motors had little power over prices, it would still have considerable economic—and political—power because of its sheer size. Note too that a firm's size is not necessarily a good indicator of the extent of its monopoly power. A small grocery store in a remote community may be a monopolist, but a large merchandising firm with many rivals may have little monopoly power.

Assets of the 100 Largest Firms

Let's look at the 100 biggest manufacturing firms in the United States. Recognizing that bigness is not the same as monopoly power, what percentage of the nation's assets do these firms control, and is this percentage increasing or decreasing over time? According to the latest available figures, the 100 largest manufacturing firms control about half of all man-

cited there. Also, see E. Mansfield, J. Rapoport, A. Romeo, E. Villani, S. Wagner, and F. Husic, *The Production and Application of New Industrial Technology,* New York: Norton, 1977.

[4] A. A. Berle, *Economic Power and the Free Society,* New York: Fund for the Republic, p. 14.

ufacturing assets in the United States, and this percentage seems to have increased considerably since the end of World War II.

Willard Mueller of the University of Wisconsin has pointed out that, of the total assets of manufacturing firms, "the share held by the top one hundred companies rose from 39.3 percent to 49.3 percent [between 1947 and 1968], and the share of the top 200 rose from 47.2 percent to 60.9 percent. In other words, by 1968 the top one hundred companies held a greater share than that held by the top 200 in 1947."[5] Thus there can be no doubt about the vast economic power of the 100 largest firms—and no doubt that, after World War II, they increased their share of the nation's manufacturing assets.

Industrial Concentration in the United States

Economists and policy makers are interested in market structure because it influences market performance. But how can one measure an industry's market structure? How can one tell how close an industry is to being a monopoly or a perfectly competitive industry? An important measure economists have devised is the **market concentration ratio,** *which shows the percentage of total sales or production accounted for by the 4 biggest firms.* The higher the market concentration ratio, the more concentrated the industry is in a very few hands. Basing this measure on 4 firms is arbitrary. You can use 5, 6, 7, or any number of firms you like. But the figures issued by the government are generally based on 4 firms.

Table 13.1 shows the market concentration ratios for selected industries. These ratios vary widely from industry to industry. At one extreme, the automobile industry is a tight oligopoly, with the concentration ratio about as high as it can get—93 percent. At the other extreme, there is very little industrial concentration in the commercial printing industry: its concentration ratio is only 6 percent. Table 13.2 shows the number of industries that have concentration ratios of various magnitudes. Over one-quarter of the manufacturing industries in the United States have concentration ratios of 50 percent or more, and about one-tenth have concentration ratios of 70 percent or more.

Most economists who have studied trends in industrial concentration seem to agree that remarkably little change has occurred in the past 70 years in the average level of concentration in the United States. As Morris Adelman of M.I.T. puts it, "Any tendency either way, if it exists, must be at the pace of a glacial drift."[6] Also, the available evidence seems to indicate that the levels of market concentration are lower in the United States than in other major industrialized countries, with the possible exception of Great Britain and Japan.

Finally, it is important to recognize that the concentration ratio is only a

Table 13.1

CONCENTRATION RATIOS IN SELECTED MANUFACTURING PRODUCT MARKETS, 1977

Industry	Market share of 4 largest firms (percent)
Automobiles	93
Photographic equipment	72
Tires	70
Aircraft	59
Blast furnaces and steel plants	45
Industrial organic chemicals	43
Petroleum refining	30
Bread and cake	33
Pharmaceuticals	24
Radio and TV equipment	20
Newspapers	19
Commercial printing	6

Source: Statistical Abstract of the United States.

Table 13.2

NUMBER OF INDUSTRIES WITH VARIOUS LEVELS OF CONCENTRATION

Concentration ratio (percent)	Number of industries	Percent of industries[a]
90–100	10	2
70–89	34	7
50–69	81	18
Less than 50	314	72
Total	439	100

[a] Because of rounding errors, figures do not sum to total.

[5] W. Mueller, *A Primer on Monopoly and Competition,* New York: Random House, 1970, p. 26. Also see W. Shepherd, *The Economics of Industrial Organization,* Englewood Cliffs, N.J.: Prentice-Hall, 1979.

[6] M. Adelman, "The Measurement of Industrial Concentration," *Review of Economics and Statistics,* 1951. Also, see B. T. Allen, "Average Concentration in Manufacturing, 1947–72," *Journal of Economic Issues,* September, 1976.

rough measure of an industry's market structure. Certainly, to provide a reasonably adequate description, it must be supplemented with data on the extent and type of product differentiation in the industry, as well as on barriers to entry. Moreover, even with these supplements, it is still a crude measure. (Among other things, it takes no account of competition from foreign suppliers.) Nonetheless, the concentration ratio has proved to be a valuable tool to economists.

The Antitrust Laws

National policies are too ambiguous and rich in contradictions to be summarized neatly and concisely. Consequently, it would be misleading to say that the United States has adopted a policy of promoting competition and controlling monopoly. To a large extent, it certainly is true that "competition is our fundamental national policy," as the Supreme Court said in 1963. But it is also true that we have adopted many measures to promote monopoly and to limit competition, as we shall see in subsequent sections (and as has already been pointed out in Chapter 11). On balance, however, we probably have gone further in promoting competition than other major industrialized countries, and the principal pieces of legislation designed to further this objective are the *antitrust laws.*

THE SHERMAN ACT

In 1890, the first antitrust law, the Sherman Act, was passed by Congress. Although the common law had long outlawed monopolistic practices, it appeared to many Americans in the closing years of the nineteenth century that legislation was required to discourage monopoly and to preserve and encourage competition. The formation of "trusts"—monopolistic combines that colluded to raise prices and restrict output—brought the matter to a head. The heart of the Sherman Act lies in the following two sections:

> Sec. 1. Every contract, combination in the form of trust or otherwise, or conspiracy, in restraint of trade or commerce among the several states or with foreign nations, is hereby declared to be illegal. Every person who shall make any such contract or engage in any such combination or conspiracy, shall be deemed guilty of a misdemeanor....
>
> Sec. 2. Every person who shall monopolize, or attempt to monopolize or combine or conspire with any other person or persons, to monopolize any part of the trade or commerce among the several States, or with foreign nations shall be deemed guilty of a misdemeanor.

THE CLAYTON ACT

The first 20 years of experience with the Sherman Act were not very satisfying to its supporters. The ineffectiveness of the Sherman Act led in 1914 to passage by Congress of two additional laws—the Clayton Act and the Federal Trade Commission Act. The Clayton Act tried to be more specific than the Sherman Act in identifying certain practices that were illegal because they would "substantially lessen competition or tend to create a monopoly." In particular, the Clayton Act outlawed unjustified *price discrimination,* a practice whereby one buyer is charged more than another buyer for the same product. It also outlawed the use of a *tying contract,* which makes the buyers purchase other items to get the product they want. Further, it outlawed mergers that substantially lessen competition; but since it did not prohibit one firm's purchase of a competitor's plant and equipment, it really could not stop mergers. In 1950, this loophole was closed by the Celler-Kefauver Anti-Merger Act.

THE FEDERAL TRADE COMMISSION ACT

The Federal Trade Commission Act was designed to prevent undesirable and unfair competitive practices. Specifically, it created a Federal Trade Commission to investigate unfair and predatory practices and to issue cease-and-desist orders. The act stated that "unfair methods of competition in commerce are hereby declared unlawful." However, the commission—composed of 5 commissioners, each appointed by the president for a term of 7 years—was given the unenviable task of defining exactly what was "unfair." Eventually, the courts took away much of the commission's power; but in 1938, the commission acquired the function of outlawing untrue and deceptive advertising. Also, the commission has authority to carry out economic investigations of the structure and conduct of American business.

The Role of the Courts

The antitrust laws, like any laws, are enforced in the courts. Typically, charges are brought against a firm or group of firms by the Antitrust Division of the Department of Justice, a trial is held, and a decision is reached by the judge. In key cases, appeals are made that eventually reach the Supreme Court. The real impact of the antitrust laws depends on how the courts interpret them. And the judicial interpretation of these laws has changed considerably over time.

The first major set of antitrust cases took place in 1911 when the Standard Oil Company and the American Tobacco Company were forced to give up a large share of their holdings of other companies. In these cases, the Supreme Court put forth and used the famous *rule of reason*—that only unreasonable combinations in restraint of trade, not all trusts, required conviction under the Sherman Act. In 1920, the rule of reason was used by the Supreme Court in its finding that U.S. Steel had not violated the antitrust laws even though it had tried to monopolize the industry—since the Court said it had not succeeded. Moreover, U.S. Steel's large size and its potential monopoly power were ruled beside the point since "the law does not make mere size an offense. It . . . requires overt acts."

During the 1920s and 1930s the courts, including the conservative Supreme Court, interpreted the antitrust laws in such a way that they were as toothless as a new-born babe. Although Eastman Kodak and International Harvester controlled very substantial shares of their markets, the

Court, using the rule of reason, found them innocent on the grounds that they had not built up their near-monopoly position through overt coercion or predatory practices. Moreover, the Court reiterated that mere size was not an offense, no matter how great the unexerted monopoly power might be.

In the late 1930s, this situation changed very greatly, with the prosecution of the Aluminum Corporation of America (Alcoa). This case, decided in 1945 (but begun in 1937), reversed the decisions in the *U.S. Steel* and *International Harvester* cases. Alcoa had achieved its 90 percent of the market by means that would have been considered "reasonable" in the earlier cases—keeping its price low enough to discourage entry, building capacity to take care of increases in the market, and so forth. (Recall our discussion of Alcoa in Chapter 11.) Nonetheless, the Court decided that Alcoa, because it controlled practically all the industry's output, violated the antitrust laws. Thus, to a considerable extent, *the Court used market structure rather than market conduct as a test of legality.*

The Role of the Justice Department

The impact of the antitrust laws is determined by the vigor with which the Antitrust Division of the Justice Department prosecutes cases. If the Antitrust Division does not prosecute, the laws can have little effect. Like the judicial interpretation of the laws, the extent to which the Justice Department has prosecuted cases has varied from one period to another. Needless to say, the attitude of the political party in power has been an important determinant of how vigorously antitrust cases have been prosecuted. When the Sherman Act was first passed, it was of singularly little value. For example, President Grover Cleveland's attorney general did not agree with the law and would not prosecute under it. "Trust-busting" was truly a neglected art until President Theodore Roosevelt devoted his formidable energies to it. In 1903, he established the Antitrust Division of the Justice Department. Moreover, his administration started the major cases that led to the *Standard Oil, American Tobacco,* and *U.S. Steel* decisions.

Subsequently, there was a long lull in the prosecution of antitrust cases, reflecting the Supreme Court's rule-of-reason doctrine and a strong conservative tide in the nation. The lull continued for about 25 years, until 1937, when there was a significant upsurge in activity on the antitrust front. Led by Thurman Arnold, the Antitrust Division entered one of the most vigorous periods of antitrust enforcement to date. Arnold went after the glass, cigarette, cement, and other industries, the most important case being that against Alcoa. The Antitrust Division attempted in this period to reopen cases that were hopeless under the rule-of-reason doctrine. With the change in the composition of the Supreme Court, Arnold's activism turned out to be effective.

Post-World-War-II Developments

The period since World War II generally has been a vigorous one from the viewpoint of antitrust, with at least six notable developments.

1. One of the biggest cases in the history of antitrust occurred in 1961 when, as you will recall from the previous chapter, the major electrical equipment manufacturers were convicted of collusive price agreements. Executives of General Electric, Westinghouse, and other firms in the industry admitted that they met secretly in hotels and communicated by mail in order to maintain prices, share the market, and eliminate competition. Some of the executives were sentenced to jail on criminal charges, and the firms had to pay large amounts to customers to make up for the overcharges. In particular, 1,800 triple damage suits against the firms resulted in payments estimated at between $400 and $600 million. Even the most zealous antitrusters will admit that this was no slap on the wrist!

2. Following the enactment of the Celler-Kefauver Anti-Merger Act, horizontal mergers—mergers of firms making essentially the same good—became increasingly likely to run afoul of the antitrust laws. In 1962, Chief Justice Earl Warren went so far as to say that a merger that resulted in a firm having 5 percent of the market might be undesirable. In the *Von's Grocery* case in 1965, the Court disallowed a merger between two supermarkets that together had less than 8 percent of the Los Angeles market. (In this case, the Court emphasized the trend toward increasing concentration in grocery retailing in Los Angeles.) Also, vertical mergers—mergers of firms that supply or sell to one another—have been viewed with a jaundiced eye by the courts. For example, in the *Brown Shoe* case, the Supreme Court said that the merger of Brown with R. G. Kinney would mean that other shoe manufacturers would be frozen out of a substantial part of the retail shoe market.

3. A leading problem confronting the Justice Department in the 1960s was conglomerate mergers—mergers of firms in unrelated industries. Conglomerate firms like Litton industries, International Telephone, and Ling-Temco-Vought were regarded very highly by investors during the 1960s. Inspired by their apparent success, other firms began to merge with firms in other industries in order to become conglomerates themselves. Supporters of these mergers claimed that they enabled weak companies to be revitalized by superior management, bigger research facilities, and so on. However, this merger movement was opposed by many other observers on the grounds that conglomerates were obtaining too much power in the economy. To some extent, this problem has diminished in importance since the conglomerates began to show relatively disappointing earnings in the late 1960s. But the Justice Department continues to keep a watchful eye on conglomerate mergers. In 1967 it succeeded in preventing a conglomerate merger between Procter & Gamble, the big soap manufacturer, and Clorox, a maker of liquid bleach. And in 1971 it made some attempt to force ITT to divest itself of the Hartford Fire Insurance Company, but the case was dropped.

4. In 1982, a government antitrust suit (begun in 1974) against the American Telephone and Telegraph Company (AT&T) was settled. According to the settlement, AT&T divested itself of 22 companies that provide most of

Basic Idea #25: The antitrust laws are designed to discourage monopoly and foster competition. Their effectiveness depends greatly on the Justice Department (which has the task of prosecuting) and the courts (which must interpret them). Without question, they have had an effect on the structure of American industry, but many observers feel that they have not been as effective as they might have been.

the nation's local telephone service, and kept its Long Lines division, Western Electric, and the Bell Laboratories. While many observers worried that one result was likely to be an increase in local telephone rates, there was also considerable feeling that, after the telephone industry was restructured in this way, AT&T would be a leaner and more dynamic firm. One immediate effect of this divestiture was a great deal of confusion among customers and costly adjustments within AT&T, but by 1985 many observers believed that it was resulting in faster introduction of new technologies and services and lower long-distance phone rates.

5. *The Antitrust Division sued IBM Corporation under Section 2 of the Sherman Act in January 1969, thus starting one of the biggest and costliest antitrust cases in history.* The government charged that IBM held a monopoly and that the firm's 360 line of computers was introduced in 1965 in a way that eliminated competition. IBM's defense was that its market position stemmed from its innovative performance and economies of scale, that its pricing was competitive, and that its profit rate really had not been high. Once the trial began in 1975, it took the government almost three years to present its case. In early 1982, on the same day that it settled the antitrust case against AT&T, the Reagan administration dropped the IBM case. It said the case was "without merit and should be dismissed."

6. *As the outcome of the IBM case indicated, antitrust policy changed in 1981 when President Reagan took office.* His Antitrust Division believed that a fair number of activities that had been deemed antitrust violations in the past not only were legal, but also were beneficial to the economy. According to this view, business decisions should be free of antitrust interference unless they are unequivocally anticompetitive. Given the huge costs (about $1 billion to IBM, according to some estimates) of the IBM case, and the feeling among some economists that economies of scale were sometimes underestimated, it is not surprising that such a change in emphasis and direction occurred. But economists who favor an aggressive antitrust policy have tended to regard this change with suspicion.

Test Yourself

1. "Perfect competition results in optimal efficiency and an optimal distribution of income. This is why the United States opts for a perfectly competitive economy." Comment and evaluate.

2. "The real impact of the antitrust laws depends on judicial interpretation." Comment and evaluate.

3. Suppose that an industry is composed of five firms. The market share of each firm is given in the table on the right:

Firm	Market share (percent)
A	10
B	10
C	20
D	25
E	35

What is the concentration ratio for this industry?

4. Suppose that firm E loses half of its sales to firm C. If the sales of the other firms remain constant, what is the effect on the concentration ratio in Question 3?

Standards for Antitrust Policy

There are at least two fairly distinct approaches to antitrust policy. *The first looks primarily and directly at* **market performance**—*the industry's rate of technological change, efficiency, and profits, the conduct of individual firms, and so on.* Advocates of this approach argue that, in deciding antitrust cases, one should review in detail the performance of the firms in question to see how well they have served the economy. If they have served well they should not be held in violation of the antitrust laws simply because they have a large share of the market. This test, as it is usually advocated, relies heavily on an evaluation of the technological "progressiveness" and "dynamism" of the firms in question. Although this approach seems quite sensible, it has a number of disadvantages. In particular, it is very difficult to tell at present whether a particular industry's performance is "good" or "bad." Economists simply do not have the sorts of measuring rods that would be required to obtain reasonably accurate and well-accepted readings on an industry's performance. In view of the vagueness of the criteria and the practical realities of the antitrust environment, adopting this approach would probably invite nonenforcement of the laws.

The second approach emphasizes the importance of an industry's **market structure**—*the number and size distribution of buyers and sellers in the market, the ease with which new firms can enter, and the extent of product differentiation.* According to this approach, one should look to market structure for evidence of undesirable monopolistic characteristics. The basic idea behind this approach, as George Stigler puts it, is that "an industry which does not have a competitive structure will not have competitive behavior." Two leading authorities on antitrust law, Carl Kaysen of M.I.T. and Donald Turner of Harvard (and formerly head of the Antitrust Division under President Johnson), are strong advocates of this approach. They believe that, if for 5 years or more, one firm has accounted for 50 percent or more of annual sales in a market, or if 4 or fewer firms have accounted for 80 percent of such sales, it should be presumed that "market power" exists. And they propose that such "market power" be declared illegal, unless such concentration can be defended by economies of scale or some other such justification. If it cannot be defended, divestiture and dissolution would constitute possible remedies.[7]

Although respected economists favor each of these approaches, the second is probably preferred by most experts in this field. However, this does not mean that the market structure approach does not have lots of critics. On the contrary, many economists and lawyers feel that the relationship between market structure and market performance is so weak that it is a mistake to choose, more or less arbitrarily, some level of concentration and to say that, if concentration exceeds this level, market performance is likely to be undesirable.

[7] C. Kaysen and D. Turner, *Antitrust Policy,* Cambridge, Mass.: Harvard University Press, 1959.

The Effectiveness of Antitrust Policy

How effective have the antitrust laws been? Obviously it is difficult to tell with any accuracy, since there is no way to carry out an experiment in which American history is rewritten to show what would have happened if the antitrust laws had not been on the books. Many experts seem to feel that the antitrust laws have not been as effective as they might—or should—have been, largely because they do not have sufficient public support and there is no politically powerful pressure group pushing for their enforcement.

But this does not mean that the antitrust laws have had no effect. As Edward Mason of Harvard University has pointed out, their effectiveness is due "not so much to the contribution that particular judgments have made to the restoring of competition as it is to the fact that the consideration of whether or not a particular course of action may or may not be in violation of the antitrust acts is a persistent factor affecting business judgment, at least in large firms."[8] This same idea is summed up in the old saying that the ghost of Senator Sherman sits as an *ex officio* member of every firm's board of directors.

Some indication of the effects of our antitrust laws can perhaps be obtained by looking at experience in other countries, since Britain, Germany, and many other European countries (as well as Japan) took a very tolerant view of monopoly power for a long time. After World War II, there was pressure to break up some of the powerful combines in Germany and Japan, but this pressure has been somewhat relaxed more recently—although antitrust practices seem to be gaining ground in the European Common Market. Foreign experience seems to indicate that the antitrust laws have helped prevent American firms from adopting many restrictive and predatory practices common elsewhere.

The *Pabst* Case: Antitrust in Action

Perhaps the most effective way to learn certain things about the antitrust field is to try to decide an actual antitrust case. Suppose that, over the protests of the American Bar Association, you are appointed a district court judge and that your first job is to hear a case (actually brought by the government in 1958) to prevent Pabst Brewing Company from acquiring the Blatz Brewing Company. According to the government, the effect of this merger "may be substantially to lessen competition, or to tend to create a monopoly" in the production and sale of beer in the state of Wisconsin, the three-state area of Wisconsin, Illinois, and Michigan, and the United States.

A fundamental issue in any case of this sort is the definition of market and industry boundaries. Market boundaries must be broad enough to include all relevant competitors but not so broad as to include products that are

PABST QUALITY.
IT'S A TRADITION THAT KEEPS GROWING.

---

[8] Edward Mason, Preface to Carl Kaysen and Donald Turner, *Antitrust Policy* (and reprinted in E. Mansfield, *Monopoly Power and Economic Performance,* 4th ed. New York: Norton, 1978).

not reasonable substitutes. The delineation of market and industry boundaries—in terms of "line of commerce" and "section of the country"—is bound to involve judgment, there being no simple, mechanical rule to settle it.

In the *Pabst* case, both the government and Pabst agreed "that the line of commerce involved the production, sale, and distribution of beer and that the continental United States is a relevant geographic market." However, there was disagreement over the government's use of Wisconsin and the three-state area of Wisconsin, Illinois, and Michigan as separate geographical markets. Pabst and Blatz claimed that there was no good reason to single out these particular areas as distinct markets. The government, on the other hand, claimed that they were distinct markets because the two firms competed most intensively in these areas. Pabst was the nation's eleventh largest seller of beer; its sales were 2.67 percent of the national market and about 11 percent of the sales in Wisconsin. Blatz was the nation's thirteenth largest seller of beer, its sales being 2.04 percent of the national market and about 13 percent of the sales in Wisconsin. Thus, *if you look at the smaller geographical area (Wisconsin and the three-state area), the two firms account for a substantial proportion of the market— about 24 percent in Wisconsin. But if you look at the national market as a whole, they account for a small proportion—less than 5 percent.*

As the district judge how should you decide the case? Should you agree with the government that Wisconsin and the three-state area are relevant markets? Or should you agree with Pabst and Blatz that they are not relevant markets in themselves, but just parts of a market? Moreover, if you agree with the government concerning the market definition, should you also agree that two firms with a total of 24 percent of Wisconsin sales should not be allowed to merge? Or if you agree with Pabst and Blatz concerning the market definition, should you allow a merger between two firms that together account for about 5 percent of the national market? It is a tough problem, isn't it? To demonstrate just how tough it is, the district judge decided one way, while the Supreme Court decided the other way. The district court, agreeing with Pabst and Blatz that Wisconsin and the three-state area should not be treated as distinct relevant areas, dismissed the government's complaint. But the district court's decision was reversed by the Supreme Court, which agreed with the government's position that the smaller areas should be treated as relevant, distinct markets.

The antitrust field is characterized by many complexities and uncertainties, as well as by legal and economic vagueness and ambiguity. This case illustrates how difficult it is even to decide what the relevant market is!

The Patent System

In a previous section, we pointed out that our national economic policies are by no means free of contradiction. In particular, although many of our policies are designed to promote competition and limit monopoly, one should not assume that all of them are meant to promote these objectives. On the contrary, quixotic as it may seem, some are designed to do just the opposite—to restrict competition. Among the most important of these pol-

Basic Idea #26: Although it is sometimes claimed that government policy supports competition and discourages monopoly, many of our laws are designed to do just the opposite. For example, the patent laws grant a temporary monopoly to inventors.

icies are our laws concerning patents, which grant inventors exclusive control over the use of their inventions for 17 years. That is, inventors are given a temporary monopoly over the use of their inventions.

THE PROS

Since Congress passed the original patent act in 1790, the arguments used to justify the existence of the patent laws have not changed very much. First, *these laws are regarded as an important incentive to induce the inventor to put in the work required to produce an invention.* Particularly in the case of the individual inventor, it is claimed that patent protection is a strong incentive. Second, *patents are regarded as a necessary incentive to induce firms to carry out the further work and make the necessary investment in pilot plants and other items that are required to bring the invention to commercial use.* If an invention became public property when made, why should a firm incur the costs and risks involved in attempting to develop, debug, and perfect it? Another firm could watch, take no risks, and duplicate the process or product if it were successful. Third, it is argued that because of the patent laws, *inventions are disclosed earlier than otherwise, the consequence being that other inventions are facilitated by the earlier dissemination of the information.* The resulting situation is often contrasted with the intense secrecy about processes that characterized the medieval guilds and which undoubtedly retarded technological progress and economic growth.

THE CONS

Not all economists agree that the patent system is beneficial. A patent represents a monopoly right, although as many inventors can testify, it may be a very weak one. Critics of the patent system stress the social costs arising from the monopoly. After a new process or product has been discovered, it may cost very little for other persons who could make use of this knowledge to acquire it. The patent gives the inventor the right to charge a price for the use of the information, with the result that the knowledge is used less widely than is socially optimal. Critics also point out that patents have been used to create monopoly positions, which were sustained by other means after the original patents had expired. They cite as examples the aluminum, shoe machinery, and plate-glass industries. In addition, the cross-licensing of patents often has been used by firms as a vehicle for joint monopolistic exploitation of their market.

Critics also question the extent of the social gains arising from the system. They point out that the patent system was designed for the individual inventor, but that over the years most research and development has been institutionalized. They assert that patents are not really important as incentives to the large corporation, since it cannot afford to fall behind in the technological race, whether or not it receives a patent. Also, they say that because of long lead times, most of the innovative profits from many innovations can be captured before imitators have a chance to enter the market, whether or not the innovator is granted a patent. Finally, they claim that firms keep secret what inventions they can, and patent those they cannot.

These questions concerning the effects and desirability of the patent

Cross-Chapter Case/Part Four
BERKEY PHOTO INC. V. EASTMAN KODAK CO.

One of the most celebrated antitrust cases of recent years involved Eastman Kodak and Berkey Photo. Eastman Kodak has long been a dominant producer of cameras and film. Berkey Photo competes with Kodak as a photofinisher, and less successfully (until 1978) as a camera manufacturer. Berkey buys much of its film and photofinishing equipment and supplies from Kodak. In 1973, Berkey filed suit, saying that Kodak had violated the antitrust laws when in 1972 it introduced its new 110 "Pocket Instamatic" camera. Because the camera was introduced with no advance notice to Kodak's competitors, Berkey could not introduce its own version of the new camera until late 1973, and did not reach a substantial sales volume until 1974. Berkey claimed that Kodak's failure to disclose the innovation to its competitors before introducing it violated section 2 of the Sherman Act.

The jury was instructed that if it found monopoly power in the relevant markets (cameras or film), it could then consider "whether in the light of other conduct [it] determine[d] to be anticompetitive, Kodak's failure to predisclose was on balance an exclusionary course of conduct,"[1] and thus in violation of section 2. The jury found that Berkey should be awarded damages, after trebling, of $45,750,000 for lost profits on the 110 camera and $167,100 for lost profits on photofinishing services. The court also instructed Kodak to disclose (before introduction) to competitors all camera and film innovations that it provides its own photofinishing division.

Eastman Kodak appealed the decision, and the Second Circuit Court reversed the damage awards. The court pointed out that "withholding from others advance knowledge of one's new products . . . ordinarily constitutes valid competitive conduct."[2] To insist on such disclosure would reduce the incentives to innovate. Regardless of whether Kodak had monopoly power in cameras or in film, Kodak did not have a duty to predisclose information about the 110 camera to its competition. "Because, as we have already indicated, a monopolist is permitted, and indeed encouraged . . . to compete aggressively on the merits, any success that it may achieve through the process of invention and innovation is clearly tolerated by the antitrust laws."[3]

In addition, Berkey claimed that Kodak engaged in two separate conspiracies, with General Electric and with Sylvania, to restrain trade in the use of new flash devices with amateur cameras. In 1963, Sylvania approached Kodak with a prototype of a new battery-powered light device: the flashcube. Berkey said that Kodak, although it did not make any real technical contributions to the flashcube, required Sylvania not to provide information concerning this invention to other camera producers. Thus Kodak was for some time the only firm able to sell cameras using this device. Similarly, Kodak insisted that Sylvania not disclose its magicube invention and that General Electric not disclose its flipflash invention. Consequently, Kodak's cameras were for a time the only ones that used these new devices.

[1] *Berkey Photo, Inc. v Eastman Kodak Co.*, 603 F. 2d 263 (1979), p. 281.
[2] Ibid.
[3] Ibid.

While the circuit court did not conclude that joint development projects between monopolists and manufacturers of complementary products are per se violations of section 1 of the Sherman Act, it did find that the secrecy agreements in this case were unreasonable restraints of trade. In the words of the circuit court judge, "Kodak and GE, of course, are not direct competitors, and Kodak and Sylvania were at best potential competitors when the magicube was being developed. Nevertheless, because of Kodak's market power over cameras, the exclusionary potential of horizontal research pools was present. In the case of the flipflash, for example, GE indicated early in 1971 that it could be at maximum production in two years. Kodak, however, counselled delay, at one point urging GE project officials to make a show of progress, "even if all you do is 'paint the red base black,' " so that "we'll feel free to work with you." Otherwise, Kodak said, GE could not be assured of being part of Kodak's future flash plans, for "we would then have to ask all [lamp] manufacturers" to submit ideas. A few months later, the two firms executed the formal agreement binding them to join development of flipflash and nondisclosure to rival lamp and camera manufacturers. From this and other evidence, the jury could have found in the verdict it returned that, without any technological justification, GE kept a desirable innovation off the market for two years solely to suit Kodak's convenience. There is a hollow ring to a claim of justification by appeal to the need to promote innovation, where the result of the conduct was such a clear loss to consumers."

system have proven extremely difficult to settle. But most observers seem to agree that, despite its faults, it is difficult to find a realistic substitute for the patent system. However, over the past 30 years, there has been a discernible trend for the courts and Congress to resolve conflicts between the patent system and antitrust policy in favor of the latter. The courts have found more and more patents invalid; Congress has set higher standards of patentability; and the courts have curtailed the extension of the effects of the patent beyond the invention described in the patent claim.

Other Policies Designed to Restrict Competition

The reasons why laws are enacted to restrict, rather than promote, competition are not difficult to understand. People want competition for the other guy, but not for themselves. Moreover, certain sectors of the economy seem to need help, and have the political muscle to get it—partly in the form of laws designed to take some of the competitive heat off them.

ROBINSON-PATMAN ACT

A case of this sort is retail trade, where the small independent retailers felt threatened by the advent of the chain store. The chain stores were able to reduce the costs of distribution below those of the smaller retailers, with the result that the total number of grocery stores and drug stores fell considerably in the 1920s and 1930s. The small retailers charged that their smaller numbers were due to the predatory tactics of the chain stores. They took their charges to Congress and succeeded in getting the Robinson-Patman Act enacted in 1936.

The Robinson-Patman Act says that sellers must not discriminate in price among purchasers of similar grade and quality where the effect might be to drive competitors out of business. The act was aimed at preventing price discrimination in favor of chain stores that buy goods in large quantities. Most economists do not regard the Robinson-Patman Act with enthusiasm because it attempts to keep competitors in existence even if they are inefficient. (The social virtues of the competitive system do not lie in maintaining a lot of inefficient small businessmen in operation.) Moreover, most observers seem to believe that the act has had the effect of reducing the vigor of price competition in retail trade.

MILLER-TYDINGS ACT

Another law designed to limit competition in U.S. retail trade was the Miller-Tydings Act of 1937, which exempted from the antitrust laws the use of resale price maintenance agreements in states permitting such agreements. *Resale price maintenance agreements* permitted manufacturers of a trademarked or branded item to establish the retail price of the item by contracts with retailers. Moreover, the Miller-Tydings Act permitted the manufacturer to bind *all* retailers in a state to a contract simply by signing such a contract with *any one* of the retailers in the state. The result was to reduce the amount of price competition in retail trade. In 1975, Congress passed a bill nullifying such agreements.

OTHER POLICIES LIMITING COMPETITION

Finally, you should recognize that policies designed to limit competition are found in many other areas besides retail trade. In Chapter 4, we saw that our national farm policies have been aimed at keeping the prices of agricultural products at a level exceeding what they would be under competition. In Chapter 14, we shall see that the government has promoted the growth of strong labor unions, which try to raise wages above competitive levels. In

Example 13.1   Resale Price Maintenance and Cosmetics

Until 1975, resale price maintenance agreements allowed manufacturers of a trademarked item to establish a floor under the retail price of the item. Suppose that the manufacturer of a cosmetic established OP as its minimum retail price, and that D_0 is the demand curve for this cosmetic at a particular drugstore. The drugstore's average costs are also shown in the diagram.

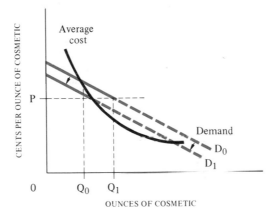

(a) Only the solid portion of demand curve D_0 is relevant to the drugstore. Why? (b) Can the drugstore make a profit on the sale of the cosmetic? (c) Will there be a change in the number of drugstores selling the cosmetic? What sort of a change? Why? (d) As changes occur in the number of drugstores selling the cosmetic, the demand curve eventually moves to D_1. Why? At this point, can a drugstore make a profit on the sale of the cosmetic?

SOLUTION

(a) Because the drugstore cannot sell the cosmetic at a price less than OP without running afoul of the resale price maintenance agreements. (b) Yes. If it sells between OQ_0 and OQ_1 ounces of the cosmetic, the price it receives will exceed its average cost. (c) Yes. Because profits are made on this cosmetic, other stores will begin to sell it, the result being that the number of stores selling it will increase. (d) Because more and more stores sell the cosmetic, the total volume is spread more thinly among the stores. In other words, the demand curve facing a particular drugstore shifts to the left. When the demand curve reaches D_1, a drugstore can no longer make a profit from the sale of the cosmetic. Thus entry ceases.*

* For further discussion, see L. Weiss, *Case Studies in American Industry,* New York: Wiley, 1980.

the field of international trade, the Webb-Pomerene Act of 1918 allowed American exporters to get together to form export trade associations, which, according to some observers, may have tended to reduce competition. Even in the bituminous coal industry, which we looked at in some detail in Chapter 10. Congress passed the Bituminous Coal Act of 1937 to establish minimum prices and reduce "cutthroat" competition, though in 1943 the act was not renewed.

Thus it is erroneous to think that the United States has opted decisively for competition. On the contrary, although the antitrust laws are clearly designed to promote competition and limit monopoly, a number of other laws are designed to do just the opposite. In many of the industries where laws designed to restrict competition have been enacted—for example, agriculture, retail trade, and bituminous coal—the basic problem has been that too many people and too much capital were tied up in the industry. Economists generally believe that it would be wiser to encourage people and capital to leave these industries than to attempt to limit competition. (Recall our discussion in Chapter 4 of American farm policies.)

Test Yourself

1. According to John Kenneth Galbraith, "The antitrust laws effectively protect the large business from social pressure or regulation by maintaining the myth that the market does the regulating instead." Do you agree? Why or why not?

2. On November 4, 1985, *Business Week* reported that, "In the Antitrust Division, with enforcement in the doldrums, many senior lawyers want to leave but can't find jobs at private firms because the lack of enforcement activity has reduced private practice, as well." Is this necessarily bad? Why or why not?

3. Chief Justice Hughes observed, "Good intentions will not save a plan otherwise objectionable, but knowledge of actual intent is an aid in the interpretation of facts and prediction of consequence." Relate this to the construction of standards for antitrust policy.

4. What are the arguments in favor of the patent system? What are the arguments against it? Is there currently considerable political support for the abolition of the patent system?

Summary

1. A monopolistic industry produces too little of the monopolized good. Society is less well off than it could be. Oligopoly can be as bad as monopoly if oligopolists engage in collusion; and even if they don't collude, inefficiencies are likely to result. Monopolistic competition can also be a socially wasteful form of market organization.

2. In defense of monopoly power, some economists, such as Galbraith, have asserted that the rate of technological change is likely to be greater in an imperfectly competitive industry than under perfect competition. It does seem unlikely that a perfectly competitive industry would be able—and have the incentive—to carry out the research and development required to promote a rapid rate of technological change in many sectors of the economy.

3. Contrary to the allegations of Galbraith and others, there is little evidence that giant firms are needed to insure rapid technological change in a great many sectors of the economy. The situation is much more complex than such statements

indicate, and the contributions of smaller firms are much greater than is commonly recognized.

4. Economic power in the United States is distributed very unevenly; 100 corporations control about half the total manufacturing assets of the economy. Moreover, many individual industries are dominated by a few firms. This concentration of power is viewed with concern by some economists and lawyers.

5. In 1890, the Sherman Act was passed. It outlawed any contract, combination, or conspiracy in restraint of trade and made it illegal to monopolize or attempt to monopolize. In 1914, Congress passed the Clayton Act, and the Federal Trade Commission was created. A more recent antitrust development was the Celler-Kefauver Anti-Merger Act of 1950.

6. The real impact of the antitrust laws depends on the interpretation placed on these laws by the courts. In its early cases, the Supreme Court put forth and used the famous rule of reason—that only unreasonable combinations in restraint of trade, not all trusts, required conviction under the Sherman Act. The situation changed greatly in the 1940s when the Court decided that Alcoa, because it controlled practically all of the nation's aluminum output, was in violation of the antitrust laws.

7. There are at least two fairly distinct approaches to antitrust policy. One looks primarily and directly at market performance; the other emphasizes market structure. Although there are respected economists in favor of each of these approaches, the second is probably preferred by most experts in this field.

8. Many observers seem to feel that the antitrust laws have not been as effective as they might—or should—have been, largely because they do not have sufficient public support. At the same time, many feel that the evidence, although incomplete and unclear, suggests that they have had a nonnegligible effect on business behavior and markets.

9. Not all our laws are designed to promote competition and restrict monopoly. On the contrary, some laws are designed to do just the opposite. The patent system confers a temporary monopoly on inventors. And the Robinson-Patman Act and many other laws have been designed to restrict competition. The truth is that, despite some protests to the contrary, our nation is by no means fully committed to promoting competition and preventing monopoly.

Concepts for Review

Market concentration ratio	Tying contract	Patent system
Antitrust laws	Rule of reason	Resale price maintenance
Price discrimination	Market performance	
	Market structure	

PART FIVE

Distribution of Income

CHAPTER 14

Determinants of Wages

Everyone has a healthy—indeed, sometimes an unhealthy—interest in income. Organizations as holy as the church and as unholy as the Mob exhibit an interest in this subject. Surely we all need to look carefully at the social mechanisms underlying the distribution of income in our society. Most income is in the form of wages and salaries; that is, it is labor income. What determines the price paid for a particular kind of labor? Why is the wage rate for surgeons frequently in the neighborhood of $100 an hour, while the wage rate for relatively unskilled labor is frequently in the neighborhood of $4 or $5 an hour? Or why is the wage rate for a secretary higher in 1986 than in 1960?

Economists frequently classify inputs into three categories—labor, capital, and land. The disadvantage of this simple classification is that each category contains an enormous variety of inputs. Consider the services of labor, which include the work of a football star like Eric Dickerson, a salesman like Willy Loman, and a knight like Don Quixote. But it does have the important advantage of distinguishing between different classes of inputs. In this chapter, we are concerned with the determinants of the price of labor. The next chapter will deal with the determinants of the prices of capital and land, as well as profits.

The Labor Force and the Price of Labor

At the outset it is important to note that, to the economist, labor includes a great deal more than the organized labor that belongs to trade unions. The secretary who works at IBM, the young account executive at Merrill Lynch, the auto mechanic at your local garage, the professor who teaches molecular

Table 14.1

OCCUPATIONAL COMPOSITION OF THE EMPLOYED LABOR FORCE, UNITED STATES, AUGUST 1984[a]

		Percent of employed labor force
Managerial and professional workers		22.9
Executive	11.0	
Professional	11.9	
Technical, sales, and administrative support workers		30.9
Technicians	3.0	
Sales	12.1	
Administrative support	15.8	
Service workers		13.4
Private household	0.9	
Protective service	1.6	
Other service	10.8	
Precision production, craft, repair workers		12.8
Operators, fabricators, and laborers		16.1
Machine operators	7.6	
Transportation and material moving	4.2	
Handlers and laborers	4.3	
Farming, forestry, and fishing		3.9
Total		100.0

[a] Because of rounding errors, figures may not sum to total.
Source: Bureau of Labor Statistics.

Table 14.2

AVERAGE WEEKLY EARNINGS, SELECTED INDUSTRIES, 1955–84 (DOLLARS)

Year	Manufact- uring	Construction	Retail trade
1955	76	91	49
1960	90	113	58
1965	108	138	67
1970	134	195	82
1975	190	265	108
1980	289	368	147
1984	373	455	177

biology, all put forth labor. Table 14.1 shows the occupational distribution of the labor force in the United States. You can see that almost two-thirds of the people employed are white collar workers (such as salesmen, doctors, secretaries, or managers) and service workers (such as waiters, bartenders, or cooks), while only about one-third are blue-collar workers (such as carpenters, mine workers, or foremen) and farm workers.

It is also worthwhile to preface our discussion with some data concerning how much people actually get paid. As shown in Table 14.2, average weekly earnings vary considerably from one industry to another. For example, in 1984, workers in manufacturing averaged about $373 a week, while construction workers averaged $455 a week, and workers in retail trade averaged $177 a week. Also, average weekly earnings vary considerably from one period to another. Table 14.2 shows that average weekly earnings in manufacturing in 1965 were only $108, as contrasted with $373 in 1984. In subsequent sections, we shall investigate the reasons for these differences in wages, both among industries and among periods of time.

More broadly, we shall be concerned in subsequent sections with the price of labor, which includes a great many forms of renumeration other than what are commonly regarded as wages. As noted above, economists include as labor the services performed by professional people (such as lawyers, doctors, and professors) and self-employed businessmen (such as electricians, mechanics, and barbers). Thus the amount such people receive per unit of time is included here as a particular sort of price of labor, even though these amounts are often called fees or salaries rather than wages.

Finally, it is important to distinguish between *money* wages and *real* wages. Whereas the money wage is the amount of money received per unit of time, the real wage is the amount of real goods and services that can be bought with the money wage. The real wage depends on the price level for goods and services as well as on the magnitude of the money wage. In recent years (particularly during the late 1970s and early 1980s), the inflation we have experienced has meant that real wages have increased less than money wages; thus the increases in earnings in Table 14.2 exaggerate the increase in real wages. In subsequent sections, since we shall assume that product prices are held constant, our discussion will be in terms of real wages.

The Equilibrium Wage and Employment Under Perfect Competition

THE FIRM'S DEMAND CURVE FOR LABOR

Let's begin by discussing the determinants of the price of labor under perfect competition. That is, we assume that firms take the prices of their products, as well as the prices of all inputs as given; and we assume that owners of inputs take input prices as given. Under these circumstances, what determines how much labor an individual firm will hire (at a specified wage rate)? Once we answer this question, we can derive a firm's demand curve for labor. A *firm's demand curve for labor* is the relationship between the price of labor and the amount of labor utilized by the firm. That is, it shows, for each price, the amount of labor that the firm will use.

THE PROFIT-MAXIMIZING QUANTITY OF LABOR

Let us assume that we know the firm's production function, and that labor is the only variable input. Given the production function, we can determine the marginal product of labor when various quantities are used. The results of such a calculation are as shown in Table 14.3. If the price of the firm's product is $10. let's determine the value to the firm of each additional worker it hires per day.[1] According to Table 14.3, the firm achieves a daily output of 7 units when it hires the first worker; and since each unit is worth $10, this brings the firm's daily revenues up to $70. By hiring the second worker, the firm increases its daily output by 6 units; and since each unit is worth $10, the resulting increase in the firm's daily revenues is $60. Similarly, the increase in the firm's daily revenues from hiring the third worker is $50, the increase from hiring the fourth worker is $40, and so on.

How many workers should the firm hire per day if it wants to maximize profit? It should hire more workers as long as the extra workers result in at least as great an addition to revenues as they do to costs. If the price of a

Table 14.3

THE FIRM'S DEMAND FOR LABOR UNDER PERFECT COMPETITION

Number of workers per day	Total output per day	Marginal product of labor	Value of marginal product (dollars)
0	0		
		7	70
1	7		
		6	60
2	13		
		5	50
3	18		
		4	40
4	22		
		3	30
5	25		

Basic Idea #27: How much labor a firm finds it profitable to hire depends on labor's productivity and price. If the value of the marginal product of labor is greater than labor's price, a firm can increase its profit by hiring more labor; otherwise, it is not profitable to do so.

[1] For simplicity, we assume that the number of workers that the firm hires per day must be an integer, not a fraction. This assumption is innocuous, and can easily be relaxed.

worker is $50 per day, it is profitable for the firm to hire the first worker since this adds $70 to the firm's daily revenues but only $50 to its daily costs. Also, it is profitable to hire the second worker, since this adds $60 to the firm's daily revenues but only $50 to its daily costs. The addition of the third worker does not reduce the firm's profits. But beyond 3 workers per day, it does not pay the firm to hire more labor. (The addition of a fourth worker adds $50 to the firm's daily costs but only $40 to its daily revenues.)

THE VALUE OF THE MARGINAL PRODUCT OF LABOR

Thus the optimal number of workers per day for this firm is 3. Table 14.3 shows that this is the number of workers at which the value of the marginal product of labor is equal to the price of labor. What is the *value of the marginal product of labor?* It is the marginal product of labor multiplied by the product's price. In Table 14.3, the value of the marginal product of labor is $70 when between 0 and 1 workers are used per day. Why? Because the marginal product of labor is 7 units of output, and the price of a unit of output is $10. Thus this product—7 times $10—equals $70.

To maximize profit, the value of the marginal product of labor must be set equal to the price of labor, because if the value of the marginal product is greater than labor's price, the firm can increase its profit by increasing the quantity used of labor; while if the value of the marginal product is less than labor's price, the firm can increase its profit by reducing the quantity used of labor. Thus *profits must be at a maximum when the value of the marginal product is equal to the price of labor.*

Given the results of this section, it is a simple matter to derive the firm's demand curve for labor. Specifically, its demand curve must be the value-of-marginal-product schedule in the last column of Table 14.3. If the daily wage of a worker is between $51 and $60, the firm will demand 2 workers per day; if the daily wage of a worker is between $41 and $50, the firm will demand 3 workers per day; and so forth. Thus *the firm's demand curve for labor is its value-of-marginal-product curve,* which shows the value of labor's marginal product at each quantity of labor used. This curve is shown in Figure 14.1.[2]

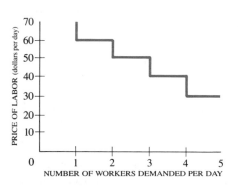

Figure 14.1

The Firm's Demand Curve for Labor under Perfect Competition *The firm's demand curve for labor is the firm's value-of-marginal-product curve, which shows the value of labor's marginal product at each quantity of labor used. The data for this figure come from Table 14.3.*

The Market Demand Curve for Labor

In previous sections, we were concerned with the demand curve of a single firm for labor. But many firms, not just one, are part of the labor market, and the price of labor depends on the demands of all of these firms. The situation is analogous to the price of a product, which depends on the demands of all consumers. *The market demand curve for labor shows the relationship between the price of labor and the total amount of labor demanded in the market. That is, it shows, for each price, the amount of labor*

---

[2] Strictly speaking, the firm's demand curve is the same as the curve showing the value of the input's marginal product only if this input is the only variable input. For a discussion of the more general case, see my *Microeconomics: Theory and Applications,* 5th ed., New York: Norton, 1985, Chapter 12.

that will be demanded in the entire market. The market demand curve for labor, like any other input, is quite analogous to the market demand curve for a consumer good, which we discussed in detail in Chapter 6.

But there is at least one important difference. *The demand for labor and other inputs is a **derived demand,** since inputs are demanded to produce other things, not as an end in themselves.* This fact helps to explain why the price elasticity of demand is higher for some inputs than for others. In particular, the larger the price elasticity of demand for the product the input helps produce, the larger the price elasticity of demand for the input. (In addition, the price elasticity of demand for an input is likely to be greater in the long run than in the short run, and greater if other inputs can readily be substituted for the input in question.)

The Market Supply Curve for Labor

We have already seen that a product's price depends on its market supply curve as well as its market demand curve. This is equally true for labor. Its *market supply curve* is *the relationship between the price of labor and the total amount of labor supplied in the market.* When individuals supply labor, they are supplying something they themselves can use, since the time that they do not work can be used for leisure activities. (As Charles Lamb, the English essayist, put it, "Who first invented work, and bound the free and holiday-rejoicing spirit down . . . to that dry drudgery at the desk's dead wood?"[3]) Because of this fact, the market supply curve for labor, unlike the supply curve for inputs supplied by business firms, may be *backward bending,* particularly for the economy as a whole. That is, *beyond some point, increases in price may result in smaller amounts of labor being supplied.*

An example of a backward-bending supply curve is provided in Figure 14.2. What factors account for a curve like this? Basically, the reason is that as the price of labor is increased, individuals supplying the labor become richer. And when they become richer, they want to increase their amount of leisure time, which means that they want to work less. Even though the amount of money per hour they give up by not working is greater than when the price of labor was lower, they nonetheless choose to increase their leisure time. This sort of tendency has shown up quite clearly in the last century. As wage rates have increased and living standards have risen, the average work week has tended to decline.

Note that there is no contradiction between the assumption that the supply curve of labor or other inputs *to an individual firm* is horizontal under perfect competition and the fact that the *market* supply curve for the input may not be horizontal. For example, unskilled labor may be available to any firm in a particular area at a given wage rate in as great an amount as it could possibly use. But the total amount of unskilled labor supplied in this area may increase relatively little with increases in the wage rate. The situation is similar to the sale of products. As we saw in Chapter 6, any firm under perfect competition believes that it can sell all

Figure 14.2

Backward-bending Supply Curve for Labor *Beyond some point, increases in the price of labor may result in smaller amounts of labor being supplied. The reason for a supply curve of this sort is that, as the price of labor increases, the individual supplying the labor becomes richer and wants to increase his amount of leisure time.*

The graph has y-axis labeled PRICE OF LABOR and x-axis labeled QUANTITY OF LABOR SUPPLIED, with origin 0.

[3] The answer to Lamb's question is perhaps to be found in Genesis 3:19.

281

it wants at the existing price. Yet the total amount of the product sold in the entire market can ordinarily be increased only by lowering the price.

Equilibrium Price and Quantity of Labor

Labor's price (or wage rate) is determined under perfect competition in essentially the same way that a product's price is determined—by supply and demand.

The price of labor will tend toward equilibrium at the level where the quantity of labor demanded equals the quantity of labor supplied. Thus, in Figure 14.3, the equilibrium price of labor is *OP*. If the price were higher than *OP*, the quantity supplied would exceed the quantity demanded and there would be downward pressure on the price. If the price were lower than *OP*, the quantity supplied would fall short of the quantity demanded and there would be upward pressure on the price. By the same token, *the equilibrium amount of labor utilized is also given by the intersection of the market supply and demand curves.* In Figure 14.3, *OQ* units of labor will be utilized in equilibrium in the entire market.

Graphs such as Figure 14.3 are useful, but it is important to look behind the geometry, and to recognize the factors that lie behind the demand and supply curves for labor. Consider the market for surgeons and that for unskilled labor. As shown in Figure 14.4, the demand curve for the services of surgeons is to the right of the demand curve for unskilled labor (particularly at high wage rates). Why is this so? Because an hour of a surgeon's services is worth more to people than an hour of an unskilled laborer's services. In this sense, surgeons are more productive than unskilled laborers. Also, as shown in Figure 14.4, the supply curve for the services of surgeons is far to the left of the supply curve for unskilled labor. Why is this so? Because very few people are licensed surgeons, whereas practically everyone can do un-

Figure 14.3

Equilibrium Price and Quantity of Labor *The equilibrium price of labor is* OP, *and the equilibrium quantity of labor used is* OQ.

Surgeons

P_S

Supply — Demand

PRICE OF LABOR

0   Q_S

QUANTITY OF LABOR

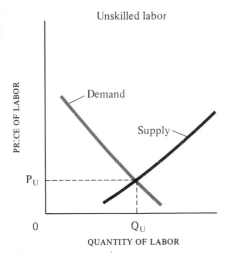

Unskilled labor

Demand

Supply

PRICE OF LABOR

P_U

0   Q_U

QUANTITY OF LABOR

Figure 14.4

***The Labor Market for Surgeons and
Unskilled Labor*** *The wage for surgeons
is higher than for unskilled labor because
the demand curve for surgeons is farther
to the right and the supply curve for
surgeons is farther to the left than the
corresponding curves for unskilled labor.*

skilled labor. In other words, surgeons are much more scarce than unskilled laborers.

For these reasons, surgeons receive a much higher wage rate than do unskilled laborers. As shown in Figure 14.4, the equilibrium price of labor for surgeons is much higher than for unskilled labor. If unskilled laborers could quickly and easily turn themselves into competent surgeons, this difference in wage rates would be eliminated by competition, since unskilled workers would find it profitable to become surgeons. But unskilled workers lack the training and often the ability to become surgeons. Thus surgeons and unskilled labor are examples of ***noncompeting groups.*** Wage differentials can be expected to persist among noncompeting groups because people cannot move from the low-paid to the high-paid jobs. But this is not the only reason for wage differentials, as we shall see in the next section.

Wage Differentials

Everyone realizes that, even in the same occupation, some people get paid more than others. Why is this true?

Differences in Ability or Skill. One reason for such wage differentials is that people differ in productive capacity; thus each worker differs from the next in the value of his or her output. Under these circumstances, the difference in wages paid to workers equals the difference in their marginal products' value. Consider the case of two lathe operators—Roberta and Leo. Roberta works for firm X and Leo works for firm Y. Roberta (together with the appropriate tools and materials) can produce output worth $2,000 per month and Leo (with the same tools and materials) can produce output worth $1,900 per month. In equilibrium, Roberta will earn $100 more per month than Leo. If the difference in wages were less than $100, Leo's employer would find it profitable to replace Leo with Roberta, since this would increase the value of output by $100 and cost less than $100. If the difference were more than $100, Roberta's employer would find it profitable to replace Roberta with Leo; although this would reduce the value of output by $100, it would reduce costs by more than $100.

Differences in Training. Besides differences in productive capacity and ability, there are many other reasons for wage differentials. Even if all workers were of equal ability, these differentials would still exist to offset differences in the characteristics of various occupations and areas. Some occupations require large investments in training, while other occupations require a much smaller investment in training. Chemists must spend about eight years in undergraduate and graduate training. During each year of training, they incur direct expenses for books, tuition, and the like, and they lose the income they could make if they were to work rather than go to school. Clearly, if their net remuneration is to be as high in chemistry as in other jobs they might take, they must make a greater wage when they get through than persons of comparable age, intelligence, and motivation whose job requires no training beyond high school. The difference in wages must be at least sufficient to compensate for their investment in extra training.

Other Differences. Similarly, members of some occupations must bear larger occupational expenses than others. A psychologist may have to buy testing materials and subscribe to expensive journals. For net compensation to be equalized, such workers must be paid more than others. Also, some jobs are more unstable than others. Some types of construction workers are subject to frequent layoffs and have little job security, whereas many government employees (but not the top ones) are assured stable and secure employment. If the former jobs are to be as attractive as the latter, they must pay more. In addition, other differences among jobs must be offset by

Example 14.1   Millionaire Geologists

On April 16, 1981, the *Wall Street Journal* reported that "many geologists earn more than many chief executive officers. Salaries of $1 million a year are routine for the experienced geologists who are in greatest demand. An independent [oil] company recently offered a senior exploration man at another company $1.5 million; he turned down the offer."

  (a) What factors were responsible for the sharp rise in the wage rate for geologists? (b) During the late 1950s and 1960s, when the U.S. began to rely more heavily on foreign crude oil, domestic exploration fell. What do you think was the effect on the number of people entering petroleum engineering? Why? (c) In 1976, the University of Pittsburgh reinstated its petroleum program as part of chemical engineering, but had trouble obtaining faculty for it. Why do you think this trouble developed?

SOLUTION

(a) Because of the hefty increase in the price of crude oil, there was in 1981 a boom in oil drilling, which pushed the demand curve for geologists far to the right (from D_1 to D_2), as shown below. The result is that the wage of a geologist increased from OP_1 to OP_2. (b) Since there was a reduction in the demand for petroleum engineers, less jobs were available, and people turned to other fields. (c) Because potential faculty members were reluctant to leave lucrative jobs in industry to take teaching jobs.*

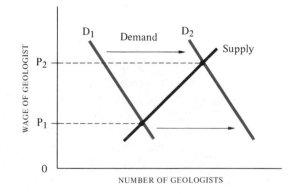

* For further discussion, see "Heated Energy Search Creates Class of Millionaire Oil-Firm Geologists," *Wall Street Journal,* April 16, 1981.

wage differentials if the net remuneration is to be equalized. For instance, there are differences among regions and communities in the cost of living. (Living costs are generally lower in small towns than in big cities.)

The All-Volunteer Army: A Case Study

In recent years there has been considerable controversy concerning the advantages and disadvantages of an all-volunteer army, the system used in this country since the early 1970s. Many economists have argued that recruiting an all-volunteer army is more efficient and equitable than relying on the draft, which through a complicated system of deferments and exemptions, as well as a lottery system, selected a certain number of young men for military service. Proponents of an all-volunteer army point out that it is more compatible with freedom of choice than the draft. In addition, they say that military personnel are used more effectively because the price of such personnel is a more realistic indicator of its value in alternative uses. Further, they point out that the cost of military manpower is distributed more equitably among the members of society. Under the draft a small group of draftees bore a large share of the cost, because they received less in wages than would have been required to induce them to volunteer.

Other economists and social observers oppose an all-volunteer army. They point out that the present system can hardly be expected to produce the necessary military manpower in a full-scale war. They also contend that an army of "paid mercenaries" might constitute a political danger by attempting to gain improper power. Some claim too that an all-volunteer army relies disproportionately on the black population, since young blacks constitute a much larger percentage of those without civilian jobs than their white counterparts.

How did the all-volunteer army come into being? In 1964, President Johnson asked that a study be made to determine whether it would be possible to shift from reliance on the draft to a system in which defense manpower needs would be met entirely by volunteers. A team of economists attempted to learn what it would cost.[4] Essentially they applied the kind of analysis described in this chapter. The basic approach was to estimate the supply curve for labor to the Department of Defense.

Figure 14.5 shows the relationship between the proportion of the male population that enlists and the level of military pay (as a percent of civilian pay), the unemployment rate being held constant at two alternative levels. As would be expected, the number of enlistments increases with the level of military pay and the unemployment rate. Using this supply curve, which was estimated by the economists, one could determine (for given values of the unemployment rate) the level of military pay that was required to bring forth the number of extra enlistments needed to eliminate the draft.

According to the economists, a 60 to 90 percent increase in enlistments

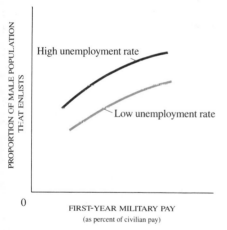

Figure 14.5

Relationship between Military Pay and Number of Enlistments *Holding the unemployment rate constant, the proportion of the male population that enlists is directly related to the level of military pay (as a percent of civilian pay). Using this supply curve, economists determined the level of military pay required to bring forth the extra enlistments needed to eliminate the draft.*

[4] See S. Altman and A. Fechter, "The Supply of Military Personnel in the Absence of a Draft," *American Economic Review*, May 1967; and literature cited there.

An interesting development in recent years, due to Harvard's Michael Spence, is the theory of market signaling. In 1981, Spence received the John Bates Clark medal (given every two years by the American Economic Association to the most distinguished economist under 40 years of age), in part for his seminal work on this topic. To illustrate what signaling is, suppose for simplicity that there are two distinctly different types of workers (high ability and low ability) that an employer can hire. The marginal product of high-ability workers is greater than that of low-ability workers. However, the employer cannot be sure whether a particular worker is high-ability or low-ability until after the worker has been hired. This is because it takes time on the job for the employer to determine the capabilities and productivity of the worker.

Michael Spence

If the employer regards the educational level of a job applicant as a signal, or indicator, of the worker's ability, it may pay workers to invest in their education in order to signal the employer that they in fact are able. Of course, Mary Stuart, in getting an education, may not think of herself as signaling. She will invest in education if there is sufficient return, which will depend on how much more the employer is willing to pay for highly educated than for poorly educated workers.

Assuming that the difficulty (and thus the cost) of attaining a higher educational level is less for high-ability than for low-ability people, it is clear that high-ability people will have more incentive than low-ability people to get high levels of education. Thus the employer's belief that educational level is an effective indicator, or signal, of ability and productivity will be reinforced by experience. Consequently, the employer will continue to find it profitable to offer a higher wage to job applicants with relatively high levels of education, since such applicants are more likely to be high-ability people. Thus high-ability individuals will continue to find it economically worthwhile to invest relatively heavily in their educations.

An important thing to note is that, to the individual, it appears that higher education is a prerequisite to a high-paying job. After all, under these circumstances, the employer pays more for people with more education. Also, to an outside observer, it appears that education enhances the productivity of the worker. This seems to be true because the better-educated people have higher productivity and earn bigger wages than the less-educated people. In fact, however, even if education has no effect on productivity and is only a signal of a person's ability, there will be a direct relationship between a person's education, on the one hand, and his or her productivity and wages, on the other.

was needed to eliminate the draft. To bring forth these extra enlistments, they estimated on the basis of the supply curve that first-term military pay for enlisted men had to be increased by about 110 percent (if the unemployment rate were 5.5 percent). Using 1964 military earnings as a base, increases in first-term pay for enlisted men had to be about $3,000 to attract enough volunteers to maintain a 2.65-million-man defense force. Multiplying 2.65 million men by the average increase in pay, the economists estimated that the increased cost to the Defense Department would be about $5 billion per year.[5] This estimate was very crude, as the economists stressed, since many noneconomic factors influenced the enlistment rate and the data and underlying assumptions were rough.

By 1973, the draft was no longer being used to obtain military manpower. Whether it will be reactivated in the near future is hard to say. For present purposes, the important point is that economic analysis, based on the fundamental concepts in this chapter, played a very significant role in the discussion and resolution of this major issue. And if conditions or attitudes change so that this issue must be reconsidered, you can be sure that economists will continue to play a significant role in its resolution.

Monopsony

In previous sections, we have assumed that perfect competition exists in the labor market. In some cases, however, *monopsony* exists instead. *A monopsony is a market structure where there is a single buyer.* Thus a single firm may hire all the labor in an isolated "company town," such as exists in the coal-mining regions of West Virginia and Kentucky. What determines the price of labor under monopsony? Suppose the firm's demand curve for labor and the supply curve of labor are as shown in Figure 14.6. Because the firm is the sole buyer of labor, it takes into account the fact that to acquire more labor it must pay a higher wage to *all* workers, not just the extra workers. For example, if the firm wants to increase the number of workers it employs from 5 to 6, it may have to pay the sixth an hourly wage of $5. If the supply curve of labor slopes upward to the right, this wage is more than was required to obtain the first 5 workers. Since the firm must pay all workers the same wage to avoid labor unrest, it must raise the wages of the first 5 workers to the level of the sixth, if it hires the sixth worker. Thus *the cost of hiring the sixth worker exceeds the wage that must be paid this worker.*

The supply curve for labor in Figure 14.6 shows the cost of hiring an additional worker, if workers already employed do *not* have to be paid a higher wage when the additional worker is hired. Thus this supply curve does *not* show the true additional cost to the monopsonist of hiring an additional worker, for the reasons given in the previous paragraph. Instead, curve *A,* which includes the extra wages that must be paid to the workers already employed, shows the true additional cost. For the reasons given above, curve *A* lies above the supply curve.

---

[5] Note that the average increase in pay is less than the average increase in first-term pay. The way Altman and Fechter proceed from the latter to the former is described in their work. Also, note that the costs to the Defense Department, which are estimated here, may be quite different from the social costs of switching to an all-volunteer army.

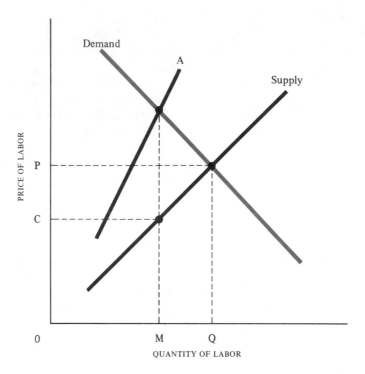

Figure 14.6

Equilibrium Wage and Quantity of Labor under Monopsony *The monopsonistic firm, if it maximizes profit, will hire laborers up to the point where the extra cost of adding an extra laborer, shown by curve A, equals the extra revenue from adding the extra laborer, shown by the demand curve for labor.*

If profit is maximized, the monopsonistic firm will hire labor up to the point at which the extra cost of adding an additional laborer (shown by curve *A*) equals the extra revenue from adding the additional laborer (shown by the demand curve). Thus the quantity of labor purchased will be *OM* and the price of labor will be *OC* in Figure 14.6. In contrast, under perfectly competitive conditions the equilibrium quantity and price would be at the intersection of the demand and supply curves. That is, the quantity of labor purchased would be *OQ* and the price of labor would be *OP*.

What is the effect of monopsony on the wage rate and the amount of labor hired? In general, *the wage rate, as well as the quantity hired, is lower under monopsony than under perfect competition.* This is the case in Figure 14.6, and it will generally hold true. This makes sense. One would expect a monopsonist, free from the pressures of competition, to pay workers less than would be required under perfect competition.

Test Yourself

1. Suppose that a perfectly competitive firm's production function is as follows:

Quantity of labor (man-years)	Ouput per year (thousands of units)
0	0
1	3.0
2	5.0
3	6.8
4	8.0
5	9.0

The firm is a profit maximizer, and the labor market is competitive. Labor must be hired in integer numbers and for a year (no more, no less). If the firm hires 4 man-years of labor, and if the price of a unit of the firm's product is $3, one can establish a range for what the annual wage prevailing in the labor market must be. What is the maximum amount it can be? What is the minimum amount? Why? Do these numbers seem realistic? Why or why not?

2. Based on the data in Question 1, plot the marginal product of labor at various utilization rates of labor. Also, plot the value of labor's marginal product at each quantity of labor used.

3. Suppose that the firm in Question 1 were a monopsonist. Do you think that it would pay a lower, higher, or the same wage rate as under the conditions described in Question 1? Why?

4. Suppose that the marginal product of skilled labor to a perfectly competitive firm is 2 units and the price of skilled labor is $4 an hour, while the marginal product of unskilled labor is 1 unit and the price of unskilled labor is $2.50 an hour. Is the firm minimizing its costs? Explain. (*Hint:* Regard skilled labor and unskilled labor as two separate inputs, and apply the cost-minimization rule in Chapter 8.)

Labor Unions

About 1 in 6 nonfarm workers in the United States belongs to a union, and the perfectly competitive model does not apply to these workers any more than it does to monopsonistic labor markets. There are about 200 national unions in the United States; the biggest are the Teamsters, the National Education Association, and the Food and Commercial Workers, each with 1.3 million members or more. Next come the United Auto Workers, the United Steel Workers, the Electrical Workers, the Machinists, the Carpenters, the State, County, and Municipal Employees, and the Service Employees, each with over 800,000 members.

The **national unions**[6] are of great importance in the American labor movement. The supreme governing body of the national union is the convention, which is held every year or two. The delegates to the convention have the authority to set policy for the union. However, considerable power is exercised by the national union's officers. Union presidents—men like Owen Bieber of the Auto Workers and Jackie Presser of the Teamsters—exercise great power.

A national union is composed of **local unions,** each in a given area or plant. Some local unions have only a few members, but others have thousands. The local union, with its own president and officers, often plays an important role in collective bargaining. The extent to which the local unions maintain their autonomy varies from one national union to another. In industries where markets are localized (like construction and printing), the locals are more autonomous than in industries where markets are national (like steel, automobiles, and coal).

Finally, there is the AFL-CIO, a federation of national unions created by the merger of the American Federation of Labor and the Congress of Industrial Organizations in 1955. The AFL-CIO does not include all national unions. The United Mine Workers refused to join the AFL-CIO, the Auto Workers left it in 1968, and the Teamsters were kicked out (because of corruption). The AFL-CIO is a very important spokesman for the American labor movement; but because the national unions in the AFL-CIO have given up relatively little of their power to the federation, its authority is limited.

[6] Sometimes they are called international unions because some locals are outside the United States—for example, in Canada.

The American Labor Movement

EARLY HISTORY OF AMERICAN LABOR UNIONS

To understand the nature and behavior of labor unions, it is necessary to look briefly at the history of the American labor movement. Unions arose because workers recognized that acting together gave them more bargaining power than acting separately. They frequently felt that they were at the mercy of their employers, and they formed fraternal societies and unions to promote economic and social benefits for the members. The first recorded case of collective bargaining in the United States took place in 1799, when Philadelphia shoemakers negotiated collectively with their employers.

However, until the 1930s unions in the United States were not very strong, partly because of employers' efforts to break up unions, and partly because the courts held that the unions' attempts to increase wages and influence working conditions were conspiracies in restraint of trade. It is not difficult to understand the antiunion feelings of management, but it is difficult to exonerate the ruthlessness with which some managements attempted to stamp out unionism. Not only were prounion workers fired and blacklisted; they were sometimes beaten up or locked out of the plant. And when strikes occurred, strike breakers were sometimes hired to teach the striking workers a lesson.

The courts were also hostile to unions. The prevailing doctrine in much of the nineteenth century was that unions were criminal conspiracies, and even when this doctrine was abandoned, the courts frequently regarded strikes, picketing, and other such union tactics as illegal. In addition, they sometimes used the Sherman Act of 1890 to stop unions, on the grounds that unions were conspiracies to restrain trade. Moreover, the courts often issued **injunctions,** which are cease-and-desist orders, to prevent unions from striking, boycotting, picketing, or carrying out other activities against the interests of their employers. In this way, the courts prevented unions from utilizing their potential power effectively.

THE AMERICAN FEDERATION OF LABOR

In 1886, the **American Federation of Labor** came into existence. In contrast to many early unions, which were aimed at political goals, the AFL, led by Samuel Gompers, concentrated on economic issues. Basically, the AFL was an association of national **craft unions,** each of which was autonomous; but although it had limited power over the national unions, Gompers was a very important spokesman for the American labor movement.

The AFL came to be the dominant federation in American labor history, and its philosophy exerted great influence on the development of trade unionism in the United States. This philosophy was built on several tenets. First, *Gompers and his associates felt that it would be a mistake to promote the development of a labor party in the United States.* The AFL would try to elect its friends and defeat its enemies, but it would not form a third party and it would not align itself with either of the two major political parties. Second, *the AFL would concentrate its efforts on bread-*

and-butter economic issues, not on attempts to alter the basic form of society. Higher wages and better working conditions, not social revolution or elimination of private property, were its aims. Third, *the AFL was suspicious of government regulation.* It felt that the interests of labor would be served best if the government interfered as little as possible in collective bargaining.

The AFL was relatively successful in increasing union membership; total union membership was about 2 million in 1904 and about 5 million in 1920. In part, this increase resulted from tight labor markets and the government's support of collective bargaining during World War I in return for labor's help in the war effort. After the war, union membership dropped from more than 5 million to about 2.6 million in 1933 (due in part to the onset of the Great Depression). The period after World War I was marked by strong antiunion sentiments. Employers resisted unions strenuously—and successfully. For example, in 1919 the U.S. Steel Corporation—led by our old friend from Chapter 12, Elbert Gary—crushed a strike resulting from an attempt to organize its plants. Firms pushed hard for an "American Plan" under which union members would not be hired. Certainly the 1920s were a difficult period for American labor unions.

THE NEW DEAL AND WORLD WAR II

During the early 1930s, the tide began to turn. To a great extent, this was because of government encouragement of unions, in which the first important step was the *Norris-La Guardia Act* of 1932. This act made it much more difficult for courts to issue injunctions against unions, and it made *yellow-dog contracts*—agreements in which workers promised their employers not to join a union—unenforceable in federal courts. The next important step occurred in 1935, when Congress passed the *Wagner Act,* which made it an unfair labor practice for employers to refuse to bargain collectively with unions representing a majority of their workers, or to interfere with their workers' right to organize. In addition, this act established the *National Labor Relations Board* to investigate unfair labor practices, to issue orders enforceable in federal courts, and to hold elections to determine which, if any, union would represent various groups of employees. The Wagner Act was a very important factor in encouraging the growth of labor unions in the United States—so important that it has often been called American labor's Magna Carta.

Another important factor in the growth of unions during the 1930s was the emergence of *industrial unions.* The more favorable atmosphere for union organization and growth led to the creation in 1935 of a new federation, the *Congress of Industrial Organizations.* The unions that created and formed the CIO rebelled against the AFL's apparent inability to take advantage of the opportunity to organize the mass-production industries like autos and steel. The AFL was composed primarily of unions organized along craft lines. The carpenters had one union, the machinists had another union, and so on for other crafts. This is in contrast to industrial unions, which include all workers in a particular plant or industry.

The young CIO, led by the United Mine Workers' president John L. Lewis, set out to establish industrial unions in the mass-production industries.[7] The CIO was very successful in its organization drives during the late 1930s. In 1937 U.S. Steel, formerly a bulwark of antiunionism, recognized the Steelworkers as bargaining agent for its more than 200,000 workers. Using the sit-down strike—in which strikers occupy the plant—as a weapon, workers in the automobile and rubber industries organized CIO unions too. In addition, the CIO organized unions in electrical machinery, petroleum refining, textiles, meat packing, longshoring, and other industries.[8]

The 1930s were a period of spectacular union growth. Aided by the prounion attitude of the Roosevelt administration, the new legislation, and the energy of its leaders, total union membership rose from less than 3 million in 1933 to more than 10 million in 1941. World War II witnessed a further growth in total union membership. Stimulated by the increase in total employment and the government's favorable attitude toward their growth, unions increased their membership from over 10 million in 1941 to almost 15 million—or about 36 percent of all nonfarm workers—in 1945. As in World War I, the government helped unions gain recognition in exchange for union cooperation in promoting war production. By the end of World War II, labor unions were conspicuous and powerful features of the economic landscape.

Postwar Developments

CREATION AND STRUCTURE OF THE AFL-CIO

In 1955, a merger occurred between the AFL and the CIO. Given the acrimony marking the relationship between these two organizations in the 1930s, the merger may seem surprising. But the differences in their attitudes toward the question of organization along industrial versus craft lines had diminished in importance over the years. And the old leaders, including those like Lewis of the Mine Workers and Hutcheson of the Carpenters who had traded blows in earlier days, had died—or, as in Lewis's case, were no longer in either federation.[9]

Moreover, the merger had advantages. The labor movement, despite large-scale organization drives in the south after the war, was unable to increase union membership appreciably during the 1950s. Many unions attributed this fact to the rivalry between the AFL and the CIO and argued that a united front would result in increased membership. Also, and perhaps most important, Congress passed several pieces of legislation, including the Taft-Hartley Act of 1947, that were heartily disliked by the

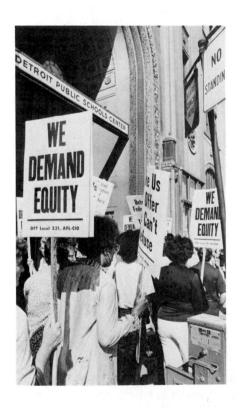

[7] Before leaving the AFL, Lewis emphasized the strength of his convictions by knocking down and bloodying up his principal opponent, William Hutcheson, president of the Carpenters' Union, on the floor of the 1935 AFL convention.

[8] Confronted with the CIO's successes, the AFL also organized new industrial unions, although craft unions remained by far the most important part of the federation.

[9] Lewis resigned from the presidency of the CIO because workers would not follow his lead and vote for Wendell Willkie for president of the United States in 1940. Later he took his union back into the AFL, but withdrew from the AFL in 1947 because the AFL did not boycott the National Labor Relations Board in an effort to defeat the Taft-Hartley Act.

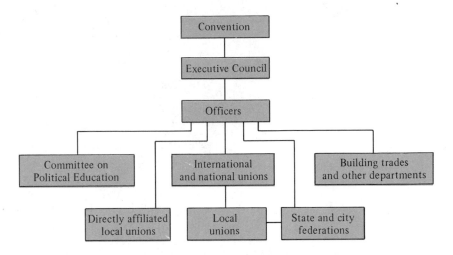

Figure 14.7
Structure of AFL-CIO *The AFL-CIO, which resulted from a merger of the AFL and CIO in 1955, is organized with the governing power in the hands of a biennial convention.*

unions, and it was felt that the merger would increase labor's political clout.

The AFL-CIO is organized along the lines indicated in Figure 14.7. The organization closely resembles that of the AFL (the larger of the merging federations). The constitution of the AFL-CIO puts supreme governing power in the hands of a biennial convention. The national unions are represented at these conventions on the basis of their dues-paying membership. Between conventions, the AFL-CIO's business is directed by its president (Lane Kirkland in 1985) and secretary-treasurer, as well as by various committees and councils composed of representatives of various national unions or people elected at the convention. The AFL-CIO contains seven trade and industrial departments, such as building trades, food and beverage trades, maritime trades, and so forth. Also, as indicated by Figure 14.7, a few local unions are not affiliated with a national union, but are directly affiliated with the AFL-CIO.

INTERNAL PROBLEMS IN LABOR UNIONS

As unions have grown older and more secure and powerful, there has been more and more concern about the nature of their internal practices and leadership. After all, they are no longer the underdogs that they were 50 years ago. They are huge organizations with immense power. Both in this country and in Europe, observers have charged that unions are often far from democratic. Members are frequently apathetic, for there is less interest in union affairs now than in the early days when unions were fighting for survival; and the leadership of some unions has become entrenched and bureaucratic. Moreover, there are frequent charges that unions engage in racial and other forms of discrimination.

Another problem is *corruption within labor unions.* In the 1950s, a Senate committee—the so-called McClellan Committee—conducted lengthy and revealing investigations which showed that the leaders of the Teamsters Union had misused union funds, had questionable relations with the underworld, and had "shamefully betrayed their own members." Other unions were also accused of corrupt practices. It is important, however, to avoid smearing the entire labor movement. Although racketeering and fraud unquestionably are problems, they tend to be localized in relatively few industries—particularly the building trades, trucking, longshoring, laundries, and hotels. Many responsible and honest leaders of the labor movement have tried hard to rid the labor movement of these unsavory practices.

POSTWAR LABOR LEGISLATION

After World War II, public sentiment turned somewhat against unions. Strikes and higher prices got under the skin of the consumer as well as the employer, and there began to be a lot of talk in Congress and elsewhere about the prewar Wagner Act having been too one-sided, giving the advantages to labor and the penalties to the employer. In 1947, despite bitter labor opposition, the *Taft-Hartley Act* was passed, with the purpose of redressing the balance between labor and employers. The act established standards of conduct for unions as well as employers, defined unfair union practices, and stated that unions can be sued for acts of their agents. Also, the act outlawed the closed shop, which requires that firms hire only workers who are already union members, and stipulated that, unless the workers agree in writing, the **checkoff** is illegal. (The checkoff is a system in which the employer deducts union dues from each worker's pay and hands them over to the union.)

In addition, the act tried to increase protection against strikes in which the public's safety and health are involved. If the president decides that an actual or impending strike imperils the national health or safety, he can appoint a fact-finding committee to investigate the situation. After receiving the committee's report, he can tell the attorney general to obtain an injunction forbidding a strike for 80 days, during which the parties can continue to negotiate. A Federal Mediation Service was established to help the parties settle such negotiations. The act does not forbid a strike at the end of the 80 days, if no agreement has been reached.

In response to the evidence of union corruption presented by the McClellan Committee, Congress passed the *Landrum-Griffin Act* in 1959. This act attempts to protect the rights of individual union members from abuse by union leaders. It contains a "bill of rights" for labor, guaranteeing that each member can participate in union elections, that elections be held by secret ballot, and that other steps be taken to protect the rights of the members. It also requires unions to file financial reports, forbids payments (beyond wages) by employers to union representatives, and prohibits loans exceeding $2,000 by unions to union officials.

Recent Trends in Union Membership

In recent years, union membership has increased rather modestly; indeed, during the late 1950s and early 1960s, it didn't increase at all. To some extent, this has been due to dissension within the labor movement and to a diminution of the zeal that characterized the movement in earlier years. Also, rightly or wrongly, unions have lost a certain amount of public sympathy and respect because of racial discrimination, unpopular strikes, evidence of corruption, and the belief that they are responsible in considerable part for cost-push inflation. But these factors only partly explain this lack of growth. In addition, important changes in the labor force have tended to reduce union membership.

Specifically, the increasing proportion of *white-collar workers* seems to have raised important problems for unions. To date, unions have made relatively little progress in organizing white-collar workers. In the early 1960s, only about 3 percent of engineers, and about 9 percent of office workers were union members. One reason for this lack of progress is that white-collar employees tend to identify with management. Also, the increasing proportion of *women* in the labor force seems to raise important problems for unions. It is sometimes claimed that female workers are harder to organize because they do not stay in the labor force very long

Example 14.2   Can a Union Increase Employment?

In many isolated areas, a single firm is the only employer of a certain kind of labor. Suppose that a textile firm is in this position, and that its demand curve for labor, as well as the supply curve for labor, are shown below. Curve A shows the extra cost to the firm of adding an extra laborer.

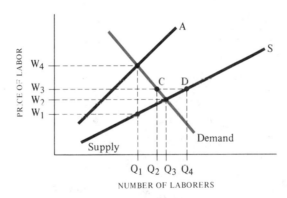

(a) How many laborers will the firm hire, and how much will each be paid? (b) Suppose that a union enters the market and that it sets a wage of OW_3. What now is the supply curve for labor? (c) How many laborers will the firm hire now? Is employment higher than before the union entered? (d) Will there be involuntary unemployment now?

SOLUTION

(a) The firm will hire OQ_1 laborers and pay a wage of OW_1, in accord with our discussion of monopsony. (b) It is W_3DS, because the firm cannot pay a wage below OW_3 under the assumed circumstances. (c) The firm will hire OQ_2 workers, since the extra cost of hiring an extra worker equals OW_3 so long as less than OQ_4 workers are hired. Employment is higher than before the union entered (when it was OQ_1). (d) Yes. At a wage of OW_3, OQ_4 workers will seek employment but only OQ_2 workers will be hired. Thus $(OQ_4 - OQ_2)$ workers will be involuntarily unemployed.

and because they are concentrated in jobs—clerical and sales positions—that are difficult to organize. Nonetheless, almost 1 in 5 union members in 1962 were women; and the majority of the Retail Clerks, the Clothing Workers, and the International Ladies' Garment Workers were women.

However, even though union membership has not been growing in recent years, it would be a mistake to jump to the conclusion that the American labor movement is stagnant or that unions are declining in importance. For one thing, membership is not a very good measure of power. A small union can sometimes bring an enormous amount of pressure to bear if it is located strategically in the economy. Also, union membership has been growing rapidly in some areas, notably *public employment.* Between 1956 and 1968, union membership among public employees grew from 915,000 to 2,155,000, with the bulk of the membership in six unions, three of federal employees and three of state and local employees.[10] For many years, there was a tradition, as well as legal prohibitions, against strikes by public employees. But during the 1960s, when these workers seemed to be left behind economically, various executive orders and legislative enactments encouraged unionism among public employees.

STRIKES BY PUBLIC EMPLOYEES

A nettlesome problem regarding the unionization of public employees is related to strikes. Since such employees man vital public services, a strike can bring a community or state to its knees. In four states—Pennsylvania, Hawaii, Oregon, and Vermont—strikes of this sort are legal. But the fact that they are forbidden by law in other states, such as New York, does not prevent walkouts by teachers, sanitation workers, or other state and local employees from being a fairly common occurrence. The public, naturally, becomes indignant when strikes of this sort occur, and the question of whether or not public employees should be able to walk off the job provokes heated debate.

In 1981, there was a well-publicized confrontation between a public-employee union and the government. When the Professional Air Traffic Controllers Organization (PATCO) went on strike, President Reagan responded by saying that the strike was illegal, and he ultimately fired the striking controllers. The nation managed to get along with only 10,000 controllers—supervisors, nonstrikers, military personnel, and new trainees. In October 1981, the Federal Labor Relations Authority stripped the union of its right to represent controllers. This was a stern message to unionized public employees, and one that has not been forgotten. In the immediate future, it seems likely that they will be less likely to call strikes of this sort.

[10] The three unions of federal employees are the American Federation of Government Employees, the National Association of Letter Carriers, and the United Federation of Postal Clerks. The three unions of state and local employees are the American Federation of State, County, and Municipal Employees; the American Federation of Teachers; and the International Association of Firefighters.

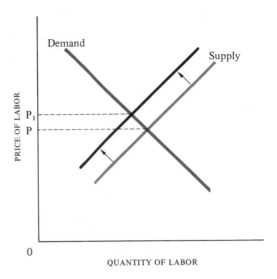

Figure 14.8

Shift of Supply Curve for Labor *A union may shift the supply curve to the left by getting employers to hire only union members and then restricting union membership, or by other techniques.*

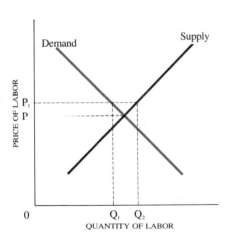

Figure 14.9

Direct Increase in Price of Labor *A union may get the employer to raise the wage from OP to OP₁, and let the higher wage reduce the opportunity for work. This is commonly done by strong industrial unions.*

How Unions Increase Wages

Unions wield considerable power, and economists must include them in their analysis if they want their models of the labor market to reflect conditions in the real world. We shall now see how this is done. Let us begin by supposing that a union wants to increase the wage rate paid its members. How can it accomplish this objective? In other words, how can it alter the market supply curve for labor, or the market demand curve for labor, so that the price of labor—its wage—will increase?

1. The union may try to shift the supply curve of labor to the left. It may shift the supply curve, as shown in Figure 14.8, with the result that the price of labor will increase from *OP* to *OP₁*. How can the union cause this shift in the supply curve? Craft unions have frequently forced employers to hire only union members, and then restricted union membership by high initiation fees, reduction in new membership, and other devices. In addition, unions have favored legislation to reduce immigration, shorten working hours, and limit the labor supply in other ways.

2. The union may try to get the employers to pay a higher wage, while allowing some of the supply of labor forthcoming at this higher wage to find no opportunity for work. In Figure 14.9, the union may exert pressure on the employers to raise the price of labor from *OP* to *OP₁*. At *OP₁*, not all of the available supply of labor can find jobs. The quantity of labor supplied is *OQ₂*, while the amount of labor demanded is *OQ₁*. The effect is the same as in Figure 14.8, but in this case the union does not limit the supply directly. It lets the higher wage reduce the opportunity for work. Strong industrial unions often behave in this fashion. Having organized practically all the relevant workers and controlling the labor supply, the union raises the wage to *OP₁*. This is a common and important case.

3. The union may try to shift the demand curve for labor upward and to the right. If it can bring about the shift described in Figure 14.10, the price of labor will increase from *OP* to *OP₂*. To cause this shift in the demand for labor, the union may resort to *featherbedding.* That is, it may try to restrict

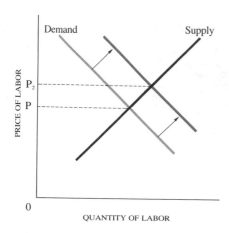

Figure 14.10
Shift in Demand Curve for Labor *A union may shift the demand curve for labor to the right by featherbedding or other devices, thus increasing the wage from OP to OP₂.*

output per worker in order to increase the amount of labor required to do a certain job. (To cite but one case, the railroad unions have insisted on much unnecessary labor.) Unions also try to shift the demand curve by helping the employers compete against other industries, or by helping to make Congress pass legislation that protects the employers from foreign competition.

Collective Bargaining

Collective bargaining is the process of negotiation between the union and management over wages and working conditions. Representatives of the union and management meet periodically to work out an agreement or contract; this process generally begins a few months before the old labor contract runs out. Typically, each side asks at first for more than it expects to get, and compromises must be made to reach an agreement. The union representatives take the agreement to their members, who must vote to accept or reject it. If they reject it, they may vote to strike or to continue to negotiate.

Collective bargaining agreements vary greatly. Some pertain to only a single plant while others apply to an entire industry. However, an agreement generally contains the following elements. It specifies the extent and kind of recognition that management gives the union, the level of wage rates for particular jobs, the length of the work week, the rate of overtime pay, the extent to which seniority will determine which workers will be first to be laid off, the nature and extent of management's prerogatives, and how grievances between workers and the employer will be handled.

Historically, industries and firms have extended recognition to unions by accepting one of three arrangements—the closed shop, the union shop, or the open shop. In a *closed shop,* workers must be union members before they can be hired. This gives the union more power than if there is a *union shop,* in which the employer can hire nonunion workers who must then become union members in a certain length of time after being hired. In an *open shop,* the employer can hire union or nonunion labor, and nonunion workers need not, once employed, join the union. As we have seen, the closed shop was banned by the Taft-Hartley Act. The Taft-Hartley Act also says that the union shop is legal unless outlawed by state laws; and in about 20 states there are "right to work" laws that make the union shop illegal. Needless to say, these right-to-work laws are hated by organized labor, which regards them as a threat to its security and effectiveness.

BASIC FORCES AT WORK

Collective bargaining is a power struggle. At each point in their negotiations, both the union and the employer must compare the costs (or benefits) of agreeing with the other party with the costs (or benefits) of continuing to disagree. The costs of disagreement are the costs of a strike, while the costs of agreement are the costs of settling on terms other than one's own. These costs are determined by basic market forces. For example, during periods when demand is great, employers are more likely to

Basic Idea #28: Unions were organized because workers recognized that acting together gave them more bargaining power than acting separately. To increase wages, unions frequently have shifted the supply curve for labor to the left, and shifted the demand curve for labor to the right. Besides higher wages, unions have tried to promote job security and other benefits for their members.

298

grant large wage increases because the costs of disagreement seem higher (a strike will prove more costly) than those of settlement. The outcome of the negotiations will depend on the relative strength of the parties. The strength of the employers depends on their ability to withstand a strike. The strength of the unions depends on their ability to keep out nonunion workers and to enlist the support of other unions, as well as on the size of their financial reserves.

In the early 1980s, many important unions cut back on their wage requests. In the automobile industry, American firms were finding it difficult to compete with their Japanese rivals, and many experts attributed this partly to the very high wages in the U.S. auto industry. In the trucking industry, unionized firms were finding it increasingly difficult to compete with nonunion firms. More and more union members in industries like autos, trucking, steel, rubber, and the airlines began to worry about the effects of hefty wage increases on whether or not they would have jobs. The climate for collective bargaining was quite different than in earlier years.

To illustrate, consider the labor negotiations in the auto industry in 1984. In September 1984, after two months of bargaining, the United Auto Workers struck 13 General Motors plants. About a week later, a settlement was reached, which called for wage increases of only about 2 percent per year. However, General Motors agreed to put $1 billion into a pool to pay workers whose jobs have been eliminated due to automation or the movement of production to overseas plants.

The Pros and Cons of Big Unions

Finally, we should discuss briefly some of the criticisms that are made of the big unions. These criticisms are based largely on their monopoly power. Critics charge that by exerting such power, unions push up the price of labor and reduce the level of employment in various industries. This results in badly allocated resources, since wage rates no longer signal accurately the relative scarcity of labor of various types. Moreover, it is argued that the resulting upward pressure on wages is an important element in cost-push inflation. Opponents of big unions have proposed at least four policies designed to reduce their power—first, that the antitrust laws be applied to unions as well as firms; second, that industry-wide bargaining, which allows a union to shut down an entire industry, be banned; third, that the union shop be banned; and fourth, that big unions be broken up into a number of smaller ones.

On the other hand, many economists feel that labor unions are an important positive force in the American economy. They argue that it is foolish to believe that without unions labor markets would be perfectly competitive—and that the price of labor would be the proper one from the point of view of resource allocation. They point out that unions tend to be an antidote to the monopsonistic power held by some employers in the labor market. And they argue that unions are not really the prime movers in cost-push inflation, but rather that unions often respond to prior price increases by firms. Thus economists are divided in their attitudes toward the growth and power of big unions.

Test Yourself

1. "The unions should not be exempt from the antitrust laws." Comment and evaluate.

2. State the principal provisions of (a) the Wagner Act, (b) the Taft-Hartley Act, (c) the Landrum-Griffin Act, and (d) the Norris-La Guardia Act.

3. Suppose that you were the president of a small firm that hired nonunion labor. How would you go about estimating the marginal product of a certain worker, or of certain types of workers? Would it be easy? If not, does this mean that the theory of wage determination is incorrect or useless?

4. Describe the various ways that labor unions can influence the wage rate. Do you think that they attempt to maximize the wage rate? If not, what do you think their objectives are?

Summary

1. Assuming perfect competition, a firm will employ each type of labor in an amount such that its marginal product times the product's price equals its wage. In other words, the firm will employ enough labor so that the value of the marginal product of labor equals labor's price.

2. The firm's demand curve for labor—which shows, for each price of labor, the amount of labor the firm will use—is the firm's value-of-marginal-product curve (if labor is the only variable input). The market demand curve for labor shows the relationship between its price and the total amount of labor demanded in the market.

3. Labor's price depends on its market supply curve as well as on its market demand curve. Labor's market supply curve is the relationship between the price of labor and the total amount of labor supplied in the market. (Labor's market supply curve may be backward bending.)

4. An input's price is determined under perfect competition in essentially the same way that a product's price is determined—by supply and demand. The price of labor will tend in equilibrium to the level at which the quantity of labor demanded equals the quantity of labor supplied. By the same token, the equilibrium amount of labor utilized is also given by the intersection of the market supply and demand curves.

5. If there are qualitative differences among workers, the differential in their wages will reflect the differential in their marginal products. Also, even if all workers were of equal ability, there would still be differences in wage rates to offset differences among occupations in the cost of training and stability of earnings, and geographical differences in the cost of living.

6. There are about 200 national unions in the United States, the biggest being the Teamsters. Each national union is composed of local unions, which operate within the context of the constitution of the national union.

7. The AFL-CIO is a federation of national unions created by the merger in 1955 of the American Federation of Labor and the Congress of Industrial Organizations. The AFL-CIO is a very important spokesman for the American labor

movement, but because the national unions in the AFL-CIO have given up relatively little of their power to the federation, its authority is limited.

8. There are several ways that unions can increase wages—by shifting the supply curve of labor to the left, by shifting the demand curve for labor to the right, and by influencing the wage directly. Collective bargaining is the process of negotiation between union and management over wages and working conditions. An agreement generally specifies the extent and kind of recognition that management gives the union—such as the union shop or open shop. In addition, it specifies the level of wage rates for particular jobs, the length of the work week, the rate of overtime pay, the extent to which seniority will determine which workers will be first to be laid off, the nature and extent of management's prerogatives, and how grievances between workers and the employer will be handled. The union's power is based to a considerable extent on its right to strike.

9. Critics of big unions charge that they possess considerable monopoly power, and that, by pushing up the price of labor and reducing the level of employment, they cause a misallocation of resources and contribute to cost-push inflation. Opponents of big unions often suggest that the antitrust laws be applied to them and that other measures be adopted to curb their power. Supporters of big unions reply that it is foolish to believe that the price of labor would be the proper one from the point of view of resource allocation if there were no big unions. Moreover, they argue that unions are needed to offset the monopsonistic power of employers, and they deny that unions are the prime movers in cost-push inflation.

Concepts for Review

Firm's demand curve for labor	Noncompeting groups	Congress of Industrial Organizations
Value of the marginal product of labor	Monopsony	Checkoff
Market demand curve for labor	National union	Featherbedding
Derived demand	Local union	Collective bargaining
Market supply curve for labor	Injunction	Closed shop
Backward-bending supply curve	American Federation of Labor	Union shop
	Craft union	Open shop
	Yellow-dog contract	Strike
	Industrial union	

CHAPTER 15

Interest, Rent, and Profits

Not all income is received in the form of wages. The school teacher who has a savings account at the Bank of America receives income in the form of *interest*. The widow who rents out 100 acres of rich Iowa land to a farmer receives income in the form of *rent*. And the engineer who founds and owns a firm that develops a new type of electronic calculator receives income in the form of *profit*. All of these types of income—interest, rent, and profit—are forms of property income. That is, they are incomes received by owners of property. In this chapter, we are concerned with the determinants of interest, rent, and profit. Also, we try to explain the social functions of each of these types of property income.

The Nature of Interest

Charles Lamb, the English essayist, said, "The human species, according to the best theory I can form of it, is composed of two distinct races, the men who borrow and the men who lend." Whether or not such a cleavage exists, most of the human species, at one time or another, are borrowers or lenders of money. Thus practically everyone is familiar with **interest,** which is a payment for the use of money. More specifically, *the **rate of interest** is the amount of money one must pay for the use of a dollar for a year*. Thus, if the interest rate is 8 percent, you must pay 8 cents for the use of a dollar for a year.

Everyone who borrows money pays interest. Consumers pay interest on personal loans taken out to buy appliances, mortgages taken out to buy houses, and many other types of loans. Firms pay interest on bonds issued to purchase equipment and on short-term bank loans taken out to finance inventories. And governments pay interest on bonds issued to finance schools, highways, and other public projects.

Interest rates vary, depending on the nature of the borrower and the type of loan. One of the most important determinants of the rate of interest charged borrowers is the *riskiness* of the loan. If lenders have doubts about their chances of getting their money back, they will charge a higher interest rate than if they are sure of being repaid. Thus small, financially rickety firms have to pay higher interest rates than large blue-chip firms; and the large, well-known firms have to pay higher interest rates than the federal government. Another factor that influences the interest rate is the *cost of bookkeeping and collection.* If a firm makes many small loans and must hound the borrowers to pay up, these costs are a great deal larger than if it makes one large loan. Consequently the interest rate that must be charged for such small loans is often considerably higher than for bigger loans.

Despite the diversity of interest rates encountered at any point in time in the real world, it is analytically useful to speak of the **pure rate of interest,** which is the interest rate on a riskless loan. The rate of interest on U.S. government bonds—which are about as safe as one can get in this world—comes close to being a pure rate of interest. Actual interest rates will vary from the pure rate, depending on the riskiness of the loan together with other factors, but the configuration of actual interest rates will tend to move up and down with the pure interest rate.

The Determination of the Interest Rate

THE DEMAND FOR LOANABLE FUNDS

Since the interest rate is the price paid for the use of loanable funds, it—like any price—is determined by demand and supply. The **demand curve for loanable funds** shows the quantity of loanable funds demanded at each interest rate. The demand for loanable funds is a demand for what these funds will buy. Money is not wanted for its own sake, since it cannot build factories or equipment. Instead, it can provide command over resources—men and equipment and materials—to do things like build factories or equipment.

As shown in Figure 15.1, the demand curve slopes downward to the right, indicating that more loanable funds are demanded at a lower rate of interest than at a higher rate of interest. A very large demand for loanable funds stems from firms who want to borrow money to invest in capital goods like machine tools, buildings, and so forth. At a particular point in time a firm has available a variety of possible investments, each with a certain rate of return, which indicates its profitability or net productivity. At higher interest rates, a firm will find it profitable to borrow money for fewer of these projects than if interest rates are lower.

To be more specific, *an asset's* **rate of return** *is the interest rate earned on the investment in the asset.* Suppose that a piece of equipment costs $10,000 and yields a permanent return to its owner of $1,500 per year.[1] (This

---

[1] It is unrealistic to assume that the yield continues indefinitely, but it makes it easier to understand the principle involved.

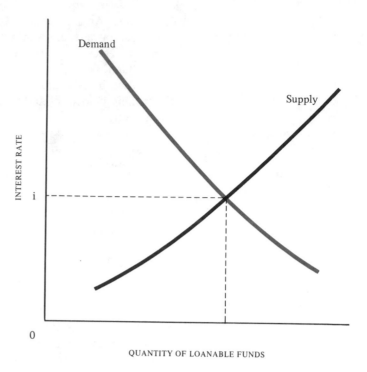

Fig. 15.1

Determination of Equilibrium Rate of Interest *The interest rate is determined by the demand and supply of loanable funds, the equilibrium level of the interest rate being Oi.*

return allows for the costs of maintaining the machine.) The rate of return on this piece of capital is 15 percent. Why? Because if an investment of $10,000 yields an indefinite annual return of $1,500, the interest rate earned on this investment is 15 percent.

If a firm maximizes profit, it will borrow to carry out investments where the rate of return, adjusted for risk, exceeds the interest rate. For example, it is profitable for a firm to pay 10 percent interest to carry out a project with a 12 percent rate of return, but it is not profitable to pay 15 percent interest for this purpose. (More will be said on this score in a subsequent section.) Consequently, the higher the interest rate, the smaller the amount that firms will be willing to borrow.

Large demands for loanable funds are also made by consumers and the government. Consumers borrow money to buy houses, cars, and many other items. The government borrows money to finance the building of schools, highways, housing, and many other types of public projects. As in the case of firms, the higher the interest rate, the smaller the amount that consumers and governments will be willing to borrow. Adding the demands of firms, consumers, and government together, we find the aggregate relationship at a given point in time between the pure interest rate and the amount of funds demanded—which is the demand curve for loanable funds. For the reasons given above, this demand curve looks the way a demand curve should. It is downward-sloping to the right.

THE SUPPLY OF LOANABLE FUNDS

The **supply curve for loanable funds** is the relationship between the quantity of loanable funds supplied and the pure interest rate. The supply of loanable funds comes from households and firms that find the available rate of

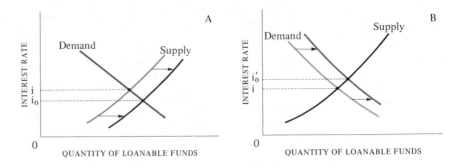

Figure 15.2

Effects on the Equilibrium Interest Rate of Shifts in the Demand or Supply Curves for Loanable Funds *If people become more willing to postpone consumption to future time periods, the supply curve will shift to the right, and the equilibrium interest rate will fall from i to i_0.*

If very profitable new investment opportunities are opened up, the demand curve will shift to the right, and the equilibrium interest rate will rise from i to i'_0.

interest sufficiently attractive to get them to save. In addition, the banks play an extremely important role in influencing the supply of loanable funds. Indeed, banks can actually create or destroy loanable funds (but only within limits set by the Federal Reserve System, our central bank).

The equilibrium value of the pure interest rate is given by the intersection of the demand and supply curves. In Figure 15.1 the equilibrium rate of interest is *Oi*. Factors that shift the demand curve or supply curve for loanable funds tend to alter the interest rate. If people become more willing to postpone consumption to future time periods, the supply curve for loanable funds will shift to the right, and the interest rate will decline. Or if inventions result in very profitable new investment possibilities, the demand curve will shift to the right and the interest rate will increase. (See Figure 15.2.)

However, this is only part of the story. Because of the government's influence on both the demand and supply sides of the market for loanable

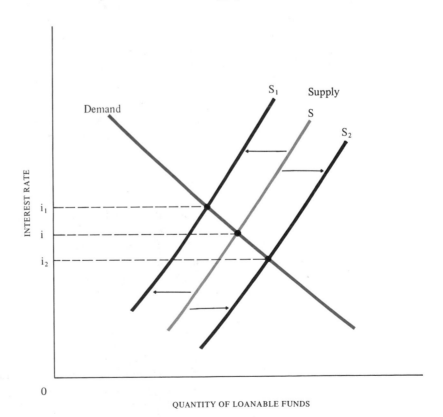

Figure 15.3

Effects on the Equilibrium Interest Rate of Federal Reserve Policies Influencing the Supply Curve for Loanable Funds *When the Federal Reserve pushes the supply curve to the right (from S to S_2), the equilibrium interest rate falls from i to i_2. When the Federal Reserve pushes the supply curve to the left (S to S_1), the equilibrium interest rate increases from i to i_1.*

funds, the interest rate at any point in time is to a considerable extent a matter of public policy. A nation's monetary policy can have a significant effect on the level of the interest rate. More specifically, when the Federal Reserve pursues a policy of easy money, this generally means that interest rates tend to fall in the short run because the Fed is pushing the supply curve for loanable funds to the right. On the other hand, when the Federal Reserve pursues a policy of tight money, interest rates generally tend to rise in the short run because the Fed is pushing the supply curve for loanable funds to the left. (See Figure 15.3.)

The government is also an important factor on the demand side of the market for loanable funds, because it is a big borrower, particularly during wartime. (Between 1941 and 1945, it borrowed almost $200 billion to help finance World War II.) During the early 1980s, it borrowed huge amounts to finance the mammoth federal deficits. At the present time, total federal debt (excluding the debt of state and local governments) held by the public is over $1 trillion.

Finally, note that the equilibrium level of the pure interest rate can be determined by John Maynard Keynes's *liquidity preference theory*, as well as by the loanable funds theory described in this section. The liquidity preference theory focuses attention on all money, not just loanable funds, and says that the interest rate is determined by the demand and supply of all money in the economy. The two approaches are not contradictory; rather, they complement one another.

Functions of the Interest Rate

Interest has often been a relatively unpopular and somewhat suspect form of income. Even Aristotle, who was hardly noted for muddle-headedness, felt that money was "barren" and that it was improper to charge interest. And in the Middle Ages, church law outlawed usury, even though interest continued to be charged. In real life and in fiction, the money lender is often the villain, almost never the hero. Yet it is perfectly clear that *interest rates serve a very important function. They allocate the supply of loanable funds.*

At a given point in time, funds that can be used to construct new capital goods are scarce, and society faces the problem of allocating these scarce funds among alternative possible uses. One way to allocate the loanable funds is through freely fluctuating interest rates. When such funds are relatively scarce, the interest rate will rise, with the result that only projects with relatively high rates of return will be carried out since the others will not be profitable. On the other hand, when such funds are relatively plentiful, the interest rate will fall, and less productive projects will be carried out because they now become profitable.

CHOOSING THE MOST PRODUCTIVE PROJECTS

The advantage of using the interest rate to allocate funds is that only the most productive projects are funded. To see why, assume that all investments are riskless. *If firms can borrow all the money they want (at the prevailing interest rate), and if they maximize their profits, they will buy all capital goods and accept all investment opportunities where the rate of return on these capital goods or investment opportunities exceeds the interest rate at which they can borrow.*[2] The reason for this is clear enough. If one can borrow money at an interest cost that is less than the rate of return on the borrowed money, clearly one can make money. Thus, if you borrow $1,000 at 3 percent per year interest and buy a $1,000 machine that has a rate of return of 4 percent per year, you receive a return of $40 per year and incur a cost of $30 per year. Since you make a profit of $10 per year, it obviously pays to buy this machine.

At a particular point in time, there is a variety of possible capital goods that can be produced and investment projects that can be carried out. Their rates of return vary a great deal; some goods or projects have much higher rates of return than others. Suppose that we rank the capital goods or projects according to their rates of return, from highest to lowest. If only a few of the goods or projects can be accepted, only those at the top of the list will be chosen. But as more and more can be accepted, society and private investors must go further and further down the list, with the consequence that projects with lower and lower rates of return will be chosen. How many of these capital goods and investment projects will be carried out? As noted above, firms will continue to invest as long as the rate of return on these goods or projects exceeds the interest rate at which they can borrow. Thus it follows that *the most productive projects—all those with rates of return exceeding the interest rate—will be carried out.*

SOCIALISM AND THE INTEREST RATE

Although interest is sometimes represented as a product of greedy capitalists, even socialist and Communist economies must use something like an interest rate to help allocate funds. After all, the socialists and Communists face the same sort of allocation problem that capitalists do. And when they try to screen out the less productive projects and to accept only the more productive ones, they must use the equivalent of an interest rate in their calculations, whether they call it that or not. (However, they do not pay interest income.) In the Soviet Union there have been published acknowledgments that a misallocation of resources resulted from decisions made in earlier years when interest rates—or their equivalent—were ignored. At present, Soviet decision makers use what amounts to interest rates in their calculations to determine which capital investments should be made and which should not.

Finally, besides its role in allocating the supply of loanable funds, the interest rate plays another important part in our economy: *It influences the level of investment, and thus the level of net national product.* Increases in the interest rate tend to reduce aggregate investment, thereby reducing total spending, whereas decreases in the interest rate tend to increase aggregate investment, thereby increasing total spending. Through its monetary policies, the government attempts to influence the interest rate

---

[2] We assume here that the investment opportunities are independent in the sense that the rate of return from each opportunity is not influenced by whether some other opportunity is accepted.

(and the quantity of money) so that total spending pushes net national product toward its full-employment level with reasonably stable prices.

Capital Budgeting

The principles discussed in the previous section can be applied to individual firms as well as entire societies. In particular, they help to indicate how a firm should make decisions on the choice of investment projects. Suppose that the Bugsbane Music Box Company believes that it will have $10 million from internal sources—primarily retained earnings and depreciation allowances—to invest next year. *To decide which investment projects to accept, it should estimate the rate of return from each one.* Suppose that it finds that it can invest $2 million in projects with rates of return of 30 percent, that it can invest $4 million in projects with rates of return of 25 percent, and so on, as shown in Table 15.1. Applying the principles just discussed, Bugsbane can maximize its profits by allocating the $10 million available from internal sources as follows. All projects yielding rates of return of 20 percent or more should be accepted; and all projects yielding less than 20 percent should not be undertaken. In other words, the projects with the highest rates of return—and with a total cost of $10 million—should be chosen.

This is a very useful step toward solving the firm's problem, but it assumes that the firm is unable or unwilling to borrow. If this is true, then nothing more needs to be said. But, as shown in Table 15.1, the firm has investment opportunities yielding 15 percent per year that it is not undertaking. It would pay the firm to undertake these projects even if it had to pay 10 or 12 percent interest—or anything less than 15 percent, for that matter. If the firm can borrow all the money it wants (within reason), but must pay 12 percent interest, what investment opportunities should it accept? All whose rate of return exceeds 12 percent. Thus, looking at Table 15.1, we see that the firm should invest its $10 million from internal sources and borrow an additional $6 million in order to undertake projects totaling $16 million.

This is an extremely simple case, but it illustrates how the interest rate and the concept of an asset's rate of return are used in practical business situations. *Capital budgeting*—the term applied to this area—has become an extremely important part of a firm's operations, as managers have relied more and more on economic concepts in allocating their firms' resources. Unaided hunch and intuition will no longer do in most major firms. Instead, most big firms insist that the prospective rate of return be estimated for each proposed investment, and that, making allowances for differences in risk, funds be allocated to the projects with the highest rates of return.[3] It is often difficult to make such estimates, but if funds are to be allocated rationally, it is essential that an analysis of this sort be carried out, formally or on the back of an envelope.

Table 15.1

INVESTMENT OPPORTUNITIES FOR BUGSBANE MUSIC BOX COMPANY

Rate of return (percent)	Amount of money the firm can invest at given rate of return (dollars)
30	2 million
25	4 million
20	4 million
15	6 million
10	7 million

[3] In practice, firms often base their decisions on discounted cash flow rather than rates of return. The present discussion is necessarily simplified. For a more complete treatment, see any managerial economics text.

Capital and Roundabout Methods of Production

Labor and land are often called the **primary inputs** because they are produced outside the economic system. Labor is created by familiar biological processes (which usually are not economically oriented, one would hope), and land is supplied by nature. *Capital,* on the other hand, *consists of goods that are created for the purpose of producing other goods.* Factory buildings, equipment, raw materials, inventories—all are various types of capital. In contrast to labor and land, capital is an input produced by the economic system itself.[4] A machine tool is capital; so is a boxcar or an electric power plant. These inputs are produced by firms, and they are purchased and used by firms. But they are not final consumption goods; instead, they are used to produce the final goods and services consumed by the public.

Our economy devotes a considerable amount of its productive capacity to the production of capital. The giant electrical equipment industry produces generators used by the electric power industry. The machine tool industry produces the numerically controlled tools used by the automobile, aircraft, and hundreds of other industries. The result in many sectors of the economy is a *roundabout method of production.* Consider the stages that lead to the manufacture of an automobile. Workers dig iron ore to be used to make pig iron to be used to make steel to be used to make machine tools to be used to make cylinders to be used to make a motor to be used to make the automobile.

Why Capital?

Why does the economy bother to product capital? After all, it may seem unnecessarily circuitous to construct capital to produce the goods and services consumers really want. Why not produce the desired goods and services—and *only* the desired goods and services—directly? Why produce plows to help produce agricultural crops? Why not forget about the plows and just produce the crops the consumers want? The answer is that the other inputs—labor and land—can produce more of the desired consumer goods and services when they are used in combination with capital than when they are used alone. A given amount of labor and land can produce more crops when used in combination with plows than when used alone.

The production and use of lots of capital make the other inputs—labor and land—more productive. But this does not mean that any society would be wise to increase without limit its production and use of capital. After all, the only way a society can produce more capital is to produce less goods and services of direct use to consumers. (For society as a whole, there are no free lunches, if resources are used fully and efficiently.) As the production of capital increases, consumers must cut further and further into their level of consumption at the present time in order to increase their capacity to produce in the future. Beyond a point, the advantage of

---

[4] Obviously, this distinction requires qualification. After all, land can be improved, and the quality of labor can be enhanced (by training and other means). Thus land and labor have some of the characteristics of capital since to some extent they can be "produced"—or at least enhanced—by the economic system.

having more in the future is overbalanced by the disadvantage of having less now. At this point, a society should stop increasing its production of capital goods.

The process by which people give up a claim on present consumption goods in order to receive consumption goods in the future is called *saving.* Just as a child may (infrequently) give up a lollipop today in order to get a lollipop and a candy cane next week, so an entire society may give up the present consumption of automobiles, food, tobacco, clothing, and so forth in order to obtain more of such goods and services later on.[5]

Capitalization of Assets

In a capitalist economy, each capital good has a market value. How can we determine what this value is? How much money is a capital good worth? To keep things reasonably simple, suppose that you can get 5 percent on various investments open to you; specifically, you can get 5 percent by investing your money in the stock of a local firm. That is, for every $1,000 you invest, you will receive a permanent return of $50 a year—and this is the highest return available. Now suppose that you have an opportunity to buy a piece of equipment that will yield you a permanent return of $1,000 per year. This piece of equipment is worth $1,000 ÷ .05 = $20,000 to you. Why? Because this is the amount you would have to pay for any other investment open to you that yields an equivalent amount—$1,000—per year. (If you must invest $1,000 for every $50 of annual yield, $20,000 must be invested to obtain an annual yield of $1,000.)

In general, if a particular asset yields a permanent amount—X dollars—each year, how much is this asset worth? In other words, how much should you be willing to pay for it? If you can get a return of $100 \times r$ percent per year from alternative investments, you would have to invest $X \div r$ dollars in order to get the same return as this particular asset yields. Consequently, this asset is worth

$$\frac{\$X}{r}.$$

This process of computing an asset's worth is called *capitalization.*

Thus, if the rate of return on alternative investments had been 3 percent rather than 5 percent in the example above, the worth of the piece of equipment would have been $1,000 ÷ .03 = $33,333 (since $X = \$1,000$ and $r = .03$). This is the amount you would have to pay for any other investment open to you that yields an equivalent amount—$1,000—per year. To see this, note that, if you must invest $1,000 for every $30 (not $50, as before) of annual yield, $33,333 (not $20,000, as before) must be invested to obtain an annual yield of $1,000.

[5] In a more poetic vein, this process of saving has been described as follows by William M. Thackeray:

Though small was your allowance,
   You saved a little store;
And those who save a little
   Shall get a plenty more.

If it does nothing else, the foregoing helps explain why Thackeray is better known as a novelist than a poet.

Effects on an Asset's Value of Changes in the Rate of Return on Other Investments

Note one important point about an asset's capitalized value. Holding constant an asset's annual returns, the asset's worth is higher the lower the rate of return available on other investments. Thus the piece of equipment discussed above was worth $33,333 when you could get a 3 percent return on alternative investments, but only $20,000 when you could get a 5 percent return on alternative investments. This makes sense. After all, the lower the rate of return on alternative investments, the more you must invest in them in order to obtain annual earnings equivalent to those of the asset in question. Thus the more valuable is the asset in question.

This principle helps to explain why in securities markets bond prices fall when interest rates rise, and rise when interest rates fall. As we pointed out in Chapter 5, a bond is a piece of paper that states that the borrower will pay the lender a fixed amount of interest each year (and the principal when the bond comes due). Suppose that this annual interest is $100, and that the interest rate equals $100 \times r$ percent per year. Then, applying the results of the previous paragraphs, this bond will be worth $100 \div r$ dollars, if the bond is due a great many years hence. Suppose the interest rate is 5 percent. Then it is worth $2,000. But if the interest rate rises to 10 percent, it will be worth only $1,000; and if the interest rate falls to 4 percent, it will be worth $2,500. Securities dealers make these sorts of calculations all the time, for they recognize that the value of the bond will fall when interest rates rise, and rise when interest rates fall.

The Present Value of Future Income

In the previous section, we determined the value of an asset that yields a perpetual stream of earnings. Now let's consider a case where an asset will provide you with a single lump sum at a certain time in the future. Suppose that you are the heir to an estate of $100,000, which you will receive in two years. How much is that estate worth now?

To answer this question, we must recognize the basic fact that *a dollar now is worth more than a dollar later.* Why? Because one can always invest money that is available now and obtain interest on it. If the interest rate is 6 percent, a dollar received now is equivalent to $1.06 received a year hence. Why? Because if you invest the dollar now, you'll get $1.06 in a year. Similarly, *a dollar received now is equivalent to $(1.06)^2$ dollars two years hence.* Why? Because if you invest the dollar now, you'll get 1.06 dollars in a year; and if you reinvest this amount for another year at 6 percent, you'll get $(1.06)^2$ dollars.

Consequently, if the interest rate is 6 percent, the estate is worth $100,000 \div (1.06)^2$ dollars now. Since $(1.06)^2 = 1.1236$, it is worth

$$\frac{\$100,000}{1.1236} = \$88,100.$$

In general, *if the interest rate is $100 \times r$ percent per year, a dollar received now is worth $1 \div (1 + r)^2$ dollars two years from now.* Thus, whatever the

311

WHAT DOES THAT DREAM HOUSE REALLY COST?

The biggest investment you'll probably ever make is in a house. The ordinary procedure is for a house buyer to take out a mortgage, often from a savings and loan association or a bank. A mortgage is a loan; the house itself becomes security (or collateral) for the loan. If you fail to meet the mortgage payments, the lender can foreclose the mortgage, which means that the lender is entitled to take possession of the house.

To figure out how much your payments must be each month, the lender determines how much you must pay so that, when the mortgage terminates, you will have repaid the amount you borrowed and paid the stipulated interest on your debt. The size of the monthly mortgage payment depends on three things—(1) the amount you borrow, (2) how long the mortgage extends, and (3) the interest rate. The more that you borrow, the higher your monthly payment, holding all other things equal. And the higher the interest rate and the shorter the period of the mortgage, the higher your monthly payment.

To be more specific, look at the accompanying table, which shows the monthly payment per $1,000 borrowed. As you can see, the monthly payment is $9.66 per $1,000 borrowed, if the mortgage extends for 20 years and the interest rate is 10 percent. Thus, if you take out a $60,000 mortgage (at 10 percent for 20 years), the monthly payment is 60 times $9.66, or $579.60.

MONTHLY MORTGAGE PAYMENTS (PER $1,000 BORROWED)

Interest rate	Length of mortgage (years)			
	15	20	25	30
(percent)		(dollars)		
7	8.99	7.76	7.07	6.66
7½	9.28	8.06	7.39	7.00
8	9.56	8.37	7.72	7.34
8½	9.85	8.68	8.06	7.69
9	10.15	9.00	8.40	8.05
9½	10.45	9.33	8.74	8.41
10	10.75	9.66	9.09	8.78

As noted above, much of the monthly payment is used to repay part of the principal of the loan. The rest goes for interest on the portion of the loan that is not yet repaid. Over the lifetime of a mortgage, a very substantial amount is paid by the borrower for interest. If you take out a 20-year, $60,000 mortgage at an interest rate of 10 percent, you will pay $79,104 in interest over the life of the mortgage. And the higher the interest rate, the bigger the amount that you will pay in interest. Thus, if the interest rate is 9½ percent (rather than 10 percent), you will pay $74,352 (rather than $79,104) in interest over the life of a 20-year, $60,000 mortgage. As you can see, *a difference of ½ percentage point in the interest rate increases the total interest payments by about $5,000!*

value of the interest rate may be, the estate is worth

$$\frac{\$100,000}{(1 + r)^2} .$$

The principle that a dollar now is worth more than a dollar later is of fundamental importance. If you don't understand it, you don't understand a basic precept of the world of finance. Although the example considered in previous paragraphs pertains only to a two-year period, this principle remains valid no matter how long the period of time we consider. Table 15.2 shows the present value of a dollar received at various points of time in the future. As you can see, its present value declines with the length of time before the dollar is received (so long as the interest rate remains constant).

Table 15.2
PRESENT VALUE OF A FUTURE DOLLAR

Number of years hence (that dollar is received)	Interest rate (percent)			
	4	6	8	10
	(cents)			
1	96.2	94.3	92.6	90.9
2	92.5	89.0	85.7	82.6
3	89.0	83.9	79.4	75.1
4	85.5	79.2	73.5	68.3
5	82.3	74.7	68.1	62.0
10	67.6	55.8	46.3	38.5
15	55.5	41.7	31.5	23.9
20	45.6	31.1	21.5	14.8

Test Yourself

1. Suppose that the demand curve for loanable funds is as follows:

Quantity demanded (billions of dollars)	Interest rate (percent)
50	4
40	6
30	8
20	10

Plot the demand curve on a graph. Describe the various kinds of borrowers that are on the demand side of the market for loanable funds.

Suppose that the supply curve for loanable funds is as follows:

Quantity supplied (billions of dollars)	Interest rate (percent)
20	4
25	6
30	8
35	10

Plot the supply curve on the same graph you used to plot the demand curve. What is the equilibrium rate of interest? If usury laws do not permit interest rates to exceed 6 percent, what do you think will happen in this market?

2. Describe the social functions of the interest rate. Do you agree with Aristotle that it is improper to charge interest?

3. Suppose that you can get 10 percent per year from alternative investments and that, if you invest in a particular business, you will get $1,000 per year indefinitely. How much is this investment worth to you?

4. If a firm can borrow money at 10 percent per year and will accept only (riskless) investments that yield 12 percent per year or more, is the firm maximizing profit? Explain.

Rent: Nature and Significance

Besides interest, another type of property income is rent. To understand rent, one must understand what economists mean by land. **Land** is defined by economists as *any input that is fixed in supply, its limits established by nature.* Thus, since certain types of minerals and natural resources are in relatively fixed supply, they are included in the economist's definition of land. Suppose that the supply of an input is completely fixed. Increases in its price will not increase its supply and decreases in its price will not decrease its supply. Following the terminology of the classical economists of the nineteenth century, *the price of such an input is **rent**.* Note that rent means something quite different to an economist than to the man in the street, who considers rent the price of using an apartment or a car or some other object owned by someone else.

If the supply of an input is fixed, its supply curve is a vertical line, as shown in Figure 15.4. Thus the price of this input, its rent, is determined entirely by the demand curve for the input. If the demand curve is D_0, the rent is OP_0; if the demand curve is D_1, the rent is OP_1. Since the supply of the input is fixed, the price of the input can be lowered without influencing the amount supplied. Thus *a rent is a payment above the minimum necessary to attract this amount of the input.*[6]

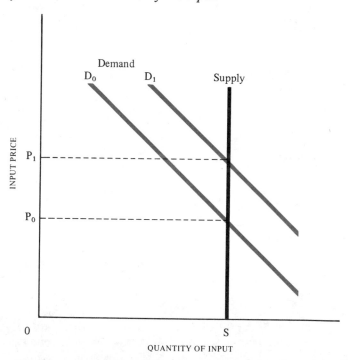

Figure 15.4

Rent *Rent is the price of an input in fixed supply. Since its supply curve is vertical, the price of such an input is determined entirely by the demand curve for the input. If the demand curve is D_0, the rent is OP_0; if the demand curve is D_1, the rent is OP_1.*

[6] In recent years, there has been a tendency among economists to extend the use of the word *rent* to encompass all payments to inputs above the minimum required to make these inputs available to the industry or to the economy. (See Example 15.1.) To a great extent these payments are costs to individual firms; the firms must make such payments to attract and keep these inputs, which are useful to other firms in the industry. But if the inputs have no use in other industries, these payments are not costs to the industry as a whole (or to the economy as a whole) because the inputs would be available to the industry whether or not these payments are made.

Why is it important to know whether a certain payment for inputs is a rent? Because a reduction of the payment will not influence the availability and use of the inputs if the payment is a rent; whereas if it is not a rent, a reduction of the payment is likely to change the allocation of resources. If the government imposes a tax on rents, there will be no effect on the supply of resources to the economy.

THE VIEWS OF HENRY GEORGE

In 1879, Henry George (1839–97) published a book, *Progress and Poverty,* in which he argued that rents should be taxed away by the government. In his view, owners of land were receiving substantial rents simply because their land happened to be well situated, not because they were doing anything productive. Since this rent was unearned income and since the supply of land would not be influenced by such a tax, George felt that it was justifiable to tax away such rent. Indeed, he argued that a tax of this sort should be the only tax imposed by the government.

Critics of George's views pointed out that land can be improved, with the result that the supply is not completely price-inelastic. Moreover, they argued that if land rents are unearned so are many other kinds of income. In addition, they pointed out that it was unrealistic to expect such a tax to raise the needed revenue. George's single-tax movement gained a number of adherents in the last decades of the nineteenth century, and he even made an unsuccessful bid to become mayor of New York. Arguments in favor of a single tax continue to surface from time to time.

RENT: AN EXAMPLE

To make the concept of rent more concrete, consider the following example. There is a lot at the corner of Third Avenue and Winchester Street in a California suburb; this property is on the edge of the town. What will be the rent for this lot? It has various possible uses. It could be the location of a store or restaurant, a small farm, a site for an apartment building, or used for some other purpose. In each possible use, this lot has a certain value as an input.

In a competitive market, this lot will tend to rent for an amount equal to its value in its most productive use. That is, if the value of its marginal product is highest when it is used as the location for a store, a store will be built on it, and the lot will command a rent equal to the value of its marginal product. In this way, the lot will be drawn into the use that seems to yield the highest returns to the renter. From society's point of view, this has much to recommend it, since the use that yields the highest returns is likely to be the one consumers value most highly.

Classical economists viewed rent as a differential that had to be paid for the utilization of better rather than poorer land. They argued as follows. If land becomes scarce, the better lands will receive a nonzero price before the poorer lands. The rent on any acre will rise to the point where it is equal to the difference in productivity between this acre and an acre of no-rent land. Why? Because, as we saw in Chapter 14, the price differential between two inputs will equal the differential in their marginal products.

Henry George

Profits

Besides interest and rent, another important type of property income is profit. Profit is not new to us. In Chapter 5, we discussed at some length the economist's concept of profit and how it varies from the accountant's concept. According to accountants, profit is the amount of money the owner of a firm has left after paying wages, interest, and rent—and after providing proper allowance for the depreciation of buildings and equipment. Economists dissent from this view; their position is that the opportunity costs of the labor, capital, and land contributed by the owner should also be deducted.

PROFIT STATISTICS

Available statistics concerning profits are based on the accountant's concept, not the economist's. Before taxes, corporation profits average about 10 percent of gross national product. Profits—expressed as a percent of either net worth or sales—vary considerably from industry to industry and from firm to firm. (For example, the drug industry's profits in the postwar period have frequently been about 15–20 percent of net worth—considerably higher than in most other manufacturing industries.) Also, profits vary greatly from year to year, and are much more erratic than wages. They fall more heavily in recessions and rise more rapidly in recoveries than wages do. Table 15.3 shows profit as a percent of stockholders' equity in manufacturing in the United States in 1980–84.

To some extent, the measured differences in profits among firms come about because the profit figures are not corrected for the value of the inputs contributed by the owners. Because they are smarter and more resourceful, some owners provide managerial labor of a much higher quality than other owners do. Profits arising from this fact are, at least in part, wages for superior management. Similarly, some owners put up a lot of the capital and work long hours. Profits arising from these sources are, at least in part, interest on capital and wages for time spent working in the firm.

INNOVATION, UNCERTAINTY, AND MONOPOLY POWER

Why do profits—as economists define them—exist? Three important factors are innovation, uncertainty, and monopoly power. Suppose that an economy was composed of perfectly competitive industries, that entry was completely free, and that no changes in technology—no new processes, no new products, or other innovations—were permitted. Moreover, suppose that everyone could predict the future with perfect accuracy. Under these conditions, there would be no profits, because people would enter industries where profits exist, thus reducing these profits eventually to zero, and leave industries where losses exist, thus reducing these negative profits eventually to zero. This sort of no-profit equilibrium has already been discussed in Chapter 10.

But in the real world, innovations of various kinds are made. For example, Du Pont introduces a new product like nylon, or Henry Ford introduces the assembly line, or Marconi introduces the radio. The people who carry out these bold schemes are the *innovators,* those with vision and

Table 15.3

ANNUAL PROFIT (AFTER TAXES) AS A PERCENTAGE OF STOCKHOLDERS' EQUITY, UNITED STATES, 1980–84

Year	All manu-facturing corpor-ations	Durable goods industries	Non-durable goods industries
	(percent)		
1980	13.9	11.2	16.3
1981	13.6	11.9	15.2
1982	9.2	6.1	11.9
1983	10.6	8.1	12.7
1984	11.9	11.3	12.4

Source: Economic Report of the President, 1985. The 1984 figures pertain to the third quarter.

the daring to back it up. The innovators are not necessarily the inventors of new techniques or products, although in some cases the innovator and the inventor are the same. Often the innovator takes another's invention, adapts it, and introduces it to the market. According to economists like the late Joseph Schumpeter of Harvard, profits are the rewards earned by innovators. The profits derived from any single innovation eventually erode with competition and imitation, but other innovations replace them, with the result that profits from innovation continue to be made.

Example 15.1   Exodus of Scientists and Engineers from Teaching

D. Allan Bromley, president of the American Association for the Advancement of Science, has pointed out that, in mathematics, physics, and engineering, many college teachers have been leaving their jobs to work in industry.

(a) Why do you think that this has been occurring? (b) What might be the effect of such a trend on the size and quality of *future* supplies of scientists and engineers? (c) If society feels that more scientists of a particular type are needed, one way of achieving an increase in supply is to shift the supply curve for this type of scientist to the right, as shown in the graph above. How can the government effect such a shift? (d) Suppose that the supply curve does not shift to the right. If the demand curve for this type of scientist shifts to the right, as shown in the graph above, does this result in some scientists of this sort receiving a higher salary than they would be willing to work for? If so, is this a rent?

SOLUTION

(a) Because new Ph.D.'s have been offered higher salaries by industry than by universities. (b) If the quality and number of college teachers were reduced, there might well be an adverse effect on the size and quality of future supplies of scientists and engineers. (c) By scholarship and other programs subsidizing the training of such scientists. (d) If the supply curve does not shift to the right, the equilibrium salary increases from OW_0 to OW_1, and those scientists that were willing to work for a salary of OW_0 receive a windfall of $(OW_1 - OW_0)$. Thus it is a rent in the sense that it is a payment above the minimum necessary to attract this amount of this input. But it is not a rent in the sense that the supply curve is vertical. (See footnote 6.)*

* For further discussion, see D. Allan Bromley, "The Fate of the Seed Corn," *Science,* July 10, 1981.

Frank Knight

In the real world, uncertainty also exists. Indeed, one of the real hazards in attempting to be an innovator is the *risk* involved. According to a theory set forth several decades ago by Frank Knight of the University of Chicago, all economic profit is due to uncertainty. Profit is the reward for risk bearing. Assuming that people would like to avoid risk, they will prefer relatively stable, sure earnings to relatively unstable, uncertain earnings—*if the average level of earnings is the same.* Consequently, to induce people to take the risks involved in owning businesses in various industries, a profit—a premium for risk—must be paid to them. This is similar to the higher wages that, according to the previous chapter, must be paid for jobs where earnings are unstable or uncertain.

Still another reason for the existence of profits is the fact that markets are not perfectly competitive. Under perfect competition, there will be a tendency in the long run for profits to disappear. But, as we have seen, this will not be the case if an industry is a monopoly or oligopoly. Instead, profits may well exist in the long run in such imperfectly competitive industries. And, as we know from Chapter 13, much of our entire economy is composed of imperfectly competitive industries. Monopoly profits are fundamentally the result of "contrived scarcities." Since a firm's demand curve is downward-sloping if competition is imperfect, it pays the firm to take account of the fact that the more it produces, the smaller the price it will receive. In other words, the firm realizes that it will spoil the market if it produces too much. Thus it pays firms to limit their output, and this contrived scarcity is responsible for the existence of the profits they make as a consequence.

The Functions of Profits

To many people, profit seems to be "something for nothing." They do not recognize the innovative or risk-bearing functions of the owners of the firm, and consequently see no reason for the existence of profits. Other people, aware that profits arise because of imperfect competition, ignore the other functions of profit and regard it as entirely the ill-gotten gain of fat monopolists, often smoking big cigars and properly equipped with a rapacious leer. But no group is more hostile to profits than the followers and disciples of Karl Marx. According to Marx, laborers in a capitalist system receive a wage that is barely enough to cover the minimum amount of housing, food, clothing, and other commodities needed for survival. The difference between the amount the employers receive for their products and the amount they pay the laborers that produce them is "surplus value." And, according to Marx, this "surplus value," which includes what we would call profit, is a measure of, and consequence of, exploitation of labor by owners of firms.

Marx's views and those of others who look on profits with suspicion and even distaste are rejected by most economists, who feel that profits play a legitimate and very important role in a capitalistic system. In such a system, consumers, suppliers of inputs, and firms, try to advance their own interests. Workers try to maximize their earnings, capitalists look for the highest interest returns, landlords try to get the highest rents, and firm owners seek to maximize their profits. At first glance, this looks like a chaotic, dog-eat-dog situation; but, as we have seen, it actually turns out to be an orderly and efficient system—if competition is present.

PROFITS AND LOSSES: MAINSPRINGS OF A CAPITALISTIC SYSTEM

Profits and losses are mainsprings of this system for several reasons.

1. They are signals that indicate where resources are needed and where they are too abundant. When there are economic profits in an industry, this is the signal for resources to flow into it; when economic losses exist in an industry, this is the signal for resources to leave it.

2. Profits are very important incentives for innovation and for betting on the future. For an entrepreneur like Joseph Wilson of Xerox, profits are the bait society dangles before him to get him to take the risks involved in marketing a new product, like xerography. If his judgment turns out to be faulty, losses—negative profits—are the penalties society imposes on him.

3. Profits are society's reward for efficiency. Firms that use inefficient techniques or produce an inappropriate amount or type of product are penalized by losses. Firms that are particularly alert, efficient, and adaptive receive profits. Further, profits enable firms to embark on new projects. Thus the profits that Xerox earned on xerography are currently being used to support its new ventures into other types of business machines.

The importance of profits in a free-enterprise economy is clear enough. However, this does not mean that all profits are socially justified or that the system as a whole cannot be improved. Monopoly profits may not be socially justified, and a competitive system, despite its advantages, may produce many socially undesirable effects—for example, an undesirable income distribution. Much more will be said on this score in the next chapter.

The Functional Distribution of Income

In this and the previous chapter, we have been concerned with wages, interest, rent, and profit. How is the total income of the nation as a whole divided among these categories? In other words, what proportion of all income goes to employees? What proportion goes for interest? For rent? For profits? In this section, we take up these questions.

Table 15.4 shows the proportion of national income going for (1) wages and salaries, (2) proprietors' income, (3) corporate profits, (4) interest, and (5) rent.[7] It is clear that wages and salaries are by far the largest of these five income categories. In 1984, about three-fourths of national income went for wages and salaries (including employer contributions to Social Security and pensions). Moreover, this is an understatement of the share of employee compensation in national income, because part of proprietors' income is really wages. As we pointed out in an earlier section, a portion of what the proprietor of the corner drugstore or the local shoestore makes is compensation for the proprietor's labor, not profit as defined by the economist.

[7] The concept of rent on which these figures are based is different from the one presented in this chapter, but this does not affect the conclusions presented below.

Table 15.4

PERCENTAGE SHARES OF NATIONAL INCOME, 1900–84

Period	Wages and salaries	Proprietors' Income	Corporate profits (percent)	Interest	Rent	Total
1900–09	55	24	7	5	9	100
1910–19	54	24	9	5	8	100
1920–29	60	18	8	6	8	100
1930–39	67	15	4	9	5	100
1939–48	65	17	12	3	3	100
1949–58	67	14	13	3	3	100
1963–70	70	12	11	4	3	100
1984	73	5	10	10	2	100

Source: I. Kravis, "Income Distribution: Functional Share," *International Encyclopedia of the Social Sciences,* New York: Macmillan, 1968, and *Annual Reports of the Council of Economic Advisers.* These figures may not be entirely comparable over time, but they are sufficiently accurate for present purposes.

The figures in Table 15.4 indicate a marked reduction over time in the proportion of national income going to proprietors, and a marked increase over time in the proportion going for wages and salaries. Part of this shift is due to the fact that the corporation has become a more dominant organizational form, with the result that many people who would have been individual proprietors owning their own small businesses 50 years ago now work as employed managers for corporations. Another fact that may help to explain this shift is the long-term shift from agriculture (where labor's share of income is low) to manufacturing and services (where labor's share is higher).

Some economists are impressed by the constancy of the share of national income going to labor. Using definitions that are somewhat different than those underlying Table 15.4, they come up with numbers indicating that labor's share has not varied much over time. Other economists, using somewhat different definitions, conclude that labor's share has varied considerably. But one thing is for sure. There is no evidence that a bigger share of the economic pie is going to capitalists in the form of interest, rent, or profits. Perhaps the figures in Table 15.4 exaggerate the extent to which labor's share has increased, but there is certainly no evidence that it has decreased.

Test Yourself

1. Assume that you inherit $1,000, which will be paid to you in two years. If the interest rate is 8 percent, how much is this inheritance worth now? Why?

2. "The supply curve for iron ore is horizontal, so its price is a rent." Comment.

3. "Based on the available data concerning changes over time in labor's share of total income in the United States, it is evident that labor is getting so powerful that it is receiving more and more of the total. This is an important reason for the shortage of capital in the United States." Comment and evaluate.

4. Suppose that a candidate for president proposes that all profits be taxed away. Would you support this proposal? Why or why not?

Summary

1. Interest is a payment for the use of money. Interest rates vary a great deal, depending on the nature of the borrower and the type and riskiness of the loan. One very important function of interest rates is to allocate the supply of loanable funds.

2. The pure interest rate—the interest rate on riskless loans—is, like any price, determined by the interaction of supply and demand. However, because of the influence of the government on both the demand and supply sides of the market, it is clear that the pure interest rate is to a considerable extent a matter of public policy.

3. Capital is composed of inputs produced by the economic system itself. Our economy uses very roundabout methods of production and devotes a considerable amount of its productive capacity to the production of capital.

4. If more and more capital is produced during a particular period, consumers must cut further and further into their consumption during that period. This process is called saving.

5. In a capitalist system, each capital good has a market value that can be determined by capitalizing its earnings. Holding constant an asset's annual return, the asset's worth is higher, the lower the rate of return available on other investments.

6. Any piece of capital has a rate of return, which indicates its net productivity. An asset's rate of return is the interest rate earned on the investment in the asset. If firms maximize profits, they must carry out all projects where the rate of return exceeds the interest rate at which they can borrow.

7. Rent is the return derived by inputs that are fixed in supply. Since the supply of the input is fixed, its price can be lowered without influencing the amount supplied. Thus, if the government imposes taxes on rents, there will be no effect on the supply of resources to the economy.

8. Another important type of property income is profits. Available statistics on profits are based on the accountant's concept, not the economist's, with the result that they include the opportunity costs of the labor, capital, and land contributed by the owners of the firm. Profits play a very important and legitimate role in a free enterprise system.

9. Two of the important factors responsible for the existence of profits are innovation and uncertainty. Profits are the rewards earned by innovators and a payment for risk-bearing. Still another reason for the existence of profits is monopoly power; due to contrived scarcity, profits are made by firms in imperfectly competitive markets.

Concepts for Review

Interest	Supply curve for	Saving
Rate of interest	loanable funds	Capitalization
Pure rate of interest	Liquidity preference theory	Land
Demand curve for	Capital budgeting	Rent
loanable funds	Primary inputs	Innovator
Rate of return	Capital	Risk

CHAPTER 16

Income Inequality, Poverty, and Discrimination

Although the United States is one of the richest countries on earth, it is not a land of milk and honey to all its inhabitants. Some Americans are poor—so poor that they suffer from malnutrition—and while poverty may not be a sin, it is no less an inconvenience to the poor. Given the affluence of American society, one is led to ask why poverty exists and whether it cannot be abolished by proper public policies. One purpose of this chapter is to examine these questions.

Poverty does not exist in a social vacuum; for one thing, it is intimately bound up with the problems of discrimination that have played an important role in American life for many years. Unquestionably, discriminatory barriers have tended to depress the incomes of females, nonwhites, and other minority groups. Besides looking at poverty in the United States, this chapter also discusses some relevant aspects of discrimination.

How Much Inequality of Income?

We don't have to be very perceptive social observers to recognize that there are great differences in income levels in the United States. But our idea of what the distribution of income looks like depends on the sort of family and community we come from. A child brought up in Lake Forest, a wealthy suburb of Chicago, is unlikely to be as aware of the incidence of poverty as a child brought up on Chicago's poor South Side. For a preliminary glimpse of the extent of *income inequality* in the United States, scan Table 16.1,

Table 16.1

PERCENTAGE DISTRIBUTION OF FAMILIES, BY INCOME, 1983

Money income (dollars)	Percent of all families	Percent of total income received	Percent of families with this and lower incomes	Percent of income received by families with this and lower incomes
Under 11,629	20	5	20	5
11,629–20,059	20	11	40	16
20,060–29,203	20	17	60	33
29,204–41,823	20	24	80	57
41,824–67,325	15	27	95	84
67,326 and over	5	16	100	100
Total	100	100		

Source: Department of Commerce.

which shows the percentage of all families in the United States that were situated in various income classes in 1983. According to the table, the bottom fifth of the nation's families received an income of less than $11,629 in 1983. On the other hand, the top fifth of the nation's families received an income of $41,824 or more in 1983.

It may come as a surprise to some that so large a percentage of the nation's families made less than $11,629. The image of the affluent society projected in the Sunday supplements and on some television programs is strangely out of tune with these facts. Yet, to put these figures in world perspective, it should be recognized that Americans are very rich relative to other peoples. This fact is shown clearly by Table 16.2, which gives for various countries the 1983 level of income per person, which is the total in-

Table 16.2

SELECTED COUNTRIES GROUPED BY APPROXIMATE LEVEL OF INCOME PER CAPITA, 1983[a]

I. Countries with income per capita exceeding $6,000

United States	Denmark	Sweden
Australia	France	Japan
Canada	Germany	Switzerland

II. Countries with income per capita between $2,500 and $6,000

Argentina	Greece	Yugoslavia
Ireland	Hong Kong	Italy
Soviet Union	United Kingdom	Venezuela

III. Countries and regions with income per capita between $1,000 and $2,500

Algeria	Congo	Guatemala
Brazil	Malaysia	Turkey

IV. Countries and regions with income per capita less than $1,000

India	El Salvador	Most of Africa
Indonesia	Haiti	Much of Asia

[a] Where 1983 figures are not yet published, the most recent available data are used. Note that all figures are expressed in 1975 dollars.

come of each nation divided by its population. The United States is among the leaders in this table.

Why Inequality?

Nonetheless, recognizing that our poor are better off than the bulk of the population in many other countries, the fact remains that there is substantial inequality of income in this country. Why is this the case? Based on our discussion of labor and property incomes in previous chapters, this question is not hard to answer. One reason is that some people possess greater abilities than others. Since Ozzie Smith and Dave Winfield have extraordinary skill as baseball players, it is easy to understand why they make a lot of money. Another reason is differences in the amount of education and training people receive. Thus physicians or lawyers must receive a higher income than people in occupations requiring little or. no training. (Otherwise it would not pay people to undergo medical or legal training.) Still another reason is that some people own large amounts of property. Thus, because of a shrewd choice of ancestry, the Fords, Rockefellers, and Mellons get high incomes from inherited wealth. Still other reasons are that some people have managed to obtain monopoly power, and others have had an extraordinary string of good luck.

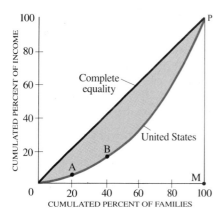

Figure 16.1
Lorenz Curve for Family Income, United States, 1983 OP *is the Lorenz curve if income were distributed equally. The shaded area between this hypothetical Lorenz curve and the actual Lorenz curve is a measure of income inequality.*

A Measure of Income Inequality

To what extent has income inequality in the United States decreased? Some people say that because of the advent of the "welfare state" the nation has moved rapidly toward greater equality of income. Others say that the rich are getting richer and the poor are getting poorer. Who is right? To answer this question, we need some way to measure the degree of income inequality. The most commonly used technique is the **Lorenz curve,** which plots the percentage of people, going from the poorest up, on the horizontal axis, and the percentage of total income they get on the vertical axis.

The Lorenz curve based on the figures in Table 16.1 is shown in Figure 16.1. To see how this diagram was constructed, note that in Table 16.1 families with incomes under $11,629 accounted for 20 percent of all families, but only 5 percent of all income. Thus, plotting 20 percent on the horizontal axis against 5 percent on the vertical axis, we get point A. The table also indicated that families with incomes under $20,060 accounted for 40 percent of all families, but only 16 percent of all income. Plotting these figures in the same way, we get point B. Connecting up all points like A and B, we obtain the Lorenz curve in Figure 16.1.

Case 1: No Inequality. Two extreme cases must be understood to see how the Lorenz curve is used. First, suppose that *incomes were the same for all families* (or whatever kinds of recipients are under consideration). Then the Lorenz curve would be a straight line connecting the origin of the diagram with its upper right-hand corner. That is, it would be *OP* in Figure 16.1. To see this, note that, if incomes are distributed equally, the lowest 10 percent of the families receive 10 percent of the total income, the lowest 20 percent

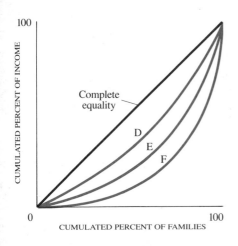

Lorenz Curves for Countries D, E, and F *Income inequality is greater in country F than in country E, and greater in country E than in country D.*

of the families receive 20 percent of the total income, and so forth. Plotting 10 percent on the horizontal axis against 10 percent on the vertical axis, 20 percent on the horizontal axis against 20 percent on the vertical axis, and so forth, one gets a Lorenz curve of *OP*.

Case 2: Complete Inequality. Suppose that *incomes were distributed completely unequally*—that is, one person has all of the income and the rest have none. In this case, the Lorenz curve would lie along the horizontal axis from *O* to *M* and along the vertical line from *M* to *P*. It would be *OMP* in Figure 16.1. Why? Because the lowest 10 percent of the families have zero percent of the total income, the lowest 20 percent of the families have zero percent of the total income, and so, in fact, do the lowest 99 percent of the families. Plotting 10 percent on the horizontal axis against zero percent on the vertical axis, 20 percent on the horizontal axis against zero percent on the vertical axis, and so on, one gets a Lorenz curve that lies along the horizontal axis from *O* to *M*. But since 100 percent of the families must receive 100 percent of the income, the Lorenz curve must then jump up from *M* to *P*.

The Importance of the Shaded Area. These two cases make it clear that *the shaded area in Figure 16.1*—the deviation of the actual Lorenz curve from the Lorenz curve corresponding to complete equality of income—*is a measure of income inequality.* The larger this shaded area, the greater the extent of income inequality. Figure 16.2 shows the Lorenz curve for the income distributions in three countries—*D, E,* and *F.* As reflected in the Lorenz curves, income inequality is greater in *F* than in *E,* and greater in *E* than in *D.* Why? Because the area between the actual Lorenz curve and the Lorenz curve corresponding to complete equality is greater in *F* than in *E,* and greater in *E* than in *D.*

Trends in Income Inequality

Let us now return to the question posed at the beginning of the previous section: To what extent has income inequality in the United States decreased? Figure 16.3 shows the Lorenz curves for the income distributions in 1929 and 1962. These curves make it clear that there was a considerable reduction in income inequality. The share of income going to the top 20 percent declined by one-fifth between 1929 and 1962. This change, described by some writers as an "income revolution," did not occur gradually throughout the period. Instead, essentially all the reduction in income inequality occurred before the end of World War II. Since then, there has been little change in the degree of income inequality.

One of the reasons for the reduction in income inequality between 1929 and the end of World War II was the increased importance of wages and salaries relative to other sources of income. Wages and salaries are more equally distributed than income from self-employment and property. Also, many public programs were established to provide income for the poor. (The details of these programs are described below.) In addition, the shift from substantial prewar unemployment to the full employment of World War II narrowed wage differentials among various types of workers. Further, the inequality in the distribution of wealth was reduced during this period.

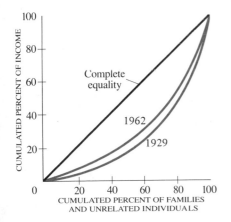

Changes over Time in Lorenz Curves for Family Income in the United States *Income inequality in the United States has decreased over time, as indicated by the Lorenz curves for 1929 and 1962.*

325

Example 16.1   Economic Effects of Illegal Aliens

In recent years, the number of illegal aliens in the United States has been estimated to be between 2 and 12 million. Most of the apprehended aliens have been Mexican nationals. Suppose that the value-of-marginal-product curve for labor in the U.S. market is as follows:

(a) If S_1 is the supply curve for labor *without* immigration of illegal aliens, what would be total labor income under these circumstances? (b) If S_2 is the supply curve for labor *with* immigration of illegal aliens, what would be the total labor income of the native U.S. population under these circumstances? (c) Will the owners of U.S. capital and land benefit from this immigration? Why or why not? (d) Why does La Raza Unidad, a farm labor union representing many Spanish-speaking American citizens, oppose such immigration?

SOLUTION

(a) Total labor income will equal the area of rectangle $OW_0 AL_0$, since it will equal the wage (OW_0) times the quantity of labor employed (OL_0). (b) Since the total supply of native U.S. labor is OL_0, total labor income will equal the area of rectangle $OW_1 BL_0$, since it will equal the wage (OW_1) times OL_0. (c) Yes. The value of the marginal product of the extra ($OL_1 - OL_0$) workers exceeds their wage, OW_1, as can be seen in the above graph. Also, the owners of U.S. capital and land benefit from the fact that they can pay native U.S. labor a lower wage. (d) One reason may be that such immigration lowers the wage received by American citizens engaged in farm labor.*

* For further discussion, see B. Chiswick, "Immigrants and Immigration Policy," in W. Fellner, ed., *Contemporary Economic Problems, 1978,* Washington, D.C.: American Enterprise Institute, 1978.

Effects of the Tax Structure on Income Inequality

So far we have looked at the distribution of before-tax income. But we must also consider the effect of the tax system on income inequality.

A tax is ***progressive*** if the rich pay a higher proportion of their income for the tax than do the poor. A tax is ***regressive*** if the rich pay a smaller proportion of their income for the tax than do the poor.

Needless to say, people who feel that the tax system should promote a

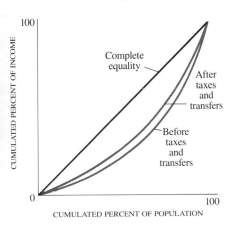

Figure 16.4

Effect of Federal Income Tax and Transfer Payments on Lorenz Curve, United States, 1980 In the United States, inequality of income after taxes and transfers is less than inequality of income before taxes and transfers.

redistribution of income from rich to poor favor progressive, not regressive taxes. Obviously, the personal income tax is progressive, since the tax rate is greater for high-income people than for low-income people. Other progressive taxes are inheritance or estate taxes. (The federal government levies a gift tax to prevent wealthy people from circumventing the estate tax by giving their money away before death.) This is applauded by reformers who oppose accumulation and preservation of inherited wealth. But, as in the case of the personal income tax, the portion of an estate subject to taxes can be reduced through clever use of various loopholes, all quite legal. Thus the estate tax is not as progressive as it looks.

Not all taxes are progressive; examples of regressive taxes are not hard to find. General sales taxes of the sort used by most states and some cities are regressive, since high-income people pay a smaller percentage of their income in sales taxes than do low-income people. The Social Security tax is also regressive. It is difficult to tell whether the corporation income tax is progressive or regressive. At first glance, it seems progressive because the owners of corporations—the stockholders—tend to be wealthy people; and to the extent that the corporate income tax is paid from earnings that might otherwise be paid to the stockholders, one might conclude that it is progressive. But this ignores the possibility that the corporation may pass the tax on to the consumer by charging a higher price; in this case the tax may not be progressive.

WHO PAYS THE TAXES AND RECEIVES THE TRANSFER PAYMENTS?

To get a better picture of the extent to which the government—in terms of both the money it spends and the taxes it levies—takes from the rich and gives to the poor, studies have been carried out to determine how much people in various income brackets pay in taxes and receive in transfer payments (social security, welfare payments, food stamps, medicare, and medicaid). The results of one important study of this sort are shown in Figure 16.4. As you can see, the effect of taxes (federal, state, and local) and transfers is to reduce income inequality. However, this is due largely to the fact that transfer payments go mainly to the poor. Taken by itself, the tax system is only mildly progressive or slightly regressive, depending on the study's assumptions. Moreover, there is evidence that the tax system is less progressive (or more regressive) in 1985 than in 1966.[1]

Estimates of this sort are interesting, but it is difficult to predict the *incidence* of some taxes—that is, it is difficult to know who *really* pays them. The incidence of certain taxes is relatively easy to determine, as we saw in Chapter 4. It is generally accepted that the personal income tax is paid by the person whose income is taxed. But there are other cases—such as the corporation income taxes we just mentioned—where it is difficult to tell how much of the tax burden the firm shifts to the consumer.[2] For these and

[1] J. Pechman, *Who Paid the Taxes, 1966–85?*, Washington, D.C.: Brookings Institution, 1985. Based on different assumptions about tax incidence, E. Browning and W. Johnson have concluded that the tax system is more progressive than Pechman concludes.

[2] To see how the burden of a tax can be shifted, recall our discussion in Chapter 4 of the effects of an *excise* tax—a tax imposed on each unit sold of a particular product. The federal government imposes excise taxes on liquor and tobacco, among many other products. The im-

(continued)

other reasons, there is considerable controversy over the extent to which the spending and taxing activities of the government really are progressive or regressive.

Income Inequality: The Pros and Cons

THE CASE AGAINST INCOME INEQUALITY

Many distinguished social philosophers have debated the merits and demerits of making the income distribution more equal. We cannot consider all the subtler points, but those who favor greater equality make four main arguments.

1. They say that inequality of income lessens total consumer satisfaction because an extra dollar given to a poor man provides him with more extra satisfaction than the loss of a dollar takes away from a rich man. According to A. C. Pigou, "It is evident that any transference of income from a relatively rich man to a relatively poor man of similar temperament, since it enables more intense wants to be satisfied at the expense of less intense wants, must increase the aggregate sum of satisfactions."[3]

A problem in this very appealing argument is its assumption that the rich man and the poor man have the same capacities to gain enjoyment from income. Most economists believe that there is no scientific way to make such comparisons (as emphasized in Appendix D). They deny that the satisfaction one person derives from an extra dollar of income can be measured against the satisfaction another person derives from an extra dollar. Although such comparisons may be drawn, they rest on ethical, not scientific, grounds.

2. It is argued that income inequality is likely to result in unequal opportunities for young people to gain advanced education and training. The children of the rich can get an education, while the children of the poor often cannot. The result is that some able and productive people may be denied an education simply because their parents are poor. This is a waste of resources.

3. It is argued that income inequality is likely to lead to political inequality. The rich may well influence legislation and political decisions more heavily than the poor, and there is likely to be one kind of justice for the rich and another kind for the poor.

4. In the past few years, the arguments for income equality have been carried a step forward by John Rawls, the Harvard philosopher. He says

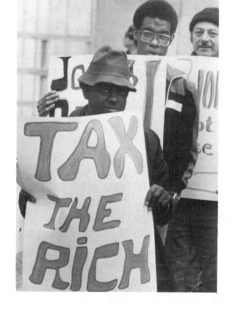

---

mediate effect of these taxes is to raise the price of the commodity since the supply curve will be shifted upward and to the left. If demand is price inelastic, most of the burden of the tax is shifted to the consumer. Under these circumstances, firms sell almost as many units of the product as before the tax was imposed, despite the higher price induced by the tax. On the other hand, if supply is relatively inelastic, the burden is borne mainly by the producer. Usually, the aim of excise taxes is to put the burden on consumers. In the case of liquor and tobacco there clearly is a feeling that drinking and smoking smack of sin, and sinners should pay, in this world and the next. For a discussion of excise taxes, see J. Pechman, *Federal Tax Policy,* 3d ed., Washington, D.C.: The Brookings Institution, 1977.

[3] A. C. Pigou, *Economics of Welfare,* 4th ed., London: Macmillan, 1948, p. 89.

that, *if people were framing a constitution for society without knowing what their class position would be, they would opt for equality.* And he argues that "all social values . . . are to be distributed equally unless an unequal distribution . . . is to everyone's advantage"—that is, unless an unequal distribution is to the advantage of society's least privileged group. Although Rawls's book, *A Theory of Justice,* has had considerable impact, many economists have pointed out that his prescription for society might not appeal to people who were willing to take risks. Suppose that you were framing a social constitution and that you could establish a society that guaranteed every family $15,000 a year (no more, no less) or one where 99 percent of all families would receive $20,000 and 1 percent would receive $12,000. You might choose the latter kind of society because, although there is a small chance that you would do worse than in the egalitarian case, the chance of doing better seems worth this risk.

THE CASE FOR INCOME INEQUALITY

In general, people who favor income inequality also make four arguments.

1. They argue that income inequality is needed to give people an incentive to work and create. After all, if everyone receives the same income, why bother to increase your production, or to try to invent a new process, or to work overtime? Whatever you do, your income will be the same. This is an important point, though it overlooks the fact that nonmonetary incentives like pride in a job well done can be as important as monetary incentives.

2. Advocates of income inequality claim that it permits greater savings, and thus greater capital formation. Although this seems reasonable, it is not hard to cite cases where countries with greater inequality of income invest less, not more, than countries with less inequality of income. Thus some Middle Eastern countries with great income inequality have not had relatively high investment rates.

3. Advocates of income inequality say that the rich have been important patrons of new and high-quality products that benefit the entire society. They argue that there are social advantages in the existence of certain people with the wherewithal to pioneer in consumption and to support art and culture. In their view, a completely egalitarian society would be a rather dull affair.

4. Advocates of income inequality point out that even if everyone received the same income, the poor would not be helped a great deal, because the wealthy are relatively few. If the riches of the rich were transferred to the poor, each poor person would get only a little, because there are so many poor and so few rich.

The Tradeoff between Equality and Efficiency

In trying to decide how much income inequality you favor, it is important to recognize that measures taken to reduce inequality are likely to decrease economic efficiency. In other words, *if we reduce inequality, we may well cut society's total output.* Why? Because, as pointed out in the previous section, people are likely to have less incentive to produce if their incomes

are much the same regardless of how much they produce. This does not
mean that all measures designed to reduce income inequality are bad.
What it does mean is that, if you want to reduce income inequality, you
should be sensitive to the effects on output. In particular, you should try to
find policies that will attain a given reduction in inequality at a minimum
cost in terms of reduced output.

In view of the strong feelings of many advocates and opponents of
reduced income inequality, it is not surprising that they sometimes make
extreme statements about the nature of the tradeoff between equality and
efficiency. Some egalitarians deny that there is any tradeoff at all. They
claim that inequality can be reduced without any cut in output. Some
opponents of reductions in income inequality assert that there will be a
catastrophic fall in output if the existing income distribution is tampered
with. Although far too little is known about the quantitative character of
this tradeoff, there seems to be general agreement among economists that
the truth lies somewhere between these two extremes.

People vary considerably in their evaluation of how much society
should pay (in terms of decreased total output) for a particular reduction
in income inequality. The late Arthur Okun of the Brookings Institution
suggested that, to characterize your own feelings on this score, it is useful
to view money as a liquid and to visualize a bucket which carries money
from the rich to the poor.[4] The bucket is leaky, so only part of what is
taken from the rich can be given to the poor. If the leak is very small, a
dollar taken from the rich may result in 99 cents going to the poor. Many
people would accept a loss of this magnitude. If the leak is very large, a
dollar taken from the rich may result in only 5 cents going to the poor.
Few people would accept this big a loss. How big a loss would you accept?
The larger the leak that you would find acceptable, the more willing you
are to accept output losses in order to attain decreases in income inequality.

The argument between the advocates and opponents of reduced income
inequality involves much more than economics. Whether you favor
greater or less income inequality depends on your ethical and political
beliefs. It is not a matter economics alone can settle. What economists can
do is assess the degree of income inequality in a country and suggest ways
to alter the gap between the haves and have-nots in accord with the
dictates of the people or their leaders. In recent years, economists in and
out of government have devoted much effort to designing programs aimed
at reducing poverty. To understand these programs, we must discuss what
poverty is, and who the poor are.

*Basic Idea #31: Attempts to promote
economic equality may well result in a
reduction in national output, since such
attempts are likely to weaken incentives
to work hard, save, and invest
productively. Conversely, attempts to
increase national output via the
strengthening of such incentives may
result in more inequality.*

What Is Poverty?

Some people are fond of saying that everything is relative. Certainly this is
true of poverty. Relative to the Mellons or Rockefellers, practically all of us
are poor; but relative to the homeless who sleep in railroad and bus termi-

[4] Arthur Okun, *Equality and Efficiency,* Washington, D.C.: Brookings Institution, 1975. For
an excerpt from this book, see E. Mansfield, *Principles of Microeconomics: Readings, Issues,
Cases,* 4th ed., New York: Norton, 1983.

nals, practically all of us are rich. Moreover, poverty is certainly subjective. Consider the average young executive making $50,000 a year. After a bad day at the office or a particularly expensive family shopping spree, he is likely to tell anyone who will listen that he is as poor as a church mouse.

There is no well-defined income level that can be used in all times and places as a touchstone to define poverty. Poverty is partly a matter of how one person's income stacks up against that of others. What most people in America today regard as stark poverty would have seemed like luxury to many Americans of 200 years ago—and would seem like luxury in parts of Asia and Africa today. Consequently, one must be careful not to define poverty in such a way that it cannot be eliminated—and then try to eliminate it. If poverty is defined as being in the bottom 10 percent of the income distribution, how can a war against poverty ever be won? Regardless of what measures are taken, there will always be a bottom 10 percent of the income distribution, unless all income inequality is eliminated (which is highly unlikely).

Perhaps the most widely accepted definition of *poverty* in the United States today is the one developed by the Social Security Administration, which began by determining the cost of a *minimal* nutritionally sound food plan (given by the Department of Agriculture). Then, since low-income families spend about one-third of their incomes on food, this food cost was multiplied by 3 to obtain an income level that was used as a criterion for poverty. Families with less income were regarded as "living below the poverty level."

Based on such computations, an urban family of four needed an income of about $10,178 to make it barely over the Social Security Administration's poverty line in 1983. (Since farm families typically have lower food costs, the estimates for them are somewhat lower.) Although one could quarrel with this figure on various counts, most people probably would agree that families with income below this level are poor.[5]

TWO CASE STUDIES

Particular cases of poverty are generally more illuminating and impressive than discussions in the abstract. Consider the following two actual cases in New York City (the names are fictitious).

The Smith Family. The Smiths—Christopher, 47, and Irene, 35—opened a small restaurant after years of saving. Within a month, Christopher had a severe heart attack and was laid up in the hospital. The Smiths lost the restaurant, and Irene went to work as a nurse's aide to supplement her husband's small disability benefits. After about a year of working and trying to take care of her husband and two children—John, 13, and Deborah, 12—Irene collapsed from the strain and had to enter a mental hospital. While she was away, a relative took care of Christopher and the children. After getting out of the hospital, Irene learned that her husband

---

[5] The basic figures come from the Department of Commerce's *Current Population Reports,* which explain in detail the way in which these figures are derived. The method described in the text is crude, but it provides results that are quite close to those of more complicated methods. Since 1969, the poverty line has been calculated on the basis of the Consumer Price Index, not the price of food.

had cancer and required expensive surgery. She became so upset that the doctor called in one of the city's charity agencies, which tried to help this troubled and impoverished family as best it could.

The Jones Family. Jean Jones, 35, is trying to raise seven children. Her husband, an unskilled laborer, never made much money. He drank a lot, terrified Mrs. Jones and the children with his abuse, and was an unfaithful husband. Four years ago, Mrs. Jones separated from him. She gets along as best she can on public assistance, but is having a difficult time. Two of the children have been arrested for theft; two others are in trouble in school; and one daughter is pregnant out of wedlock. Mrs. Jones feels beaten. In recent months, through the help of neighbors, she has consulted a community service bureau where the social workers have given her help and encouragement. But she obviously needs a great deal of aid if she and her family are to get their heads above water.

Neither of these cases is typical. Since they were cited by the *New York Times* as being among New York's 100 neediest cases, it is fair to say that their plight is probably worse than that of the great bulk of America's poor. But they provide some idea of just how bad things can get; and one has to be hardhearted indeed not to feel compassion for people like the Smiths and Mrs. Jones.

Declining Incidence of Poverty

Because college students tend to come from relatively well-off families, they often are unaware of the number of families in the United States whose incomes fall below the Social Security Administration's poverty line. According to estimates made by the federal government in 1984, about 15 percent of the population in the United States was below this line. In absolute terms, this means that over 35 million people were poor—usually not as poor as the Smiths or Mrs. Jones, but poor enough to fall below the criterion described above.

Fortunately, the incidence of poverty (measured by this criterion) generally has been declining in the United States. In 1947, about 30 percent; in 1960, about 20 percent; and in 1977, about 12 percent of the people were poor by this definition. This is what we would expect. As the average level of income rises, the proportion of the population falling below the poverty line (which is defined by a relatively fixed dollar amount of income) will tend to decrease. Nonetheless, the fact that poverty is being eliminated in the United States does not mean that this process is going on as fast as it should. Many observers feel, as we shall see in subsequent sections, that poverty could and should be eradicated more rapidly.

Characteristics of the Poor

Naturally, the poor are not confined to any particular demographic group, but some types of families are much more likely than others to be below the poverty line. In particular, *nonwhites are much more likely to be poor than whites.* In 1983, 36 percent of nonwhites were poor, whereas 12 percent of whites were poor. Also, *families headed by females are much more likely to be poor than families headed by males.* In addition, very large families—7 persons and over—are much more likely than others to be poor.

Poverty strikes a particularly hard blow at children. Even the most hardhearted citizens are prone to agree that the young should be shielded from the crippling impact of dire poverty. According to a government survey carried out in 1975, *over 8 million children under 16 in the United States were being raised in families below the poverty line.* This is a very striking fact indeed.

Reasons for Poverty

To a considerable extent, the reasons why families are poor lie beyond the control of the families themselves. About one-third of the poor adults have suffered a disability of some sort, or the premature death of the family breadwinner, or family dissolution. Some have had to face a smaller demand for their occupation (because of technological or other change) or the decline of their industry or geographical area. Some have simply lived "too long"–their savings have given out before their minds and bodies did. Another instrumental factor in making some families poor is discrimination of various kinds. The most obvious type is racial, but others exist as well–discrimination based on sex, religion, age, residence, education, and seniority. In addition, some people are poor because they have very limited ability or little or no motivation. These factors should not be overlooked.

There are important barriers which tend to separate the poor from the rest of society. As the University of Wisconsin's Robert Lampman points out,

> Barriers, once established, tend to be reinforced from the poverty side by the alienated themselves. The poor tend to be cut off from not only opportunity but even from information about opportunity. A poverty subculture develops which sustains attitudes and values that are hostile to escape from poverty. These barriers combine to make events nonrandom; e.g., unemployment is slanted away from those inside the feudalistic walls of collective bargaining, disability more commonly occurs in jobs reserved for those outside the barriers, the subculture of poverty invites or is prone to self-realizing forecasts of disaster.[6]

Judging from the available evidence, poverty tends to be self-perpetuating. Families tend to be poor year after year, and their children tend to be poor. Because the families are poor, the children are poorly educated, poorly fed, and poorly cared for, and poverty is transmitted from one generation to the next. It is a vicious cycle.

---

[6] Robert Lampman, "Approaches to the Reduction of Poverty," *American Economic Review,* May 1965.

Test Yourself

1. Suppose that the following data pertain to the income distribution in the nation of Upper Usher in 1984:

Income (dollars)	Percent of families with indicated income
2,000	40
4,000	30
6,000	20
10,000	10

Plot the Lorenz curve for this nation in 1984.

2. In 1985, suppose that the income distribution in Upper Usher is as follows:

Income (dollars)	Percent of families with indicated income
2,000	20
4,000	40
6,000	35
10,000	5

Plot the 1985 Lorenz curve, and compare it with the 1984 curve. Did income inequality in this nation increase or decrease between 1984 and 1985?

3. People are classified as poor on the basis of their current money income. Should the following items also be taken into account? (a) The assets of the person or family; (b) the existence of rich relatives of the person or family; (c) the person's or family's income over a period of years, not a single year.

Social Insurance

OLD-AGE INSURANCE

Until about 50 years ago, the federal government played little or no role in helping the poor. Private charity was available in limited amounts, and the state and local governments provided some help, but the general attitude was "sink or swim." Self-reliance and self-support were the watchwords. The Great Depression of the 1930s, which changed so many attitudes, also made a marked change in this area. In 1935, with the passage of the Social Security Act, the federal government established a social insurance system providing compulsory old-age insurance for both workers and self-employed people, as well as unemployment insurance. By 1984, about 36 million Americans were receiving well over $100 billion in benefits from the resulting system of old-age and survivors' insurance.

Every wage earner covered under the Social Security Act pays a tax, which in 1984 amounted to 7 percent of the first $37,800 of his or her annual earnings. The employer also pays a tax, which is equal to that paid by the employee. The amount that one can expect to receive each month in *old-age insurance* benefits depends on one's average monthly earnings. Also, the size of the benefits depends on the number of years one has worked. Table 16.3 shows the maximum monthly benefits in 1984. The benefits in the table are a retirement annuity. In other words, they are paid to the wage earner from the date of retirement to the time he or she dies. In addition, when a wage earner dies, *Social Security* provides payments to his or her spouse, to dependent parents, and to children until they are about 18 years of age. Further, payments are made to a wage earner (and dependents), if he or she is totally disabled and unable to work.

Table 16.3

MAXIMUM INITIAL SOCIAL SECURITY BENEFITS, 1984

	Monthly payment
Retired worker alone	
65 years old	$703
62 years old	559
Retired worker with spouse	
65 years old	908
62 years old	821

Source: World Almanac.

CONTROVERSIES OVER SOCIAL SECURITY

There are a number of controversial aspects of the Social Security program.

1. *If you work past the retirement age of 65, you can be penalized considerably.* For every dollar in wages that you earn above and beyond $6,960 in 1984, you lose 50 cents in Social Security benefits. Thus, since you must pay taxes on your earnings, you get to keep well under one-half of every extra dollar that you earn in wages (over $6,960 per year). But you can earn any amount of interest or dividends or pensions without your Social Security benefits being reduced. To some observers, this is unfair discrimination against older people who want to hold down jobs.

2. *The Social Security tax is regressive,* since those with annual earnings above $37,800 pay a smaller proportion of their income in Social Security taxes than do those with annual earnings below $37,800. For this and other reasons, many observers believe that the system is not as generous to the poor as it should be.

3. *Some people are disturbed that the Social Security system is not really an ordinary insurance system at all.* An ordinary insurance program must have assets that are sufficient to finance all of the benefits promised to the people in the program. This is not the case for Social Security. But this does not mean that you won't receive your Social Security benefits. What it does mean is that the Social Security system is a means of transferring income each year from the working young and middle-aged to the retired old people. It will be up to future Congresses to determine what these benefits will be. (In 1983, Congress made a number of important changes: for example, up to half of the Social Security benefits of the well-to-do will be taxable under the personal income tax.) Perhaps you will receive much more than the amounts in Table 16.3—but then again, perhaps you won't. Only time will tell.

4. *Some people are disturbed that Social Security is mandatory.* Milton Friedman is concerned that the government interferes with an individual's freedom to plan for the future by forcing him or her to be a member of the Social Security system. (Workers might be able to obtain larger pensions by investing the money that they contribute to Social Security in investments of their own choosing.) Other observers retort that without a mandatory system, some workers would make inadequate provision for their old age and might become public charges.

5. *Some people are concerned that Social Security is an impediment to saving and capital formation.* Martin Feldstein, former chairman of President Reagan's Council of Economic Advisers, feels that Americans save relatively little because they depend on Social Security to take care of their old age. This, he believes, tends to depress capital formation in the United States, since savings can be used to build factories, expand old plants ,and add in various ways to the nation's stock of capital. He favors a slowdown in the rate of growth of Social Security, and more reliance on private pensions and personal savings.

MEDICARE, UNEMPLOYMENT INSURANCE, OTHER PROGRAMS

In 1965, the Congress extended the Social Security program to include **Medicare,** a compulsory hospitalization insurance plan plus a voluntary insurance plan covering doctors' fees for people over 65. The hospitalization insurance pays for practically all the hospital costs of the first 90 days of each spell of illness, as well as some additional costs. The voluntary plan covers about 80 percent of doctors' fees after the first $60. The cost of the compulsory insurance is included in the taxes described above.

Besides instituting old-age, survivors, and medical insurance, the Social Security Act also encouraged the states to set up systems of *unemployment insurance.* Such systems now exist in all states, financed by taxes on employers. Once an insured worker is unemployed, he can obtain benefits after a short waiting period, generally a week. The average weekly benefits differ from state to state; in 1982 they ranged from about $150 in Michigan to about $80 in Mississippi. (Since these benefits are not subject to income taxes, these figures understate the value of the benefit to the recipient.) In most states, there is a 26-week ceiling on the duration of benefits, but in 1975, there was a temporary extension of benefits to a maximum duration of 65 weeks. Clearly, unemployment insurance is another important device to keep people from falling below the poverty line.

Finally, in 1974, a new program was created to replace federal grants to the states to help the aged, the blind, and the disabled. This program, called the *Supplemental Security Income* program, establishes a uniform national minimum income for people in these categories who are unable to work. (Also, many states supplement these federal payments.) In 1984, about 4 million people received income from this program.

Antipoverty Programs

According to the English poet and essayist Samuel Johnson, "A decent provision for the poor is the true test of civilization." There is general agreement that our social insurance programs, although useful in preventing and alleviating poverty, are not an adequate or complete antipoverty program. For one thing, they focus largely on the elderly, which means that they do not aid many poor people. They do not help the working poor; and even for the unemployed, they provide only limited help for a limited period of time.

Consequently, the government has started a number of additional programs specifically designed to help the poor, although many of them are aimed more at the symptoms of poverty than at its basic causes. There are programs that provide goods and services to the poor. Perhaps the most important of these are the *food programs,* which distribute food to needy families. (Before 1973, this food generally came from surpluses due to the farm programs described in Chapter 4.) The federal government gives *stamps* that can be used to buy food to local agencies, which sell them (at less than the equivalent of market prices) or give them to low-income families. In 1983, the cost of this program to the federal government exceeded $11 billion. On the whole, this program has reached people who were truly needy, but critics have pointed out that some recipients, like college students from well-off families, qualified for the program and received this subsidy.

More important in quantitative terms than programs that give particular commodities to the poor are programs that provide them with cash. These are what people generally have in mind when they refer to *welfare.* There are advantages to cash payments. They allow a family to adapt its purchases

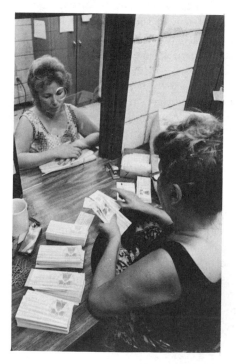

to its own needs and circumstances. There are obvious disadvantages too, since the money may be spent on liquor and marijuana rather than on food and milk. The most important single program of cash payments gives *aid to families with dependent children*. In 1984, this program alone paid out over $13 billion.

To qualify for this program, a family must contain dependent children who are without the support of a parent (usually the father) through death, disability, or absence (and in some states, through unemployment as well). The amount paid to a family under this program varies from state to state, since each state administers its own program and sets its own schedule of payments—as well as contributes part of the cost of the program, with the federal government providing the balance. In 1980, the average payment was about $3,400, but it was higher in states like New York and Massachusetts and lower in states like Mississippi and Alabama. To determine eligibility, the family's affairs are examined; and while receiving aid the family may be under the surveillance of a social worker who supervises its housekeeping and child care.

In 1981, President Reagan cut back the food stamp program, aid to families with dependent children, and other such programs. With regard to aid for families with dependent children, the changes reduced or eliminated the benefits for some low-income people who work. With regard to food stamps, the changes stiffened income eligibility requirements. Liberals tended to be angry at these cuts; many conservatives tended to view them as overdue.

THE NEGATIVE INCOME TAX

There is widespread dissatisfaction with current antipoverty—or welfare—programs. The cost of these programs has risen alarmingly; the programs themselves are judged by many experts to be inefficient; and, in some people's view, the welfare recipients are subjected to unnecessary meddling and spying. Moreover, there is little incentive for many people to get off welfare. Both Republicans and Democrats seem to agree that current welfare programs need improvement. What changes might be made? One suggestion that has received serious consideration is the negative income tax, an idea proposed by Stanford University's Milton Friedman (an adviser to presidential candidate Barry Goldwater in 1964 and to President Nixon) and Yale's James Tobin (an adviser to President Kennedy).

A *negative income tax* would work as follows: Just as families with reasonably high incomes *pay* taxes, families with low incomes would *receive* a payment. In other words, the poor would pay a *negative* income tax. Figure 16.5 illustrates how a negative income tax might work; it shows the amount a family of four would pay—or receive—in taxes for incomes at various levels. According to Figure 16.5, $4,000 is the *break-even income*—the income at which a family of four neither pays nor receives income taxes. Above $4,000, a family pays taxes. Thus a family with an income of $6,000 pays $500 in taxes. Below $4,000 a family receives a payment. Thus a family with an income of $1,000 is paid $1,500.

There are several advantages of a negative income tax.

1. It would give people on welfare more incentive to work. As indicated in Figure 16.5, for every extra dollar it earns, the family receives only 50

Figure 16.5

Example of Negative Income Tax *A family with more than $4,000 in income pays taxes. Thus a family with an income of $6,000 pays $500 in taxes. A family with an income less than $4,000 receives a payment. Thus a family with an income of $1,000 is paid $1,500.*

cents less from the government under this kind of negative income tax. Thus the family gets to keep half of every extra dollar (up to $4,000) it earns, which is a larger portion of this extra dollar than under the present system.

2. There would be no intrusion into the internal affairs of families on welfare and no regulations that cut off welfare payments if the husband remains with his family. In the past, the welfare system has given families an incentive to break up, and encroached on the dignity of poor people.

3. It might cost less to administer the negative income tax than the present system, and differences among states in benefits might be reduced.

Despite these advantages, many citizens remain skeptical about the negative income tax. For one thing, they are antagonistic to the idea of giving people an income without requiring any work in return. They also are unwilling to transfer large amounts from rich to poor. This amount would depend on how high the break-even income was set and on the negative tax rates. In the late 1960s, it was estimated that a negative income tax based on the sort of plan described in Figure 16.5 would have meant that those above the break-even income level would transfer about $25 billion to those below the break-even level. Despite the attractive features of a negative income tax, a transfer of this magnitude has proved unacceptable in many quarters.

Also, some economists regard the results of the experiments with a negative income tax in Seattle and Denver to have been disappointing. These experiments, carried out with a sample of households, seem to indicate that under a negative income tax people work less, apparently because they are more willing to quit work, and less willing to search hard for a new job.

HAS THE WAR ON POVERTY BEEN WON?

The official government statistics concerning the incidence of poverty do not recognize the fact that many people below the official poverty line receive noncash benefits from the government, such as food stamps, subsidized school lunches, public housing, Medicaid, and Medicare. These benefits accounted in 1980 for more than two out of every three dollars of government assistance. According to a report published by the U.S. Bureau of the Census in 1984, the percentage of the U.S. population below the poverty line is much smaller than the official statistics indicate, when these government noncash benefits are taken into account. Specifically, the figure according to official statistics is about 10 percent. When underreporting of incomes is taken into consideration, some economists conclude that only about 4 percent of the population have fallen below the poverty line in recent years. Based on these statistics, some observers claim that the war on poverty in the United States has been won. But it is important to recognize that, even if only 4 percent fall below the poverty line, this means that about 9 million people remain poor. And among blacks, the percentage of poor people is much higher than 4 percent. Also, the statistics themselves are subject to a great many limitations, and should be viewed with caution.

Example 16.2   Why Not Cure Poverty with a Check?

If the United States government were to mail checks to all poor families to raise their incomes to the poverty level, these checks would amount to less than 1 percent of our gross national product. Suppose that the government decides to solve the poverty problem in this way.

(a) If the poverty level is $5,000 per year, what is the relationship between a family's income before subsidy and its income after subsidy? (b) Up to $5,000, does a family's earnings influence its income after subsidy? (c) For people whose pre-subsidy earnings are below the poverty level, what would be the effect of this program on the incentive to work? (d) For people whose pre-subsidy earnings are slightly above the poverty level, what would be the effect of this program on the incentive to work? (e) Would the cost of this program be greater than the amount of the checks mailed to the poor?

SOLUTION

(a) This relationship is shown below:

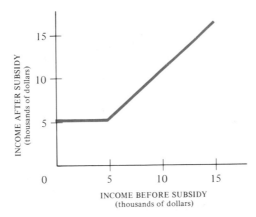

(b) No. (c) Because they can get $5,000 without working, some would be likely to quit working, or to work less hard. (d) Because they can get almost as much as their current income without working, some would be likely to quit working, or to work less hard. (e) Yes. There would be the additional costs due to the diminished incentives to work. For reasons discussed above, people would work less, and fewer goods and services would be produced.

Table 16.4

ECONOMIC CHARACTERISTICS OF WHITES AND NONWHITES, UNITED STATES, 1983

	White	*Non-white*
Median family income (dollars)	25,757	14,506
Percent of persons in poverty	12.1	35.7
Percent unemployed (males)	6.4	16.4
Percent unemployed (females)	6.5	15.4
Percent unemployed (male teenagers)	16.8	42.7
Percent of people (25 years and over) with 4 years or more of college	19.5	9.5

Source: Economic Report of the President, 1985, and World Almanac. Unemployment rates pertain to 1984.

Although they suggest that considerable progress against poverty has been made, these statistics do not indicate that poverty is no longer of concern to the American people.

The Problems of Discrimination

RACIAL DISCRIMINATION

Poverty, discrimination, and race are closely intertwined. Despite recent improvements, the sad fact is that racial discrimination occurs in many walks of life in many areas of the United States. Table 16.4 shows certain aspects of the relative position of the white and nonwhite populations in the United States. The average income of nonwhites is less than two-thirds that of whites. About one-third of the nonwhite population is below the poverty line, compared to only about one-eighth of the white population. On the average, whites complete more years of schooling than nonwhites, and a larger percentage of whites than of nonwhites are college graduates.

There is considerable agreement that at least part of these economic differences is the result of discrimination. Nonwhites are often prevented from reaching certain occupational or managerial levels. It is rare to find a black in the higher reaches of management in a major corporation. To a considerable extent they are cut off from job opportunities at this level by lack of education. But even at much lower levels, they are kept out of certain occupations by union policy (the building trades are a good example); and even when nonwhites do essentially the same kind of work as whites, there is sometimes a tendency to pay nonwhites less.

EFFECTS OF DISCRIMINATION

Some important effects of racial discrimination can be demonstrated by using the theory of wages discussed in Chapter 14. (The general point of this discussion holds true whether discrimination is on racial or other grounds.) The important thing to recognize at the outset is that nonwhite labor is not allowed to compete with white labor. This results in two different labor markets, one for whites and one for nonwhites. As shown in Figure 16.6, the demand curve for nonwhite labor is quite different from the demand curve for white labor, reflecting the fact that nonwhites are not allowed to enter many of the more productive occupations. Because of the difference in the demand (and supply) curves, the equilibrium wage for nonwhites, P_B, is lower than for whites, P_W.

How does this equilibrium differ from a situation of no discrimination? If nonwhites and whites competed in the same labor market, the total demand for labor—regardless of color—and the total supply of labor—regardless of color—would be as shown in panel B of Figure 16.6, and the wage for all labor—regardless of color—would be P_T. A comparison of P_T with P_B shows that the wage rate of nonwhites would be increased considerably. A comparison of P_T with P_W shows that the wage rates of whites would be decreased slightly. The slight cut in white wages would be much smaller than the considerable increase in nonwhite wages, since the nation's total production

A. The case of discrimination

B. No discrimination

Figure 16.6

Racial Discrimination *Under discrimination, the demand curve for white labor is quite different from that for nonwhite labor, and the supply curve of white labor is quite different from that of nonwhite labor, so that the equilibrium wage for nonwhites, P_B, is lower than for whites, P_W. If there were no discrimination, the wage for all labor, nonwhite or white, would be P_T.*

(and income) would increase because nonwhites could be put to more productive use.

Thus the effect of discrimination is to exploit nonwhites—by reducing their wages relative to whites—and to lower the nation's total output. Fortunately, there is evidence that racial discrimination is lessening. In part because of changing attitudes among whites, the growing restiveness of the nonwhites, and the coming of age of new leadership, the old patterns of segregation and discrimination are breaking down. Blacks are now being recruited actively by many prestigious colleges, and they are being hired and promoted to responsible positions in firms where formerly they remained at a relatively menial level. Progress is slow, but it unquestionably exists.

DISCRIMINATION AGAINST WOMEN

Needless to say, discrimination is not limited to nonwhites. There is also some discrimination against older workers. Even more widespread is discrimination against women. Holding age and education constant, women earn much less than men. To some extent, this difference in earnings arises because women work shorter hours and often have less experience in their jobs than men. But even after adjusting for factors such as education, work experience during the year, and lifetime work experience, there remains a differential of about 20 percent between the earnings of men and women. To a considerable extent, this differential is probably the result of discrimination, the nature of which has been described in the following terms by the Council of Economic Advisers:

There is clearly prejudice against women engaging in particular activities. Some patients reject women doctors, some clients reject women lawyers, some customers reject automobile saleswomen, and some workers reject women bosses. Employers also may have formulated discriminatory attitudes about women, exaggerating the risk of job instability or client acceptance and therefore excluding women from on-the-job training which would advance their careers. In fact, even if employers do estimate correctly the average job turnover of women, women who are strongly committed to their jobs may suffer from "statistical discrimination" by being treated as though their own behavior resembled the average. The extent to which this type of discrimination occurs depends on how costly it is for employers to distinguish women who will have a strong job commitment from those who will not. Finally, because some occupations restrict the number of newcomers they take in and because women move in and out of the labor force more often, more women than men tend to fall into the newcomer category and to be thus excluded. For example, restrictive entry policies may have kept women out of the skilled crafts.

On the other hand, some component of the earnings differential and of the occupation differential stems from differences in role orientation which start with differences in education and continue through marriage, where women generally are expected to assume primary responsibility for the home and subordinate their own outside work to their household responsibilities. It is not now possible to distinguish in a quantitative way between the discrimination which bars women from jobs solely because of their sex, and the role differentiation whereby women, either through choice or necessity, restrict their careers because of the demands of their homes. Some may label the

341

Cross-Chapter Case/Part Five

HOW THE MINIMUM WAGE AFFECTS TEENAGE UNEMPLOYMENT

The minimum wage goes back almost half a century in the United States. In 1938, the Congress passed the Fair Labor Standards Act, which established a minimum wage of 25 cents per hour. With inflation and changes in social attitudes and values, the minimum wage has been increased. Between 1938 and 1981 it was increased 15 times. Moreover, it has been extended to more and more workers. By 1984, it reached $3.35 an hour, and was applicable to more than 80 percent of all jobs.

At first glance, the minimum wage seems to be a sensible way to help the poor. After all, it seems reasonable to believe that people in very low-paying jobs tend to be poor, and a minimum wage would seem to increase their income. But a superficial analysis of this sort can be very misleading. As a matter of fact, many economists are convinced that the minimum wage has harmed many of the nation's poor. Few economists, if any, would argue that the minimum wage is the optimal way to fight poverty.

The difficulties with a minimum wage are demonstrated in the following figure, which shows the demand and supply curves for unskilled labor in a competitive labor market. Without the minimum wage, the equilibrium wage rate is $3.00 per hour, and OL_2 hours of labor are hired. If a minimum wage of $4.00 per hour is put into effect, employers will cut back on the amount of labor that they hire. Rather than employing OL_2 hours of labor, they will employ only OL_1 hours of labor. Unemployment will be created. Whereas workers would like to work OL_3 hours, they will only be able to work OL_1 hours. Not all of this unemployment will be reflected in the government's unemployment statistics, since some people who are unable to find jobs may give up looking for work (and thus not be counted in the government's figures).

Clearly, the unskilled workers who keep their jobs are better off because of the minimum wage; they get $4 an hour rather than $3 an hour. But those who lose their jobs or are unable to find jobs are worse off. In general, one would expect that the least skilled and most disadvantaged would be the ones that would be hardest hit by the minimum wage. Specifically, one would expect the unemployment rate among teenagers, particularly black teenagers, to be increased by the minimum wage—and by increases in the minimum wage.

To illustrate how increases in the minimum wage can affect teenage employment, consider the fast-food industry (including firms like McDonald's), a leading employer of teenagers. When the minimum wage increased from $2.30 to $2.65 per hour in the late 1970s, the fast-food chains reduced their employees' average hours (by closing earlier and opening later), and introduced new equipment (like computerized cash registers) to save labor. Also, they sometimes substituted adults for teenagers. The overall result of the increase in the minimum wage was a decrease in the employment of teenagers.

Statistical studies have been carried out by economists to estimate the extent to which increases in the minimum wage affect the employment of teenagers. Dozens of such studies have been done. Although the results vary from study to study, most such investigations have found that a 10 percent increase in the minimum wage causes about a 1 to 3 percent reduction in teenage employment.[1]

Many observers, including President Reagan, favor a lower minimum wage for teenagers than for other workers. According to Daniel Hamermesh of Michigan State University, if the minimum wage for teenagers were reduced to $2.50 an hour, the unemployment rate for teenagers could be reduced considerably. Indeed, among black teenagers, the unemployment rate might be cut in half.[2]

In 1977, the House of Representatives established a Minimum Wage Study Commission, which was asked to investigate the effects of increasing the minimum wage on inflation, employment, and unemployment; and the ability of the minimum wage to combat poverty. In May 1981, the Commission issued a 250-page report summarizing its findings. Two principal recommendations were that the minimum wage should be indexed to adjust for inflation, and that there should not be a lower minimum wage for young workers than for older workers. Some observers, particularly conservatives, were critical of the Commission for its generally favorable attitude toward the minimum wage.[3]

As indicated above, many economists feel that the minimum wage is a poor way to fight poverty. One reason is that it creates unemployment. Another reason is that relatively few families seem to be poor because their

[1] C. Brown, C. Gilroy, and A. Kohen, "The Effect of the Minimum Wage on Employment and Unemployment," *Journal of Economic Literature,* June 1982.

[2] J. Shaw, "The Case for Paying Teenagers A Lower Minimum Wage," *Business Week,* April 2, 1984.

[3] M. Eccles and R. Freeman, "What! Another Minimum Wage Study?," *American Economic Review,* May 1982.

343

members earn low wages. (Instead, most do not have jobs or work only part-time.) Thus the minimum wage can have only a limited positive effect on the incomes of the poor. Nonetheless, some powerful groups, including organized labor, are strong believers in the minimum wage, and there is little prospect of fundamental changes in the minimum wage laws in the immediate future.

latter as a pervasive social discrimination which starts in the cradle; nonetheless, it is useful to draw the distinction.[7]

In various ways, the government has set out to discourage discrimination against women. The Equal Pay Act of 1963 requires employers to pay men and women equally for the same work, and Title VII of the Civil Rights Act of 1964 bars discrimination in hiring, firing, and other aspects of employment. In addition, a number of women have been appointed to high-ranking government jobs, including economists Juanita Kreps (who has been secretary of commerce), Marina Whitman (who has served as member of the President's Council of Economic Advisers), Alice Rivlin (who has headed the Congressional Budget Office), and Nancy Teeters (who has been a member of the Federal Reserve Board). All these measures undoubtedly will have a beneficial effect, but it must be recognized that eliminating discrimination of this kind will require basic changes in the attitudes of both males and females. The problem of discrimination against women is likely to be with us for a long time.

[7] *The Economic Report of the President,* 1973, pp. 106–7.

Test Yourself

1. "Since there cannot be two different prices for a homogeneous input, the existence of discrimination can be expected to disappear over time due to market forces." Comment and evaluate.

2. "The Social Security system is actuarially unsound. The amounts currently collected in Social Security taxes do not equal the amounts currently paid out in benefits. We cannot keep this up!" Comment and evaluate.

3. According to some economists, Social Security should be voluntary, not mandatory. Present the arguments on each side of this issue in as much detail as you can.

4. Do the official government statistics concerning poverty recognize that many people below the poverty line receive non-cash benefits from the government? If not, does this mean that these statistics are useless? Explain.

Summary

1. Lorenz curves are used to measure the extent of income inequality. They make it clear that there has been a considerable reduction in income inequality in the United States since the late 1920s. Practically all this reduction occurred before the end of World War II.

2. Many factors are responsible for existing income differentials. Some people are abler, better educated, or luckier than others. Some people have more property, or more monopoly power, than others.

3. Critics of income inequality argue that it lessens total consumer satisfaction because an extra dollar given to the poor provides them with more extra satisfaction than the loss of a dollar taken away from the rich. Also, they argue that income inequality leads to social and political inequality.

4. Defenders of income inequality point out that it is scientifically impossible to make interpersonal comparisons of utility, and argue that income inequality is needed to provide incentives for people to work and create, and that it permits greater capital formation.

5. There is no well-defined income level that can be used in all times and all places to determine poverty. Perhaps the most widely accepted definition of poverty in the United States today is the one developed by the Social Security Administration, according to which about 15 percent of the population in the United States—over 35 million people—fall below the poverty line. In recent decades, the incidence of poverty has been declining in the United States.

6. Nonwhite families, families headed by a female, and very large families are more likely than others to be poor. To a considerable extent, the reasons for their poverty lie beyond the control of the poor people. About one-third of poor adults have suffered a disability of some sort, or the premature death of the family breadwinner, or family dissolution. Most heads of poor families do not have jobs.

7. Because private charity is judged to be inadequate, the nation has authorized its government to carry out various public programs to aid the poor. There are programs to provide them with goods and services—food-stamp programs, for instance. Other programs, like aid to families with dependent children, give them cash. When these programs are taken into account, the percentage of the population falling below the poverty line is reduced considerably.

8. There is widespread dissatisfaction with existing antipoverty—or welfare—programs. They are judged to be inefficient; their costs have been increasing at an alarming rate; and they provide little incentive for people to get off welfare. One suggestion to remedy these problems is a negative income tax. In most of the forms put forth it involves a transfer of income that may be beyond the realm of political feasibility.

9. Despite recent improvements, the sad fact is that racial discrimination occurs in many walks of life in many areas of the United States. Nonwhites often are cut off from educational and job opportunities; and even when nonwhites do essentially the same kind of work as whites, there is sometimes a tendency to pay them less. The effects of discrimination are to reduce the wages of nonwhites relative to whites and to lower the nation's total output.

10. There is also much discrimination against women, making them less likely than men to enter the better-paying occupations. Even after adjusting for factors such as education and work experience, women earn about 20 percent less than men.

Concepts for Review

Income inequality	Old-age insurance	Welfare
Lorenz curve	Social Security	Aid to families with
Progressive tax	Medicare	dependent
Regressive tax	Unemployment insurance	children
Tax incidence	Supplemental Security	Negative income tax
Poverty	Income Program	Break-even income
	Food programs	Discrimination

PART SIX

Energy and the Environment

CHAPTER 17

Environmental and Energy Problems

Environmental pollution and energy have been two important problems in the United States, and both are related to economic growth. According to many scientists and social observers, one of the costs of economic growth is environmental pollution. For a long time, people in the United States paid relatively little attention to the environment and what they were doing to it, but this attitude changed markedly in the last twenty years. The public became genuinely concerned about environmental problems. However, in the effort to clean up the environment, choices are not always clear, nor solutions easy. In particular, the energy crisis of the 1970s brought home the fact that a cleaner environment is not costless. Many measures that would reduce pollution would increase the demand for energy.

America's energy problems have been related only partly to environmental matters. To a considerable extent, they stem from the fact that oil reserves in this country are being depleted, and that foreign sources of oil have banded together in an international cartel which raised the price of crude oil enormously in 1974 and 1979. In this chapter, we consider the economic aspects of both environmental decay and the nation's energy needs. Our purpose is to indicate the extent of these problems, the factors that are responsible for them, and the sorts of public policies that might be adopted to help deal with them.

Our Environmental Problems

WATER POLLUTION

To see what we mean by environmental pollution, let's begin with one of the most important parts of man's environment, our water supplies. As a result of human activities, large amounts of pollutants are discharged into streams, lakes, and the sea. Chemical wastes are released by industrial plants and mines, as well as by farms and homes when fertilizers, pesticides, and detergents run off into waterways. Oil is discharged into the waters by tankers, sewage systems, oil wells, and other sources. Organic compounds enter waterways from industrial plants and farms, as well as from municipal sewage plants; and animal wastes, as well as human wastes, contribute substantially to pollution.

Obviously, we cannot continue to increase the rate at which we dump wastes into our streams, rivers, and oceans. A river, like everything else, can bear only so much. The people of Cleveland know this well. In 1969, the Cuyahoga River, which flows through Cleveland, literally caught fire, so great was its concentration of industrial and other wastes. Of course, the Cuyahoga is an extreme case, but many of our rivers, including the Hudson and the Ohio, are badly polluted. Water pollution is a nuisance and perhaps a threat.[1]

AIR POLLUTION

If clean water is vital to man's survival, so too is clean air. Yet the battle being waged against air pollution in most of our major cities has not been won. Particles of various kinds are spewed into the air by factories that utilize combustion processes, grind materials, or produce dust. Motor vehicles release lead compounds from gasoline and rubber particles worn from tires, helping to create that unheavenly condition known as smog. Citizens of Los Angeles are particularly familiar with smog, but few major cities have escaped at least periodic air pollution. No precise measures have been developed to gauge the effects of air pollution on public health and enjoyment, but some rough estimates suggest that perhaps 25 percent of all deaths from respiratory disease could be avoided by a 50 percent reduction in air pollution.

One of the most important contributors to air pollution is the combustion of fossil fuels, particularly coal and oil products: by-products of combustion comprise about 85 percent of the total amount of air pollutants in the United States. Most of these pollutants result from impure fuels or inefficient burning. Among the more serious pollutants are sulphur dioxide, carbon monoxide, and various oxides of nitrogen.

At present, the automobile is the principal source of air pollution in the United States. According to some estimates, human activities pump into the air over 200 million tons of waste each year, and automobiles can be credited with the dubious honor of contributing about 40 percent of this

[1] See *Fortune,* February 1970; D. Rohrer, D. Montgomery, M. Montgomery, D. Eaton, and M. Arnold, *The Environment Crisis,* Skokie, Ill.: National Textbook, 1970; and Environmental Protection Agency, *The Economics of Clean Water,* 1973, Washington, D.C.: Government Printing Office, 1973.

figure. Spurred on by the public interest in pollution control, some technologists have been hard at work on substitutes for the internal combustion engine. Attempts have been—and are being—made to devise economical and convenient electric and steam-driven automobiles. To date, however, these efforts have not succeeded. Thus it seems likely that in the near future at least, we shall have to rely heavily on modifications of the internal combustion engine and its fuel to reduce air pollution.[2] (More use of nonpolluting transport like bicycles and feet would help too.)

The Important Role of External Diseconomies

The reason why our economic system has tolerated pollution of the environment lies largely in the concept of external diseconomies, which we mentioned in Chapter 4. An *external diseconomy* occurs when one person's (or firm's) use of a resource damages other people who cannot obtain proper compensation. When this occurs, a market economy is unlikely to function properly. The price system is based on the supposition that the full cost of using each resource is borne by the person or firm that uses it. If this is not the case and if the user bears only part of the full costs, then the resource is not likely to be directed by the price system into the socially optimal use.

To understand why, we might begin by reviewing briefly how resources are allocated in a market economy. As we saw in Chapter 3, resources are used in their socially most valuable way because they are allocated to the people and firms who find it worthwhile to bid most for them, assuming that prices reflect true social costs. Under these circumstances, a firm that maximizes its profits will produce the socially desirable output and use the socially desirable amounts of labor, capital, and other resources. Under these circumstances, there is no problem.

PRIVATE COST ≠ SOCIAL COST

Suppose, however, that because of the presence of external diseconomies people and firms do not pay the true social costs for resources. For example, suppose that some firms or people can use water and air for nothing, but that other firms or people incur costs as a consequence of this prior use. In this case, the *private costs* of using air and water differ from the *social costs: the price paid by the user of water and air is less than the true cost to society.* In a case like this, users of water and air are guided in their decisions by the private cost of water and air—by the prices they pay. Since they pay less than the true social costs, water and air are artificially cheap to them, so that they will use too much of these resources, from society's point of view.

Note that the divergence between private and social cost occurs if, and only if, the use of water or air by one firm or person imposes costs on other

---

[2] Ibid. Also, see L. Lave and E. Seskin, *Air Pollution and Human Health,* Baltimore: published for Resources for the Future by The Johns Hopkins University Press, 1977.

firms or persons. Thus, if a paper mill uses water and then treats it to restore its quality, there is no divergence between private and social cost. But when the same mill dumps harmful wastes into streams and rivers (the cheap way to get rid of its by-products), the towns downstream that use the water must incur costs to restore its quality. The same is true of air pollution. If an electric power plant uses the atmosphere as a cheap and convenient place to dispose of wastes, people living and working nearby may incur costs as a result, since the incidence of respiratory and other diseases may increase. In such cases, there may be a divergence between private and social cost.

We said above that pollution-causing activities that result in external diseconomies represent a malfunctioning of the market system. At this point, the nature of this malfunctioning should be clear. *Firms and people dump too much waste material into the water and the atmosphere. The price system does not provide the proper signals because the polluters are induced to use our streams and atmosphere in this socially undesirable way by the artificially low price of disposing of wastes in this manner. Moreover, because the polluters do not pay the true cost of waste disposal, their products are artificially cheap, so that too much is produced of them.*

Consider two examples. Electric power companies do not pay the full cost of disposing of wastes in the atmosphere. They charge an artificially low price, and the public is induced to use more electric power than is socially desirable. Similarly, since the owners of automobiles do not pay the full cost of disposing of exhaust and other wastes in the atmosphere, they pay an artificially low price for operating an automobile, and the public is induced to own and use more automobiles than is socially desirable.

Public Policy Toward Pollution

Pollution is caused by defects in our institutions, not by malicious intent, greed, or corruption. In cases where waste disposal causes significant external diseconomies, economists generally agree that government intervention may be justifiable. But how can the government intervene? Perhaps the simplest way is **direct regulation,** through the issuance of certain enforceable rules for waste disposal. For example, the government can prohibit the burning of trash in furnaces or incinerators, or the dumping of certain materials in the ocean; and make any person or firm that violates these restrictions subject to a fine, or perhaps even imprisonment. Also, the government can ban the use of chemicals like DDT, or require that all automobiles meet certain regulations for the emission of air pollutants. Further, the government can establish quality standards for air and water.

The government can also intervene by establishing effluent fees. An **effluent fee** is a fee a polluter must pay to the government for discharging waste. In other words, a price is imposed on the disposal of wastes into the environment; and the more firms or individuals pollute, the more they must pay. The idea behind the imposition of effluent fees is that they can bring the private cost of waste disposal closer to the true social costs.

Wastewater treatment plant

Basic Idea #33: *A free-enterprise economy is likely to result in too much pollution because the firms and individuals who dump waste materials into the water and the atmosphere are guided by the artificially low prices they pay for disposing of wastes in this way. The true costs to society of such waste disposal are greater than the prices they pay. To remedy the situation, economists argue that polluters should be made to pay the true social costs of polluting (for example, through effluent fees).*

Faced with a closer approximation to the true social costs of their activities, polluters will reduce the extent to which they pollute the environment. Needless to say, many practical difficulties are involved in carrying out this seemingly simple scheme, but many economists believe that this is the best way to deal with the pollution problem.[3]

Still another way for the government to intervene is to establish **tax credits** for firms that introduce pollution-control equipment. There are, of course, many types of equipment that a plant can introduce to cut down on pollution—for example, "scrubbers" for catching poisonous gases, and electrostatic precipitators for decreasing dust and smoke. But such pollution-control equipment costs money, and firms are naturally reluctant to spend money on purposes where the private rate of return is so low. To reduce the burden, the government can allow firms to reduce their tax bill by a certain percentage of the amount they spend on pollution-control equipment. Tax incentives of this sort have been discussed widely in recent years, and some have been adopted.

DIRECT REGULATION

Let's look more closely at the advantages and disadvantages of each of these major means by which the government can intervene to remedy the nation's pollution problems. At present we rely mostly on direct regulation of waste disposal (and the quality of the environment); and despite the many problems involved, it has undoubtedly done much good. As Allen Kneese, one of the country's top experts in this area, says about water pollution, "The control of water discharges through administrative orders regulating individual waste disposers has been a useful device and cannot be abandoned until we have a better substitute."[4]

However, economists agree that direct regulation suffers from some serious disadvantages:

1. Such regulations have generally taken the form of general, cross-the-board rules. For example, if two factories located on the same river dump the same amount of waste material into the river, such regulations would probably call for each factory to reduce its waste disposal by the same amount. Unfortunately, although this may appear quite sensible, it may in fact be very inefficient. Suppose that it is much less costly for one factory to reduce its waste disposal than for the other. In such a case, it would be more efficient to ask the factory that could reduce its wastes more cheaply to cut down more on its waste disposal than the other factory. For reasons of this sort, *pollution reductions are likely to be accomplished at more than minimum cost, if they are accomplished by direct regulation.*

2. To formulate such regulations in a reasonably sensible way, the responsible government agencies must have access to much more information than they are likely to obtain or assimilate. Unless the government agencies

[3] Another possibility is for the government to issue a certificate or license to pollute. The government might issue a limited number of certificates, to be auctioned off to the highest bidders.

[4] A. Kneese, "Public Policy toward Water Pollution." in E. Mansfield, *Microeconomics: Selected Readings,* 3d ed., New York: Norton, 1979.

351

have a detailed and up-to-date familiarity with the technology of hundreds of industries, they are unlikely to make sound rules. Moreover, unless the regulatory agencies have a very wide jurisdiction, their regulations will be evaded by the movement of plants and individuals from localities where regulations are stiff to localities where they are loose. In addition, the regulatory agencies must view the pollution problem as a whole, since piecemeal regulation may simply lead polluters to substitute one form of pollution for another. For example, New York and Philadelphia have attempted to reduce water pollution by more intensive sewage treatment. However, one result has been the production of a lot of biologically active sludge that is being dumped into the ocean—and perhaps causing problems there.

EFFLUENT FEES

The use of effluent fees is the approach most economists seem to prefer, for the following reasons. First, *it obviously is socially desirable to use the cheapest way to achieve any given reduction in pollution. A system of effluent fees is more likely to accomplish this objective than direct regulation, because the regulatory agency cannot have all the relevant information* (as we noted above), *whereas polluters, reacting in their own interest to effluent fees, will tend to use the cheapest means to achieve a given reduction in pollution.*

To see why this is the case, consider a particular polluter. Faced with an effluent fee—that is, a price it must pay for each unit of waste it discharges—the polluter will find it profitable to reduce its discharge of waste so long as the cost of doing so is less than the effluent fees it saves. Thus, if this firm can reduce its discharge of wastes relatively cheaply, it will be induced to make such a reduction by the prospect of increased profits. On the other hand, if it cannot reduce its discharge of wastes at all cheaply, it will not make such a reduction, since the costs will exceed the saving in effluent fees. Thus a system of effluent fees induces firms that can reduce waste disposal more cheaply to cut down more on their waste disposal than firms where such a reduction is more expensive. This means that a given reduction of pollution will occur at a relatively low cost.

Economists also favor effluent fees because this approach requires far less information in the hands of the relevant government agencies than does direct regulation. After all, when effluent fees are used, all the government has to do is meter the amount of pollution a firm or household produces (which admittedly is sometimes not easy) and charge accordingly. It is left to the firms and households to figure out the most ingenious and effective ways to cut down on their pollution and save on effluent fees. This too is a spur to inventive activities aimed at developing more effective ways to reduce pollution. Also, economists favor the use of effluent fees because financial incentives are likely to be easier to administer than direct regulation.

While economists tend to favor the use of effluent fees, they are not always against direct regulation. Some ways of disposing of certain types of waste are so dangerous that the only sensible thing to do is to ban them. For example, a ban on the disposal of mercury or arsenic in places where human beings are likely to consume them—and die—seems reasonable enough. In effect, the social cost of such pollution is so high that a very high penalty—imprisonment—is put on it. In addition, of course, economists favor direct regulation when it simply is not feasible to impose effluent fees—for example, in cases where it would be prohibitively expensive to meter the amount of pollutants emitted by various firms or households.

THE RUHR: A CASE STUDY[5]

Let's consider a well-known case of effluent fees in use: the Ruhr valley in West Germany. The Ruhr is one of the world's most industrialized areas. It includes about one-third of West Germany's industrialized capacity, and about 70 to 90 percent of West Germany's coal, coke, and iron and steel outputs. It contains about 10 million people and about 4,300 square miles. Water supplies in the Ruhr are quite limited. Five small rivers supply the area. The amazing amount of waste materials these rivers carry is indicated by the fact that the average annual natural low flow is less than the volume of effluent discharged into the rivers. Yet the local water authorities have succeeded in making this small amount of water serve the needs of the firms and households of this tremendous industrial area, and at the same the streams have been used for recreation. Moreover, all this has been achieved at a remarkably low cost. The success of water management in the Ruhr seems to be due in considerable part to institutional arrangements that allowed the German water managers to plan and operate a relatively efficient regional system. Collective water quality improvement measures are used. Water quality is controlled by waste treatment in over 100 plants, regulation of river flow by reservoir, and a number of oxidation lakes in the Ruhr itself.

Effluent fees are an integral part of the institutional arrangements governing water quality. The amount a firm has to pay depends upon how much waste—and what kind—it pumps into the rivers. A formula has been devised to indicate how much a polluter must pay to dispose of a particular type of waste. In simple terms, the formula bases the charge on the amount of clean water needed to dilute the effluent in order to avoid harm to fish. Using this formula, the local authorities can determine, after testing the effluent of any firm, the amount the firm should pay. Specifically, the amount depends on the amount of suspended materials that will settle out of the effluent, the amount of oxygen consumed by bacteria in a sample of effluent, the results of a potassium permanganate test, and the results of a fish toxicity test. You need not understand the nature or specific purposes of these measurements and tests. The important thing is that you understand their general aim—which is to measure roughly the amount of pollution caused by various kinds of wastes. Having made these measurements and tests, the local authorities use their formula to determine how much a firm must pay in effluent fees.

TAX CREDITS FOR POLLUTION-CONTROL EQUIPMENT

Many tax inducements to encourage firms and individuals to install pollution-control equipment have been proposed. A typical suggestion is that the

View of the Ruhr valley, Germany

[5] This section is based on A. Kneese and B. Bower, *Managing Water Quality: Economics, Technology, Institutions,* Washington, D.C.: Resources for the Future, 1968, Chapter 12.

government offer a **tax credit** equal to 20 percent of the cost of pollution-control equipment, and allow a firm to depreciate such equipment in only one to five years. In this way, the government would help defray some of the costs of the pollution-control equipment by allowing a firm that installed such equipment to pay less taxes than if no such tax inducements existed.

However, such schemes have a number of disadvantages:

1. Subsidies to promote the purchase of particular types of pollution-control equipment may result in relatively inefficient and costly reductions in pollution. After all, other methods that don't involve special pollution-control equipment—such as substituting one type of fuel for another—may sometimes be a more efficient way to reduce pollution.

2. Subsidies of this sort may not be very effective. Even if the subsidy reduces the cost to the firm of reducing pollution, it may still be cheaper for the firm to continue to pollute. In other words, subsidies of this sort make it a little less painful for polluters to reduce pollution; but unlike effluent fees, they offer no positive incentive.

3. It seems preferable on grounds of equity for the firms and individuals that do the polluting—or their customers—to pay to clean up the mess that results. Effluent fees work this way, but with tax credits for pollution-control equipment, the government picks up part of the tab by allowing the polluter to pay lower taxes. In other words, the general public, which is asked to shoulder the additional tax burden to make up for the polluters' lower taxes, pays part of the cost. But is this a fair allocation of the costs? Why should the general public be saddled with much of the bill?

Pollution-Control Programs in the United States

In recent decades, there has been considerable growth in government programs designed to control pollution. To take but one example, federal expenditures to reduce water pollution increased in the period from the mid-1950s to 1970 from about $1 million to $300 million annually. To curb water pollution, the federal government has for years operated a system of grants-in-aid to state, municipal, or regional agencies to help construct treatment plants; and grants are made for research on new treatment methods. In addition, the 1970 Water Quality Improvement Act authorized grants to demonstrate new methods and techniques and to establish programs to train people in water control management. (The federal government has also regulated the production and use of pesticides.) The states, as well as the federal government, have played an important role in water pollution control. They have set standards for allowable pollution levels, and many state governments have provided matching grants to help municipalities construct treatment plants.

In 1969, the Congress established a new agency—the Council on Environmental Quality—to oversee and plan the nation's pollution control programs. Modeled to some extent on the Council of Economic Advisers, the Council on Environmental Quality, which has three members, is supposed to gather information on considerations and trends in the quality of the environment, review and evaluate the federal government's programs in this area, develop appropriate national policies, and conduct needed surveys and research on environmental quality. The tasks assigned to the council are obviously important ones.

In 1970, the federal government established another new agency, the Environmental Protection Agency (EPA). Working with state and local officials, this agency establishes standards for desirable air and water quality, and devises rules for attaining these goals. The 1970 Clean Air Amendments directed EPA to establish minimum ambient standards for air quality, and it set limits on the emission of carbon monoxide, hydrocarbons, and nitrous oxides from automobiles. But after a number of clashes between EPA and the auto makers, the EPA relaxed the deadlines when these limits were supposed to be met. In 1972 amendments to the Water Pollution Act authorized EPA to set up effluent standards for both privately and publicly owned plants. A stated goal of the amendments was to eliminate the discharge of pollutants into water by 1985, but, for reasons discussed in the next section, this goal was unrealistically stringent. In general, recent legislation has emphasized direct regulation, although there has been some study of the use of effluent fees. For example, the government has considered imposing a fee on the emission of sulphur oxide into the air.

Some people believe that public policy is moving too rapidly in this area: others believe that it is moving too slowly. It is not easy to determine how fast or how far we should go in attempting to reduce pollution. Those who will bear the costs of reducing pollution have an understandable tendency to emphasize (and perhaps inflate) the costs and discount the benefits of such projects. Those who are particularly interested in enjoying nature and outdoor recreation—like the Sierra Club—are understandably inclined to emphasize (and perhaps inflate) the benefits and discount the costs of such projects. Politics inevitably plays a major role in the outcome of such cases. The citizens of the United States must indicate, through the ballot box as well as the market place, how much they are willing to pay to reduce pollution. We must also decide at what level of government the relevant rules are to be made. Since many pollution problems are local, it often seems sensible to determine the appropriate level of environmental quality locally. (However, there are obvious dangers in piecemeal regulation, as pointed out above.)

How Clean Should the Environment Be?

One of the most fundamental questions about pollution control is: How clean do we want the air, water, and other parts of our environment to be? At first glance, it may seem that we should restore and maintain a pristine pure environment, but this is not a very sensible goal, since the costs of achieving it would be enormous. The Environmental Protection Agency has estimated that it would cost about $60 billion to remove 85 to 90 percent of water pollutants from industrial and municipal sources. This is hardly a trivial amount, but it is far less than the cost of achieving zero discharge of pollutants, which would be about $320 billion—a truly staggering sum.

Example 17.1 How to Reduce the Costs of Cleaning Up

According to estimates made by Allen Kneese and Charles Schultze, the cost of achieving a one-pound reduction in the amount of pollutants emitted at a petroleum refinery and a beet-sugar plant are as shown below:

(a) Suppose that it is decided that the total amount of pollutants discharged by both plants should be reduced by 50 percent. If the government decrees that each plant should cut its discharge by 50 percent, what would be the cost of a one-pound reduction at each plant? (b) Can you suggest a way in which this total reduction in pollution can be achieved more efficiently? (c) To achieve this reduction most efficiently, which plant (the petroleum refinery or the beet-sugar plant) should reduce its discharge by the greater percentage? (d) Would an effluent fee achieve this reduction at less cost than the regulation in (a)?

SOLUTION

(a) The petroleum refinery would operate at point *U*, where the cost of a one-pound reduction in pollution is 6 cents. The beet-sugar plant would operate at point *V*, where the cost of a one-pound reduction would be 1 cent. (b) Since the beet-sugar plant can reduce pollution at less cost than the petroleum refinery (1 cent per pound rather than 6 cents per pound), it should cut its pollution more and the petroleum refinery should cut its pollution less. (c) The beet-sugar plant, for the reasons given in (b). (d) Yes. If an effluent fee were established, the cost of a one-pound reduction in pollution would tend to be the same at both plants.*

* See A. Kneese and C. Schultze, *Pollution, Prices, and Public Policy,* Washington, D.C.: The Brookings Institution, 1975; and W. Baumol and W. Oates, *Economics, Environmental Policy, and the Quality of Life,* Englewood Cliffs, N.J.: Prentice-Hall, 1979.

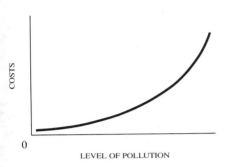

Figure 17.1

Costs to Society of Pollution *The costs to society of pollution increase with the level of pollution.*

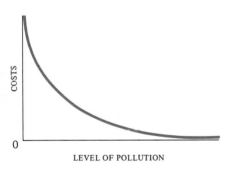

Figure 17.2

Costs to Society of Pollution Control *The more pollution is reduced, the higher are the costs to society of pollution control.*

Fortunately, however, there is no reason to aim at so stringent a goal. *It seems obvious that, as pollution increases, various costs to society increase as well.* Some of these costs were described at the beginning of this chapter. For example, we pointed out that increases in air pollution result in increased deaths, and that increases in water pollution reduce the recreational value of rivers and streams. Suppose that we could get accurate data on the cost to society of various levels of pollution. Of course, it is extremely difficult to get such data, but if we could, we could determine the relationship between the amount of these costs and the level of pollution. It would look like the hypothetical curve in Figure 17.1. The greater the level of pollution, the higher these costs will be.

But these costs are not the only ones that must be considered. *We must also take into account the costs of controlling pollution.* In other words, we must look at the costs to society of maintaining a certain level of environmental quality. These costs are not trivial, as we saw at the beginning of this section. To maintain a very low level of pollution, it is necessary to invest heavily in pollution-control equipment and to make other economic sacrifices.[6] If we could get accurate data on the cost to society of controlling pollution, we could find the relationship between the amount of these costs and the level of pollution. It would look like the hypothetical curve in Figure 17.2; the lower the level of pollution, the higher these costs will be.

A GOAL OF ZERO POLLUTION?

At this point, it should be obvious why we should not try to achieve a zero level of pollution. *The sensible goal for our society is to minimize the sum of the costs of pollution and the costs of controlling pollution.* In other words, we should construct a graph, as shown in Figure 17.3, to indicate the relationship between the sum of these two types of costs and the level of pollution. Then we should choose the level of pollution at which the sum of these two types of costs is a minimum. Thus, in Figure 17.3, we should aim for a pollution level of *A*. There is no point in trying for a lower level; such a reduction would cost more than it would be worth. For example, the cost of achieving a zero pollution level would be much more than it would be worth. Only when the pollution level exceeds *A* is the extra cost to society of the additional pollution greater than the cost of preventing it. For example, the cost of allowing pollution to increase from *A* to *B* is much greater than the cost of prevention.

It is easy to draw hypothetical curves, but not so easy actually to measure these curves. Unfortunately, no one has a very clear idea of what the curves in Figure 17.3 really look like—although we can be sure that their general shapes are like those shown there. Thus no one really knows just how clean we should try to make the environment. Under these circum-

---

[6] It is important to recognize that the costs of pollution control extend far beyond the construction of more and better water treatment plants, or the more extensive control of gas emission, or other such steps. A serious pollution-control program can put firms out of business, put people out of work, and bring economic trouble to entire communities. Further, a pollution-control system can result in a redistribution of income. For example, automobiles, electric power, and other goods and services involving considerable pollution are likely to increase in price relative to other goods and services involving little pollution. To the extent that polluting goods and services play a bigger role in the budgets of the poor than of the rich, pollution controls hurt the poor and help the rich.

Figure 17.3
Determining Optimal Level of Pollution
The optimal level of pollution is at point
A, *since this is where the total costs are a*
minimum. Below point A, *the cost to*
society of more pollution is less than the
cost of preventing it. Above point A, *the*
cost to society of more pollution is
greater than the cost of preventing it.

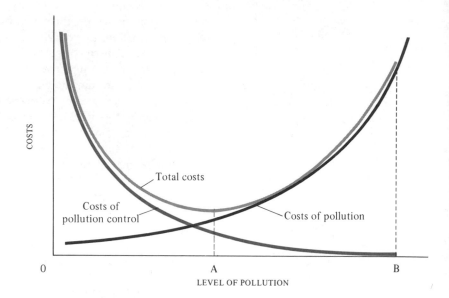

stances, expert opinion differs on the nature and extent of the programs that should be carried out. Moreover, as pointed out in a previous section, political considerations and pressures enter in. But one thing is for sure: we will continue to live with some pollution—and that, for the reason just given, will be the rational thing to do.

Recent Directions of Environmental Policy

In the late seventies and early eighties, policy makers became increasingly concerned that regulatory agencies like EPA had been paying too little attention to the costs involved in reducing pollution. For example, a government study found that a relaxation of EPA's 1977 standard for water-pollution control in the steel industry *with no change in its more stringent 1983 standard* would allow savings in capital costs of $200 million. As President Carter's Council of Economic Advisers pointed out, "In making regulatory decisions on the speed of attaining standards, we should explicitly make a qualitative judgment about whether the gains from earlier attainment are worth the costs."

Going a step further, some experts, like Lester Lave and Gilbert Omenn of the Brookings Institution, have concluded from their studies that the Clean Air Act has not been very effective. In their view, "the application of pollution controls to existing plants and older cars has been limited, and costs have been excessive, largely because Congress has failed to confront [many of] the difficult issues . . ."

During the 1980s, environmentalists and others charged that the Reagan administration was dismantling, or at least emasculating, EPA. Anne Gorsuch resigned in 1983 as head of EPA, as criticism of the agency continued to build. James Watt, former Secretary of the Interior, also angered environmentalists. Administration officials retorted to such criticism by claiming that they were trying to promote and restore balance between environmental objectives and economic growth.

In 1985 a political battle raged over the superfund, the fund authorized by federal legislation to clean up sites where chemical wastes have been dumped. Environmentalists wanted a fund of $10 billion; the Reagan administration proposed $5 billion. Some observers wanted the oil and chemical firms to contribute more to the fund, while these firms bitterly opposed such a move.

Test Yourself

1. Suppose that the paper industry emits wastes into rivers and streams, and that municipalities or firms downstream must treat the water to make it usable. Do the paper industry's private costs equal the social costs of producing paper? Why or why not?

2. Suppose that each ton of paper produced results in pollution that costs municipalities and firms downstream $1.00, and that a law is passed that requires the paper industry to reimburse the municipalities and firms downstream for these costs. Prior to this law, the supply curve for paper was:

Price of paper (dollars per ton)	Quantity supplied (million tons)
1.00	10.0
2.00	15.0
2.50	17.5
3.00	20.0
4.00	25.0

After the law takes effect, what will be the quantity supplied at each price?

3. In Question 2, which output—the one prevailing before the industry has to reimburse others, or the one prevailing afterward—is socially more desirable? Why?

4. If the demand curve for paper is as shown below, what will be the equilibrium output of paper before and after the paper industry has to reimburse the municipalities and firms downstream (as indicated in Question 2)?

Price of paper (dollars per ton)	Quantity demanded (million tons)
1.00	30.0
2.00	25.0
3.00	20.0
3.50	17.5
4.00	15.0

5. Suppose that the social cost (in billions of dollars) due to pollution equals $5P$, where P is the level of pollution, and that the cost (in billions of dollars) of pollution control equals $10-2P$. What is the optimal level of pollution? Is this a typical case?

Our Energy Problems

OPEC AND THE ENERGY CRISIS

During the early 1970s, even as it began to dawn on Americans that our environment was not indestructible, other urgent concerns arose about our national resources. A nation that had taken its abundant energy supplies for granted suddenly was confronted by the prospect of shortages. In late 1973, there was the Arab oil embargo; then in 1974, there was a tremendous increase in the price of imported crude oil. In September 1973, imported crude oil cost American petroleum refiners about $4.50 per barrel; a year later, it cost them about $12.50 per barrel. This great and sudden increase in the price of imported crude oil had a very substantial effect on both the national and international economy. It helped to create inflation at home, and it transferred tens of billions of dollars from the United States to the oil-producing nations. (See Figure 17.4.) Further, this big price increase was by no means the end. For example, in 1979, after Iran began cutting its oil output, the price of oil went up about 50 percent.

Why did the price of imported crude oil increase so spectacularly? Because the Organization of Petroleum Exporting Countries (OPEC) upped the price of crude oil. OPEC is an international cartel—that is, an association of national petroleum producers that gets together and sets prices for oil.[7] Formed in the early 1960s, OPEC's charter says that "members shall study and formulate a system to ensure the stabilization of prices by, among other means, the regulation of production, with due regard to the interests of the producing and the consuming nations, and to the necessity of securing a steady income to the producing countries." In the 1960s, OPEC gained strength; in the 1970s, it lowered the boom on the oil-consuming nations.

The Arab oil embargo in late 1973 called attention to another aspect of our energy problems: the fact that the United States was coming to depend to an increasing extent on foreign sources of supply of crude oil. Oil imports supplied almost one-half of domestic petroleum demand in 1977, as compared to about one-quarter in 1965. Some people worried that our national security might be imperiled by a cutoff of foreign oil.

The argument that we should try to avoid being dependent on foreign sources of oil was by no means new. Until 1973, this argument was used to justify the adoption of oil import quotas in the united States. These import quotas set a limit on the amount of foreign oil that could be imported. Many economists were opposed to these quotas because they increased the price of petroleum and petroleum products to consumers. (See Chapter 18.) Whether self-sufficiency with regard to energy is as important a goal as some policy makers seem to believe is hard to say. But the Arab oil embargo made the potential threat much more credible.

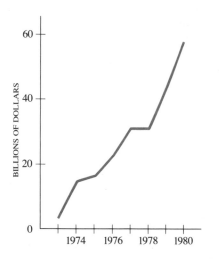

Figure 17.4

Total U.S. Payments for Crude Oil Imports, 1973–80 *Because the price of oil skyrocketed after 1973, the amount that America paid for imported oil skyrocketed too.*

ENERGY AND ECONOMIC GROWTH

Responding to the oil crises of the 1970s, U.S. policy makers proclaimed the importance of guaranteeing energy supplies that would meet the nation's growing energy demands. According to some observers, such as the authors of the *Limits to Growth,*[8] this could not be done. Why? Because there's only a finite supply of energy resources like oil and coal. If economic growth continues, the demand for these resources will increase exponentially. Eventually, according to these observers, we shall run out of such resources, with the result that both output and production will decline. Moreover, although this outcome is not around the corner, it is not so far off either. In their view, it will occur in the next 100 years.

Many people regard this as one of the most serious and fundamental of our energy problems. However, few economists accept the assumptions underlying these arguments. In the first place, economists charge that the authors of *Limits to Growth* underestimate very substantially the amount of the world's energy resources. Between 1944 and 1969, total world economic reserves of crude oil increased by about 12 times, due to producers'

---

[7] Although many of the oil-exporting countries are in the Middle East, OPEC also includes countries in Africa, Latin America, and other continents.

[8] D. Meadows *et al., The Limits to Growth,* New York: New American Library, 1972.

efforts to find and develop new sources of supply. Since annual world consumption rose about 6 times, this meant that reserves more than kept pace with oil consumption. Yet the authors of *Limits to Growth* assumed that known economic reserves of energy resources would increase only 5 times between now and the year 2100.

More fundamentally, economists charge that the authors of *Limits to Growth* do not take proper account of the workings of the price system. When the supply of a resource becomes tight, its price rises, with the result that firms have a greater financial incentive to find more of it. Also, as the price of this resource rises, firms have an incentive to develop new technology that permits less of this resource to be used. These mechanisms have resulted in the elimination of many apparent shortages in the past, and most economists tended to believe that they would play a major role in attacking our energy problems as well.

Public Policy Toward Energy

REDUCTION OF ENERGY DEMAND

During the 1970s economists put forth a number of suggestions concerning ways to solve our energy problems. One suggestion was that we should reduce our demand for energy. Without question, there are many areas where energy could be saved with little inconvenience. One way that a reduction in energy demand could be accomplished is through the imposition of a tax on fuel. A number of economists suggested such a measure. To see how it might work, consider Figure 17.5, which shows the demand and supply curves for fuel. Without tax, the price of fuel would be OP_0, and the quantity consumed would be OQ_0.

Suppose that a tax of \$.20 per gallon[9] of fuel were imposed. If so, the supply curve would shift upward by the amount of the tax. To see why, note that, if the pretax price had to be OP_0 per gallon to induce sellers to supply OQ_0 gallons of fuel, the posttax price would have to be \$.20 higher to induce the same supply. Similarly, if the pretax price had to be OP_1 per gallon to induce sellers to supply OQ_1 gallons of fuel, the posttax price would have to be \$.20 higher to induce the same supply. The reason why the sellers require \$.20 more per gallon to supply the pretax amount is that they must pay the tax of \$.20 per gallon to the government. Thus they need the extra \$.20 to wind up with the same amount as before.

Since the tax shifts the supply curve upward by \$.20, the posttax equilibrium price and quantity are OP_2 and OQ_2, respectively. The effect of the tax on the quantity of fuel consumed is just what one would expect. It reduces fuel consumption. In Figure 17.5, the reduction is from OQ_0 to OQ_2. According to calculations by Dale Jorgensen of Harvard University and Edward Hudson of Data Resources, Inc., a tax equal to 3 percent of sales in 1985 and increasing gradually to about 15 percent in the year 2000 would result in no growth whatsoever in the quantity of energy consumed between 1985 and 2000. However, it is by no means clear that the United States

---

[9] We assume here that fuel is measured in gallons. For some fuels (like coal), this is not the case; but this simplification can easily be removed. It is used here only for convenience.

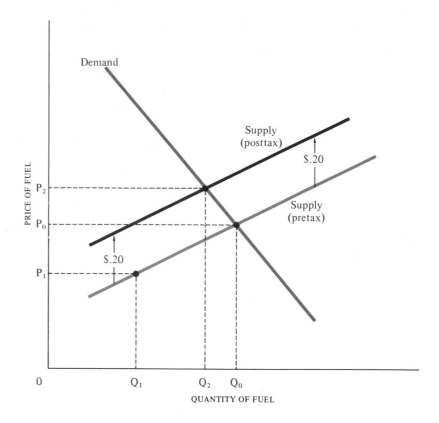

Figure 17.5

*Effect of a Tax on Fuel If a tax of $.20
per gallon is imposed on fuel, the supply
curve for fuel shifts upward, as shown
here. Thus the quantity of fuel consumed
is cut from OQ_0 to OQ_2.*

should seek to maintain energy consumption at a constant level. For one
thing, such a policy would reduce our rate of economic growth, although
considerable growth would still occur.

DEVELOPMENT OF NEW ENERGY TECHNOLOGIES

Economists and others also suggested that, to avoid increased dependence
on foreign oil, we might develop new technologies that can produce energy
economically from our domestic resources. One important resource of this
kind is shale, which is found in Colorado, Wyoming, and Utah. For many
years, shale has been regarded as a promising source of synthetic oil, but so
far the costs of producing oil by this route have been too high to make it
economical. Also, there are many unresolved environmental problems,
since it is difficult to dispose of the spent shale. In Canada, a potentially
important source of synthetic oil is the tar sands located in Alberta. Here
too, the costs of producing oil in this way are relatively high, but some production is occurring. In both the cases of shale and tar sands, perhaps additional investments in research and development can solve the problems that
presently prevent these resources from being a more economical source of
synthetic oil.

The United States has vast quantities of coal. To some extent, it might be
possible to substitute our relatively plentiful coal for other fuels. However,
one important problem with much of our Eastern coal is that it contains a
great deal of sulphur, with the result that its combustion leads to a rise in
the emission of sulphur dioxide, an important air pollutant. One way to
cope with this problem is to scrub most of this chemical from power plants'

BUBBLES, OFFSETS, AND BANKS

Attempts to maintain an acceptable level of air quality in the United States are based on the direct regulation of individual sources of pollution. A source is defined as any installation which emits at least one pollutant; thus a single industrial plant can have several distinct sources. Each polluter is supposed to obey rules, set by the government, stipulating both the necessary amount of pollution abatement and the technology to be employed at each source. This process has proved cumbersome and time-consuming. Many studies must be made by both the regulators and the regulated. Hearings are often necessary. Moreover, for reasons discussed in this chapter, direct regulation of this sort has been inefficient. The reduction in pollution has been more costly than necessary.

In the late 1970s, the Environmental Protection Agency (EPA) began to experiment with market-like schemes for pollution control. Rather than directly controlling the behavior of each source of pollution, these schemes introduced financial incentives for firms to use their own expertise to achieve air quality levels relatively cheaply. To date, the EPA has moved very cautiously in this direction; direct regulation has not been abandoned. Only limited use of financial incentives has been approved. Three incentive schemes—bubbles, offsets, and banks—have been developed, each of which is discussed below.

The concept of a *bubble* is meant to take account of the fact that the costs of controlling pollution differ among processes within a particular plant and among plants and firms. A "bubble" is put around an entire plant or area, and it is viewed as a single source of pollution rather than several distinct sources. Regulators establish emission limits for a plant (or area) as a whole, and managers can allocate pollution abatement in any way they like as long as the overall emission target is attained. Since the managers' decisions affect their firms' profits, they have an incentive to reduce pollution in a least-cost way. The bubble concept can only be applied to existing firms, not to potential sources of pollution.

Experience with bubbles indicates that they can result in significant savings. For example, Armco Steel substituted dust-reducing actions for pollution controls in its steel-making process, the result being a saving of $20 million in capital costs and $2.5 million per year in operating costs. In Providence, Rhode Island, the New England Electric System has used different fuels at two power plants included within a bubble, and reports savings of $4 million in 2½ years. However, there are many restrictions on the use of bubbles. For example, as noted above, they can only be used by existing sources of pollution, not by new entrants.

The concept of an *offset* was developed to permit new plants to open and old ones to expand in areas that do not meet the national environmental standards, while at the same time ensuring that air quality does not get worse. Whereas bubbles apply only to existing sources of pollution, offsets apply to new sources. Offsets permit construction of new pollution sources (and enlargement of existing sources) if the resulting new emissions are *less than* the reduction in emissions from existing sources. The offset program allows firms that want to introduce new sources of pollution to negotiate with existing firms to purchase emission reductions from them. Also, firms can offset the increases in pollution stemming from their new sources by reducing the emissions from other sources that they own in the area.

The offset program began in 1977. According to EPA, there have been hundreds of offsets, most of which have occurred within a single firm. For example, in Brazoria County, Texas, Phillips Petroleum Company added new sources of pollution in order to enlarge the capacity of its refinery. The pollution from these new sources was offset by doing a more complete job of controlling hydrocarbon emissions from Phillips's existing storage tanks and other facilities. Through 1980, only 32 offsets involving negotiations between different firms had taken place, as shown in the table below. This seemed to be due in part to the bureaucratic difficulties in carrying out offsets.

The concept of a *bank* is an extension of an offset, the idea being to promote greater flexibility with regard to the timing of the trade of emission reductions. If a firm pushes its daily emissions below the mandated standards, it can hold these reductions in reserve at a clearinghouse, and it can trade them at some date in the future. In other words, it can "bank" these reductions. One advantage is that the basic offset program is made more efficient because firms that want to purchase emission reductions from other firms can find potential sellers of such reductions by consulting the clearinghouse inventory.

Bubbles, offsets, and banks are very partial steps toward the use of market incentives to help promote efficiency in pollution control. The United States is very far from having a system of marketable pollution rights. But as Robert Crandall of the Brookings Institution has put it, "We are surely closer to a system of economic incentives in air pollution control . . . than we were a decade ago, when a proposed sulfur tax disappeared without even serious legislative debate."[1]

| Pollutant | *Number of offset transactions through 1980* | |
	Approved	*Pending, withdrawn, or uncertain*
Hydrocarbons	20	8
Total suspended particulates	8	3
Sulfur dioxide	4	1
Carbon monoxide	0	1
Nitrogen oxides	2	0
Total	32	12

Source: Wes Vivian and William Hall, "An Examination of U.S. Market Trading in Air Pollution Offsets," Institute of Public Policy Studies, University of Michigan, 1981.

[1] R. Crandall, *Controlling Industrial Pollution,* Washington, D.C.: Brookings Institution, 1983, p. 98.

Example 17.2   Oil Price Decontrol and Imports

From 1971 to early 1981, the government imposed controls on the price of crude oil. Suppose that the domestic supply and demand curves for crude oil were as shown below:

The price of imported foreign oil was OP_1 dollars per barrel. Government controls enabled buyers of crude oil to pay OP_2 dollars per barrel, but domestic suppliers received only OP_3 dollars per barrel.

(a) How much will domestic producers of crude oil supply? (b) How much will domestic buyers of crude oil demand? (c) How much crude oil will be imported? (d) If the price of crude oil were decontrolled, how much crude oil would be imported? (e) In early 1981, the price of crude oil was decontrolled. The American Petroleum Institute reported that imports of crude oil in the first six months of 1981 plunged 20 percent, to an average of 5.9 million barrels per day. Is this what would be expected, based on the above model?*

SOLUTION

(a) OQ_0 barrels per day. (b) OQ_5 barrels per day. (c) $(OQ_5 - OQ_0)$ barrels per day. (d) Under decontrol, the domestic price would have to equal the price of imported oil, OP_1. Thus the domestic producers would supply OQ_2 barrels per day, and domestic buyers would demand OQ_4 barrels per day, which means that $(OQ_4 - OQ_2)$ barrels per day would be imported. (e) Yes. The model predicts that imports will fall from $(OQ_5 - OQ_0)$ to $(OQ_4 - OQ_2)$ barrels per day under decontrol.

* See R. Leftwich and A. Sharp, *Economics of Social Issues,* Dallas: Business Publications, 1978; and "Economic Gains Tied to Ending Oil Price Curbs," *New York Times,* September 8, 1981.

flue stacks. Unfortunately, however, there does not seem to be any technology that can do this effectively and economically. Another way to cope with the problem is to convert coal to a clean gas. A number of technologies have been developed to do this, but many are still in the pilot-plant stage. Here is another area where research and development have a promising role to play.

Still another promising source of energy is the sun. Techniques for harnessing solar energy have been known for a long time. For example, flat plate collectors can be used to heat water or air, which can then be used to heat buildings. But solar energy is still very costly, and there are problems in storing it for use on cloudy days and at night. According to some experts, solar energy is potentially of great economic significance, and too little has been invested to try to develop it and reduce its cost. This is an obvious area for further research and development.

The Weakening of OPEC

During the 1980s, the power of the OPEC oil cartel was substantially reduced, for several reasons.

1. Oil consumption was reduced. Faced with the greatly increased oil prices, consumers cut back on their demand for oil. In part, this was due to the adoption of oil-saving technologies and more fuel-efficient cars. For example, a Buick Electra gets 17 miles a gallon in city driving, compared with about 10 miles that similar models got in the 1970s.

2. OPEC's share of world oil output fell. Due in part to the substantial increase in oil output by Britain, Norway, Mexico, and other non-OPEC countries, OPEC's share fell from 54 percent in 1973 to 32 percent in 1983. Countries like Britain and Norway cut oil prices, forcing OPEC producers to follow suit. In October 1984, Norway, followed by Britain, cut the price of its crude oil by $2 a barrel.

3. Some OPEC members refused to abide by the cartel agreements. In particular, Nigeria, badly needing cash, reduced its price below that set by the cartel. To help ease Nigeria's problems, other OPEC countries, such as Saudi Arabia, are reported to have allowed Nigeria to sell more oil, while cutting back their own output.

In 1983, OPEC—faced with declining demand for oil, increased competition from non-OPEC sources of oil, and price cuts within its own ranks—agreed to reduce its price from $34 to $29 a barrel. In 1984, the cartel, faced with a world oil glut and the fact that oil was trading on the world market for only about $27 a barrel, tried to muster more discipline, but without apparent success. Oil experts and analysts seemed to believe that further price declines were in the cards and that OPEC would not regain its former economic power in the foreseeable future.

However, some observers still worry about the vulnerability of the United States to oil-supply disruptions. For example, it is argued that the Soviet threat to oil-producing facilities in the Middle East is great enough to warrant the preparation of alternative energy options to supplement military contingency plans. Thus, although our energy supplies have been the subject of less worry in 1985 than in the middle and late 1970s, they continue to be the subject of some public concern.

Test Yourself

1. "A tax on fuel will reduce the quantity consumed by a greater amount if the quantity of fuel demanded is relatively insensitive to its price than if it is relatively sensitive to it." Comment and evaluate.

2. According to *Business Week,* August 19, 1985, "Falling prices have trimmed Exxon's sales, but higher profits and cash flow have fueled dividend hikes and massive share buybacks that have sent Exxon stock soaring." Interpret. Is this evidence of a crisis? If so, why?

3. During the 1970s, some economists suggested that a tax on fuel might help to solve America's energy problems. What are the disadvantages of such a tax?

4. In 1981, President Reagan decontrolled the price of oil, which had been kept below world levels by federal controls. What are the disadvantages of keeping the U.S. price of oil artificially low?

Summary

1. One of the major social issues of the 1980s is environmental pollution. To a considerable extent, environmental pollution is an economic problem. Waste disposal and other pollution-causing activities result in external diseconomies.

2. Firms and individuals that pollute the water and air (and other facets of the environment) often pay less than the true social costs of disposing of their wastes in this way. Part of the true social cost is borne by other firms and individuals, who must pay to clean up the water or air, or who must live with the consequences.

3. Because of the divergence of private from social costs, the market system does not result in an optimal allocation of resources. Firms and individuals create too much waste and dispose of it in excessively harmful ways. Because the polluters do not pay the full cost of waste disposal, their products are artificially cheap, with the result that too much is produced of them.

4. The government can intervene in several ways to help remedy the breakdown of the market system in this area. One way is to issue regulations for waste disposal and other activities influencing the environment. Another is to establish effluent fees, charges a polluter must pay to the government for discharging wastes. In recent decades, there has been considerable growth in government programs designed to control pollution.

5. It is extremely difficult to determine how clean the environment should be. Of course, the sensible goal for society is to permit the level of pollution that minimizes the sum of the costs of pollution and the costs of controlling pollution; but no one has a very clear idea of what these costs are, and to a large extent the choices must be made through the political process.

6. Another major issue has been energy. The Arab oil embargo in late 1973 and OPEC's huge price increase in early 1974 called attention to the growing dependence of the United States on foreign sources of crude oil. Billions of dollars were transferred to the oil-producing countries. A cutoff of foreign oil could disrupt our economy.

7. A variety of policy measures were proposed to help deal with our energy problems. One proposal was that we enact a tax on fuel to reduce energy demand. Another approach was to develop new energy technologies that can produce energy economically from our domestic energy resources. During the 1980s, OPEC was weakened by falling demand for oil and increased supplies. Oil prices fell, and America's energy problems seemed much less urgent.

Concepts for Review

External diseconomy	**Direct regulation**	**Bubbles**
Private costs	**Effluent fees**	**Offsets**
Social costs	**Tax credits**	**Banks**

PART SEVEN

International Economics and the Communist Economies

CHAPTER 18

International Trade

Practically all human beings realize that they are not islands unto themselves, and that they benefit from living with, working with, and trading with other people. Exactly the same is true of nations. They too must interact with one another, and they too benefit from trade with one another. No nation can be an island unto itself—not even the United States. To understand how the world economy functions, you must grasp the basic economic principles of international trade.

This chapter discusses many of the fundamental questions about international trade. What is the nature of American foreign trade? What are the effects of international trade? What determines the sorts of goods a nation will import or export? What are the advantages of free trade and the arguments against it? What are the social costs of tariffs and quotas, and what has been their history in the United States? What are some of the major issues regarding protectionism in the United States today? Some of these questions have occupied the attention of economists for hundreds of years; some are as current as today's newspaper.

America's Foreign Trade

America's foreign trade, although small relative to our national product, plays a very important role in our economic life. Many of our industries depend on other countries for markets or for raw materials (like coffee, tea, or tin). Our *exports*—the things we sell to other countries—amount to about 10 percent of our gross national product, which seems small relative to other countries like Germany, France, Italy, and the United Kingdom,

Table 18.1

U.S. MERCHANDISE EXPORTS, 1984

Product	Amount (billions of dollars)
Food, feed, and beverages	32
Industrial supplies and materials	63
Machinery	62
Automotive vehicles and parts	22
Aircraft	10
Other	31
Total	220

Source: Survey of Current Busness, March 1985.

Table 18.2

PERCENT OF U.S. EXPORTS, BY AREA, 1984

Country	Percent
Japan	10
Western Europe	26
Latin America	14
Canada	24
Eastern Europe	2
Other	24
Total	100

Source: See Table 18.1.

Table 18.3

U.S. MERCHANDISE IMPORTS, 1984

Product	Amount (billions of dollars)
Food, feed, and beverages	21
Petroleum and oil products	57
Other industrial supplies and materials	67
Capital goods	60
Automotive vehicles and parts	55
Consumer goods (excluding autos)	60
Other	8
Total	328

Source: See Table 18.1.

where exports are about 15 to 20 percent of gross national product. But this is because our domestic market is so large. In absolute terms, our exports (and imports) are bigger than those of any other nation. Without question, our way of life would have to change considerably if we could not trade with other countries.

When we were a young country, we exported raw materials primarily. During the 1850s about 70 percent of our exports were raw materials and foodstuffs. But the composition of our exports has changed with time. More are now finished manufactured goods and less are raw materials. In the 1960s, about 60 percent of our exports were finished manufactured goods, and only about 20 percent were raw materials and foodstuffs. Table 18.1 shows the importance of machinery and industrial supplies in our merchandise exports. Table 18.2 indicates to whom we sell. Western Europe and Canada take about one-half of our exports, and Latin America takes over 10 percent.

What sorts of goods do we buy from abroad? About 10 percent of our *imports* are agricultural commodities like coffee, sugar, bananas, and cocoa. Almost 20 percent are petroleum and its products. But a considerable proportion is neither raw materials nor foodstuffs. Over one-half of our imports, as shown in Table 18.3, are manufactured goods like bicycles from England or color TVs from Japan. Just as we sell more to Canada and Western Europe than any other area, so we buy more from these countries too (see Table 18.4). But the pattern varies from product to product. Thus Canada is our leading foreign source for wood pulp and nonferrous metals, while Latin America is our leading source of imported coffee and sugar.

Specialization and Trade

We have discussed the extent and nature of our trade with other countries, but not *why* we trade with other countries. Do we—and our trading partners—benefit from this trade? And if so, what determines the sorts of goods we should export and import? These are very important questions, among the most fundamental in economics. The answers are by no means new. They have been well understood for considerably more than a century, due to the work of such great economists as David Hume, David Ricardo, Adam Smith, and John Stuart Mill.

WHY DO INDIVIDUALS TRADE?

As a first step, it is useful to recognize that the benefits *nations* receive through trade are essentially the same as those *individuals* receive through trade. Consider the hypothetical case of John Barrister, a lawyer, with a wife and two children. The Barrister family, like practically all families, trades continually with other families and with business firms. Since Mr. Barrister is a lawyer, he trades his legal services for money which he and his wife use to buy the food, clothing, housing, and other goods and services his family wants. Why does the Barrister family do this? What advantages does it receive through trade? Why doesn't it attempt to be self-sufficient?

Table 18.4

PERCENT OF U.S. IMPORTS, BY AREA, 1984

Country	Percent
Japan	17
Western Europe	22
Latin America	15
Canada	21
Eastern Europe	1
Other	25
Total[a]	100

Source: See Table 18.1.

[a] Because of rounding errors, figures do not sum to total.

To see why the Barrister family is sensible indeed to opt for trade rather than self-sufficiency, let's compare the current situation—where Mr. Barrister specializes in the production of legal services and trades the money he receives for other goods and services—with the situation if the Barrister family attempted to be self-sufficient. In the latter case, the Barristers would have to provide their own transportation, telephone service, foodstuffs, clothing, and a host of other things. Mr. Barrister is a lawyer—a well-trained, valuable, productive member of the community. But if he were to try his hand at making automobiles—or even bicycles—he might be a total loss. Thus, if the Barrister family attempted to be self-sufficient, it might be unable to provide many of the goods it now enjoys.

WHY DO NATIONS TRADE?

Trade permits specialization, and specialization increases output. This is the advantage of trade, both for individuals and for nations. In our hypothetical case, it is obvious that, because he can trade with other families and with firms, Mr. Barrister can specialize in doing what he is good at—law. Consequently, he can be more productive than if he were forced to be a Jack-of-all-trades, as he would have to be if he could not trade with others. The same principle holds for nations. Because the United States can trade with other nations, it can specialize in the goods and services it produces particularly well. Then it can trade them for goods that other countries are especially good at producing. Thus both we and our trading partners benefit.

Some countries have more and better resources of certain types than others. Saudi Arabia has oil, Canada has timber, Japan has a skilled labor force, and so on. *International differences in resource endowments, and in the relative quantity of various types of human and nonhuman resources, are important bases for specialization.* Consider countries with lots of fertile soil, little capital, and much unskilled labor. They are likely to find it advantageous to produce agricultural goods, while countries with poor soil, much capital, and highly skilled labor will probably do better to produce capital-intensive, high-technology goods. We must recognize, however, that the bases for specialization do not remain fixed over time. Instead, as technology and the resource endowments of various countries change, the pattern of international specialization changes as well. As we saw in the previous section, the United States specialized more in raw materials and foodstuffs about a century ago than it does now.

Absolute Advantage

To clarify the benefits of trade, consider the following example. Suppose that the United States can produce 2 electronic computers or 5,000 cases of wine with 1 unit of resources. Suppose that France can produce 1 electronic computer or 10,000 cases of wine with 1 unit of resources. Given the production possibilities in each country, are there any advantages in trade between the countries? And if so, what commodity should each country export, and what commodity should each country import? Should

France export wine and import computers, or should it import wine and export computers?

To answer these questions, assume that the United States is producing a certain amount of computers and a certain amount of wine—and that France is producing a certain amount of computers and a certain amount of wine. If the United States shifts 1 unit of its resources from producing wine to producing computers, it will increase its production of computers by 2 computers and reduce its production of wine by 5,000 cases of wine. If France shifts 1 unit of resources from the production of computers to the production of wine, it will increase its production of wine by 10,000 cases and reduce its production of computers by 1 computer.

Table 18.5 shows the *net* effect of this shift in the utilization of resources on *world* output of computers and of wine. World output of computers increases (by 1 computer) and world output of wine increases (by 5,000 cases) as a result of the redeployment of resources in each country. Thus *specialization increases world output.*

Moreover, if world output of each commodity is increased by shifting 1 unit of American resources from wine to computers and shifting 1 unit of French resources from computers to wine, it follows that world output of each commodity will be increased further if each country shifts *more* of its resources in the same direction. This is because the amount of resources required to produce each good is assumed to be constant, regardless of how much is produced.

Thus, in this situation, one country—the United States—should specialize in producing computers, and the other country—France—should specialize in producing wine. This will maximize world output of both wine and computers, permitting a rise in both countries' standards of living. Complete specialization of this sort is somewhat unrealistic, since countries often produce some of both commodities, but this simple example illustrates the basic principles involved.

Table 18.5

CASE OF ABSOLUTE ADVANTAGE

	Increase or decrease in output of:	
	Computers	Wine (thousands of cases)
Effect of U.S.'s shifting 1 unit of resources from wine to computers	+2	− 5
Effect of France's shifting 1 unit of resources from computers to wine	−1	+ 10
Net effect	+1	+ 5

Comparative Advantage

The case just described is a very special one, since one country (France) has an absolute advantage over another (the United States) in the production of one good (wine), whereas the second country (the United States) has an absolute advantage over the first (France) in the production of another good (computers). What do we mean by the term *absolute advantage?* Country A has an **absolute advantage** over Country B in the production of a good when Country A can produce a unit of the good with less resources than can Country B. Since the United States can produce a computer with fewer units of resources than France, it has an absolute advantage over France in the production of computers. Since France requires fewer resources than the United States to produce a given amount of wine, France has an absolute advantage over the United States in the production of wine.

But what if one country is more efficient in producing both goods? If the United States is more efficient in producing both computers and wine, is there still any benefit to be derived from specialization and trade? At first glance, you are probably inclined to answer no. But if this is your inclination, you should reconsider—because you are wrong.

Table 18.6

CASE OF COMPARATIVE ADVANTAGE

	Increase or decrease in output of:	
	Computers	Wine (thousands of cases)
Effect of U.S.'s shifting 2 units of resources from wine to computers	+4	−10
Effect of France's shifting 3 units of resources from computers to wine	−3	+12
Net effect	+1	+2

Basic Idea #35: Trade between two countries can be mutually beneficial even if one country is more efficient at producing everything than the other country. Each country can specialize in products where it has a comparative advantage and import those where the other country has a comparative advantage. What is important in determining what a country should produce is comparative, not absolute, advantage.

A NUMERICAL EXAMPLE

To see why specialization and trade have advantages even when one country is more efficient than another at producing both goods, consider the following example. Suppose the United States can produce 2 electronic computers or 5,000 cases of wine with 1 unit of resources, and France can produce 1 electronic computer or 4,000 cases of wine with 1 unit of resources. In this case, the United States is a more efficient producer of both computers and wine. Nonetheless, as we shall see, world output of both goods will increase if the United States specializes in the production of computers and France specializes in the production of wine.

Table 18.6 demonstrates this conclusion. If 2 units of American resources are shifted from wine to computer production, 4 additional computers and 10,000 fewer cases of wine are produced. If 3 units of French resources are shifted from computer to wine production, 3 fewer computers and 12,000 additional cases of wine are produced. Thus the combined effect of this redeployment of resources in both countries is to increase world output of computers by 1 computer and to increase world output of wine by 2,000 cases. Even though the United States is more efficient than France in the production of both computers and wine, world output of both goods will be maximized if the United States specializes in computers and France specializes in wine.

Basically, this is so because, although the United States is more efficient than France in the production of both goods, it has a greater advantage in computers than in wine. It is twice as efficient as France in producing computers, but only 25 percent more efficient than France in producing wine. To derive these numbers, recall that 1 unit of resources will produce 2 computers in the United States, but only 1 computer in France. Thus the United States is twice as efficient in computers. On the other hand, 1 unit of resources will produce 5,000 cases of wine in the United States, but only 4,000 cases in France. Thus the United States is 25 percent more efficient in wine.

TRADE DEPENDS ON COMPARATIVE ADVANTAGE

A nation has a *comparative advantage* in those products where its efficiency relative to other nations is highest. Thus, in this case, the United States has a comparative advantage in the production of computers and a comparative disadvantage in the production of wine. So long as a country has a comparative advantage in the production of some commodities and a comparative disadvantage in the production of others, it can benefit from specialization and trade. A country will specialize in products where it has a comparative advantage, and import those where it has a comparative disadvantage. The point is that *specialization and trade depend on comparative, not absolute advantage.* One of the first economists to understand the full significance of this fact was David Ricardo, the English economist of the early nineteenth century.

A Geometric Representation of Comparative Advantage

The principle of comparative advantage, like so many important economic concepts, can be displayed diagrammatically. Again, we suppose that in the United States 1 unit of resources will produce 2 electronic computers or 5,000 cases of wine. Consequently, the ***production possibilities curve*** in the United States—the curve that shows the maximum number of computers that can be produced, given various outputs of wine—is the one in panel A of Figure 18.1. The United States must give up 1 computer for every additional 2,500 cases of wine that it produces; thus the slope of the American production possibilities curve is $-\dfrac{1}{2,500}$.[1]

Also, as in the previous section, we suppose that in France 1 unit of resources will produce 1 electronic computer or 4,000 cases of wine. Thus the production possibilities curve in France is as shown in panel B of Figure 18.1. France must give up 1 computer for every additional 4,000 cases of wine it produces; thus the slope of France's production possibilities curve is $-\dfrac{1}{4,000}$.

Now suppose that the United States uses all its resources to produce computers and that France uses all its resources to produce wine. In other words, the United States operates at point A on its production possibilities curve and France operates at point B on its production possibilities curve. Then suppose that the United States trades its computers for France's wine. AC in panel A of Figure 18.1 shows the various amounts of computers and wine the United States can end up with if it specializes in computers and trades them for French wine. AC is called the ***trading possibilities curve*** of the United States. The slope of AC is minus 1 times the ratio of the price of a case of wine to the price of a computer, since this ratio equals the number of computers the United States must give up to get a case of French wine. Similarly, the line BD in panel B of Figure 18.1 shows France's trading possibilities curve. That is, BD represents the various amounts of computers and wine France can wind up with if it specializes in wine and trades it for U.S. computers.

The thing to note about both panels in Figure 18.1 is that each country's trading possibilities curve—AC in panel A, BD in panel B—lies above its production possibilities curve. This means that *both countries can have more of both commodities by specializing and trading than by trying to be self-sufficient*—even though the United States is more efficient than France at producing both commodities. Thus Figure 18.1 shows what we said in the previous section: If countries specialize in products where they have a comparative advantage and trade with one another, each country can improve its standard of living.

Figure 18.1
Benefits of Specialization and Trade
AC *represents the various amounts of computers and wine that the United States can end up with, if it specializes in computers and trades them for French wine. The slope of* AC *equals* − *1 times the ratio of the price of a case of wine to the price of a computer, assumed to be* $\dfrac{1}{3,333}$*.* BD *represents the various amounts of computers and wine that France can wind up with, if it specializes in wine and trades for U.S. computers.* AC *lies above America's production possibilities curve and* BD *lies above France's production possibilities curve. Thus both countries can have more of both commodities by specializing and trading than by attempting to be self-sufficient.*

The Terms of Trade

The ***terms of trade*** are defined as the quantity of imported goods that a country can obtain in exchange for a unit of domestic goods. Thus, in Figure 18.1, the terms of trade are measured by the ratio of the price of a

---

[1] As we know from Chapter 2, the production possibilities curve shows the maximum amount of one commodity that can be produced, given various outputs of the other commodity. Since the United States must give up 1/2,500 computer for each additional case of wine that it produces, the slope must be − 1/2,500.

computer to the price of a case of wine—since this ratio shows how many cases of French wine the United States can get in exchange for an American computer. In Figure 18.1, we asume that this ratio equals 3,333:1. It is important to note that this ratio must be somewhere between 2,500:1 and 4,000:1. By diverting its own resources from computer production to wine production, the United States can exchange a computer for 2,500 cases of wine. Since this is possible, it will not pay the United States to trade a computer for less than 2,500 cases of wine. Similarly, since France can exchange a case of wine for 1/4,000 of a computer by diverting its own resources from wine to computers, it clearly will not be willing to trade a case of wine for less than 1/4,000 of a computer.

But where will the price ratio lie between 2,500:1 and 4,000:1? The answer depends on *world supply and demand for the two products.* The stronger the demand for computers (relative to their supply) and the weaker the demand for wine (relative to its supply), the higher the price ratio. On the other hand, the weaker the demand for computers (relative to their supply) and the stronger the demand for wine (relative to its supply), the lower the price ratio.

Incomplete Specialization

Figure 18.1 shows that the United States should specialize completely in computers, and that France should specialize completely in wine. This result stems from the assumption that the cost of producing a computer or a case of wine is constant. If, on the other hand, the cost of producing each good increases with the amount produced, the result is likely to be incomplete specialization. In other words, although the United States will continue to specialize in computers and France will continue to specialize in wine, each country will also produce some of the other good as well. This is a more likely outcome, since specialization generally tends to be less than complete.

International Trade and Individual Markets

We have emphasized that nations can benefit by specializing in the production of goods for which they have a comparative advantage and trading these goods for others where they have a comparative disadvantage.[2]

[2] The principle of comparative advantage is useful in explaining and predicting the pattern of world trade, as well as in showing the benefits of trade. For example, consider the exports of Great Britain and the United States. Robert Stern of the University of Michigan compared British and American exports of 39 industries. In 21 of the 24 industries where our labor productivity was more than three times that of the British, our exports exceeded British exports. In 11 of the 15 industries where our labor productivity was less than three times that of the British, our exports were less than British exports. Thus, in 32 out of 39 industries, the principle of comparative advantage, as interpreted by Stern, predicted correctly which country would export more. This is a high batting average, since labor is not the only input and labor productivity is an imperfect measure of true efficiency. Moreover, as we shall see in subsequent sections, countries raise barriers to foreign trade, preventing trade from taking place in accord with the principle of comparative advantage.

Figure 18.2

Determination of Quantity Imported and Exported under Free Trade *Under free trade, price will equal $4.20 or £3. The United States will export* XY *units, the English will import* UV *units, and* XY = UV.

A. United States

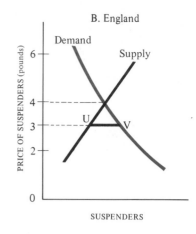

B. England

But how do a nation's producers know whether they have a comparative advantage or disadvantage in the production of a given commodity? They do not call up the local university and ask the leading professor of economics (although that might not always be such a bad idea). Instead, as we shall see in this section, the market for the good provides the required signals.

To see how this works, let's consider a new (and rather whimsical) product—bulletproof suspenders. Suppose that the Mob, having run a scientific survey of gunmen and policemen, finds that most of them wear their suspenders over their bulletproof vests. As a consequence, the Mob's gunmen are instructed to render a victim immobile by shooting holes in his suspenders (thus making his trousers fall down and trip him). Naturally, the producers of suspenders will soon find it profitable to produce a new bulletproof variety, an innovation which, it is hoped, will make a solid contribution to law and order. The new suspenders are demanded only in the United States and England, since the rest of the world wear belts. The demand curve in the United States is as shown in panel A of Figure 18.2, and the demand curve in England is as shown in panel B. Suppose further that this product can be manufactured in both the United States and England. The supply curve in the United States is as shown in panel A, and the supply curve in England is as shown in panel B.

Take a closer look at Figure 18.2. Note that prices in England are expressed in pounds (£) and prices in the United States are expressed in dollars ($). This is quite realistic. Each country has its own currency, in which prices in that country are expressed. As of 1985, £1 was equal to about $1.40. In other words, you could exchange a pound note for $1.40—or $1.40 for a £1 note. For this reason, the two panels of Figure 18.2 are lined up so that a price of $2.80 is at the same level as a price of £2, $4.20 is at the same level as £3, and so on.

NO FOREIGN TRADE

To begin with, suppose that bulletproof suspenders cannot be exported or imported, perhaps because of a very high tariff (tax on imports) imposed on them in both the United States and England. (One can readily imagine members of both Congress and Parliament defending such a tariff on the grounds that a capacity to produce plenty of bulletproof suspenders is important for national defense.) If this happens, the price of bulletproof suspenders will be $2.60 in the United States and £4 in England. Why? Because, as shown in Figure 18.2, these are the prices at which each country's demand curve intersects its supply curve.

FOREIGN TRADE PERMITTED

Next, suppose that international trade in this product is permitted, perhaps because both countries eliminate the tariff. Now what will happen? Since the price is lower in the United States than in England, people can make money by sending this product from the United States to England. After all, they can buy it for $2.60 in this country and sell it for £4 (= $5.60) in England. But they will not be able to do so indefinitely. As more and more suspenders are supplied by the United States for the English market, the price in the United States must go up (to induce producers to produce the additional output) and the price in England must go down (to induce consumers to buy the additional quantity).

When an equilibrium is reached, *the price in the United States must equal the price in England.* If this did not happen, there would be an advantage in increasing American exports (if the price in England were higher) or in decreasing American exports (if the price in the United States were higher). Thus only if the prices are equal can an equilibrium exist.

At what level will this price—which is common to both countries—tend to settle? Obviously, *the price must end up at the level where the amount of the good one country wants to export equals the amount the other country wants to import.* In other words, it must settle at $4.20 or £3. Otherwise, the total amount demanded in both countries would not equal the total amount supplied in both countries. And any reader who has mastered the material in Chapter 3 knows that such a situation cannot be an equilibrium.

THE SIGNAL OF MARKET FORCES

At this point, we can see how market forces indicate whether a country has a comparative advantage or a comparative disadvantage in the production of a certain commodity. *If a country has a comparative advantage, it turns out—after the price of the good in various countries is equalized and total world output of the good equals total world demand for it—that the country exports the good under free trade and competition.* In Figure 18.2, it turns out—as we've just seen—that the United States is an exporter of bulletproof suspenders under free trade, because the demand and supply curves in the United States and England take the positions they do. The basic reason why the curves take these positions is that the United States has a comparative advantage in the production of this good. Thus, to put things in a nutshell, a nation's producers can tell (under free trade) whether they have a comparative advantage in the production of a certain commodity by seeing whether it is profitable for them to export it. If they can make a profit, they have a comparative advantage.[3]

---

[3] In reality things are not quite so simple. For one thing, high transport costs are often involved in moving goods from one country to another. These costs can impede trade in certain commodities. Also, tariffs or quotas can be enacted by governments to interfere with free trade. Much more will be said on this score in later sections.

Economies of Scale and Learning

Specialization and trade may be advantageous even if there is no difference among countries in the efficiency with which they can produce goods and services. In a case like this, although no nation has a technological advantage over any other, specialization and trade may still be of benefit, because there may be economies of scale in producing some commodities. Thus, if one country specializes in one good and another country specializes in another good, firms can serve the *combined* markets of both countries, which will make their costs *lower* than if they could only reach their domestic markets. This is a major argument for forming an international economic association like the European Common Market, discussed later in this chapter.

Another reason for specialization is that it may result in learning. It is well known that the cost of producing many articles goes down as more and more of the articles are produced. In the aircraft and machine tool industries, producers are well aware of the reduction in costs from learning. The unit costs of a new machine tool tend to be reduced by 20 percent for each doubling of cumulated output, due to improved efficiency through individual and organizational learning. If such learning is an important factor in an industry, there are advantages in having one nation's producers specialize in a certain good. Specialization can reduce costs to a lower level than if each nation tries to be self-sufficient. Longer production runs cut costs since *the more a producer makes, the lower the unit costs.*

Innovation and International Trade

International trade also arises because of technological change. Suppose that a new product is invented in the United States and an American firm begins producing and selling it in the American market. It catches on, and the American innovator decides to export the new product to Europe and other foreign markets. If the new product meets European needs and tastes, the Europeans will import it from the United States; and later, when the market in Europe gets big enough, the American firm may establish a branch plant in Europe. For a time at least, European firms do not have the technological know-how to produce the new product, which is often protected to some extent by patents.

Trade of this sort is based on a *technology gap* between countries. Consider the plastics industry. After the development of a new plastic, there generally has been a period of 15 to 25 years when the innovating country has had a decisive advantage and has been likely to lead in per capita production and exports. It has had a head start, as well as the benefits of patents and commercial secrecy. Production has been licensed to other countries, but often on a limited scale and only after a number of years. Soon after the patents expire, a different phase begins. Imitation is easier, technical know-how spreads more readily, direct technical factors lose importance, and such other factors as materials costs become much more important. Industry from other countries may challenge the innovator in export markets, and sometimes in the innovator's home market as well, although the innovating firm still benefits to some extent from its accumulated knowledge and experience and its ongoing research and development.

The United States tends to export products with a high technological component—relatively new products based on considerable research and development. If the 5 U.S. industries with the largest research programs are compared with the 14 other major industries, it turns out that the high-research industries export 4 times as much per dollar of sales as the others.[4] During the 1960s, Europeans expressed considerable concern over the technological gap between the United States and Europe. They asserted that superior know-how stemming from scientific and technical development in the United States had allowed American companies to obtain large shares of European markets in areas like aircraft, space equipment, computers, and other electronic products. More recently, our technological lead has narrowed considerably in many industries, as the Japanese, Germans, and others have upgraded their technology. Indeed, in some areas, their technology now surpasses our own. According to many observers, some American exports will be, and are being, hurt as a consequence.[5]

Multinational Firms

One of the most remarkable economic phenomena of the last 30 years has been the growth of **multinational firms**—firms that make direct investments in other countries and produce and market their products abroad. For example, Coca-Cola is produced and bottled all over the world. Most multinational firms are American, but companies like Shell in petroleum and Hoffman-La Roche in drugs are examples of foreign-based multinational firms. The available data indicate that the multinational firms have grown by leaps and bounds, and that their shipments have become a bigger proportion of international trade.

The reasons why firms have become multinational are varied. In some cases, firms have established overseas branches to control foreign sources of raw materials. In other cases, they have invested overseas in an effort to defend their competitive position. Very frequently, firms have established foreign branches to exploit a technological lead. After exporting a new product (or a cheaper version of an existing product) to foreign markets, firms have decided to establish plants overseas to supply these markets. Once a foreign market is big enough to accommodate a plant of minimum efficient size, this decision does not conflict with economies of scale. Moreover, transport costs often hasten such a decision. Also, in some

---

[4] Charles Kindleberger, *International Economics,* Homewood, ill.: Irwin, 1968, p. 67. Also, see R. Vernon, "International Investment and International Trade in the Product Cycle," *Quarterly Journal of Economics,* May 1966; and R. Caves and R. Jones, *World Trade and Payments,* 2d ed., Boston: Little, Brown, 1977.

[5] Besides differences in technology, another reason for trade is a difference in national tastes. If Country A likes beef and Country B likes pork, it may pay both countries to produce beef and pork, and Country A may find it advantageous to import beef from Country B and Country B may find it advantageous to import pork from Country A.

cases, the only way a firm can introduce its innovation into a foreign market is through the establishment of overseas production facilities.

EFFECTS OF MULTINATIONAL FIRMS

By carrying its technology overseas, the multinational firm plays a very important role in the international diffusion of innovations. A firm with a technological edge over its competitors often prefers to exploit its technology in foreign markets through wholly owned subsidiaries rather than through licensing or other means. To some extent, this is because of difficulties in using ordinary market mechanisms to buy and sell information. The difficulties of transferring technology across organizational, as well as national, boundaries also contribute to the decision. For these and other reasons, the innovating firm may find it advantageous to transfer its technology to other countries by establishing subsidiaries abroad.

One of the most important effects of the multinational firm has been to integrate the economies of the world more closely into a worldwide system. In other words, multinational firms have tended to break down some of the barriers between nations. Besides speeding the diffusion of new technology, they have linked the capital markets of many countries and promoted the international transfer of important managerial labor.

Particularly in the less developed countries, there has been an impassioned debate over the pros and cons of the multinational firm, which sometimes is viewed with suspicion by the nation-states in which it operates. These nation-states feel that their sovereignty is threatened by the great power of the multinational firm over their national economies. And the tragedy at Bhopal, India, where thousands of people were killed in 1984 by an accident at a plant owned by a major multinational firm— Union Carbide Corporation—has caused further conflict of this sort. Also, some observers are wary of multinational firms because of the possibility that they will attain undesirable monopoly power.

Test Yourself

1. Suppose that the United States can produce 3 electronic computers or 3,000 cases of wine with 1 unit of resources, while France can produce 1 electronic computer or 2,000 cases of wine with 1 unit of resources. Will specialization increase world output?

2. Suppose that the United States has 100 units of resources while France has 50 units. Based on the data in Question 1, draw the production possibilities curve in each country. Without international trade, what will be the ratio of the price of an electronic computer to the price of a case of wine in each country?

3. Given the information in Questions 1 and 2, how will firms in France and the United States know whether they should produce wine or electronic computers? Must the government instruct them on this score? Why or why not?

4. Under the circumstances described in Questions 1 and 2, will each country specialize completely in the production of one or the other good? Why or why not? What factors result in incomplete specialization in the real world?

Tariffs and Quotas

WHAT IS A TARIFF?

Despite its advantages, not everyone benefits from free trade. On the contrary, the well-being of some firms and workers may be threatened by foreign competition; and they may press for a *tariff,* a tax the government imposes on imports. The purpose of a tariff is to cut down on imports in order to protect domestic industry and workers from foreign competition. A secondary reason for tariffs is to produce revenue for the government.

To see how a tariff works, consider the market for wristwatches. Suppose that the demand and supply curves for wristwatches in the United States are as shown in panel A of Figure 18.3, and that the demand and supply curves for wristwatches in Switzerland are as shown in panel B. Clearly, Switzerland has a comparative advantage in the production of wristwatches, and under free trade the price of a wristwatch would tend toward $10 in the United States and toward 25 Swiss francs in Switzerland. (Note that 1 Swiss franc is assumed to equal 40 cents.) Under free trade, the United States would import 10 million wristwatches from Switzerland.

Now if the United States imposes a tariff of $10 on each wristwatch imported from Switzerland, the imports will completely cease. Any importers who buy watches in Switzerland at the price (when there is no foreign trade) of 15 Swiss francs—which equals $6—must pay a tariff of $10; this makes their total cost $16 per watch. But this is more than the price of a watch in the United States when there is no foreign trade (which is $15). Consequently, there is no money to be made by importing watches—unless Americans can be persuaded to pay more for a Swiss watch than for an identical American watch.

THE SOCIAL COSTS OF TARIFFS

What is the effect of the tariff? The domestic watch industry receives a higher price—$15 rather than $10—than it would without a tariff. And the workers in the domestic watch industry may have more jobs and higher

Figure 18.3

Effect of a Tariff on Swiss Watches
Under free trade, price would equal $10, or 25 Swiss francs. If a tariff of $10 is imposed on each watch imported from Switzerland, there will be a complete cessation of imports. Price in the United States will increase to $15, and price in Switzerland will fall to 15 Swiss francs.

381

wages than without the tariff. The victim of the tariff is the American consumer, who pays a higher price for wristwatches. Thus the domestic watch industry benefits at the expense of the rest of the nation. But does the general public lose more than the watch industry gains? In general, the answer is yes. The tariff reduces the welfare of the nation as a whole.

The tariff in Figure 18.3 is a *prohibitive tariff*—a tariff so high that it stops all imports of the good in question. Not all tariffs are prohibitive. (If they were, the government would receive no revenue at all from tariffs.) In many cases, the tariff is high enough to stop some, but not all, imports; and, as you would expect, the detrimental effect of a nonprohibitive tariff on living standards is less than that of a prohibitive tariff. But this does not mean that nonprohibitive tariffs are harmless. On the contrary, they can do lots of harm to domestic consumption and living standards.

The detrimental effects of tariffs have long been recognized, even in detective stories. Thus, in the course of solving the mystery concerning the Hound of the Baskervilles, Sherlock Holmes expressed his enthusiastic approval of a newspaper editorial that read as follows:

> You may be cajoled into imagining that your own special trade or your own industry will be encouraged by a protective tariff, but it stands to reason that such legislation must in the long run ... lower the general conditions of life on this island.

Of course, Holmes considered this point elementary (my dear Watson) but worth hammering home.

WHAT IS A QUOTA?

Besides tariffs, other barriers to free trade are *quotas,* which many countries impose on the amount of certain commodities that can be imported annually. The United States sets import quotas on sugar and exerts pressure on foreigners to get them to limit the quantity of steel and textiles that they will export to us. To see how a quota affects trade, production, and prices, let's return to the market for wristwatches. Suppose the United States places a quota on the import of wristwatches: no more than 6 million wristwatches can be imported per year. Figure 18.4 shows the effect of the quota. Before it was imposed, the price of wristwatches was $10 (or 25 Swiss francs), and the United States imported 10 million wristwatches from Switzerland. The quota forces the United States to reduce its imports to 6 million.

What will be the effect on the U.S. price? The demand curve shows that, if the price is $12, American demand will exceed American supply by 6 million watches; in other words, we will import 6 million watches. Thus, once the quota is imposed, the price will rise to $12, since *this is the price that will reduce our imports to the amount of the quota.* A quota—like a tariff—increases the price of the good. (Note too that the price in Switzerland will fall to 20 francs. Thus the quota will reduce the price in Switzerland.)

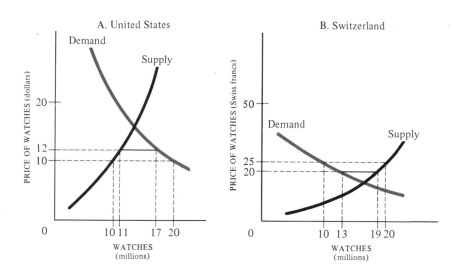

Figure 18.4
Effect of a Quota on Swiss Watches
Before the quota is imposed, the price is
$10, or 25 Swiss francs. After a quota of 6
million watches is imposed, the price in
the United States rises to $12, and the
price in Switzerland falls to 20 Swiss
francs.

THE SOCIAL COSTS OF QUOTAS

Both a quota and a tariff reduce trade, raise prices, protect domestic industry from foreign competition, and reduce the standard of living of the
nation as a whole. But most economists tend to regard quotas with even
less enthusiasm than they do tariffs. Under many circumstances, a quota
insulates local industry from foreign competition even more effectively
than a tariff does. Foreigners, if their costs are low enough, can surmount
a tariff barrier; but if a quota exists, there is no way they can exceed the
quota. Moreover, a (nonprohibitive) tariff provides the government with
some revenue, while quotas do not even do that. The windfall price increase from a quota accrues to the importer who is lucky enough or influential enough—or sufficiently generous with favors and bribes—to get an
import license. (However, if the government auctions off the import licenses, it can obtain revenue from a quota.)

EXPORT SUBSIDIES AND OTHER NONTARIFF BARRIERS TO FREE
TRADE

Finally, **export subsidies,** another means by which governments try to give
their domestic industry an advantage in international competition, are
also a major impediment to free trade. Such subsidies may take the form
of outright cash disbursements, tax exemptions, preferential financing or
insurance arrangements, or other preferential treatment for exports. Export subsidies, and other such measures, frequently lead to countermea-
sures. Thus, to counter foreign export subsidies, the U.S. government has
imposed duties against such subsidies on goods sold here.
   Other nontariff barriers to free trade include licensing requirements and
unreasonable product quality standards. By granting few licenses (which
are required in some countries to import goods) and by imposing unrealistically stringent product quality standards, governments discourage imports.

Arguments for Tariffs and Quotas

Given the disadvantages to society at large of tariffs and other barriers to free trade, why do governments continue to impose them? There are many reasons, some sensible, some irrational.

THE NATIONAL DEFENSE ARGUMENT

One of the most convincing arguments is the desirability of maintaining a domestic industry for purposes of *national defense.* Thus, even if the Swedes had a comparative advantage in producing airplanes, we would not allow free trade to put our domestic producers of aircraft out of business if we felt that a domestic aircraft industry was necessary for national defense. Although the Swedes are by no means unfriendly, we would not want to import our entire supply of such a critical commodity from a foreign country, where the supply might be shut off for reasons of international politics. (Recall the Arab oil embargo of 1973.)

This is a perfectly valid reason for protecting certain domestic industries, and many protective measures are defended on these grounds. To the extent that protective measures are in fact required for national defense, economists go along with them. The restrictions entail social costs (some of which were described in previous sections), but these costs may well be worth paying for enhanced national security. The trouble is that many barriers to free trade are justified on these grounds when in fact they protect domestic industries only tenuously connected with national defense. Moreover, even if there is a legitimate case on defense grounds for protecting a domestic industry, subsidies are likely to be a more straightforward and efficient way to do so than tariffs or quotas.

Besides national defense, there are other noneconomic reasons for protecting particular domestic industries. Some countries—Canada, for one—use a tariff to protect certain industries that they feel help them to be more independent of foreign domination and influence. Many Canadians, for understandable reasons, are intent on maintaining their traditions and values, and on resisting the penetration of American ways. Such noneconomic reasons for protection are perfectly reasonable if the nation as a whole understands the economic cost and agrees that the game is worth the candle (and if the reasons are sufficiently understood by foreigners that the measures do not provoke retaliation).

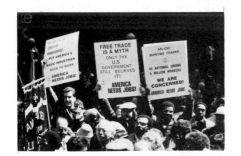

OTHER ARGUMENTS FOR TARIFFS

Besides national defense, several other arguments for tariffs or quotas can make sense.

1. Tariffs or other forms of protection can be justified to foster the growth or development of young industries. Suppose that Japan has a comparative advantage in the production of a certain semiconductor, but Japan does not presently produce this item. It may take Japanese firms several years to become proficient in the relevant technology, to engage in the learning

described in a previous section and to take advantage of the relevant
economies of scale. While this industry is "growing up," Japan may impose a tariff on such semiconductors, thus shielding its young industry
from competition it cannot yet handle. This "infant industry" argument
for tariffs has a long history; Alexander Hamilton was one of its early
exponents. Needless to say, it is *not* an argument for *permanent* tariffs,
since infant industries are supposed to grow up—and the sooner the better.
(Moreover, a subsidy for the industry would probably be better and easier
to remove than a temporary tariff, according to many economists.)

*2. Tariffs sometimes may be imposed to protect domestic jobs and to
reduce unemployment at home.* In the short run the policy may succeed, but
we must recognize that other nations are likely to retaliate by enacting or
increasing their own tariffs, so that such a policy may not work very well in
the long run. A more sensible way to reduce domestic unemployment is to
use the tools of fiscal and monetary policy rather than tariffs. If workers are
laid off by industries that cannot compete with foreign producers, proper
monetary and fiscal policy, together with retaining programs, should enable
these workers to switch to other industries that can compete.

*3. Tariffs sometimes may be imposed to prevent a country from being too
dependent on only a few industries.* Consider a Latin American country that
is a major producer of bananas. Under free trade, this country might
produce bananas and little else, putting its entire economy at the mercy of
the banana market. If the price of bananas fell, the country's national
income would decrease drastically. To promote industrial diversification,
this country may establish tariffs to protect other industries—for example,
certain types of light manufacturing. In a case like this, the tariff protects
the country from having too many eggs—or bananas (if you want to avoid
mixing a metaphor)—in a single basket.

*4. Tariffs may sometimes improve a country's terms of trade—that is, the
ratio of its export prices to its import prices.* The United States is a major
importer of bananas. If we impose a tariff on bananas, thus cutting down
on the domestic demand for them (because the tariff will increase their
price), the reduction in our demand is likely to reduce the price of bananas
abroad. Consequently, foreign producers of bananas will really pay part of
the tariff. However, other countries may retaliate; and if all countries
pursue such policies, few, if any, are likely to find themselves better off.

FREQUENTLY ENCOUNTERED FALLACIES

Although, as we have just seen, tariffs can be defended under certain
circumstances, many of the arguments for them frequently encountered in
political oratory and popular discussions are misleading. Although no
field of economics is free of popular misconceptions and fallacies, this one
is particularly rich in pious inanities and thunderous *non sequiturs.*

Fallacy 1. One frequently encountered fallacy is that, if foreigners want
to trade with us, they must be benefiting from the trade. Consequently,
according to this argument, we must be giving them more than we get—
and it must be in our interest to reduce trade. This argument is entirely
erroneous in its assumption that trade cannot be beneficial to *both* trading
partners. On the contrary, as we have seen, the heart of the argument for
trade is that it can be mutually beneficial.

Fallacy 2. Another fallacy one often encounters in polite conversation—and not-so-polite political debate—is that a tariff is required to protect our workers from low-wage labor in other countries. According to this argument, since American labor (at $8 an hour) clearly cannot compete with foreign labor (which works at "coolie" wage levels), we have no choice but to impose tariffs. If we do not, cheap foreign goods will throw our high-priced laborers out of work. This argument is wrong on two counts. First, *high wages do not necessarily mean high unit costs of production.* Because the productivity of American workers is high, unit labor costs in the United States are roughly in line with those in other countries. Unit labor cost equals the wage rate divided by labor productivity. Thus unit labor cost may be no higher here than abroad, even though the wage rate here is much higher, if labor productivity here is also much higher than abroad.) Second, *if our costs were out of line with those of other countries, there should be a change in exchange rates, which would tend to bring them back into line.* That is, exchange rates should move to bring our exports and imports into balance.

Fallacy 3. Still another fallacy that makes the rounds is that it is better to "buy American" because then we have both the goods that are bought and the money, whereas if we buy from foreigners we have the goods but they have the money. Like some jokes, this fallacy has an ancient lineage—and one that borders on respectability, since Abraham Lincoln is supposed to have subscribed to it. Basically, the flaw is the implicit assumption that money is somehow valued for its own sake. In reality, all foreigners can do with the money is buy some of our goods, so that really we are just swapping some of our goods for some of theirs. If such a trade is mutually advantageous, fine.

WHY SO MUCH NONSENSE?

Why do politicians (both Democrats and Republicans) sometimes utter these fallacies? No doubt an important reason is simply ignorance. There is no law that prevents people with little understanding of economics from holding public office. But this may not be the only reason. Special-interest groups—particular industries, unions, and regions—have a lot to gain by getting the government to enact protective tariffs and quotas. And Congress and the executive branch of the government are often sensitive to the pressures of these groups, which wield considerable political power.

Faced with a choice between helping a few powerful, well-organized groups and helping the general public—which is poorly organized and often ignorant of its own interests—politicians frequently tend to favor the special-interest groups. After all, these groups have a lot to gain and will remember their friends, while the general public—each member of which loses only a relatively small amount—will be largely unaware of its losses anyhow. Having decided to help these groups, representatives or senators may not exert themselves unduly to search out or expose the weakness in some of the arguments used to bolster their position. Thus there is the story of a well-known senator who, about to deliver a certain oration, wrote in the margin of one section of his speech: "Weak point here. Holler like hell."

Finally, it is important to recognize once again that, although the majority of citizens benefit from free trade, some are likely to be hurt by it. A reduction in the tariff on shoes is likely to hurt people who own and work in American shoe factories. If our domestic shoe industry cannot compete with foreign producers, workers will be laid off and plants will close. The result will be a considerable loss to domestic shoe producers and workers. Most people believe that society as a whole, which benefits from free trade, should help the minority that is victimized by it. To promote this objective, the United States has established "adjustment assistance" for firms or workers who, because of government agreement to reduce barriers to free trade, have suffered idleness or unemployment due to an increase in imports. Workers can enter retraining programs and can obtain allowances to help pay for moving to other jobs.

Tariffs in the United States

How high are American tariffs, now and in the past? In our early years, we were a very protectionist nation. The argument for protecting our young industry from the competition of European manufacturers was the "infant industry" argument, which, as we saw above, can be perfectly sensible. However, our own industries understandably found it advantageous to prolong their childhood for as long as possible—and to press for continuation of high tariffs. During the nineteenth century and well into the twentieth, the industrial Northeast was particularly strong in its support of tariffs. Furthermore, the Republican party, which generally held sway in American politics between the Civil War and the New Deal, favored a high tariff. Thus, as shown in Figure 18.5, the tariff remained relatively high from about 1870 until the early 1930s. With the exception of the period around World War I, average tariff rates were about 40 to 50 percent. With the enactment of the Smoot-Hawley Tariff of 1930, the tariff reached its peak—about 60 percent. Moreover, these tariff rates understate the extent to which the tariff restricted trade: Some goods were completely shut out of the country by the tariff, and do not show up in the figures.

Figure 18.5

Average American Tariff Rates *The tariff generally remained high from about 1870 to the early 1930s; in recent decades it has decreased substantially.*

With the Democratic victory in 1932, a movement began toward freer trade. The Trade Agreements Act of 1934 allowed the president to bargain with other countries to reduce barriers to trade. He was given the power to lower U.S. tariffs by as much as 50 percent. In 1945, he was given the power to make further tariff reductions. Between 1934 and 1948, tariff rates fell substantially, as shown in Figure 18.5. By 1948, the United States was no longer a high-tariff country; the average tariff rate was only about 10 percent.[6]

THE KENNEDY ROUND

During the 1950s, there were no further decreases in the tariff—but there were no substantial increases either. The movement toward freer trade was continued by President Kennedy in 1962, and during the 1960s, the "Kennedy Round" negotiations took place among about 40 nations in an attempt to reduce tariffs. In 1967, the United States agreed to cut tariffs by about one-third on a great many items.

The negotiations during the 1960s were prompted by the establishment of the *European Economic Community*—or *"Common Market."* The EEC was composed originally of Belgium, France, West Germany, Holland, Italy, and Luxembourg; and in the late 1970s, Britain, Denmark, and Ireland joined. When the EEC was formed, the member countries agreed to reduce the tariff barriers against one another's goods—but not against the goods of other nations, including the United States.

The formation and success of the Common Market—and the likelihood that other European countries would join—posed a problem for the United States. The Common Market is a large and rich market, with over 200 million people and a combined gross national product in the trillions of dollars. With the reduction of tariff barriers *within* the Common Market, trade *among* the members of the Common Market increased rapidly, and prices of many items were cut. But American exporters were less than ecstatic about all of this, because the members of the Common Market still maintained their tariff barriers against American goods. While the "Kennedy Round" negotiations succeeded in reducing some of the tariff barriers between the United States and the Common Market, important tariff barriers remained, particularly for agricultural products.

THE TRADE REFORM ACT AND THE TOKYO ROUND

In 1974, the Congress passed the Trade Reform Act of 1974, which enabled the president, after international negotiations, to reduce any tariff presently above 5 percent by three-fifths and to abolish any tariff presently equal to 5 percent or less. Also, the act allowed workers, firms, and communities that are hurt by import competition to obtain payments and other forms of assistance. As pointed out in a previous section, such as-

---

[6] In 1947, the United States and 22 other nations signed the *General Agreement on Tariffs and Trade* (GATT), which calls for all participating countries to meet periodically to negotiate bilaterally on tariff cuts. Any tariff cut negotiated in this way will be extended to all participating nations.

Example 18.1   The Effects of a Tariff on Shoes

The quantity of shoes demanded in the United States at each price of a pair of shoes is shown below. In addition, the quantities of shoes supplied by American producers and by foreign producers at each price are shown too.

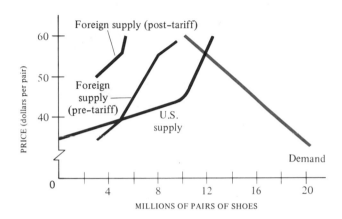

(a) Assuming that the market for shoes is competitive, what is the equilibrium price of a pair of shoes in the United States? (b) What proportion of the U.S. market goes to foreign producers of shoes? (c) Suppose that the United States imposes a tariff of $15 per pair of shoes. How many pairs of shoes will foreign producers now supply if the price is (1) $50, (2) $55, (3) $60. (Note that a $50 price together with a $15 tariff means that the price to the foreign producer is $50 − $15, or $35.) (d) After the imposition of the tariff, what is the equilibrium price? (e) After the imposition of the tariff, what proportion of the U.S. market goes to foreign producers of shoes? (f) How much revenue does the U.S. government get from this tariff?

SOLUTION

(a) $45, since at this price U.S. supply (10 million pairs) plus foreign supply (6 million pairs) equals the quantity demanded (16 million pairs). (b) 6/16. (c) 3 million pairs (since this is what would have been supplied at a price of $35 without the tariff), 5 million pairs (since this is what would have been supplied at a price of $40 without the tariff), 6 million pairs (since this is what would have been supplied at a price of $45 without the tariff). (d) $50, since at this price U.S. supply (11 million pairs) plus foreign supply (3 million pairs) equals the quantity demanded (14 million pairs). (e) 3/14. (f) 3 million × $15, or $45 million.

sistance is a way of helping the minority of workers and firms that may be victimized by freer trade.

In 1973, over 100 nations met in Tokyo to plan a new round of trade negotiations. The aim was to make progress toward the reduction of both tariffs and nontariff barriers to trade. (In recent years, tariffs have been replaced to some extent by nontariff barriers to trade.) After over 5 years of difficult negotiations, an agreement was approved in April 1979. This agreement called for the industrial nations to reduce tariffs on thousands of goods by an average of about 33 percent during an 8-year period. It also tried to reduce export subsidies, phony technical standards for imports (used to keep out foreign goods), and barriers to international bidding for government contracts.

INCREASED PROTECTIONISM

Recent years have seen a marked increase in protectionist feelings in the United States. As Western Europe and Japan have become more formidable competitors abroad and at home, many industries have begun to press for quotas and higher tariffs. The automobile, steel, and textile industries have been among the most frequent petitioners for protection. In 1981, the Japanese agreed to limit import of Japanese autos into the U.S. to 1.68 million per year; in 1984, the ceiling was raised to 1.85 million per year, and the agreement called for the industrial nations to reduce tariffs on thousands of goods by an average of about 33 percent during an 8-year period. It also tried to reduce export subsidies, phony technical standards for imports (used to keep out foreign goods), and barriers to international bidding for government contracts.

In the mid-1980s, hundreds of petitions have been filed by industry and labor, asking the federal government to protect them from imports. In considerable part, this was due to the very strong dollar. As we shall see in the following chapter, the dollar's value relative to other currencies rose markedly from 1980 to 1983, the result being that foreign goods became much cheaper to American buyers. Also, in some industries like semiconductors, the quality of foreign goods sometimes exceeded that of American suppliers. Faced with very stiff competition from imports, American firms asked the government for protection.

As indicated in earlier sections of this chapter, the American consumer is the loser. Robert Crandall of the Brookings Institution has estimated that in 1983 the auto import quotas resulted in about a $400 per car increase in the price of U.S. cars and a $1,000 per car increase in the price of Japanese imports, the total cost to American consumers being over $4 billion in 1983 alone. According to Crandall, "The cost per job saved, therefore, was nearly $160,000 per year. Employment creation at this cost is surely not worth the candle."[7]

Most economists feel that the upsurge in protectionism in the mid-1980s

[7] R. Crandall, "Import Quotas and the Automobile Industry," *The Brookings Review*, Summer 1984, p. 16.

The EEC, born in the embers of World War II, was fathered by a desire to bind Germany to the rest of Europe. The success of the European Steel and Coal Community and the Benelux union encouraged the "Europeanists," and in 1957 the Treaty of Rome formally proclaimed the birth of a six-country free-trade area in which labor, capital, and goods were to move freely. None of this was to happen instantaneously, but the six countries—France, Germany, Italy, Belgium, the Netherlands, and Luxembourg—did agree on a timetable for the removal of centuries-old barriers and on a commission and council to manage the details of the process.

Headquarters of the European Economic Community, Brussels

There are ample statistics to tell what happened after the EEC was formed—relatively high growth rates, increased competitiveness by European firms, increases in per capita incomes, and increased membership (including Great Britain). But the flavor of this customs union comes through best by seeing what it has meant to three prototype economic people.

Nino T. was born in southern Italy, where reported unemployment has been 14 percent. If disguised unemployment were included, the rate might run as high as double that. Wages, for those with jobs, averaged about $20 per week. In 1965, he migrated to Germany to work in an automobile plant in Frankfort, where he could make $75 a week, and send back $40 to his family. He planned to stay for another two years—perhaps until he had saved enough to buy a small business.

Elizabeth C. works for a leather-goods firm in London. When Britain joined the Common Market, her chief worry was that it would mean higher food prices. Why? Because the technologically inefficient but politically powerful French farmer demanded protection from cheap American and Canadian food. Thus, while French wheat would flow freely into Great Britain, the high external tariff would now keep out North American wheat.

Richard B., an American businessman, now lives in Paris, managing the French subsidiary of a large New York-based corporation. He was moved to Paris about 20 years ago, when company officials decided that the removal of internal barriers by the EEC would allow U.S. companies to operate on the scale to which they were accustomed. To stay competitive in the European market, they decided to build production facilities inside the EEC, rather than producing in the U.S. and shipping abroad. Richard now finds himself very much at home in France, and seriously considers living out his days in Paris.

E.A.

is an unfortunate development. Although they understand that it will be difficult to beat back the protectionist tide, they hope that this upsurge of protectionist spirit will be short-lived, and that developments here and abroad will enable us and our trading partners to move closer to the realization of the benefits of free trade.

Test Yourself

1. According to Hendrik Houthakker, "Our workers get high real income not because they are protected from foreign competition, but because they are highly productive, at least in certain industries." Do you agree? Why or why not?

2. According to Richard Cooper, "Technological innovation can undoubtedly strengthen the competitive position of a country in which the innovation takes place, whether it be one which enlarges exports or displaces imports." Give examples of this phenomenon, and discuss various ways that one might measure the effects of technological innovation on a country's competitive position.

3. "The principle of comparative advantage doesn't work. The U.S. exports electronic computers to Japan and imports electronic consumer goods like TV sets from Japan." Comment and evaluate.

4. Would you favor a high tariff on imported steel if you were (a) an automobile worker, (b) a steel worker, (c) an automobile buyer, (d) a plastics worker? Explain your reasoning in each case.

Summary

1. International trade permits specialization, and specialization increases output. This is the advantage of trade, both for individuals and for nations.

2. Country A has an absolute advantage over Country B in the production of a good when Country A can produce a unit of the good with less resources than can Country B. Trade can be mutually beneficial even if one country has an absolute advantage in the production of all goods.

3. Specialization and trade depend on comparative, not absolute, advantage. A nation is said to have a comparative advantage in those products where its efficiency relative to other nations is highest. Trade can be mutually beneficial if a country specializes in the products where it has a comparative advantage and imports the products where it has a comparative disadvantage.

4. If markets are relatively free and competitive, producers will automatically be led to produce in accord with comparative advantage. If a country has a comparative advantage in the production of a certain good, it will turn out—after the price of the good in various countries is equalized and total world output of the good equals total world demand—that this country is an exporter of the good under free trade.

5. Specialization may occur because of economies of scale and learning. Also, some countries develop new products and processes, which they export to other countries until the technology becomes widely available.

6. A tariff is a tax imposed by the government on imports, the purpose being to cut down on imports in order to protect domestic industry and workers from foreign competition. Tariffs benefit the protected industry at the expense of the general public, and, in general, a tariff costs the general public more than the protected industry (and its workers and suppliers) gains.

7. Quotas are another barrier to free trade. They too reduce trade, raise prices, protect domestic industry from foreign competition, and reduce the standard of living of the nation as a whole.

8. Tariffs, quotas, and other barriers to free trade can sometimes be justified on the basis of national security and other noneconomic considerations. Moreover, tariffs and other forms of protection can sometimes be justified to protect infant industries, to prevent a country from being too dependent on only a few industries, and to carry out other national objectives. But many arguments for tariffs are fallacious.

9. In our early years, we were a very protectionist country. Our tariffs remained relatively high until the 1930s, when a movement began toward free trade. Between 1934 and 1948, our tariff rates dropped substantially. Again during the 1960s, there was a significant reduction in our tariffs. But more recently, as some of our industries (like steel) have been hit hard by imports, there has been a tendency to push for more protectionist measures. During the 1980s, the protectionist tide was very strong.

10. Although it has equaled only about 10 percent of our gross national product, foreign trade is of very considerable importance to the American economy. Many of our industries rely on foreign countries for raw materials or for markets, and our consumers buy many kinds of imported goods. In absolute terms, our exports and imports are larger than those of any other nation.

Concepts for Review

Exports
Imports
Absolute advantage
Comparative advantage
Production possibilities
  curve

Trading possibilities
  curve
Terms of trade
Multinational firm
Tariff
Prohibitive tariff

Quota
Export subsidy
European Economic
  Community
  (Common Market)

CHAPTER 19

The Communist Countries and Marxism

Everybody talks and reads about *communism.* You hear the word frequently on television and see it frequently in the newspapers, but if you really know what it means, you are in the minority. It is a safe bet that most people have only a vague and distorted idea of what communism is, partly because the relationship in recent years between the Communist and non-Communist countries has been marked by suspicion, dissension, and sometimes war. Yet about a third of the world's population lives under Communist rule. The Soviet Union, China, Yugoslavia, Cuba, and many other countries are Communist. You should know something about the nature of communism to understand what is going on in a large part of the world.

In this chapter we describe and analyze the nature and workings of the economic system in various Communist countries, with our major emphasis on the Soviet Union. After a brief discussion of the doctrines of Karl Marx, the intellectual father of communism, we describe how the Soviet economy works. Since economic planning plays a major role in its functioning, the USSR's planning system is described in some detail. Next, we turn to the economy of China, and to some of the major differences between communism and democratic socialism. Finally, we describe briefly the nature of radical economics, a recent, and still very small, movement in the United States that draws heavily on Marx's views.

The Doctrines of Karl Marx

THE CLASS STRUGGLE

The name Karl Marx probably makes you think of revolutionaries meeting by candlelight in damp cellars to plot the overthrow of nineteenth-century European governments. If this is the picture you associate with the name, you are quite right! Karl Marx was a revolutionary who wanted the masses to revolt against the existing social order. In 1848, he and Friedrich Engels published the famous *Communist Manifesto,* the spirit of which is given by its closing lines:

> Communists ... openly declare that their ends can be attained only by the forcible overthrow of all existing social conditions. Let the ruling classes tremble at a Communist revolution. The proletarians have nothing to lose but their chains. They have a world to win. Workers of the world, unite!

Karl Marx

This is stirring language, no doubt about it. But why did Marx preach revolution, and what goals do the communists want to achieve?

To understand their aims, it is helpful to look at Marx's famous treatise, *Capital* (the first part of which was published in 1867), which states much of his economic and political thought. According to Marx, the fundamental causes of political and social change are socioeconomic factors. Changes in the ways goods and services are produced and distributed—and in the ways in which people enter into "productive relations" with one another (the feudal lord with the serf under feudalism, or the capitalist with the worker under capitalism)—are responsible for the great political and social movements of history. History can be viewed as a series of class struggles. In ancient times, the struggle was between masters and slaves. In feudal times, it was between lords and serfs. And in modern times, it is between the **capitalists,** who own the means of production, and the workers, or **proletariat.**

According to Marx, every economic system—ancient, feudal, or modern—develops certain defects or internal contradictions, which eventually cause it to give way to a new system. As the old system begins to weaken, the new system gains strength. Thus the feudal system grew out of the ancient system, and the modern system grew out of the feudal system. In Marx's view, *the struggle between the capitalists and the proletariat will eventually result in the defeat of the capitalists. This will set the stage for a new economic system—socialism, a transitional phase toward communism.* Communism, according to Marx, is the ultimate, perfect form of economic system.

THE THEORY OF VALUE AND WAGES

The reasons for Marx's belief that in modern times there must be a struggle between capitalists and workers lie in his theory of value and wages. *According to Marx, the* **value** *of any commodity—that is, its price relative to other commodities—is determined by the amount of labor time used in its manufacture.* In other words, if a shirt requires twice as much labor time to produce as a tie, its price is twice that of a tie. By labor time, Marx meant both the amount of labor used in making a commodity and the amount of labor time "congealed" in the machinery used to make the commodity. According to Marx, wages tend to equal the lowest level consistent with the subsistence of the workers, because capitalists, driven by the profit motive, pay the lowest wage they can.

Combining his theory of value and his theory of wages, Marx concluded that workers produce a *surplus value*—a value above and beyond the subsistence wage they receive—which is taken by the capitalists. This surplus value arises because the capitalists make the workers labor for longer hours than are required to produce an amount of output equal to their wage. Consider the worker who may be made to work 10 hours a day, even though her output in 6 hours equals the value of her wage. The output produced in the remaining 4 hours is surplus value.

According to Marx, surplus value is what makes the capitalist world tick. Indeed, the reason why capitalists engage in production is to make this surplus value, which they steal from the workers. Capitalists also use some of it to purchase new capital. Thus capital formation, in Marx's view, comes about as a consequence of surplus value. If the capitalist class is exploiting the workers in the way Marx visualized, it is not difficult to see why he felt that a class struggle between capitalists and workers was inevitable, and even easier to see why he was on the workers' side.

MARX'S VISION OF THE FUTURE

In Marx's view, capitalism would eventually reveal certain fundamental weaknesses that would hasten its demise. As more and more capital is accumulated, Marx felt that the profit rate would be driven down, that unemployment would increase (because of a rise in technological unemployment), that business cycles would become more severe (depressions becoming more devastating), and that monopoly would grow more widespread. As these developments imposed greater and greater hardships on the working class, the chance of revolution would increase. Eventually the workers, recognizing that they "have nothing to lose but their chains," would throw off the yoke of capitalism.

However, Marx did not visualize an immediate progression to communism. Instead, he saw socialism as a way station on the road to communism. *Socialism would be a "dictatorship of the proletariat."* The workers would rule. Specifically, they would control the government, which, according to Marx, is merely a tool of the propertied class under capitalism. Moreover, the socialist government would own the means of production—the factories, mines, and equipment. Under socialism each person would receive an amount of income related to the amount he or she produced.

Finally, after an unspecified length of time, Marx felt that socialism would give way to communism, his ideal system. Communism would be a classless society, everyone working, and no one owning capital or exploiting the other person. Under communism, the state would become obsolete and wither away. The principle of income distribution would be, "From each according to his ability, to each according to his needs." Marx was a visionary and a social prophet, and communism was his promised land, the ultimate goal for which he prodded the workers to revolt—and the land into which the forces of history would ultimately propel them.

CRITICISMS OF MARX

Since Marx's doctrines have captured the imagination of huge numbers of people, and hundreds of millions now march under his banners, it is clear that Marx was a remarkable success as a social philosopher and political activist. But what about Marx the economist? Most economists feel that his economic theories have basic flaws, and that many of his economic predictions have gone badly astray. Although there is almost universal admiration for the power and originality of his mind, few economists in the non-Communist world buy his economic doctrines.

Specifically, there are the following problems with his theories:

1. His labor theory of value simply will not hold water. As we have seen in previous chapters, the price of a commodity depends on nonlabor costs as well as labor costs. In particular, capital, land, and entrepreneurship contribute to production. Moreover, the price of a commodity depends on the demand for it as well as on its costs. (You will recall that price is determined by the intersection of the demand curve and the supply curve.)

2. Marx's subsistence theory of wages has long been discredited. It simply isn't true that wages are set at the subsistence level. Far from being barely sufficient to keep the worker alive, wages in the United States are high enough to provide the typical worker with a car, television, travel, and a variety of other conveniences. Further, Marx's prediction that the working class would experience greater and greater misery has not been fulfilled. On the contrary, the standard of living of workers in the West has increased at a remarkable rate in the century since Marx wrote *Capital.*

3. His prediction that the rate of profit would fall has been wrong. Instead, the rate of profit has moved up and down, with no clear trend in either direction. And his prediction of greater warfare between capitalists and workers has not materialized either. On the contrary, workers have tended to buy shares in corporations, thus joining the capitalist class. And the lines of demarcation between the working class and the capitalist class have been blurred, not accentuated, by time.

Nonetheless, despite these and other flaws in his theories, Marx was a very important figure in economics. He recognized some of the most important problems of capitalism—in particular the problems of unemployment, income inequality, and monopoly power—and analyzed these problems forcefully and originally. One need not agree with his ideas, or sympathize with some of his followers, to recognize his remarkable talents.

The Soviet Economy

COMMUNISM IN THE USSR

The economy of the Soviet Union provides an important example of the application of Marxian theories. By the beginning of the twentieth century, **Marxism** was an international political force of some significance. In 1917,

---

Basic Idea #37: *According to Marx, socialism would be characterized by government ownership of the means of production. The workers would rule, and each person would receive an income related to the amount he or she produced. Eventually, in Marx's view, socialism would lead to communism, in which everyone would work, no one would own capital, the state would wither away, and income would be distributed according to need.*

May Day in Moscow

a Marxist-oriented party established itself in Russia. This was the first time any major country went communist. With V. I. Lenin at its helm, the Communist party overthrew the Russian government in November 1917, and set up the Union of Soviet Socialist Republics several years later. The stated goal of the party was to establish Marxian socialism—and eventually communism—in the USSR. When Lenin died in 1924, his place was taken by Josef Stalin, who ruled until his death in 1953. Since the USSR is now by far the most economically advanced and militarily strongest Communist country, we need to understand how its economy works.

Two characteristics of the Soviet economy should be stressed at the outset:

1. Although Marx seemed to want the state eventually to wither away, the Soviet government is a remarkably hardy perennial. The Kremlin's influence over Russian life is well known. Power is centralized in the hands of a relatively few Communist officials who make the big decisions about what is to be produced, how it is to be produced, and who is to receive how much. This contrasts with capitalist economies like ours, where these decisions are made largely in the market place.

2. In accord with Marx's views, most productive resources in the Soviet Union are publicly owned. The government owns the factories, mines, equipment, and so on. This too is quite different from the situation in the United States, where most productive resources are privately owned. Specifically, the Soviet government owns practically all industry, most retail and wholesale stores, and most urban housing. Some farms are government-owned, but most are collective farms. The principal case of private ownership in the Soviet Union is the small strip of land each family on a collective farm is allowed to work for itself. In addition, people are allowed to own furniture, clothing, utensils, and sometimes houses.

Soviet Economic Planning

The Soviet Union's central planners decide what the country will produce. How do they go about making these decisions, what steps do they follow, and who is involved in this process? Before trying to answer these questions, it is important to recognize that the procedures followed by the central planners change from time to time as they recognize their mistakes and try to rectify them. Planning and controlling a vast economy like the Soviet Union's is enormously complicated. In the period immediately after the Russian Revolution of 1917, the Communists made some whopping mistakes, but as time went on, the planners became better able to carry out their jobs.

This is the general procedure that evolved. First, the principal officials of the Communist party made the fundamental decisions as to how much output would be allocated for consumption and how much for investment, which industries would be expanded and which would be cut back. Once these decisions were made, people at a lower level decided the details concerning how various plants should be operated. Then these decisions were transmitted to and carried out by managers, engineers, and workers. This decision-making process is clearly very centralized. During the 1960s,

Table 19.1

THE ELEVENTH FIVE-YEAR PLAN FOR THE SOVIET UNION, 1981–85

Item	Actual output in 1980	Planned output for 1985
Electric power (billions of kilowatt hours)	1,295	1,550–1,600
Oil (million tons)	603	620–645
Natural gas (billion M³)	435	600–640
Coal (million tons)	716	770–800
Steel (million tons)	148	n.a.
Grain (million tons)	205	238–243
Meat (million tons)	14.9	17–17.5
Cement (million tons)	125	140–142

Source: D. Bond and H. Levine, "The Eleventh Five-Year Plan, 1981–85," 1981.

the Russians began to experiment with greater decentralization, delegating more of the planning to the individual plants and industries, and doing less of it centrally. But these reforms met with resistance, as we shall see below.

Several groups are involved in planning. The top officials of the Communist party establish the overall goals for the economy. These goals are generally enunciated in a *five-year plan,* which shows where the economy should be in five years. Table 19.1 shows part of the Soviet Union's Eleventh Five-Year Plan, for 1981–85. One goal was to increase electric power production by about 22 percent (about 4 percent per year). When the broad goals are decided, the detailed production plans are drawn up by *Gosplan,* the State Planning Commission. Gosplan obtains enormous amounts of data from the ministries responsible for the performance of particular industries. These data describe production capacities of various productive units and available productive resources. On this basis, Gosplan formulates a tentative production plan.

Once Gosplan's tentative plan is formulated, a host of other groups enters the picture. A number of ministries, each concerned with a particular industry, reports to Gosplan in the Soviet administrative hierarchy. These ministries review Gosplan's tentative plan, as do individual plant managers. The purpose of this evaluation is to make sure that the plan is realistic and feasible. Some plant managers will argue that the amount they are asked to produce is too high or that the amount of labor and materials they are allocated is too low. Negotiations take place, and suggestions for revision are sent back to Gosplan. Eventually Gosplan produces the final five-year plan.

ECONOMIC PLANNING: A SIMPLE ILLUSTRATION

The job faced by the Soviet planners is difficult and complex. Unless you have some appreciation of how tough it is, you cannot understand the difficulties any planned economy must face. Suppose you are handed the job of planning the performance of a small economy consisting of a chemical industry, a coal industry, and an electric power industry. To produce electric power, one needs coal, chemicals, electric power, and

Table 19.2

AMOUNT OF EACH INPUT USED PER DOLLAR OF OUTPUT

| Type of input | Type of output | | |
	Electric power	Coal	Chemicals
	(dollars)		
Electric	0.1	0.3	0.0
Coal	0.5	0.1	0.0
Chemicals	0.2	0.0	0.9
Labor	0.2	0.6	0.1
Total	1.0	1.0	1.0

labor as inputs. To produce coal, one needs electric power, coal, and labor as inputs. To produce chemicals, one needs chemicals and labor as inputs. Suppose that the country's political rulers have said that in five years they want the country to consume $100 million of electric power, $50 million of coal, and $50 million of chemicals.

It is not easy to decide what production targets to establish for each industry. For one thing, the output set for one industry must depend on the output set for another industry because each industry uses another's output. Thus, if you are not careful, one industry will be unable to achieve its target because another industry has produced too little. Suppose that each industry uses the products of the other industries in the proportions shown in Table 19.2. (The second column of figures, for example, states that every dollar's worth of coal requires $.30 worth of electric power, $.10 worth of coal, and $.60 worth of labor.) Under these circumstances, what should the production targets be? The answer isn't obvious. Try it and see. (It can be shown that the production targets must be as follows. In five years, $144 million of coal, $159 million of electric power, and $818 million of chemicals must be produced. For a proof, see pp. A13–A14.)

This illustration gives you some inkling of the problems faced by the Soviet planners—but only an inkling. Our illustration has only three industries, while in fact the Russians have to deal with thousands. In the illustration, the input-output coefficients (in Table 19.2) were assumed known. In fact, these coefficients change over time and are not very accurately known. In this simple illustration, we can work out the production target for each industry, using straightforward mathematical techniques. The Soviet planning problem is so much bigger and more complicated that it is impossible, even with the most sophisticated mathematical techniques and the biggest computers, to solve their planning problem the way we could solve it for the three-industry economy.

Priorities and Performance

To make the planning problem more tractable, the Soviets set higher priorities for certain production goals than for others. Thus they may set a goal for the production of houses and a goal for the production of missiles, but the production of missiles may be given higher priority. If trouble arises in meeting this production goal, the planners may take resources away from the housing industry to make sure the higher-priority goal is achieved. This makes the planner's job a little easier, but does not guarantee that the economy will be very efficient.

The best-laid plans can go awry. To make sure theirs do not, the Russians have a number of important organizations to check on the performances of plants and managers. First, there is the *Gosbank,* the state-run banking system. When the plan is published, the Gosbank gives the managers of each plant enough money to buy the resources—labor, materials, and so on—allocated to their plant. If the managers run out of money, they are using more resources than the plan called for. Also, when the managers sell the plant's output, the receipts must be deposited in the Gosbank. If the deposit is less than the value of output specified in the plan, it is clear that the plant has produced less than the plan called for. In this way, the Gosbank keeps close tabs on the performance of various plants. Second, the *State Control Commission* has inspectors who visit plants and go over the records of the Gosbank. Third, officials of the Communist party are expected to report poor performance to the party bosses.

SOVIET MANAGERS AND WORKERS

The Soviet economy is a **command economy**—people are told what to do. The managers of an industrial plant are told that to fulfill the plan, they must produce a certain amount, their **quota.** Moreover, they are authorized to spend a specific amount on wages (they are free to hire labor in the labor market), and to purchase a specified amount of raw materials and equipment. Their job is to carry out these orders, but they are not told *how* to run their plant. That is up to them. The Soviets have introduced managerial incentives not too different from those in the West. If managers are resourceful and diligent, they may be able to exceed their quota. In this case the Soviets—like good capitalists—reward them with extra pay, honors, and perhaps a promotion. If they are lazy, foolish, or unlucky, they may fall short of their quota, which may lead to a pay cut or disgrace.

However, because managers have generally been judged on whether they have met their quotas, certain problems have arisen. Managers have tried to underestimate what their plants could produce in order to get easy quotas. They have tried to hoard and conceal materials and labor so that they would appear to use less resources than they did. And they have sometimes allowed the quality of their product to decline in order to meet their quota. Moreover, managers have been loath to introduce new methods or other innovations because of the risks involved. If a new method did not pan out, it could mean Siberia for the manager. Better play it safe, even though this hurts productivity over the long run.

Soviet workers have considerable freedom to determine where they work. However, farm workers are not allowed to leave the farms, and personnel are not allowed to leave certain projects of great importance to the government. To get work of the right kind done to fulfill the plan, the planners set up wage differentials to induce people to do the needed work. This is quite similar to the sorts of incentives that prevail under capitalism. In addition, however, other pressures are used to get people to work hard and in accord with the plan. The government provides medals and awards to workers who do very well. The labor unions, which are really part of the state, push for higher productivity. And people who perform poorly may be fined or penalized in other ways. Nonetheless, labor problems of various kinds exist. There are many complaints that Soviet workers are unnecessarily late and absent from their jobs, and that labor turnover is far higher than it should be.

Prices in the USSR

As we have seen in earlier chapters, prices in a market economy allocate resources in a way that promotes the goals and satisfactions of the con-

State Department Store, Moscow

sumers. Obviously, prices in the Soviet Union do not function like this. On the contrary, they are set by the government to promote the goals of the state. Note that there are two fundamental differences here between the United States and the Soviet Union. Prices are set largely by the market in the United States; they are set by the government in the USSR. And prices should promote the goals of consumers in the United States, but promote the goals of the government in the USSR.

PRICES TO PRODUCERS

More specifically, how are prices set—and how are they used—in the Soviet Union? The answer varies depending on whether one adopts the point of view of a producer or a consumer. First, consider a producer—a plant producing shoes, say. The government sets the price of the shoes, as well as the prices of the labor, materials, and other inputs the producer uses. The government tries to set these prices so that a firm of average efficiency will run neither a profit nor a loss. Thus the system of prices is used to determine whether a producer is relatively efficient or relatively inefficient. If a plant makes a profit, this is evidence that it is efficient; a loss is evidence that it is inefficient.

This is no different from capitalism. But in the USSR, prices of inputs do not reflect the relative scarcity of inputs, as they do in capitalistic economies. Moreover, the price system in the USSR does not determine the output of each commodity, as it does under capitalism. Instead, as we saw in the previous section, government planning determines target output levels.

PRICES TO CONSUMERS

Next, let's consider the prices consumers must pay for goods and services. The function performed by these prices is quite different from that performed by the prices that producers must pay. While the prices facing producers are used to gauge the producers' efficiency (and how well they perform according to the plan), the prices facing consumers are used to ration the consumer goods that are produced. Thus the price of a commodity to the producer is likely to be quite different from its price to the consumer. For example, the price of a pair of shoes may be 10 rubles to the producer and 20 rubles to the consumer. Why 20 rubles to the consumer? Because 20 rubles is the price the government feels will equate the amount demanded with the amount being produced.

Consumer prices are set with an eye toward raising the planned revenue needed for investment. The gap between the price to the consumer and the price to the producer is the **turnover tax.** The turnover tax rate—100 percent in the case of the shoes, since the difference between the two prices, 10 rubles, is the same as the price to the producer—varies considerably from commodity to commodity. It provides a good deal of the Soviet government's revenue, and is a way to reduce inflationary pressures and make consumer spending fit in with the government's economic plan.

The Distribution of Income

At this point, recall that one of the fundamental tasks of any economic system is to distribute the society's output among the people. Do citizens in the Soviet Union receive income in accord with their needs, as Marx envisioned? The answer clearly is no. The Soviet planners set incomes in accord with the type of work people do, how hard they work, and how productive they are. The result is a great deal of income inequality in the Soviet Union. If we look only at income from labor, the extent of income inequality is about as great there as in the United States. However, for all types of income (including interest, dividends, and capital gains, none of which exist in the Soviet Union), there is more income inequality in the United States.

Example 19.1   A Peek Behind Soviet Price Tags

Consider two goods, X and Y, produced and sold in the Soviet Union. The average production cost, factory profit margin, turnover tax, wholesalers' margin and retail margin of each good is shown below (in rubles):

	Good X	Good Y
Average cost of production	100	100
Factory's profit margin	5	5
Factory wholesale price	105	105
Turnover tax	50	15
Wholesalers' margin	5	5
Retail margin	10	10
Retail price	170	135

(a) Do consumers value an extra unit of good X more or less than an extra unit of good Y? (b) Is the cost of producing a unit of good X more or less than that of producing a unit of good Y? (c) Given that the ratio of retail price to cost of production is so much higher for good X than for good Y, will the planners increase the output of good X relative to that of good Y? (d) Why is the turnover tax higher for good X than for good Y?

SOLUTION

(a) They value an extra unit of good X more than an extra unit of good Y, since they are willing to pay 170 rubles for an extra unit of good X but only 135 rubles for an extra unit of good Y. (b) The cost is 100 rubles for both a unit of good X and a unit of good Y. (c) Not if this is counter to their objectives. Output levels are determined to promote the goals of the state. (d) Because the government feels that it must be higher for good X in order to equate the amount demanded with the amount being produced.*

* For further discussion, see Alec Nove, *The Soviet Economy,* New York: Praeger, 1968.

It is important to recognize that about three-fourths of all Soviet industrial workers are paid according to *piece rates.* The amount these workers receive is determined by how much output they turn out. Thus, to a much greater extent than in the United States, income is tied directly to a person's production. This is an important reason for the considerable income inequality in the USSR. Moreover, the Soviet labor unions do not play the same role American unions do. Whereas wage differentials in the United States have often been narrowed by union pressures, such pressures have not been exerted by unions in the USSR. It is very interesting, and understandable, that the Communists have emphasized monetary incentives to coax people to produce more.

INCOME DIFFERENTIALS

In the Soviet Union, as in the United States, occupations differ greatly in pay and status. Distinguished Soviet scientists and professors, leading ballet and opera stars, and important government officials and industrial managers are at the top of the heap. Their incomes are perhaps 20 times as high as that of an unskilled laborer, and they have the good housing, the plush vacations, the cars, and other luxuries that are scarce in the Soviet Union. The unskilled and semiskilled workers get the lowest incomes in the Soviet Union, as they do elsewhere. This doesn't mean, however, that various occupations cannot change their position in the salary scale. On the contrary, the Soviet planners push wages for various types of work up or down in order to get the labor required to help fulfill the plan.

To put a floor under the living standards of the poor, the Soviet government provides many free services, including education and health care. Also, the government provides other services at a very low price. For example, very low-rent housing—most of which is government-owned—is available. These programs help reduce income inequality by supplementing the incomes of the poor. The turnover tax, discussed above, is used to finance these programs.

Soviet Economic Growth

A nation's rate of economic growth is often used as an indicator of its performance. Has the Soviet economy been growing more rapidly than the economies of the United States and other non-Communist countries? Before trying to answer this question, it is essential to recognize that the United States is far in front of the Soviet Union economically. *Our gross national product (in real terms) is about double that of the Soviet Union. Consequently, since our population is smaller than theirs, per capita gross national product in the United States is more than twice that in the Soviet Union.* When comparing the growth rates of the two countries, keep these facts in mind.

The Fifties. In the 1950s, the Soviet Union achieved a very rapid rate of economic growth. American observers watched with some uneasiness as the

Soviet gross national product increased at about 7 percent per year, while our own increased much more slowly. This remarkable Soviet performance was partly responsible for President Kennedy's decision in the early 1960s to attempt to increase our own growth rate. One important reason for the rapid Soviet growth was the heavy investment by the Russians in plant and equipment. Investment constituted about 30 percent of gross national product, in contrast to about 15 percent in the United States. Soviet planners kept a tight lid on consumption. Indeed, consumption per capita grew little, if at all, from the late 1920s to the late 1950s. Soviet consumers were not allowed to increase their standard of living. The increases in production went primarily to build factories and equipment and to build military power. Other reasons for the high Soviet growth rate were the fact that the Soviets could—and did—borrow Western technology, and that the Soviet system does not tolerate unemployment.

The Sixties and Seventies. In the 1960s and 1970s, the Soviet growth rate seemed to slump. This, together with the fact that many people began to place somewhat less emphasis on the growth rate as a measure of economic performance, resulted in less concern in the United States over the Soviet growth rate, less pressure for government measures to increase our growth rate, and less talk about "growthmanship." According to leading Kremlin watchers, an important reason for the decline in the Soviet growth rate was the greater emphasis on consumption in the post-Stalin Soviet Union. The Communist leaders began to allocate more to the consumer, and this increase in consumption goods meant a decrease in the production of investment goods, which in turn lowered the growth rate.

The Eighties and Beyond. According to the best available estimates, the Soviet growth rate has remained relatively low during the 1980s, a fact which has caused considerable concern among Soviet leaders. At this point, it should be clear that the social mechanisms determining the rate of economic growth in the Soviet Union are entirely different from those that determine the rate of economic growth in the United States. In the Soviet Union, the central planners attempt to determine the growth rate by their decisions on the rate of investment in various industries, the amount spent on research and development, and the rate of expansion of the educational system. In the United States, on the other hand, decision making is decentralized. The American growth rate is determined largely by countless decisions by consumers and producers attempting to reach their own goals.

Since per capita gross national product is so much lower in the Soviet Union than in the United States, it seems extremely doubtful that the Soviet Union will catch up with us for a long time. Even if the Soviet growth rate were to exceed ours by a full percentage point, it would be sometime in the twenty-first century before their GNP catches up with ours, and since their population exceeds ours, it would be even further in the future before their per capita GNP equals ours. In addition, an even more fundamental question is whether any real tragedy would ensue if the Russians did narrow the income gap considerably. Since gross national product is a poor measure of military power, an increase in Soviet GNP by itself certainly would not imperil American security.

Soviet industry in the 1980s

Evaluation of the Soviet Economy

SOVIET ECONOMIC PERFORMANCE

In previous sections, we've described the salient features of the Soviet economy. Now let's try to evaluate its performance. Needless to say, any such evaluation must be incomplete. And since we look at the Soviet economy through American eyes, it is sure to be biased—at least in the eyes of the Soviets and other Communists. But we cannot avoid trying to make such an evaluation, despite the many formidable problems involved.

Freedom. One's evaluation of the Soviet economy must depend fundamentally on the value one places on freedom. The USSR is a command economy; to us, its economy is not free. The planners decide what is produced, how it is produced, and who is to get what. A centrally planned economy of this sort may be able to push industrialization and economic growth at a rapid rate, but at a great cost in economic freedom and in living standards. The Soviet planners have decided to build tractors, not cars; dams, not housing; and blast furnaces, not refrigerators. This emphasis on investment has increased future living standards, but that may be small comfort to those called on to make these sacrifices—people who, it should be recalled, have had a much lower standard of living than their counterparts in the industrialized Western countries.

Equity. It is difficult to say much about the equity of the income distribution, since there is no scientifically valid way to say that one income distribution is better than another. This is an ethical question, which people must answer for themselves. Perhaps the most interesting aspect of the income distribution in the Soviet Union is that it contains so much inequality. There is less difference between the Soviet Union and the Western industrialized countries in the extent of income inequality than one might expect. Thus those who favor more income equality may find less to say for the Soviet economy than might be expected.

Efficiency. It is clear that the Russian economy works—and that in many respects it works very well indeed. However, it is also plagued by problems. First, as noted above, incentives for innovation have been weak. Managers, fearful of not meeting their quotas, often resist new techniques. Second, since the planners, not the market, dictate what will be produced, goods consumers do not want are sometimes produced. The link between consumers and producers is not as firm as in the Western economies. Third, the use of production quotas and targets has led to inefficiency. Thus, if the quota for a pencil factory is expressed in terms of number of pencils, the manager of the factory may reduce the quality or size of the pencils in order to meet the quota. Fourth, since input prices do not reflect relative scarcities, they may give improper signals to producers. Fifth, the Soviet Union has had many setbacks in agriculture. Its farms produced about 6 percent less in 1975 than in 1974, and about 4 percent less in 1974 than in 1973. In 1979, its wheat crop was about 25 percent less than expected, due largely to bad weather. In 1980 and 1981, its grain production was considerably less than its grain consumption. To some extent, the poor performance of Soviet agriculture seems due to the fact that many farms are too big, and that there are too few incentives for efficiency.[1]

[1] Responding to this situation, the United States, as well as Canada, Australia, and other countries, has sold many billions of dollars of grain to the Soviets.

Mikhail Gorbachev

CHANGES IN THE SOVIET ECONOMY

The Soviet economy experienced a substantial decrease in its growth rate in the early 1960s. This led to a considerable amount of self-criticism by Soviet economists. Many of the problems just cited—resistance to innovation, mismatches between what is produced and what consumers want, inefficiency due to the stress on production quotas—were admitted by some Soviet economists, and there was much discussion of possible solutions. Among the most influential economists arguing for economic reforms was Professor Y. Liberman of Kharkov University, who proposed several kinds of changes. First, he favored more decentralized decision making. Plant managers should be allowed to decide on their work force, the wages they want to pay, the supplies they want to use, and the improvements they want to make in their equipment. Second, a plant's efficiency should be gauged by the ratio of its profit to its capital investment—a dangerously capitalistic concept. To prod managers and workers to increase efficiency, the bonuses received by managers and the benefits received by workers should vary with the plant's profits. Third, to promote a better match between the goods produced and what consumers want, the profits of a plant should be linked to the amount of goods sold rather than the amount of goods produced. Fourth, interest—long banished from the Communist world—should be resurrected. Recognizing that the interest rate is a device to ration scarce capital, Liberman proposed that interest charges, imposed as a tax, be made for the use of capital by plants.

During the early 1960s, the Communists began to experiment with changes of this sort. As favorable results were achieved by the decentralized decision making and emphasis on "profits" that Liberman proposed, these innovations spread throughout the economy. By 1968, perhaps one-fourth of the Soviet economy was characterized by this "new look"—a remarkable shift toward decentralization and Western economic concepts. But the Soviets have had difficulties in operating an economy that is part planned and part market-oriented, and many of the Soviet central planners distrust the "new look." When the Soviet economy fell short of its production goals in the late 1960s, there was a shift back toward centralization.

In 1983, the late Yuri Andropov, who briefly was head of the Soviet government, made some sweeping criticisms of the inefficiencies in the Soviet economic system. He called for greater authority for local plant managers and increased labor discipline (e.g., less absenteeism and drunkenness). In 1985, Mikhail Gorbachev, a protégé of Andropov, became leader of the Soviet government, after the death of Konstantin Chernenko. In his acceptance speech, he called for "restructuring the material and technical base of production." But the extent of the changes he will bring about, and the future direction of the Soviet economy, remains uncertain. It may move further toward greater decentralization and Western economic concepts, or it may revert to its older style of operation. In his first months in office, Gorbachev seemed to encourage manager autonomy, pay incentives, and the full-scale use of computerization. The authority of Gosplan seemed to be curtailed.

1. In recent years, has the Soviet Union's rate of economic growth tended to decline? Has its rate of productivity growth (that is, the rate of growth of output relative to input) tended to decline as well? If so, why?

2. Describe the system of economic planning in the Soviet Union. To what extent is this system to be found in the writings of Karl Marx?

3. Discuss the differences between the United States and the Soviet Union in the way in which prices are determined. What are some of the most important economic effects of these differences?

4. Has the state "withered away" in the Soviet version of communism? Explain. What are some of the problems in Soviet planning?

The Chinese Economy

In 1949, another of the world's major powers—China—joined the Communist ranks. With Mao Tse-tung at its head, the Communist army entered Peking, the capital of a nation containing one-fourth of the world's population. China was a poor country, with little capital, little technology, and little education—a less developed country par excellence, despite its ancient civilization. Further, the Communists inherited an economy marred by many years of war with the Japanese. The country needed as much economic growth as possible, and quickly.

THE FIRST FIVE-YEAR PLAN

The Chinese Communists responded with a ruthless drive toward industrialization. China's Five-Year Plan of 1952–57 emphasized investment in heavy industry like steel and machinery and some expansion of light industry. It also called for a massive reorganization of agriculture, involving collective ownership of some farms and transfer of land from the rich to the poor. To permit the high rate of investment called for by the plan, the Chinese government pared consumption to the bone. The Chinese people were asked to work long and hard—for little return in goods and services.

Most observers agree that the plan achieved its goal of rapid economic growth. Even though China's population increased considerably, output per capita increased by about 4 or 5 percent per year during the 1950s. This was an enormous achievement for a country whose economy had been stagnant for centuries. To accomplish these objectives, China adopted measures that seem stern even when compared with the Soviet Union. (China, like the USSR, operates a command economy, but this has not prevented the development of considerable tension between them. To buttress its own position, each nation claims that the other has abandoned the true faith of Marxism.)

THE GREAT LEAP FORWARD

Having succeeded in pushing the economy ahead in the Five-Year Plan of 1952–57, in 1958 China's leaders launched a more ambitious plan, called the Great Leap Forward. Its aim was to increase per capita output by 25 percent. The large number of underemployed workers in China were to be swept into the employed labor force, and there was to be a great increase in investment. It all sounded very impressive on paper, but it turned out to be a disaster. Despite all the slogans and propaganda, the plan was unrealistic. Literally millions of people were asked to produce steel in primitive furnaces in their back yards. The result was a lot of unusable scrap metal. Also, poor planning directed millions of workers to produce other goods of little or no value. And too many people were ordered to leave agriculture and enter factories, with the result that far too little food was produced.

By 1960, the Great Leap Forward was obviously a failure of catastrophic proportions, and China's leaders had little choice but to alter their policies. In 1961, they published their new economic plan, which called for more emphasis on agriculture and less on industry. Industries that contributed to agricultural productivity—like the tractor industry—would receive more capital, while less would be devoted to industries that did not affect agriculture. Also, higher priority was given to the production of consumer goods for the peasants. Despite the new emphasis, the gains in agricultural production and efficiency seem to have been modest during the 1960s. Apparently, the Great Leap Forward had wreaked so much havoc that it was difficult to get agriculture moving ahead.

THE CULTURAL REVOLUTION

The so-called Cultural Revolution that began in 1968 saw large-scale political disorders in Communist China. Because the data on Chinese economic performance are meager and unreliable, even the experts find it difficult to estimate the effects of this social turmoil on the economy. But by 1971, it seemed likely that the economy had recovered in large part from the economic disorders arising from the Cultural Revolution. According to recent estimates by Thomas Rawski, Chinese industrial production in 1971 was perhaps double what it had been in 1963.

MOVEMENTS TOWARD DECENTRALIZATION

During the late 1970s and early 1980s, China, under the leadership of Vice-Premier Teng Hsiao-p'ing, began to move toward a more decentralized economic system where market forces were allowed to play an important role. In December 1978, China's Central Committee approved a new system of incentives for China's 800 million peasants, under which those that produced more were rewarded. The result was a sharp increase in farm output, and China's communes began to break up as individual households became the basic agricultural unit.

In October 1984, China announced sweeping changes in its urban economy. About a million state-owned enterprises were to be given greater independence—and the necessity to compete to survive. Extensive government subsidies for consumer products like food and clothing were to be phased out. Central planning was to be limited, and the prices of many products and services were to be determined by supply and demand. Unquestionably, this was a very important shift in China's economic system, but whether these changes will be permanent or temporary remains to be seen.

In any event, during 1983 and 1984, China's real economic growth was

Workers in a farm equipment factory

about 8 percent per year, which was impressive. According to many reports, the new emphasis on decentralization and greater economic freedom was having beneficial results.

Economic Life in China

Despite the economic gains it has achieved, China is still a less developed country. In 1980, its per capita income was less than one-seventh that in the United States. Over 50 percent of the typical wage earner's income goes for food, and many consumer goods, like rice and cloth, have been rationed, so that a family could buy only a certain amount per month. Automobiles are uncommon in China; the bicycle is the usual means of private transportation in cities. Workers have been divided into a number of strata, and wages have been uniform within each strata. The government has played an important role in determining where and in what position a particular person works. Labor markets have not been nearly as free as in the United States. In 1979, the government, in an attempt to control population growth, adopted a policy limiting each couple to one child.

CAPITAL FORMATION

To step up its rate of economic growth, China has devoted about 25 percent of its national output to capital formation. This is a high rate of investment, relative to developed countries as well as to other less developed countries. However, it must be recognized that this does not come from voluntary saving. Instead, it is due to government action. Because the educational and skill level of the population is low, it is difficult to invest this forced saving as productively as would otherwise be the case. The Russians, when they were on better terms with the Chinese, provided some technical assistance, but those days are long gone. At present, China finds it difficult to absorb the technology it so badly needs.

INDUSTRY AND AGRICULTURE

About four-fifths of China's population is engaged in agriculture, which contributes about 40 percent of GNP. Industrial production has been growing more rapidly than agricultural output. In 1983, industrial output increased by about 10 percent; in 1984, it increased by over 13 percent, according to Chinese officials.

INCOME DISTRIBUTION

The distribution of income in China is much less unequal than it was 30 years ago. Some economists, like John Gurley of Stanford University, believe that China has been able to eradicate abject poverty despite her economic adversities. According to Gurley,

> The basic, overriding economic fact about China is that for twenty years she has fed, clothed, and housed everyone.... Millions have not starved; sidewalks and

streets have not been covered with multitudes of sleeping, begging, hungry, and illiterate human beings; millions are not disease-ridden.[2]

It is difficult, however, to obtain reliable information about living conditions in so huge and diverse a country, particularly when very few Americans were allowed in China before President Nixon's visit in 1972. Many economists are less enthusiastic than Gurley about China's economic performance.[3] Also, some call attention to the price the Chinese have paid in what we would regard as regimentation and lack of political and social freedom.

U.S.-CHINA RELATIONS

In 1979, Chinese Vice-Premier Teng Hsiao-p'ing visited the United States —this being the first official visit by a high government official of China in about 30 years. The American government agreed to sell China a communications satellite system, among other things; and Teng expressed the hope that further American credit and technology would be made available to his country.

According to some estimates, U.S. exports to China in 1980 were about $3 billion, and China's exports to the U.S. were about $1 billion. During the early 1980s, the United States and China engaged in a variety of scientific and technological exchange programs. The Reagan administration and American firms tried in many ways to promote trade with China. Although Sino-American relations may not have improved as rapidly as some optimists forecasted in the late 1970s, they are certainly much warmer than they were several decades ago.

Democratic Socialism

We have described two brands of Communism—Russian and Chinese. And in previous chapters, we have described capitalism. Now we must stress that there are other types of economic systems besides capitalism and Communism. One of the most important of these is **democratic socialism,** which has included France's and Sweden's socialist governments and Britain's Labor government, among others. In many ways, the democratic socialist economies occupy a middle ground between our more capitalist system and the Communist systems. They generally favor government ownership of heavy industry like coal and steel (although the fervor for nationalization of such industries has died down in recent years); heavy taxation of the rich; and extensive welfare programs (social security, medical care, and so on); as well as a certain amount of economic planning, rather than the unfettered play of market forces.

But in contrast to the Communists, the democratic socialists generally do not favor violent revolution. Instead, they believe that democratic

[2] John Gurley, "Maoist Economic Development," in E. Mansfield, *Principles of Microeconomics: Readings, Issues, and Cases,* 4th ed., New York: Norton, 1983.

[3] For example, see James Tobin, "The Economy of China: A Tourist's View," in Mansfield, *Principles of Microeconomics: Readings, Issues, and Cases,* 4th ed.

means should be used to obtain power. A good example is the British Labor government, which came into office after World War II. During the 1920s and 1930s, the Labor party had worked within the existing political system and gained strength. Finally, after the war it got its hands on the reins. Since then the Labor party has remained a major influence in British politics (although it has been in and out of office). As it has gathered further experience, its goals have changed somewhat. Thus, because government ownership of industry seems to have been inefficient, the socialists are much more tolerant of private property, and less interested in nationalizing industry, than they were 25 years ago.

CHANGES IN THE U.S.

To a considerable extent, the more capitalist countries—like the United States—have taken over many of the socialist programs. The United States has moved a long way toward heavy taxation of the rich and toward extensive welfare programs. If Calvin Coolidge could be retrieved from the Great Beyond—and if Silent Cal could be induced to comment—he surely would be impressed (and perhaps dismayed) by how far the United States has traveled toward socialism since his presidency in the 1920s. Even though *planning* is viewed with suspicion in the United States, the government has become more and more involved in various aspects of our economic life, as we have seen in earlier chapters. The adoption by essentially capitalistic countries of many of their programs has taken some of the appeal—and some of the vitality and direction—from the socialists.

Radical Economics

RADICAL ECONOMICS AND THE NEW LEFT

In the United States in recent years, a new force in economics has appeared: *radical economics.* The radical economists, mainly young and still in the process of shaping their own contributions to the field, draw heavily on the views of Karl Marx. Looking at the urban, racial, environmental, and poverty problems of today, they argue that the conventional tools of economics are too biased toward maintaining the *status quo* to analyze many of these problems properly. They challenge the methods and assumptions of conventional economics, criticize conventional economists for neglecting many important social problems, and question the reasonableness of many of our society's economic goals.

The analytical framework underlying radical economics consists largely of the following hypotheses. First, following Marx, the radical economists argue that the structure of any society is determined principally by the society's dominant mode of production, and that the most distinctive features of the mode of production under capitalism is the use of the wage-contract, the dominance of impersonal markets, and the private ownership of capital. Second, according to the radical economists, the pressure under capitalism for capital accumulation and riches tends to create a momentum in and of itself, which creates important contradictions and social problems. Third, according to the radical economists, the United States

THE MAMMOTH DEBT PROBLEMS OF ARGENTINA, BRAZIL, AND MEXICO

During the early 1980s, the financial pages of the newspapers (and the front pages and editorials as well) were full of stories concerning the very severe debt problems of third-world countries, particularly Argentina, Brazil, and Mexico (which together owed over $200 billion). In 1982, Mexico announced that it was unable to meet its obligations to foreign creditors. The U.S. government responded by mounting a rescue operation involving banks (to whom much of the debt was owed) and the International Monetary Fund. Subsequently, Brazil and Argentina also found it necessary to look for debt relief from their creditors, and ways were found to keep them afloat, at least temporarily.

The major American banks have lent an enormous amount of money to these countries. For example, Manufacturers Hanover, a major New York bank, has lent over $1 billion—40 percent of its capital—to Argentina alone. During the 1970s, the banks increased their loans to these countries at a rapid rate. Because their exports were growing fast, the banks felt that these countries would be able to earn the dollars to pay off the loans. (As shown in Table 1, the ratio of debt to exports was lower in 1980 than in 1974.) However, during 1980–82, the real rate of interest increased, thus increasing the interest payments on these loans. Moreover, the 1980–82 world recession reduced the export earnings of the debtor countries. Because of these and other factors, including major mistakes made by the debtor nations themselves, each of these nations was unable to meet its financial obligations.

Should these countries be granted new loans? According to some observers, this is throwing good money after bad, since the loans will never be repaid. In their opinion, the debt should be written off, at least in part. But others, including President Reagan's Council of Economic Advisers, argue that the problem is only temporary, and that continued lending is justified. Among other things, they stress the importance of avoiding unnecessary damage to the economies of the debtor nations. The banks to whom the debts are owed are anxious, of course, to collect as much as they can, while the debtor countries want to have the interest rates and fees on the loans reduced.

Table 1

DEBT, RATIO OF DEBT TO EXPORTS, AND INTEREST PAYMENTS OF ARGENTINA, BRAZIL, AND MEXICO COMBINED, 1974–83

	1974	1977	1980	1981	1982	1983
Debt (billions of dollars)	43.4	75.7	143.2	185.1	205.3	213.9
Debt divided by exports	2.1	2.7	2.4	2.7	3.2	3.2
Interest payments (billions of dollars)	2.7	4.9	15.1	22.6	28.4	26.2

By 1983, interest payments were over $26 billion, and banks were reluctant to extend enough new loans to these countries to cover these payments. There was a widespread feeling that the banks had made unwise loans, and that they should reap the consequences. After all, an important aspect of the price system is that firms should accept the losses imposed by the market place, not go hat in hand to the government. But the government, faced with what it regarded as an extremely hazardous situation, helped to put together a set of actions and policies aimed at improving the situation. As part of this cooperative effort, the banks granted about $9 billion in new loans to Argentina, Brazil, and Mexico in 1983.

The debtor countries themselves improved their aggregate trade balance in goods and services (excluding interest) by $28 billion between 1981 and 1983. Imports were cut by about 52 percent in Argentina, 30 percent in Brazil, and 66 percent in Mexico. Each of these countries experienced severe recessions that resulted in a cut in expenditures on traded goods. According to the debtors, they have accepted bitter medicine to help pay their debts. In some quarters, there is a fear that, if pushed too hard, some of these countries might repudiate their debts. Although such a drastic step would result in the ostracism of the country from the world banking community, it cannot be ruled out completely.

The International Monetary Fund (IMF), established by 40 nations at the end of World War II to ensure reasonable stability of exchange rates, has played a major role in trying to manage the debt problem. The IMF lends money to any of its member governments that is having difficulties with its balance of payments. In 1983, Congress approved the U.S. share of an increase in resources for the IMF. In that same year, the IMF lent about $4 billion to Argentina, Brazil, and Mexico. But the size of the loans made by the IMF is often less significant than its role as a catalyst. If a debtor country agrees to follow particular policies, the IMF can give the country a "seal of approval," which enables it to borrow from banks and elsewhere. In recent years, in order for such a seal of approval to be given, the banks to which the country owes money must also agree to extend new loans.

The governments of the creditor countries have also extended credit directly to the debtor countries. Because of the lack of private credit, some U.S. firms that normally export to these countries are unable to do so. The U.S. Export-Import Bank can raise its levels of credit in such circumstances. Other countries have similar agencies. In 1983, government financing for Argentina, Brazil, and Mexico was about $3 billion.

This combination of actions by the banks, the IMF, and the governments of the creditor and debtor countries has thus far kept the situation from deteriorating further, but the mammoth debt problems of these countries will continue to haunt them and their creditors for many years to come.[1]

---

[1] For further discussion, see 1984 Annual Report of the Council of Economic Advisers, and *Business Week*, February 6, 1984.

has reached a state of economic development where class struggles are not necessary or rational, since there is enough productive capacity so that all citizens can share adequately in wealth and leisure. To solve existing social problems, the radicals argue that the basic institutions of our society must change. In their eyes, nothing less will suffice.

The flavor of the radical position is well conveyed by this quotation from David Gordon:

> Radicals criticize capitalist society essentially because it evolves irrationally. Its basic mode of production and the structures of its institutions create conflicts which do not need to exist. In the language of economics, it forces "trade-offs" that are not necessary. Fundamentally, radicals argue, capitalism forces a conflict between the aggregate wealth of society (and obviously the enormous wealth of some individuals) and the freedom of most individuals. In another, truly democratic, humanist and socialist society, radicals argue, conditions could be forged in which increases in aggregate social wealth complemented the personal freedom of all individuals. Edwards and Mac-Ewan mention some of the other unnecessary conflicts created (or sustained) by capitalist societies: "income growth versus a meaningful work environment, employment versus stable prices, private versus social costs, public versus private consumption, and income versus leisure." Other conflicts can be specified, but the criticisms gain force in the context of the radical vision of a "better" society. It should be emphasized in discussing the radical vision that many modern socialist radicals, though socialist, do not view most modern socialist countries with great approval. To many Western radicals, the purposes and the realities of the socialist revolution in Cuba provide the closest manifest approximation to their ideals. Che Guevara, in many ways a more important ideologue of that revolution than Fidel Castro, has often expressed those ideals most eloquently.[4]

RESPONSE TO RADICAL ECONOMICS

As you would expect, the economics profession has responded in a variety of ways to the emergence of radical economics, with its relatively small number of followers. Some economists have chosen to ignore them, while others, like Robert Solow of M.I.T., have responded sharply. In Solow's view,

> Radical economics may conceivably be the wave of the future, but I do not think that it is the wave of the present. In fact, to face the issue head on, I think that radical economics as it is practiced contains more cant, not less cant; more role-playing, not less role-playing; less facing of the facts, not more facing of the facts, than conventional economics. In short, we neglected radical economics because it is negligible. There is little evidence that radical political economics is capable of generating a line of normal science, or even that it wants to.[5]

Since radical economists are still engaged in the work that will tell whether theirs is really a contribution to science, it is premature to attempt to evaluate the accuracy or importance of their efforts. Admittedly, they

[4] D. Gordon, *Problems in Political Economy: An Urban Perspective,* Boston: Heath, 1971, p. 7.

[5] R. Solow, "The State of Economics," *American Economic Review,* May 1971.

415

have attracted considerable attention, despite the smallness of their numbers, but attention and agreement are two different things. The vast majority of the economics profession unquestionably would disagree with their conclusions. Most economists do not believe that capitalism should be replaced. Nor do they agree with the radicals' view of how our society works, or with their indictment of conventional economics.

Does Capitalism Have a Future?

Basic Idea #38: The major capitalist economies in Asia, Europe, and North America have shown great vitality in recent decades. The Marxist prediction that the lot of the workers would get worse and worse seems completely out of tune with the facts. Although we do not lack challenges, our kind of economic system seems to be performing effectively.

Most economists today do not seem to believe that our modern version of capitalism is about to wither on the vine. This is particularly noteworthy, since at the end of World War II, many distinguished non-Marxist economists and social seers, as well as the Marxists, were predicting the demise of capitalism and the rise of socialism. One of the most significant developments of the past 40 years has been the extent to which these prophecies have fallen flat on their faces.

The essentially capitalistic economies of the West have shown a tremendous vitality, have grown at a relatively rapid rate, and have avoided any deep depressions (although stagflation has proved to be a persistent difficulty). This is a tremendous achievement, and one that should be recognized and appreciated. It does not mean that we do not have many problems. On the contrary, much of this book has been devoted to the discussion of our important social problems. But it does mean that our modern version of capitalism seems to be more than holding its own in today's world.

Test Yourself

1. "In a field where controlled experimentation is impossible, the relative performance of India and China gives some idea of whether a Communist or a democratic system results in faster economic development." Comment and evaluate.

2. There have been complaints in Chinese newspapers that the centralized system of job allocation has been unable to find work for all the entrants into the labor force. According to some estimates, about 20 million people were waiting for job assignments. Does this amount to what would be called unemployment in the West? Explain.

3. According to some critics, like Assar Lindbeck, whereas either markets or centralized power can be used to organize a modern economy, the radical economists are against both. How then can an economy like ours be organized?

4. Compare the economic systems of the Soviet Union and China. To what extent have they departed from Marx's teachings? To what extent are their economic institutions much the same? What are the major differences in the way economic decisions are made? Which of them seems to be performing best economically? Which of them seems to be performing worst?

Summary

1. Karl Marx viewed history as a series of class struggles, the present class struggle being between the capitalists, who own the means of production, and the workers. In Marx's view, capitalists and workers struggle because the workers are exploited. Marx, who subscribed to a labor theory of value, believed that the workers create a surplus value, the difference between the value of what they produce and the subsistence wage they receive. Capital formation, in Marx's view, comes about as a consequence of this surplus value.

2. According to Marx, the lot of the workers would inevitably get worse. Consequently, capitalism would eventually be overthrown and succeeded by socialism, then by communism. Socialism would be a "dictatorship of the proletariat." After an unspecified period of time, Marx felt that socialism would give way to communism, which would be characterized by a classless society, the withering away of the state, and the distribution of income according to the principle: "From each according to his ability, to each according to his needs."

3. The Soviet Union, the first country to embrace Marxian socialism, has a command economy where power is concentrated in the hands of a relatively few Communist officials who make the big decisions on what is to be produced, how it is to be produced, and who is to receive how much. The government owns the factories, mines, equipment, and other means of production—and gives no evidence of withering away.

4. The top officials of the Communist party establish the overall goals for the economy. The detailed production plans to realize these broad goals are drawn up by Gosplan, the State Planning Commission. These plans are reviewed by individual industries and plants, and after negotiations and revision, Gosplan issues the final plan.

5. In the Soviet Union, the government, not the market, sets prices. Prices facing producers are set in such a way that a firm of average efficiency will make neither a profit nor a loss. Prices facing consumers are set to ration the consumer goods produced and to raise the planned revenue needed for investment. The difference between the price to the consumer and the price to the producer is the turnover tax.

6. Another type of Communist system is found in China, which is a very poor country despite its ancient civilization. China's first Five-Year Plan was an ambitious drive toward industrialization that seemed to achieve its objectives, but Mao's Great Leap Forward was a disaster that set back the country's economic development. More recently, China's industrial output seems to have grown relatively rapidly.

7. In the United States, a new force in recent years has been radical economics, which is based largely on Marxism. The radical economists challenge the methods and assumptions of conventional economics, and advocate basic institutional change. Many economists question whether radical economics is a contribution to science at all. At present, it is difficult to say, since radical economics is so new.

8. The essentially capitalist economies of the West have shown great vitality in the postwar period. They have grown at a relatively rapid rate, and have managed to avoid any deep depressions. Contrary to many predictions of over 40 years ago by some distinguished social seers, our modern version of capitalism seems to be more than holding its own in the world of today, although it obviously is beset by many serious problems.

Concepts for Review

Communism

Capitalist

Proletariat

Socialism

Value

Surplus value

Marxism

Five-year plan

Gosplan

Gosbank

Command economy

Quota

Turnover tax

Piece rates

Democratic socialism

Radical economics

APPENDICES

Digging Deeper into the Economist's Tool Box

In this final section of the book, we present four appendices, each of which contains important material that is sometimes considered too advanced for the elementary course. Appendix A deals with isoquants, isocost curves, and the optimal input combination. Appendix B is concerned with linear programming. Appendix C deals with general equilibrium analysis and input-output models. Appendix D is concerned with welfare economics, optimal resource allocation and perfect competition.

Appendix A: Isoquants, Isocost Curves, and the Optimal Input Combination[1]

In this Appendix, we present a somewhat different way of finding a firm's optimal input combination. This approach is based on the use of isoquants and isocost curves. There are advantages in being acquainted with this approach, as well as the one presented in Chapter 8.

ISOQUANTS

In the case of a crude-oil pipeline, a given amount of oil can be carried per day either by using a large diameter of pipe and relatively small horse-power or by using a smaller diameter of pipe and greater horsepower.

[1]To understand this Appendix, the reader should have covered Chapter 8.

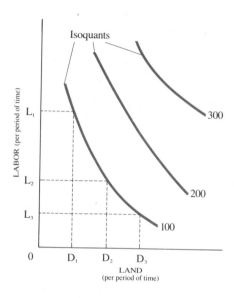

Figure A.1
*Isoquants, Wheat Farm   An isoquant
shows all possible efficient combinations
of inputs capable of producing a certain
quantity of output. These isoquants show
the various combinations of inputs that
can produce 100, 200, and 300 bushels of
wheat per period of time. For example,
100 bushels of wheat can be produced
with OL₁ units of labor and OD₁ units of
land, with OL₂ units of labor and OD₂
units of land, or with OL₃ units of labor
and OD₃ units of land.*

Figure A.2
*Isoquants for 100,000, 200,000, and
300,000 Barrels of Crude Oil Carried
per Day, Crude-Oil Pipeline   This graph
shows the isoquants in an actual case.
Note that they are shaped as economic
theory would predict.*

Similar opportunities to vary inputs to achieve a given output rate exist in
practically all industries. To describe these opportunities, economists use
the concept of an isoquant. *An **isoquant** is a curve showing all possible
efficient combinations of inputs capable of producing a certain quantity of
output.* An *inefficient* combination of inputs is one that includes more of at
least one input, and as much of other inputs, as some other combination of
inputs that can produce the same quantity of output. Inefficient combinations cannot minimize costs or maximize profits. On a wheat farm, it may
be possible to produce 1 unit of output with 2 units of land and 3 units of
labor. It may also be possible to produce 1 unit of output with 3 units of
land and 3 units of labor. The second input combination—which is inefficient—cannot be the least-cost input combination, so long as land has a
positive price. Only *efficient* input combinations are worth bothering with
in the present circumstances, and they alone are included in an isoquant.

There is an isoquant pertaining to each level of production. Figure A.1
shows some isoquants for a wheat farm. These isoquants show the various
combinations of inputs that can produce 100, 200, and 300 bushels of
wheat per period of time. Consider the isoquant for 100 bushels of wheat
per period of time. According to this isoquant, the farm can attain this
output rate if OL_1 units of labor and OD_1 units of land are used per period
of time. Alternatively, this output rate can be attained with OL_2 units of
labor and OD_2 units of land—or OL_3 units of labor and OD_3 units of
land—per period of time.

The shape and position of a firm's isoquants are derived from the firm's
production function. Indeed, one way to represent the firm's production
function is by showing its isoquants. Thus the firm's isoquants, like its
production function, show the firm's technological possibilities—the various efficient input-output combinations that can be achieved with existing
technology. The shape of an isoquant is typically like that shown in Figure
A.1; that is, it slopes downward to the right, but *its slope becomes less and
less steep.*

To illustrate what isoquants in an actual firm look like, consider once
again our crude-oil pipeline. Figure A.2 shows the isoquants corresponding
to 100,000, 200,000, and 300,000 barrels of crude oil carried per day. For

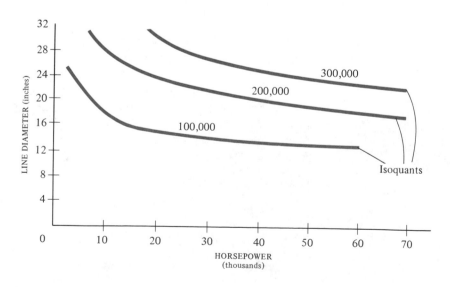

example, the isoquant corresponding to 100,000 barrels per day shows all the combinations of line diameter and horsepower that permit a pipeline to carry 100,000 barrels per day (for 1,000 miles). Note that each of these isoquants slopes downward to the right. Moreover, comparing these isoquants with Table 8.2, you can readily see that, if Table 8.2 contained more detailed data on the production function, it would be simple to derive the isoquants from the data regarding the production function in Table 8.2. How? By determining from this more detailed version of Table 8.2 the various input combinations that can produce each output rate. For example, to derive the isoquant corresponding to 100,000 barrels of crude oil carried per day, one could determine from such a table the various input combinations that can produce this output rate.

ISOCOST CURVES AND THE OPTIMAL INPUT DECISION

To determine the combination of inputs that will minimize the firm's costs, one can use the isoquant concept. All input combinations that can efficiently produce the specified level of output can be represented by the isoquant corresponding to this level of output. For example, the isoquant in Figure A.3 shows all the input combinations a wheat farm can use to produce a certain amount of wheat. The optimal input combination must lie on this isoquant, but where? A simple way to determine the optimal input combination is to draw a number of *isocost curves,* as shown in Figure A.3. *Each isocost curve shows the input combinations the firm can obtain for a given expenditure.* Consider the isocost curves corresponding to expenditures of $12,000, $16,200, and $20,000, shown in Figure A.3.

In Figure A.3 the price of labor is $8,000 per man-year, and the annual price of using land is $2,000. Given the price of each input, it is a simple matter to draw each isocost curve. Take the case of the isocost curve corresponding to annual expenditures of $12,000. If this expenditure were devoted entirely to labor, 1½ man-years could be hired. Thus this isocost curve must cut the horizontal axis in Figure A.3 at 1½ man-years of labor. Similarly, if this expenditure were devoted entirely to land, 6 acres of land could be hired. Thus this isocost curve must cut the vertical axis at 6 acres of land. Finally, if we connect the point where the isocost curve cuts the vertical axis to the point where it cuts the horizontal axis, we obtain the entire isocost curve.

Given both the isoquant and the isocost curves, one can readily determine the input combination that will minimize the firm's costs. This input combination corresponds to *that point on the isoquant that lies on the lowest isocost curve*—in other words, point *A* in Figure A.3. Input combinations on lower isocost curves (like that corresponding to $12,000) that lie below *A* are cheaper than *A*, but cannot produce the desired output. Input combinations on isocost curves (like that corresponding to $20,000) that lie above *A* will produce the desired output but at a higher cost than *A*.

What is the relationship between the input combination determined in this way and the input combination determined by means of the rule described in Chapter 8? Reassuringly enough, these input combinations will always be the same, since the rule described in Chapter 8 will always give the same answer as this geometric technique. In general, *if you find the combination of inputs where the marginal product of a dollar's worth of any one input equals the marginal product of a dollar's worth of any other input*

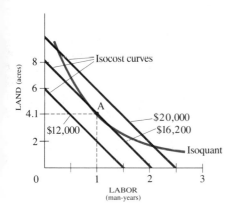

Figure A.3

Least-Cost Input Combination The least-cost input combination is at point A, where 4.1 acres of land and 1 man-year of labor are used. The isoquant shows all input combinations that can be used to produce the required amount of wheat, and the isocost curves show the input combinations costing $12,000, $16,200, and $20,000, respectively.

used, this will give you the same answer as if you find the point on the isoquant that lies on the lowest isocost curve.

FINDING THE OPTIMAL INPUT COMBINATION: A CASE STUDY

To illustrate the use of isoquants and isocost curves to identify optimal input combinations, let's go back to Earl Heady's study of the production of corn, discussed in Chapter 8. Figure A.4 shows an isoquant that Heady and his coworkers estimated from the production of corn on Kansas Verdigras soil. This isoquant shows the amounts of land and fertilizer that will produce 82.6 bushels of corn. It indicates that this amount of corn can be produced if 1.19 acres of land and no fertilizer are used, or if 1.11 acres of land and 20 pounds of fertilizer are used, or if .99 acres of land and 60 pounds of fertilizer are used, and so forth. (The same data are shown in Table 8.5.)

After estimating isoquants of this sort, Heady and his coworkers derived the optimal input combination farmers should use to minimize their costs. Suppose that a pound of fertilizer costs .003 times as much as an acre of land. Then the isocost curves would be as shown in Figure A.4. Under these circumstances, the minimum-cost combination would be 40 pounds of fertilizer and 1.04 acres of land. (This finding agrees with the results obtained in Chapter 8, where we took up this same case.) No matter what the ratio of the price of fertilizer to the price of land may be, the least-cost input combination can be derived this way.

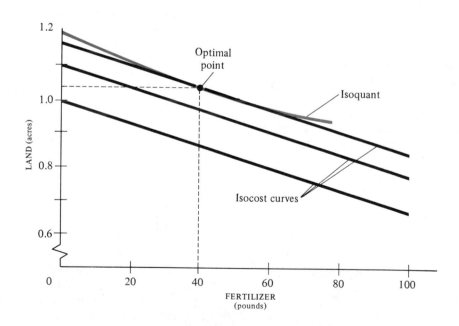

Figure A.4

Isoquant for the Production of 82.6 Bushels of Corn in Kansas *This graph shows how economic analysis has been used to help farmers make better production decisions. Given the assumed conditions, the optimal input combination would be 40 pounds of fertilizer and 1.04 acres of land.*

Appendix B: Linear Programming[2]

In this Appendix, we look at the firm's production problems from a somewhat different angle—that of **linear programming.** Linear programming is

[2]To understand this Appendix, the reader should have covered Chapter 8 and Appendix A.

the most famous of the mathematical programming methods that have come into existence since World War II. It is a technique that permits decision makers to solve maximization and minimization problems where there are certain constraints on what can be done. First used shortly after World War II to help schedule the procurement activities of the United States Air Force, linear programming has become an extremely important part of economic analysis and a very powerful tool for solving managerial problems. Its remarkable growth has been helped along by the development of computers, which can handle the many computations required to solve large linear programming problems.

There are at least two reasons why it is important to re-examine the theory of the firm in terms of linear programming:

1. The programming analysis is more fundamental in one respect than the conventional analysis presented up to this point. The conventional theory is based on the production function, which assumes that the efficient production processes have been determined and given to economists before they attack the problem. But in the real world, economists are usually confronted with a number of *feasible* production processes, and it is very difficult to tell which ones—or which combinations—are *efficient.* The choice of the optimal combination of production processes is an extremely important decision, and it can be analyzed more fully by linear programming.

2. The programming analysis seems to conform more closely to the way managers view production. The language and concepts of linear programming, though abstract and by no means the same as those of management, seem to be closer to those of managers and engineers than the ones used by conventional theory. This means that often it is easier to apply linear programming to many types of production problems in industry and government.

THE LINEAR-PROGRAMMING VIEW OF THE FIRM

To economists who use linear programming, *the technology available to a firm consists of a finite number of* **processes,** *each of which uses inputs and produces one or more outputs.* IBM can choose among a number of different processes to manufacture a computer, and U.S. Steel can use a number of processes to manufacture steel. Typically, a firm can use various alternative processes to do a particular job. An important assumption in linear programming is that *each process uses inputs in fixed proportions.* Consider the case of an automobile manufacturer that, among other things, assembles truck engines. Suppose that one process it can employ is Process X, which uses 10 hours of labor and 1 hour of machine time to assemble 1 truck engine. If this process uses inputs in fixed proportions—as assumed in linear programming—this 10:1 ratio of labor time to machine time must be maintained. It cannot be altered.

Any process can be operated at various activity levels; *the **activity level** of a process is the number of units of output produced with the process.* If Process X is used to assemble 3 truck engines, its activity level is 3; if it is used to assemble 100 truck engines, its activity level is 100. If the output of any process is varied, it is assumed that the inputs used by the process vary proportionately with the output of the process. Consequently, the amount of any input used by a process equals the activity level of the process—i.e., the number of units of output produced with the process—times the number of units of input the process requires to produce a unit of output. In our example, the amount of labor used by Process X to assemble 5 truck engines is 50 man-hours, since the process is operated at an activity level of 5, and Process X requires 10 man-hours of labor to assemble each truck engine.[3]

Linear programming views the firm's production problem as follows. *The firm has certain fixed amounts of a number of inputs at its disposal. Thus a manufacturing firm has available a limited amount of land, managerial labor, raw materials, and equipment of various kinds.* (These limitations on the amounts of various inputs that the firm can use are called **constraints**.) *Each unit of output resulting from a particular process yields the firm a certain amount of profit. This amount of profit varies in general from process to process. Knowing the profit to be made from a unit of output from each process and bearing in mind the limited amounts of inputs at its disposal, the firm must determine the activity level at which each process should be operated to maximize profit.* This is the firm's problem in a nutshell—a linear-programming nutshell, that is.

REMOVING DEFECTS FROM SHEET METAL: AN EXAMPLE

No general description of linear programming can give more than a very incomplete idea of the nature of linear programming and its power to solve real-life problems. We can get a somewhat better idea from a simple case study which concerns a metalworking firm that removes defects from sheet metal. Suppose that there are three processes the firm can use—Processes A, B, and C. Process A requires 2 man-hours of labor and 1 hour of machine time to remove the defects from 1 square foot of sheet metal, Process B does the same job with 1.5 man-hours of labor and 1.5 hours of machine time, and Process C requires 1.1 man-hours of labor and 2.2 hours of machine time. The same kind of machine is used for each process.

Assume that the firm has contracted to remove the defects from 100 square feet of sheet metal per week, and that it will receive a price of $10 a square foot for this service. Also assume that the firm must pay $3 per man-hour for labor and that the cost of an hour of machine time is $2. Given these circumstances, the firm must decide which process or processes it should use to satisfy this contract. Should it use any single process to remove the defects from all 100 square feet of sheet metal per week? If so, which process should it use? Should it use some combination of processes, such as Process A for 50 square feet and Process B for the rest? Which of the myriad of possibilities will maximize the firm's profits?

Since the firm receives $1,000 a week for the work (100 square feet × $10 per square foot) regardless of which processes it uses, the firm will maximize its profit by minimizing its costs. Thus, in this simple case,[4] the problem boils down to determining which process or processes can do the job at least cost. We begin by assuming that the firm can hire all the

---

[3]It is also assumed that, when two or more processes are used simultaneously, they do not interfere with one another or make each other more productive.

[4]In general the problem of maximizing profit does not boil down to the minimizing of cost because the firm's total revenue is not fixed as it is in this simple case.

labor that it wants and that it has plenty of the necessary machines. (This assumption is contrary to our earlier statement that linear programming views the firm as having limited amounts of certain inputs, but we relax this assumption in a later section.) Letting Q_1 be the number of square feet of sheet metal subjected to Process A, Q_2 be the number of square feet subjected to Process B, and Q_3 be the number of square feet subjected to Process C, *the firm's problem can be regarded as the following simple linear programming problem. Choose the lowest possible value for*

$$\text{total cost} = \quad 8.0\ Q_1 + 7.5\ Q_2 + 7.7\ Q_3 \tag{B.1}$$

subject to the constraints—

$$Q_1 + Q_2 + Q_3 = 100 \tag{B.2}$$

$$Q_1 \geq 0;\ Q_2 \geq 0;\ Q_3 \geq 0. \tag{B.3}$$

Why should the firm seek the lowest possible value for the expression in Equation (B.1)? Because this expression equals the firm's total weekly costs of doing the job. The cost of each square foot of sheet metal subjected to Process A is $8.00, since Process A requires 2 man-hours of labor (at $3 per man-hour) and 1 hour of machine time (at $2 per hour). Thus the total cost of the sheet metal subjected to Process A is 8.0 Q_1. Similarly, the total cost of sheet metal subjected to Process B is 7.5 Q_2, since the cost of each square foot of sheet metal subjected to Process B is $7.50. And the total cost of the sheet metal subjected to Process C is 7.7 Q_3, since the cost of each square foot subjected to Process C is $7.70. Clearly, the total cost of the job is the sum of whatever costs are incurred using each of the processes, which is the expression in Equation (B.1).

Why must the firm conform to the constraints in Equation (B.2) and Inequality (B.3)? Equation (B.2) must hold if the firm is to meet its contract, since it states that the sum of the amounts of sheet metal subjected to each process must equal 100 square feet. That is, $Q_1 + Q_2 + Q_3$ must equal 100. Also, the inequalities in (B.3) must hold. All they say is that the number of square feet of sheet metal subjected to each process must be either zero or more than zero, which certainly must be true. (If you wonder why such an obvious constraint must be specified, remember that electronic computers won't recognize it as being true unless they are told.)

SOLVING THE PROBLEM: NO CONSTRAINTS ON INPUTS

It is convenient to begin solving the problem by providing a graphic representation of each of the three processes. Since a process is defined to have fixed input proportions and since all points where input proportions are unchanged lie along a straight line through the origin, we can represent each process by such a line, or **ray.** In Figure B.1, the ray OA represents Process A. Process A uses 2 man-hours of labor and 1 hour of machine time per square foot of sheet metal—in other words, 2 man-hours of labor for every hour of machine time. Consequently, the ray OA includes all points where labor time is combined with machine time in the ratio of 2:1.

Figure B.1

Graphical Representation of Process A
The ray OA *includes all points where labor time is combined with machine time in the ratio of 2:1, since this is the ratio used by Process A. The point* U_A *corresponds to an output of 100 square feet of sheet metal per week. (Why? Because Process A uses 2 man-hours of labor and 1 hour of machine time per square foot of sheet metal. Thus 200 man-hours of labor and 100 hours of machine time are required to produce an output of 100 square feet.)*

Graphical Representation of Processes A, B, and C *Ray* OA *pertains to Process A, ray* OB *to Process B, and ray* OC *to Process C. Based on these rays, we derive the isoquant corresponding to an output of 100 square feet per week,* $U_A U_B U_C$. *(Since Process B uses 1.5 man-hours of labor and 1.5 hours of machine time per square foot of sheet metal, point* U_B *is at 150 man-hours of labor and 150 hours of machine time. Since Process C uses 1.1 man-hours of labor and 2.2 hours of machine time per square foot of sheet metal, point* U_C *is at 110 man-hours of labor and 220 hours of machine time.)*

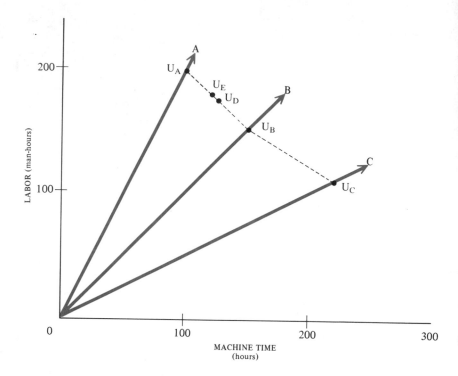

Two things should be noted about ray *OA*. First, *each point on this ray implies a certain output level.* For example, point U_A, where 200 man-hours of labor and 100 hours of machine time are used, implies an output of 100 square feet of sheet metal per week. Second, *every possible output rate corresponds to some point on this ray.* This is true because all possible points at which labor time is combined with machine time in the ratio of 2:1 are included in the ray *OA*.

In Figure B.2, we show the rays corresponding to all three processes: *OA* corresponds to Process A, *OB* to Process B, and *OC* to Process C. Each ray is constructed in the same way. Using these rays, we can draw the isoquant corresponding to the output of 100 square feet of sheet metal processed—the curve that includes all input combinations that can produce this amount of output. Focusing first on Processes A and B, point U_A is the point corresponding to an output of 100 square feet of sheet metal with Process A, and point U_B corresponds to an output of 100 square feet with Process B. Thus U_A and U_B *are points on the isoquant corresponding to an output of 100 square feet of sheet metal.*

Moreover, *any point on the line segment joining* U_A *and* U_B *is also on this isoquant,* because the firm can simultaneously use both Process A and Process B to remove defects from a total of 100 square feet of sheet metal. For example, point U_D corresponds to the case in which Processes A and B are each used to remove defects from 50 square feet of the metal; and point U_E corresponds to the case in which Process A is used for 60 square feet and Process B for 40 square feet. By varying the proportion of the total output subjected to each of these two processes, one can obtain all points on the line segment that joins U_A to U_B.

To complete the isoquant, we must recognize the existence of Process C,

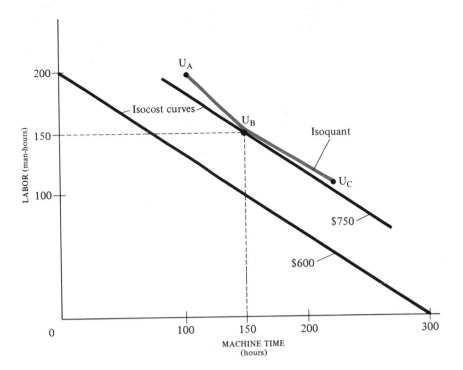

Figure B.3

Isoquant and Isocost Curves *The point on the isoquant* $U_A U_B U_C$ *that is on the lowest isocost curve is point* U_B. *(The $600 isocost curve shows all combinations of labor and machine time that can be obtained for $600. The $750 isocost curve shows all combinations of labor and machine time that can be obtained for $750.)*

too. In Figure B.2, U_C is the point corresponding to the use of Process C to remove defects from 100 square feet of sheet metal. Thus U_C *is also a point on this isoquant.* Moreover, *any point on the line segment joining* U_B *and* U_C *is also on this isoquant,* because the firm can simultaneously use both Process B and Process C to remove defects from a total of 100 square feet of sheet metal.[5] Consequently, *the entire isoquant is* $U_A U_B U_C$. Note that this isoquant, like all in linear programming, consists of connected line segments, and, while not smooth, has the same basic shape as the isoquants of conventional theory.

Given the isoquant $U_A U_B U_C$, it is simple to solve the firm's problem. All we have to do is construct Figure B.3, which contains this isoquant as well as some isocost curves, each of which shows all input combinations that cost the firm the same amount. The isocost curves corresponding to $600 and $750 are shown in Figure B.3. To find the input combination that minimizes the cost of removing defects from 100 square feet of sheet metal, we need only follow the procedure recommended in Appendix A: *find the point on the isoquant that is on the lowest isocost curve.* This is U_B—the point corresponding to the use of Process B alone. Thus the firm should use only Process B, its total costs will be $750, and it will make a profit of $250 per week on the contract, which is the best it can do.

---

[5] At first glance, one might wonder why the line segment joining U_A to U_C is not part of the isoquant. After all, it too represents various combinations of labor time and machine time that can remove the defects from 100 square feet of sheet metal. This line segment is excluded because the points on it are inefficient. They use as much of one input and more of the other input than some point on $U_A U_B U_C$. Recall from Appndix A that an isoquant contains only efficient combinations of inputs.

SOLVING THE PROBLEM: CONSTRAINT ON MACHINE TIME

The foregoing problem is simple—so simple that it can easily be solved outside the framework of linear programming.[6] Let's complicate the problem a bit and make it somewhat more realistic. In the previous section, we assumed that the firm could use all the machine time it wanted—at $2 per hour. But in the short run, the firm is likely to have only a certain number of machines available. It therefore is constrained to use no more than a certain number of machine hours per week. Specifically, suppose that the firm can use no more than 120 hours of machine time per week; this is the maximum capacity of the machines it owns or to which it has access. Now which process or processes should be used to satisfy the contract?

This problem recognizes that the firm has limited amounts of certain inputs in the short run; thus it contains constraints of the sort visualized in the linear-programming view of the firm. The objective is still to minimize the expression in Equation (B.1), and the constraints in Equation (B.2) and Inequality (B.3) must still be met, but there is now a new contraint—

$$Q_1 + 1.5 \ Q_2 + 2.2 \ Q_3 \leq 120. \tag{B.4}$$

Why? Because the number of hours of machine time per week must be less than (or equal to) 120, and the total number of hours of machine time used per week equals $Q_1 + 1.5 Q_2 + 2.2 Q_3$.

To see that this is so, recall that the removal of defects from each square foot of sheet metal by Process A requires 1 hour of machine time; thus, since Q_1 is the number of square feet of sheet metal treated per week by Process A, the number of hours of machine time per week used on Process A must also equal Q_1. Similarly, the number of hours of machine time per week used on Process B must equal $1.5 \ Q_2$ since the removal of defects from each square foot of sheet metal by Process B requires 1.5 hours of machine time. Moreover, the number of hours of machine time per week used on Process C must equal $2.2 \ Q_3$ since Process C requires 2.2 hours of machine time per square foot of metal. Thus the *total* amount of machine time used per week on *all* processes must be $Q_1 + 1.5 Q_2 + 2.2 Q_3$.

How can this problem be solved? The constraint in Inequality (B.4) means that many of the points in Figure B.3 are no longer feasible, because they require more than 120 hours per week of machine time. These nonfeasible points are shown in the shaded area of Figure B.4. To solve the problem, we must find that *feasible* point on the isoquant $U_A U_B U_C$ that is on the lowest isocost curve. The feasible points on this isoquant are all on line $U_A U_E$ in Figure B.4. Isocost curves representing costs of $600 and $780 are shown in Figure B.4. It is evident that the point on $U_A U_E$ that is on the lowest isocost curve is U_E. Thus the firm should use 180 man-

---

[6] All this problem really entails is a choice among three methods of production, the cost of producing a unit of output being constant for each process and no constraint being placed on the amount that can be produced with a certain process. In such a case, the answer is obvious. Produce the required volume of output with the process with the lowest cost per unit of output. The simplicity of this case does not detract from its usefulness as a first step in the discussion of the nature of linear programming.

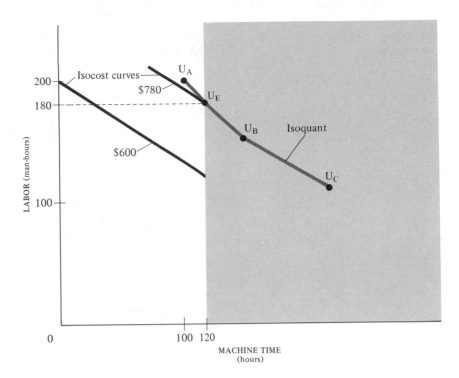

Figure B.4

Isoquant (with Constraint on Machine Time) and Isocost Curves *If the firm cannot use more than 120 hours of machine time per week, the shaded area is no longer feasible, so the feasible point on the isoquant that is on the lowest isocost curve is U$_E$. (The $780 isocost curve, which is the lowest isocost curve touching the line U$_A$U$_E$, shows all combinations of labor and machine time that can be obtained for $780.)*

hours of labor and 120 machine hours per week—which means that Process A should be used on 60 square feet of sheet metal per week and Process B on 40 square feet.[7] The firm's total cost is $780, and it makes $220 per week—which is the best it can do under these circumstances.

LINEAR PROGRAMMING AND MANAGEMENT SCIENCE

Linear programming is only one of a number of analytical tools that have been developed in the past 30 years to aid decision making in the private and public sectors of the economy. These techniques form the core of **management science** or **operations research,** a very rapidly growing and exciting field that draws on economics and other disciplines. Although management is still very much an art, the development and application of techniques like linear programming are making it more and more a science. Many problems that were "solved" only 10 or 20 years ago by guesswork and seat-of-the-pants judgment are now being handled by linear programming and other such techniques, with the result that decisions are better, firms are more efficient, and society gets more out of its available resources.

---

[7] Since the total amount of man-hours used equals 180 hours, $2Q_1 + 1.5Q_2 = 180$. And since the total amount of machine time used equals 120 hours, $Q_1 + 1.5Q_2 = 120$. Solving these two equations simultaneously, $Q_1 = 60$ and $Q_2 = 40$. Thus Process A should be used on 60 square feet and Process B on 40 square feet.

Appendix C: General Equilibrium Analysis and Input-Output Models[8]

PARTIAL EQUILIBRIUM VERSUS GENERAL EQUILIBRIUM ANALYSIS

In this book, we looked in detail at the behavior of individual decision-making units and the workings of individual markets. We looked at consumers, at firms, and at various types of product markets and input markets. We almost always viewed each single market in isolation. According to the models we have used, the price and quantity in each such market are determined by supply and demand curves, with these curves drawn on the assumption that other prices are given. Each market is regarded as independent and self-contained for all practical purposes. In particular, it is assumed that *changes in price in the market under consideration do not have serious repercussions on the prices in other markets.* This is *partial equilibrium analysis.*

General equilibrium analysis recognizes that *changes in price may affect other prices, and that the changes in other prices may have an impact on the market under consideration.* No market can adjust to a change in conditions without causing *some* change in other markets, and in some cases this change may be substantial. Suppose that an upward shift occurs in the demand for barley. In previous chapters, it was generally assumed that when the price and output of barley changed in response to this change in conditions, the prices of other products would remain fixed. However, the market for barley is not sealed off from the markets for rye, corn, wheat, and other foodstuffs. (For that matter, it is not completely sealed off from the markets for nonfood products like sewing machines and autos.) Thus the market for barley cannot adjust without disturbing the equilibrium of other markets *and having these disturbances feed back on itself.*

Both partial and general equilibrium analyses are very useful, each in its own way. Partial equilibrium analysis is perfectly adequate when a change in conditions in one market has little repercussion on prices in other markets. Thus, in studying the effects of a proposed excise tax on the production of a certain commodity, we often can assume that prices of other commodities are fixed and remain close to the truth. However, if a change in conditions in one market has important repercussions on other prices, a general equilibrium analysis may be required.

INPUT-OUTPUT ANALYSIS

Input-output analysis, due largely to Nobel laureate Wassily Leontief, puts general equilibrium analysis in a form that is operationally useful to governments and firms faced with a variety of important practical problems. An important feature of input-output analysis is its emphasis on the *interdependence* of the economy. Each industry uses the outputs of other industries as its inputs, and its own output may be used as an input by the same industries whose output it uses. Recognizing this interdependence,

---

[8]To understand this Appendix, the reader should have covered Chapter 10.

input-output analysis attempts to determine the amount each industry must produce so that a specified amount of various final goods will be turned out by the economy. This type of analysis has been used to help predict production requirements to meet estimated demands. Economic planners have applied it to military mobilization, to problems of economic development in less developed countries, and to many other areas.

To put general equilibrium analysis in a usable form, input-output analysis makes a number of simplifying assumptions. Thus it generally uses as variables the *total* quantity of a particular good demanded or supplied, rather than the quantity demanded by a particular consumer or supplied by a particular firm. This reduces enormously the number of variables and equations in the analysis. Also, in the simpler versions of input-output analysis, it is assumed that consumer demand for all commodities is known. Input-output analysis attempts to find out what can be produced, and the amount of each input and intermediate good that must be employed to produce a given output. It views these questions as largely a matter of technology.

Finally, input-output analysis assumes that inputs are used in *fixed proportions* to produce any product and that there are *constant returns to scale*. This is a key assumption of Leontief's input-output system. In the production of steel, Leontief would assume that, for every ton of steel produced, a certain amount of iron ore, a certain amount of coke, a certain amount of fuel, and so on would be required. The amount of each input required per unit of output is assumed to be the same, whatever the level of output. If a certain amount of iron ore is required to produce 1 million tons of steel, it is assumed that 10 times that amount is required to produce 10 million tons of steel.[9]

A NUMERICAL EXAMPLE

With some basic algebra, the essentials of input-output analysis are quickly grasped. Suppose that the economy consists of only three industries—coal, chemicals, and electric power. Each industry uses the products of the other industries in the proportions shown in Table C.1. Thus the second column of Table C.1 states that every dollar's worth of coal requires $.30 worth of electric power, $.10 worth of coal, and $.60 worth of labor. (One could just as well carry out the analysis with inputs and outputs measured in physical units—labor-hours or tons per year—as in money.)

This economy has set consumption targets of $100 million of electric power, $50 million of coal, and $50 million of chemicals. Input-output analysis takes up the question: *How much will have to be produced by each industry in order to meet these targets?* Let's begin with coal. If electric power output is E, chemical output is C, and coal output is X (E, C, and X are measured in millions of dollars), it follows from Table C.1 that

Table C.1

AMOUNT OF EACH INPUT USED PER DOLLAR OF OUTPUT (DOLLARS)

| Type of input | Type of output | | |
	Electric power	Coal	Chemicals
Electric power	.10	.30	.00
Coal	.50	.10	.00
Chemicals	.20	.00	.90
Labor	.20	.60	.10
Total	1.00	1.00	1.00

[9] In previous chapters, we said that the proportion in which inputs are combined can generally be altered. This is a direct contradiction of the assumption of fixed proportions in input-output analysis. But it often takes a fair amount of time for changes to be made and they are often gradual, with the result that Leontief's assumption of fixed proportions may work reasonably well in the short run.

$$X = .5E + .1X + 50 \qquad \text{(C.1)}$$

if the target is met. Why? Because the electric power industry needs an amount of coal equal in value to $.5E$, the coal industry needs an amount equal in value to $.1X$, and an amount equal in value to 50 must be produced for consumption. Thus the total output of coal must be equal to the sum of these three terms, as shown in Equation (C.1).

If we construct similar equations for electric power output and chemical output, we find that

$$E = .1E + .3X + 100 \qquad \text{(C.2)}$$

$$C = .2E + .9C + 50 \qquad \text{(C.3)}$$

if the targets are to be met. For example, Equation (C.3) must hold because chemical output must equal the amount needed by the electric power industry ($.2E$) plus the amount needed by the chemical industry itself ($.9C$) plus 50 for consumption.

WHAT'S THE ANSWER?

Since Equations (C.1) to (C.3) are three equations in three unknowns, X, E, and C, we can solve for the unknowns, which turn out to be $X = 144$, $E = 159$, and $C = 818$. We have answered our question—*$144 million of coal, $159 million of electric power, and $818 million of chemicals must be produced to meet the consumption targets.* We can also find out how much labor will be required to meet these targets, since (according to Table C.1) the total value of labor required equals

$$.2E + .6X + .1C. \qquad \text{(C.4)}$$

Substituting the 144, 159, and 818 for X, E, and C, respectively, in Equation (C.4), will find that $200 million of labor is required. If this does not exceed the available labor supply, the solution is feasible; otherwise the targets must be scaled downward.

This simple example illustrates the fundamentals of input-output analysis. It also suggests why the assumption that inputs are used in fixed proportions is so convenient. Without this assumption, the input-output table in Table C.1 would not hold for each output level of the industries. Instead, the numbers in the table would vary depending on how much of each commodity was produced. The added complexity that would arise (without this assumption) is obvious. Even with this assumption, the computational and estimation problems involved in solving large input-output models can be substantial. Government agencies, such as the Departments of Commerce and Labor, have constructed a model of the U.S. economy involving several hundred industries. Usually, however, far fewer industries are included in such models.

APPLICABILITY OF INPUT-OUTPUT ANALYSIS

Whether input-output analysis can be applied fruitfully in a particular situation depends in part on whether the **production coefficients**—the numbers in Table C.1—remain constant. (See footnote 9.) There are at least two important factors that might cause changes over time in such coefficients. First, changes in technology may change the relative quantities of input used. For this reason, among others, the amount of coal required to produce many goods decreased considerably in the years since World War II. Second, changes in the relative prices of inputs may result in changes in production coefficients as cheaper inputs are substituted for more expensive ones.

Since World War II, much has been done to implement and extend input-output analysis. Basic research has been conducted by academic economists interested in the quantitative significance of various types of economic interdependence. Applied research has been devoted to formulating techniques that would be useful in decision making in government and business. In 1973–74, Anne Carter of Brandeis University and Clopper Almon of the University of Maryland used input-output analysis to estimate the effect of the Arab oil embargo on the level of unemployment in various industries. Other countries have used input-output analysis to determine the relationship of imports and exports to domestic production, as well as to analyze various problems of economic development. Also, business firms have used input-output analysis to forecast their sales.[10]

Appendix D: Optimal Resource Allocation and Perfect Competition[11]

THE NATURE OF WELFARE ECONOMICS

One of the great goals of economics is to determine how best to allocate society's scarce resources. Questions concerning the optimal allocation of inputs among industries and the optimal distribution of commodities among consumers are general equilibrium problems, since the optimal usage of any input cannot be determined by looking at the market for this input alone, and the optimal output of any commodity cannot be determined by looking at the market for this commodity alone. On the contrary, the optimal allocation of resources between two products depends on the relative strength of the demands for the products and their relative production costs.

The term *welfare economics* covers the branch of economics that studies policy issues concerning the allocation of resources. (Do not confuse welfare economics with the various government "welfare" programs you read about in Chapter 16.) It should be stressed from the start that welfare economics, although useful, is certainly no panacea. By itself, welfare economics can seldom provide a clear-cut solution to issues of public policy. But in combination with other disciplines, it can frequently show useful ways to structure and analyze these issues.

INTERPERSONAL COMPARISONS OF UTILITY

Perhaps the most important limitation of welfare economics stems from the fact that *there is no scientific way to compare the utility level of different*

---

[10]W. Leontief, *Input-Output Economcs,* New York: Oxford University Press, 1966; and H. Chenery and P. Clark, *Interindustry Economcs,* New York: Wiley, 1959.
[11]To understand this Appendix the reader should have covered Chapters 6 to 11 of this book.

individuals. There is no way to show scientifically that a bottle of Château Haut-Brion will bring you more satisfaction than it will me, or that your backache is worse than mine. This is because there is no scale on which we can measure pleasure or pain so that interpersonal comparisons can be made scientifically. For this reason, the judgment of whether one distribution of income is better than another must be made on ethical, not scientific, grounds. If you receive twice as much income as I do, economists cannot tell us whether this is a better distribution of income than if I receive twice as much income as you do. This is an ethical judgment.

However, most problems of public policy involve changes in the distribution of income. A decision to increase the production of jet aircraft and to reduce the production of railroad locomotives may mean that certain stockholders and workers will gain, while others will lose. Because it is so difficult to tell whether the resulting change in the distribution of income is good or bad, it is correspondingly difficult to conclude whether such a decision is good or bad.

Faced with this problem, economists have adopted a number of approaches, all of which have significant shortcomings. Some economists have simply paid no attention to the effects of proposed policies on the income distribution. Others have taken the existing income distribution as optimal, while still others have asserted that less unequal income distributions are preferable to more unequal ones. Purists have argued that we really cannot be sure a change is for the better unless it hurts no member of society, while others have suggested that we must accept the judgment of Congress (or the public as a whole) on what is an optimal distribution of income.

For now, the major thing to note is that the conditions for an optimal allocation of resources, described in the following sections, are incomplete, since they say nothing about the optimal income distribution. Whatever the income distribution you or I may consider best on ethical or some other (nonscientific) grounds, the conditions below must be met if resources are to be allocated optimally. Remember, however, that there may be many allocations of resources that meet these conditions, and the choice of which is best will depend on one's feelings about the optimal income distribution.

OPTIMAL RESOURCE ALLOCATION: CONDITION 1

Fundamentally, there are three necessary conditions for optimal resource allocation. The first pertains to the optimal allocation of commodities among consumers, and states that *the ratio of the marginal utilities of any two goods must be the same for any two consumers who consume both goods.* That is, if the marginal utility of good A is twice that of good B for one consumer, it must also be twice that of good B for any other consumer who consumes both goods. The proof that this condition is necessary to maximize consumer satisfaction is quite simple. We need only note that, if this ratio were unequal for two consumers, both consumers could benefit by trading.

Thus assume that the ratio of the marginal utility of good A to that of good B is 2 for one consumer, but 3 for another consumer. This means that the first consumer regards an additional unit of good A as having the same utility as 2 extra units of good B, whereas the second consumer regards an additional unit of good A as having the same utility as 3 extra units of good B. Then, if the first consumer trades 1 unit of good A for 2.5 units of good B from the second consumer, both are better off. (Why? Because the first consumer receives 2.5 units of good B, which he prefers to 1 unit of good A, and the second consumer receives 1 unit of good A, which she prefers to 2.5 units of good B.)

OPTIMAL RESOURCE ALLOCATION: CONDITION 2

The second condition, which pertains to the optimal allocation of inputs among producers, states that *the ratio of the marginal products of two inputs must be the same for any pair of producers that use both inputs.* That is, if the marginal product of input 1 is twice that of input 2 in one firm, it must also be twice that of input 2 in any other firm that uses both inputs. If this condition does not hold, total production can be increased merely by reallocating inputs among firms.

To illustrate this, suppose that for the first producer the marginal product of input 1 is twice that of input 2, whereas for the second producer the marginal product of input 1 is three times that of input 2. Then, if the first producer gives 1 unit of input 1 to the second producer in exchange for 2.5 units of input 2, both firms can expand their output. To see this, suppose that the marginal product of input 1 is M_1 for the first producer and M_2 for the second producer. Then the output of the first producer is reduced by M_1 units because of its loss of the unit of input 1, but it is increased by $2.5 \times M_1/2$ units because of its gain of the 2.5 units of input 2, so that on balance its output increases by $M_1/4$ units because of the trade. Similarly, the output of the second producer is increased by M_2 units because it gains the 1 unit of input 1, but it is decreased by $2.5 \times M_2/3$ units because it loses the 2.5 units of input 2, with the consequence that on balance its output increases by $M_2/6$ units because of the trade.

OPTIMAL RESOURCE ALLOCATION: CONDITION 3

The third condition pertains to the optimal output of a commodity. It states that *any commodity's output level, if it is optimal, must be such that the marginal social benefit from an extra unit of the commodity is equal to its marginal social cost.* If this condition is violated, social welfare can be increased by altering the output level of the commodity. Specifically, if the marginal social benefit from an extra unit of the commodity exceeds its marginal social cost, an increase in the output of the commodity will increase social welfare. (Why? Because the extra social benefit resulting from an extra unit of the commodity outweighs the extra social cost.) And if the marginal social benefit from an extra unit of the commodity is less than marginal social cost, a decrease in the output of the commodity will increase social welfare.

OPTIMAL RESOURCE ALLOCATION: A CASE STUDY

Let's turn now to a case study of how these conditions can be applied to one of our most important commodities—water. If the first condition is to hold, the ratio of the marginal utility of water to that of any other good must be the same for all consumers. To be specific, suppose that the other good is money. Then the ratio of the marginal utility of water to the marginal utility of money must be the same for all consumers. That is, if resources are allocated optimally, *the amount of money a consumer will give up to obtain an extra unit of water must be the same for all consumers.* This follows because the ratio of the marginal utility of good A to the marginal utility of good B equals the number of units of good B that the consumer will give up to get an extra unit of good A.

The common sense underlying this condition has been described well in a study of water resources done at the RAND Corporation:

> Suppose that my neighbor and I are both given rights (ration coupons, perhaps) to certain volumes of water, and we wish to consider whether it might be in our mutual interest to trade those water rights between us for other resources—we might as well say for dollars, which we can think of as a generalized claim on other resources like clam chowders, babysitting services, acres of land, or yachts. . . . Now suppose that the last acre-foot of my periodic entitlement is worth $10 at most to me, but my neighbor would be willing to pay anything up to $50 for the right. . . . Evidently, if I transfer the right to him for any compensation between $10 and $50, we will both be better off in terms of our own preferences. . . . But this is not yet the end. Having given up one acre-foot, I will not be inclined to give up another on such easy terms (and) my neighbor is no longer quite so anxious to buy as he was before, since his most urgent need for one more acre-foot has been satisfied. . . . Suppose he is now willing to pay up to $45 (for another acre-foot), while I am willing to sell for anything over $15. Evidently, we should trade again. Obviously, the stopping point is where the last (or marginal) unit of water is valued equally (in terms of the greatest amount of dollars we would be willing to pay) by the two of us. . . . At this point no more mutually advantageous trades are available—and efficiency has been attained.[12]

If people can trade water rights freely—as in this hypothetical case—an efficient allocation of water rights will be achieved. But what if water rights cannot be traded freely, because certain kinds of water uses are given priority over other types of uses, and it is difficult, even impossible, for a low-priority user to purchase water rights from a high-priority user? The effect is to prevent water from being allocated so as to maximize consumer satisfaction. Unfortunately, this question is not merely an academic exercise. It focuses attention on a very practical problem. In fact, there is a wide variety of limitations on the free exchange of water rights in the United States. Thus some legal codes grant certain types of users priority over other types of users, and free exchange of water is limited. Experts believe that these limitations are a serious impediment to the optimal allocation of water resources.

PERFECT COMPETITION AND WELFARE MAXIMIZATION

One of the most fundamental findings of economic theory is that a perfectly competitive economy satisfies the three sets of conditions for welfare

[12]J. Hirshleifer, J. Milliman, and J. DeHaven, *Water Supply,* Chicago: University of Chicago Press, 1960, p. 38.

maximization set forth in previous sections. An argument for competition can be made in various ways. Some people favor it simply because it prevents the undue concentration of power and the exploitation of consumers. But to the economic theorist, the basic argument for a perfectly competitive economy is that such an economy satisfies these three conditions. In this section we prove that this is indeed a fact.

Condition 1—The Ratio of the Marginal Utilities of any Pair of Commodities Must Be the Same for All Consumers Buying Both Commodities. Recall that under perfect competition consumers choose their purchases so that the marginal utility of a commodity is proportional to its price. Since prices, and thus price ratios, are the same for all buyers under perfect competition, it follows that the ratio of the marginal utilities between any pair of commodities must be the same for all consumers. If every consumer can buy bread at $.50 a loaf and butter at $1 a pound, each one will arrange his or her purchases so that the ratio of the marginal utility of butter to that of bread is 2. Thus the ratio will be the same for all consumers—2 for everyone.

To make sure you understand this point, let's consider any two goods, A and B. Based on our discussion in Chapter 7, we know that each consumer will buy amounts of these goods so that

$$\frac{MU_A}{P_A} = \frac{MU_B}{P_B},$$

where MU_A is the marginal utility of good A, MU_B is the marginal utility of good B, P_A is the price of good A, *and* P_B is the price of good B. Multiplying both sides of this equation by $P_A \div MU_B$, it follows that

$$\frac{MU_A}{MU_B} = \frac{P_A}{P_B}.$$

Since $P_A \div P_B$ is the same for all consumers, $MU_A \div MU_B$ must also be the same for all of them, which means this condition is satisfied.

Condition 2—The Ratio of the Marginal Products of any Pair of Inputs Must Be the Same for All Producers Using Both Inputs. We have already seen in Chapter 8 that under perfect competition producers will choose the quantity of each input so that the ratio of the marginal products of any pair of inputs equals the ratio of the prices of the pair of inputs. Since input prices, and thus price ratios, are the same for all producers under perfect competition, it follows that the ratio of the marginal products must be the same for all producers. If every producer can buy labor services at $4 an hour and machine tool services at $8 an hour, each one will arrange the quantity of its inputs so that the ratio of the marginal product of machine tool service to that of labor is 2. Thus the ratio will be the same for all producers: 2 for each.

To make sure you understand this point, let's consider any two inputs, X and Y. Based on our discussion in Chapter 8, we know that each firm will buy amounts of these inputs so that

$$\frac{MP_X}{P_X} = \frac{MP_Y}{P_Y},$$

where MP_X is the marginal product of input X, MP_Y is the marginal product of input Y, P_X is the price of input X, and P_Y is the price of input Y. Multiplying both sides of the equation by $P_X \div MP_Y$, it follows that

$$\frac{MP_X}{MP_Y} = \frac{P_X}{P_Y}.$$

Since $P_X \div P_Y$ is the same for all firms, $MP_X \div MP_Y$ must also be the same for all of them, which means this condition is satisfied.

Condition 3—The Marginal Social Benefit From an Extra Unit of any Commodity Must Be Equal to Its Marginal Social Cost. Recall from Chapter 10 that under perfect competition firms will choose their outputs so that price equals marginal cost. If a commodity's price is an accurate measure of the marginal social benefit from producing an extra unit of it, and if its marginal cost is an accurate measure of the marginal social cost of producing an extra unit of it, the fact that price is set equal to marginal cost insures that this condition will be met.

Thus, in summary, *all three conditions for optimal resource allocation are satisfied under perfect competition.* This is one principal reason why many economists are so enamored of perfect competition and so wary of monopoly and other market imperfections. If a formerly competitive economy is restructured so that some industries become monopolies, these conditions for optimal resource allocation are no longer met. As we know from Chapter 11, each monopolist produces less than the perfectly competitive industry that it replaces would have produced. Thus too few resources are devoted to the industries that are monopolized, and too many resources are devoted to the industries that remain perfectly competitive. This is one of the economist's chief charges against monopoly. It wastes resources because it results in overallocation of resources to competitive industries and underallocation of resources to monopolistic industries. The result is that society is less well off. Similarly, oligopoly and monopolistic competition are charged with wasting resources, since the conditions for optimal resource allocation are not met there either.

However, in evaluating this result and judging its relevance, one must be careful to note that it stems from a very simple model that ignores such things as technological change and other dynamic considerations, risk and uncertainty, and external economies and diseconomies. Also, there is the so-called *theory of the second-best,* which states that unless *all* of the conditions for optimal resource allocation are met, it may be a mistake to increase the number of such conditions that are fulfilled. Thus piecemeal attempts to preserve or impose competition may do more harm than good.

Brief Answers to Odd-Numbered Test-Yourself Questions*

Chapter 1 (p. 8)

1. (a) Iron ore that is still in the ground is included in land. (b) The 747 is capital. (c) These inventories are capital, as explained on p. 6. (d) Unless the University owns the telephone, it is not part of the university's capital, but it is capital to the telephone company.

3. Yes, use of the catalyst alters the relationship between inputs of crude oil and the refined oil output. By making the refining process more efficient, the catalyst allows a larger volume of refined oil to be gleaned from a barrel of crude oil. The services of engineers and scientists, as well as research laboratories, were used to obtain the invention.

Chapter 1 (p. 16)

1. Preparing the meal costs the family $25.00, assuming that Ms. Harris could see patients during that hour.

3. The $1,000 figure is correct because the remaining cost of room and board must be met whether the student goes to college or works instead.

* The answers provided here are meant only to be brief guides, not complete or exhaustive treatments. Many were contributed by Michael Claudon of Middlebury College, who is responsible for the *Instructor's Manual* accompanying this book.

Chapter 2 (p. 23)

1. 2 million bushels generates $2 million; 1 million bushels generates $2 million. No, I would produce 1 million bushels since I can sell it for as much as I can get for 2 million bushels.

3. The demand curve in Figure 2.2 shifts to the right when preferences change in favor of playing tennis.

Chapter 2 (p. 35)

1. (a) No. (b) Yes. (c) The combination of 20 million tons of food and 6 million tractors is inside the curve. Contributory factors: unemployment, inefficiency, or bad weather.

3. Yes, it is on the new curve. The horizontal intersection is 24 million tons, and the vertical one is 60 million tractors.

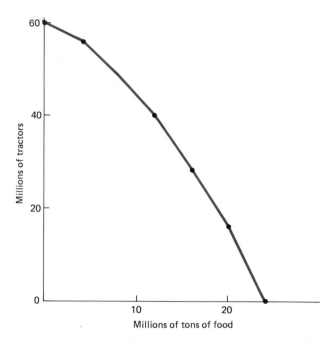

5. This statement is true. Of course, it is also important to note that not all individuals have the same number of votes, because of income inequality.

Chapter 3 (p. 47)

1. This is a direct relationship. Supply curves are generally direct relationships.

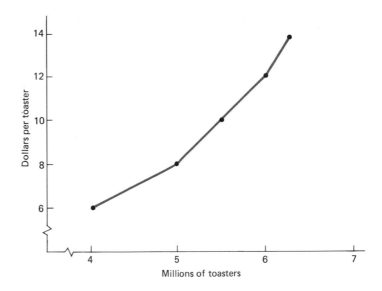

3. No, quantity demanded will exceed quantity supplied. Black markets and queues may arise. If black markets develop, the price may rise above the official price of $8. Such a ceiling might be introduced as part of an anti-inflationary program or to help the poor.

5. Equilibrium price = $3.33, and equilibrium quantity = 6.67 million pounds.

Chapter 3 (p. 61)

1. The toaster demand curve shifts: (a) right; (b) right; (c) left; (d) right; (e) no shift.

3. The impact on price is ambiguous. Equilibrium quantity rises.

5. The demand for beets and beet growers' profits rise. The opposite happens for string beans. Bean growers spy beet growers' high profits and plant beets instead of beans. Beet supply rises and string bean supply falls.

Chapter 4 (p. 75)

1. It is very difficult in many cases to know whether a certain activity can be performed better by government than private citizens can do for themselves. But the first half of this chapter indicates a number of areas where most economists believe the government has legitimate functions.

3. You can consume the services provided by national defense without depriving me of also doing so simultaneously. A rifle is not a public good; the hallmark of a public good is that it can be consumed collectively or jointly.

5. Such activities result in external economies.

Chapter 4 (p. 83)

1. The socially optimal output of paper is less than OQ. The supply curve reflecting true social costs lies to the left of the one shown because the latter neglects part of the social cost of paper production.

3. Government programs supported prices of dairy and grain farmers. The result has been excess supply of dairy and grain products, and huge government purchases of the excesses to support prices. Federal government programs have not solved the problem. See the section of the text on "Evaluation of Government Farm Programs."

5. The essential point here is one shared by many government programs, be they protective tariffs or farm subsidies. The benefits of the programs are concentrated on a relatively small and highly organized group of people, while the programs' costs are spread across the population at large.

Chapter 5 (p. 96)

1. The new olefins plant is not a firm; it is part of Exxon, which is a firm. A proprietorship is unlikely to build such a plant due to a lack of resources.

3. (a) and (b) are false because neither the University of Texas nor Massachusetts General Hospital are run to make profits. (c) is false because many firms are individual proprietorships with only one owner. (d) is false because many stockholders or partners do not participate in the management of the firms of which they are part owners.

5. Bondholders are not owners of the corporation, but stockholders are. Bondholders have lent money to the corporation at an agreed-upon interest rate, whereas stockholders' returns are based upon the profitability of the corporation they own.

Chapter 5 (p. 106)

1. All but (h).

3. Column 1: $700,000; Column 2: $1,100,000 and $2,000,000. The owners owe $1,600,000. The owners have contributed $400,000. The difference between current assets and fixed assets is the length of time before they will be converted into cash.

Chapter 6 (p. 120)

1. About 0.4. About 1.4. Teenagers have lower income than adults.

3. It is price elastic.

Chapter 6 (p. 125)

1. (a) not true; (b) not true for some goods; (c) true.

3. Because of changes in tastes and incomes, and greater familiarity with cars, the demand curve may have shifted to the right between 1914 to 1916. Also, the price elasticity of demand may have been different then than in more recent years.

Chapter 7 (p. 135)

1. 2 utils. 1 util. Yes.

3. Air is cheap because its marginal utility is quite low. In general, people are willing to pay relatively higher prices for commodities having higher marginal utilities.

Chapter 7 (p. 142)

1. The quantity demanded is 26 at a price of $1, 23 at a price of $2, 19 at a price of $3, 14 at a price of $4, and 11 at a price of $5.

3. Bill's consumer's surplus = 6 cents. This number tells us how much more Bill would have been willing to spend on the two apples per day he consumes.

Chapter 8 (p. 156)

1.

3. Labor is a variable input since the amount of labor is not fixed. Machines are a fixed input; their number cannot be changed during the period.

Chapter 8 (p. 161)

1. The price of a unit of capital is $8.00.

3. This does not seem sensible. For one thing, it denies the existence of diminishing marginal returns in the short run.

Chapter 9 (p. 173)

1. Total fixed costs = $20,000. The total variable cost of 4 units of output is $500.

3. The average costs are: $20,100, $10,100, $6,767, $5,125, and $4,160.

5. The marginal cost increases with output, since each extra unit of output increases total variable cost by more than the previous one does.

Chapter 9 (p. 181)

1. (a) False, the statement describes increasing returns to scale. (b) False, the statement confuses the short run (decreasing marginal returns) with the long run (returns to scale). (c) False, what is important in determining the optimal number of firms in an industry is the shape of the long-run average cost function.

3. No. A linear total cost curve implies constant marginal cost. If the actual marginal costs rise quickly with output, the breakeven chart is not likely to be very accurate.

Chapter 10 (p. 194)

1. Between 3 and 4 is the optimal output.

3. Marginal cost is unchanged since the total variable cost function is unchanged.

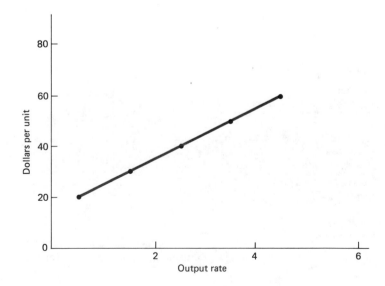

Chapter 10 (p. 204)

1. Quantity supplied increases by about 0.1 percent.

3. Price = ½. The market period supply curve is vertical.

5. For the effects on indoor tennis courts, see Example 3.2.

Chapter 11 (p. 219)

1. No, because marginal revenue is negative when demand is price inelastic. Thus a reduction in output will raise total revenue. Since it is also likely to reduce total cost, it will increase profits.

3. Marginal cost equals average variable cost over this range of output. Output will be between 2 and 3 units per year, and price will be between $6,000 and $7,000.

5. Output falls to between 1 and 2 units of output, and price increases to between $7,000 and $8,000.

Chapter 11 (p. 228)

1. See the sections in the text on "Perfect Competition and Monopoly: A Comparison" and "The Case Against Monopoly."

3. Perfectly competitive firms can earn high accounting profits if they are more efficient than are other firms. Also, in the short run, they may earn large profits.

Chapter 12 (p. 241)

1. As the slope of the demand curve becomes closer and closer to horizontal, it is tangent to the long-run average cost curve at a point that is closer and closer to the minimum point.

3. It is true that oligopolists may behave in this way.

Chapter 12 (p. 251)

1. Cartel output is 3,000 units per year.

3. If other members of the cartel hold their prices fixed (in accord with the agreement), each firm has a strong motive for lowering price, expanding sales, and increasing its profits.

Chapter 13 (p. 265)

1. The statement is incorrect. One cannot prove that perfect competition results in an optimal distribution of income. Also, the United States really hasn't opted for perfect competition, which is an abstract model.

3. The four-firm concentration ratio is 90 percent.

Chapter 13 (p. 274)

1. The issue is whether firms can escape the discipline of the market. Galbraith argues that they can: many (probably most) economists take a different view.

3. The answer should touch on the difficulties of establishing intent and, in some circumstances, its irrelevance.

Chapter 14 (p. 288)

1. The maximum is $3,600, since if the wage exceeded this amount, the firm would hire 3, not 4, man-years of labor. The minimum is $3,000, since if the wage were below this amount, the firm would hire 5, not 4, man-years of labor. These wage rates seem unrealistically low for the United States at present.

3. It would pay a lower wage. See pp. 287–288.

Chapter 14 (p. 300)

1. The focus of the answer should be upon whether the unions can be considered as monopolizers of a service.

3. This is not an easy task, as you would need data relating output responses to changes in various types of labor. No, the theory is not useless. Employers must form judgments of some sort on this score.

Chapter 15 (p. 313)

1. Borrowers might include: consumers purchasing durable goods, businesses financing inventories, and local, state, and federal governments financing expenditures.

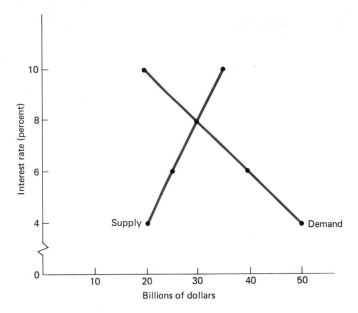

Eight percent is the equilibrium interest rate. If usury laws put a 6 percent ceiling on interest rates, there would be an excess demand for loanable funds.

3. The capitalized value of the asset is $1,000 \div .10 = $10,000$.

Chapter 15 (p. 320)

1. $1,000 \div (1.08)^2 = 857.34.

3. As indicated in the chapter, much of the apparent increase in labor's share may have little to do with the growth of labor's power. Moreover, in recent years, it is not clear that labor's power has grown. The links to the alleged shortage of capital also are unclear.

Chapter 16 (p. 334)

1. The proportion of total income received by families with incomes of $2000 equals $40 \times 2,000 \div (40 \times 2,000 + 30 \times 4,000 + 20 \times 6,000 + 10 \times 10,000) = 19.0$ percent. The proportions received by families with incomes of $4,000, $6,000, and $10,000 are 28.6 percent, 28.6 percent, and 23.8 percent, respectively. Thus the Lorenz curve is as follows:

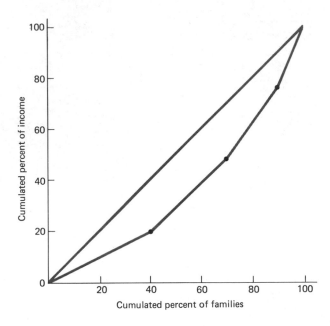

3. (a) Yes, since people can sell assets to maintain consumption. (b) No. (c) Yes.

Chapter 16 (p. 345)

1. If nonwhite and white labor are homogeneous, one would expect market forces to set the same price for them. But there are many factors that can interfere with, and postpone, such an outcome.

3. See p. 335 on "Social Insurance."

Chapter 17 (p. 359)

1. No, the private costs are less than the social costs because of the required downstream water treatment.

3. The output prevailing after the industry has to reimburse others is more desirable, because it reflects the social costs of paper manufacture.

5. The total cost equals $10 - 2P + 5P = 10 + 3P$. Thus it is minimized when $P = 0$. No.

Chapter 17 (p. 367)

1. The statement is incorrect. The tax raises the price, and therefore has a greater influence on consumption the greater is the sensitivity of demand to price.

3. One disadvantage of such a fuel tax is that it might reduce our rate of economic growth.

Chapter 18 (p. 380)

1. Yes, since the domestic opportunity cost of a computer is 1,000 cases of wine in the United States and 2,000 cases in France. The United States has a comparative advantage in computers, and France has one in producing wine. The United States is three times as efficient as France in computers, but only 50 percent more efficient in wine production.

3. No, forces of supply and demand will set the price of each good in world markets so that U.S. firms will find it profitable to make and export computers, while French firms will find it profitable to make and export wine.

Chapter 18 (p. 392)

1. Yes, protection is likely to reduce, not increase, a country's standard of living. On the other hand, a country's standard of living tends to be directly related to its productivity.

3. The United States may have a comparative advantage in computers, but not in TV sets.

Chapter 19 (p. 408)

1. Both have declined due to more emphasis on consumption rather than investment, inefficiencies inherent in the planning process, and a lack of incentive to perform, either as managers or workers.

3. The response should focus on the differences between the price mechanism and planning in solving the basic economic problems (what, how, for whom, and how much growth). See the section on "Prices in the USSR."

Chapter 19 (p. 416)

1. Some people have stated this view, but so many factors are not held equal that it is hard to see that very much can be learned from this simple comparison. Nonetheless, comparative studies of this sort, if conducted carefully, can be valuable.

3. For the views of the radical economists on this score, see pp. 412–416 on "Radical Economics."

Glossary of Terms

Absolute advantage the ability of one country to produce a good or service more cheaply than another country.

Aid to Families with Dependent Children (AFDC) an antipoverty program that provides cash payments to families with children.

Alternative cost the value of what certain resources could have produced had they been used in the best alternative way; also called **opportunity cost.**

American Federation of Labor-Congress of Industrial Organizations (AFL-CIO) a federation of national labor unions formed in 1955 by the merger between the American Federation of Labor (originally a federation of unions organized along craft lines) and the Congress of Industrial Organizations (originally a federation of unions organized along industrial lines).

Antitrust laws legislation (such as the Sherman Act, the Clayton Act, and the Federal Trade Commission Act) intended to promote competition and control monopoly.

Average fixed cost the firm's total fixed cost divided by its output.

Average product of an input total output divided by the amount of input used to produce this amount of output.

Average product of labor total output per unit of labor.

Average total cost the firm's total cost divided by its output; equal to average fixed cost plus average variable cost.

Average variable cost the firm's total variable cost divided by its output.

Backward-bending supply curve for labor a supply curve for labor inputs showing that, beyond some point, increases in price may result in smaller amounts of labor being supplied.

Balance sheet an accounting statement showing the nature of a firm's assets, the claims by creditors on those assets, and the value of the firm's ownership at a certain point in time.

Balanced budget a budget in which tax revenues cover government expenditures.

Barometric firm in an oligopolistic industry, any single firm that is the first to make changes in prices, which are then generally accepted by other firms.

Bond a debt (generally long-term) of a firm or government.

Break-even chart a chart that plots a firm's total cost and total revenue, and that shows the output level that must be reached if the firm is to avoid losses.

Budget a statement of the government's anticipated expenditures and tax revenues for a fiscal year.

Budget deficit a budget in which tax revenues fall short of government expenditures.

Budget line a line showing the market baskets that the consumer can purchase, given his or her income and prevailing prices.

Budget surplus a budget in which tax revenues exceed government expenditures.

Capital resources (such as factory buildings, equipment, raw materials, and inventories) that are created within the economic system for the purpose of producing other goods.

Capital formation investment in plant and equipment.

Capital goods output consisting of plant and equipment that are used to make other goods.

Capitalism an economic system characterized by private ownership of the tools of production; freedom of choice and of enterprise whereby consumers and firms can pursue their own self-interest; competition for sales among producers and resource owners; and reliance on the free market.

Capitalization of assets a method of computing the value of an asset by calculating the present value of the expected future income this asset will produce.

Cartel an open, formal collusive arrangement among firms.

Checkoff a system whereby an employer deducts union dues from each worker's pay and hands them over to the union.

Closed shop a situation where firms can hire only workers who are already union members.

Collective bargaining process of negotiation between the union and management over wages and working conditions.

Collusion a covert arrangement whereby firms agree on price and output levels in order to decrease competition and increase profits.

Common stock certificate of ownership of a corporation. Holders of common stock are owners of the corporation.

Comparative advantage the law that states that a nation should produce and export goods where its efficiency *relative to other nations* is highest; specialization and trade depend on comparative, not absolute advantage.

Complements commodities that tend to be consumed together, i.e., commodities with a negative cross elasticity of demand such that a decrease in the price of one will result in an increase in the quantity demanded of the other.

Constant dollar amounts amounts measured in base-year dollars (i.e., according to the purchasing power of the dollar in some earlier year), in order to express value in a way that corrects for changes in the price level.

Constant returns to scale a long-run situation where, if the firm increases the amount of all inputs by the same proportion, output increases by the same proportion as each of the inputs.

Consumer an individual or household that purchases the goods and services produced by the economic system.

Consumer goods output consisting of items that consumers purchase, such as clothing, food, and drink.

Consumer Price Index a measure of U.S. inflation, calculated by the Bureau of Labor Statistics, originally intended to measure changes in the prices of goods and services purchased by urban wage earners and clerical workers; in 1978, expanded to cover all urban consumers.

Consumer's surplus the difference between the maximum amount that a consumer would pay for a good or service and what he or she actually pays.

Corporate profits the net income of corporations (i.e., corporate profits before income taxes), including dividends received by the stockholders, retained earnings, and the amount paid by corporations as income taxes.

Corporation a fictitious legal person separate and distinct from the stockholders who own it, governed by a board of directors elected by the stockholders.

Cost function the relationship between cost and a firm's level of output, i.e., how much cost a firm will incur at various levels of output.

Council of Economic Advisers a group established by the Employment Act of 1946, whose function is to help the president formulate and assess the economic policies of the government.

Craft union a labor union that includes all the workers in a particular craft (such as machinists or carpenters).

Creeping inflation an increase in the general price level of a few percent per year that gradually erodes the value of money.

Cross elasticity of demand the percentage change in the quantity demanded of one commodity resulting from a one percent change in the price of another commodity; may be either positive or negative.

Decreasing returns to scale a long-run situation where, if the firm increases the amount of all inputs by the same proportion, output increases by a smaller proportion than each of the inputs.

Demand curve for loanable funds a curve showing the quantity of loanable funds that will be demanded at each interest rate.

Depreciation the value of the capital (i.e., plant, equipment, and structures) that is worn out in a year; also called a **capital consumption allowance.**

Derived demand demand for labor and other inputs not as ends in themselves, but as means to produce other things.

Differentiated oligopoly a market structure (such as those for automobiles and machinery) where there are only a few sellers of somewhat different products.

Direct regulation government issue of enforceable rules concerning the conduct of firms.

Dominant firm in an oligopolistic industry, a single large firm that sets the price for the industry but lets the small firms sell all they want at that price.

Economic profits the excess of a firm's profits over what it could make in other industries.

Economic resources resources that are scarce and thus command a nonzero price.

Economics the study of how resources are allocated among alternative uses to satisfy human wants.

Economies of scale efficiencies that result from carrying out a process (such as production or sales) on a large scale.

Effluent fee a fee that a polluter must pay to the government for discharging waste.

Equilibrium a situation in which there is no tendency for change.

Equilibrium price a price that shows no tendency for change, because it is the price at which the quantity demanded equals the quantity supplied; the price toward which the actual price of a good always tends to move.

Excise tax a tax imposed on each unit sold of a particular product, such as cigarettes or liquor.

Explicit cost the cost of resources for which there is an explicit payment.

Exports the goods and services that a nation sells to other nations.

External diseconomy an uncompensated cost to one person or firm resulting from the consumption or output of another person or firm.

External economy an uncompensated benefit to one person or firm resulting from the consumption or output of another person or firm.

Featherbedding a practice whereby a union restricts output per worker in order to increase the amount of labor required to do a certain job.

Firm an organization that produces a good or service for sale in an attempt to make a profit.

Firm's demand curve for labor a curve showing the relationship between the price of labor and the amount of labor demanded by a firm, i.e., the amount of labor that will be demanded by a firm at various wage rates.

A35

Firm's supply curve a curve, usually sloping upward to the right, showing the quantity of output a firm will produce at each price.

Fixed input a resource used in the production process (such as plant and equipment) whose quantity cannot be changed during the particular period under consideration.

Food programs federal antipoverty programs that distribute food to the poor, either directly from surpluses produced by farm programs or indirectly via stamps that can be exchanged for food.

Free resources resources (such as air) that are so abundant that they can be obtained without charge.

Historical cost of assets what a firm actually paid for its assets.

Implicit cost the cost (for which there may not be an explicit payment) of the resources that are provided by the owner of a firm, measured by what these resources could bring if they were used in their best alternative employment.

Imports the goods and services that a nation buys from other nations.

Income effect the change in the quantity demanded by the consumer of a good due to the change in the consumer's level of utility resulting from a change in the price of the good.

Income elasticity of demand the percentage change in the quantity demanded of a commodity resulting from a one percent increase in total money income (all prices being held constant).

Income statement an accounting statement showing a firm's sales, costs, and profits during a particular period (often a quarter or a year).

Income tax a federal, state, or local tax imposed on personal income and corporate profits.

Increasing returns to scale a long-run situation where, if a firm increases the amount of all inputs by the same proportion, output increases by a larger proportion than each of the inputs.

Indifference curve a curve representing market baskets among which the consumer is indifferent.

Individual demand curve a curve showing the relationship between individual consumer demand and prices, i.e., how much of a good an individual consumer will demand at various prices.

Industrial union a labor union that includes all the workers in a particular plant or industry (such as autos or steel).

Inflation an increase in the general level of prices economy-wide.

Innovation the first commercial application of a new technology.

Innovator a firm that is first to apply a new technology.

Input any resource used in the production process.

Interest the payment of money by borrowers to suppliers of money capital.

Interest rate the annual amount that a borrower must pay for the use of a dollar for a year.

Isocost curve a curve showing the input combinations the firm can obtain for a given expenditure.

Isoquant a curve showing all possible efficient combinations of inputs capable of producing a certain quantity of output.

Labor human effort, both physical and mental, used to produce goods and services.

Labor force the number of people employed plus the number of those unemployed (i.e., actively looking for work and willing to take a job if one were offered).

Labor productivity the average amount of output that can be obtained for every unit of labor.

Land natural resources, including minerals as well as plots of ground, used to produce goods and services.

Law of diminishing marginal returns the principle that if equal increments of a given input are added (the quantities of other inputs being held constant), the resulting increments of product obtained from the extra unit of input (i.e., the marginal product) will begin to decrease beyond some point.

Law of diminishing marginal utility the principle that if a person consumes additional units of a given commodity (the consumption of other commodities being held constant), the resulting increments of utility derived from the extra unit of the commodity (i.e., the commodity's marginal utility) will begin to decrease beyond some point.

Law of increasing cost the principle that as more and more of a good is produced, the production of each additional unit of the good is likely to entail a larger and larger opportunity cost.

Liabilities the debts of a firm.

Loanable funds funds (including those supplied by households and firms that find the rate of interest high enough to get them to save) that are available for borrowing by consumers, businesses, and government.

Local unions labor unions, organized around either craft or industrial lines, that are set up in particular geographical areas or plants, and which may or may not belong to a larger national union.

Long run the period of time during which all of a firm's inputs are variable, i.e., during which the firm could completely change the resources used in the production process.

Long-run average cost function a representation of the minimum average cost of producing various output levels when any desired type or scale of plant can be built.

Lorenz curve a curve that measures income inequality by showing what percentage of the people receive what percentage of total income.

Marginal cost the addition to total cost resulting from the addition of the last unit of output.

Marginal cost pricing a pricing rule whereby the price of a product is set equal to its marginal cost.

Marginal product of an input the addition to total output that results from the addition of an extra unit of input (the quantities of all other inputs being held constant).

Marginal product of labor the additional output resulting from the addition of an extra unit of labor.

Marginal revenue the change in total revenue that results from the addition of one unit to the quantity sold.

Marginal tax rate the proportion of an extra dollar of income that must be paid in taxes.

Marginal utility the additional satisfaction derived from consuming an additional unit of a commodity.

Market a group of firms and individuals that are in touch with each other in order to buy or sell some good or service.

Market demand curve a curve, usually sloping downward to the right, showing the relationship between a product's price and the quantity demanded of the product.

Market demand curve for labor a curve showing the relationship between the price of labor and the total amount of labor demanded in the market.

Market period the relatively short period of time during which the supply of a particular good is fixed and output is unaffected by price.

Market structure the type or organization of a market. Markets differ with regard to the number and size of buyers and sellers in the market, the ease with which new firms can enter, the extent of product differentiation, and other factors.

Market supply curve a curve, usually sloping upward to the right, showing the relationship between a product's price and the quantity supplied of the product.

Market supply curve for labor a curve showing the relationship between the price of labor and the total amount of labor supplied in the market.

Markup in cost-plus pricing, an addition to a product's estimated average cost that is meant to include certain costs that cannot be allocated to any specific product, and to provide a return on the firm's investment.

Medicare a compulsory hospitalization program plus a voluntary insurance plan for doctors' fees for people over 65, included under the Social Security program.

Model a theory composed of assumptions that simplify and abstract from reality, from which conclusions or predictions about the real world are deduced.

A37

Money income income measured in current dollars (i.e., actual money amounts).

Monopolistic competition a market structure in which there are many sellers of somewhat differentiated products, where entry is easy, and where there is no collusion among sellers. Retailing seems to have many of the characteristics of monopolistic competition.

Monopoly a market structure (such as those for public utilities) in which there is only one seller of a product.

Monopsony a market structure (such as that for the single firm that employs all the labor in a company town) in which there is only a single buyer.

Multinational firm a firm that makes direct investments in other countries, and produces and markets its products abroad.

National debt the amount owed by the government. To cover the difference between its expenditures and its tax revenues, the government sells bonds, notes, and other forms of IOUs.

Natural monopoly an industry in which the average costs of producing the product reach a minimum at an output rate large enough to satisfy the entire market, so that competition among firms cannot be sustained and one firm becomes a monopolist.

Negative income tax a system whereby families with incomes below a certain break-even level would receive, rather than make, a government income tax payment.

Net exports the amount spent by foreigners on a nation's goods and services (exports) minus the amount a nation spends on foreign goods and services (imports).

Nominal expressed in current dollars (i.e., actual money amounts).

Normative economics economic propositions about what ought to be, or about what a person, organization, or nation ought to do.

Old-age insurance benefits paid under the Social Security program to retired workers, from taxes imposed on both workers and employers.

Oligopoly a market structure (such as those for autos and steel) in which there are only a few sellers of products that can be either identical or differentiated.

Open shop a situation where a firm can hire both union and nonunion workers, with no requirement that nonunion workers ever join a union.

Opportunity cost the value of what certain resources could have produced had they been used in the best alternative way; also called **alternative cost.**

Parity the principle that a farmer should be able to exchange a given quantity of farm output for the same quantity of nonfarm goods and services he would have been able to purchase at some point in the past; in effect, the principle that farm prices should increase at the same rate as the prices of the goods and services that farmers buy.

Partnership a form of business organization whereby two or more people agree to own and conduct a business, with each party contributing some proportion of the capital and/or labor and receiving some proportion of the profit or loss.

Perfect competition a market structure in which there are many sellers of identical products, where no one seller or buyer has control over the price, where entry is easy, and where resources can switch readily from one use to another. Many agricultural markets have many of the characteristics of perfect competition.

Positive economics descriptive statements, propositions, and predictions about the economic world that are generally testable by an appeal to the facts.

Price discrimination the practice whereby one buyer is charged more than another buyer for the same product.

Price elastic the demand for a good if its price elasticity of demand is greater than one.

Price elasticity of demand the percentage change in quantity demanded resulting from a one percent change in price; by convention, always expressed as a positive number.

Price elasticity of supply the percentage

change in quantity supplied resulting from a one percent change in price.

Price inelastic the demand for a good if its price elasticity of demand is less than one.

Price leader in an oligopolistic industry, a firm that sets a price that other firms are willing to follow.

Price supports price floors imposed by the government on a certain good.

Price system a system under which every good and service has a price, and which in a purely capitalistic economy carries out the basic functions of an economic system (determining what goods and services will be produced, how the output will be produced, how much of it each person will receive, and what the nation's growth of per capita income will be).

Primary inputs resources (such as labor and land) that are produced outside of the economic system.

Private cost the price paid by the individual user for the use of a resource.

Product differentiation the process by which producers create real or apparent differences between products that perform the same general function.

Product group a group of firms that produce similar products that are fairly close substitutes for one another.

Product market a market where products are bought and sold.

Production function the relationship between the quantities of various inputs used per period of time and the maximum quantity of output that can be produced per period of time, i.e., the most output that existing technology permits the firm to produce from various quantities of inputs.

Production possibilities curve a curve showing the combinations of amounts of various goods that a society can produce with given (fixed) amounts of resources.

Profit the difference between a firm's revenue and its costs.

Progressive tax a tax whereby the rich pay a larger proportion of their income for the tax than do the poor.

Prohibitive tariff a tariff so high that it prevents imports of a good.

Property tax a tax imposed on real estate and/or other property.

Proprietorship a firm owned by a single individual.

Public goods goods and services that can be consumed by one person without diminishing the amount of them that others can consume. Often there is no way to prevent citizens from consuming public goods whether they pay for them or not.

Public sector the governmental sector of the economy.

Pure oligopoly a market structure (such as those for steel, cement, tin cans, and petroleum) in which there are only a few sellers of an identical product.

Pure rate of interest the interest rate on a riskless loan.

Quota a limit imposed on the amount of a commodity that can be imported annually.

Rate of return the annual profit per dollar invested that business can obtain by building new structures, adding new equipment, or increasing their inventories; the interest rate earned on the investment in a particular asset.

Regressive tax a tax whereby the rich pay a smaller proportion of their income for the tax than do the poor.

Rent in the context of Chapter 15, the return derived from an input that is fixed in supply.

Reproduction cost of assets what the firm would have to pay to replace its assets.

Resource market a market where resources are bought and sold.

Resources inputs used to produce goods and services.

Retained earnings the total amount of profit that the stockholders of a corporation have reinvested in the business, rather than withdrawing as dividends.

Rule of reason the idea that not all trusts, but only unreasonable combinations in restraint of trade, require conviction under the antitrust laws.

Runaway inflation a very rapid increase in the general price level that wipes out practically all of the value of money.

Sales tax a tax imposed on the goods consumers buy (with the exception, in some states, of food and medical care).

Short run the period of time during which at least one of a firm's inputs (generally its plant and equipment) is fixed.

Social Security a program that imposes taxes on wage earners and employers, and provides old-age, survivors, disability, medical, and unemployment benefits to workers covered under the Social Security Act.

Substitutes commodities with a positive cross elasticity of demand (that is, a decrease in the price of one commodity will result in a decrease in the quantity demanded of the other commodity).

Substitution effect the change in the quantity demanded (by a consumer) of a commodity resulting from a change in the commodity's price, if the consumer's level of utility is held constant.

Supply curve for loanable funds a curve showing the relationship between the quantity of loanable funds supplied and the pure interest rate.

Tariff a tax imposed by the government on imported goods (designed to cut down on imports and thus protect domestic industry and workers from foreign competition).

Tax avoidance legal steps taken by taxpayers to reduce their tax bill.

Tax evasion misreporting of income or other illegal steps taken by taxpayers to reduce their tax bill.

Technological change new methods of producing existing products, new designs that make it possible to produce new products, and new techniques of organization, marketing, and management.

Technology society's pool of knowledge concerning how goods and services can be produced from a given amount of resources.

Terms of trade the ratio of an index of export prices to an index of import prices.

Total cost the sum of a firm's total fixed cost and total variable cost.

Total fixed cost a firm's total expenditure on fixed inputs per period of time.

Total revenue a firm's total dollar sales volume.

Total variable cost a firm's total expenditure on variable inputs per period of time.

Trading possibilities curve a curve showing the various combinations of products that a nation can get if it specializes in one product and trades that specialty for foreign goods.

Tying contract the practice whereby buyers must purchase other items in order to get the product they want.

Unemployment according to the definition of the Bureau of Labor Statistics, joblessness among people who are actively looking for work and would take a job if one were offered.

Unemployment rate the number of people who are unemployed divided by the number of people in the labor force.

Union shop a situation where firms can hire nonunion workers who must then become union members within a certain length of time after being hired.

Unitary elasticity a price elasticity of demand equal to one.

Utility a number representing the level of satisfaction that a consumer derives from a particular masket basket.

Value of the marginal product of labor the marginal product of labor (i.e., the additional output resulting from the addition of an extra unit of labor) multiplied by the product's price.

Variable input a resource used in the production process (such as labor or raw material) whose quantity can be changed during the particular period under consideration.

Wage and price controls limits imposed by the government on the amount by which wages and prices can increase, in order to reduce the inflation rate at a given unemployment rate.

Wage rate the price of labor.

Photograph Credits

Bureau of Land Management (6, 68); U.S. Department of Labor (6); Sperry New Holland (7); Warder Collection (13, 30, 51, 269, 375, 395, 398, 402); Free-Lance Photo Guild, photo by Kerwin B. Roche (33); photo by Amanda Adams (40); photos by Jeremy Townsend (58, 91); Food and Drug Administration (66); Official U.S. Coast Guard Photo (68); U.S. Air Force Photo (73); AP/Wide World (75, 292, 407); Caterpillar Tractor Company (76); IBM (88); Wide World (93); Edward C. Topple, NYSE Photographer (94); Uniphoto (116); Ford Archives (118); Historical Pictures Service (130); Courtesy of Gary Becker (140); Courtesy of Ken Scala — Century 21/ Scala and Clark Co., Inc. (159); Chicago Mercantile Exchange (186); Courtesy of Charles Plott (198); United Nations/Carlton Read (226); Harvard University News Office (236); Burk Uzzle, Magnum Photos (237); Courtesy of William Baumol (249); Harvard University Archives (257); Photo © by Jim Kalett (258); Department of Justice (263); © Pabst Brewing Company, Milwaukee, Wisconsin (267); Courtesy of Michael Spence (286); AFL-CIO News Photo (291); Jacques E. Levy (312); NYPL Ford Collection (315); Reprinted from the *Journal of Political Economy,* Vol. 81, No. 3, May/June 1973. Copyright © 1973 by the University of Chicago (318); UPI/ Bettmann Newsphotos (328); United Nations/S. Potner (332); U. P. Laffont/Sygma (336); National Archives, photo by Joseph Sterling (350); E. I. Du Pont de Nemours & Co. (351); German Information Center (353, 391); Burt Glinn/Magnum Photos (378); The Picture Group (379); United Nations (396, 405); Sygma Photos (409).

Index

Definitions of terms appear on pages set in **boldface** type.